The Journey West

The Journey West

The Mormon Pioneer Journals of HORACE K. WHITNEY
with Insights by HELEN MAR KIMBALL WHITNEY

RICHARD E. BENNETT
EDITOR

RSC
BYU

DESERET
BOOK

Published by the Religious Studies Center, Brigham Young University, Provo, Utah, in cooperation with Deseret Book Company, Salt Lake City.

Visit us at rsc.byu.edu.

Printed in the United States of America by Sheridan Books, Inc.

Visit us at DeseretBook.com.

Cover and interior design by Emily V. Strong.

Front cover: Glen S. Hopkinson, *Leaving Nauvoo—Packing the Wagon.*
Back cover: Greg Olsen, *Winter Quarters.*

ISBN: 978-1-9443-9434-9

Library of Congress Cataloging-in-Publication Data

Names: Whitney, Horace K. (Horace Kimball), 1823-1884, author. | Whitney, Helen Mar, 1828-1896, author. | Bennett, Richard Edmond, 1946- editor.
Title: The journey West : the Mormon pioneer journals of Horace K. Whitney with insights by Helen Mar Kimball Whitney / Richard E. Bennett, editor.
Other titles: Pioneer journals of Horace K. Whitney with insights by Helen Mar Kimball Whitney | Woman's exponent.
Description: Provo, Utah : Religious Studies Center, Brigham Young University ; Salt Lake City : Deseret Book Company, [2018] | Includes bibliographical references and index.
Identifiers: LCCN 2017059339 | ISBN 9781944394349
Subjects: LCSH: Mormon pioneers--West (U.S.)--Diaries. | Whitney, Horace K. (Horace Kimball), 1823-1884--Diaries. | Whitney, Helen Mar Kimball--Diaries. | Mormon pioneers--West (U.S.)--History--Sources. | Overland journeys to the Pacific--Sources. | Frontier and pioneer life--West (U.S.)--Sources. | Pioneers--West (U.S.)--Diaries. | Pioneers--West (U.S.)--History--19th century--Sources. | West (U.S.)--Description and travel--Sources. | West (U.S.)--History--To 1848--Sources.
Classification: LCC F592 .W58 2018 | DDC 978/.02--dc23 LC record available at https://lccn.loc.gov/2017059339

Contents

Acknowledgments

This editorial project is an "IOU" of sorts that I have been intending to complete for a long time. I made up my mind over thirty-five years ago that someday I would edit and publish the Horace K. Whitney journals. I was convinced that this unpublished resource that had proven to be of such great value to me surely would benefit others. Despite my best intentions, however, life's interruptions, six other books, and scores of articles got in the way. However, with the help and support of many people and an excellent publisher in the Religious Studies Center of Brigham Young University, that day has finally come!

I first became aware of the significance of the Whitney journals when working as a research assistant for Leonard J. Arrington, who had been recently appointed as church historian. I will ever look back upon this remarkable scholar, friend, and mentor as one of the richest blessings of my professional life. His love for Mormon history and for those engaged in researching and writing it was contagiously inspiring and so very encouraging. Likewise, I will ever owe a debt of gratitude to Marvin S. Hill, who taught me how to utilize primary source documents in evidential ways. Later, while a PhD student at Wayne State University, I was once again tutored by one of the finest gentleman-scholars in the land—Professor Philip Mason, director of the Walter P. Reuther Library of Labor and Urban Affairs. With his encouragement, I wrote my dissertation on the Mormon exodus and, in the process, came to understand and appreciate the professional world of archival science and the power of the manuscript.

After completing my course work at Wayne State University, I spent the next twenty years in Winnipeg at the University of Manitoba as head of the Department of Archives and Special Collections. While sundry career priorities inevitably got in the way, I never lost interest in the Whitney project. I want to thank my library directors through those years, who encouraged me to work on this labor of love as time permitted. With their encouragement and support, I received funding from the Social Sciences and Research Council of Canada to continue work on this project. Later, after joining the faculty at Brigham Young University in 1997, I continued to receive institutional support from the Department of Church History and Doctrine and from Religious Education in the form of research grants and occasional time off to continue in this work. Finally, a generous grant from the Frederick W. and Jolene Edmunds Rockwood Family Foundation greatly facilitated the hiring of student editorial support staff, expedited the tedious work of carefully editing, proofreading, and digitizing these journals, and made possible the aquisition of several images herein. Without the foundation's financial assistance, this project would still be years away from completion.

I also need to thank the Horace K. Whitney family for preserving and donating the Whitney journals in the first place to the Church History Library of the Church of Jesus Christ of Latter-day Saints so many years ago. Long after their donation, Edyth Jenkins Romney, longtime editorial assistant and secretary to what was then called the Church Historian's Office, spent months making a remarkably accurate initial transcription of these ofttimes very hard to read journals, a wonderful time-saving transcription which has proven very valuable to the present project. Of course, I appreciate the Church History Library for permission to edit and publish these journals after these many years. I wish also to thank the staff at the LDS Church History Library, the Church History Museum of the Church of Jesus Christ of Latter-day Saints, the L. Tom Perry Special Collections in the Harold B. Lee Library at Brigham Young University, Special Collections and Archives at the Merrill-Cazier Library at Utah State University, the Wyoming State Archives, the Nebraska State Historical Society, and the Wisconsin Historical Society for their valuable assistance.

Many student research assistants have also assisted me through the years on this project, some whose names I have forgotten. My thanks especially to the following: Hugh Hannesson, who was me with me at the very beginning; Natalie Larson, who spent the better part of a year proofreading the text and typing the original typescript copy on the computer; and Wendy Top, my current research assistant, who has been particularly helpful in ensuring the quality of the glossary of names. Finally, I owe a special, more recent debt of gratitude to the editorial staff of the Religious Studies Center at Brigham Young University. These include Thomas A. Wayment, publications director, who agreed to take on this project; Joany O. Pinegar, publications supervisor; editors Devan Jensen, Tyler Balli, and Megan Judd; designer Emily Strong; and Brent Nordgren, production supervisor.

Above all, I thank my wife, Patricia, who once again has put up with the other love of my life—writing and editing works of church history. She has been a wonderfully patient, uncomplaining partner, going where I have gone, listening, encouraging, and ever supporting.

INTRODUCTION

There are many unwritten incidents which could be related with profit, and prove interesting reading to those who pioneered across the barren, trackless wastes of the great American desert to these once lone and dreary vales of the Rocky Mountains, as well as scores who are not of that number and even many strangers would enjoy reading of those early scenes among the "Mormons." . . . I mention this as a stimulus to prompt others to write and give to the world the benefit of their travels and experience with this people.

—Helen Mar Whitney, *Woman's Exponent*, vol. 15, no. 6, 15 August 1886, pp. 46–47

One of the ironies of Mormonism is that, although it is an American religion, the United States of America has struggled to accept it. In fact, the early history of the Church of Jesus Christ of Latter-day Saints is one long chapter of rejection, persecution, and expulsion. For years after its founding in upstate New York under the hand of Joseph Smith Jr. in April 1830, the church was on the run from pillar to post: first, New York; then Kirtland, Ohio; Independence and Far West, Missouri; Nauvoo, Illinois; and finally, the Rocky Mountains. Scholars have long argued over what poisoned the mix. Perhaps it was its radical claim of being the only true and restored church of Christ upon the earth. Or its adamant belief in the divine authenticity of the Book of Mormon, which Smith translated from ancient golden plates that he discovered in upstate New York. Furthermore, its fervent expectation in the imminent Second Coming of Christ to its new Zion in Jackson County, Missouri, seemed peculiar at best to local citizens bent on establishing a new home in the West.

Whatever the case, many Americans came to believe that the allegiance of most early Mormons was more to their prophet than to the president, more to revealed scripture than to the American Constitution. There may have been too much talk of a kingdom of God for a restless republic of the people to accept. And when large concentrations of Latter-day Saint "Yankees" began moving to the slave state of Missouri in the early 1830s intent on establishing their Zion, it inevitably created a climate of suspicion and distrust amidst a clash of cultures that eventually led to their undoing. The sad fact is Mormonism could not have chosen a more difficult time, a less promising place, amidst a more unwelcoming people to establish their New Jerusalem than in Missouri in the early 1830s.

The tragic expulsion of the Mormons from Missouri in the winter of 1838–39 under the threat of "extermination" as decreed by Governor Lilburn W. Boggs led to a forced two-hundred-mile march of several thousand Mormons from the far west of Missouri to Quincy, Adams County, in the more accepting "free" state of Illinois. There, over the next seven years, they finally established a home in their beloved Nauvoo, where they hoped to build a permanent settlement and to live and worship as they pleased. By 1844, some twelve thousand Latter-day Saints from the eastern United States, Canada, and Great Britain were crowding into their new surroundings in Nauvoo, and for a time, their future looked promising.

But by 1844 the Saints were again facing all kinds of trouble. Many Missourians continued to hold grievances against them and plotted to recapture their prophet-leader. With Nauvoo threatening to become an economic powerhouse, other slower-growing nearby river towns, like Warsaw, stood to lose valuable business. And when rumors began to fly that Joseph Smith and a few other Mormon leaders were secretly practicing polygamy, many former friends and members turned suspicious and began speaking of conspiracy and kingdom building. "Saintly scoundrels" such as John C. Bennett, former mayor of Nauvoo, falsely charged that the city militia—the Nauvoo Legion—was plotting militarily against the very existence of the nation. When Joseph Smith announced in 1844 that he would seek the presidency of the United States in large measure to seek redress for Missouri's depredations upon the Saints, his growing chorus of critics branded him a political and religious megalomaniac, a prophet without constraint, one certainly "without honor" in his own country. In short, the anti-Mormon press tried every which way to label Mormonism as an anti-American, anti-Christian, and anti-family religion—a lethal triplet of unfounded charges which nonetheless led inexorably to the murder of Joseph Smith and his brother Hyrum in Carthage Jail in June 1844. Many expected their death would put an end to Mormonism once and for all.

Although Sidney Rigdon, James Strang, and others laid claim to Smith's mantle of prophetic leadership, Brigham Young eventually held sway. As shrewd a leader as he was sympathetic to the plights of his people, "Brother Brigham," in his capacity as president of the Quorum of the Twelve Apostles, recognized that there was no future for the church in Illinois. By 1845, he and the Council of Fifty, a highly influential political advisory body to church leadership, were quietly laying plans for a departure west to some new home far away where they could finally live their peculiar religion in peace. On behalf of the entire council, Orson Spencer indicated that the Saints were "willing to accept of any eligible location within any part of the Territory of the U. States" so long as it was large enough to accommodate at least five hundred thousand people.[1] Faced with the threat of his own assassination, the possible interference of their westward march by a United States Army of the West, and potential defections in greater numbers, Brigham Young began to lead his people out of Nauvoo in the teeth of a very cold February of 1846. Their plan was to reach Council Bluffs on the Missouri River in a matter of weeks, establish farms and way stations at Grand Island and elsewhere in what is today Nebraska,[2] and from there dispatch a speedy vanguard company of pioneers over the mountains to some large valley all in 1846, that memorable "Year of Decision," as historian Bernard DeVoto so aptly termed it.[3]

Alas, it was not to be. Instead of an express vanguard company of one or two hundred handpicked pioneers, soon 2,500 Saints rapidly crowded around their leader. Such a large, relatively unprepared company hedged up his way. Instead of leaving their Sugar Creek encampments just across the river from Nauvoo in early March, they languished there until mid-April. When finally they did begin to roll out across Iowa Territory, the rains came, incessant and torrential, so much so that instead of making their planned fifteen miles a day, they barely made one. With wagons sunk to their axles in mud day after weary day, many began to wonder whose side God was on after all. Desperately seeking his way across a three-hundred-mile-long Iowa mudhole, Brigham Young ordered most of his struggling, rain-soaked followers to start building their proposed way stations much sooner than anticipated. They first identified Garden Grove (just 143 miles west of Nauvoo) and then Mount Pisgah, Iowa (192 miles west) as places to build habitations and put in spring crops for the thousands yet to follow. Later that summer he instructed others to return to Nauvoo with vacated wagons to bring on the "poor camps" of refugees being hounded out of Nauvoo by mad militia mobs intent on destroying whatever vestige of Mormonism there remained. Under miserable skies, miscommunications, and misunderstandings and one failed timetable after another, their entire plan of exodus was in disarray. Many of his followers were sick and about to die from near starvation, sheer exhaustion, and the cruel and unrelenting exposure to the elements. Not only were their westering plans in doubt, but the very salvation of the church was at stake.

The Army of the United States did indeed come as earlier feared, but instead of interfering, it came inviting. With the expansionist-minded President James K. Polk anxious to declare war against Mexico to ensure the annexation of California, Captain James Allen of Stephen W. Kearny's Army of the West caught up with the Mormons at Mount Pisgah in early June of 1846 and there asked for a battalion of five hundred of their strongest, healthiest men to enlist. Indignant to serve a nation many felt had consented to driving them out, the "Mormon Battalion" ultimately listened to the persuasions of one Colonel Thomas L. Kane

1. Council of Fifty, Minutes, 4 February 1845, in Matthew J. Grow et al., eds., *Council of Fifty, Minutes, March 1844–January 1846*, vol. 1 of the Administrative Records series of *The Joseph Smith Papers*, ed. Ronald K. Esplin, Matthew J. Grow, and Matthew C. Godfrey (Salt Lake City: Church Historian's Press, 2016), 243.
2. Nebraska did not become a territory of the United States until 1854, nor a state until 1867. Iowa, on the other hand, became a territory in 1838 and a state in 1846.
3. Bernard DeVoto, *The Year of Decision: 1846* (Boston: Little, Brown and Company, 1943).

of Philadelphia, a friend of both Polk and the Mormons. At his assurances, they embarked upon one of the longest overland marches in military history: from Fort Leavenworth to San Diego, a distance of 1,618 miles, where many were honorably discharged having never fired a shot in hostile action. Several, however, reenlisted and marched another five hundred miles north, where they participated in finding gold at Sutter's Fort, near Sacramento, in 1848. Yet, instead of staying on and making their fortunes, most of them headed east several hundred more miles to rejoin their families either in the Salt Lake Valley or, as was the case with many, somewhere back along the Mormon Trail. Thus some of the Mormon Battalion men marched more than three thousand miles!

Meanwhile, back in Iowa, Brigham Young and his vanguard company finally reached the Missouri River in mid-June, much too late—as every trader and mountain man knew well—to make a dash for the Rocky Mountains, a sad truth that the Donner-Reed party would learn the hard way that same year. In the fall of 1846, with reluctant permission from military officials to settle on Indian lands located on the west banks of the Missouri River in what today is Omaha, the Mormons established their Winter Quarters settlement, Nebraska's first city. By the end of the year, four to five thousand were settled there, with a comparable number across the river in Council Bluffs (which they renamed Kanesville) and another three to four thousand strewn all across Iowa clear back to the Mississippi. Some stayed in St. Louis and in other Missouri river towns. While some murmured and more than a few defected, the vast majority of the Saints remained faithful to the leadership of Brigham Young.

After enduring a winter of suffering and death, the long-hoped-for spring of 1847 finally arrived. Brigham Young wasted no time in leading out his handpicked, hearty band of pioneers to find a new home in the West. His pioneer company of 148 (143 men, 3 women, and 2 children) left the Elkhorn River in early April and pioneered their own trail north of the Platte River so as not to interfere with the more crowded Oregon and California Trail followers on the south side, many of whom were from Missouri. Enjoying much better weather than the year before, they reached Chimney Rock (the approximate halfway point) on 28 May, Fort Laramie by 2 June, and Independence Rock by 21 June, from whence they followed the South Pass down and across the Green River to Fort Bridger. From there, they decided to travel down Echo and other canyons westward to scout out the Valley of the Great Salt Lake, where, on 24 July 1847 Brigham Young, though sick with Rocky Mountain spotted fever, declared it to be "the right place. Drive on!"[4] Their long journey now at an end, the word soon went out for all to come. And come they did. Eventually, tens of thousands of new

4. Manuscript History of Brigham Young, 23 July 1847, Church History Library, The Church of Jesus Christ of Latter-day Saints. Later, on 8 August and as affirmed in the Horace Whitney journals, Brigham Young referred to the Salt Lake Valley specifically when he said, "This is the spot that I had anticipated." The term "spot," and more specifically "consecrated spot," is in consonance with the early revelations of the church referring to Zion in Missouri as the "spot" to build the temple and establish a righteous people" (D&C 57:3; 84:31).

converts from Great Britain, Scandinavia, and elsewhere found their way by ship, wagon, and even handcarts to their new mountain Zion.

The Mormon exodus was that of an entire believing people fleeing out of Babylon to a new mountain home "far away in the West" (to borrow William Clayton's phrase),[5] where they could worship without fear of persecution. They came to believe, as Brigham Young's "Word and Will of the Lord" revelation at Winter Quarters stated, that they would find their place if they followed their God. In the process, they forged a character and an identity that to this day sets the Latter-day Saints apart from the rest of America, if not in an ethnic way, then certainly in a religious one. It is within this rich and unfolding drama that the Horace K. Whitney journals and the accompanying selective reminiscences of his wife must be understood and appreciated.

Children of the Restoration

Horace Kimball Whitney and Helen Mar Kimball (Smith) Whitney are a unique couple in Latter-day Saint history. While most early Mormon diarists and correspondents converted to the church later in life and migrated to join the fledgling Latter-day Saint movement, Horace and Helen were children of the Restoration, childhood acquaintances, if not sweethearts, from two of the most prominent convert families in Kirtland, Ohio. Born in 1823, Horace was the oldest son of Newel K. Whitney, the second presiding bishop of the church. Helen Mar, daughter of Heber C. Kimball, a member of the original Quorum of the Twelve, was five years his junior. The two grew up together in the shadow of the Kirtland Temple, moved on to Nauvoo with their parents, and eventually married one another in the Nauvoo Temple just one day before the Mormon exodus to the Salt Lake Valley began in early February 1846. One might say they saw it all in that they lived through the exciting, if not deeply troubling, growing pains of the young Church of Jesus Christ under the leadership of their prophet, Joseph Smith Jr. They suffered along with the rest of their fellow believers, losing their first three children to the rigors of the exodus, but their sorrows never gave way to faithlessness, hopelessness, or despair. Instead, they chose to see life and its incessant challenges through the confident lens of youthful love and abiding optimism, full of hope and faith. As Joseph Conrad once penned about such youthful exuberance and adventure, "I remember my youth and the feeling that will never come back any more—the feeling that I could last for ever, outlast the sea, the earth, and all men; . . . the triumphant conviction of strength, the heat of life in the handful of dust."[6] For Helen and Horace, the sea that they were about to cross was what many then called the Great American Desert.

---

5. William Clayton, "Come, Come, Ye Saints," *Hymns* (Salt Lake City: The Church of Jesus Christ of Latter-day Saints, 1985), no. 30.
6. Joseph Conrad, *Youth: A Narrative and Two Other Stories* (Edinburgh: William Blackwood and Sons, 1903), 41.

Horace Kimball Whitney

Horace Kimball Whitney was born in Kirtland, Ohio, 25 July 1823, the oldest child of Newel K. and Elizabeth Ann (Smith) Whitney. His father, a prominent and successful store owner and operator, and his mother, a goodly woman full of Christian faith and integrity, converted to Mormonism in November 1830 when Parley P. Pratt, Oliver Cowdery, Ziba Peterson, and Peter Whitmer Jr. came to town with their message of the Book of Mormon and the restored gospel of Jesus Christ. In early February 1831, Horace first met Joseph Smith Jr., the Mormon prophet, who upon arriving in Kirtland said to Horace's father, Newel K. Whitney, "You prayed me here. What do you want of me?" Joseph Smith soon afterwards called Brother Whitney as bishop of the church in Kirtland. Baptized when nine years old by Reynolds Cahoon, Horace ever revered Joseph Smith as the prophet of God. Many a night by the hearth of the Whitney home as the fire crackled and the candles flickered, he listened to Joseph Smith tell of his spiritual quests, his visions and blessings, and the translation of the Book of Mormon, believing with the total trust of a young boy.

Horace's parents, more well-to-do than most, made sure that their son received a first-rate education, providing him with every advantage of schooling that his time and environment could afford. Because of it, he acquired a thirst for learning that would last a lifetime. When his bedroom candles burned out at night, he would often open his window with his books in hand to read by the light of the moon. "Ask Horace" became a proverb among his boyhood friends when seeking information upon almost every topic. He ever looked back with fondness upon the opportunity he had of learning from Joseph Smith, Heber C. Kimball (his future father-in-law), Brigham Young, and other church leaders in the Hebrew school held in the upstairs of his own home where he learned Hebrew, Latin, and Greek as well as English. Blessed with a quick and impressionable mind, he learned faster than most and received one ribbing after another from those who loved and admired him for racing ahead of them. A careful notetaker and observer, Horace loved literature, history, and the study of books. His memory was, as one put it, "like hooks of steel."

While others may have sought him out, Horace was never one to seek the limelight. He was a sensitive, unassuming, and rather modest young lad, and though a lively conversationalist, he shunned popularity and position. He was most comfortable as a follower, not the ambitious leader, and had a reputation for honesty and integrity. A better writer than a preacher, Horace once admitted, "Were preaching an employment by which to earn one's livelihood, and I had chosen it as such, my nervous excitement on attempting to speak would warn me that I had mistaken my calling."[7]

Growing up, young Horace witnessed the many ups and downs of Kirtland. New converts by the hundreds continued to pour into the city from all over the eastern United States. Meanwhile, the Prophet proclaimed a spate of visions and revelations, established new

7. Horace K. Whitney to Helen Mar Kimball Whitney, 24 December 1869, Helen Mar Kimball Whitney Papers, MSS 179, Merrill-Cazier Library, Special Collections and Archives Division, Utah State University Logan, UT.

positions in the church, and made exciting new proclamations, foremost of which was his call for the Saints to construct the Kirtland Temple in their poverty, beginning in 1833. Now a strapping young man, Horace helped out as much as he could. In April 1836, with the temple's dedication, several claimed to see celestial beings surround the structure in what has gone down in church history as a Pentecostal season of spiritual manifestations.

In vivid contrast, he also witnessed the rise of rancor, bitterness, and finger-pointing among the Saints with the collapse of the Kirtland Safety Society Anti-Banking Company, an economic hardship largely attributable to the nationwide Panic of 1837. Once harmonious feelings deteriorated into acrimony, distrust, defection, and persecution, so much so that the Whitney family felt compelled to quit their city for their own safety and join in with some five hundred others in the so-called "Kirtland Camp" of 1838 for a new "Zion" home in Missouri.

Fifteen-year-old Horace, however, never made it to Missouri. Upon arriving in St. Louis and hearing that the Saints in Missouri were facing an extermination and expulsion order courtesy of Governor Lilburn W. Boggs in the late fall of 1838, the Whitney family decided to spend the winter in Carrollton, Greene County, Illinois, some twenty-five miles north of St. Louis. There Horace obtained employment as a country teacher, despite his youthful age. Being large in stature and slightly bearded, Horace came off older and more mature looking than most others his age. When the examining trustee queried, "I should say you were about twenty-one, Mr. Whitney," he replied, "You needn't guess again," and the examination closed.

Within a year, however, the Whitney family was on the move again, this time north to join the Saints in their settlement of Commerce, Illinois, which Joseph Smith—fresh out of Liberty Jail—rechristened Nauvoo, the "City Beautiful." While his father took up his duties as presiding bishop of the church, Horace once again taught school for a season, teaching reading, writing, and arithmetic to a handful of students at a fee of three dollars a quarter.[8] Once settled in Nauvoo, he also learned the printer's trade and was employed with the *Times and Seasons* newspaper as a compositor. A lover of music and the theater, Horace learned to play the flute, a talent he continued to foster throughout his life. In 1843, soon after being ordained an elder by Joseph Smith, he served a mission to the east with Amasa Lyman. Upon his return to Nauvoo, he began thinking seriously about a future companion. Who better, perhaps, than his childhood friend and sweetheart, Helen Mar Kimball? But courting Helen Mar would pose serious unforeseen difficulties, and marrying her would come at a most unusual cost.

Helen Mar Kimball

Helen Mar Kimball was born in Mendon, Monroe County, New York, ten miles west of Palmyra, on 22 August 1828, the fourth child and oldest daughter of Heber Chase and Vilate Murray Kimball. Her parents converted to Mormonism in April 1832 and

8. Handwritten memorandum of Horace K. Whitney, 22 November 1840, Helen Mar Kimball Whitney Papers, MSS 179.

Horace K. Whitney (1823–84). Courtesy of Church History Library.

Helen Mar Kimball Whitney (1823–96). Courtesy of Church History Library.

removed to Kirtland in the fall of 1833, when she was but five years old. Her father, totally devoted to the cause and a hardworking farmer, potter, and blacksmith, had traveled with Joseph Smith on the Zion's Camp expedition of 1834 to Jackson County, Missouri. His unswerving commitment to the Mormon prophet led to him being called as one of the original Twelve Apostles in February 1835. He would later serve in the First Presidency of Brigham Young for more than thirty years. In the spring of 1836, Helen Mar attended Eliza R. Snow's school in a house connected to Joseph Smith's dwelling, where she remembered using the Book of Mormon as a textbook. "Uncle" Brigham Young, a very close friend of the Kimballs, baptized her a member of the church in the frozen Chagrin River in 1837, cutting a hole in the ice to perform the ordinance. Unbothered by the cold water, she said of it later, "I had longed for this privilege and though I had some distance to walk in my wet clothes I felt no cold or inconvenience from it."[9]

When her parents decided to move west to Missouri, "I was delighted," she remembered, "although some of my little mates tried to frighten me with awful tales about being eaten alive by the Missourians, who were cannibals with horns."[10] Very much like her father in faith and disposition, she was seen by many as his "best representative." Shortly thereafter, nine-year-old Helen Mar left for Missouri with her parents, arriving in Far West on 25 July 1838. Unfortunately, they arrived in a hurricane of persecution. Six months later, the Kimballs fled for their lives, along with thousands of other Saints, to Illinois, settling first in Atlas, Illinois, later in Quincy, and finally in Commerce (Nauvoo), arriving there in the summer of 1839.

Life in Nauvoo was never easy. Her father, Heber, was soon called on a mission to Great Britain, leaving his family behind for eighteen months. The success of that apostolic mission led to thousands of new British converts eventually migrating to Zion.[11] That remarkable achievement, nevertheless, must be weighed against the sufferings and deprivations of family loved ones and "church widows" left behind. Although Heber built a primitive log home upon arriving from Quincy and a newer house just before he left for England, life in Nauvoo ever proved challenging and unpredictable. Although Joseph Smith called their city "Nauvoo the Beautiful," he later said it was at first "a deadly sickly hole," and, while painting as bright a picture as possible for would-be emigrants, he admitted that "although we have been keeping up appearances, and holding out inducements to encourage immigration, that we scarcely think justifiable in consequence of the mortality that almost invariably awaits those who come from far distant parts."[12] Many sickened and died from

9. Helen Mar Whitney, *Woman's Exponent*, vol. 9, no. 22, 15 April 1881, p. 170.

10. Helen Mar Whitney, *Woman's Exponent*, vol. 9, no. 6, 15 August 1880, p. 42.

11. James B. Allen, Ronald K. Esplin, and David J. Whittaker, *Men with a Mission, 1837–1841: The Quorum of the Twelve Apostles in the British Isles* (Salt Lake City: Deseret Book, 1992). See Carol Wilkinson and Cynthia Doxey Green, *The Field Is White: Harvest in the Three Counties of England* (Provo, UT: Religious Studies Center; Salt Lake City: Deseret Book, 2017).

12. Joseph Smith to Horace R. Hotchkiss, 25 August 1841, Church History Library. Don Carlos, Joseph and Emma Smith's own son, died less than a month later at fourteen months of age.

Newel K. Whitney store, Kirtland, Ohio, circa 1907. Photograph by George Edward Anderson. Courtesy of Church History Library. Original in the George Edward Anderson Collection, Brigham Young University.

malaria, ague, and other diseases. Money was always scarce; food, shoes, and clothing were in short supply; and visitors were not always sensitive. Helen remembers receiving two toy china dolls from her father as a gift, which she put on salt cellars for display. When Joseph Smith dropped by one day to visit the family, he accidentally broke the head off one of them and merely remarked, "'As that has fallen, so shall the heathen gods fall.' I stood there a silent observer, unable to understand or appreciate the prophetic words, but thought them a rather weak apology for breaking my doll's head off." [13]

The Prophet came by for another reason when Helen was but fourteen years old. It is a well-established fact in Mormon history that Joseph Smith claimed to have received a revelation as early as 1831 on the eternality, as well as the plurality, of the marriage covenant under certain prescribed conditions. Fearing resistance and a harmful backlash if publicly announced, he had introduced the "principle" of plural marriage in secret difficulty and deft denial.[14] Evidence suggests that he took his first plural wife, Fanny Alger, in 1835. And well before he informed his first wife, Emma, he also had married Louisa Beaman, his first plural wife in Nauvoo, in April 1841.[15] That same month, he also married nineteen-year-old Emily and twenty-two-year-old Eliza Partridge, two sisters whom Emma may have given to her husband in marriage. By that time, Joseph Smith had already married as many as eighteen other women. In all, he may have married as many as thirty women, some for "time"

13. Helen Mar Whitney, *Woman's Exponent* 10, no. 5, 1 August 1881, 34.

14. Address of Brigham Young, 8 October 1866, Brigham Young Papers, Church History Library.

15. See the LDS Church website essay on plural marriage entitled "Plural Marriage in Kirtland and Nauvoo," https://www.lds.org/topics/plural-marriage-in-kirtland-and-nauvoo?lang=eng.

and others for "time and eternity."[16] His brother Hyrum was at first a reluctant believer in the practice, but eventually he also accepted it, marrying at least three women. Wanting to support her husband but unwilling to share his affections with other wives, Emma found polygamy to be "an excruciating ordeal." She not only "vacillated" in her support of it but eventually denied that her husband had ever countenanced the practice. The intensely difficult matter of plural marriage contributed to her decision not to go west with the Saints in 1846 and in significant ways contributed to the establishment of the Reorganized Church of Jesus Christ of Latter Day Saints in 1860.[17]

The Prophet also instructed several others to enter quietly into the practice, although to speak little if anything about it, with most plural marriages performed in private homes. One of the first was Helen's own father, Heber C. Kimball. In early 1842 he married two spinster sisters, Laura Pitkin and Abigail Pitkin, both of whom were friends of the family, and soon afterwards the much younger Sarah Peak (Noon). [18] Vilate, Heber's original wife and devoted

16. To date, no solid evidence has been located to indicate that he had any children from any of his plural wives. See Ugo A. Perego, Natalie M. Myers, and Scott R. Woodward, "Reconstructing the Y-Chromosome of Joseph Smith: Genealogical Application," *Journal of Mormon History* 31, no. 2 (Summer 2005): 70–88.

17. At least twenty-nine other men married a total of fifty plural wives in Nauvoo before Joseph's death. Some scholars have estimated that as many as nine hundred plural marriages were performed in Nauvoo.

18. Stanley B. Kimball, *Heber C. Kimball: Mormon Patriarch and Pioneer* (Urbana: University of Illinois Press, 1986), 95.

Kirtland Temple, circa 1907. Photograph by George Edward Anderson. Courtesy of Church History Library.

Twenty-five sons and daughters of Heber C. Kimball, 14 June 1887. Helen Mar Whitney, middle row, fourth from left. Courtesy of Church History Library.

follower of the Prophet, after struggling with the principle, is on record as receiving a revelation dispelling her doubts and encouraging her not only to accept but also to promote plural marriage. Heber was eventually sealed to at least forty-three women before he died in 1868, with children from seventeen of them. Still, according to his biographer, "It was always Vilate who remained the center of his emotional life."[19]

Meanwhile, underscoring the secrecy of the practice, when Sarah Peak had a child in December 1842 (or early January 1843), Helen, who was now her stepdaughter, "had no knowledge then of the plural order," as she later recorded, "and therefore remained ignorant of our relationship to each other until after his [the infant's] death, as he only lived a few months. It's true I had noticed the great interest taken by my parents in behalf of Sister Noon [Peak] but . . . I thought nothing strange of this." [20]

Then on 27 July 1842, Bishop Newel K. Whitney and Elizabeth Ann gave their seventeen-year-old daughter, Sarah Ann Whitney, Horace's younger sister, to Joseph Smith in yet another plural marriage, with her father, Bishop Whitney, performing the ceremony and her

19. Kimball, *Heber C. Kimball*, 99.

20. Helen Mar Whitney, *Woman's Exponent*, vol. 11, no. 4, 15 July 1882, 26.

Daguerreotype of the Nauvoo Temple, ca. 1847. Photograph by Louis R. Chaffin. Original in the Cedar City Daughters of Utah Pioneers Museum. Used with permission.

Tithing Office, Salt Lake City, 1861. Charles W. Carter Collection, Church History Library.

mother standing by. "They willingly gave to him their daughter," said Helen of this event, "which was the strongest proof that they could possibly give of their faith and confidence in him as a true Prophet of God."[21]

Horace, however, was not so impressed. Though he soon afterwards accepted the call to serve a short-term mission east with Amasa Lyman, he remained unreconciled to the matter until later. According to Helen, "He had some slight suspicion that the stories about Joseph were not all without foundations, but had never told them, nor did he know the facts till after his return to Nauvoo, when Sarah hastened to tell him all. It was no small stumbling-block to him."[22]

In May 1843, Helen Mar Kimball was two or three months shy of her fifteenth birthday when Joseph Smith approached her parents seeking permission to marry their daughter. Anxious to have his family sealed to that of the Prophet's, Heber encouraged his daughter to accept the proposition. Astounded, Helen vacillated for the next twenty-four hours. "I was skeptical—one minute believed, then doubted," she later wrote. "I thought of the love and tenderness that he felt for his only daughter, and I knew that he would not cast her off, and this was the only convincing proof that I had of its being right. I knew that he loved me too well to teach me anything that was not strictly pure, virtuous and exalting in its tendencies; and no one else could have influenced me at that time or brought me to accept of a doctrine so utterly repugnant and so contrary to all of our former ideas and traditions."[23] In what might be termed a "dynastic" sealing between two of the most prominent families in early Mormonism, the Smith and Kimball houses would now be eternally linked together. Nevertheless, it almost broke her mother's heart. "She had witnessed the sufferings of others, who were older & who better understood the step they were taking," Helen later recalled. "& to see her child, who had scarcely seen her fifteenth summer, following in the same thorny path, in her mind she saw the misery which was as sure to come as the sun was to rise and set: but it was all hidden from me."[24]

With Joseph Smith's death in June 1844, Helen became a very young widow without child, sealed for eternity to the Prophet but with a full life ahead of her. Horace was then

21. Helen Mar Whitney, *Woman's Exponent*, vol. 11, no. 19, 1 March 1883, p. 146.
22. Helen Mar Whitney, *Woman's Exponent*, vol. 11, no. 19, 1 March 1883, p. 146.
23. Helen Mar Whitney, *Woman's Exponent*, vol. 11, no. 5, 1 August 1882, p. 39.
24. Autobiography of Helen Mar Kimball Whitney, 30 March 1881, MS 744, Church History Library.

twenty years old and looking for a companion. The two began dating and, putting all their doubts, questions, and misgivings aside, made plans to marry—eventually. Their courtship may have been shortened by circumstance, but they had long recognized they had much in common—by faith, interests, and disposition. And theirs was more than a platonic relationship. In one of his letters written somewhere along the Mormon Trail in Nebraska, Horace remembered some of those quieter, more intimate times: "I think of you all the time, and God knows, that my thoughts are frequently wafted home to the old chapel fireside, when we so much enjoyed each other's society at eventide."[25] However, the intense persecution surrounding the Saints in Nauvoo in late 1845 and the decision of church leaders to leave Nauvoo sooner rather than later led them to move quickly. Better to be married during the harrowing journey west, they figured, than to try to find one another in an unknown somewhere in the wilderness. Helen received her endowment on New Year's Day 1846, and on 3 February, just one day before the commotion of the Mormon exodus began, she and Horace went to the not-yet-dedicated Nauvoo Temple to exchange vows on their very special day.

What happened next was a strange twist. On their wedding day, Helen was sealed to Joseph Smith for eternity, with Horace standing proxy for the Prophet; then Horace and Helen were sealed together for time. The next day, Helen stood proxy as Horace was sealed to an Elizabeth Sykes, deceased. Todd Compton, in his book on Joseph Smith's many wives, refers to this as a "wistful sadness," a "bittersweet, paradoxical marriage" for young sweethearts that would go through life expecting to spend eternity with other companions.[26]

One would err, however, in concluding that their marriage for time would be an unhappy one. As Helen wrote in a short autobiography, "I loved and married your father. . . . We have lived happily together for over 35 years."[27] And despite the fact that they lost their first three children to the rigors of the exodus, they would have eight more. A staunch believer in the sanctity of plural marriage, Helen encouraged her husband, Horace, to take other wives, which he did. Nonetheless, Horace was never a strong supporter of polygamy. He obeyed it out of his enduring devotion to the Prophet Joseph but did so reluctantly. Like his father-in-law's marriage to Vilate, his first wife was preeminent. "You will always be the one, and the only one to whom I shall resort to pour out my griefs," he wrote in April 1849, "and from whom I shall expect that consolation which man sometimes stands in need of, and which can only be administered with effect by a dutiful and affectionate companion, which you have always proved yourself to be. . . . As long as you are mine, Helen, you shall continue to stand at the head."[28]

25. Horace K. Whitney to Helen Mar Kimball Whitney, 15 April 1847, Helen Mar Kimball Whitney Papers.

26. Todd Compton, *In Sacred Loneliness: The Plural Wives of Joseph Smith* (Salt Lake City: Signature Books, 1997), 486–87.

27. Autobiography of Helen Mar Kimball Whitney, 30 March 1881.

28. Horace K. Whitney to Helen Mar Kimball Whitney, 17 April 1849, Helen Mar Kimball Whitney Papers.

Departing Nauvoo in the vanguard company of the Twelve, and as their writings will attest, their honeymoon was more of a "honeymud," as they and their fellow Saints crossed Iowa together, victims of one of the wettest springs on record. Taken together, Horace's daily journal entries and Helen's reflective commentaries bring to life the love they shared one for another, their mutual faith in God and in Mormonism, and their hope for a new life with fellow believers in a new home "far away in the West."

In the years following their arrival in the Salt Lake Valley—Horace with the Brigham Young company of the Twelve in July 1847, and Helen in 1848, after Horace had visited Winter Quarters in the fall of '47—the two went on to live a happy married life. Horace worked as a clerk in the Tithing Office for twenty years. To augment his meager income, he also worked as one of the original compositors for the church-owned *Deseret News*, beginning in 1853. He fostered his love for music and the theater by becoming a member of various bands and orchestras and by serving as an officer in the Deseret Dramatic Association. He also served a second mission for the church, this one back to the Ohio of his childhood, in 1869–70. Ever faithful to the church, he once penned the following: "My intention is to live humbly and prayerfully, bear a faithful testimony to the truth, and in all things honorably acquit myself before God and man."[29] Horace Whitney married at least two other women—including Lucy Amelia Bloxham in 1850, by whom he had one child; and Mary Cravath in 1856. He and Mary had fourteen children, making a grand total of twenty-six children. He successfully passed that legacy of faith on to his children, one of whom, Orson F. Whitney, himself a very gifted writer and speaker, served twenty-nine years in the Quorum of the Twelve Apostles, from 1906 to 1935. Horace died in Salt Lake City on 22 November 1884 at age sixty-one.

Helen Mar lived on to publish a series of reminiscences of the Mormon exodus in her later life in the *Woman's Exponent*, a literary magazine aimed at the Mormon female audience, that constitutes a fine complement to her husband's diaries. Together, these two records form one of the most comprehensive records of the Mormon exodus extant and certainly the best husband-wife account available. She also published two booklets in defense of polygamy and of her teenage marriage to Joseph Smith.[30] Concerning her defense of plural marriage, she later wrote: "It was to be a life-sacrifice for the sake of an everlasting glory and exaltation," a principle "calculated to purify and exalt the human family."[31] And, speaking of her own teenage marriage to the Prophet and of those many women who married Joseph Smith, she wrote the following late in her life: "We may read the history of martyrs and mighty conquerors, and of many great and good men and women, but that of the noble women and fair daughters of Zion, whose faith in the promises of Israel's God enabled them to triumph over self and obey His higher law, and assist His servants to establish it upon the earth, though

29. Horace K. Whitney to his family, 26 November 1869, Helen Mar Kimball Whitney Papers.

30. Helen Mar Whitney, *Plural Marriage as Taught by the Prophet Joseph Smith: A Reply to Joseph Smith, Editor of the Lamoni (Iowa) Herald* (Salt Lake City: Juvenile Instructor Office, 1882), and Helen Mar Whitney, *Why We Practice Plural Marriage* (Salt Lake City: Juvenile Instructor Office, 1884).

31. *Woman's Exponent*, vol. 9 no. 15, 1 January 1881, p. 114, and vol. 11, no. 19, 1 March 1883, p. 146.

buried in the past, I feel sure there was kept by the angels an account of their works which will yet be found in the records of eternity, written in letters of *gold*."[32] Faithful to the Latter-day Saint cause, Helen Mar died in Salt Lake City a half century later, on 15 November 1896, twelve years after the death of her husband, and six years after President Wilford Woodruff's Manifesto signaling an end to the Mormon practice of polygamy.

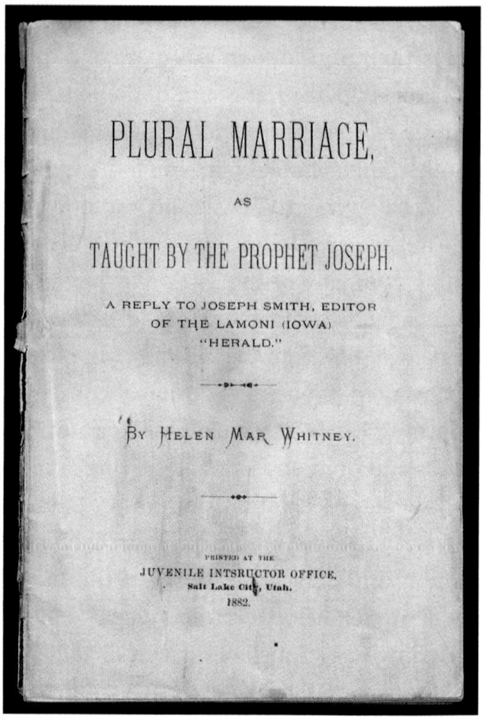
PLURAL MARRIAGE,

AS

TAUGHT BY THE PROPHET JOSEPH.

A REPLY TO JOSEPH SMITH, EDITOR OF THE LAMONI (IOWA) "HERALD."

BY HELEN MAR WHITNEY.

PRINTED AT THE
JUVENILE INTSRUCTOR OFFICE,
Salt Lake City, Utah.
1882.

Helen Mar Whitney, Plural Marriage as Taught by the Prophet Joseph. *Church History Library.*

Scope

Returning now to the larger story of the Mormon exodus of 1846–47, it might be helpful to view it in its five distinct phases:

1. Departure from Nauvoo, Illinois, and the crossing of Iowa Territory, February–August 1846
2. Winter Quarters (Nebraska) settlement, fall 1846–spring 1847 (and later in Kanesville, Iowa, just across the Missouri River)
3. Vanguard company journey of the original Mormon pioneers under the direction of Brigham Young from the Missouri River Valley to the Valley of the Great Salt Lake, 1 April–24 July 1847
4. Original summer settlement in the Salt Lake Valley, complete with the building of fortifications, planting crops, and establishing colonization priorities, 25 July–31 August 1847
5. Return trip of the company of the Twelve Apostles and other church leaders from the Salt Lake Valley back to Winter Quarters, late August–31 October 1847

Several excellent journals have been published over the years that document this exciting chapter in Mormon history, including those of Thomas Bullock, William Clayton, Orson Pratt, Hosea Stout, Howard Egan, Norton Jacob, and Wilford Woodruff. Each has its own unique strengths and limitations. It is in comparison to these journals that the writings of

32. Helen Mar Whitney, *Woman's Exponent*, vol. 10, no. 11, 1 November 1881, p. 83.

Horace K. Whitney and Helen Mar take on special significance. Some of these pioneer journals cover only portions of the Mormon exodus as diagramed below.

DIARISTS	SEGMENTS (TAKEN FROM THE ABOVE FIVE DISTINCT PARTS)				
	1	2	3	4	5
Thomas Bullock			x	x	x
Wilford Woodruff			x	x	x
Hosea Stout	x	x			
Orson Pratt	x	x	x		
William Clayton	x	x	x	x	x
Norton Jacob	x	x	x	x	x
Howard Egan	x	x	x	x	x
Horace K. Whitney	x	x	x	x	x
Appleton Milo Harmon			x		

The Whitney journals also cover all five segments and provide a very complete account of the entire story. When Helen Mar's reminiscences are included, they provide not only a woman's essential perspective but a very personal, very faithful view as well. And although it is true that her reflections have twice before been published, never have they been so carefully aligned, as they are herein, to the everyday life on the Mormon Trail.[33] His and her writings are wonderfully synergetic, revealing, and supportive, and, when read in tandem one with another, like looking through a pair of binoculars, they clarify the many stories of the exodus, illuminate our understanding, and provide focus and a fuller, clearer, and more correct viewing of this important moment in time.

PHASE 1: CROSSING IOWA

Everything was supposed to happen in 1846.[34] The vanguard companies of approximately 2,500 left Nauvoo in early February 1846. The original plan was to cross Iowa in four to six weeks, get across the Missouri river, and then for Brigham Young and a handpicked number of the best pioneers to head west and find a suitable valley somewhere in "the tops of the Rocky Mountains." However, "Brother Brigham" might have been able to escape his enemies

33. Helen Mar's accounts have been published in the *Woman's Exponent* and in *A Woman's View: Helen Mar Whitney's Reminiscences of Church History*, ed. Jeni Broberg Holzapfel and Richard Neitzel Holzapfel (Provo, UT: Religious Studies Center, 1997). The reminiscences of Helen Mar herein included are selective, not exhaustive, and are included to amplify and illustrate her husband's journals.

34. "It being the intention at that time to cross over the Rocky Mountains the same year." Whitney Journals, 31 March 1846.

but he could never get away from his people. At one point, in exasperation he said to his followers who were afraid of being left behind:

> The Saints have crowded on us all the while, and have completely tied our hands by importuning and saying: Do not leave us behind. Wherever you go, we want to go, be with you, and thus our hands and feet have been bound which has caused our delay to the present time, and now hundreds at Nauvoo are continually praying . . . that they may overtake us and be with us. . . . They are afraid to let us go on and leave them behind, forgetting that they have covenanted to help the poor away at the sacrifice of all their property.[35]

This matter of covenant points to the fact that the Latter-day Saint leaders saw their exodus as an extension of the law of consecration and that if they lived in obedience to that promise, all would go well. However, such crowding, delays, and insufferable heavy rains during that spring of 1846 impeded their progress. Hundreds were left back at Garden Grove and Mount Pisgah, their hastily erected way stations in Iowa Territory that they established to preserve their health and strength and to put in crops for the thousands yet to follow. As a result, instead of crossing Iowa in four to six weeks, it took them three months! When Brigham Young and his advance company finally reached the Missouri on 14 June 1846, it was all but too late to make a dash for the Rockies.

Whitney's journal attests abundantly to the trials and travails of crossing Iowa. Writing on 11 April, he noted the following: "Some of my fathers' teams got stuck in the mud, and had to stop a mile or two back and none reached us except J. C. K[ingsbury] with the buggy, the one horse wagon, and Sarah Ann's wagon. Bro. Pond broke his harness in attempting to extricate himself from a mud-hole." Upon reaching the Grand River on 1 May, he wrote this entry: "The weather has been so inclement since our arrival that our stay here will necessarily be protracted beyond the time originally intended." Whitney not only speaks corroboratively of their well-known troubles crossing Iowa but likewise offers a farm-hand's observations into the building of both Garden Grove and Mount Pisgah, insights not always afforded by other diarists. For instance, the following is his description of the early days at Garden Grove: "There are a hundred men assigned to this business, 10 laying up rails, 48 to building houses, 12 to each house – 10 herding cattle, 12 digging wells, 10 building a bridge across the river for to pass over on our journey west, 10 stocking ploughs and making drays, 5 or 6 blacksmith shops started, the remainder to attend to the business of farming, etc. etc."[36]

Phase 2. Winter Quarters, September 1846–April 1847

Horace's and Helen's writings reflect the fresh vantage point of a young, highly committed Mormon pioneer couple, which lends a unique spirit of anticipation and faith to their

35. Journal History of the Church of Jesus Christ of Latter-day Saints, 3 May 1846 (hereafter Journal History).

36. Whitney Journals, 27 April 1846.

observations. Contrasted with some other journals—like the writings of Hosea Stout, which tend to be critical, suspicious, and dark—the Whitneys wrote with a certain youthful alacrity.[37] Nevertheless, his writing style and sense of detail ofttimes are of the mundane, everyday variety, often lacking the emotion of the moment, a dimension his wife often added to complete the story.

Their insights are particularly revealing about the trying and very difficult Winter Quarters segment of the exodus, that period extending from the fall of 1846 until April the following year. The Saints' first priority was planting spring crops, hay cropping, branding, and otherwise taking care of the thousands of head of cattle and sheep that were mostly confined in the "rush bottoms" some hundred miles upriver. They then turned their attention to fashioning crude living quarters. More than any other observer, Horace explains how they survived that difficult winter. He informs us on what cabins they built, how they were constructed, how they were aligned throughout their makeshift community, and much more pertaining to the social life of their new city. While many passed the fall and early winter living in tents with wind-torn canvases, in caves dug out of the side of the Missouri riverbanks, or in wagons exposed to the elements, Horace speaks of the tireless energy required to build lifesaving, if hastily erected, cabins for as many as possible: "Saturday the 7th: Fine day. Engaged in roofing and sodding the second house into one room of which we [he and wife, Helen Mar] moved this evening, the other room being occupied by Sister Kimball [his mother-in-law] and Mary Kimball. We congratulated ourselves considerably upon being able to live in a house once again, as we have got thoroughly tired of living in tents."[38]

His journals also speak of digging thirty-five-feet-deep wells and building, chinking, and daubing dozens of hastily built log cabins, often one or more in a day or two, each five to seven feet high with sod chimneys, tent awnings supporting dirt-covered roofs with freshly cut wooden shingles, and dirt floors. They erected their cabins very close to each other and in a "compact body" so that they might be "better able to defend ourselves against [Indian] encroachments."[39]

These lodgings were not only drafty and often cold; they were not always the safest things to live in. "This evening a fire was discovered under the hearth in Bro. K[imball]'s room," Horace recorded in January 1847. "We took down the better part of the chimney in order to get at the fire, which we put out, and rebuilt the chimney, this taking till half past 4 in the morning. Bro. K. felt very thankful that the fire did not occur in the night when we were all asleep, as there was 5 or 6 lbs of powder in a chest near the fire place, in addition to the danger incurred by the fire otherwise."[40]

37. For the best study of Hosea Stout, see *On the Mormon Frontier: The Diary of Hosea Stout*, ed. Juanita Brooks, 2 vols. (Salt Lake City: University of Utah Press, 1974).

38. Whitney Journals, 7 November 1846.

39. Whitney Journals, 13 December 1846.

40. Whitney Journals, 18 January 1847.

Horace likewise provides us with much information on the construction of the Winter Quarters Council House, which, much like the Newel K. Whitney store back in Kirtland, Ohio, would serve as the mercantile establishment and central gathering place for the Mormon settlement. Highly frugal in his own personal expenditures, Horace gives more financial details than most other diarists, complete with costs and expenditures. Such information allows us to reconstruct and understand the Winter Quarters economy.

He also describes the many dances, balls, and festive occasions that the Mormons held during that winter, as if to defy and stave off the darkness and sadness of that fateful time. A member of the Nauvoo brass band that now had been revived in Winter Quarters, Whitney also tells of one round of parties after another, whether with the bishops charged with taking care of the wives of the Mormon Battalion, the quorums of high priests, the "Silver Greys" of older folks, or some other group. "Ellis Eames, a player on the violin, came up from the Point [Council Point]," he recorded on 1 March 1847. "A number of [the] Band including him and myself went round in a sleigh this evening, (Porter driving) and serenaded several places in the town. Bro. K. was along with us. We stopt at Bishop Hunter's and played a tune and then by invitation of Bro. K., went to his house, where we spent some time in dancing, etc. and retired." [41]

Yet Horace and Helen Whitney were not oblivious to the sufferings and agonies of many around them that fateful winter. Sometimes referred to as Mormonism's Valley Forge, the Latter-day Saints' stay at the Missouri River in the winter of 1846–47 was a testing point of faith. William Clayton's hymn of sacrifice and endurance—"Come, Come, Ye Saints"—spoke of holding on despite every challenge. This prairie anthem of the exodus said in part, "And should we die before our journey's through, happy day! All is well!"—a foreboding of worse times to come. Because of their long exposure to the elements, their poor and substandard housing once they reached the Missouri, and the outbreak of such deadly diseases as malaria and scurvy, the Mormons began to perish in epidemic numbers. At least 1,200 died (one in ten) within two years of their arrival at Council Bluffs. These were frightening times among a people who believed they were on God's errand. And Horace speaks much about it, although without criticism, rancor, or disbelief. His accounts of life at Winter Quarters are incomparably rich and detailed and unbelievably positive for such a dire moment, striking a tone of deliberate faithfulness in their furnace of affliction.

A good example of this is his characteristically matter-of-fact entry in October 1846:

> Commenced raining this afternoon. . . . Forgot to mention that Eliza Ann Pierson, a niece of Dr. Willard [Richards] died last evening at his tent. She had left father and mother far behind, to join the saints of God in the wilderness, to suffer and die among them for the gospel's sake. She was a worthy, exemplary young person, and the remembrance of the many happy hours I have passed in her society, together with her sisters and friends, will never be obliterated, while time shall last. She was from Richmond,

41. Whitney Journals, 1 March 1847.

> Massachusetts, where I became acquainted with her during my sojourn in the E[astern] States.

Not content to dwell on such sadness, he ends his entry thus: "This afternoon the brethren drove into camp all the cattle they found during their search yesterday which covered a large space of ground."[42]

Indeed, most of his entries are as cheerful and upbeat as they are contemporary in the sense that they were usually recorded the day, or the day after, the events occurred. For example, in the midst of profound sickness, serious privations, and enormously hard work, Horace continuously sees the positive as indicated in the following entry: "William, Porter and myself took a walk around the city [Winter Quarters] this afternoon, the first time that we three have had a social walk and 'chat', since we left the city of Nauvoo. There seems to be a particular dispensation of Providence in our behalf; for although, we have had several cold nights and frosty ones, the weather had been remarkably mild for winter, and we have not, as yet, experienced the first snow storm." [43] This silver lining descriptive approach, written at a time when they knew so many were perishing, permeates much of his descriptions.

Writing in December 1846, Horace makes reference without elaboration to the tragedy that struck Stillman Pond, who eventually lost his wife and four children: "Rather cool today. Today Abigail Pond died, her two sisters, Harriet and Jane died a day or two ago."[44] Writing months later of a time when hundreds of others had perished, he records: "Fine day. Nothing of importance to-day. . . . There is a disease, called by the folks here, the 'black-leg,' getting quite prevalent in the camp. It commences with a sharp pain in the ankles, swells, and finally the leg gets almost black, and in many cases it proves fatal. There have a great many died, within the last month. It is caused, in a great measure, by the want of vegetable food, and having to eat salt food."[45]

Thus Horace takes time to mention the sad and the sorrowful but never gives in to it or provides it undue time or space. While we may regret the lack of intense emotion in his diaries, one senses from them a sheer determination not to surrender to the darkness and discouragements closing in around them. Their everyday efforts at survival drive from off the page any lengthy gloomy ruminations of how bad things had become.

Phase 3: To the Valley of the Great Salt Lake, April–July 1847

Horace Whitney's fascination with the American Indian is well covered in his accounts. These include the Otoe, Omaha, Ponca, Pottawattamie, Pawnee, Sioux, Shoshone, and Ute tribes. He speaks in a fair-minded way of their habits, tribal warfare, trading practices, lodgings, hunting patterns, fears, and frustrations. Occasionally, he writes of how they were

42. Whitney Journals, 11 October 1846.

43. Whitney Journals, 22 November 1846.

44. Whitney Journals, 7 December 1846.

45. Whitney Journals, 18 March 1847.

mistreated and misunderstood by others. For example, the following entry tells of the government payments made for certain Indian land properties at the Missouri.

> Bro. C. [Layton] informs me he never saw such a swindling operation as that practiced on the Indians down there, they receiving their payments in money and then followed by a gang of sharpers who watch their opportunity, get them drunk and then gamble with them and cheat them out all their money. Bro. John Kay came down here from the Punkaw [Ponca] nation. He has been out with them hunting since he left here and will rejoin them in 6 weeks from this time.[46]

And then there is this very sad observation:

> This evening, the [Omaha] Indians encamped near Brigham's, had a great powwow among them, screeching and yelling in a horrible manner on account of their having just received intelligence that a large number of their warriors, who went on the hunting expedition a short time since, having been killed off by the Sioux.[47]

A member of Brigham Young's 148 handpicked pioneers who left Winter Quarters in April 1847, Horace constantly tells of their encounters with other tribes. For instance, their deliberate calculation to make their own trail on the north side of the Platte rather than to follow the California and Oregon Trail on the south side brought them square into Pawnee country and right through the heart of the Pawnee Indian villages. The belief was that it was better to make peace with them up front. Writing in late April near the Pawnee Indian villages on the north side of the Platte, he records: "Pres't Young . . . said that if we had an attack from Indians, it would be from the Sioux, not the Pawnees, for the latter knew that the former were in the country and were watching them – that the Sioux when they came to make an attack, always [down] a little ravine that lies north-east of us." [48]

Horace describes what he saw upon reaching the Pawnee village: "Orson and myself went and took a view of the ruins of the Pawnee village which was an interesting sight, indeed, and gave me singular feelings. The village is situated on the northern bank of and immediately fronting the river – it is irregularly formed, or laid out, is 1¼ a mile in extent and comprised upwards of 200 lodges, a great share of which have been burnt down by the Sioux." [49] One reason the Mormons brought a cannon with them was to scare off possible Indian attacks, attacks that never came.

All across Nebraska and Wyoming, Horace offers daily insights on the weather, the Platte River, buffalo—"the plain is perfectly black with them"—and their many hunting expeditions, accidents along the trail, camp life, Sunday sermons, daily mileages, and multiple creek and river crossings. As with the authors of most other overland trail journals, he is impressed with the changing topography and gives ample attention to such trail landmarks

46. Whitney Journals, 6 November 1846.

47. Whitney Journals, 12 December 1846.

48. Whitney Journals, 22 April 1846.

49. Whitney Journals, 24 April 1846.

as Ash Hollow, Chimney Rock (which they reached in late May), Scott's Bluff, Fort Laramie, Independence Rock, South Pass, Fort Bridger, and ultimately the Salt Lake Valley.

His journals are unexceptional in their daily accounts. The Orson Pratt and William Clayton journals are more explicit and more exciting in this regard. The major contribution of Horace's journals is providing us with an understanding of the organization of the companies of the Saints and the doctrinal underpinnings surrounding it. Although not the official clerk of any of the pioneer companies, young Horace K. Whitney, as the son of presiding Bishop Newel K. Whitney, was a trusted secretary to Brigham Young and knew well the inner operations of the church for several years. Though still young, Horace was tasked by Brigham Young and other prominent leaders to keep their records, provide secretarial services, and record carefully and legibly the comings and goings of the Saints. For instance, it was Horace who recorded Joseph Smith's revelation on eternal/celestial (plural) marriage (now section 132 of the Doctrine and Covenants). Having grown up in the church, he and his wife knew the operations of church leadership firsthand, were highly trusted, and were more seasoned in the doctrine, culture, and family practices of Mormonism than most others were.

Another deficiency of Horace's journals is that, unlike the Wilford Woodruff journals, they are not generally given to spiritual ruminations. As a young husband, laborer, sheepherder, and all-around construction worker, Horace is much closer to the hands-on, basic everyday survival activities of the camps. These routine but essential duties included herding sheep and cattle, working with the various Indian tribes, hunting and fishing, putting in crops and successfully establishing the new Salt Lake settlement in the summer of 1847, and undertaking a myriad of other life-sustaining responsibilities. Helen Mar's reminiscences often provide the spiritual flavor and perspective that her husband's daily recordings sometimes miss.

Yet the careful observer will also see much more in his journals than merely descriptions of the physical. Carefully tucked away within them are keys to a remarkable understanding of unique Mormon doctrines and practices as they were beginning to play out on the outer edges of the great American wilderness. As mentioned above, Joseph Smith had introduced the concept of the eternality of the marriage covenant shortly before his death in 1844 and along with it the practice of "celestial" or plural marriage. Not nearly so well understood was the "law of adoption," also revealed in Nauvoo and played out here along the Mormon Trail.[50]

This principle had both a doctrinal and a social application. The doctrine of the law of adoption based itself upon the belief that salvation in the next life was partly dependent upon one's actions in this sphere. These included being "sealed" to someone who held the

50. For a good introduction to the law of adoption, see Gordon Irving, "The Law of Adoption: One Phase of the Development of the Mormon Concept of Salvation, 1830–1900," *BYU Studies* 14, no. 3 (Spring 1974): 291–314. See also Richard E. Bennett, *Mormons at the Missouri, 1846–1852: "And Should We Die"* (Norman: University of Oklahoma Press, 1987). For the most current study of the topic, see Jonathan A. Stapley, *The Power of Godliness: Mormon Liturgy and Cosmology* (New York: Oxford, 2018).

power or priesthood of God and more specifically to someone who held such priesthood "keys" and authorities. And as with their trek west, which demanded the consecration and cooperation of everyone working together in camp, the Latter-day Saint view of salvation was arguably less an individual concern and more a group or family matter. As they wended their way west, it was, as William Clayton reminded them in his song, always a matter of "*we'll* find the place" and of "should *we* die" rather than going it alone. Either they make it in the company of others in this life or in the next, or they do not.

The law of adoption was an early expression of this group salvation concept. The uniquely Mormon doctrine of baptisms for the dead, practiced in Nauvoo since 1841, was based upon the belief that families must somehow be "linked" together in one great family chain extending back into the mists of earthly time and that such extended and extensive earthly families could be welded together by priesthood authority and ordinances hereafter. As Joseph Smith's revelations put it: "The earth will be smitten with a curse unless there is a welding link of some kind or other between the [ancestral] fathers and the children, upon some subject or other—and behold what is that subject? It is the baptism for the dead" (D&C 128:18). To speak of baptisms for the dead without intergenerational family sealings is to miss a critical point of their belief.

A problem in this developing doctrine of salvation at this very early formative time was that deceased ancestors and ancestral families had died and gone on without the saving power of the priesthood. To be sealed to a man who had not the gospel in his life and who had never received the priesthood was not yet clear or convincing in Mormon thinking. In fact, it would not be until 1877 in the St. George (Utah) Temple that endowments for the dead and multigenerational *family* sealings began.[51] Until then, the Saints' understanding was that they should be sealed or "adopted" into *priesthood* families, represented best by church leaders or general authorities, living or dead.

The essential thing was for the male head of the family—and his plural marriage wives and families—to be sealed or "adopted" to those priesthood leaders over him who held the keys of authority and eternal life in a vertical interconnected chain of priesthood-based, assured salvation. The practice of plural marriage, by which additional wives were sealed or married to the same man, was an extension or appendage to this doctrinal understanding, the horizontal branches to the ever-expanding vertical kingdom or tree of family salvation. And for a man to be an adopted son of such a family, or a woman to be sealed through being married, plurally if need be, provided an expectation of a more economically secure living in this world and the assurance of an eternal one hereafter complete with family and friends. Small wonder such practices were of great importance to this growing number of Latter-day Saints, many of whom wondered if they would survive their impending trials.

---

51. For more on this subject, see Richard E. Bennett, "'Line upon Line, Precept upon Precept': Revelations on the 1877 Commencement of the Performance of Endowments and Sealings for the Dead," *BYU Studies* 44, no. 2 (2005): 38–77.

The practice of the law of adoption also influenced both the social order of the Winter Quarters community as well as its travel patterns. It often dictated social spheres of influence and one's circle of friends and associates, even the locale of their tents or cabins. One's place in the family hierarchy provided some kind of social stratification. Those in Brigham Young's expanding family lived fairly close to one another, as did those in Heber C. Kimball's family, Wilford Woodruff's, Willard Richards's, and those of other prominent church leaders. The expectation was that in return for spiritual blessings and eternal inheritances due from their spiritual fathers, adopted sons and families owed them physical support.

Occasionally large adopted-family or tribal-family meetings convened in Winter Quarters and along the trail for instructional purposes. Brigham Young remarked as follows in one such meeting:

> Those that are adopted into my family . . . I will preside over them throughout all eternity and will stand at their head. Joseph [Smith] will stand at the head of this Church and will be their president, prophet and god to the people in this dispensation. When we locate [in the mountains] I will settle my family down in the order and teach them their duties. They will then have to provide temporal blessings for me instead of my boarding from 40 to 50 persons as I do now, and will administer spiritual blessings for them.[52]

Homes of Horace K. Whitney's wives (Helen Mar and Mary Cravath) and families, 26 E. North Temple, Salt Lake City. Courtesy of Church History Library.

52. Journal of John D. Lee, 16 February 1847, as quoted in Bennett, *Mormons at the Missouri*, 192.

Here, then, is a key reason why the Horace Whitney diaries take on increasing significance. His biological father and presiding bishop over the entire Church, Newel K. Whitney, was an adopted son—in the priesthood lineage sense described above—of apostle Heber C. Kimball, who coincidentally was also the biological father of Horace's wife, Helen Mar Kimball (Smith) Whitney. Thus he belonged to the Kimball family before being married into it. Horace identifies by name a large number of three or four dozen men and their families who also belonged by the law of adoption to Heber Kimball: Jackson Redding, Asa Davis, Howard Egan, Dan Davis, Ellis Sanders, J. M. Grant, Alfred Randall, to name but a few.[53] He even spent most of one day and part of the next in early January making out a list of the entire Kimball clan.[54] Many of the Kimball family log cabins were erected in close proximity one to another, a Kimball enclave within an already tightly drawn Mormon wilderness community. By extension, the whole of Winter Quarters was "familyized" or "tribalized" in similar fashion. Horace's diaries, therefore, provide us with a fuller understanding of the complicated social order among the Latter-day Saints and of developing doctrines and practices attendant to the exodus.

The original plan of their travels west was supposed to have followed after this tribal pattern. During wintertime deliberations in mid-January at the newly constructed Council House, Brigham Young drew up plans to have the first company or "division" of one hundred be drawn from his adopted/spiritual family, the second hundred from Heber C. Kimball's, and so forth, with a liberal sprinkling of Mormon Battalion family members.[55] Though this plan was eventually discarded in favor of a handpicked crew of well-skilled teamsters, farmers, fishermen, surveyors, explorers, and other pioneers, several of those in the vanguard company identified themselves as belonging to one family clan or another.

In unofficially recording the essence of some of these large adopted family meetings, Horace Whitney provides invaluable insights into the need for such adoptions and the intergenerational linkages they entailed. Said father Heber C. Kimball after listening to comments from his adopted son, presiding bishop Newel K. Whitney:

> I have been much edified by the conversation of Brother Whitney, and we always had the same feelings in common and our views always met, and our thoughts flow in the same channel. . . . I am your head, your lawgiver, and king, and will be, to all eternity, and I am responsible to my head and President and you are responsible to me, your file leader. I believe that some of my old progenitors, of whom I have no knowledge, will appear and tell me when the time shall come for me to rise up and administer in the ordinances for them, and I shall receive a great deal of knowledge from them. . . . I want to have power, when I see my brother and sister, to tell Death to depart.[56]

53. Whitney Journals, 19 October 1846.
54. Whitney Journals, 1 and 2 January 1847.
55. Whitney Journals, 18–22 January 1847.
56. Whitney Journals, 14 February 1847.

Thus from time to time, whether at Winter Quarters or at various resting places along the trail, Horace and Helen Mar provide profound doctrinal insights into Mormon thought and social practices as they were developing along their way west.

Phase 4: The Salt Lake Valley Settlement, 25 July–31 August 1847

Unfortunately, upon reaching the Salt Lake Valley on 24 July 1847, Horace Whitney says nothing about what Brigham Young may or may not have said when he first saw the future home of the Mormon people. For his part, he writes, "Going down several steep descents, we at length emerged from the pass (having come 4 miles) and were highly gratified with a fine view of the open country and the 'Great Salt Lake,' whose blue surface could be seen in the distance with a lofty range of mountains in the background." Not given to hyperbole, Horace stoops to discover something closer by, something that will later come to discomfort the Mormon settlements like little else could. "One thing I omitted to mention, viz. there are numerous black crickets of an enormous size to be seen here."[57] He does, however, record in early August, just prior to their return to Winter Quarters, that Brigham Young decided that the Salt Lake Valley was indeed the right place to locate their city and to build their temple. Said he: "This is the spot that I had anticipated. They will not have a hard winter here. The highest mountains are near 1¼ miles high. We will find that sugar cane and sweet potatoes will grow here. . . . There never was a better or richer soil than this."[58]

Reaching the floor of the valley on his twenty-fifth birthday, Horace speaks of the need for immediate irrigation efforts, early scouting expeditions, Brigham Young's satisfaction with the valley as their "promised land," edifying sermons in celebration of finding their place, hunting expeditions, floating on the Great Salt Lake, and feverishly planting crops in soil better than they had anticipated—all with the excitement of a young child on a Christmas morn. He also tells of surveying their new city under the direction of Henry G. Sherwood; fencing and building stockades, adobe houses, log cabins, and a bowery; and their first encounters with the Shoshone and Eutaw Indians.

More optimistic than he had been in Winter Quarters, Horace permeates his writings with a spirit of redemption, a promise now fulfilled, a place sought after and now discovered. To that end, he records Heber C. Kimball's 22 August 1847 sermon in detail: "I wish to God, we had not got to return. If I had my family here, I would give anything I have. This is a Paradise to me. It is one of the most lovely places I ever beheld. I hope none of us will be left to pollute this land."[59]

57. Whitney Journals, 24 July 1847.

58. Whitney Journals, 8 August 1847.

59. Whitney Journals, 22 August 1847.

Phase 5: Return to Winter Quarters, September–October 1847

But return they must. The account of the return of 108 men, including Brigham Young, Heber C. Kimball, and most of the other leading authorities of the church, is not well documented in most other leading Mormon exodus journals. However, it is a story amply documented in Horace's writings, as he was among the few directed to return. Leaving the valley on 26 August 1847, the return company made much faster mileage going back than they ever did coming out. Often they covered twenty-two to twenty-eight miles per day, compared to fifteen on the outbound journey. Some reasons for this were their knowledge of the trail, much lighter and fewer wagons, the use of horses rather than oxen, their knowledge of the best camping spots, and shallower creeks and rivers because of the lateness of the season. Among the highlights of their return trip was meeting the so-called Emigrant Camp or "Big Camps" of Mormons heading west under the direction of Parley P. Pratt and John Taylor.

Upon reaching Winter Quarters on 30 October after traveling over two thousand miles over a trackless wilderness, finding a new city and a new hope for the Saints, and enduring privations of almost every kind, the matter-of-fact Horace K. Whitney ended his voluminous journals with the following:

> An expression was then taken whether we should all remain in a body, horsemen and all, and go into town together or otherwise; which resulted in the affirmative. Pres't Young and Bro. Heber then spoke briefly, stating that they were satisfied with the conduct of the Pioneers during the journey of the past season, and blessed them in the name of the Lord; and soon after we were dismissed with the injunction to provide plenty of cotton wood for our horses during the night. Bro. Heber let me have a little flour to-night, as my provisions had all given out.[60]

Conclusion

In summary, the Horace K. Whitney journals and the Helen Mar Whitney reminiscences which accompany them are a two-part history. A young husband–wife duo of writings, they add a freshness and vitality to a well-worn story. While his writings are given more to the nondescript details of everyday living, hers are more of the reflective, ruminating variety. Taken together, they provide remarkably candid insights into the peculiar beliefs, customs, and practices of their people. And, while discussing the negative and the forlorn, they both maintain a cheerful, youthful tone and honest perspective. Combined into one, they are a lasting tribute to those men and women who made so many sacrifices in the cause of their faith and in the hope of a new life "far away in the West."

60. Whitney Journals, 30 October 1847.

Editor's Notes

Editing and annotating the six 1846–47 pioneer journals of Horace K. Whitney, which cover 631 pages and contain some two hundred thousand handwritten words, has been a daunting challenge. The leather-bound journals themselves are remarkably well preserved some 170 years later. And, fortunately for modern readers, Whitney was a well-educated person, a preferred scribe in the camps, with a good command of the English language; however, he often wrote on the fly, in a hurry, and usually at night, with only the flicker of a lonely candle to light his way. Thus, his prairie trail penmanship is not always easy to read. Fortunately, his entries were recorded almost always in ink, with very little fading of the original. Nevertheless, at least three pairs of eyes have carefully compared his original to the typescript and our final digitized version, often with the aid of a magnifying glass.

The addition of the reminiscent writings of his wife, Helen Mar Kimball Whitney, will greatly contribute to the value of his journals. Whereas every word of his journals has been copied, transcribed, and carefully edited, Helen Mar's reminiscences are selectively chosen based upon their relevancy to her husband's accounts. Though published previously, they have never before been coupled with her husband's journals. Together, they take on a unique male/female, contemporary/reflective perspective on the many stories and details of the early Mormon exodus. Her entries are italicized after her husband's daily journal entries.

To further enrich this work, I have added a substantial number of footnotes that explain events, places, significant experiences, and Mormon doctrines and practices that should assist the reader. Very few names are included in the footnotes (with the exception of non–Latter-day Saints met on the trail); however, virtually every other name mentioned in the Whitney journals is briefly described with dates of birth and death and lifetime highlights. These are located in the glossary of names found near the end of the book. It represents one of the more complete listings of Latter-day Saints who were moving west in 1846–47 and that alone may be worth the "cost of admission."

The following editing guidelines and procedures have been followed:

- The precise spelling, grammar, and capitalization of the original journals and reminiscences have been preserved, including incorrect place-names and other errors of fact; however, in cases of an obvious or egregious error, I have occasionally included the intrusive term *sic*, meaning "as found in the original work." Editorial insertions, when deemed necessary for clarification within the texts, have been made within [square brackets] as opposed to (parenthesis) originally inserted by the Whitneys themselves.
- The many explanatory footnotes that I have added to the text and inserted at the bottom of the page are provided to add color, commentary, elucidation, and valuable related information; they are usually placed at the end of sentences and daily entries.
- The use of **** in Helen Mar's reminiscences reflects her own redactions and original omissions of text.
- Time references in the journals are "a.m." and "P. M." in the original text and have been retained accordingly.
- Columns of names, ledger and accounting entries, mileages, etc., have been preserved as closely as possible to the originals, although with some slight variations.
- In almost all cases, periods, commas, apostrophes, dashes, and underlines are retained, regardless of their grammatical correctness; however, occasionally punctuation has been added or altered for clarification—[,] or [.].
- Occasionally, first names have been added in [square brackets] within the text where confusion may exist because of duplication of names or other incongruities.
- The dashes found in the original journals have been preserved, though they are somewhat out of style today.
- Occasionally, years have been added to the original entry for clarification purposes.
- The pagination found herein is continuous throughout all six of the Whitney journals, whereas, in the originals, each journal has its own separate pagination, if at all.

In sum, every effort has been made to ensure accuracy, clarity, and completeness so that the reader can rest assured that what is offered here is a faithful representation of what Horace Whitney and Helen Mar recorded by hand in his journals and in her reminiscences.

Illustrations

A
Journal,

Kept by H. K. Whitney,
during the journey and
sojourn of the Church
of Jesus Christ of
Latter-day Saints
in the wilderness,
Anno Domini,

1846.

Journal 1

15 February–15 July 1846

A

JOURNAL

Kept by H. K. Whitney,

during the Journey and

sojourn of the church

of Jesus Christ of

Latter-day Saints

in the wilderness,

Anno Domini,

1846.

Sunday, the 15th of February 1846

President Brigham Young, with his family, crossed the river at Nauvoo, and repaired to the encampment on Sugar Creek, I. T. seven miles from the opposite side.[1]

In that first exodus there was such a great desire among the people and such a determination to emigrate with the first company that there were hundreds started without the necessary outfit. They could neither procure sufficient teams nor provisions, which retarded our progress, and was the cause of a greater amount of suffering than there would otherwise have been. And my father, in speaking of it, said, under the circumstances it would take years to reach the mountains.

Woman's Exponent, vol. 12, no. 13
1 December 1883, pp. 102–3

Monday the 16th

Elder Heber C. Kimball and family left their home also and departed to the same place.

I see by my husband's journal that it was Monday the 16th that "Heber C. Kimball and family left their home and repaired to the encampment on Sugar Creek," and that President Young had gone the day before. The wagons father had sent ahead as fast as they were loaded, and he with mother and family were invited to stop and take dinner with Hiram Kimball and wife, our respected sister, Sarah M. Kimball. The day was pleasant, but the weather freezing. My husband returned and came over to camp next day.

At Sugar Creek father's men had pitched a tent and put up a sheet iron stove at one end, and great log fires were burning all through the camp. When we had warmed ourselves we made our beds upon the ground and laid down with grateful hearts for so comfortable a shelter, and slept soundly till morning. The snow was deep so that paths had to be made with spades between the wagons and tents. Camping out increased our appetites so that our picnic was very nearly consumed before the camp was ready to leave Sugar Creek. We had cooked up a great amount of provisions, consisting of roasted chicken, beef, boiled hams, pork and beans, bread, rusks and many other eatables, beside sea biscuits and crackers, which we could eat and eat and still be hungry.

Woman's Exponent, vol. 12, no. 11,
1 November 1883, p. 81

Tuesday the 17th

Bro. Joseph C. Kingsbury and myself went over to the camp – he returned, I staid all night.

1. Ever since the Black Hawk Indian War of 1830–32, eastern Iowa had been open to settlement. In 1838, it separated from Wisconsin and became a relatively small territory. From 1838 to 1846, its population tripled from thirty thousand to ninety-six thousand, most of whom were settlers clustered in the eastern counties along the Mississippi and Des Moines Rivers.

Nauvoo, from the Mississippi, Looking Down the River. *In* [Frederick] Gleason's Pictorial Drawing-Room Companion *(Boston, 1854), 36. Courtesy of Church History Library.*

WEDNESDAY THE 18TH

President Young called the people of the camp together for the purpose of organization – I returned the same day to Nauvoo to assist father in removing – In the afternoon Bros. B.[righam] Young and H. C. Kimball came back to assist Joseph Kingsbury to procure teams.

THURSDAY THE 19TH

It being very stormy, they did not recross the river to the camp – next day my wife [Helen Mar Kimball Whitney] came back intending to remain with us till we start – Nothing of notice transpired till.

On the 19th it began storming, and it was dismal enough to give even a saint the blues.

Woman's Exponent, vol. 12, no. 11,
1 November 1883, p. 81

[***Editor's note***: Horace's journal inexplicably jumps to Sunday the 22nd.]

SUNDAY THE 22D

Bros. Brigham and Heber went over to the camp. [***Editor's note***: no entries for 23rd to the 26th.]

FRIDAY THE 27TH

Father [Cornelius Peter] Lott with his team left Nauvoo with the women and children crossed the river on the ice and took them to the camp.[2] – I accompanied them on horseback Father Lott staid with us all night.[3]

---

2. For most of the month of February 1846, the Saints crossed the river on ferryboats and other watercraft, sometimes navigating around ice chunks. However, from 24 February until 1 March the river froze solid between Nauvoo and Montrose. At best, no more than two hundred to three hundred crossed on solid ice. Many crossed back and forth on the river fetching last-minute supplies, attending meetings, and completing last-minute details. For the most recent scholarship on this topic, see William G. Hartley, "The Nauvoo Exodus and Crossing the Ice Myths," *Journal of Mormon History* 43, no. 1 (January 2017): 30–58.
3. Of their first night sleeping on the frozen Iowa ground, Emmeline B. Wells recorded the following in her journal: "Mrs. Whitney, Sarah Ann and myself crossed the river to go to the encampment of the saints.

Friday, the 27th of February, I bade my last adieu to our home and city and recrossed the Mississippi with Bishop Whitney's family, whom he sent to camp in charge of Father C. P. Lott, the bishop remaining behind to see his own and church teams over, and he came to the camp next day. Brother Joseph C. Kingsbury and Wm. Clayton stayed back in Nauvoo to assist in winding up the church business. During that time Wm. Clayton composed a parody on the song, "Dido and I," and though I have forgotten the words, the burthen of it was that the chores had been left for the "bishop and I," which was afterwards sung in camp with much gusto by the boys.

Woman's Exponent, vol. 12, no. 12,
15 November 1883, pp. 89–90

Saturday the 28th

Bro W[illia]m. Kimball and myself returned to the City – before crossing over found father's teams had all just got over the river they proceeded to the camp, we transacted some business which we had in the city, [Nauvoo] and returned – reached our quarters about sunset –

Camp-life in February was quite a novel experience, and might be called a pleasant one at Sugar Creek when compared with what was laying before us; more especially the youthful portion—they feeling no particular responsibilities resting upon them, nor any great hardships as yet. The band played every evening, and Hans C. Hanson, an adopted son of my parents, was very fond of playing his violin. My husband would often join him with his flute, and there being quite a number of young people in my father's family we could form a cotillion or French four by the big log fire, and often we did so at evening, and danced to amuse ourselves as well as to keep our blood in proper circulation. I there took my first lesson in the Danish waltz. The weather was so cold that it was impossible to keep warm without exercise. Many declared that they had never suffered so much from the cold as they did at Sugar Creek, and we were informed that nine children were born the first night the Saints camped there. Feb. 5th, 1846.[4] *The inspiring music by William Pitt's brass band, which was organized into companies of tens to travel*

Br. Lot and his wife took Mrs. W. and myself in their carriage. We crossed the river a part of the way on foot, and then went on to the encampment about 7 miles beyond; we reached the destined place about sunset when we came in view it looked like pictures I have seen of the ancients pitching their tents and journeying from place to place with their cattle and their goods. We repaired immediately to Br. H. C. Kimball's tent, . . . took supper and slept for the first time on the ground. There was a snow-storm without yet all was peace and harmony within." Emmeline B. Wells, journal, 27 February 1846, L. Tom Perry Special Collections, Harold B. Lee Library, Brigham Young University, Provo, UT.

4. The long-standing myth of nine children being born on one single night does not hold up to scholarly scrutiny. It may be that nine were born while the Saints headed west across Iowa but not on one single night. Thomas L. Kane, in his crusading, humanitarian style of describing the Mormon sufferings after having witnessed them himself, was probably responsible for this exaggeration. See Carol Lynn Pearson, "'Nine Children Were Born': A Historical Problem from the Sugar Creek Episode," *BYU Studies* 21, no. 4 (1981): 441–44. See also Thomas L. Kane, *The Mormons: A Discourse Delivered before the Historical Society of Pennsylvania* (Philadelphia: King and Baird, printers, 1850).

C. C. A. Christensen, Sugar Creek. *Church History Museum, Salt Lake City.*

Modern photograph of Sugar Creek. Courtesy of Kenneth R. Mays.

together, often gladdened the hearts of the Saints, and helped greatly to keep their spirits from sinking. They appointed Wm. Cahoon and Howard Egan captains over them.

Woman's Exponent, vol. 12, no. 13,
1 December 1883, pp. 102–3

Sunday the 1st of March

about noon Bro. Kimball and father with the majority of the camp left Sugar Creek encampment – travelled about 6 miles and encamped for the night on a small creek about 15 miles from Farmington – the same evening brother Brigham arrived with the remainder of the camp (except the artillery) who came up late in the evening[5]

Our difficulties commenced the first day that we started from Sugar Creek; and my trials as well. My father had one large family carriage in which mother and the children and most of the women folks were obliged to ride or else walk, as his wagons were all so heavily loaded; I did not consider that my marrying had lessened my claims, nor given anyone else the right to my place by the side of my mother, and it was something of a surprise and a trial to my faith to find that my father's family had become so large that he had not conveyances for them. One of his wives (Christine Golden) who came from Philadelphia and was living with the family of Bro. Jedediah Grant at Sugar Creek, was unknown to me until I met her there. She was a very proud-spirited woman, and that morning father sent her to his carriage, but finding it crowded full she turned without a word and went and rode that day with Sister Grant. After becoming acquainted we made our confessions, and many a time we have referred to that day and laughed heartily over it, as well as other things that once vexed and tried us.[6] *At every bad place the teams had to be doubled, and the first day we were detained, it seemed to me hours, while they crossed over a deep ravine and drew the loaded wagons up a steep hill on the other side. The rest had all got out of the carriage, and while I sat holding the reins the wind was so cold and piercing that it seemed to me as if I should perish. We only made six miles and encamped for the night on a small creek about fifteen miles from Farmington. . . . The snow had to be cleaned away to pitch the tents, and our beds were made upon the frozen ground. We were not blessed with a stove in our tent that night and it was impossible to get warm by the campfire; so that night I laid nothing off, not even my hood or josie. But the weather moderated before morning and*

5. Farmington, Iowa, was settled in 1833 and officially incorporated in 1841. Named for Farmington, Connecticut, it is the oldest village in Van Buren County and was the first county seat. It was a major center for milling, manufacturing, and trading.

6. Heber C. Kimball's first wife was Vilate Murray, whom he married in 1822, well before they joined the church. He married his first plural wife, Sarah Peak Noon, in 1842 in Nauvoo. Stanley B. Kimball, Heber Kimball's biographer, estimated that by the beginning of the exodus Heber had married at least thirty-eight wives, many of whom were widows of Joseph Smith or of other men. Once in Utah he married an additional five more wives, for a total of forty-three. At least seven of his wives refused to come west. Seventeen bore children, for a combined posterity numbering fifty-seven children. See Stanley B. Kimball, *Heber C. Kimball: Mormon Patriarch and Pioneer* (Urbana: University of Illinois Press, 1981), 95, 122, 227–44, 307–16.

the backbone of winter was broken. We started from there about noon and traveled only seven miles in consequence of the badness of the road.

Woman's Exponent, vol. 12, no. 13,
1 December 1883, pp. 102–3

Monday the 2[d]

Left our place of encampment about noon and travelled 7 miles only in the consequence of the badness of the roads – encamped on another small creek this night Bro. Brigham having preceded us and encamped 3 miles ahead.

Tuesday the 3[d]

Proceeded about 10 miles and encamped three miles beyond Farmington through which we passed[7] – very muddy bad travelling to-day. overtook Brother Brigham here – also Bishop [George] Miller who, with his company, had been here about a week.

We passed through Farmington on the 3rd and encamped three miles Beyond—making ten miles that we traveled that day—the mud made traveling almost impossible. We overtook President Young here, also Bishop Miller, who with his company had been encamped about a week.

Woman's Exponent, vol. 12, no. 13,
1 December 1883, pp. 102–3

Wednesday the 4th

To day we remained here in our tents – In the afternoon the Band, [William Pitt's brass band] having received an invitation from the people of Farmington, went there and played[8] – Wm. and myself accompanied them – were treated with great respect and kindness by the inhabitants – returned to the camp about 9 P. M.– This day also Bishop Miller and his company left the camp and went ahead to seek a new place. – Bro. Kimball's family and our own all continue well hearty and in good spirits.

There was a great amount of sympathy manifested by the people as we traveled through Iowa. Many visited our camps, and wherever the companies stopped our men were able to find employment. The splendid music made by the Nauvoo Brass Band quite surpassed anything that had been heard in that part and they were cordially invited to play at every settlement, and requested to give a number of concerts—this they did after consulting the Presidency, and

7. George Miller was then associate presiding bishop to Newel K. Whitney.
8. William Pitt (1813–73), a British convert, was a well-known musician in Nauvoo who organized a small brass ensemble in 1842. It played at many festive occasions and included trumpets, trombones, baritones, and other instruments. William Clayton was also a member. Pitt's brass band performed evening concerts in various settlements along the Des Moines River, the proceeds of which proved very beneficial to the migrating companies.

for which they were generously recompensed. Thus we see that God did fulfill the predictions made that day by my father, and truly His angels went before us, and He was the breaker up of our way.

Woman's Exponent, vol. 12, no. 13,
1 December 1883, pp. 102–3

We remained in our tents. Early that morning the band came and played for the benefit of President Young and brethren. In the afternoon, they having received an invitation from the people of Farmington to play, went after obtaining the mind of the President, where John Kay, our favorite songster, sang one of his best, "The sea, the sea." They were treated with the greatest respect and kindness, and given an excellent supper at the Gait House, and afterwards escorted a mile towards the camp.

The following little incident occur[r]ed in the early part of our journey. Two or more of father's young wives were walking behind the wagons when night overtook them and the wagons being out of sight, and, not daring to proceed alone, they stopped at a farmhouse where they were kept all night and treated to the best the house afforded. The nicest room they had—belonging to their only son—was given them to sleep in, and after breakfast he escorted them to the camp, which though but a little distance off was hidden under a high hill to the left of the road. Father had cautioned his wives and folks from about lingering behind, and this had a tendency to make them remember it.

Woman's Exponent, vol. 12, no. 14,
15 December 1883, pp. 110–11

Thursday the 5th

Struck our tents about 10 a.m. – had not proceeded more than 10 or 15 rods when the axle-tree of one of our wagons was broken – in consequence had to leave the wagon behind and put the load on our other wagons. – I went ahead 2 miles with [Orrin] Porter [Rockwell] on horseback to a little place called Bonaparte – we stopped till our folks came up;[9] At this place we crossed the Des Moines River and encamped, after going a short distance having made only 3 miles this day – I then proceeded 2 miles further to Bro. Kimball's encampment who with several others including the artillery had stopt on the open prairie – About 11 o'clock was awakened by Joseph K. who came for Bro. Kimball, stating tha [*sic*] S.[arah] Ann [Whitney] [Horace's younger sister] was very sick – the next morning.

9. Bonaparte, Iowa, named after Napoleon Bonaparte, was originally settled by William Meek, who established a woolen mill there in 1837. His mill later became internationally renowned for the quality of wool it produced. It is located in Van Buren County, on the banks of the Des Moines River.

FRIDAY THE 6TH

After having struck our tents and being about ready to start, Bro. Kimball returned from father's encampment bringing the news that Sarah Ann was much better. Bro. Kimball, and family then went on – I remained till our folks came up and proceeded about 6 miles to Indian Creek, where we arrived at 2 P. M. and took up our quarters for the night, they having made 8 miles to day – Very bad muddy going, but not so much so as yesterday.

Sarah Ann Whitney (Kingsbury) Kimball (1825–73), younger sister to Horace K. Whitney. Courtesy of Church History Library.

SATURDAY THE 7TH

Before starting this morning a man living in the neighborhood 4 miles south of Keosauqua by the name of Cochran came to our camp and laid claim to one yoke of father's oxen, saying that they had strayed or been stolen from him three years previously.[10] To avoid disturbance father paid him 30 dollars in gold and about 10 o'clock a.m. struck our tents and travelled about 9 miles and encamped on a small creek by the side of the road, Bro. Kimball's family having preceded us and stopped 3 miles ahead. – About 4 o'clock in the morning was awakened by hearing Sarah Ann cry – appeared to be in great pain – Bro. Kimball was sent for – arrived about daylight – I went on foot to Bro. Kimball's camp – had not been there long before Bro. [Stephen] Markham arrived, bringing the news of the birth of S. Ann's child, which happened at 8 minutes past 7 o'clock on this 8th day of March 1846. – The child was called David as also the valley where he was born. It is located in Jackson Township Van Buren Co. I. T. [Iowa Territory][11] Towards evening Brigham and Heber went to father's camp blessed the child and returned home – This evening Bro. W[illia]m Clayton with the Band came up and camped with us.

---

10. Keosaqua is the largest village and county seat of Van Buren county, Iowa. Established in 1839, it is located on the Big Bend of the Des Moines River. Its name translates from Meskwaki and Sauk to "Bend in the river."

11. Iowa did not become a state of the Union until 28 December 1846. Thus technically in February it was still a territory of the United States.

Monday the 9th

This afternoon about 3 o'clock father's family left the Valley of David and went to the place where Bro. K. was encamped which is called Richard's Point on the borders of a small wood Bro. B. Young is also here with the majority of the camp.[12] – The number of souls in Zion's camp this side the Mississippi River at the present time somewhat exceeds 2000. – Wm. conveyed Sarah Ann in an easy carriage to the camp this day, before leaving the Valley of David father had the good luck to exchange a span of horses for two yoke of oxen and 30 bushels of corn with a man living in the vicinity.[13]

Towards morning father was sent for to return to Bishop Whitney's camp. Next day Bro. Markham arrived, bringing the news of the birth of a son to my father's wife, Sarah Ann. This was the eighth day of March, and the child was called David, as also the valley where he was born. Next day towards evening father and President Young went to Bishop Whitney's camp and blessed the child. The same evening Bro. Wm. Clayton with the band came up and camped with us, for which we were all glad, as they entertained us every evening when in camp. This place where we were camped was called Richard's Point, on the borders of a small wood. The majority of the camp of Israel were there, where we were obliged to remain over a week in consequence of stormy weather.

Woman's Exponent, vol. 12, no. 14,
15 December 1883, pp. 110–11

Tuesday the 10th

This day in consequence of a heavy fall of rain we did not strike our tents – The Band having received a invitation from the people of Keosauqua to come and play, went and returned receiving an invitation to repeat their visit the next night. – This place the county seat of Van Buren county lies about 10 miles east from our present place of encampment on the Des Moines about 15 or 16 miles above Farmington

Wednesday the 11th

In accordance with their invitation the Band went to Keosauqua – Wm. and myself accompanied them – started about noon – returned at 2 a.m. on [the 12th]

---

12. Richardson's Point is located in Van Buren county, Iowa, fifty-six miles west of Nauvoo. The Saints encamped there for several days, waiting for the roads to become more passable.

13. The well-advised came with a solidly built wagon, a harness, a dependable team of horses or preferably oxen, some cows, a thousand pounds of flour, a hundred pounds of sugar, farming and mechanical tools, cooking utensils, seeds, clothing, a musket, and other necessities.

Thursday the 12th

Very stormy. – The rain has fallen almost incessantly since Tuesday last, To-day received a letter from W.[illiam Wines] Phelps stating the general news in Nauvoo, among which was that W[illia]m. Smith and [George] Adams had arrived there and were about to reorganize the church, that John E. Page and Rufus Beach had joined the Strangites, that Luke Johnson was again received into the church on Sunday the 8th, that Cain was to leave on the 10th inst. that the ice had got out of the river, that steamboats were running, &c &c. –[14]

Richards' Point, where we are now located, is situated on Chequest Prairie, and here we are likely to remain for some time at least, as the roads were almost impassable.

This was quite a newsy letter, and all these things were interesting to a people who were traveling away from their homes, never more to behold them. But there was no mourning nor lamentations, we felt too glad to have made our escape. And the first evening after the warm sun had dried the earth, the young people were out dancing by moonlight—determined upon being happy, or at least to snatch all the pleasant moments and enjoy them as they came along. Some of the camp were already prostrated with chills and fever in consequence of want and exposure. It now rained almost incessantly, and Bishop Whitney's daughter Sarah Ann, was in a critical state part of the time while there. And Mother Whitney, who stayed with her daughter, and, like all the rest was exposed to cold and wet, took the rheumatism, and it settled in her left wrist, which had been broken the previous winter by jumping from a buggy when the horse became frightened one evening as she was returning from the temple. She could not be convinced that it was broken, although the bishop's father, who was a doctor, told her that it was broken, and that she ought to have a doctor to set it, he being then too old to attend to it himself. Her hand and arm commenced to wither away, and one day while on the journey Father John Smith called to her

James J. Strang (1813–56), contender for church leadership. Daguerreotype, 1856.

14. James Strang (1813–56), a relatively recent convert to Mormonism, laid claim to succession as president of the church after Joseph Smith's martyrdom. Professing prophetic authority from a letter Joseph Smith allegedly had written him appointing him to be "President," Strang opposed Brigham Young's plan for exodus in favor of a resettlement of the Saints in Wisconsin. Proclaiming new scripture, visions and revelations, Strang believed in an immediate reorganization of the First Presidency. He was temporarily successful in drawing away the allegiance of approximately 1,500 Latter-day Saints, primarily in areas removed from Nauvoo. Among his many followers were Martin Harris, William Smith (Joseph Smith's younger brother), Clark Lyman Whitney (Bishop Newel K. Whitney's brother), George Miller, and apostle John E. Page. Strang eventually moved to Beaver Island, Michigan, where in 1856 he was assassinated. Many of his followers eventually drifted into the Reorganized Church of Jesus Christ of Latter Day Saints (Community of Christ). The Church of Jesus Christ of Latter-day Saints (Strangite) continues in small congregations in Wisconsin and New Mexico to this day.

tent to see her, and noticing her hand and wrist enquired into the cause and seemed to feel greatly interested in her behalf. He called for a bottle of consecrated oil and administered it with prayer and mighty faith, and he prophesied that flesh should come upon that arm and hand, which was literally fulfilled, though the wrist was out of place.

Woman's Exponent, vol. 12, no. 14,
15 December 1883, pp. 110–11

FRIDAY THE 13TH.

The clouds having cleared away this morning the weather assumes a near smiling aspect; which, after 3 days of incessant rain and storm is very acceptable. – This afternoon Porter and myself took a short ride of about 3 miles on horseback into the country.

SATURDAY THE 14TH.

This morning about 10 a.m. Porter and Edwin Cutler Started on horseback for Nauvoo. – [Clark] Lyman W.[hitney] and myself took a short excursion into the country for the purpose of trading for oxen – returned, having partially effected an exchange – the tolerably fair to-day [*sic*] though evening set in as if for a storm.

SUNDAY THE 15TH.

This morning, notwithstanding the inauspicious appearance of the weather last evening, the sun arose cloudless and beautiful – In the afternoon Wm. and myself accompanied by several others went to a small place called Stringtown, took dinner and returned home about sunset.[15]

MONDAY THE 16TH

This day remained in camp – the weather continues favorable – fair prospect of being able to renew our journey in a few days.

TUESDAY THE 17TH

To day quite cloudy but no rain – about 11 o-clock in the night began a slow drizzly rain which continued the remainder for the night were intending to start to morrow had it not been for the rain. To-day the Band again went to Keosauqua by invitation.

WEDNESDAY THE 18TH

The weather continued showery through the day till evening when it cleared off pleasant. – The corpse of Bro. Edwin Little was brought into camp and interred to-day. He was taken

15. Still a small town in eastern Iowa, Stringtown is known today for its Amish-style grocery stores.

sick here a few days ago and conveyed into the country in order to have the advantage of skillful treatment and to be shielded from the inclemency of the weather; but notwithstanding all was done for his relief that human aid could afford he died today while in the wagon on the way to the camp His disease was the quick consumption [tuberculosis] – he appeared to be reconciled to his death, and died in the full faith of the Gospel.

Thursday the 19th

This morning about 11 o'clock struck our tents and proceeded on our journey having been encamped 9 days, the weather fine and pleasant, though rather cool – the roads quite smooth, and improving all the time – travelled about 2 miles and pitched our tents on a small creek, which also bears the name of Chequest, on the land of a widow, name unknown. – We are now travelling through Davis County, which joins Van Buren county Bro. Kimball's family and our own are all well – Sarah Ann gaining rapidly.

Friday the 20th

This morning about half past 9 started over again our route being chiefly on the prairie the roads were very bad – crossed Fox River to-day – travelled 14 miles and encamped about 4 P. M. in the edge of a small piece of timber – very poor muddy camping plain being destitute of a name, consequently gave it one, viz: – Slough of Discontent – The prairie through which we have been travelling to-day and shall be for a day or two is called the "New Purchase" or the "Fox Divide"[16]

Saturday the 21st

Started at half past 7 this morning – had a good road – proceeded 11 miles and encamped on the brow of a hill, in the vicinity of a creek in the edge of the timber about 4 miles from the river Chariton – reached this place at 2 P. M.

That evening the band overtook us, and before retiring they played a few tunes before President Young's tent and father's. Oh, what dismal days those were! And the next day was Sunday—cloudy and disagreeable—as we started in the morning and crossed the bottom, which intervened between us and the Chariton River. We had considerable difficulty in crossing that stream, on account of the steepness of the descent on its banks. After crossing there was a very bad hill to ascend, and they were obliged to double team in both places, besides the assistance of a number of men to hold back, and push up hill. This labor consumed the greater part of the

16. In 1839 a federal highway or "agency road" opened from the Mississippi northwestward to the Sac and Fox Indian agency near Ottumwa on the Des Moines River. Along this route sprang a number of river communities the Mormons had been passing through. But beyond these frontier settlements, farms and fledgling, intermittent settlements were connected by the poorest of roads (more aptly described as surveyed trails) in southeast and south-central Iowa as far as the Knoxville meridian, or Red Rock line, in central Iowa. See Richard E. Bennett, *Mormons at the Missouri, 1846–1852: "And Should We Die"* (Norman: University of Oklahoma Press, 1987 and 2004), 30.

day. We encamped on the top of the hill in a small piece of timber. How fresh in my mind are some of those tedious days of rain, sleet and mud, and sometimes hunger, for already were our rations poor and pinched, it being the intention at that time to cross over the Rocky Mountains the same year. One important event transpired that dismal morning, while we were crossing the bottom between our camping ground and Chariton River, which was indelibly written upon my memory. We passed the wagon of Sister Zina D. H. Young, which had halted upon the east bank, where she had a beautiful son born, and he was named Chariton. I have never met that son nor heard his name without its reminding me of Chariton River, and the circumstances attending our sojourn there.

Woman's Exponent, vol. 12, no. 14,
15 December 1883, pp. 110–11

Sunday the 22D

Cloudy disagreeable morning but no rain started at half past 9 crossed the bottom which intervened between us and the Chariton River had considerable difficulty in crossing that stream on account of the steepness of the descent on its banks – after crossing had a very bad hill to ascend – were obliged to double team in both places – besides the assistance of a number of men to hold back and push up hill – this labor consumed the greater part of the day – encamped on the top of the hill, having only made 4 miles to day. Rec'd a letter from Sarah Foot.

I remember how nearly forlorn I felt some of the time during those dismal, stormy days; being in Bp. Whitney's camp I was separated from my dear mother by an almost impassable road of mud, and was all of a quarter of a mile away from father's camp. So one morning I undertook the disagreeable and perilous journey on the back of a little white Ginnie, which Father Lot had given to one of the Bp's little boys in Nauvoo, and, by the by, she had carried me over the Mississippi the last time that I crossed it to Sugar Creek, accompanied by Horace on his pony.

Ginnie stood about three feet from the ground, and the mud being so deep, I felt some dubiety about our accomplishing the journey that day in safety, but being stimulated by a touch of homesickness I persevered without regard to appearance or the mud, with which I was generously bespattered. On the opposite side of the road from father's camp was the camp of the Nauvoo Brass Band, and O! their woebegone appearance I could never forget; and how I looked over at them with a pitying gaze from the door of my mother's wagon. They were actually swamped in mud; but what was most surprising, under the circumstances, not a sad face did I behold. The women were out around, and would give me a cheerful nod as they were attending to their domestic duties, and all the camps were in a similar condition. The following incident was related to me concerning Br. Wm. Pitt and wife, who, like some of the rest, were sick with the ague, caused by the cold and wet weather, and one night they were left behind in the mud, and were not missed till late the next morning when some of the band went back and

Brigham Young (1801–77). Courtesy of Church History Library.

found them. Those were sorry times, but who, besides the Latter-day Saints, can understand or explain the reasons for such patience, and even cheerfulness under like circumstances, having been expelled, though they were law-abiding citizens, from their homes, and at that time of the year, enduring such hardships and privation, that would have disheartened any but the true Saints, who were willing to make sacrifice and to be tried, even though it be seven times in the furnace of affliction.

Woman's Exponent, vol. 12, no. 15,
1 January 1884, pp. 117–18

Monday the 23^D^

Remained within pitched tents – This afternoon about 2 o'clock had quite a hail storm – they fell as large or larger than buckshot Continued stormy with rain and hail alternately through the day & night Yesterday Bro. John Butler came from Bishop Miller's camp which is seven miles ahead – he seems to like to be in advance of the main body as he always pulls up stakes at our approach and goes ahead with his company [17] – Bro. Butler thinks it would be a good idea to go back 20 miles or so in order to get on a road which goes thro' the settlements as the country through which we are now travelling affords us scarcely any provender for our cattle.

Tuesday the 24TH

Commenced snowing and continued with little cessation through the day – In the afternoon Bros. [Stillman] Pond and [Thomas] Burns went into the country about 8 miles and bought 20 bushels of corn at 25 cts. a bushel – rather scarce at that price – some of the cattle in camp have had no sustenance since day before yesterday with the exception of what they could browse in the woods – To-day – saw three deer carried by our tent that had been killed by the hunters – first that we have seen on our journey, – the roads very muddy and almost impassable – fair probability of being obliged to remain here a number of days –

Wednesday the 25TH

Continued snowing through the day till evening when it cleared off pleasant – This afternoon Bro. Pond took my colt and two of our team horses into the country with the intention of exchanging them for oxen – did not return to-day –

17. Bishop George Miller was one of the principal scouts during the Iowa crossing. He had been across Iowa Territory previously and probably knew the terrain better than anyone else. As we shall see, however, he was not one to take counsel or direction very well and eventually would break with the church and with Brigham Young at Winter Quarters.

Thursday the 26th

Tolerably fair to-day – hail fell a little this after-noon saw Bishop Miller, P[arley] P Pratt, O.[rson] Pratt and G.[eorge] A.[lbert] Smith pass by our tent on their way home – they came up from Bro Miller's camp by request to hold council –

Friday the 27th

Quite windy to-day though the sky cloudless and serene. This forenoon Bros. Brigham and Heber went ahead about 7 miles to a place where they were met by Bishop Miller's company, and where he had formerly been encamped but which place he had left a few days before and gone a few miles ahead – Here they proceeded to make a new organization of the Companies – B. Young, H.C. Kimball, P. P. Pratt, John Taylor , Peter Hawes , and Bishop Miller, who had formerly been captains of companies, were promoted to the office of President and their places filled by others – In our company the vacancy of the office of Capt. was filled by Stephen Markham an able and efficient officer – In each company there was appointed 2 commissaries and a clerk – In our company the leading commissary is David Yearsly – His business is to go ahead and engage grain, procure jobs for the company &c.– Our distributing commissary is Jedediah Grant whose business it is to distribute corn oats &c. when bro't into the camp. Our clerk is John Pack, whose business is to record all essential matters pertaining to the company.

Saturday the 28th

To-day a council was held – but little was done, however, except ratifying what was done yesterday at Father Smith's camp. The weather continues favorable and the roads are improving, though there are some very bad places ahead yet, as we learn from our men who occasionly [*sic*] go out in pursuit of game – which in this section consists principally of deer and turkeys. There has been a number of the former already bro't into the camp.

Bishop Whitney disposed of a feather bed at this place valued at $9.00 in exchange for a cow, with a man living six or seven miles in the country. Brother Pond returned, having disposed of the colt and another team horse for two yoke of oxen. He had been over in the state of Missouri where he made the trade, and one of the oxen proving lame Brother Pond swapped him for another, giving $9.00 "to boot." On the 31st O. P. Rockwell returned from Nauvoo. My husband and brother Wm. received some papers from Phineas Kimball, brother-in-law to Sarah M. Kimball. Porter started back to Nauvoo in a few days.

Woman's Exponent, vol. 12, no. 15,
1 January 1884, pp. 117–18

Sunday the 29th

To-day father disposed of a feather bed, valued at $9 in exchange for a cow with a man living some six or seven miles in the country – Bro. Pond also returned to-day having disposed of the colt and another team horse for 2 yoke of oxen which are also in the country with the rest of our oxen sent out to feed about the same distance – He has been over in the State of Missouri about 20 miles when he made the trade.[18]

Monday the 30th

To-day Bro. Parley G.A. Smith Orson and Bishop Miller again came here to hold council with the brethren – the result was the camp concluded to move on Wednesday. One of the oxen that Bro. Pond got proving lame he swapped him for another giving $9 to "boot"–

Tuesday the 31st

To-day Porter returned from Nauvoo. Wm. and myself received through him 2 papers from [Heber] P. Kimball also a letter for me from Mr. [Noah] Rogers. To day the boys also brought the oxen in from the country 7 miles where we have been keeping them to feed, as also the cow which father purchased last Sunday – Porter intends starting back to-morrow or next day.

Wednesday the 1st of April

Brigham with all the camp except our "Fifty" started on their journey – they intended going only 6 miles to Father Smith's camp where they intended to wait till we come up in order to hold a council. To-day Father's company employed themselves in making ox yokes and other chores necessary for the journey – To-day a Thomas Burns one of our teamsters left us to return to Nauvoo, in consequence had to hire another by the name of David Taylor, whom we found with Dr. Bealy here in the camp – This evening H. C. K. wrote 2 letters to Nauvoo for a friend –

Thursday the 2d

This morning about half past 8 struck our tents and proceeded to Father Smith's camp on Shoal Creek about 7 miles where we found Bro. Brigham, who had encamped here yesterday.

---

18. The Mormons first settled in Independence, Jackson County, Missouri in 1831. For a variety of religious, cultural, and economic reasons, they were driven north into Clay County in 1833 and later into Caldwell and Daviess Counties. Hostilities so intensified during the "Mormon Missouri War" of 1838–39 that Governor Lilburn W. Boggs issued an "extermination order" in late 1838, driving some five thousand Mormon settlers from Far West, Missouri to Quincy, Illinois. Thus in 1846 Mormon-Missouri relations were at an all-time low. Two excellent studies on the Mormon difficulties in Missouri are Alexander L. Baugh, *A Call to Arms: The 1838 Mormon Defense in Northern Missouri* (Provo, UT: Joseph Fielding Smith Institute for Latter-day Saint History and BYU Studies, 1996); and Stephen C. LeSueur, *The 1838 Mormon War in Missouri* (Columbia: University of Missouri Press, 1984).

When we arrived they were holding a council – Bro Kimball went to it and returned with the news that we were going on, consequently Bro. K's. company, the artillery and some others went on 5 miles further and encamped on Prairie Creek a branch of Shoal Creek, leaving Bro. B's. company behind – were piloted a short distance by Bishop Miller and another brother who then rode on to his camp, which is 3 miles ahead of our present place of encampment. Took leave of Porter at Bro. B's camp who returns to Nauvoo to-day the bearer of several letters – This day quite cloudy but not rain the roads improving, though rather bad yet in some places – Before leaving Shoal Creek camp unloaded 1 of our wagons and sent it after corn in company with 1 or 2 others – putting the load on our other wagons – Crossed the Missouri State line this afternoon just before coming to this place –[19]

Friday the 3D

This morning, soon after breakfast, Bro. Brigham's company over took us and after stopping a few minutes went on to Bro. Miller's camp where they intend to feed – During last night three of our oxen strayed away, consequently were detained after the rest of our company had left – I proceeded on foot to Bro. M's. camp – had not gone far before it commenced raining, which continued through the greater part of the day and night. Bro. M. is encamped on the South Fork of Shoal Creek, after crossing which, and ascending the opposite hill, Bro. K. encamped – Thinking the rain might hinder father from coming on I started back – had not gone far before I met Bro. Johnson of the artillery who informed me that father had recovered his cattle, the men sent out in pursuit having found a man in the act of driving them off – Bro. Johnson informed me as near as he could find out that his name is John Shaddon, living about 12 miles from here. He is said to have been seen in our camp this morning – Father started about 1 o' clock and reached here at 3 P. M. when he encamped by the rest of Bro. K's company

We had not been here more than a hour before the teams, which had been sent out in pursuit of corn arrived bringing 51 bushels – After ascending the hill, Bro Brigham with his company continued on – we suppose they have gone on to the next creek which is 13 miles ahead, Joseph K. broke one of the thills of his buggy, this morning, soon after starting – occasioned by the horse jumping suddenly. –

---

19. At stake in this long-standing dispute were 2,600 square miles of fertile farm land. It stemmed from a discrepancy between an 1816 survey and an 1820 survey over the location of a set of river rapids that were to mark the northeastern boundary of Missouri, which claimed the valuable land when seeking statehood in 1820. Since Missouri came into the Union as a slave state, the slavery question was also at issue. The two sides almost went to war (the so-called "Honey War") in 1839 over it but at the last moment agreed to submit the matter to Congress, which, in turn, passed it on to the Supreme Court. In 1849, the Court ruled in Iowa's favor. See Caroll J. Krauss, "A Study in Border Confrontation: The Iowa-Missouri Boundary Dispute," *Annals of Iowa* 40, no. 2 (Fall 1969): 81–107. See also Spencer M. Thomas, "'Demand Nothing but What Is Strictly Right and Submit to Nothing That Is Wrong': Governor Lilburn Boggs, Governor Robert Lucas, and the Honey War of 1839," *Missouri Historical Review* 103, no. 1 (October 2008): 22–40.

Saturday the 4th

From the rains of the previous day and night the little creek on which we are encamped, is much swollen continued also raining thro' this day and night with but little cessation, consequently had to remain within pitched tents.

Sunday the 5th

This morning the sun arose in unclouded splendor – Bro. Kimball called the people of the camp together and exhorted them to observance of several duties which had been hitherto neglected – one of which was that the captain of each Ten should call his company together and partake of the sacrament, which was accordingly done – The weather continued beautiful thro' the day but the ground dried very little or none.[20]

Monday the 6th

On waking up this morning was astonished to find it raining, the more so as yesterday closed so auspiciously – it continued raining without intermission till evening when it had the appearance of clearing off when all at once the sky was obscured with dark heavy clouds the distant roaring of the wind was heard, which accompanied by a cold rain soon burst upon us in all its fury blowing off hats & prostrating the tents of which but few were found standing in the morning – Tho the storm or rather hurricane continued the most of the night but little other damage was sustained, except the inconvenience of being wet by the constant dripping of the rain thro' the covers of the wagons where we slept, or rather passed the night. Today the company again sent into the country after corn, Jacob W.[etherbee] went with one of our wagons, also Father Durfee with one of Joseph Kingsbury's wagons. – From information the course which we are now pursuing is very little south of west –

I remember this very well. The camps were about ready to retire to rest when the storm overtook us; some were in the act of evening worship and others were preparing their beds or closing their tents and wagons for the night, when the hurricane overtook us "as a thief in the night," and not a wagon cover or tent could withstand it except the ones that were fastened down. Those who had no covering sought shelter with the ones that had till morning, when the

20. Unlike the practices of many of their fellow overlanders, Mormon devotion to the Sabbath was a mixture of Puritan devotion and New England practicality. Invariably they rested on Sundays, except when travel for a better campground made it necessary to move on. Hunting was not allowed, unless they were totally without food. And worship services, complete with makeshift pews, choirs, and speeches, were held as occasion allowed. Admitted Isaac Pettijohn, part of an Illinois company that later caught up to the Mormons west of Fort Laramie: "I saw and talked with [William] Vance, a son of Mr. Vance from McDonough Co. Illinois. Unlike us they had stopped to spend the Sabbath." See Richard E. Bennett, *We'll Find the Place: The Mormon Exodus, 1846–1848* (Norman: University of Oklahoma Press, 2009), 155.

tents were pitched and things righted. Next day it was very cold and windy, though tolerably fair. The day previous men had again been sent into the country for corn.

Woman's Exponent, vol. 12, no. 15,
1 January 1884, pp. 117–18

Tuesday the 7th

Very cold & windy day – but tolerably fair – To-day a messenger came from Brigham 12 miles ahead requesting the brethren to come on – To-day Helen and myself succeeded in getting a wagon for ourselves to ride and sleep in – one that father gave up for that purpose – Our teams which were sent out after corn we understand have come as far as Shoal creek, which they are unable to cross in consequence of the late rains which have considerably swollen that stream – they will probably be in tomorrow, when we contemplate pursuing our journey –

On the 7th a message came from President Young, who was twelve miles ahead, requesting my father and the rest to come on. That day Horace succeeded in getting a wagon for us and also a gentle yoke of oxen. Previously we had had no place in particular. I had traveled mostly with my mother, and our lodging had been, like that of hundreds of others, on the ground. But here was a new lesson for Horace, who from a schoolboy in Kirtland had done little else but printing and school teaching—yoking up and driving oxen he had never before undertaken.

Woman's Exponent, vol. 12, no. 16,
16 January 1884, pp. 126–27

Wednesday the 8th

No rain, but cold and cloudy – This afternoon P. P. Pratt, Amasa Lyman, and G. A. Smith, came up with us – Our teams also came up with 30 bushels of corn – a council was called in the evening and a letter from Brigham read, requesting us to come on.

Thursday the 9th

Started this morning about 8 o' clock – took my first lesson in the science of Oxology[21] – On taking the team to drive, I went into Bro. Kimball's company – had not gone far before it began to rain, which continued thro' the day and night – travelled 7 miles and encamped about 6 P. M. on the open prairie in one of the most disagreeable muddy places I remember ever to have seen – drove our horses and cattle about a mile to the nearest wood, which consisted principally of elm trees, and afforded them an excellent opportunity for browsing – Some of my father's teams got stuck in the mud, and had to stop a mile or two back and none reached us except J. C. K. [Kingsbury] with the buggy, the one horse wagon, and Sarah

21. Those who did not know that oxen would hold up along the trail much better than horses would soon find such to be the case. Slower and much more deliberate than horses, oxen nevertheless proved far more

Photographer unknown, "The Next Thing to Paradise." Interior of a covered wagon, circa 1858. Kerosene lamps came into popularity in the early 1850s. Wyoming State Archives.

Ann's wagon. Bro. Pond broke his harness in attempting to extricate himself from a mud-hole – Bro. Lorenzo Young and other of the company were also unable to come up, as also Parley and his company.

On the 9th, after leaving this place, he wrote, "Started this morning about eight o'clock—took my first lesson in the science of oxology." On taking the ox whip to drive, the first thing he did was to go on the wrong side, and then had to endure the roars of laughter from several of the boys who were standing ready to witness his first effort, but some of them were quite as green as himself in the practice of ox driving. But after seeing his chagrin one of them took the whip and drove a little ways to give him an idea how it was done, and he soon became as handy in yoking, unyoking and driving ox-teams as any of the boys, and even some of our sisters were schooled in the same science before we got to our journey's end, as numbers of our brethren who came out from Nauvoo as teamsters, returned after a little, some of them taking their teams with them, after we had obtained some from other quarters. We had doors, generally, cut on

durable and dependable, could pull much heavier loads, were much less fussy about what to eat, and, if necessary, provided better meat.

the left side of the wagon covers. Boxes and bags of grain, etc., were packed in the rear part of our wagon, upon which our bed was made. We had our provision chest in front, which served as a table, and between was just room for my chair—this being my only piece of furniture—the most of our household chattels having been left in our house in Nauvoo. I could now knit and read as we traveled, and Horace could read or play his flute as he liked, and none, I think, but those who had a like experience can form the slightest idea of the appreciation and happiness it gave us, to have a little wagon all to ourselves, which, under the circumstances, was next thing to paradise. . . .

The muddy camping place, mentioned by Horace, was one not easily to be forgotten. The dismal places were the ones that seemed to impress themselves the most indelibly upon my memory, but this one really had its pleasant side, for I remember how grateful I felt there to be under a tight wagon cover, where we were comfortable and secure from the cold and beating rain, which, falling upon the cover, served as a kind of lullaby to soothe us to sleep. And in the morning my cousin Netty, the head cook, brought us some warm eatables, requesting me to stay in the wagon, as she would rather bring our breakfast to us than have me bothering around in the mud, to which arrangement we very cheerfully submitted.

Woman's Exponent, vol. 12, no. 16,
16 January 1884, pp. 126–27

Friday the 10th

This morning on rising, found the rain had not ceased falling, but, on the contrary, pouring down with redoubled vigor – Getting our cattle from the woods we started about noon doubling teams when it cleared off leaving J. C. K. behind, as also 3 of Bro. Kimball's teams in the care of Hans [Hanson] travelled 3½ miles and encamped at 3 P. M. on the East Fork of Locust Creek near where Brigham had previously encamped – one of the most beautiful locations for an encampment my eyes ever beheld – in fact it seems as if expressly designed for our use, and, in contrast with the place where we last stopt a perfect paradise –

Saturday the 11th

Bro. Kimball's horse and ox teams, including myself, went back after the wagons left behind Wm put 4 of his horses on Sarah Ann's wagon and our ox teams went back a mile further to pull one of father's teams out of a mud-hole and the folks all got to the camp about 3½ o-clock the same time we did with the ox teams – When we arrived found Brigham here with 2 or three other brethren they were in council – Bro. B's camp is only 2 miles from here on the W. Fork of Locust To-day made a coal pit that we might be able to do some blacksmithing –

Sunday the 12th

To-day a meeting was called at 12 M. – Present – B. Young, H. C. Kimball, P. P. Pratt, O. Pratt, A. Lyman, G. A. Smith, J Taylor, Bishops [Newel K.] Whitney and Miller, and several others. Bro. Young spoke, gave some good instruction, and concluded with a plan for our future movements – that was to send 50 men ahead to the source of Grand River and then to make some improvements – fence in about a mile square build some huts plant some grain and garden seeds then by saving their garden seeds which would not otherwise keep any length of time – after that for the main body to follow them – from here the place where we now are we aim to take a north west course. till we arrive at the head of Grand River – from thence proceed to Council Bluffs on the Missouri River – thence over the mountains, leaving behind at our new settlement those that have not the means to prosecute the Journey – thereby furnishing a sojourning place for those that may hereafter come on from the States[22] – Bro Brigham and the brethren with him went back to his camp, after having taken dinner – In the afternoon at 4½ P. M. Bro. R. called a meeting, gave some good advice to the brethren, partook of the sacrament and dismissed with prayer – I did not attend, being absent with the cattle up the creek a little ways where I had taken them to feed – The weather has continued fine since Friday last – To-day a number of our teams, as also 2 of Bro. Kimballs to bring up the remainder of our co. viz: – Bro. Lorenzo, Young, L. Whitney [Clark Lyman Whitney], and a wagon father had left behind – We are now in Putnam County, Missouri and have been since we left the South Fork of Shoal Creek –

Monday the 13th

Remained in camp today – Bro. [Hosea] Cushing [William] King, and Orson and myself put a new set of hoops on my wagon – Bro. C. is to put his horses on my wagon when we start, and my oxen to be put on another wagon which does not run so easy

Tuesday the 14th

Struck our tents and proceeded to Bro. B's. Camp on the W. Fork of Locust Creek where we arrived late in the afternoon – Bro. Perry [Fitzgerald] drove team for me to day, he had been driving for Bro. [Rufus] Allen who left us and went back a day or two ago. Had to double our

22. The original plan of Brigham Young and the Quorum of the Twelve Apostles was to reach a destination and forge a new settlement somewhere in the Rocky Mountains in the summer of 1846. The extremely wet weather they were now facing in Iowa threatened to postpone this original plan. A new revision of the plan would now force them to leave behind a large number of the Saints at two or more waystations in Iowa and to send an "express company" to Council Bluffs, Grand Island, and up the Platte River to their destination somewhere in the Rocky Mountains. For much more on the planning and preparations for the exodus, see Matthew J. Grow et al., eds., *Council of Fifty, Minutes, March 1844–January 1846*, vol. 1 of the Administrative Records series of *The Joseph Smith Papers*, ed. Ronald K. Esplin, Matthew J. Grow, and Matthew C. Godfrey (Salt Lake City: Church Historian's Press, 2016); see also Matthew J. Grow and R. Eric Smith, eds., *The Council of Fifty: What the Records Reveal about Mormon History* (Provo, UT: Religious Studies Center; Salt Lake City: Deseret Book, 2017), especially chapter 13.

teams some distance across the bottom – as also the hill on which we encamped after we left the creek – soon after arriving went to Bro. Willard Richard's tent which is called by us the Post Office of the Camp of Israel where Charles Decker had just arrived from Nauvoo the bearer of a number of messages and letters – he however had none for me –

That evening the band also came up and they played for President Young and father before retiring. All remained at this place till Thursday, except Bishop Miller and company, they went ahead next morning.

Woman's Exponent, vol. 12, no. 16,
16 January 1884, pp. 126–27

Wednesday the 15th

Bishop Miller, and his company left this morning and went ahead – we staid behind – tolerably fair weather to-day – it rained a little however during the night, but not enough to impair the roads for traveling This afternoon the pioneers of our company consisting of about 20 men with others from Brigham's camp, started for the head of Grand River – on arriving they are to take jobs of work in order to procure corn and provisions – Bro. Kimball gave them a great deal of good advice, such as never to involve themselves in any quarrels, strifes, or contentions with the inhabitants, but on the contrary to court their favor by every possible means in their power – Bros. Kimball and Markham accompanied them a short distance on their route, and gave them other good counsel about conducting themselves – Hans Hanson took his cow and went with them – In the evening there was a grand christening held at Bro. Claytons camp in celebration of the birth of his child in Nauvoo when the band was encamped a short distance from us just at the top of the hill[23] –

As I learned, through the mail, that Wm. Clayton was the father of a child by his wife, Diantha Farr, who was left with her parents in Nauvoo. I bore the tidings to Wm., whose delight knew no bounds, and that evening Horace, myself and a number were invited over to their camp, Wm. being one of the band, whose encampment was only a short distance from ours.

Woman's Exponent, vol. 12, no. 16,
16 January 1884, pp. 126–27

Thursday the 16th

Left our place of encampment at half past 9 a.m. proceed about 6 miles and encamped at 2 P. M. on the prairie near where Bro Taylor G A Smith A Lyman had encamped the night previously To-day 8 rattlesnakes were killed by our company, and 2 of the oxen in the same were bitten – One of Willard's horses' lips was swelled considerably supposed also to be

---

23. Mormonism's 'anthem of the exodus', "Come, Come Ye Saints," was composed by William Clayton at a site twelve miles southeast of present-day Corydon, Iowa. An instant favorite, this memorable hymn, while predicting eventual rest in the west, also foreshadowed the inevitable loss of life among the Saints.

occasioned by the bite of a rattlesnake – To-day is the first time we have seen any of these reptiles on our journey – as we progress on our route game grows quite plenty more especially deer and turkey of which there are several almost daily bro't into our camp – vegetation also is now commencing to spring up around us which we consider as quite a blessing as we have had no corn for our cattle for two or three days – Bro. Brigham and the Band is also encamped on the prairie within 1½ a mile of our place – on arriving here had to drive our cattle a mile or two to give them a good chance – to feed – while absent saw 3 large turkeys but had no gun

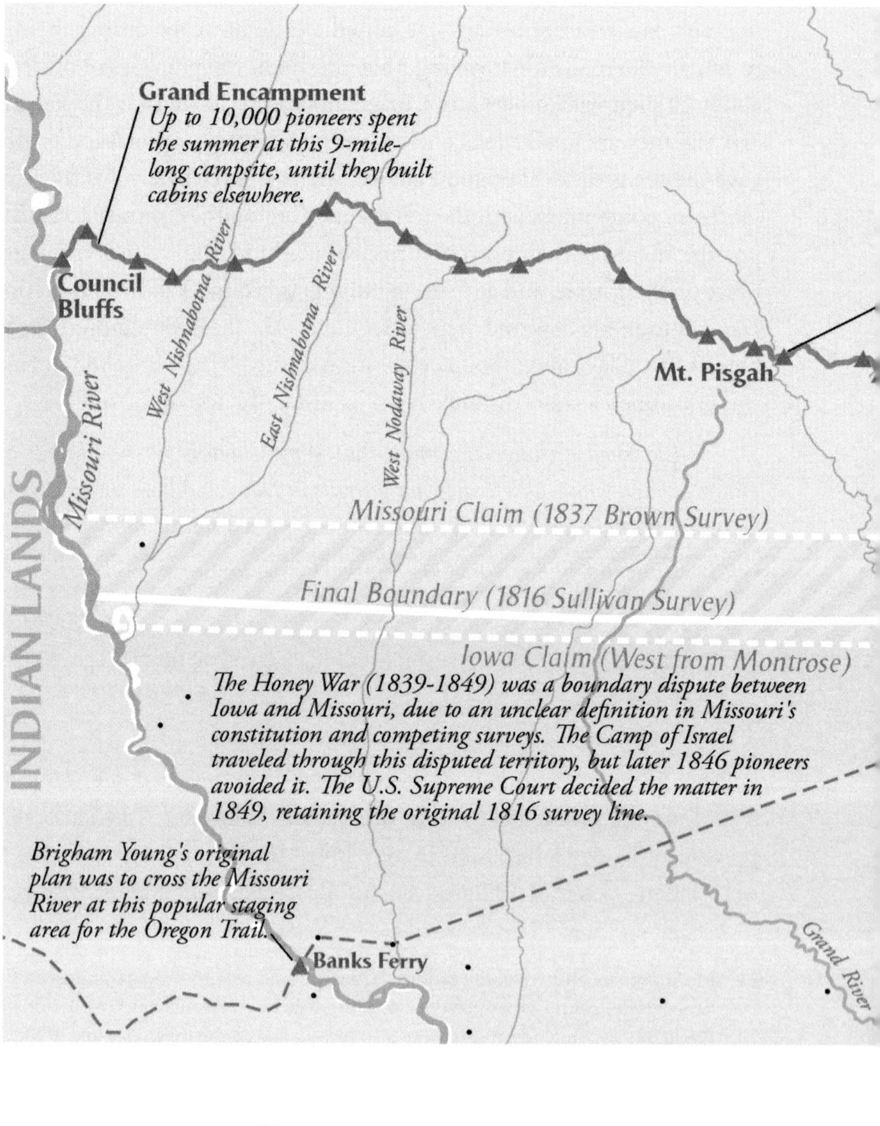

Map of Mormon crossing of Iowa Territory, February–June 1846. Courtesy of Brandon S. Plewe, ed., Mapping Mormonism: An Atlas of Latter-day Saint History, 2nd ed. *(Provo, UT: BYU Press, 2014), 75.*

I remember that day, and of seeing our men killing snakes in the grass, where our tents were afterwards pitched, and it was enough to give one nervous spasms to see them, and then to think of sleeping in the neighborhood of such dangerous enemies.

Woman's Exponent, vol. 12, no. 16, 16 January 1884, pp. 126–27

FRIDAY THE 17TH

Started this morning at 8½ a.m. – proceeded about 8 miles and encamped in a grove of hickory, bordering on the prairie on the Medicine Creek. Father, – Bro. Yearsly, and others of our company instead of joining us went down the hill crossed the creek, proceeded about 3/4 a mile and encamped in the vicinity of a small piece of timber, where Brigham and the Band also encamped. Bro. Kimball learning this, determined to go on – accordingly we started

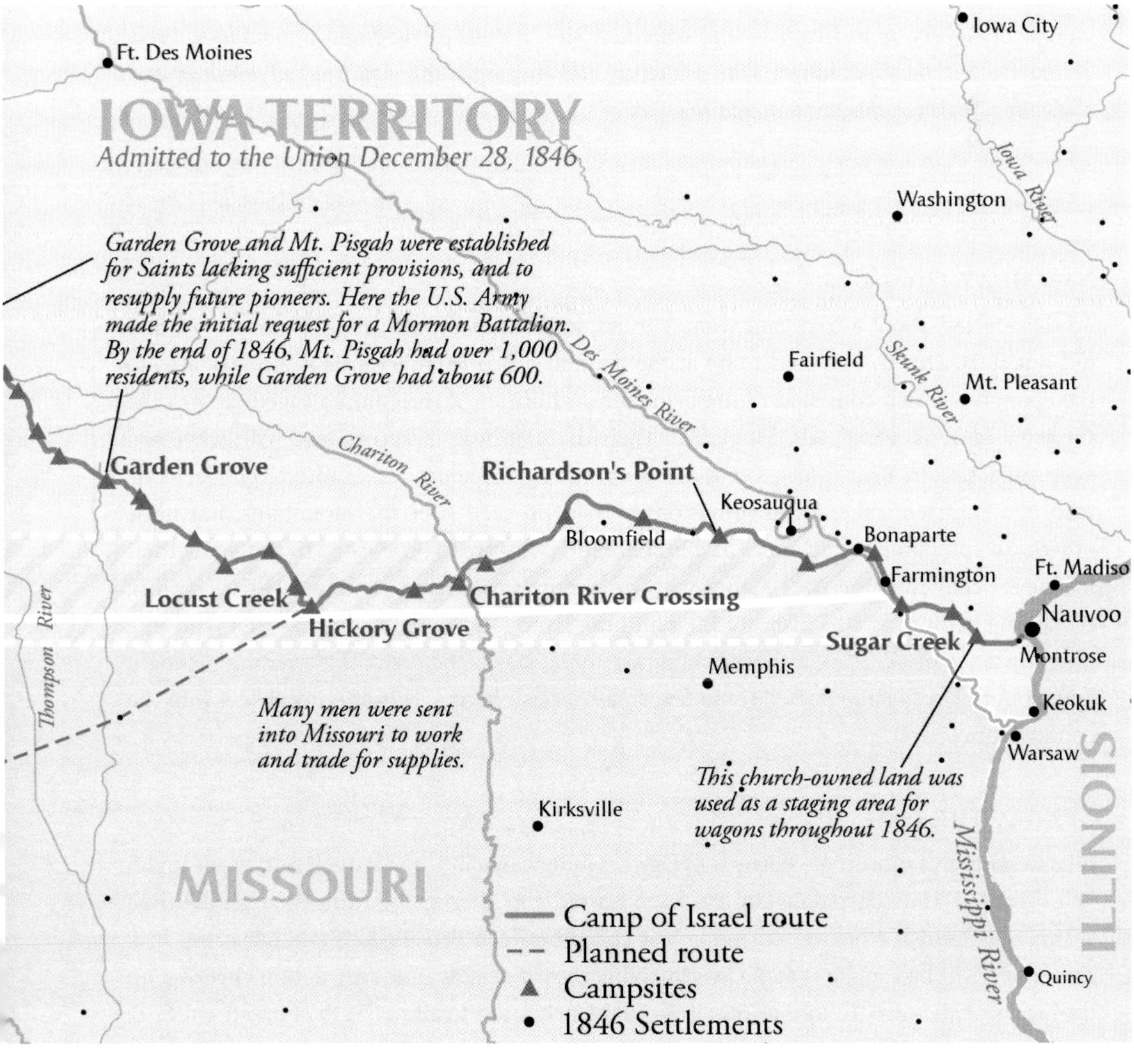

about 5 P. M. – after descending the hill and crossing the creek, we were detained by the fire on the prairie about 3/4 of an hour, and a number of us were obliged to stand by with sticks to whip out the fire in order to make ourselves a road, or passage thro' it – we then went on without interruption to the place where the rest of our company were and encamped – Here also, we overtook Bishop Miller's Co. Our two principal hunters, Bros. [Isaac] Higbee and Smith went out before starting this morning, and cut down two bee-trees bringing in to the Commissary 3 pails full of first rate honey – they also killed 2 deer and 2 turkeys during the day, which were distributed to the company – To-day I for the first time saw a rattlesnake – he was in the road – had just been killed – This evening we met Bro Averett [Addison Everett] who had just come from Grand River, from here distant 15 miles – he tells us there is abundance of corn in that region, and that some of the brethren have taken a job, building a double log barn –

On the morning of the 17th our company proceeded about eight miles and encamped in a grove of hickory on a stream called Medicine Creek, named by the Indians, no doubt. Prest. Young, Bp. Whitney and others, with the band, had encamped three quarters of a mile ahead, and father, learning this, determined to go on.

Woman's Exponent, vol. 12, no. 16,
16 January 1884, pp. 126–27

Saturday the 18th

To day started about 8 a.m. and went 2 miles, and camped on E. F. of Madison – father did not start with us but staid to be at the council – Bro K. afterwards went back also to the council – which consisted of the principle authorities of the Church together with the Captains of Tens, Hundreds, Fiftys, &c. Their decision was in accordance with what had been suggested by Bro. Young, viz: that after reaching the source of Grand River every one who had sufficient means and provisions should proceed over the mountains, but none others, except, indeed, Mechanics of different kinds who are to be assisted to prosecute their journey – council being over Father with his family started and came up with us, Bro B. remaining behind, as also Bishop Miller and the Band – Bro. Taylor is encamped with in a short distance of us. Took a short fishing excursion down the creek this evening – caught 3 fish but not very large ones – some few small cat fish here – This afternoon sent into the country for corn –

Sunday the 19th

Fine weather this morning – Porter and Edwin Cutler came in with the mail to-day – Nauvoo Left there last Thursday some families have started and are starting from there all the time – This afternoon at 4 o'clock a meeting was called between Bro. Taylor's and our camp Bro. Taylor and Kimball spoke at some length giving a great deal of good instruction cheering up the hearts of all – Bro. K. told us that it would be necessary to allow 1½ lb of bread-stuff per day to each individual for 500 days – in going 1500 miles over the Mountains Had a letter from our pioneers stating that they had a job to do of building a jail and storehouse – worth $250, on the E. Fork of Grand River 30 miles from here – Yesterday wolves were seen round the camp

Monday the 20th

Beautiful day the birds begin to sing, grass to grow and every thing assumes a pleasing aspect – Bro Back [Pack?] came in with one of the teams sent out after corn – Wm and Cushing and King did not come – they had to pay 20cts. per bushel – Bro. [Daniel] Spencer who has been a long while back just came up with us this afternoon In the last mail Bro. R. Received a number of the Hancock Eagle – Bro. K. and father went back to Bro B's camp to day to attend the general Council –

Tuesday the 21st

To day Bros Cushing and King came in bringing in 22 bushels of corn – Wm. did not come with them but they supposed had gone to the place where Hans is – Brigham's and Bishop Miller's companys passed our camp this forenoon – Bro K. will start as soon as Wm arrives, and as soon as he can arrang [*sic*] his loading. An Indian was seen passing by our camp – there is said to be an Indian encampment somewhere in the vicinity – Porter went on ahead to Bro. B's. camp – he intends starting back to-morrow or next day – In the little woods on the little creek where we are now camped a person can discover evident signs of Indians having been here – While fishing the other day I noticed a kind of hut or wigwam made of boughs of trees, very ingeniously interwoven together, having been formerly covered with bark – it had the appearance of having been erected last autumn probably used as a temporary sojourn while they were hunting in the vicinity – Heard day before yesterday that Bro. Wilford Woodruff had returned to Nauvoo. Bro. Markham, L. Young, [Aaron] Farr, W.[illiam] Walker with their families went ahead to-day –

Wednesday the 22d

William does not come yet consequently we are unable to start – Porter came back from Brigham's camp which is 6 miles the nearest way tho' the way they went it is 10 or 15 miles – part of our company that went ahead yesterday had overtaken them Porter intends starting to morrow for the city, as also Bro. Pond and Durfee whom further has released with their teams – father intends taking back the 2 yoke of oxen he gave to me, and Bro. K. has made an arrangement for another yoke and intends to get another yoke still in the place of them – it has been somewhat cloudy, but did not rain till evening when it commenced and rained most of the night accompanied by considerable thunder and lightning. – Bro. K. and father have been busy arranging their loading, taking out such things as they wish to dispose of for provisions to the inhabitants – wrote 4 letters for Bro. K. to-day – to Bro. Winchester, Sister

Orson, Amanda, and O[rson] Hyde, and W. Woodruff – intends sending them by Porter to Nauvoo –

Thursday the 23[d]

This afternoon Wm. came back having explored most of the country as far as Grand River – saw our pioneers there, who he says find plenty of work to do – cattle are rather scarce there, an Oregon company having traversed the region round and engaged above 500 yoke of cattle previously to his arrival – Bro. Pond, Porter, W[illia]m. [Lathrop] Cutler and Father Durfee started back to-day taking 2 buggies with them. Porter took my watch with him to get fixed. Start 8 o clock P. M. We started and went about 4 miles and encamped about sunset on the edge of a ravine in the open prairie, where there was beautiful feed for our oxen and horses, the grass being of very high and thick growth – I drove 1 yoke of oxen to-day on Wm's wagon he having swapped wagons with his father – Bro. W[illia]m. Cahoon, with part of the Band is camped within a short distance of us Bro. Taylor and Spencer have gone ahead, probably to Brighams camp – tolerable weather thro the day tho' it commenced raining soon after our arrival, which, however, did not last long. Bro. Perry left us also to-day and went back to Nauvoo.

Friday the 24th

Bro. Markham came back from his camp, which is 3 miles ahead near where Brigham had firmly encamped with 15 or 16 yoke of oxen to assist us along which was very acceptable as during the last night 4 of Bro. K's. horses had strayed away – a number of the boys went out in pursuit of them – we went on to Bro M. camp and stopt – This afternoon Bro. Yearsly who went ahead with the pioneers a few days ago to the Grand River, came back and told us that he had seen the boys and told them where to find the horses – they found them at the place where they had last bo't corn some 15 miles distant, and came back to us about 9 P. M. we run on another small creek, name unknown Bro Hosea Stout is camped within a short distance from us – Bro. [Charles] Dalton's h[orse]; was bitten by a rattlesnake to day – we have a civilized Indian of the ancient Delaware tribe with us who is of great service to us in such cases[24] – also this morning noticed a heifer be longing to Bro. Pack which had been bitten – These reptiles are getting so plenty as to be quite dangerous for those traveling on foot tho' I believe as yet no person has [been?] bitten – the other day one of Bro. K's horses being bitten, he laid his hand on the part affected and rebuked the sickness occasioned by the poison in the name of the Lord which prayer was almost immediately answered – Bro. K. says it is just as proper to lay hands on a horse or an ox and administer – to them in the name of the Lord,

24. Whitney is likely referring to Lewis Dana. See glossary of names.

and of as much utility as it is to a human being, both being creations of his creation, both consequently having a claim to his attention[25]

Saturday the 25th

Travelled about 7 miles this day and encamped on quite a large creek the name unknown – called it Mt. Pleasant This day by the advice and arrangement of Bro. K Helen and myself commenced "keeping house" or tent rather by ourselves, taking Cushing King, [Helen Janet] Jenette [Murray] F.[rancis] Whitney and Heber, thus by this means more equalizing the number for the other 2 tents rained a little during the night so much so as to render it somewhat slippery the next day. To-day news came to Bro K. from Brigham that he was 5 miles ahead of us on one of the forks of G. River our present place of destination and that the calculation is to commence splitting rails &c in order to enclose some farms, also to lay out a town plat &c.,[26] For the last 2 days have been driving 1 yoke of oxen –

When hearing the rehearsal of trials, privations and hardships endured by the camp of Israel, while journeying from the Mississippi River to the Missouri, my mind inadvertently turns to that portion between Nauvoo and Garden Grove, as the darkest in my memory. We were poorly prepared for such an exodus; and many joining us who were anxious to come, but had little or nothing of the necessaries for their own sustenance, ours had to be divided among them. We had many weeks of cold, stormy weather, and our teams being insufficient to draw the loads, rendered traveling over those soft prairies next thing to an impossibility; expecting, as we did, to go over the mountains that year we were put on rations, and had to lengthen out our flour and provisions in the most economical manner. During that time our sea biscuit, crackers, parched cornmeal, etc., which were among the luxuries, molded, until finally they were fed out to our horses and cattle. At the beginning of the journey the crackers went very well to eat dry, but I'll never forget the first time I saw a meal made of sea biscuit broken into milk. I had called at Uncle Brigham's tent—I had always addressed him by that title—where he was just taking some for dinner, and he invited me to have a bowl; but I declined, with thanks, and a feeling of

25. Latter-day Saints believed in the laying on of hands for the healing of the sick. While male members of the church exercised priesthood authority to perform such blessings, women also performed healing ministrations through the gift of faith. See Bennett, *Mormons at the Missouri*, 175–79.

26. Recognizing that their plans to reach the Missouri River would now have to be postponed, and aware that thousands of other Saints would soon be leaving Nauvoo in their wake, Brigham Young established a way station near Weldon Creek (the east fork of "Grand River") Iowa. On 27 April 1846, the Saints began to establish a farm site and a community of forty-eight log houses. Eventually named Garden Grove, this farm settlement would provide not only relief for the struggling advance company immigrants but also provisions, crops, and sustenance for later companies yet to leave Nauvoo. See Paul and Karla Gunzenhauser, "Decatur County: Garden Grove—A Mormon Frontier Community," in *The Iowa Mormon Trail: Legacy of Faith and Courage*, ed. Susan Easton Black and William G. Hartley (Orem, UT: Helix Publishing, 1997), 219–28. For an excellent demographic study of Garden Grove, see Jill N. Crandell, "Garden Grove, Iowa: From Mormon Way Station to Permanent Settlement, 1846–1852" (master's thesis, Brigham Young University, 2010). See also Bennett, *Mormons at the Missouri*, 39–51.

wonder how he could relish it. When it came to sitting down daily to milk and water porridge and crackers in it, it became so nauseous that hunger could not tempt me to eat it.

At this period the young, and even aged people were forced to walk, if it were possible, a goodly portion of the way to save the teams, no matter what the weather might be, storms, or excessive heat, or how weary, faint and footsore we became, there was no alternative but to endure till we had reached the spot called Garden Grove. Here they unpacked and sent out many valuables into the Missouri settlements and exchanged them for provisions and the most needful articles. They also traded horses for oxen and milk cows, and from that time our living was more comfortable. Father's and Bishop Whitney's families were divided up into messes, each tent having one or two women to cook for the teamsters, and wagons were provided for all the women and their little children to ride and to sleep in at night. Although we were not rid of hardships and vexations, consequent upon the moving of a great camp, and the intense heat of the weather, we certainly had little cause for complaint compared with what we had experienced previously, and the rest of our journey was made with comparative ease.

The whooping cough, which had so sorely afflicted my mother's babe, Brigham Willard, previous to starting from Nauvoo, grew lighter from the time we commenced camping out at Sugar Creek, and Mother Whitney's babe, Mary, which had been sick unto death, improved rapidly from that date. There were others, and even some of the most feeble and delicate women, that grew stronger for a time, until after the hot weather set in. Some of the strongest, who were more exposed, became prostrated with fever and ague, etc., before arriving at Chariton River, where we stopped a time for the weather to settle. My mother's little one had commenced to run down with teething, etc., and her own health, which was never good, failed to that degree that Mary Ann Sheflin, one of father's wives, who had lived with her in Nauvoo, being anxious to relieve her, took the child, and she loved and cared for him as tenderly as though he had been her own, till after we arrived at the end of our journey.

Woman's Exponent, vol. 14, no. 9,
1 October 1885, p. 66

Sunday the 26th

This morning notwithstanding our beautiful location we are forced to go ahead in consequence of there being no good range for our cattle to feed – went on to Bro B's camp – Before starting heard Bro [John] Scott telling a circumstance that happened about 15 miles from here in the Weldon Settlement, near where Wm found his horses – this man, (Weldon) being notorious for his Mobocratic principle A portion of the artillery had gone there and taken jobs of work[27] – they had earned about $26 of our men, when they were waited on by

27. With reference to the artillery, it should be noted that this advanced company of the Twelve brought with it at least three canons. Their primary purpose, as was the case with many other non-Mormon companies moving west, was to intimidate Indian war parties and scare off possible Indian attacks. A large number of men in the company had also served in the Nauvoo Legion and carried with them military titles such as "captain," "colonel," etc.

a committee, professing to be a deputation of the people, who told them they must leave immediately – the man who owed them the $26 seemed disposed to pay them but on manifesting a disposition to do so, he was told by his neighbors that he should "pack his duds and leave" accordingly he paid them nothing

travelled 5 miles and overtook the remainder of Zions Camp – at this place the fitting out of those who intend going over the Mountains, will take place – here it is said we will remain above a week in order to enclose grounds plant seeds &c &c. This evening Bro. S.[hadrach] Roundy came from the City bringing the mail – father received a letter from Bro. Tho[ma]s. Burdick dated April 22 at Nauvoo, stating that he had just received a letter from his brother-in-law Reuben McBride living in Kirtland, announcing the death of Grandfather [Samuel] Whitney, which happened soon after his arrival there. This morning by the kindness of Bro. S. of the artillery we were furnished with some pull pork, some of his company having killed 2 wild hogs in this vicinity, of which they saw quite a drove –

Monday the 27th

On waking this morning found it raining, which continued thro' the day and night, a slow drizzly rain – consequently the brethren could not do much at splitting rails &c. There are a hundred men assigned to this business, 10 laying up rails, 48 to building houses, 12 to each house – 10 herding cattle, 12 digging wells, 10 building a bridge across the river for us to pass over on our journey west 10 stocking ploughs and making drays, 5 or 6 blacksmith shops started the remainder to attend to the business of farming &c, &c.

It seems that for two days there was not much done on account of the rains, which continued incessantly day and night till Wednesday evening, when it cleared off pleasant. By the last mail father had received a letter from Bro. Joseph L. Heywood, at Nauvoo, announcing the sale of our place there for thirty-five yoke of oxen, to which Horace wrote an answer on the 28th.

Woman's Exponent, vol. 12, no. 17,
1 February 1884, pp. 135–36

Thursday the 28th

Not much done, to-day on account of the rains – a company of about 100 is about being fitted out for the expedition over the mountains – which I heard Brigham say to-day must start by Monday or Tuesday next – A general council of all hands to take place to morrow noon – it continued raining incessantly through the day and night – Wrote a letter for Bro. K. to-day to Bro. [Joseph L.] Haywood in answer to one from him announcing Bro. K's place was sold for 35 yoke of oxen –

Wednesday the 29th

Rained till evening when it cleared off pleasant, and the moon and stars shone out beautifully – continued pleasant thro' the night – This evening Orson and Geo.[rge Pierce] Billings and

Lyman came in from the last camp but one being 15 miles distant where they had been two or three days taking care of 2 of J. K.'s teams A meeting was called about noon of all hands, in order to do some business necessary to fitting out an expedition over the mountains – Bro. O. Pratt made an estimate of the number of wagons, grain, implements of farming such as hoes, shovels, &c. that would be necessary for 100 men on this expedition which I have not in possession – The bill he made out varied considerably from those made by others – We are on the E. F. of G. River

Thursday the 30th

On rising this morning found it raining again – considered it rather surprising last evening closed so beautifully – the sky continued lowery thro. the day and night – Bishop Miller with a number of others went out peddling (Bro [James] Smithies among) the other day – the Quadrille Band the number also went out Tuesday on the same business – Father Roundy and Edwin Cutler started back today R. C. Moon also went with them – Bro. R. took two of J. C. K's wagons back, and one span of horses belonging to himself – one of the wagons Sarah Ann had rode in since we started from Nauvoo

Friday the 1st of May

Rather cloudy, but no rain – This forenoon Bro. Yearsley, John Davenport and Francis Whitney went into the country with a wagon and 2 yoke of oxen, taking a harness, double-tree, crockery &c. &c., in order to make exchange for bacon and other provisions, which we stand much in need of – I suppose they will go somewhere near where Hans is on Grand River, some 46 miles distant from this place – We are now engaged in repairing the wagons that we intend taking with us when we shall start again – The weather has been so inclement since our arrival that our stay here will necessarily be protracted beyond the time originally intended – there is however, now, a prospect of fair weather. –

He also speaks of his father and mother, Prest. Young and wife Mary Ann, and my father and mother going to Lorenzo Young's tent that same day to dine, where they had quite a family meeting. While stopping there there was not more than one or two days till about the 13th that we did not have a shower; some of the time hail and rain, and on the night of the 5th had a heavy thunderstorm, and there was some sickness in consequence, but we had very few deaths in our camp during that part of our journey, for which we had great cause to be thankful. Numbers of the brethren, who had come that far with teams and to drive, return to Nauvoo.

Woman's Exponent, vol. 12, no. 17,
1 February 1884, pp. 135–36

Saturday the 2[d]

The sun rose cloudless and beautiful tho' about 10 it became cloudy – Had a small shower about 1 P. M. at the place where I was, 3 miles from here, watching cattle – the sun went down behind a cloud this evening. –

Sunday the 3[d]

Remained quite pleasant till the afternoon when we had quite a shower of rain which lasted till evening – there was a meeting held to-day – did not attend in consequence of illness – all the boys except Peter and myself went out on the prairie 2½ miles where the oxen are in order to erect a temporary hut for the herdsmen to stay in, also, a yard to put the cattle in nights –

Monday the 4th

Rather cloudy by spells, but no rain – Abram Hatch one of J.C.K.'s teamsters went back with Houston's team – I went out where the boys are herding the cattle – returned again in the evening – one of father's horses on being driven up to night was discovered to be very badly bitten in two or three places on the head – we immediately resorted to our family horse physician, the Delaware who has been very successful hitherto in such cases, and under his

Garden Grove site. *Photograph by Kenneth R. Mays.*

hands we look for a speedy and permanent cure – Forgot to mention that on the 1st day of May, Brigham and wife Heber and wife and father and mother went to Lorenzo Youngs tent and dined and had quite a family meeting.

TUESDAY THE 5TH

The weather fair thro' the day – the warmest day we have yet experienced – as the night set in had quite a thunder storm, engendered by the heat during the day – raised the creek considerably – Stephen Winchester started back this morning with his team, in order to assist his father to come up with us – To-day Bro. K. made some arrangements about the loading of the wagons – Helen and myself changed – took a wagon which H.[orace] Rockwell had formerly had – more convenient still than the Murray wagon, which we had last –

WEDNESDAY THE 6TH

This morning the sun rose cloudless and beautiful – towards night however a storm with hail and rain somewhat similar to the one of last evening arose, accompanied by considerable wind which prostrated 2 trees a short distance from our tent the tops falling on a mule that happened to be in the way and knocking him down – he could not rise till we took the limbs from off him, what is quite surprising he was not injured in the least – Bro. J. M. Grant returned from the county, where he has been for the purpose of trading – he exchanged a horse for 1 yoke of 3 year old steers, a cow & calf J. C. K. has been quite unwell for a number of days – a number are complaining of the diarrhea, probably owing to their drinking the creek water – I myself have not been well for a few days past –

THURSDAY THE 7TH

Somewhat cloudy it cleared off however towards night – Wm wrote a letter to day to P. Kimball, intend sending it by the first opportunity – we are still continuing to fix the wagons we intend taking with us when we start – The brethren are mostly engaged in drawing rails cutting house logs, building fence, blacksmithing digging wells, repairing wagons, &c.– while quite a number are gone into the country engaged in peddling off such things as they cannot take with them on the Journey for bacon, flour, meal, corn, and other necessaries of life – these things we stand much in need of – we have had no meat of any kind, (except a little we borrowed the other day) for a number of weeks, but have subsisted principally on sea biscuit, and milk porridge Father's horse, spoken of as being bitten by a rattlesnake on Monday, died today contrary to our expectations, as we had began to hope he was getting well – this was owing to inattention on the part of the boys who neglected to take care of him – Father considers it quite a loss as it breaks up one of his teams –

FRIDAY THE 8TH

Beautiful day sky cloudless and serene – Jacob with 5 yoke of Bro. K's. oxen came in and went to drawing rails this afternoon. The brethren finished their fencing to day. having enclosed 300 acres, leaving a surplus of 10,000 rails – they have besides a sufficient number of house logs cut to build 30 or 40 buildings. This afternoon A.[ndrew] Cahoon came in from Nauvoo – brought the mail – the 5th No. of the Eagle for Brigham, and the news that Porter was arrested, while asleep, by [Sheriff Jacob] Backenstos in Nauvoo, for the murder of [Frank] Warrell, that he was taken to Carthage, stood trial on the charge and was acquitted – he was no sooner liberated, however, than he was taken up on another accusation – that of threatening a man's life, and committed to Quincy Jail there to await his trial[28] – The wife of Bro. [John Hyrum] Green, Captain of a company of pioneers died lately. – she was buried here yesterday –

SATURDAY THE 9TH

Beautiful day – about noon I started out and got the cattle – put 4 yoke on my wagon 3 on Bro. Smithies, and 1 on the Carriage and went out 3 or 4 m. and encamped where our cattle have been kept – took the little tent with us. Wm and King went with us and helped us drive the teams and went back to the camp – we got here about sunset. We are in a great distance of the hut which the boys built the other day, where John Smith and Jacob Frazier stay nights There is a wolf's den about a ¼ of a mile from here which Wm found the other day – the boys chased a wolf into it and put fire at the entrance, but could not scare the wolf out and on repairing them the next day discovered the sticks they had made it of carefully laid aside Besides Helen and myself there are 6 of us John, Jacob, Jenette Sister Smithies, and her 2 children –

SUNDAY THE 10TH

The weather is beautiful this morning, but I being unwell did not attend the meeting at Garden Grove, which is the name given to the new settlement – understood there were some resolutions passed at the meeting – one was, that the land which has been enclosed, and all that pertains thereto, should be considered as belonging to the Church, or church property – Each man, or family, is allotted a certain portion of land to till, and if he neglect it it is to be taken from him and given to another[29] – Father [Samuel] Bent is to be left as President

28. Lieutenant Frank A. Worrell of the Carthage Greys, the militia that failed to protect the prophet Joseph Smith the day he was murdered, was himself shot to death in a bitter altercation on 16 September 1845, by one of Smith's most loyal bodyguards, Orrin Porter Rockwell.

29. The Garden Grove settlement represented an important feature in the Mormon belief in the law of consecration. No private properties existed in Garden Grove since all belonged to "The Lord" (i.e., the church), and properties were divvied out based on family size and other needs. Many of the wagons the Saints had been traveling in also belonged to the church, and were surrendered on demand to help with later migrations of other companies leaving Nauvoo.

of the Stake or Br. assisted by 2 counsellors and the most implicit obedience to his orders is enforced on the brethren who remain by Prest. Young Bro. Grant preached in the forenoon on the first principles of the gospel – a number of Missionaries were present. Feel a little worried to day about Mother's health in consequence of what father told me yesterday that her arm, which she hurt last winter in getting into a wagon, is gradually perishing away and it pains her so much that it affects her whole system – All the rest of the folks, like myself staid out here on the prairie, in our wagons, the most of the day, which was rather lonesome Caught quite a number of fish to day out of the little creek which flows by our camp –

This day the sky was cloudless and beautiful, and I was happy because the few days spent there were so quiet and peaceful, and I looked forward with a feeling of dread to the time that it must be broken in upon and again be forced to mingle with the crowd and unavoidable noise and bustle of a large camp. Our tent was pitched on a gentle slope, and below, some distance away, was a crystal stream of water babbling over the rocks down through a little grove of trees and willows, where I accompanied Horace the next day, Sunday, to fish, taking along our books to read. This was his favorite pastime, and in which he indulged every opportunity. This was the most delightful spot we had seen, the whole landscape around us was lovely, they called it rolling prairie, and it had such a variety of hills and dales, all dressed anew in their bright velvety robes of spring.

The first morning I took an early stroll to enjoy the scene, and I was almost enchanted as I stood there alone gazing at the glorious sight as the sun was peeping over the hills—and to lend more to the scene of enchantment here came a beautiful fawn and also an antelope, skipping fearlessly over hill and dale and out of sight, with naught to disturb them nor the peace and tranquility of my thoughts, but the knowledge that the spell was so soon to be broken.

I was a romantic girl, not yet eighteen, and naturally an admirer of the beauties of God's handiwork, and I thought, like the "Minstrel,"

"O nature, how in every charm supreme! Whose votaries feast on raptures ever new! O, for the voice and lire of seraphim, To sing thy glories with devotion due!"

Woman's Exponent, vol. 12, no. 17,
1 February 1884, pp. 135–36

Monday the 11th

The weather still continues fair – The intention is to make a start again in a day or two – Bro. Parley, with his company started to day, some of them encamped a little way beyond us the rest about a mile back – Bro. K this morning sent out for 4 yoke of oxen – Jacob went in with them and returned in the evening bringing Wm's wagon, with him and Mary – to-morrow the rest of the folks are coming out here – heard more news from Porter – Bro. Scott told Bro. K. that he heard that he had been shot in an attempt to escape from Quincy Jail, whether this is true or false, we know not. But judge and hope it is an idle rumor – took another fishing excursion down the creek to day – caught a dozen or more of very decent size –

Next day another fishing excursion was taken, where Horace caught a dozen or more. These substantials were very acceptable, as we had had no meat, except a little that had been given to us and some we had borrowed a few days previous, for a number of weeks, but had subsisted principally on sea biscuits and that sort of fare. When the sun did shine the heat was intense, and the reason for my remembering it was that we were compelled to walk all that was possible to favor the teams, as they were fast giving out, and the most aggravating part was the slow progress that we made, it taking us over three months to accomplish what would have been a week's journey under ordinary circumstances.[30]

Sometimes our camping place would be in sight of the one that we had started from in the morning, being on the prairie and having to follow the crooked ravines, there being no roads or bridges unless we stopped to build them. The most trying part of the journey, at least to me, was when we had to walk, and the scorching sun at times beating down upon us, until my little strength and patience would be quickly exhausted. There were times when we girls would drop down by the roadside and vow that we would not rise again till we saw the tents pitched, then we would take a straight line to the camp. I had not yet obtained sufficient religion to assist me and as my strength failed me so did my faith, but when the teams were ahead our only alternative was to get up and travel on. But after they decided to peddle off such things as they could not take with them over the mountains and we got more teams and provisions, we were much more comfortable. I shall never forget how I feasted at Garden Grove upon my mother's first white bread and fresh churned butter. I had been famishing for a fortnight or more for the want of nourishment, or the lack of appetite to eat such as was set before us. At Garden Grove we had our first trial at eating cakes made of parched cornmeal, one meal of which sufficed me. At the beginning of our journey the crackers went very well for lunch, but after laying in the boxes, as they did through that long siege of wet weather, they became more or less mouldy and tainted with the pine wood, so that the greater part were fit only to be thrown away.

I remember one evening at our pleasant camping place, after leaving the main camp, when our little circle had knelt for prayers, I happened to bow by the bag of parched meal, and the effect was so unpleasant I could not center my thoughts upon worship, so I arose quietly and moved to the opposite end of the tent. Some were considerably reduced in flesh by this time. But at this place Bishop Miller and a number of the brethren went out peddling. The quadrille band, Bro. James Smith[ies] among the number, had gone on the same business in order to make exchanges for teams, flour, bacon, and other provisions, which the camp stood in great need of.

Woman's Exponent, vol. 12, no. 17,
1 February 1884, pp. 135–36

30. Helen Mar is correct in saying that it took the advance company three months to cross Iowa Territory; however, she greatly exaggerates in saying that it should have taken them "only a week." A distance of three hundred miles at an optimum speed of fifteen miles per day would have taken them at least three weeks' time. Still, she reflects accurately the original plan of the Twelve to reach the Missouri River well before the end of May.

Tuesday the 12th

The weather continues fair, till toward evening when it clouded up and rained a little during the night. Bro K's folks all got along this evening, also Bro. Grant[,] Thibbetts [Alvah Tippets] & Walker – John Davenport came in with the rest – he reached camp this morning, bringing 10 bushels of meal and 1000 weight of bacon, which the pioneers had earned – expect Hans in before long, as Bro. K has sent for him – Bro. K has just bo't two wagons, one of which he let Sarah Ann have, the other he bro't along with him – father could not start, till he had got his wagon fixed but will be along in a day or two – Understood Horace Rockwell started for the city to-day, probably to see about Porter's case –

The evening of the 12th it clouded up and rained some during the night, just at dusk came father, Bro. Jedediah Grant, and their families with others of the camp, with the loud ge-ha's of teamsters and yells of herdsmen, driving, unyoking and taking off their teams and other like noises which brought confusion, when the charm was broken, and lo, my bliss had departed.

Woman's Exponent, vol. 12, no. 18,
15 February 1884, p. 138

Wednesday the 13th

Rain and sunshine alternately thro' the day, till evening, when a tremendous cold rain storm came on – it lasted a good part of the night – Bro. Grant's tent was blown down in the gale. This forenoon Bro. K. and Wm. rode back to the camp of Garden Grove, on horseback. Bro. K. let father have 2 yoke of oxen for J. C. K. in addition to the wagon he had already given him – Bro. Brigham with his company passed by to day – we should have started to-morrow, had it not rained – took out a lot of sea-biscuit, which was in my wagon, and put it in the place thereof other articles of greater weight They are as follows: –

	lbs.
1 sack of flour	180
" " " buckwheat	152
" " " beans	120
1 box of soap	51
" " " "	52
" " " "	56
" " iron horseshoes &c.	72
" keg of alcohol	100
" coil of rope	7
" sack of boots & shoes	43
" bed, clothing, &c.	120
Total	953 lbs.[31]

This is the number and amount of the articles in the back part of the wagon Bro. Spencer is encamped about a mile beyond us – Brigham probably 5 or 6 miles ahead, where Parley is – fished a little again to-day, caught a large catfish and 2 or three small ones, of the common kind, called dace. – Bro. A. Farr, Pack, and Lorenzo Young, came up to day and camped with us.

We had rain and sunshine alternately through the day till evening, when a tremendous cold rainstorm came on and lasted a good part of the night. Bro. Grant's tent was blown down in the gale. President B. Young and company had passed us that day. Some of fathers men who had been out trading reached camp that morning, bringing 10 bushels of meal and 1,000 weight of bacon, which these pioneers had earned. Father had purchased two wagons, and before starting from Garden Grove our small one was exchanged for a larger one, and this day they had some sea biscuits taken out and articles of greater weight put in to equalize the loads, making the whole load about 1148 pounds, also another yoke of oxen was added.

Woman's Exponent, vol. 12, no. 18,
15 February 1884, p. 138

Thursday the 14th

Beautiful day – nothing of notice transpired – expect to start tomorrow if the weather is fair – Father does not yet come up with us, but is remaining at Garden Grove, repairing his wagon – In addition to the load already put into the back part of my wagon there is to be put in the fore part a chest weighing 80 lbs., our cooking utensils, about 15 lbs., a fiddle box and fiddle, 10 lbs. Bro. K's tent and mine, ours weighing 50 the other 40 lbs., making the whole load about 1148 pounds.

Friday the 15th

The weather still beautiful not a cloud to be seen in the horizon, tho' the roads somewhat muddy from the recent rain – Started this morning about 8 a.m. went about 3 miles and saw Bro. Spencer's and Dr. [Willard] Richard's place of encampment – they soon struck their tents and went on – we proceeded about 2 miles and met the Band returning from their trading expedition, as also Bishop Miller, with some of his company who had also been out trading – went on about 6 miles further and encamped, the sun about an hour high on the edge of a ravine that makes into one of the banks of Grand River on the prairie, a short distance from the timber, having made 11 miles to-day – Bro. Kimball styles it the – "Cream of

31. As per reference to the "100 lbs of alcohol," the Latter-day Saints were not then adhering to the Word of Wisdom in quite the same way as they do now. Tea, coffee, tobacco, brandy, and whisky were often consumed along the way, although moderation was enjoined. Not until the late nineteenth century, and certainly by the time of the administration of President Heber J. Grant, did a more literal living of the Word of Wisdom become binding upon the Saints. See Paul H. Peterson, *An Historical Analysis of the Word of Wisdom* (Salt Lake City: Benchmark Books, 2005); see also Thomas G. Alexander, "The Word of Wisdom: From Principle to Requirement," *Dialogue: A Journal of Mormon Thought* 14, no. 3 (1981): 80–90.

all the encampments we have hitherto had," in consequence of the beautiful "rolling" prairie, and the rich verdure for our cattle that abounds in such plenty around us – Saw what is called the "Oregon trail" to day, that is the route pursued generally by the Emigrants in their ways to that territory.[32] Dr Richards is encamped with us tonight, Bro. Spencer about a mile and a half, where Brigham encamped last night –

Saturday the 16th

Fair day again – travelled about 11 miles, and encamped on a small creek on the prairie, about a mile from timber – Bro. K. named it "Crooked Creek" After coming about half way to-day, saw the place where Brigham had encamped the night previously on a small creek by the side of the road in the prairie –

Sunday the 17th

Somewhat cloudy and sprinkled a little started at about 8 a.m. travelled 2½ miles and found Brigham encamped on a small creek in a valley – We went on by and a little way and pitched our tents on the top of an hill about 10 a.m. – Brigham and Bro. K, Amasa, G. A. Smith, and one or two others, went ahead on horseback to survey the road – returned after a short time bringing the news that they had found a good place to camp about 3 miles ahead, concluded to go on for fear it might rain; before starting father overtook us was glad to see him – Young Jasper had left him and gone back – He took two of Bro. N.[oah] Packards boys with him to assist him, on starting from Garden Grove – He would have been along sooner, but he lost his horses and was detained half a day in consequence – Lyman has lost his horses, and is yet behind – Bro. Myres came up to-day – as also Solomon Hancock, bringing the news that there were 200 tents pitched at Sugar Creek of those that had crossed the river since our departure[33] – they were 4 weeks from Nauvoo – we are encamped about an hour high at the place the brethren had selected on a small creek on the prairie having made 5 miles to-day – glad to find mother in pretty good spirits – her arm getting better J. C. K. also –

The morning of the 17th was cloudy and rained a little. We traveled about two and a half miles and found President Young encamped on a small creek in a valley. We went on a little way and pitched our tents on the top of a hill, when father, Brigham Young, Amasa Lyman, George A. Smith and one or two others went ahead on horseback to survey the road, and

---

32. Whitney's reference to the Oregon Trail may be of interest to scholars of the American West, who have long believed that the Oregon Trail began at various jumping-off spots along the Missouri River, stretching over two thousand miles to the fertile Willamette Valley. Whitney's reference here in Iowa indicates that some Oregon-bound emigrants also drove across Iowa.

33. The approximately 2,500 Saints who left Nauvoo in February 1846 in this "vanguard company" represented approximately one-sixth of the total Mormon population in and around Nauvoo. The exodus from Nauvoo also included later spring and summer departures and eventually the poor camps of September 1846. See William G. Hartley, "Spring Exodus from Nauvoo: Act Two in the 1846 Mormon Evacuation Drama," in *Iowa Mormon Trail*, 61–83.

finding a good place to camp about three miles ahead, returned and concluded to go on for fear it might rain. We made about five miles that day. Bishop Whitney and family overtook us at the place where we last stopped, and we were rejoiced to see them. He had lost some of his horses and been detained at Garden Grove. We felt considerably worried about Mother Whitney's health in consequence of her arm which was gradually perishing away, and it pained her so that it affected her whole system, but we found her getting better and in pretty good spirits, and also Bro. Joseph C. Kingsbury, who had been quite sick. Sister E. B. Whitney (the present editor of the EXPONENT) was the faithful nurse and companion of Mother Whitney in those troubling times, and continued to be like a loving daughter to her until she was laid in her last resting place. Bro. Soloman Hancock came up the same day bringing news that there were 200 tents pitched at Sugar Creek of those that had crossed the river since our departure. They were four weeks from Nauvoo.

Woman's Exponent, vol. 12, no. 18,
15 February 1884, p. 138

Monday the 18th

No rain tho' rather cloudy – Had to build a bridge this morning, before starting – A large horse apparently having formerly belonged to the Indians was caught by T[h]om[as] Williams lately – Started early this morning – stopt in the afternoon again to build a bridge – after doing which, and ascending the opposite hill, we perceived a large rock which had the appearance of having been rent in pieces either by the Indians setting fire to it, or by some convulsion of Nature – Proceeded and encamped at evening in a hickory grove on the brow of a hill, a small bottom of about half a mile in width intervening between us and the Middle Fork of Grand River, which is here about as large as the Chariton It abounds in fish, such as [blotted out]fish, sunfish, – Here it is the intention to remain some time, and make another farm – travelled 10 miles to-day –

Monday morning, 18th, the brethren had to build a bridge before starting and had to stop and build another in the afternoon. We traveled ten miles and encamped at evening in a grove on the brow of a hill—a small bottom intervening between us and the middle fork of the Grand River, which abounded in fish, such as sunfish and catfish. Here we were to remain some time and make another farm for the saints that were to follow us. This was called Mt. Pisgah.

Woman's Exponent, vol. 12, no. 18,
15 February 1884, p. 138

Tuesday the 19th

This morning Bro. Wm King and myself with 6 yoke of oxen and 1 wagon started for Garden Grove, to bring up some provisions, which we expected to get out of Bro. Yearsly – Met Lyman W. and Bro. Potts after going about 10 miles – also Bro. [Jacob Flynn] Hutchinson, who was in search of his horse – Lyman did not find his horse but came on without him

– Got to the farm on Wednesday, Met Bro. Hans also about noon – Bro Yearsley not at home – waited for him till Friday about 10 o'clock when we started back the creeks all very high and some scarcely fordable – reached home on Monday evening, accompanied by Bro. Markham Cahoon & several others – Bro't back the most of Bro. T's things in his wagon and our own, putting three yoke on his and two on ours – one yoke to let Bro. [Charles C.] Rich have to help him along who also came with us – Met J. C. K. and C. L. W. [Clark Lyman Whitney] going out to track Saturday – While we were going met a great number of emigrants just from Nauvoo – some three weeks from there and some 6 – in fact they are coming away as fast as they can get ready[34] – Bro. Kimball talks of building 3 houses here Brigham 2 – there have been 2 Indians here since we have been gone who said they had lost 3 horses – they were very glad to recognize the horse that Tom Williams found as being one of them – There were two messengers sent to their station on the West Fork about 50 miles hence to make arrangements about paying for the cultivation of the land – they returned bringing word that the Chief himself would come here and settle the terms thereof – they belong to the Pottawatomie tribe – Found Jacob Frazier very sick on our arrival two deaths – Bishop Miller's company – Bro. Wm Edwards and Bro. Farley's child. Bro. W[illia]m. Huntington has been appointed president over those who remain here assisted by Ezra Benson and Charles Rich – No whites within 45 miles of here – Bro. [John] Holman was the first man to put a plough in the ground here, notwithstanding he does not intend to remain – Our two messengers learned from the Indians that Bro. L. Wight is about 100 miles from there but do not know in what direction Bro. John Taylor has just returned from Nauvoo – he say [*sic*] that has got to be a wicked place – he makes the calculation that there are about 600 wagons on the way between here and Nauvoo – there are all sorts of reports afloat there respecting us, such as that we have been mobbed &c.–

While they were absent two Indians came to our camp belonging to the Pottawatomie tribe, who said they had lost their horses, one of which had been caught by one of the company a few days previous—they were glad to recognize the horse. They had been sent as messengers to their station on the west fork, about fifty miles hence, to make arrangements about paying for the cultivation of the land—they returned, bringing word that the chief himself would come to us and settle the terms thereof. Also learned through them that Lyman Wight was about one hundred miles from there, but could not tell the direction. Here Bishop Whitney's driver (Jacob

34. Whitney is likely referring to the so-called spring exodus of Mormons from Nauvoo. When the Camp of Israel, or Company of the Twelve, left Nauvoo in early February with approximately 2,500 souls, at least 11,000 others were still preparing to leave. The spring, or May, exodus consisted of at least 3,200 Saints, and during July and August other companies departed sporadically. A final group of less than 1,000 people, the so-called poor camps, who were driven out as a result of the Battle of Nauvoo or the Nauvoo War, left in mid-September. See Hartley, "Spring Exodus from Nauvoo," 61–83. See also Richard E. Bennett, "'Dadda, I Wish We Were Out of This Country': The Nauvoo Poor Camps in Iowa, Fall 1846," in *Iowa Mormon Trail*, 155–70.

Frazier) was very sick, which Horace mentions—also speaks of two deaths in Bishop Miller's company—Bro. Wm. Edwards's and Bro. Turley's child.

Woman's Exponent, vol. 12, no. 18,
15 February 1884, p. 138

[***Editor's note***: No entries from May 20th to May 25th]

Tuesday the 26th

Tolerable fair to-day – built a yard this afternoon to put our cattle in nights Bro. Clayton come up this evening. Mothers arm getting better – she has a rattlesnake bound on it – Bro. Geo. Herring, a Mohawk Indian arrived here today, he having been sent for some time since by the brethren – he came from Council Bluffs – he says there are a number of the brethren of [James] Emmett's company waiting for us at the State line[35] – that some had taken jobs of work near a settlement of the Pottawattomie Indians about 2000 in number – that the Indian agents by the orders of the governor of Missouri, are enjoined not to let any whites stop among them but More especially to prohibit the "Mormons" from doing so, also that they (the Mormons) should not be suffered to settle this side of the Rocky Mountains Bro Herring also told us that the United States had declared war against Mexico We hail all such things as happy events, because when the Gentiles are embroiled among themselves, they have less leisure to persecute the Saints of God[36] –

35. James Emmett, a member of the Council of Fifty, an advisory body to the Twelve Apostles, had been a persistent problem to Brigham Young for years. Never content to stay in any one place for very long, he had led one expedition after another. In September 1845 he led a group of people across Iowa to establish an unauthorized settlement among the Sioux Indians on the banks of the Vermillion River. Upon the orders of Indian agents and church leaders, Emmett moved south. Early in June 1846, the Emmett party had reached the Bluffs, intending to merge with the main companies and set up camp approximately thirty-five miles south of Mosquito Creek, on the east bank near the Missouri state line, in order to be close to trading centers. Emmett, meanwhile, had offended his wife, alienated most of his followers, and disturbed Indian agents when it was learned that he secretly had taken a Sioux Indian woman as another wife. He had also stolen several Indian horses. His heavy-handed style of leadership and impolitic actions caused most of his bedraggled followers to abandon him for the main camp, then nearing the Missouri River. See Juanita Brooks, ed., *On the Mormon Frontier: The Diary of Hosea Stout, 1844–1861* (Logan: University of Utah Press, Utah State Historical Society, 1964), 1:168; Journal of John D. Lee, 11 June 1846, Church History Library. For even more context, see Matthew J. Grow et al., eds., *The Joseph Smith Papers: Administrative Records: Council of Fifty Minutes, March 1844–January 1846* (Salt Lake City: The Church Historian's Press); also Richard E. Bennett, "Mormon Renegade: James Emmett at the Vermillion, 1846," *South Dakota History* 15, no. 3 (Fall 1985): 217–33.

36. The Mexican-American War, also known as the Mexican War (1846–48), was an armed conflict between the United States and the Centralist Republic of Mexico, brought on in part by the American annexation of Texas. The expansionist-minded administration of President James K. Polk dispatched American forces, including the Mormon Battalion, to occupy New Mexico and California, and then invade parts of northeastern Mexico and northwestern Mexico. Another American army captured Mexico City. The war ended soon thereafter in a victory for the United States. The Treaty of Guadalupe Hidalgo forced Mexican cession of California and New Mexico to the United States, in exchange for fifteen million dollars. Mexico accepted the loss of Texas and thereafter recognized the Rio Grande as its national northern border. For

This may be considered, by some, an unkind feeling, but note the orders received by those agents concerning us, and the unnatural treatment we have received from the hands of our government, which should have protected and succored us, but instead have allowed us to be persecuted, harassed and driven from state to state, and our men to be imprisoned and many slain, and also innocent women and children murdered in cold blood, and a whole people to be exiled and driven into an almost unknown wilderness, without the inquiry or understanding of the facts concerning us, and all the suffering that we were daily enduring as consequence, could they realize this, and how sorely we felt it, and then take it home to themselves, they would wonder at our patience, and that we did not join hands with the poor Indians, who would have been too glad—or with the Mexicans to fight against the nation, who had driven us out from their midst, hoping as they did and expecting that we should perish or be scattered to the four winds, regardless of our feelings and rights, and had it not been that our people were true Christians we would long since have followed our natural instinct, as others have done, who, though professing so much more enlightenment, have shown how much they were lacking in that same spirit of Christianity, which has ever governed and controlled the

Modern reconstruction of a log cabin at Mount Pisgah. Courtesy of Kenneth R. Mays.

more on the war, see Seymour V. Connor and Odie B. Faulk, *North America Divided: The Mexican War, 1846–1848* (New York: Oxford University Press, 1971).

Latter-day Saints, of whose inner lives and faith they know nothing until they are willing to become, as Jesus said, "Like little children, for of such is the Kingdom of Heaven."

Woman's Exponent, vol. 12, no. 18,
15 February 1884, p. 138

Wednesday the 27th

On rising this morning found it raining, which however did not last long – it commenced raining again towards evening which contd. till 10 oclock – To-day father presented me with a pistol – Hans arrived to day with Bro Smith – Brigham Heber father and some others went on horseback to find a suitable place for crossing the river when they shall start again they returned having found a place where they intend to build a bridge –

Thursday the 28th

Somewhat cloudy, but no rain – one of Bro. K's horses (Prince) on being found and bro't up from the prairie this evening was discovered to be bitten – went a fishing at a slough close by the river found Bro. Clayton at it also – caught quite a number of sunfish & trout, &c. Got summer cloth for 2 pair of pants of S. Ann one of which was made up today by mother also calico for 1 shirt for myself – The brethren here are busily engaged – some ploughing and putting corn into the ground others building fences and houses, making ploughs & ox yokes & c. while the rest are herding the cattle[37] – Bro. Yearsly, with his family, arrived here to day from Garden Grove – he got there the same day Bro. William King and myself came away

Friday the 29th

Fine and pleasant – the brethren have nearly completed the bridge – Bro. Brigham chastised the people last Sunday at meeting because a great many manifested a disposition to tie the hands of the twelve, as it were – neglecting to put in crops here and wanting to go ahead on their journey when they have not the means to do so, – Bro. Brigham gave them the choice of two things to do – either to fit themselves out and go ahead, and leave the Twelve here, or, by using their utmost exertion to fit out the Twelve and let them go into the wilderness and establish the kingdom – there was however no vote taken on the subject Br. K. said if the people chose to have the Twelve stay here – they (the Twelve,) would go into foreign

---

37. Located twenty-seven miles west of Garden Grove, Mount Pisgah, so named by Parley P. Pratt after an Old Testament site, was "a farm of several thousand acres." Patterned after the earlier way station of Garden Grove, Mount Pisgah was divided into five-, ten-, and twenty-acre plots and distributed by lot among individual families. Though the land was privately farmed, the effort was clearly a cooperative enterprise. There, a high council was organized to regulate both church and civic matters. A welcome respite from the dreariness of their immediate past sojourn, Ezra T. Benson said of it, "This was the first place where I felt willing in my heart to stay at, since I left Nauvoo." See Leland H. Gentry, "The Mormon Way Stations: Garden Grove and Mt. Pisgah," *Brigham Young University Studies* 21 (Fall 1981): 456–57. See also Bennett, *Mormons at the Missouri*, 40.

countries, preach the gospel and raise up a body of people who would be willing to abide by council and act as become the saints of God[38] – Got Ruth Pack to make me another pair of pants, to day – also got some leather of Sarah Ann and Abram is making me a pair of shoes – I have worn out 1 pair of shoes and 1 of boots since we have been on the journey besides an old pair I had when we started – this in consequence of having to travel so much on foot driving oxen thro the mud prairie grass &c., &c.–

Saturday the 30th

The weather fine and pleasant – nothing of moment transpired –

Sunday the 31st

A General Conference had been appointed for to-day, but as the meeting was about [to] commence, a heavy storm arose which caused the people to disperse – they met again in the afternoon but the weather being rainy they did not effect much of anything – the rain continued thro' the day and night – Bro. Noah Rogers expired to-day after an illness of 10 days – He, Bro. [Benjamin Franklin] Grouard, Bro. Addison Pratt and Bro. [Knowlton F.] Hanks were the first to introduce the gospel to the inhabitants of Toobouai and Tahiti, islands belonging to the Society Group in the Pacific Ocean – Bro. Rogers was gone about 3 years, during which time he, with his brethren, accomplished a great work and were the means of bringing many to the knowledge of the truth He has left a large family to sorrow for his loss, but one great consolation to them will be the fact that he died in full faith of the gospel and with the hope of a glorious resurrection, having the conscious satisfaction many a dark and benighted heathen had, thro' his instrumentality, been led into the "straight and narrow path that leads to eternal life"[39]

---

38. Said Brigham Young: "The Saints have crowded on us all the while, and have completely tied our hands by importuning and saying: Do not leave us behind. Wherever you go, we want to go, be with you, and thus our hands and feet have been bound, which has caused our delay to the present time, and now hundreds at Nauvoo are continually praying . . . that they may overtake us and be with us. . . . They are afraid to let us go on and leave them behind, forgetting that they have covenanted to help the poor away at the sacrifice all of their property." Journal History of the Church of Jesus Christ of Latter-day Saints, 3 May 1846, Church History Library (hereafter Journal History).

39. Addison Pratt is best known for his two missions to French Polynesia. Baptized in Kirtland, Ohio, in 1838, Pratt, along with Noah Rogers and two other companions, left on a mission to the South Pacific in May 1843, where he established the first branch of the church in the Pacific Islands on the isle of Tubuai. He established several more branches on neighboring islands before returning to America in 1847. After meeting up with the Saints in the Salt Lake Valley where he rejoined his family, Pratt returned again to the islands in 1848, accompanied by his wife and four daughters. In 1852, he made his way back to California, where he left the church and became a spiritualist. He died in Anaheim in 1872. Andrew H. Hedges, "Pratt, Addison," in *Encyclopedia of Latter-day Saint History*, ed. Arnold K. Garr, Donald Q. Cannon, and Richard O. Cowan (Salt Lake City; Deseret Book, 2000), 938. For more, see S. George Ellsworth, ed., *The Journals of Addison Pratt* (Salt Lake City: University of Utah Press, 1990).

Monday the 1st of June

Continued raining till about noon when it cleared off – was on watch with Jacob, (who is getting better,) from 11 till 1 P. M. – very cold weather indeed, for the time of year, being the first day of the first month of summer – Horace Rockwell arrived here to-day from Nauvoo, bringing the mail – he left the city last Wednesday – brot' me a paper ("Hancock Eagle") from [William] Waterman Phelps by reading which I found that Porter had taken a change of venue to Jo. Daviess Co. and is to be tried at Galena on Monday the 8th inst. – the rumors that we have heard, of his being shot in his unsuccessful attempts to escape from Quincy Jail, are entirely groundless – on the contrary he has made no effort to escape, and has declared that were even so good an opportunity to present itself he would not avail himself of a chance to escape, but would await his trial – we had formerly heard that Sheriff Backenstos sent him word that he would have to arrest him, in order to give him a chance to get beyond his circle and that Porter disdained the idea of running away, but this is not so, he never got the message – Horace says there did not seem to be much hostility manifested towards him where he has been, but rather a feeling of curiosity to behold such a noted individual, and that he had a great number of visitors who daily flocked to see him – He is treated kindly, uniformly both by the officers of the law and the people – We intend moving over the river to-morrow –

Tuesday the 2d

Rose early this morning, and went after the cattle – very cold morning – struck our tents sun about 2 hours high, crossed the river, went 2 miles and encamped on the prairie – Brigham is 3 miles ahead, he having started yesterday – Father did not start to-day, but probably will tomorrow – Sarah Ann accompanied us and intends living with Helen and myself here after – Orson drives team for her – The roads somewhat muddy, but improving

It rained a little during that night—just as we were about starting next morning a young Indian, belonging to the Pottawatomie tribe, rode up on a pony—he had a young spotted fawn in his arms, which father bought of him, giving him a dollar in silver, but it died in a couple of days after. We overtook President Young before his tents were struck, stopped there about three hours, where Bishop Whitney overtook us, having come that morning from Mt. Pisgah.

Woman's Exponent, vol. 12, no. 21,
1 April 1884, pp. 161–62

Wednesday the 3d

Notwithstanding the inauspicious appearance of the weather last evening it did not rain much during the night – as we were about starting this morning, a young Indian belonging to the Pottawatomie tribe rode up on a pony – he had a young spotted fawn in his arms which Bro. K. bought of him a dollar in silver travelled about 3 m's and overtook Brigham who had not struck his tents – here father overtook us – he left the farm to day – stopt here about 3 hours when the whole camp proceeded 6 miles and encamped on the prairie near the timber making in all 9 miles today – G. A. Smith is encamped about 2 miles back This morning, before starting wrote 2 letters (one to the Trustees in Trust, the other to Mary Smith, Hyrum [Smith]'s widow for Bro K. – he intends sending them by Bro. Markham who is shortly going back – Bro. K gave him an order on the Trustees for 4 yoke of oxen, he having given up his team to him The name of the last settlement made is Mt. Pisgah, (from the Bible –)

Day was cold and cloudy, accompanied by quite a sharp wind. We started quite early that morning, leaving Bishop Whitney behind—he had lost his cattle during that night. We went about eight miles and halted about noon, where we saw some fine looking Indians on horseback. We went ten miles further and encamped on the prairie, which we were told was eighteen miles long, being the distance we had accomplished that day; the longest day's journey since we left Nauvoo. We had just encamped when Bro. A. Fielding overtook us and remained with us all night. He was to start next day for Nauvoo. A day or two previous to this my husband's sister, Sarah Ann, commenced tenting with us, and we continued together till houses were built at Winter Quarters.

Woman's Exponent, vol. 12, no. 21,
1 April 1884, pp. 161–62

Thursday the 4th

Cold and cloudy accompanied by quite a sharp wind – started quite early this morning, leaving father behind – he had lost his cattle during the last night and could not come on – went about 8 miles and baited, about noon, went 10 miles further and encamped on the prairie near the timber and a running stream of water – Our route to day has been altogether on the prairie, which Bro. [John D.] Lee told us last night was 18 miles long, being the distance we accomplished to-day, the longest days' journey since we left Nauvoo We had just encamped when Bro. A.[mos] Fielding overtook us – he said he passed father's place of encampment about 2 o'clock and he had just found his cattle – Bro. Fielding remained with us all night – I slept with him – he is going to start back to Nauvoo to morrow

Friday the 5th

The sun some what obscured by clouds this morning and a little rain, but it soon cleared off, cloudless, and beautiful – Wrote a letter this morning for Bro. K, (and took a copy thereof,) to Bros. Huntington, Benson and Rich, at Mount Pisgah requesting 4 yoke of cattle – Started about 8, and about 10 o'clock, struck the Indian trail leading from Raccoon Forks to Council Bluffs – passed thro some very romantic spots, and quite a diversity of scenery to what we have hitherto seen on our route – passing "over hill and dale, tho' brake and bush" – We saw the remains of a great many Indian wigwams which had the appearance of being constructed sometime since – they were composed of boughs of trees curiously interwoven Just before reaching our place of encampment for the night we saw a large number of them which had fallen down, and were dried from on account of the long time that had elapsed since they were built. As we intended going on a little further before stopping and as there was nothing but prairie before us as far as the eye could extend – every man gathered a bundle for fire wood Wm. found a small breastplate that had evidently been lost by the Indians – the young fawn which Bro. K. bought lately died to day – we traveled about 14 miles to day – father does not yet come up with us – encamped on a small creek on the prairie, – Brigham also, within a short distance from us –

Unknown artist, Pottawattamie (Potawatomi) Village of Prairie Indians. *The Pottawattamie were the first Native American tribe the Saints encountered in their western trek across Iowa in 1846.*

Saturday the 6th

Rained a little during the day – travelled about 14 miles – encamped on the bottom in the vicinity of quite a large creek – the wagons were all arranged successively in a circle of about a quarter of a mile in circumference thus making an enclosure for our horses, that the Indians might not steal them – just as we were camping, father with his teams, came up – they had traveled very fast to overtake us to night, and would have overtaken us before had they not stopt to repair a wagon

Sunday the 7th

Meeting was called at 10 Bro. Brigham and Heber spoke at some length exhorting the people to the observance of the ordinances and commandments of God – A number of Indians and squaws came in to see us, mounted on their ponies and horses, and decorated and painted in their peculiar manner – they are of the Pottawatomie tribe[40] – they have a camp some 4 or 5 miles from here – About 3 P. M. got up our cattle and started on – went about 7 miles and encamped just after sunset on a small creek, near the timber after crossing the bridge.

40. The Pottawatomi (also spelled Potawatomi or Pottawatomie), originally known as Anishnabek, are a Native American tribe of the Upper Mississippi River and Western Great Lakes region. A member of the Algonquin family, they originally lived in what is now southwestern Michigan. Pottawatomi warriors took part in Tecumseh's War, the War of 1812, and the war in Peoria, siding at various times with Britain and the United States. Dispossessed of their original lands, the Pottawatomi were forced westward to lands along the Missouri River where they first encountered the Latter-day Saints in 1846. Recognizing a similarly dispossessed people, the Pottawatomi and most other tribes at the Missouri remained on relatively friendly terms with the Mormons. Today the Pottawatomie are a thriving community in southwestern Michigan. R. David Edmunds, *The Potawatomis: Keepers of the Fire*, vol. 145 of the Civilization of the American Indian Series (Norman: University of Oklahoma Press, 1978).

Brigham arranging his wagons on one side the road, Bro. Heber his on the other Had a beautiful day for travelling – the roads very good – One of Bro. Dike's [likely William Dykes (1815-1879)] oxen in Brigham's company had his neck broken, being turned loose in the yoke. Bro. Miller has built a bridge here and on a tree before crossing which, will be seen an inscription, done with a knife – "Lost Fork Bridge"

MONDAY THE 8TH

Beautiful day – started about 8 this morning travelled about 4 miles came to a river which we crossed on a bridge and passed thro the village, where the Chief of the Pottawatomies resides – immediately after crossed the same stream again which bears the name of Manottawa, or the "Sleeping Rock", probably originating from some wild legend or tradition of the Indians – here we stopt about an hour and baited our cattle – during which time we were visited by a great number of the tribe, both Indians and squaws The Chief went to Brigham and wished him to pay them – for the grass which the cattle eat, the request they were probably "put up to" by some of the whites, enemies to our people – The Pottawatomie village is situated in a bend of the river and consists, as we were told by some of the Indians, of 130 wigwams, but we did not learn the number of inhabitants – while we stopt here we had the amusement of seeing 2 or three Indian horse races – they have very fine horses and ponies among them, as we found out to our satisfaction by running with them – travelled 14 miles and encamped about sunset on another small creek near the timber – Father and Brigham had already arrived here, and encamped – Just before descending the hill to the river saw an Indian burying ground which we distinguished by a white flag which we saw fastened to a tree – The Indians appeared to be in quite a destitute condition offering us various ornaments, such as beads wampum and other trinkets in exchange for food – To day a trifling difficulty occurred between Bro. [Howard] Egan and Pack about the right of place – During the evening Bro. K. called his portion of the camp together, and admonished them to get their flintlocks ready in case of emergency – The names of those who never had been organized were then called over – there were 14 of them of whom Bro. Alva Thibbets was appointed Captain

TUESDAY THE 9TH

Beautiful day – started about 8 o clock this morning nothing worthy of notice transpired – towards evening arrived at a spot something like an inclined plane, situated on a small creek and environed by trees on each side – On account of the uncommon beauty of the place Bro. K. named it "Paradise" – We there crossed the creek, ascended a hill, proceeded about a mile and encamped on another creek in the vicinity of timber – here we found a beautiful spring of water which rivaled in sweetness any I ever saw – Did not overtake Bro. Brigham learned from Lorenzo, (whom we found lame,) that he is encamped 3 miles ahead, where Bishop Miller and company are engaged in building a bridge, which they intend finishing to-morrow – This day travelled about 13 miles

Here we found Bro. Lorenzo Young, who, as a rule, camped a little distance from the rest to favor Sister Harriet Young, who was a constant sufferer from asthma, and desired to be quiet, which was out of the question in a large camp, and as young as I was she had my sympathies. We learned from Uncle Lorenzo that President Young had encamped three miles ahead, where Bishop Miller and company were engaged in building a bridge, so we stopped here, having traveled about thirteen miles.

Woman's Exponent, vol. 12, no. 21,
1 April 1884, pp. 161–62

Wednesday the 10th

Fine day – In consequence of having to build a bridge where Bishop Miller is, we did not start to-day – A number of our camp went to assist about it – Bro. K. and father went in the carriage to Bishop Miller's camp and returned – In the afternoon Brigham and wife with his carriage came over to our camp – He, Bro. K. and father mounted their horses, while Sisters Young, K. and Mother got into the carriage and went out after strawberries – they returned towards evening bringing 3 or 4 quarts – To-night our boys returned, having finished the bridge. – Bro. Miller intended going ahead 5 or 6 miles this evening – We all intend to start to-morrow morning – had quite a pleasant time this evening which we spent in dancing on the green grass till bed time the bright orb of night shinning in all its glory over our heads –

A number of our camp went to assist in building the bridge. Father and Bishop Whitney drove over to see the President, and in the afternoon he came back in his carriage with Sister Mary Ann Young. He, with father and Bishop Whitney, mounted their horses, while sister Young, my mother and Mother Whitney got into the carriage and went after strawberries. They returned towards evening bringing three or four quarts.

Woman's Exponent, vol. 12, no. 21,
1 April 1884, pp. 161–62

Thursday the 11th

Very warm and sultry – Started about 8 a.m. crossed the creek, and on ascending the opposite hill, saw that Brigham had not yet started – therefore we stopt and waited an hour till his teams had got out of the way – we then went on, crossed the bridge which the boys finished yesterday – this, like the one at the Sleeping Rock, has no other foundation than flood wood. – Passed thro the timber about half a mile before reaching it and after crossing a small bottom and ascending a hill on the opposite side of the river, saw a grave, which had been dug apparently some 4 or 5 months since – it was covered with logs laid up in an oblong form, and about 3 feet high; something like a log building – the stream we crossed is called by the Indians the "Nishina the E. Fork Botany" River[41] – stopt again about noon, baited our cattle and waited for Bro Miller and B. Young, to cross another bridge which they had about finished when we came up with them – we then went on and encamped sun about a hour high on a "divide" near the timber, quite a large creek on one side and a branch of the same on the other, Brigham having encamped on our right, and Bro. Miller on our left, while Bro. Spencer is in front of us, on the bottom close to the creek – Bro. [James Willard] Cummings came from the Bluffs, yesterday – he says Emett's company are 30 miles below the Bluffs; on the River and have taken jobs of work there, in order to get themselves provisions to prosecute their journey – he said that there were 12 wagons (Mormon,) had come up from St. Louis lately, and that a U. S. officer, had told them that he was ordered to prohibit all

Artist unknown, Nishnabotna River Crossing. *Courtesy of Church History Library.*

41. A tributary of the Missouri River, the Nishna Botana (or Nishnabotna) River is made up of two smaller rivers (the East Nishnabotna and West Nishnabotna) originating in Fremont County, Iowa. Its name translates in Otoe to "canoe-making river." It served as the water supply for several temporary Mormon settlements in southwestern Iowa.

suspicious persons from crossing the State line, hinting that the Mormons were the persons meant. Some of the brethren tho't that the grave that we saw to-day, was that of one of the brethren in Bro. Wight's Company[42] Bro. [Henry G.] Sherwood tells me that the streams we crossed after leaving Grand River, or before reaching the Monottawa, are the head waters of the Platte – the stream where we are now is the W. Fork of the "Nishinie Botanie"

Friday the 12th

Did not start till towards noon – having to build a bridge – Bro. K. sent a large number of men to assist – the weather warm and sultry – travelled about 10 m's and encamped sun an hour high between the 2 forks of a creek, where we have, to-morrow morning to build another bridge – Bro. K. called the people of the camp together, and selected 25 men to go to work at it early in the morning, before breakfast. Bro. Brigham and Miller are encamped within a short distance of us.

Saturday the 13th

Were detained this morning, about the same length of time we were yesterday morning, in building a bridge – we then started – the weather sultry and unpleasant – stopt about 2 o'clock P. M. and baited our cattle – had to drive them about a mile to water – in fact there has been so much dry weather and so little rain in this part of the country, that there is a great drought through the country – from our stopping place, we could perceive the grand and lofty hills on the opposite side of the Missouri River, their pinnacles widely jutting up and reaching far above the surrounding scenery – Brigham is encamped for the night about a ¼ of a mile beyond – Bro. K. went ahead to look out a good camping ground – he returned, having found one – and we all started and went a mile and a half further and encamped on a creek near the timber, somewhat out of our way, in order to have a good place for our cattle – we can perceive the Missouri River from our present position, which is about 2 miles, a swampy wet bottom intervening[43] – some of the brethren tho't they could see the trader's houses sometime before we got here – on the right hand side of us is Musquitoe Creek, on our left a branch of the same with a beautiful wood in the front and the Council Bluffs are to be seen in the distance[44] – over this creek we have to build another bridge, before we can proceed

42. Lyman Wight was a disaffected member of the Council of the Twelve. For the most recent study of Wight and his Texas colony, see Melvin C. Johnson, *Polygamy on the Pedernales: Lyman Wight's Mormon Villages in Antebellum Texas, 1845 to 1858* (Logan: Utah State University Press, 2006).

43. It was well known among traders and trappers in the American West that no travelers should leave for the Rocky Mountains from the Missouri River any later than 1 June as the Donner-Reed party learned the hard way in 1846. Trapped in the snows of the High Sierras, the Donner-Reed party cannibalized itself in the winter of 1846–47.

44. The modern city of Council Bluffs, Iowa, was named after an 1804 meeting of Lewis and Clark with the Otoe Indian tribe, which occurred at Council Bluffs near present day Fort Calhoun, Nebraska. Council Bluffs became the generic name for land on both sides of the Missouri River, north of the mouth of the Platte River.

further, and then we shall have to retrace our steps and travel 6 miles south to accomplish the 2 miles across to the river – travelled about 10 miles to-day – we found another beautiful spring of water in this place, in fact the ground here appears to be full of springs The scenery around us, is entirely different from that thro' which we have hitherto been travelling abounding in hills and dales and murmuring rivulets, and considerably resembles that of the New England states –

Missouri River and Council Bluffs. *Lithograph by Frederick J. Piercy in* Route from Liverpool to Great Salt Lake Valley, *ed. James Linforth (Liverpool: Franklin D. Richards, 1855). It took Brigham Young's vanguard company over three months to cross Iowa and reach Council Bluffs, much longer than expected. Courtesy of Church History Library.*

SUNDAY THE 14TH

The weather still warm – A number of the girls went out strawberrying this forenoon – Bro. K. rode over about a mile to Brigham's camp – Bro. Miller had finished the bridge on Musquitoe creek – he had been to see the agents – they agreed to furnish spikes and pitch for the building of a ferry-boat if after the church had all crossed they would give up in the boat to them – they wished us to have nothing to say to the Indians in the way of tampering with them. Struck our tents about 2 P. M. – and went on – after crossing the creek ascending and descending a bluff travelled in a circuitous route over the bottom – after getting a short distance from the bluff – we discovered at our right hand just under the brow of the same a large farm enclosed by a fence, which extended a good way over the bottom, – also 2 or 3 houses. The whole camp of Israel encamped on the banks of the Missouri River, near the timber, about a mile above the trading houses – there is also quite a settlement on opposite side of the river to where we are – saw a number of Indians, and half-breeds, on our arrival, who accompanied by the agent were riding about on their horses – there are 3 trading houses at the settlement below – Soon after our arrival, the brethren met in council on the banks of the river to lay down certain rules for our observance while we remain here – there were as follows: – every 4th man is to assist in building the boat, 1 or 2 out of each 10 to herd cattle, while others are to go out in the country, to trade for provisions There was a committee of three appointed (viz: Father, Rockwood & Miller) to wait on the agents, and ascertain the prices of things – meanwhile no man is permitted to have any traffic with the inhabitants or Indians without having permission so to do from the proper source – and there are men hereafter to be appointed to do all the trading – so that if a person stands in need of any article he must apply to them –

The heat of the weather was now at its height, and the whole country around abounded in strawberries, raspberries and blackberries, and other fruit indigenous to the country; and the day following our arrival there, a number of our girls went out strawberrying. This was Sunday, and father rode over about a mile to President Young's camp, and learned there that Bishop Miller had been to see the agents, who agreed to furnish spokes and pitch for the building of a ferry boat; if, after the church had all crossed, they would give it up to them. They wished us to have nothing to say to the Indians in the way of tampering with them. Our companies had no disposition to do this, but it was nothing strange that they should view us, or any other white people, with suspicion, for they had generally been mean and dishonest in their dealings with the Indians; besides they had been warned by a Unites States officer to beware of us, but we had too much at stake to take advantage of the tribes, traveling as we were through their territories.

There were certain ones in camp at the early start who received severe rebukes from the presidency for being dishonest. One was the case of a young man in Bishop Miller's camp, who undertook to pass counterfeit money in pay for cattle, etc. The bishop wrote to President Young to excuse the young man, but wished him to make restitution to Mr. Cochran, the man who had been cheated by him—but for which the bishop received an awful rebuke, and was ordered to restore the property. It was soon discovered that such characters were not wanted among us, nor were they to be sustained in the camp, for the most strict laws and rules were laid down in their council held at Chariton, where they organized the camp. Here are a few words from President Young's remarks, made on the following Sabbath: "I told them I was satisfied that the course we were taking would prove to be the salvation, not only of this camp, but of the Saints left behind; but there had been things done which were wrong. Some pleaded our suffering from persecution, and the loss of our houses and property, as a justification for retaliating upon our enemies, but such a course tends to destroy the kingdom of God."[45]

The whole of the camp started in the afternoon and encamped on the bank of the Missouri River about a mile above the trading houses, where we saw a number of Indians and half-breeds, who were riding about accompanied by the agent, trading horses at the settlement below.

Woman's Exponent, vol. 12, no. 22,
15 April 1884, p. 170

Monday the 15th

Went to the slough hard by to assist the girls in washing very warm day – Wm and King went down to the settlement – this forenoon – Wm learned that there are 2200 Indians, (Pottawatomies) 100 families of whites traders [*sic*] a number of halfbreeds, that reside on the pt. below us, – Among those on the other side of the river are some Mohawks – Sioux, and other tribes – Early this morning there was a rumor thro' the camp that 2 cows had been killed by the Indians, last night, but on inquiry it turned out to be false Bro. Pack, Egan,

45. For more on counterfeiting among the Saints, see Kenneth W. Godfrey, "Crime and Punishment in Mormon Nauvoo, 1839–46," *Brigham Young University Studies* 32, no. 1 (1992): 195–227.

Grant, & L. Young and others went out into the country to day for the purpose of trading – there is some talk this evening of moving back to our old quarters on the bluff, that we last had before coming here, on account of being so crowded here with our cattle, and the other place affording so much better chance to us for fuel, good pure spring water, &c., &c.– the brethren commenced their work on the bridge to-day – Emeline [Mary Ellen] Harris (fathers family) is very sick with the fever at this time – Brigham, Bro K, father, and Bro. Miller went down to the trading house today to make some arrangements with the agents and ascertain the prices of things

Those uninteresting and unpleasant incidents I remember very distinctly, though I might have passed them over had he not made mention of this circumstance. As cleanliness is next to godliness, and having abundance of time when the weather permitted, we had no good reason for neglecting this duty. And we had plenty of boys ready and willing to hitch up a team to take us to the water if any distance away from camp; if so, we would take a picnic or send back for a warm dinner. The boys would spend their spare time fishing or as they felt inclined till the washing was done. Though our washing was not so very extensive, it was hard enough with the sun beating down, and so breathless and sultry that it appeared as though we must melt down under it, and this was not a pleasant thing to anticipate. I was not a strong girl—having grown up like a shaded plant I had little strength, and was what is generally termed lazy; one of the worst ills, I think, that can afflict humanity, if I may judge from my own experience. But we had ample time to do our washing, ironing and mending, also our sewing, besides making our daily toilet. And even our fashionable dressmakers found employment as the warm weather came on. Father had two or three wives who had learned the trade, and the same number who understood tailoring, and one of them had been brought up to the corset making trade, and all of them were trained up to some kind of useful industry, and were virtuous and worthy women, and, as a general rule, they sought the interests of one another. All had their trials and temptations—being new beginners in what might be termed an adverse school, which was calculated to bring into action faculties that might forever have lain dormant—testing everyone's nature, showing up their weak points and bringing them to the surface, to be thrown off, and learn each one to govern themselves, which was the very thing to make them saints or sinners. The "Mormon" companies were all orderly, and were truly models by the side of those who followed in their trail who were not governed by the same strict rules and religious motives and principles that our people were. Our salvation, both temporal and spiritual, depended upon this course, and our history is a wonder and a marvel to those who have taken the trouble to hunt us and review it in all its ups and downs. And my reasons for writing what many, no doubt, think rather dry and prosy reading, concerning the journey and sojourn of the Latter-day Saints in the wilderness in the year 1846, over a country which could be easily traveled in a week or ten days under ordinary circumstances, but which took us six months to accomplish, are to give to the generations that have grown up since, a little idea of the trials and hardships of those long and tedious days and months that were spent by the pioneers in making roads, building bridges and houses and making farms, etc., etc., for the comfort of the ones who were to follow;

and our experience, I think, comes nearest to that of the children of Israel after their departure out of the land of Egypt than any other people of whom we have any record, though I believe that we were a more patient people. And who have been as miraculously saved from death in many forms than they were? And the same God has fought for us while we have held our peace, and has brought us deliverance every time; and it is our wish and purpose to trust Him still.

Woman's Exponent, vol. 12, no. 23,
1 May 1884, p. 182

Tuesday the 16th

Very warm – We all started back about noon, after having retraced our steps across the bottom instead of ascending the bluff we kept 'round on the edge of it to the right hand, and built a bridge in about 2 hours, over the creek considerably further down than the one that Bro. Miller built, which we crossed and soon reached our old place, which forms a beautiful contrast to the one we just left – every thing – wood and water being more conveniently at hand than they were there – reached here in good season, and shortened the distance considerably by coming the way we did Brigham with his company soon followed us, also Bishop Miller, who arrived about 10 in the evening and encamped just behind us – he bro't a large quantity of fish, which consisted of catfish, buffalo of good size, and – a number of small ones – he gave Bro. K. about 100wt. which was distributed in the company – Bro. K. intends sending some teams into the country to-morrow after provisions – I suppose we shall remain here 2 or three weeks which time it will take to build the boat we hear there are a great many brethren on the road between here and Nauvoo and one told me that there were about 500 wagons, but I am inclined to think this account somewhat exaggerated –[46]

Wednesday the 17th

This morning, Bro. King, Hans, W.[arren] Markham and myself started into the country to get wheat, flour, corn &c. for Bro. K – father sending a number of hands with teams at the same time Went into Atchison Co. one of the border countries of Missouri, threshed out something like 160 bushels of wheat and sent 140 odd to Mill 20 miles below – bro't home about 6300 flour [*sic*]– shelled out a quantity of corn, and bro't home 42 bushels of seed wheat, Bro't 5 cows for father while gone having been absent 3 weeks to a day[47] – about a week before we came back, Bro. K. sent Daniel Davis and John Davenport down to our

46. Horace's statement about the number of wagons is not an exaggeration. By mid-June, the vast majority of Nauvoo Saints, upwards of ten thousand, were on the trail crossing Iowa and following the path of the advanced company of the Twelve.

47. For a fuller discussion of the Missouri lifeline to the Mormons, see Richard E. Bennett, "Mormons and Missourians: The Uneasy Truce," *Midwest Review* 9 (Spring 1987): 12–21. Between September 1846 and the spring of 1847, Mormon pioneers purchased a minimum of $28,000 worth of food and provisions from Missouri farmers and mercantile establishments. Furthermore, many Mormons spent the winter in northern Missouri working in stores, farms, and other establishments for a substantial amount of money.

assistance – Bro Egan, who preceded us some two or three days into the country was our principal agent, engaging our grain &c.– Returned on [missing text]

Horace, with some of my father's men and W. Markham, started on a trading expedition, also some of Bishop Whitney's men with teams. They went into Atchison Co., Missouri, where they threshed out about 120 bushels of wheat, sent it to mill about twenty miles below there to be ground, and brought back about 6,300 pounds, also shelled out a quantity of corn and brought with them—also some seed wheat. Howard Egan, who was father's principal agent, had preceded them two or three days. They were absent two weeks and returned on the 17th of July, finding President B. Young and father absent, having gone back for the purpose of raising volunteers for the Mexican expedition. From the 17th Horace had to depend on Peter Hanson's journal for facts occurring during his absence.

Woman's Exponent, vol. 12, no. 23,
1 May 1884, p. 182

Tuesday the 7th of July

[***Editor's note***: While Horace was ill for almost a month, Peter Hanson wrote in his journal for him from 17 June to 15 July.]

Found our folks encamped on the bottom some what nearer the trading house than they they were before, tho' a great number yet remain on the hill where our folks were when we left – Bro. K. and Brigham had gone back to the "Trains" to raise 500 volunteers for the Mexican expedition. In consequence of working very hard since I have been gone, and the excessive hot weather, I am quite unwell – therefore I am obliged to depend on Peter's Journal for facts occurring during my absence as well as for about a week after my arrival The following, from Wednesday the 17th of June to Wednesday the 15th of July are extracts from the same –

Wednesday the 17th [of June]

Fine cool morning – To-day the girls went about a mile to wash – very warm day – 4 of our wagons started for the Platt country for provisions – for Bro. K., Bro. King, [Chancey] Whiting Hans and Hanson for Bro. Whitney, J. Wetherbee, Orson, Abijah [likely Abiah Wadsworth] – To-day, by invitation, B. Young, Bro. K. Dr. Richards, Bro. Whitney and some of the Band went down in carriages to the settlement to take dinner – The Agent, the principal Indian chief and a number of others were there and appeared delighted with our music – This evening our company was enlarged by 5 families from Michigan – We learn that Elder Orson Hyde and John Taylor have just come up with their companies

Peter speaks of the abundance of strawberries found at that place. There was a carriage load of us went with mother on the 19th some distance from camp where they grew so thick that we could not help stepping on them. The heat was intense, being in a small valley in the woods, and having no water, only what we carried in a jug. I had been picking for quite a time and the berries looking so delicately tempting I kept reaching for them until I fell helpless, though not senseless. But the rest having gone farther away from the carriage than myself, I was alone and had to lay there till I recovered enough to crawl to the carriage where, though famishing for a cooling draught, I found nothing but tepid water. Towards sundown it grew cooler, and feeling better, I went out again. President B. Young came down with a carriage load of his family about that time and we picked berries till dusk, when we returned to camp. We had filled all our pails and pans full and eaten till we were clogged and wanted no more strawberries that year. That day an invitation had been received from the agent for the camp and Wm. Pitt's band to spend the day at the Point. This was delightful, especially to the young people, and though I was very unwell through the night, it was out of the question for me to forego such a pleasure. This was the first time that our chests had been disturbed or opened since packing them in Nauvoo, being the first time that we had needed anything but common apparel. And it was really delightful to once more see the inside of our chests and to bring out the pretty bonnets, laces, ribbons, parasols and kid shoes, etc., that had been packed away, and to think that we were again to attend a ball. And I rather think we astonished the good folks at the Point to see so many well dressed and merry hearted boys and girls and gentle people who were exiles from civilization. Peter Hanson, in his description, says of them, "They were mostly French, half breeds and Indians—the ladies of all are very interesting and quite neat in their personal appearance. Music and dancing were had, and one of the Indian ladies wished to have an introduction to Brother Kimball, that she might dance with him." This was Le Clerc's daughter, the educated chief of the Pot-towatomie tribe. She was a spoiled child, and had married a young white man of very immoral habits.

Mormon Trail Encampment. *Lithograph by Piercy,* Route from Liverpool to Great Salt Lake Valley. *Utah State Historical Society.*

She had been educated in a western city and dressed with taste and was quite accomplished in the art of coquetry and the bewitching graces characteristic of the fashionable belle of society. All of the inhabitants were warm-hearted and treated us with great hospitality. The gaiety and excitement of the day with the dancing was too much for me and I was taken home very sick, and remained so for three or four days; and afterwards received quite a reproof from my father, when I had recovered enough to bear it, for my foolishness. My husband being absent, he felt it his duty to chasten his daughter, whose only plea was ignorance and a passionate love of the dance. But the lesson came too late only as a warning with a heavy penitence for past folly. At this place we had some windy, dusty and stormy days. Five families came from Michigan—and also a large camp, called the Mississippi company, overtook us there.

Woman's Exponent, vol. 12, no. 23,
1 May 1884, p. 182

THURSDAY THE 18TH

Father [Charles W.] Hubbard joined us to-day – strawberries are found here in abundance – warm weather during the day – thunder in the distance this evening –

FRIDAY THE 19TH

Fine morning – heavy dews – warm weather thro' the day

SATURDAY THE 20TH

This forenoon Bro. K. with most of his family went 9 miles to the town in 2 carriages, together with some of the "Twelve" and families, also, some of the Band, to visit the inhabitants who were very much pleased – they are mostly French, half-breeds & Indians, and speak English F. and Indian – The ladies of all sorts are very interesting and quite neat in their personal appearance – Music and dancing was had, and one of the Indian ladies, wished to have an introduction to Bro. K. that she might dance with him – Elder G. A. Smith and A. Lyman camped within a short distance from us this afternoon – A large camp called the Mississippi company [of Latter-day Saint converts], lays about ½ a mile from O. Hyde's camp which lies east about a ¼ a mile –

SUNDAY 21ST.

Cold and windy – which makes it unpleasant, on account of the dust – A number of French and Indians came up to the camp on horseback this afternoon – Two meetings held this day –

Monday the 22d

Cold and windy – Killed one of our calves this morning this forenoon, father with some of his family went down to the village to visit and at the same time bo't some boards, salt, buffalo hides &c.

Tuesday the 23d.

Cold windy and rainy to-day – Bro. Joseph Toronto, the only Italian in the church, made mother (Sister [Vilate Murray] K.[imball]) a present of some oranges lemons and wine – he had come from the city of Joseph in 9 days – Helen been quite sick – getting well –

Wednesday the 24th

Still cold and rainy – Bro. K. is writing a letter to Nauvoo, called this place "Heber's Rest" – This day we have been glad to make even [?] of the storm –

Thursday the 25th

Warm calm and foggy this morning – Teams sent down on the flat after timber for ox yokes – News from the Society Islands – branchs [*sic*] of the church are being built up continuously, and the Queen and all the heirs to the crown have been baptized – The agent's name is Mitchell –

News was received from the "Society Islands" of branches being built up, and that the queen and all the heirs to the crown had been baptized into the Church of Jesus Christ of Latter-day Saints.

Woman's Exponent, vol. 12, no. 24,
15 May 1884, p. 186

Friday the 26th

Council held to-day – To-day George Rhodes came to drive a team for Bro. K. –

Saturday the 27th

Fine weather – To-day Bro. K. and Brigham went back 3 miles and while gone saw 14 camps of the Saints – This Morning men were sent down 10 miles to build a bridge that those returning from trading in the Platt country could thus save some 15 miles journey – rather stormy this evening –

Sunday the 28th

Meeting at our largest tent this morning – a large number of K's family being present and some others he preached to them exhorting them to love one another with a great deal of other good advice – the sacrament was then administered, and the meeting closed Bro. K. then went to public meeting which was opened with prayer by O. Hyde – B. Young then spoke at some length He spoke of the necessity of guarding our sheep from the wolves – Bro. Grant, [Samuel] Myers and some others came from the Platt county to day –

MONDAY THE 29TH

Fine morning – 2 men with 6 yoke of oxen sent to meet our teams –

TUESDAY THE 30TH

This morning Bro. K. & family started to move back to the river but it commenced raining, and so only went a little way beyond Musquito Creek bridge, and stopt – after we had took dinner it cleared off and we saw a number of the Twelve pass by on their way to the old camping ground on the river Bro. K. accordingly also went on to the river and encamped also – The reason of the Twelve's moving was this – they received intelligence that 4 officers had come from Fort Leavenworth to Mt. Pisgah, and were now on the road here, to request us to let our young and able bodied men enlist and go to the Fort, there to procure arms provisions &c., and go to Santa Fe to fight against the Mexicans and then go to California to get a location for the rest of the Mormons, in remuneration for their services after we had started to-day a messenger came up to tell us that the said officers had arrived at the camp on the hill[48] –

WEDNESDAY, JULY THE 1ST

Fine morning This morning the Presidency went back to the Bluffs to see said officers – Council was held, and their request to raise 500 volunteers from among us, taken into consideration. (Each man to be allowed $12 a month, 18 oz. bread stuff per day, and 14 oz.

48. Mustered into service in June 1846 at Council Bluffs to serve in Stephen W. Kearny's U.S. Army of the West, the "Mormon Battalion" consisted of 497 volunteers and as many as 80 women and children. Many in camp were at first reluctant to sign up but with the fortuitous arrival of Col. Thomas L. Kane of Philadelphia, a trusted associate of President James Polk, he was able to dispel a great many fears. The truth is, Jessie Little, agent for the church in Washington, DC, and acting under the authority of the Twelve, had been trying to arrange some accommodation with the U.S. government not only to manifest Mormon loyalties to the United States but also to arrange for government contracts to help allay the costs of the exodus. Designed to serve in the Mexican-American War, the Mormon Battalion marched to San Diego via Pueblo, Santa Fe, Albuquerque, Tucson, and Yuma, arriving at the shores of the Pacific Ocean on 29 January 1847. While many members of the battalion were discharged at Los Angeles in July 1847, several others continued to serve and later participated in the discovery of gold at Sutter's Mill near Sacramento in 1848, which signaled the beginning of the California gold rush the following year. Rather than staying in the gold fields, most battalion members returned to meet their families either in the new Mormon settlement of the Great Salt Lake City in the summer of 1847 or all the way back to Winter Quarters in the fall of the same year. The march of the Mormon Battalion has gone down as one of the longest in modern military history. See John F. Yurtinus, "A Ram in the Thicket: A History of the Mormon Battalion in the Mexican War" (PhD diss., Brigham Young University, 1975). See also David L. Bigler, and Will Bagley, eds., *Army of Israel: Mormon Battalion Narratives* (Logan: Utah State University Press, 2000).

meat.) If they could not raise that number they did not want any – The presidency agreed to it – on condition that the people were willing – In the afternoon, when Bro. K. came back, we started to cross the river, but on getting to the ferry we could not cross – therefore went back a about 3/4 of a mile and encamped on a slight elevation of ground, under the beautiful shade of an old elm tree – Bro. K. and Brigham are about starting back to Mt. Pisgah to raise volunteers – Colonel Scott and Dr. Richards are encamped here with us –

The mosquitoes being so troublesome near the river obliged us to move back, and as we were far from water they accordingly dug a well closeby.

As it was nearly dusk when they concluded to move from the river, and being very weary, I, with one or two others, had accepted an invitation from the chief's daughter to accompany her home; and when returning, finding the wagons gone and not feeling strong, she urged me to return and stop the night, which invitation I accepted, though I spent a somewhat nervous and wakeful night, but when morning came I felt more at ease. I learned that her parents had separated, as her mother was now living with her and did most of the work. Though dressed in her native costume she looked neat, and kept the house tidy, and could cook equal to the white women. This was quite a wood country, which abounded in blackberries and other wild fruit, and as they were getting ripe we went out in the morning and picked what we wanted to eat, after which she showed her taste and skill in braiding my hair in broad plats, after the latest French style, and put it up a la mode, and after dinner accompanied me to camp. While stopping at this place I went, by invitation, with one or two of my father's young wives, to take tea with the wife of the interpreter, who gave us a little of the history, not only of the chief and his daughter, but of the Indian tribes the Sioux and Pottawatomies, who were at war with each other. And it was only the evening of the 6th that a Pottawatomie Indian came to our camp on horseback, bringing a message, which he could only make known by signs. The import of it was that the Sioux Indians had killed a Pottawatomie, and he wanted our people to assist them in fighting the Sioux, and thus revenge their comrade's death.

Woman's Exponent, vol. 12, no. 24,
15 May 1884, p. 186

Thursday the 2[D]

We learn this morning that some cattle have been lost in the creek – As we are far from water, we went to the N. E. bend of Musquito creek to seek for springs, and a place to encamp, but as we found none, and no place high enough to be out of the reach of Musquitos, we determined to remain here, and accordingly dug a well close by under the hill an elevation on which we are encamped, the water of which proved to be very good Today Wm sold his "Cub Hare" to a man living in the village below We have our wagons so arranged as to form quite a door-yard –

On the morning of the 3rd father and President B. Young started for Mt. Pisgah on the recruiting business. When the news first came to us of the war between the United States and

Mexico we little dreamed of the requirement that the government were about to make at our hands, and congratulated ourselves that being expelled from their midst we should travel undisturbed Beyond the Rocky Mountains, where we should hear no more contentions, turmoils and strife, and we had cause to look upon this demand with suspicion, especially after the threat which was thrown out in the letter received from Sam Brannan just previous to starting on our journey. But our people proved their loyalty by kissing the hand that had driven them into the wilderness, where it was hoped, by the majority, we should utterly perish, and it was thought that by taking from us 500 of our young, able bodied men in the Indian country that it would cripple us so much that it would insure our utter destruction; but there a few honorable men like Colonel Thomas L. Kane, who, like true-hearted countrymen, rendered all the assistance that was possible to the Saints in this, their most trying hour.

Woman's Exponent, vol. 12, no. 24,
15 May 1884, p. 186

Previous to this an express had been sent by the president to Mt. Pisgah to raise one hundred men for the expedition over the mountains, and the day before their arrival brother Woodruff had called for mounted volunteers, when "sixty at once stepped out into line" But the day following the people there were thrown into consternation by the sudden cry, "The United States troops are upon us!"

But it soon proved to be Captain James Allen with three dragoons—who, after making known his business in the high council at that place, was furnished with a letter of introduction to the President and authorities at Council Bluffs and Brother Woodruff dispatched a messenger to prepare them for the business of this government agent.

Woman's Exponent, vol. 13, no. 1,
1 June 1884, p. 2

Friday the 3D

This morning, Bro. K. and Brigham started for Mt. Pisgah on the recruiting business – Wm went to the Bluffs to bring down a load of goods left there – Quite windy to day –

Saturday the 4TH

Very warm – To-day Bishop Whitney and Bro. Grant moved down here from the Bluffs Colonel Rockwood had sent word for us to come down at 9 P. M. and cross over to night, but we judged it expedient to remain here on account of the Indians – Bro. Billings, [Luman] Shirtliff and others arrived here to day from Nauvoo having been 6 weeks on the road – after dark it commenced raining very hard accompanied with considerable wind & hail – a number of tents were blown down –

Sunday the 5th

Nothing important to day – Very warm – Thunder this afternoon –

Monday the 6th

A Pottawatomie Indian came here last evening on horseback to bring a message, the import of which, as far as we could judge by his signs, was this: – That a Mormon had been shot by a mobocrat, that Mobs were gathering, and that it was better for us to go away – This afterward proved to be a mistake – Instead it appeared that the Sioux had killed a Pottawatomie, and he wanted us to assist them in fighting the Sioux and thus revenge their comrade's death This afternoon, Bro. Winchester with his family arrived –

Tuesday the 7th

Fine day – 4 wagons started to cross the river – This afternoon, our brethren, Hans, Daniel, King, Horace, John D. and Whitney & others came in no other accident than a yoke being broken and Hans' breaking his wagon tongue while alone on the prairie

That day Horace and the other boys returned from their trading trip in the Platt country, having met with no other accident than the breaking of a yoke and a wagon tongue, the latter happened to Hans Hanson while alone on the prairie. There was but one boat and that capable of holding only three wagons at a time.

Woman's Exponent, vol. 13, no. 1,
1 June 1884, p. 2

Wednesday the 8th

We drove our cows across this morning with considerable difficulty – We all intend crossing this afternoon – We have but one boat and that is capable of holding only 3 wagons at a time – The current is quite favorable – setting in almost to the opposite shore, where there is quite an eddy – the road from the landing is very steep, but it has been dug down so much as to render it quite passable – after ascending this steep declivity from the river, the road leads thro a narrow defile or ravine between two lofty hills and then begins gradually to rise to higher ground – after going about 2 miles thro woods "brake and bust" you commence anon on to the open prairie – we came down to the landing in the afternoon, but a number of teams were ahead of us, and we had to wait till 1 a.m. before we could commence crossing over –

Thomas L. Kane, Enlisting Camp of the Mormons, July 14, 1846 *(sketch). Comments on the reverse side of the sketch identify landmarks with letters: "A. Captain [James] Allen's tent. B. The road that comes from Mount Pisgah to the Missouri and continues all along the Prairie Bottom, marked here and there by waggons drawn by ox teams. . . . C. Marks the course of the Missouri." Kane's sketches are among the very few contemporary visual portrayals of the Mormons at Council Bluffs. Thomas L. Kane Collection, L. Tom Perry Special Collections, Harold B. Lee Library, Brigham Young University, Provo, Utah.*

Our cows were driven across on the 8th, and we came down to the landing in the afternoon, but a number of teams were ahead of us, and we had to wait till one a.m. before we could commence crossing over.

Woman's Exponent, vol. 13, no. 1,
1 June 1884, p. 2

THURSDAY THE 9TH

We were blessed with a fine moonlight night, which aided us greatly in crossing – This morning drove our oxen into the river to swim them across but they would not go, on account of the reflection of the sun's rays upon the water, which dazzeled their eyes – consequently had to take them over in the boat – at about 5 o'clock had every thing over but 2 oxen which were missing – Had a very heavy rain while we were going out to the camp 4 miles from the river where we all arrived to night pretty well fatigued – We just learned that Bishop Miller who has gone ahead has had his horses stolen –

FRIDAY THE 10TH

Raining this morning Bishop Whitney came up to day He crossed soon after we did – He staid in the woods last night and was detained somewhat, having lost some of his cattle but he found them again – We learn that a woman, (sister Higbee,) and a child have died lately in the camp Joseph Herring, and Indian of the Mohawk tribe has just come from the south-west, – he tells us that there is a civil war among the Cherokees on account of one party of them selling land to the United States[49] – he had to escape to save his life, and travelled 200 miles on his horse in three days – This[50] afternoon we moved about ¼ of a mile beyond and located ourselves on a small rise of ground, being much more commodious and cleanly than this place where Brigham is and where Bishop Miller has formerly encamped – Very good springs of water in the vicinity – Quite a large creek about 3/4 of a mile distant The Indians have cornfields immediately around us, and on that account we have to keep close watch over our horses and cattle lest they should break into them –

I remember the scenes he describes and the camping fires; also of going to the creek mentioned to do our washing, as well as the cornfields that we passed, they being the first we had seen; and of our purchasing some of the ears to roast. It looked good to us to once more see vegetation and cultivated land, or anything resembling civilization after traveling as we had and camped for so long a time upon wild prairie land. It was to us like an oasis to the weary traveler in the midst of a wilderness, and reminded us of our western homes, where the tall cornfields waved o'er our heads, and where we had learned the art of making hoe cake, which was our "daily bread" with hominy and the luxurious gravy from transparent pork.

Woman's Exponent, vol. 13, no. 1,
1 June 1884, p. 2

SATURDAY THE 11TH

Fine – day –

SUNDAY THE 12TH

Fine morning – Last night, Hans has the misfortune to cut his foot with an axe We have all of us been troubled with sore feet – This evening Colonel [Thomas L.] Kane made a speech here concerning the recruiting affairs – This young gentleman became acquainted with some of our presiding elders in the east, particularly Bro. [Jesse C.] Little with whom he held several interviews, and obtained knowledge of our persecutions, &c. and having sympathy for us he

---

49. With the signing of the infamous Indian Removal Act of 1830, President Andrew Jackson pushed for the removal of a large number of Indian tribes from off their ancestral lands to new, unknown territory west of the Missouri. The forcible expulsion of several southeastern tribes in particular, most notably the Cherokee in 1838, led to what is known as the "Trail of Tears," in which upwards of 6,000 of the 16,543 Cherokees perished making the move. Although the government made financial payments in exchange for the removal, numerous conflicts erupted between and among the tribes over control of such funds.

50. ***Editor's note***: At this point in the diary is the following insertion in another person's hand. It reads: "H. K. Whitney weighed 143^{lbs} on J. S. Clapp's scales on the 13th of July 1846 W. M. Rogers."

was anxious to do something for our benefit, and being intimately acquainted with the President of the U. S., he went to the city of Washington, and laid before him our case – The President knowing that the land of California stood in need of protection concluded to send an army thither, and accordingly gave Capt. Allen orders to raise a regiment of volunteers from among the Mormons, on such conditions that it would be an advantage to us – Bro. O. Pratt and G. A. Smith also made an appropriate speech ratifying what Colonel Kane had just said – Thus this young man appears to be an instrument in the hands of the Lord to bring about our salvation at the present time[51] – The U. S. fleet has taken possession of the coast of California By doing this, we establish a certain claim on the land, and once there ours will be the majority of people – A meeting is to be held to morrow morning at 10 o'clock to enlist men –

Those who could went to see them, some in carriages and some on horseback. My mother went with others of our family and I was to have gone horseback, but the boys all wanting to go, and not having horses enough, I stayed back—Horace and others returned that evening, but father and mother remained. We learned that one hundred men were yet wanting to complete the recruiting list.

Woman's Exponent, vol. 13, no. 1,
1 June 1884, p. 2

Monday the 13th

not very warm – somewhat cloudy – We learn that Bro. K and B. Young is at the camp on the Bluffs – Sister K. Wm Peter John F. John D. Hosea, Daniel, some in the carriage and some on horseback went to see them – Every thing was full of life and bustle in the camp, and over 300 enlisted and their officers were chosen by themselves – Bro. K. William and mother stayed, the rest of us returned home which we reached about dark –

Tuesday the 14th

Bro Orson Hyde had his two lost horses bro't to him by two Indians – Monday – every thing going on bravely – Bro K. does not yet come back – 100 men are yet wanting to complete their recruiting list

51. Born in Pennsylvania in 1822, Thomas L. Kane was a soldier and colonel in the U.S. military and later served in the Civil War. Though never baptized a Mormon, he nevertheless remained a friend to the Mormons for his entire life. Kane was highly instrumental in persuading the Latter-day Saints at Mount Pisgah and at Council Bluffs that President Polk's invitation to recruit a Mormon battalion was a legitimate expression of American interests. Kane rapidly gained the trust of Brigham Young and later played a crucial role in the resolution of the Utah War of 1857. Kane County, Utah, was named after him. For more on this famous "friend of the Mormons," see Matthew J. Grow, *"Liberty to the Downtrodden": Thomas L. Kane, Romantic Reformer* (New Haven: Yale University Press, 2009).

WEDNESDAY THE 15TH

This afternoon Bro. K. Wm and Mother came back   To day the requisite number of troops have been ready made up – Bro. J.[ohn] Forsgren embarked to day. News: – P. P. Pratt, Orson Hyde and John Taylor appointed to day to go to England[52] – It is said the steamboat will be up to night after the troops"

End of extract from Peter's Journal –

52. The reason for this apostolic mission to England was to gather tithing funds from the British Saints and to put an end to various embezzlement schemes that had been siphoning off donations to the church. They also wanted to purchase the best surveying and measurement instruments to aid in the exodus west. See Richard E. Bennett, "'We Might Have Gone to Vancouver's Island': The Mormon Exodus, British Emigration, and the Pacific Northwest," in *Regional Studies in Latter-day Saint Church History: Western Canada*, ed. Dennis A. Wright et al. (Provo, UT: Department of Church History and Doctrine, Brigham Young University, 2000), 13–34.

A

Journal.

Kept by H. K. Whiting, during the Journey and sojourn of the church of Jesus Christ of Latter-day Saints in the wilderness.

Anno Domini

1846.

(Continued.)

2

Journal 2

16 July–16 August 1846

A

Journal

Kept by H. K. Whitney, during

the journey and sojourn of

the church of Jesus Christ

of Latter-day Saints

in the wilderness.

Anno Domini.

1846.

(Continued.)

July 1846

Thursday the 16th

Rather cool weather The camp of Heber, where we now are contains at this time, 22 wagons, and 25 tents A meeting was called this morning – The people were told to choose whether they would go over the Mountains with Bro. Miller, to Grand Island, or to go back on the other side of the river – The most of them were for going on with Miller[53] – There was also a call made for more volunteers for the war – Bro. K. father and Brigham started to go over the river to the camp on the Bluffs, there to hold another council there they intended with some of the Twelve to go up the river some distance to seek a location for us this winter – Wm. Mary, Helen Sarah S. Harriet and myself accompanied them on mules to the Bluffs – William took the carriage back, and returned in the evening on horseback – After going about a mile and a half from the ferry on the other side, the brethren were met by a number of the Twelve and others going down to the village being near Bro. Geo. A's. camp they stopt there and held council, – I rode on with the girls, and we reached the camp late in the afternoon – found a number of our old acquaintances, here – viz: Bro. Pierce Bro. [Joseph Wellington] Coolidge and a number of others – after a while the brethren arrived – Helen and myself staid with Bro. Coolidge's folk's all night – About midnight Wm came over bringing Vilate and Nancy Green –

Here we found a number of our old acquaintances—among them were Bros. Robert Pierce and Cooledge and families. This camp was much larger than ours and consisted principally of those who left Nauvoo long after our departure. Horace, myself, and Sarah Lawrence stopped with Bro. Cooledge's folks that night.

Woman's Exponent, vol. 13, no. 1,
1 June 1884, p. 2

Friday the 17th

A meeting was called this morning, and considerable business done – there was quite a subscription taken in behalf of Brother [William] Yokum a brother who lost a limb in the

53. Central to the original 1846 exodus plan was to encamp most of the Saints at Grand Island in the summer. By the time Brigham Young and the vanguard company reached the Missouri River, it was clear that most of the Saints would be staying at Garden Grove, Mount Pisgah, and the Missouri. However, Brigham Young did instruct George Miller and his companions to explore the possibility of a late Grand Island encampment. The island proved not to be nearly as habitable as previously reported. Furthermore, travel getting there was difficult along the Platte River bottoms, and the area seemed to be a center of warfare between the Sioux and Pawnee Indian tribes. Upon arrival at the island, Miller was invited by the Punkaw (Ponca) Indian tribe to settle near their villages, some two hundred miles north on the Niobrara (Vermillion) River, which invitation he accepted. Grand Island, Nebraska, is located on the Platte River. Named "La Grande Isle" by French fur traders in the early 1800s, Grand Island is today the fourth largest city in Nebraska.

Missouri persecutions, and had suffered a great deal. Some gave money, some flour, &c.– Brigham father Bro. K. and a number of others intend starting and going 15 miles up the river this afternoon – Wm and myself and the girls took a short ride into the country this forenoon, and about 3 P. M. we started for home which we reached about sunset – The camp we visited is a much larger one than ours, and consists principally of those who left Nauvoo a long time after our departure –

George Miller (1794–1856), associate presiding bishop, member of the Council of Fifty, trail-blazer and scout, and Brigham Young antagonist. Image from H. W. Mills, "De Tal Palo Tal Astilla," Annual Historical Society of Southern California *10, no. 3 (1917), found between 112–13.*

SATURDAY THE 18TH

Warm and pleasant – towards evening father returned – Brigham and Bro. K. had got back as far as the camp on the Bluff – they had been some 15 or 20 miles up the river, but not finding any suitable place to winter, they came back, previously sending on 6 men in search of some good place to stop this winter –

SUNDAY THE 19TH

Started on foot this morning to go to the village on the other side of the river to see some old friends that had enlisted, understanding that they intend leaving to-morrow – I had not proceeded far before I met Bro. B. Y. and K. returning to the camp – overtook Peter at the Ferry who, in company with 3 of the girls had started for the Bluffs some time before I did – I went over with the girls in a skiff leaving Peter to take charge of the mules till I could raise a sufficient number of men to row the large boat with them over – I had raised a number of men, and got them down to the shore when I perceived the boat starting off from the other shore, they having succeeded in getting men on that side – Peter and the girls went on to the Bluffs where they intend to stop all night – I remained till late in the afternoon at the village and then returned home on foot in company with Bro. Egan – just at sunset as we arrived at the camp met Bro. Brigham K. and Richards on their way back over the river where they intend holding another council – they had held a meeting here to-day in order to find out who were going over the mountains, and who were not going to Grand – Island – they made out some 50 wagons, which were to go ahead, join Miller, and proceed with him over the mountains – Brigham spoke severely of the brethren who being set to watch cattle, fell asleep at their posts, and suffered them to run into the Indians' cornfields – he said that such men not fit to fill the slough holes of hell, and those found guilty of like acts again should be expelled from the camp of Israel for they were a perfect disgrace to us

MONDAY THE 20TH

Fine day – Bro. Smithies and Hutchinson, went over the river to the other camp to join the rest of the Band in a party, which they hold over there to-day – as some of us could not well go, we determined to make a party too, and accordingly got a quantity of bushes and made a bower before our tent – we commenced dancing about noon, and kept it up till supper-time, we then adjourned till evening, when we met and danced till about 10, and dismissed having had a good time, each one expressing himself satisfied with our scene of festivity – Davis' wife came back this evening – Pete does and the other two girls does not yet come To-day we were visited by two men from the village who came here on horseback. Their names are Beach and [John J.] Harding – they are old residents there – Mr. Beach informed me that the name of the creek in the vicinity is Butterfly we hear that Bishop Miller is some 150 miles distant, and is still going ahead – we heard the other day that Bro. Wm Cutler died of the Small Pox at Nauvoo, some time since, but know nothing of the truth of the report –

This was the farewell ball which Col. Kane so touchingly described to the "Historical Society of Pennsylvania."[54] *My parents and a great number were there, both old and young, but there were also many more who did not attend it. There were not horses enough for all to ride, and we being among the number who remained behind were determined to make a party, too, and accordingly the boys got a quantity of bushes and made a bower before our tent, and commenced dancing about noon and continued till supper time. We then adjourned till evening, when we met and danced till about ten o'clock, and then dismissed, having had a good time, and all expressing themselves satisfied with our scene of festivity. We could furnish our own music, and we often danced "by the light of the moon," which was then shining upon us in all its glory like one bright chandelier. I remember many an evening after the cares and bustle of the day were over, when numbers of the youth would gather outside the tents, and as chairs were rare luxuries, the majority resorted to wagon tongues, ox-yokes, provision chests and that sort of appliances in camp life, where we enjoyed a quiet entertainment of songs, music, etc. Horace excelled as a flutist, and the sweet strains that flowed soft and mellow from his instrument was owning much to his father's training. When a small boy, in Kirtland, he was presented with a fife by Orson Hyde, who was then a clerk in his father's store, but his incessant practice wearied his father and everybody within the hearing of it. And seeing his determination to learn the instrument his father bought him a flute the next time he went to New York for goods. John F. Boynton, one of the first quorum of the twelve, who stopped at his father's a great deal, gave him his first lessons on the flute, and his father would always correct him if he heard him play otherwise than smoothly. He also possessed an excellent voice for singing, as well as a generous supply of wit and humor, and telling anecdotes was one of his best fortes; and there were others of this class as well as some superior lady singers, and by this means we often drove away, dull care*

54. See Thomas L. Kane, *The Mormons: A Discourse Delivered Before the Historical Society of Pennsylvania, March 16, 1850* (Philadelphia: King & Baird, printers, 1850).

and cheered the aged and the drooping hearts, making lighter their burdens. One of the best songs that we used to hear was the "Jewish Maid," which one of our girls could sing as sweetly as did Miss Devine at the Point, the evening before the departure of the battalion boys, which was referred to by the late Thomas L. Kane, but who, it seems, was unable to obtain the song except the following lines, which he gives as "a version of the text touching to all earthly wanderers."

"By the rivers of Babylon we sat down and wept,
We wept when we remembered Zion."

Bro John Kay was the first to introduce this song to us in Nauvoo, but the chorus was changed, and instead of singing

"No more shall the children of Judah sing,"
"Again shall the children of Judah
Sing the lays of a happy time."

This was sung according to the faith of the Saints, who did not weep when they "remembered Zion," for Zion they had brought with them.[55]

The same day that we held our festival we were visited by two men from the village, who came on horseback, their names being Beach and Harding. They were old residents there. Mr. Beach informed us that the name of the creek in that vicinity was "Butterfly."

Woman's Exponent, vol. 13, no. 2,
15 June 1884, p. 10

TUESDAY THE 21ST

Commenced raining about 8 o'clock this morning, and rained till 11 o'clock a.m. – The girls got back this afternoon; also Peter – they bro't the news that 4 of the company started from the village to-day, and that the 5th is to start to-morrow – Bro. K. also came back this evening. C. L. W. [Clark Lyman Whitney] has got over the river with his team, and has sent word to us to come and help him up – for which purpose a number of teams are going down to-morrow – He abused father the other day in the vilest manner, calling him a damned scoundrel, and using other opproprobrious [*sic*] epithets of a most unmanly nature, to a man who has always tried to sustain him thro' evil and good report, and who has exerted himself in his behalf in many ways in times that are past and gone – Not to repay ingratitude with unkindness, father determined to return good for evil, and accordingly intends to-morrow sending a number of cattle to his assistance –

55. The song "Jewish Maid" had been introduced to the Saints in Nauvoo by their most popular singer and songwriter, John Kay. According to Horace Whitney, Kay changed the words to the chorus somewhat so that instead of singing "By the Rivers of Babylon we sat down and wept, we wept when we remembered Zion," it read, "Again shall the children of Judah sing the lays of happy time." See Helen Mar Whitney, "Our Travels Beyond the Mississippi," *Woman's Exponent* 13, no. 2 (15 June 1884): 10.

The folks returned home and brought the news that four companies started from the village that day, and the fifth was to start on the morrow. It is not pleasant to dwell on the dark side, nor is it my intention now to rehearse the scenes of sorrow and additional suffering of wives and children, which was forced upon them by the cruel requisition made upon our people at that time by this government, after suffering us to be ruthlessly driven out from their midst, I will only mention the case of Sister Ed. Martin, which may illustrate, the pitiful condition under which many more were left with families.

Brother Martin had just buried a newborn infant, and left his wife sick, not knowing who was to take care of her, and there was no time to make any arrangement for her comfort, and they had to leave all in the hands of God and their friends. And who are more capable of singing and sensing the full meaning of the sweet and touching song, "Hard times, hard times come again no more" than the ones who remember those gloomy days and scenes of want and suffering that were experienced by the Saints who were left in Winter Quarters.

Woman's Exponent, vol. 13, no. 2,
15 June 1884, p. 10

Wednesday the 22[D]

Rained a little this morning before we were up – continued showery thro' the day – I went ahead on the road about a mile, to watch the Indian cornfields lest the cattle shall break in to them – these are to be found on either side of Butterfly Creek for some distance up and down that stream – In the making of their fields, they have not used the plough, but selecting the softest ground (which is to be found on the margin of these streams) with little or no sod, they have simply cut down the weeds with their hoes and then put in their corn – In this way they leave it giving it no farther attention till they are ready to harvest it, or rather, when they return from their hunting expedition they resort to these fields for roasting ears, which they are very fond of:– if any is left after that, they bury it deep in the ground, where it remains during the winter – I had considerable difficulty in keeping the cattle away from the fields – another thing somewhat perplexed me, – Quite a number of teams from Brigham's camp, as well as our own, started to-day, and I had all I could do, to keep the cattle of our camp from crossing the creek, and following them off – About noon, Brigham, Bro. K., & Dr. Richards passed by me in a carriage on their way to the Elk Horn, a branch of the Platte River in order to survey the face of the country Those 6 men, before spoken of as having been sent the other day up the Missouri River on the other side to select a location returned, and reported that they had been some distance up the river but had been entirely unsuccessful in finding a suitable place to winter the country being no more favorable for that purpose than the place where we now are[56] – Accordingly Brigham advised the brethren in council

56. The Mormons first stopped at a temporary resting place, recommended by George Miller, on the Petit Papillion Creek, which they called Cold Springs or Butterfly Bluff. Situated four miles northwest of the ferry landing and fifteen miles above Bellevue, Cold Springs served as camp headquarters and provided a much needed rest during that hot, sweltering July. Local historian Gail Holmes believes that Cold Springs

on Monday last at the Bluffs, to disperse themselves among the hills and bottoms and remain there this winter – While out to-day, I set my hook and line and caught 6 very fine catfish, one of which weighed 4 or 5 lbs. The red oxen, which I have hitherto drove are about being exchanged for a yoke of 4 year old steers – that is if the man sticks to his bargain, but this is not certain. Bro. K. exchanged his horse Charly for 1 yoke of oxen a cow and heifer; and another old horse for another yoke – to-day Hans was fitted out with a wagon and team to accompany his father-in-law over the mountains – they intend starting to-morrow Geo. Billings came to drive team for Bro. K. –

Thursday the 23^D^

Fine and pleasant – tho' extremely warm – Bro. Hans, with his father-in-law, and a number of others, started for the mountains, but on coming to the creek, were obliged to build a bridge before crossing, the late rains having considerably swollen the stream – consequently had to camp on the banks on this side – Bro. K., and Brigham returned to day from the Elk-Horn[57] – Bro. K. tells me it is about 18 miles to the place where they had been – this stream is about 150 feet wide, and about 3 ft. deep and the only present means of crossing, is on a raft, composed of logs put together in a rough manner, and a very slow way it is, only one wagon going over at a time, the raft dragging on the bottom, and when they get to the other shore they are obligated to take hold of it with their hands, and pull it up on the shore in order for the teams to get off Just as Bro. K. arrived, Bro. Woodruff, Bro. Taylor, Little, and [Joseph] Horn came here in pursuance to previous arrangement to hold council, but it being so late they concluded not to hold any tonight Bro. Taylor, Woodruff, and Horn remained with us all night, Helen giving up her bed for the purpose – Bro. K. rode over to the creek to organize that company before they go on, which will be in the morning, as the bridge will be done by that time – He appointed Hiram Clark captain of fifty and Bro. Billings and N.[oah Willis] Bartholomew as his counsellors – We hear that a number of Indians rode over to see their corn this afternoon, and on discovering it to be trodden down by the cattle were very angry, and for fear that they might retaliate by taking some of our cattle, every man in the camp was ordered out to assist in driving in the cattle and yoking them up, which was done. Bro. K. intends to send the most of the camp ahead to-morrow in order to build a bridge over the Elk Horn. This is one of the objects of council to morrow –

was just north of Interstate 80, and near the corner of 61st and Patterson Streets in Omaha. See Gail George Holmes, "Winter Quarters Revisited: Untold Stories of the Seven-Year Stay of the Mormons in the Missouri Valley 1846–53," 19–20; see also Holmes's leaflet, *Historic Mormon Sites to Visit in Greater Omaha—Council Bluffs.*

57. The Elkhorn River, 292 miles long, is one of the largest tributaries of the Platte River, originating in the eastern Sandhills of Nebraska, and merging into the Platte just southwest of Omaha.

FRIDAY THE 24TH

Fine and pleasant – This morning, pursuant to agreement the Twelve, with father, met in council – they assembled on the hill, back of the camp some distance – To-day our cattle remain yoked, and two men are sent out to herd them – some have neglected, to bring in their cattle and herd them, consequently have yet to keep a watch upon the corn – I went myself on that duty this afternoon – the bridge they have built is a very good one – a number of brethren started from here to day – but 3 or 4 families remain, besides Bro. K's. and father's families –

SATURDAY THE 25TH

Warm and pleasant – This being the 23d anniversary of my birthday, Mother, Sarah Ann and Orson took supper with us at Bro. K's. tent – To-day Bro. Orson Hyde moved back over the river – where he intends to leave his family till his return from England, whither he is immediately going with Parley and Bro. Taylor[58] Bro. Woodruff is about moving over this side of the M. River Bro. K. borrowed $100 in gold of a brother by the name of Halamagh Van Wagoner [Halmagh John Van Wagoner] – I wrote the note for the amount for Bro. K., which was to be paid on demand about 11 o-clock at night it commenced raining and continued about half an hour accompanied by considerable thunder and lightning – We hear that one of the soldier-brethren has died since their departure from the village – he is said to have been the son [likely Albert Warren Dunham] of the late General [Jonathan] Dunham, of the Nauvoo Police, who died about a year ago while on a mission among the Indians Harriet Sanders is quite unwell –

SUNDAY THE 26TH

Fair weather – Bro. K. and father sent 4 yoke of oxen to the river each to assist Bro. Woodruff up – Bro. Coolidge with his Omnibus came in the afternoon, Bro. Cushing driving it for him, he being quite sick at this time – Wm and some of the rest of the boys got back from the river, where they went this afternoon about 2 o'clock in the morning bringing up the remainder of Bro. Coolidge's wagons – Brigham and Bro. K and father also went over the river to-day,

58. Apostles Parley P. Pratt and John Taylor and later Wilford Woodruff, who would join them, were dispatched to England on a very delicate mission to recover lost monies. Specifically, their mission was to recover funds embezzled by Reuben Hedlock, confront James Strang's missionaries who were then cultivating a large following, and return with the best surveying instruments possible in preparation for their spring 1847 move west. They returned in late March 1847 with 469 gold sovereigns representing a fraction of the total tithes from the British Saints. They also brought with them almost five hundred dollars' worth of astronomical and surveying instruments which would prove very useful to Brigham Young and his pioneers in their spring 1847 exodus. See Richard E. Bennett, "'We Might Have Gone to Vancouver's Island': The Mormon Exodus, British Emigration, and the Pacific Northwest," in *Regional Studies in Latter-day Saint Church History: Western Canada*, ed. Dennis A. Wright et al. (Provo, UT: Department of Church History and Doctrine, Brigham Young University, 2000), 13–34.

they did not come back to-night – Bro. Harrison Burgess took the lead of a meeting which we held here to day under our bower, in front of the tent, by Bro K's request –

MONDAY THE 27TH

Weather still fine – to-day went with the girls to the creek to wash – a number of the boys and girls went fishing at the same time – While there – saw a number of teams crossing the bridge on their way back – there were 10 wagons there proved to be the property of men who have just left the Pawnee village about 120 miles above here in consequence of the hostility of the Indians, where they have lived a number of years – they are going to the village below on this side the Missouri River, whither a number of their company had already preceded them Among those we saw, were 4 wagons and 6 men belonging to Bro. Miller, who is taking a load back for them, and receive in payment for the same 300 bushels of grain, mostly wheat I believe – the occasion of their leaving is this:– A hostile tribe of Indians, called the Punkaws, who are constantly roving about, and are much addicted to thieving have lately made their appearance at the Pawnee village, and molested them so much by their thieving operations, and otherwise, that they were obliged to leave, the Indians having previously stolen all their horses[59] – the settlement of men who have thus left formerly consisted of 8 families:– viz: 3 Missourians, 3 farmers, 1 blacksmith, and a school teacher commissioned by government

Ponca Indian Village *(undated). Wyoming State Archives.*

59. The Ponca (Cut-throat) Indians are a Midwestern Native American tribe of the Dhegihan branch of the Sioux. They originated in the Ohio River Valley. One branch moved south to Oklahoma; the other to Nebraska.

– the school teacher had under his direction some 20 Pawnee children who have left with him to go down to the said village, and whom he is educating at the expense of government – some of Bro. Miller's men told me that the Pawnee village was totally vacated, they having gone out on a hunting expedition – they told me furthermore that they were living on the fat of the land, there being plenty of garden sauce, such as potatoes, onions, peas, &c., which the settlers had left behind, not being able to bring them away[60] – the brethren who were sent on to build the bridge at the Elk Horn, have done nothing about it but have gone on – A piece of unexpected good fortune lately happened to father – When his boys went down into the country some time ago after provision, he sent 89 dollars for the same, but thro' the mismanagement of the agent, he did not get more than half he wanted, and consequently, would have been unable to prosecute the journey, had it not been, that the Lord, seemingly on purpose to repair this misfortune or injury, put forth his hand in his behalf – the circumstances were these – Bro. Hyde, being about to depart for England, just before crossing the river again with his family, let him have 2 yoke of oxen, 10 barrels of flour, and a bushel and a half of beans, which, to use his own phrase, "has completely set him on his legs again," and he is now fitted out to his heart's content – Brigham Bro. K. and father got back from the camp on the other side of the river this evening – While there, father received a wanton insult from Bro. Taylor – he happened to be at his tent at about the dinner hour, also, Brigham and Heber and one or two others – when they all set down at the table by his invitation, except father, whom he never once condescended to notice by word or look – the occasion of this was probably some personal pique, tho' father knows of no such that can possibly exist in reason – Rained a little during the night – Bro. K. says there are about 150 wagons ready to cross the river, and the passage this side is completely blocked up with wagons and intends sending down 12 or 15 yoke oxen tomorrow to assist in pulling them up the hill – Forgot to name, at the same time that Bro Hyde let father have those things above named, Parley gave him 30 dollars in gold, in exchange for the same amount of incurrent [*sic*] eastern (Maine) money What more particularly surprised father in the conduct of Bro. Taylor, is the fact, that, previous to the circumstance above mentioned he had treated him with the most uniform politeness, and the professed strongest friendship towards him in public and private, forming a great contrast to the unprovoked and wanton insult he gave him the other day in the company of their mutual friends and brethren –

60. George Miller eventually broke with the Saints at Winter Quarters after a serious disagreement with Brigham Young over which route to follow to the Rocky Mountains. Young favored the more southerly route up the Platte, to the Sweetwater, and over South Pass, while Miller preferred following the Vermillion to the Tongue River country and thence to Oregon. The real issue, however, was more personality than geography. Miller and his tagalong, James Emmett, both members of the Council of Fifty, believed they had as much authority to direct the exodus as Young did. Miller eventually drifted down to join the Lyman Wight colony in Texas, and then later James Strang in Beaver Island, Michigan. Emmett died in California, while Miller is buried in Marengo, McHenry County, northeast Illinois.

Tuesday the 28th

Beautiful Morning – About 2 o'clock P. M. it commenced raining, and continued showery thro the day and night accompanied by considerable thunder and lightning – it seemed to pour down almost perpendicularly and in perfect torrents so that there was not a wagon but that the rain penetrated thro' the cover thereof, and wet all the bed clothing &c. therein – This morning Bro. K. called a meeting to see how many of the brethren would go down the river with their teams to help those wagons on this side, out of the valley up the hill – a number volunteered, and the meeting was dismissed – About a dozen of Indians of the Otoes tribe including their chief came here this afternoon on horseback they had some moccasins, which they were very anxious to "swap,"– one of them had a quantity of beef on his horse which Brigham had given them[61] – Colonel Kane, the gentleman who negotiated with us for the troops, for the Mexican expedition left here last Monday, for Grand Island, where there is some talk of our soon going – He intends to stay with us and in our vicinity, till he can write a sketch of our history, which he intends to present to the President on his return to Washington Bro. Woodruff is encamped within a short distance of us towards Brigham's camp[62] –

This was one of the trials calculated to test one's patience, a virtue which had been considerably exercised during the five months that we had spent picking and plodding our way under difficulties which no language can describe, therefore must leave it for imagination to do.

Woman's Exponent, vol. 13, no. 3,
1 July 1884, p. 18

Wednesday the 29th

This morning fine and pleasant, the atmosphere sweet & pure, in contrast to the salty heat of yesterday – almost every wagon in the camp was unloaded in order to dry the things therein – Bro. King, Whitney, Jacob Frazier. G. Billings, and myself went over the creek after grapes, while they were gathering which I caught 3 or 4 good sized cat-fish – Bro. K. & Brigham went over the river to-day to make some arrangements about the brethren starting for England

61. The Otoe Indian tribe was once part of the Winnebago Sioux. Splitting off from the parent tribes, they migrated to areas south and west of the Great Lakes where they adopted the horse culture and nomadic lifestyle of the Great Plains, making the bison central to their diet. Between 1817 and 1841 they lived near the mouth of the Platte River. In 1854 the Otoe ceded most of the land south of that river, in eastern Nebraska, to the U.S. by treaty. Today, most Otoe Indians live in Noble and Pawnee counties in Oklahoma. The classic introduction to the history of North American Indian tribes, including the Otoe Indians, remains Thomas L. McKenney, *History of the Indian Tribes of North America*, 3 vols. (Philadelphia: J. T. Boen, 1848–50).

62. Fort Leavenworth was built in 1827 by Colonel Henry Leavenworth to protect fur traders and to keep peace with the Native Americans. The oldest active United States Army post west of Washington, D.C., it is located in Leavenworth County, Kansas. It served as the outfitting point for the Mormon Battalion in 1846. See George H. Walton, *Sentinel of the Plains: Fort Leavenworth and the American West* (Englewood Cliffs, NJ: Prentice-Hall, 1973).

Thomas L. Kane, Distant View of the Horn Campground Horseback July 29th (?) 1846. *Thomas L. Kane Collection, L. Tom Perry Special Collections, Harold B. Lee Library, Brigham Young University, Provo, Utah.*

Thomas L. Kane, My Waggon—The First Camp of the Distant Prairie of the Platte July 29th (?) 1846. *Thomas L. Kane Collection, L. Tom Perry Special Collections, Harold B. Lee Library, Brigham Young University, Provo, Utah.*

– they (Bro. Hyde Taylor & Parley) intend starting to-morrow Since we have been lying still, our cattle have suffered from the "footrot" caused either by the mud or grass getting between their hoofs – while we are travelling, we have never been troubled with it – the remedy we make use of, is to pour melted rosin into the hoof, after first pulling a rope backward and forward thro' it to get out the filth – Bro. K. returned this evening, about dark –

Thursday the 30th

Warm day – about sunset, a shower came up, and it continued raining at intervals, thro' the night – Bro. Lott, with his teams got up yesterday and to day – he has considerable church property with him, some cattle, sheep, &c., &c.– Bro. K. and wife went over the river to visit a farm – they returned this evening, – bringing quite a quantity of green corn – first that we have seen that is fit to eat – Forgot to mention, that during the storm on Tuesday evening, an ox belonging to a Bro. [Horace S.] Eldridge was struck by lightning, and instantly killed – Another meeting was held this morning, and a number of teams sent down to pull up the wagons of those who are crossing the river all the time, and are constantly swelling the size of our camp with their numbers – Bro. [Thomas] More, one of father's children, with his family arrived yesterday, and a number of others. –

Friday the 31st

Rained a little this morning – continued cloudy and warm thro' the day with considerable thunder – Another meeting called this morning, and a number of those who have not yet been were sent to the river to work – Bro. K. and Brigham went down also – while they were at the river the Steamboat "General Brooks" came down, and stopt at the village on this side, two miles below the Ferry – Bros. Parley, Hyde, Taylor, R. Pierce and Bro Little came over in the skiff, took in Brigham and Bro. K., and went down the river to overtake the boat, but when they got to the village, the steamboat had left, consequently, Bro. Taylor Hyde and Parley were obliged to go down in a flat-boat in company with some Missourians till they can overtake a steamboat – We learn, that the "General Brooks" was loaded down with the choicest kind of furs – she also had on board two grizzly bears and a young buffalo, which they caught while they were swimming the river, some 4 or 500 miles above here[63] – Father [Alpheus] Cutler, with his family, arrived to-day, and encamped on a hill a little beyond us–

Saturday the 1st of August

Quite a warm windy day – Another lot of men sent down to the river this morning with teams – Bro. Cahoon, Bro. Yearsly, and a number of others came up to day – Bro. John

63. The *General Brooks* steamboat, then under the command of Captain Joseph Throckmorton, navigated the Missouri River. The Upper Missouri River above Fort Benton (known as Fort Lewis before 1850) was considered unnavigable, so the majority of steamboats plied only the lower part of the river. See William E. Lass, *A History of Steamboating on the Upper Missouri River* (University of Nebraska Press, 1962).

Artist unknown, Steamboats on the Missouri River.

Higbee is also here – To-day a number of the Otoe Indians were here – they had a lot of corn with them which they had stolen from the cornfields of the Mohaws, close by here – The Otoes are a mean, thievery race, and are also very cunning, which they showed particularly in this case, knowing that the taking of the corn would be laid on to us by the Mohaws– Father Mother and little Carlos are quite sick to-day – Father took cold sitting up and watching with mother, who was very sick during the last night, but is a little better to-day

Sunday the 2d

Fair day – Brigham and Bro. K. and some others, took a trip up the river on this side to day, to find out a nearer road to the place where they want to go – they returned and held a council this afternoon – it is contemplated to start on to-morrow or next day and go to some place to settle down and prepare for winter – Father and mother are considerably better than they were yesterday To-day, put up my little tent again; which we have not before used since I returned from the trading expedition in the country – Sarah Ann, Helen, Mary Houston, Geo. Billings and myself, by the advice and arrangement of Bro. K. are to occupy it, and intends to take J. C. K's tent and put Wm and some others into it, thus dividing the family into 3 messes, and making it more agreeable and convenient to all –

Monday the 3d

The weather still fine and pleasant – Bro. K sent 10 yoke of oxen down to the river to help up Bro. Clayton, and family – Whitney, & myself went to the "Little Butterfly Creek, with the girls to day to assist them in washing – returned about sunset pretty well tired out – Bro Brigham let Bro. K. have a quantity of beef to-day, an ox of his having jumped off from a bridge and broke his neck this forenoon – it is the intention to take an early start to-morrow-morning, and go on – the boys, during our absence at the creek, have been unloading, and reloading, and making other arrangements necessary for our early departure. This evening, Bro. K. called the people of the camp together, told them the intention of moving in the morning, and received their vote and acquiescence in the same. He told them that he and Brigham had gone up the river 5 miles yesterday and had found out a good road on the "divide" between the Missouri, and Elk Horn Rivers, and which divide, for aught he knew, might continue 100 miles – He further told them that he intended going till he found a suitable place to stop and winter – He had no doubt of finding some good location on some of the bottoms; where we could build our houses for the winter, and our families meanwhile live on highlands or bluffs till cool weather. These bottoms abound in pea-vines, which will be first rate forage for our cattle, till winter, when he told them they could swim them over the river, or take them over on the ice, into the rush bottoms to feed[64] – Forgot to mention the death of a child [John Harris Harley] of Bro. [Edwin] Harley's which happened on Sunday –

Tuesday the 4th

Fair day – took a tolerably early start this morning, and travelled about 8 miles and encamped on the prairie about the middle of the afternoon – found a spring of water about half a mile off – from here we could see the Missouri River, about a mile off, also our former place of encampment on the opposite side on the Bluffs, where, as far as we could judge, a number of families yet remain Bro. K. and Father Cutler went ahead on horseback a short distance to discover what kind of a country was ahead – could not go further on account of its being most night – they returned bringing word that to the next timber they supposed it was 5 miles – Brigham did not come up with us to-night – don't know whether he started or not –

Wednesday the 5th

Started tolerably early this morning, travelled about 5 ms. And encamped about 1 P. M. near the beforementioned timber, and a spring at the head of a ravine close by – here we shall probably remain a day or two, till Bro. K. can make a survey of the country, and find out some good place to stop Colonel Kane arrived this evening – he had been to Grand Island, where he received a letter from Brigham informing him that the brethren had given up the idea of moving up that way; so he tho't he would come back; There is a mound in the vicinity about ¼ a mile off which Bro. K. and Colonel Kane noticed in an short ramble which they took last evening, and the Colonel expressed a desire: that some of the men should take spades, in the morning proceed thither and see what could be found by excavating it[65] – I

64. Under the direction of Asahel Lathrop, the Saints wintered most of their cattle (over ten thousand head) in a small encampment in the lush growing "pea-vines" region several miles north of Winter Quarters. Formerly part of George Miller's Ponca camp, Lathrop became disenchanted with Miller's leadership and left the Niobrara settlement with ten other families to come to Winter Quarters. Having traveled the west banks of the Missouri for two hundred miles, he recommended his tiny settlement as an ideal grazing ground for the church cattle at a spot roughly equidistant between Winter Quarters and the Niobrara River. The rush bottoms along the Missouri above Winter Quarters were covered with a growth of rushes or "jointed grass" that stayed green most of the winter. Such growth is now almost extinct. Lathrop's herd was probably located just east of Tekamah, Burt County, Nebraska. Charles Kelley, ed., *Journals of John D. Lee, 1846–1847 and 1859* (Salt Lake City: University of Utah Press, 1984), 23, editor's note.

65. Recent research conducted by the Nebraska State Historical Society, Archaeology Division, along the Papillion Creek indicates that this mound site was very likely that of Otoe Indians buried there some 250–500 years ago. For a fine introduction to the highly debatable topic of North American Indian origins see Lee Eldridge Huddleston, *Origins of the American Indians: European Concepts, 1492–1729* (Austin: University of Texas Press, 1967). More specific to Indian mound building, see Robert Silverberg, *Mound Builders of Ancient America: The Archaeology of a Myth* (New York: New York Graphic Society, 1968). For a more recent study of Pawnee Indian burial grounds and mounds, see Rodger C. Echo-Hawk and Walter R. Echo-Hawk, *Battlefields and Burial Grounds: The Indian Struggle to Protect Ancestral Graves in the United States*

understand, he intends soon leaving for the east – We formed our wagons in a circle, so to make an enclosure for our horses –

Col. Thomas L. Kane (1822–83), attorney, humanitarian, and friend of the Mormons. Utah State Historical Society.

The first time we met Col. Kane was on the 5th of August, just after our wagons were formed in a circle so as to make an enclosure for horses. The meeting was somewhat peculiar.

My sister-in-law and I being more than weary that day with the sun beating down and not a shade of any kind to screen us from its scorching rays, we were considerably out of sorts, and were just giving expression to some of our thoughts and feelings, in consequence of the unpleasant circumstances to which we were subjected, through the heartlessness of those who were allowed to wrong and oppress the weak, etc., and wondering when these trials would cease or where our lots were to be cast, etc. We were going on in this strain while washing the dust from our hands and faces preparatory to getting dinner. But our conversation came to a sudden stop, for as I went to the tent door to dash out some water, who should I see but a young stranger standing in a listening attitude by the side of his carriage, which stood hardly a yard away from our tent. He looked up as I threw out the water, and I felt my cheeks crimson as our eyes met; and I made a hasty retreat, wondering who he was and what we had said that he could take advantage of, if so disposed. Neither of us were aware of the Col.'s arrival in camp, and this young man looked a mere stripling, being delicate in form as well as features. But we soon learned who he was. He came, as it were, like an angel of mercy, and one whom the Lord, no doubt, raised up to act as a mediator in behalf of a homeless and afflicted people.

*In the trouble of 1858, called the "Mormon Rebellion," but more correctly "Buchanan's Blunder [*the Utah War*]," Col. Kane appeared again as an ambassador, though he was then in feeble health and worn down with travel. At the conclusion of Governor Young's remarks in their council, he said, "Friend Thomas, the Lord sent you here and He will not let you die—no, you cannot die till your work is done. I want to have your name live to all eternity. You have done a great work, and you will do a greater work still." Afterwards when asked by Elder Staines why he wished to be introduced as Dr. Osborne, he replied, "My dear friend, I was once treated so kindly at Winter Quarters that I am sensitive over its memories. I knew you to be a good people then, but since I have heard so many hard things about you, that I thought I would like to convince myself whether or not the people possessed the same humane and hospitable spirit that I found in them once. I thought, if I go to any of my great friends of Winter Quarters, they will treat me as Thomas L. Kane, with a remembrance of some services which I may have rendered*

(Minneapolis: Lerner Publications Company, 1994). The passage of the 1990 Native American Graves Protection and Repatriation Act has assured better protection than before of Indian burial lodges and mounds throughout America.

them. So I requested to be sent to some stranger's house as 'Dr. Osborne,' that I might know how the Mormon people would treat a stranger at such a moment as this, without knowing whether I might not turn out to be either an enemy or a spy. And now, Mr. Staines, I want to know if you could have treated Thomas L. Kane better than you have treated Dr. Osborne?"

"No, Col.," he replied, "I could not." "And thus, my friend," added Dr. Osborne, "I have proved that the Mormons will treat the stranger in Salt Lake City, as they once did Thomas L. Kane at Winter Quarters."

Woman's Exponent, vol. 13, no. 7,
1 September 1884, pp. 49–50

THURSDAY THE 6TH

Remained here to-day – Brigham came up with us, and encamped a short distance off – He, Bro. K. and others took a ride out this afternoon to see the country ahead – did not go very far, visited some springs in the woods a mile or two from here Some of the boys to-day dug into the before-mentioned mound, where they found the "skeleton form" of an Indian apparently having been buried for some time – they also found with it, quite a quantity of beads brass trinkets, &c. which formerly in life had adorned his person He [Kane] has carefully wrapt up the bones, and the cranium, which he intends taking with him to Philadelphia for the inspection of some professional friend of his who is versed in the science of Craniology. The boys received the sum of two dollars, divided among them for their services in digging – Forgot to mention, that the day we came here, Bro. K. arranged Sarah Ann's wagon and my own travel between father's and his own company, and in this order we have encamped between the two companies – The ring of wagons being too small to admit any more wagons in it, a number are encamped on the outside of it – Bro. Cahoon is encamped only two or three rods behind our wagons – Don Carlos [Whitney] is quite sick – father and mother gaining rapidly –

FRIDAY THE 7TH

Warm and pleasant – We remained here to-day also – A council held to-day in Bro. Grant's tent – the result was that we are to remain where we are, as no more more [*sic*] commodious a place can be found, and form in a hollow square[66] – Helen not very well this evening – Don C. getting better – This morning about 3 o-clock Bro D. Cahoon's wife brought forth a daughter into the world – Forgot to mention that 12 men were chosen by the Council this morning, as a committee to act for and make arrangements in behalf of the camp, who are to see executed the orders of the Council make arrangements for the winter &c. &c.– John D.

66. As they had in Kirtland and Nauvoo, church leaders organized a municipal high council in both the Winter Quarters (Nebraska) encampment and another across the river in Pottawattamie County (Iowa). However, no stake was organized on either side of the river, a clear indication that the church intended to move west the following spring and not to remain any longer than necessary at the Missouri. Each Council exercised jurisdiction over both temporal and spiritual affairs.

took two yoke of oxen and went back to the Big Springs, our former camping place, after Bro. Clayton

Saturday the 8th

Still warm and sultry – To-day the wagons were arranged as contemplated in the form of a hollow square – this bro't us still farther on the hill, and a considerable greater distance from water – Bro. Clayton arrived this afternoon – Father's and Bro. K's companies occupy one end entire of the square – to-day the teams were engaged in hauling trees to make a bowery the whole length of our wagons, which we worked at till past 11 o'clock in the night, and nearly completed – trees were also drawn for the purpose of building a bower in the center of the square – they also intend fencing in the camp so that the cattle can not get inside – there are also yards are [*sic*] to be built for them – after these things are done, it is the intention to commence cutting hay for winter – there was a lamb run over by one of our wagons while moving to-day, and broke his leg – this is the second time within a week, we have been indebted to accident for fresh meat –

Sunday the 9th

Beautiful morning – This morning, Bro. K. called his family together to hold a private family meeting.[67] There were a number of others however attended. Bro. K. spoke at some

67. In the absence of regular church-sponsored meetings or church houses in the Missouri River wilderness, the so-called Camp of Israel was divided into large, spiritually adopted family units such as the Young, Kimball, Richards, and other "family tribes" for instruction, guidance, partaking of the sacrament, and occasionally, as in this instance, for reproach and chastisement. Held rarely while toiling across Iowa due to their scattered and woe-be-gone condition, such family assemblies became much more common at Winter Quarters than ever before in church history. Thus the early vanguard companies of the Mormon exodus were far more than a string of pioneers and wagons traveling indiscriminately; rather, they were characterized by extended family units or tribes, living and moving together under strong patriarchal, priesthood, and family governing authority, all under the ultimate direction of the Quorum of the Twelve Apostles.

The law of adoption, in which faithful Saints were sealed or connected by a temple-centered priesthood ordinance to a prophet, apostle, or some other major church leader instead of to one's own ancestors, goes back in church history to at least Nauvoo. In the very early days of the church, when so many were joining without parent or family support, it was unclear how one could be safely sealed to deceased ancestors who were not members of the church. Not until President Wilford Woodruff's 1893 revelation ending the law of adoption was this practice finally revoked in favor of being sealed to one's direct progenitors. And later, with Joseph F. Smith's 1918 Vision of the Dead in which he taught that the work of redemption in the spirit world would obviate many obstacles to conversion in that sphere, the impulse to be sealed to one's own ancestors became stronger than ever before. This perception holds sway in the church to this day. See more in the introduction. For the finest scholarly work on this sometimes confusing topic, see Gordon Irving, "The Law of Adoption: One Phase of the Development of the Mormon Concept of Salvation, 1830–1900," *BYU Studies* 14 (Spring 1974): 291–314. See also Jonathan S. Stapley, "Adoptive Sealing Ritual in Mormonism," *Journal of Mormon History* 37, no. 3 (Summer 2011): 53–117. For a more specific look at how the law of adoption was practiced in Winter Quarters, see Bennett, *Mormons at the Missouri*, 91–95.

length – he spoke particularly of dissensions existing in his family – that some of the female members had spoken against him, and endeavored to propagate slandors concerning one another, and he rebuked such a spirit in the name of the Lord, and said that any person persisting in that course should not remain in his family, for he would not have them about him – and furthermore, that they should be cursed. He said he had borne such things long enough, and he would not bear them any longer – He spoke of the folly of people wishing for death for the sake of getting out of trouble and going to Heaven, when if they should have their wish they would go immediately to hell, and be damned, for every person is bound to create his own heavenly happiness by his conduct here on earth Bro. K. was followed by Father [Bishop Newel K. Whitney] and Bro. Grant, who spoke at some length in corroboration of what he had said – the sacrament was then administered, and the meeting dismissed – Council meeting was held at the new-made meeting ground in the grove where we calculate to winter – Brigham spoke at some length concerning the twelve men who were chosen to form a Church Council, and were to act as City Council, also, high council to the Church – Bro. Cutler was appointed the president thereof by a unanimous vote Samuel Russel the Clerk, and Horace S. Eldridge Marshall – President Young named our wintering

MORMON TABERNACLE CAMP.

Mormon Tabernacle Camp, Harper's Monthly, *April 1853. This camp was most likely at Cutler's Park, forerunner of Winter Quarters, fall 1846. Utah State Historical Society.*

place "Cutler's Park"[68] – The clerk then read a letter written to President [James K.] Polk – vote unanimous for it to be sent – the expediency of remaining in large camps was spoken, as affording less chance for the natives to rob and plunder upon us – also the propriety of securing the permission of the Lamanite chiefs, before cutting their timber – Colonel Kane is quite sick and has moved out a little way on to the prairie by himself –

MONDAY THE 10TH

Fine and pleasant – this morning, some of the people constituting this end of the camp, and those immediately belonging to Bro. K's family were called together for the purpose of making arrangements about cutting hay for the winter – the calculation was made to cut 800 tons, which divided among the 64 men which were counted, made 12 ½ tons apiece – there were also estimated 350 head of cattle, 31 horses and mules, and 48 sheep – To-day we busied ourselves in completing our fence on this end of the ground, and in finishing the bowery – the fence round the whole camp is not yet done Colonel Kane was bro't again into camp last evening, very ill indeed he was taken to Bro. Grant's tent – John Green is taking care of him – 40 wagons (including Bros. [Henry] Herriman's and Pack's families, who went on to the Elk Horn some time ago, [ )] came up here –

TUESDAY THE 11TH

Same weather – Busied ourselves to-day in cutting and drawing houselogs, and one or two commenced digging a well – we are building a house for the purpose of storing away provisions &c., that we may have the use of our wagons to haul hay with &c. &c.– A council of a number of the Twelve and the authorities of the Church, was held at father's tent this evening, respecting our arrangements for the winter &c., &c.– Saw Bro Parley this morning – 25 men were lately appointed to stand on guard night and day to keep the cattle out of the woods that they may not get into the pea-vines, which we depend upon considerably for our cattle this winter

68. While awaiting final word on the Grand Island plan, those pioneers already upon the west side of the Missouri River stopped at a temporary resting place, recommended by George Miller, on the Petit Papillion Creek, which they called Cold Springs. Situated four miles northwest of the ferry landing, and fifteen miles above Bellevue, Cold Springs served as a temporary camp headquarters in July 1846. Once the Mormons decided to winter at the Missouri, they sought a more suitable winter campsite, and Cold Springs became ever more crowded with new arrivals. In August they discovered a more acceptable campsite on higher ground, fourteen miles north of Cold Springs and three miles west of the Missouri River. Called Cutler's Park after Alpheus Cutler, the site was situated on a raised prairie among the gently rolling steppe lands, 2.5 miles west of the Missouri. See Bennett, *Mormons at the Missouri*, 68. Local historian Gail Holmes has conducted a tremendous amount of research on site locations in and around Winter Quarters. For just one of his several excellent works, see *Old Council Bluffs: Mormon Developments, 1846–1853 in the Missouri and Platte River Valleys of SW Iowa and E Nebraska* (Omaha: LDS Institute of Religion, 2000). See also BYU: College of Life Sciences, Brigham Young University, "Winter Quarters," winterquarters.byu.edu /Settlements/Nebraska.

WEDNESDAY THE 12TH

Cool and pleasant – the people collected this morning between this and Brigham's camp, to receive letters from their friends in the army [Mormon Battalion] – our camp as well as Brigham's now completely fenced in, and the well is in a fair state of progress – Colonel Kane yet quite sick with the fever – he has sent, or talked of sending to Fort Leavenworth, after a physician of his acquaintance –

THURSDAY THE 13TH

On waking this morning found it raining, which, however did not last long – A meeting was called this evening, in the center of the square, and captains and foremen of divisions, and companies chosen for the purpose of superintending the cutting of hay – their names the names [*sic*] or parties 16 companies read over. Bro. K's and father's companies constitute the 1st division of the 2d company of the whole camp of Israel. A report from the council was then read by Bro. Grant, requesting the people to turn out en masse to morrow-morning, gather in all their cattle, yoke them, let them remain in the yards until further orders, meanwhile furnish them with newly cut grass – also to sharpen their scythes and axes, and hold themselves in readiness to commence the work of haying

FRIDAY THE 14TH

Fine and pleasant – Pursuant to the arrangement last evening, most of the men, this morning were engaged hunting up, yoking and confining their cattle in yards, &c.– Bro. King, [Louis] Dana, and myself went to a small creek or ravine, about 2 miles back to assist the girls in washing – returned home at night very tired – during our absence the boys drew a load of hay, built up the store-house nearly 5 logs high &c.– The well they did not work at to-day – they dug at it yesterday and day before, and have sunk it to the depth of 28 feet without finding water –

Some of the brethren went to cutting and drawing house logs, and one or two commenced digging a well. In two days they had dug to the depth of twenty-eight feet without finding water. They also commenced building a house for the purpose of storing away provisions and other things, that they might have the use of the wagons to haul hay with, etc.

Woman's Exponent, vol. 13, no. 7,
1 September 1884, pp. 49–50

SATURDAY THE 15TH

To-day, the brethren busied themselves still in driving in the cattle from the woods, &c.–

Sunday the 16th

Fine day – this morning, a meeting held in the woods, about 1 mile and a half from here – also one in the afternoon – Father talks of soon going to St. Louis[69] – Porter arrived this evening, after an absence of 4 or 5 months, 10 days from Nauvoo – he was lately liberated at Galena, no one appearing against him – He bro't a watch of mine back, which he took with him to get repaired, when he last left us. Bro't also a number of [Hancock County] "Eagles," issued July 31st and letters but none for me – In the paper is announced the death of its late editor Dr. W[illia]m. E. Matlock, of whom the obituary notice speaks in the highest and most praiseworthy terms

69. Newel K. Whitney, presiding bishop of the church, was dispatched to St. Louis in late 1846 to purchase in bulk needed supplies from famous outfitting warehouses in St. Louis. These included burrstones for the flourmill, hardware merchandise, boots and shoes, clothing, textiles, grain, and other necessities, which eventually were sold in the Whitney store in Winter Quarters at favorable prices comparable to those in the East.

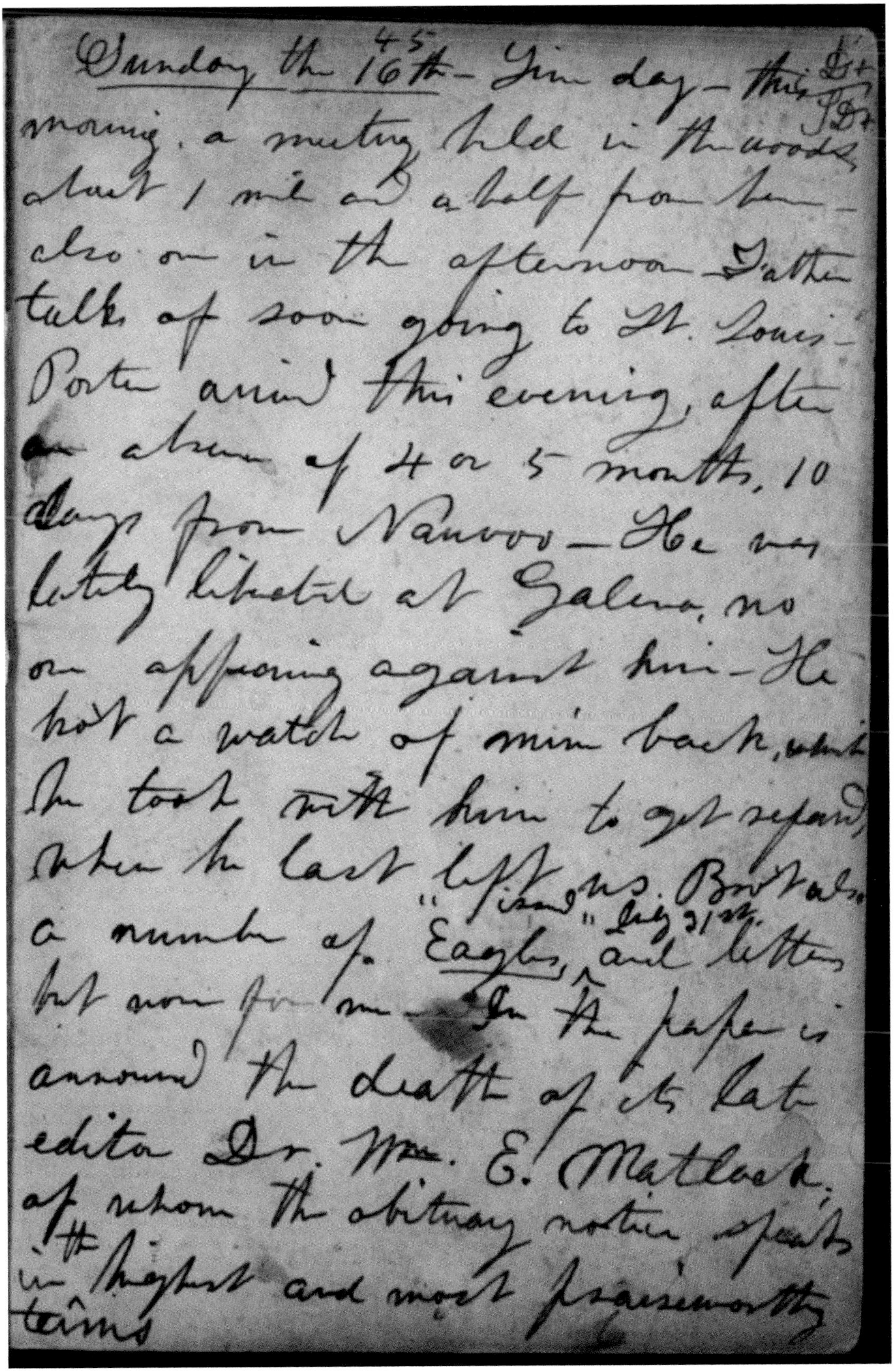

45

Sunday the 16th — Fine day — this morning, a meeting held in the woods about 1 mile and a half from here — also one in the afternoon — Father talks of soon going to St. Louis — Porter arrived this evening, after an absence of 4 or 5 months, 10 days from Nauvoo — He was lately liberated at Galena, no one appearing against him — He brot a watch of mine back, which he took with him to get repaired, when he last left us. Brot also a number of "Eagles," "issued" July 31st, and letters but none for me — In the paper is announced the death of its late editor Dr. Wm. E. Matlock, of whom the obituary notice speaks in the highest and most praiseworthy terms

Entry for 16 August 1846 from the original journal, slightly larger than the original size. Note the page number at the very top. Courtesy of Church History Library.

A

Journal

Kept by H. K. Whitney;
during the journey and
sojourn of the Church
of Jesus Christ
of Latter day Saints

Anno Domini

1846.

(Continued.)

(No. 3.)

Journal 3

17 August–27 September 1846

A

Journal

Kept by H. K. Whitney,

during the journey and

sojourn of the church

of Jesus Christ

of Latter-day Saints

Anno Domini.

1846.

(Continued.)

(No. 3.)

H. K. Whitney's Journal.[70]

Nauvoo, May 8th, 1843.

70. ***Editor's note***: This appears to be on the inside of the cover of the journal. At the beginning of this journal, there are 29 pages of Horace K. Whitney's 1843 missionary journal that are not included here.

Monday the 17th

Fine day – myself and three others engaged in digging the well – at night, it was 44 feet in depth but yet no water – Dr. Reeves, (the physician who was sent for by Colonel Kane) arrived from Leavensworth this afternoon in company with Mr. Fleming, who lives at the village below. He, (the Doctor) tho't his patient was recovering rapidly – The two gentlemen came to my tent this evening, when we sent for [William] Pitt Hutchinson and Smithies, who came with their instruments, and entertained us till about 11 o'clock, with a variety of charming music – the Doctor said it was the best music he had heard in this country – Mr. [Lucien] Woodworth (the Parson) came here from over the river to see us to day – the man whom he came with lost his horse, therefore he was obliged to stay all night – There was a council held to-day at Bro. Clayton's tent This morning, Bro. Dana and W. Markham went back to Mt. Pisgah taking three yoke of oxen and a wagon belonging to Bro. K. –

Colonel Kane, as before stated, was convalescent. The only cause of his sending to Fort Leavenworth for a physician was his anxiety for his Mormon friends, fearing that a relapse might take him off, and his death might be laid to their charge. He came among us with the intention of learning the facts concerning the strange people who had been so terribly persecuted, and were now exiles from their homes, and the spots doubly sacred—the resting place of their dear ones, and after all the sorrows and suffering endured at the hands of the government, they had willingly responded to the first call.

Thus was explained the act of his standing eavesdropping by the side of our tent, on his first arrival at the camp. There was nothing that seemed to escape his notice. The little children who came around Brother Jedediah's tent, where he was nursed during his sickness, were objects of interest. One of Mother Whitney's little ones, a beautiful, fair, curly haired boy, who was just recovering from a severe illness, was one that attracted his attention. As he was only a few rods from us the child was often seen at the tent door where he lay, or as he sat under the bower outside.

The next spring there came to his friends numerous and various tokens of remembrance. Among them was a box containing fishing tackle, etc., which was sent to the little fair-haired Whitney boy; also the old nurse who was living in Bishop Whitney's family—Aunt Sabry Granger—was remembered to [have] a large box of superior black tea. As she parted with a portion of it, my mother purchased a few pounds, and I, being among the invalids, was daily treated to this delicious beverage. None were forgotten who had made his acquaintance, or done him the slightest favor. The presents, though, did not arrive till after the pioneers had left.

Woman's Exponent, vol. 13, no. 8,
15 September 1884, p. 58

Tuesday the 18th

Worked at the well, till noon when it commenced raining, and continued with little intermission thro the day, and night – Dr. Reeves and Mr. Fleming did not return to-day, in consequence of their horses being lost in the night – my wife is quite unwell to-day –

Wednesday the 19th

Cloudy thro the day – little or no rain – the Dr. and Mr. Fleming, not finding their own horse, took Colonel Kane's to return with – they had not been gone more than 2 or 3 hours before we found their horse in the woods close by – Bro. Burgess was employed to day in making shakes for the roof of our log house – the rest of us were busied in enlarging our cattle-yard – Saw Father Isaac Morley, and Bro. Phineas Richards; they had come over the river to see the brethren; their families are on the other side. Father killed one of his calves this evening –

Thursday the 20th

Rather cloudy in the morning – rained considerably in the middle of the day – tolerably cool weather – The boys busied in shingling the house – Wm. and Porter went down to the village this morning to take down the Doctor's horse – they returned about 11 o'clock at night – Bro. N. married, this evening, a Miss Black [likely Martha (Patsy) Brown] to a Mr. [David] Boss in our camp. The choir of singers met at Bro. Clayton's this evening to practise – ground up our scythes this evening preparatory to going at the haying business to-morrow morning – Council held to-day, among the rest was considered the propriety of sending for many things by father when he goes to St. Louis. Some of Brighams camp have commenced mowing some days since.

Friday the 21st

Quite cool weather – wrote a letter for Bro. K. to John Forsgren in answer to two letters received from him and Rob[er]t. Collins – it was directed to Fort Leavensworth – Father Morley, Phineas Richards, and Bro. [Jonathan] Hale went back over the river. Two of our boys and others went out with Bro. Winchester the foreman, intending to commence mowing – the place they have selected for working in is about 3 miles north of here – Brigham and Dr. Richards, with Bro. K. and father, spent the most of the forenoon at my tent in talking over the affairs of the church. &c.–[71]

---

71. The reason why church leaders sometimes met in Horace Whitney's tent was that he was a highly trusted, dependable, if unofficial secretary to the Quorum of the Twelve Apostles. His skills as a writer, his proven ability to keep confidences, and his utter devotion to the Latter-day Saint cause made him an invaluable backup to Thomas Bullock, the official clerk of the Camp of Israel, and to William Clayton, another trusted camp recorder. Heber C. Kimball often entrusted Horace with writing entries in his own personal journal.

SATURDAY THE 22D

Cool and cloudy. This morning, felt, quite unwell – wrote a letter of exhortation and advice left by Bro. K. to his family, to be read to them this evening – He, Wm Porter, Brigham, & Dr. Richards went over the river, where they intend to hold meeting to-morrow – Most of the boys went out haying to-day – The money sent up by the brethren in the army at their first payment, amounted to $5860, besides about $800 that they give to Bro. Hyde[72] – One night, while the brethren were encamped in the woods, on the route to Leavensworth, a terrible storm or hurricane arose, which surpassed any thing of the kind within the memory of the inhabitants – But what surprised them all was, that although showers of limbs of trees were constantly falling around them, the space within which they were encamped was in perfect calmness and security. Bro. Sherwood, who arrived day before yesterday told us that father [Samuel] Bent died at Garden Grove quite lately. – the same day Bro. Brigham and wife, Kimball and wife, Father and Mother, dined at Father Lott's tent – A brother by the name of [Albert Bailey] Griffin called, and bro't intelligence from Bro. Miller's camp. He related to us an anecdote concerning two of the brethren who went out on mules armed & equip't as a kind of scouting party – were surprised by a party of Indians of the Punkaw tribe who dragged them from their mules, took from them their arms, and were about to confine them, when one of the mules suddenly turned and kicked one of their party over – this circumstance distracting their attention, afforded the men a chance to escape, which they quickly did on foot leaving their mules &c. behind in the hands of the Indians, they (the brethren) returned to their camp, and in two days after their mules came in with their saddles and bridles on – the reason was supposed to be that they ran away from the Indians, and they could not retake them – Bro. Griffin also told us, that 8 chiefs of the Punkaw tribe came to the Pawnee village (where the brethren are encamped,) to smoke the "pipe of peace" with the Pawnees, who were out on a hunting excursion – as they did not return after waiting for them some time – The Punkaw chief told Bro. Miller that they would conduct him to a good place (one of their villages) to pass the winter, which they did, it being 50 miles north on the route to Fort Laramy – they went with them and found it a beautiful place indeed, abounding in rushes, pea-vines &c. &c.[73] The Indians appeared to be very friendly and offered them corn, or any thing else they wanted, and told they were welcome to put up buildings and remain as long as they chose –

---

72. This initial payment of $5,860 represented approximately 25 percent of the total $22,000 clothing allowance promised the Mormon Battalion members in return for their service. It is important to note that the money was given first to the battalion member, who then sent his money to his family—either his mother and father or his wife and children. They, in turn, were invited to contribute as much as possible to the church so as to buy food, provisions, and equipment in bulk at cheaper prices. Records show that the average battalion family retained approximately 24 percent of the funds sent home for essential food and supplies, donating the balance to the church. See Bennett, *Mormons at the Missouri*, 124.

73. This invitation, extended by the Punkaw Indians to George Miller, was for him and his company to spend the winter at their Niobrara (Vermillion) River settlement, now on the border between South Dakota and Iowa, an invitation that he gladly accepted but that the superintendent of Indian Affairs would not have condoned.

The 22nd I well remember it being my 18th birthday. That day Horace wrote a letter of exhortation and advice left by my father to his family to be read to them that evening as he, with President B. Young, W. Richards and one or two others, went over the river to hold meetings next day it being Sunday.

Woman's Exponent, vol. 13, no. 9,
October 1, 1884, pp. 65–66

Lately, in looking over some old papers, I found a letter of exhortation and counsel to father's family, written by my husband, at his dictation, as he was about leaving Cutler's Park to go with President Young to attend to some business over the river. It is dated August 22nd, 1846, my 18th birthday, and had been preserved among father's papers. The words being as appropriate today as then, I reproduce a portion for the benefit of those who regarded him in the light of a friend and wise counselor.

"I wish to give a few words of counsel to my family and to all that belong thereto—both male and female, old and young, and what I say unto one I say unto all, and shall expect it to be heeded in the full sense of the word.

"Of late there has been a great deal of carelessness, imprudence and slothfulness with many of the members of my family as regards to taking care of themselves—going without suitable clothing and stockings in cold, chilly weather, sitting out of doors under the bower after dark, when it is cold, wet weather, exposing themselves to sickness and death, which we have suffered much of. These things have caused me much sorrow and regret, and have caused my family much toil and hardship and fatigue, which has been brought upon us by a total neglect of counsel, which would have saved us these things.

** * * * I am now about leaving you for a short time, and I improve this opportunity to address you in this manner. I love my family, and I have never faltered for the first time in seeking their welfare, to provide everything that lay in my power for their happiness, and still intend to, inasmuch as my counsel can be respected. Now, my feelings are this: That all domestic affairs, as far as women are concerned, are out of the way 'while it is called day,' for when the night cometh no man can work, for the Lord says, in a certain revelation, 'Retire to thy bed early, that thy body may be invigorated, that thy days may be many.'*

"Now, I shall require these things at your hands, except circumstances shall otherwise direct. Cease from vanity, seek humility and meekness, bow before the Lord in the morning and at eve, and in so doing your days may be many, peace and tranquility shall soothe your bosoms, health and happiness shall dwell in thy wagons, tents, wigwams and cottages, while these things are observed. Cease from murmuring or complaining, finding fault with your friends or with each other, but manifest to all men and women, by your works, and the closeness of your tongues, and the integrity of your hearts, that you are right, and that God is with us of a truth. I always do, and shall expect that those which constitute my house, will remember me before the Lord, that I may have wisdom, health, patience and endurance to endure all things, that I may always

give suitable counsel to my family, even that that shall proceed from the Holy Ghost, for I never wish to counsel by any other spirit.

"I now feel to bless you all in the name of the Lord God of Israel, with peace, prosperity and salvation, that we all may be pure in heart. These are the words and blessings I feel to communicate and leave with my dear family.

"As ever, I remain, your most affectionate husband, father and friend in the new and everlasting covenant. Amen.

"HEBER C. KIMBALL."

Woman's Exponent, vol. 14, no. 9,
1 October 1885, p. 66

Sunday the 23d

Beautiful morning; I am yet quite unwell – consequently, did not attend meeting to-day, held in the neighboring woods. Bro. Grant, I believe, preached – Father Cutler was to speak, but was hindered on account of sickness.

Monday the 24th

Cool weather – it clouded up toward evening, and had every appearance of raining, which it did during the night. – Bro. Davenport arrived this evening with his family and camped with us, and some other's, who joined Brigham's camp. The boys mostly out haying to-day, except myself and Pete, who are quite sick, and Daniel and Wm King, who are making a sort of hay stack [?] .

Tuesday the 25th

Fair day – Sister Young [likely Clarissa Clara Decker Young] who was over to our camp this evening, and took supper, said there were 6 Indians waiting for Brigham to come home, wanting to see him on business –

Wednesday the 26th

Cool, cloudy weather To-day one of father's oxen (a stag) died with the murrain. He was apparently well on Sunday morning – One of Bro. [Elijah Knapp] Fuller's oxen was killed to-day going down a hill too fast, and hitting his head against a tree, broke his neck. – Bro. K. does not yet come home – he and Brigham are raising means of the brethren on the other side the river to send to St. Louis by father, who intends going down there in about a week.

Thursday the 27th

Misty and cloudy – The haying business going on as usual – Bro. K. Wm. Porter and Brigham got back to-day – Council held this evening – Besides the 6 chiefs spoken of above there are about 150 Indians in the vicinity, waiting to make some arrangement with the brethren about the possession of the land we are now occupying, on which they the brethren are to hold a council to-morrow morning. –

Friday the 28th

Fine morning. This morning, pursuant to agreement, a Council was called, at which 150 Indians were present. An aged chief almost blind arose and requested all those who had anything to say about the land business would speak – Accordingly a number of the brethren spoke – the amount of whose words were these: – That we had been driven like themselves, the Lamanites, and now desired a resting place with them for a little season, and would render them any favor in our power, except assisting them to war against other tribes, which would involve the shedding of blood. After the brethren had all got through speaking the old chief arose and said "Have you done?" refusing to make any reply, without or until that was the case – on receiving a token of assent, he arose and said – "I love your words, and will do all the good I can, for we have been pushed and driven too, by the nations around us, and should have come out in open war against them long ago, had not our "Grandfather", (the President), said, "live in peace"– He further more said, that the land that we are now on, is in dispute between this tribe, (the Omahaws) and the (Otoes) who he said were a thievish race, but if we could move up the river 10 miles to the old Fort of Council Bluffs (where the tribes formerly met in council, and transacted business with the agents of the U. S.),[74] then we might have peace and liberty with them we might make fields for them, and they in return, would let us have young men to assist us in herding our cattle – He furthermore said we were welcome to build houses and winter there, and remain as long as we chose with them, for they had undisputed title to the land in the vicinity of it, and there were greater conveniences there than here, plenty of water, wood, &c. close at hand.[75] –

The conclusion of the council was, that some of the brethren would go up and see the country about there before deciding to remove hence – Bro. [Stephen] Markham and family arrived this afternoon – he has had the misfortune to lose one of his fingers since we saw him last

Saturday the 29th

Fine day most all in the hayfield except me. Brigham Bro. K and wife, father and mother took supper at my tent this evening and conversed on several things connected with father's going

74. The Old Fort of Council Bluffs appears to be Fort Atkinson. Located ten miles north of Winter Quarters, it was the first United States Army post established west of the Missouri River and is also credited as the first town in Nebraska. Established in 1819 by Colonel Henry Atkinson, it was abandoned in 1827. It is now a State Historical Park and a National Historic Landmark.

75. Brigham Young followed a policy of strict neutrality while at Winter Quarters with respect to Mormon-Indian relationships. The Mormons would assist the Indians in providing food, medical care, and other necessities but did not want to be seen as preferring one tribe over another.

to St. Louis – Brigham told us that he had received news of the death of Father [William Huntington] who, had died since we heard of Father Bent's death – Father H. died at Mt. Pisgah – It is very sickly on the other side the river, and it is generally conceded that it is much healthier this side than the other. – We hear the Captain [James] Allen, who, was appointed to the command of the regiment of Mormon soldiers, has lately died at Fort Leavensworth –

Sunday the 30th

Fine morning – a meeting was held this forenoon at the "Stand" in the wood, did not attend in consequence of illness – Wm. Porter, John Davenport, went back to Musquito Creek to help Bishop [Edward] Hunter up, who is quite sick – A meeting was called at 5 P. M. under the bower near our tent – Father John Smith spoke at some length – He was followed by Elder O. Pratt, who, in a clear and concise manner, pointed out to the brethren the advantages of our closing with the offer of the Omahaw Indians, and moving up the river to the Old Fort, – Father Cutler spoke a few words – the amount of them was, that the brethren were not to discontinue the haying business, because they tho't they were going to move away, but to "rush ahead" and do all they could – President Young then spoke at some length, on the order of the government of the Kingdom of God. He said, no man was fit to act as a governor or ruler, until he had first proved himself worthy of the office, by showing himself ready and willing to be governed – He also said, that it was necessary we should move as speedily as possible to our winter quarters, in order that we may be engaged in the building of houses, which it is necessary should be immediately commenced – wrote a letter for Bro. K. to John Forsgren, Cyrus Canfield, and Robt. Collins, to be conveyed by (Dr.) H. E., whose departure is a secret – Bro. John Pack's youngest child (an infant) died to-day – death occasioned by teething.

Monday the 31st

Beautiful morning. This morning, Brigham, Heber, father, Fathers Cutler and Cahoon, and several others, some on horseback, others in wagons, started to go up the river to look out our winter location. This evening Wm. arrived with the carriage, bringing Bishop Hunter with him – His family have stopt for the night 8 or 9 miles back, – John Davenport is with them – they will be up to-morrow – Porter is at the river assisting Bro. Woodworth's folks across, who are all quite sick.

Tuesday the 1st of September

Quite windy to-day – To-day paid a visit to Bro. Hutchinson's at Brigham's camp. Zebedee Coltrin's father died last night in this camp – another man also in our camp, who had been living with Dr. [Garner Godfrey] Potter whose name I do not know This evening Bro. Woodworth's folks arrived, all quite sick – We rigged a temporary bedstead in my tent, for Flora, who has been very sick, but is now slowly gaining her health – Her folks encamped on the side hill a little to the left of our camp. –

The father of Zebedee Coltron died in our camp on the night of the 31st, also another man who had traveled with Dr. Patten. On the evening of September 1st Brother Woodworth and family arrived; all sick. They encamped outside of the square a little distance from our tent. We had a temporary bedstead prepared and took their daughter, Flora Gove, into our tent, where I nursed her until she recovered her strength. Her husband was also sick with fever; she had lain helpless for many days, and her heavy raven locks were so matted together that it took me hours to comb them out. We had lived neighbors in Nauvoo, and were old schoolmates. She was older than myself and was sealed to the Prophet Joseph as his wife. This happened before I was aware of the principle. A young man boarding at her father's, after the death of Joseph not a member of the Church had sought her hand, in time won her heart, and in a reckless moment she was induced to accept his offer and they eloped to Carthage, accompanied by a young lady friend, and were there married by a justice of the peace. Flora was never happy with him as he hated the Mormons, and she felt condemned for the rash step she had taken. She made this confession to me while I was nursing her, and said she desired to cling to Joseph hereafter.

They settled at the "Point," and she paid me a visit the following winter. She still expressed herself as strong in the faith of the gospel, also her great desire to cleave to the Prophet. I never saw her again as she died at that place, leaving two or three children. Joseph Smith gave her father the title of "pagan prophet." He came with his family to the valley, where he left them and went to California and never returned. Her mother was a true saint and a very gifted woman, well known and respected by thousands of the Saints in Utah.

I have given this little incident in the life of Flora truthfully, and it ought to teach a lesson to those who read it, for no Latter-day Saint can find happiness in marriage with an unbeliever as soon as the illusion which bewildered them wears off; they find no true companionship, and remorse will come, though, alas, too late to retrace their steps.

Woman's Exponent, vol. 13, no. 11,
1 November 1884, p. 87

Wednesday the 2d

Fair weather – The brethren who went up the river, on Monday, returned to-day – there were 21 or 22 in all among which were 8 of the high council and 5 of the Twelve, besides father – They started from here about 10 o'clock on Monday Morning and took the trail which Bro. Holman and others' had made in coming from the "Horn" – they travelled 25 or 30 miles this day and stopt for the night when Bro. Pack and Herriman had encamped when they came back from the "Horn" – The next morning they retraced their steps towards the Old Fort of Council Bluffs – travelled till they came to a creek where they had to make a bridge, after crossing which, instead of ascending the ridge on their right hand, they kept on thro the bottom which was covered with very high grass which soon grew so thick that they got entangled in it and were forced to use their knives to cut a passage in some places – it was so high too that they could not see over it although they stood up on their horses. After pursuing this route for some time in momentary danger of getting "swamped," they at length emerged from it and went up on the Bluff which was so steep that they had to dismount from their horses and let them ascend it by themselves – after a while a while [*sic*] they saw the Fort in the distance apparently about 6 miles off – they soon came to another brook or ravine where they were again obliged to build a sort of a bridge throwing in stuff of different kinds that they might be enabled to cross – The sun was about a hour high when they arrived at the "Fort," which consisted of the ruins of a few old buildings the principal of which was the "Magazine" – the walls were of stone, about 8 feet high, which had been formerly arched over with brick which had mostly fallen in – they come on about a mile further and camped for the night at the head of a ravine where they found a good spring of water – The next day they returned home, but little satisfied with the result of their journey. Forgot to mention, that on Monday also, a committee of three, viz: Orson Pratt, J. M. Grant, and Bro. [Charles] Bird were sent to confer with the Omahaws and the Otoes concerning our remaining on the land here – I visited the camp this evening where Bro. Woodworth's folks are – saw the corpse of Bro. Silas Mayson there who had been dead about an hour His disease was the fever – He came on with Bro. Woodworth's family –

THURSDAY THE 3D

Continued fair till towards night, when it clouded up and rained considerably during the night – Council held this evening – The committee sent on Monday to confer with the Omahaws & Otoes bro't in their report to the same They had seen the chiefs of the Omahaws, "Big Elk" and "Standing Elk" his son who signed the article which they had drawn up requesting their consent to remain here one or two or more years – Both tribes are very anxious to have all the improvements we shall leave behind The Otoes were anxious that we should not close with the

George Catlin, Chief Big Elk *(Omaha, 1832). Wikimedia.*

offer of the Omahaws and go up the river, because then they would have no clue to the improvements we shall make, whereas if we stay where we are they consider themselves entitled to every thing we shall leave behind[76] – A committee was appointed by the council to look out a good place for cattle among the pea-vines, and to see something about the removal of the Ferry up the river near here –

Friday the 4th

Weather fine and clear – the atmosphere much purer from the rains of last night Made out a bill of things for Bro. K. to send by father to St. Louis Father Bro. [Edwin Dilworth] Wooley and [Alexander] Wright are also engaged in making out bills of goods.

Saturday the 5th

Fine morning, tho rather cool – This morning, Bro. K., accompanied by eight others, (viz: O. Pratt, W. Woodruff, J. M., Grant, Tho[ma]s. Grover, Bro. Eldridge, Bro. [Joseph] Busby, Jackson Redding ["Return Jackson Redden"], O. P. Rockwell,) set out in pursuit of a new ferrying place – they travelled 5½ miles down the river, and came to a small creek across which they built a bridge and went over it – Near here they saw 2 deer – Porter killed a turkey – they then went to the mouth of the creek, where they had agreed to meet the committee from the other side the river – they waited here some time and at last saw 4 or 5 men up the river on the other side – they took a leather boat, belonging to Bro. Eldridge, which they had brought with them in a wagon, and two of them Bro. K. and O. Pratt, went over to see the committee – on getting over, they found 5 of the brethren, (viz: – Isaac Morley, Geo. [rge] W. Harris, Phinehas Richards, W[illia]m Snow, Bro. Miller) waiting for them – they all got into the boat with them and went back making 7 in all – There being a heavy wind up stream, and the waves rolling very high, they were in momentary danger of upsetting, so Bro. K. said, who steered the boat, but they landed safe without any accident, at the place from whence they had started – Here at the mouth of the creek they built a brush bridge – 2 of them, Bro. K. and Wm Snow rode up the river about 2 miles to see if they could find any better place for the ferry than here – after a while they returned, not having found any, consequently it was agreed to establish it here – one or two of the brethren then took the others back on the river in the leather boat, and they then returned home by a different route then they had come, making it about 9 miles back – They learned from Father Morley and his brethren of the death of Jonathan Hale who died on Thursday the 3d inst. at the Bluffs – Council held this evening –

---

76. Said Chief Big Elk through Logan Fontenelle, his interpreter: "I am an old man and will have to call you all my sons. I am willing you should stop in my country but I am afraid of my great father at Washington. . . . We have been oppressed by other tribes because we were weak. We have been like the hungry dog which runs through camp in search of something to eat and meets with enemies on every side. We have been oppressed for ten years; many times we could have defended ourselves, but our great Father told us not to fight. . . . We heard you were a good people, we are glad to have you come." Winter Quarters High Council Minutes, 28 August 1846, Church History Library. See also Journal History, 28 August 1846.

Sunday the 6th

Cool fall weather – Meeting held in the grove this morning, did not attend – Council held again this evening – wrote a letter for Bro. K. to Heywood, [Almon] Babbit and [John S.] Fullmer to send back by Daniel and William who start for Nauvoo, to-morrow or next day – the brethren up to this date, have cut from 1500 to 2000 tons of hay the most of which is already stacked. Forgot to mention the arrival of Joseph Young and family on Saturday evening, there is now rising [upwards] of 800 wagons in the three camps which are situated in the form of a triangle on the different hills around

Monday the 7th

Cool fall weather – This morning, Father, Bros. Wooley, Wright, and [John] Van Cott, started for the river in Bro K's carriage, Porter going along to drive – their intention is to get aboard of a steamboat, as they had heard of being at the village, or close by – not finding any they all came back this evening, except Bro. Wright who remained at the river – their intention is to start again to-morrow, and if they do not find a boat at the river, to go thro' by land to Montrose – thence to St. Louis. – Brigham and Bro. K. went down to the New Ferry to-day the former not having yet seen it.

Tuesday the 8th

This morning cool lowery cloudy weather – Bro. K. called his family together this morning to give them a few words of good advice and counsel – He said, that in consequence of three boys having been whipt lately for improper conduct by the Marshall and others appointed for the purpose,[77] a great many persons were "up in arms" about it, and that the spirit which proceeded from the devil and even got into his own family, and the language which some of the fathers and mothers used was this: – "damn them if they attempt to whip my children, I will cut their damned throats for them" – He said furthermore that the men who executed justice on the offenders, were appointed and commanded to do it by the council and authority, which we had made a solemn covenant to uphold and sustain. Consequently we were in a state of rebellion against God when we resisted such things, "for" said he "how it looks: – they attempting to execute the commands of the authorities of the church on one hand, and you on the other, standing in their way saying 'damn you, if you do, we will cut your damned throats for you'" – He cautioned his family against talking about things they knew nothing about and told them not to listen for a moment to slanderous things said by

77. Under the direction of marshal Horace S. Eldridge and chief of police Hosea Stout, one of the three young men punished, Peletiah Brown, was whipped with "18 stripes which brought the blood in two places." Said he: "O Br Eldridge if you will only stop I'll never touch another girl again while hell's afloat." One of the other young men, Jack Clothier, received 23 stripes, "five [extra] for his mean conduct while in our hands." Juanita Brooks, ed., *On The Mormon Frontier: The Diary of Hosea Stout, 1844–1861* (Salt Lake City: University of Utah Press and Utah State Historical Society, 1982), 1:191. Many in the camps feared Stout more than they did the Indians.

others, but if they heard anyone telling tales in his tents or in his wagons to forbid it in his name – He further said, inasmuch as William and David and Orson were about starting for Nauvoo, he tho't proper to call this meeting in order to put them on their guard, that they might be wise while they were there, and not say any thing which should prove a detriment to the church – Many other things he said, and gave a great deal good advice to them all, and finally called for an expression of their minds by vote – "If," said he, "you are willing to uphold and sustain me in the remarks I have made, signify it, by the uplifted hand – the vote was unanimous – He then closed by prayer, invoking blessings upon the heads of all those who are about leaving us for Nauvoo, and St. Louis.

– To-day 25 yoke of oxen, 7 cows and heifers, belonging to Bro. K. and 5 oxen belonging to Bro. Davenport, and 11 yoke belonging to Father marked "W" were sent up the river to be put into the herd of the whole camp, all having the mark or brand of "H. C. K." – The man chosen out of this division to assist in herding them is Jack Redding – Forgot to mention that a short time ago, a market place was made for the brethren to put in cattle, in order that when a person wanted a piece of meat they would know where to go and get it. Bro. K. put in 7 (two of which are the ones I drove) Bro. Davenport l. – Father put in three intending to kill them himself when he returns from St. Louis. –

This morning Wm Colonel Kane Daniel and Orson started for Nauvoo, also. Father Bro. Wooley and Van Cott for St. Louis – Porter also, intending to go to Mt. Pisgah – He, however, this evening got back – he came after some letters which had been forwarded here to Colonel Kane by Sarpee[78] [Peter A. Sarpy] – He said the steamer "General Brooks" was or had been at the village, and the folks would have taken passage with them, had it not been that they charged too much, which was 15 dollars apiece, consequently they would go by the way of Nauvoo – The steamboat was going back down the river 80 miles to bring up the rest of the freight belonging to Sarpee – Forgot to mention, that I wrote a little on Monday for Bro. K. to Hiram Kimball commenced raining towards evening and continued the most of the night – Council held this evening at Bro. Russel's tent. A committee was chosen to select locations for the winter between 2 miles from the village and the Old Fort as sanctioned by the Indians – Committee's names; Father Eldridge, Cutler, A. P. Rockwood, W. Farr, and J. M Grant – Brigham and Heber intend accompanying them.

78. Coming from a long line of explorers, fur trappers, and traders, Peter Sarpy had been trading at the Missouri River since at least 1834. His father, Gregoire B. Sarpy, was the first man to navigate the Mississippi River in keel boats. Peter Sarpy's brothers, Thomas and John, were clerks for the American Fur Company. He had both an Indian and a white wife living on either side of the river. Eccentric and excitable, and one who loved horses and liquor, Sarpy became a wealthy trader in Indian furs, later opening stores at St. Mary's and Decatur, Nebraska, and farming large acreages near Council Bluffs, Iowa. He died in 1865. See Hiram Martin Chittenden, *The American Fur Trade of the Far West* (Lincoln: University of Nebraska Press, 1986), 1:390.

WEDNESDAY THE 9TH

Rainy bad weather; which continued thro' the day Porter waited till afternoon in hopes the rain would cease, but being disappointed therein he started back in the rain about the middle of the afternoon, Bro Grant accompanying him – He is going to confer with the Indians, on business. The rain continued thro' the day, and at intervals during the night –

Peter A. Sarpy (1805–65), fur trader, ferry operator, businessman. Courtesy of Nebraska State Historical Society.

THURSDAY THE 10TH

Commenced raining and blowing very hard towards evening, and continued showery during the night Brigham, Bro. K., O. Pratt, Father Eldridge A. P. Rockwood, Joseph and Phineas Young rode out to seek a location. They went round over the woods and bluffs in the vicinity, but found no place suitable, and as Bro. K said their minds were constantly turned back to this place, as the best they could find – Council was held this evening, at which it was resolved, that all who chose to remain on the prairie, where we now are should have the privilege, and all those who chose to seek the woods should have the same privilege Bro. K. said for his part, he was in favor of remaining where we are –

FRIDAY THE 11TH

Rather cloudy thro' the day – This forenoon a majority of the "Twelve" (7 of them) viz: – Brigham, Heber, W. Richards, O. Pratt, G. A. Smith, W. Woodruff, A. Lyman, walked out to survey the ground – and this afternoon got a compass and laid out the city plot – Brighams quarters for the winter will be on this side the road near where we now are, Bro. K's on the other side near the timber – they also selected the spot on which to build the council house, which is not far hence – About midnight Wm and Porter got back in the wagon – they came back to bring back the bedclothes, &c. belonging to Bro. Grant that were taken away by Colonel Kane – they had gone about 15 miles on their route from the village, when he told them that he did not feel able to go thro' by land, consequently, they came back, and put him on board the steamboat, letting Wm. take his horse, and agreed to meet him at Nauvoo, in which if he failed, Wm. was to keep the horse – Daniel and Orson went on – also, Father and his company –

SATURDAY THE 12TH

Fine weather – nothing worthy of notice during the day – wrote a letter this evening for Bro. K. to Laura and Abigail Pitkin for whom he is going to send by William – also wrote again an order for Bro. Winchester or Lorenzo Young for two dollars worth of beef – Wm and Porter did not start to-day and probably will not before Monday. Council held this evening, at which the following resolutions were made –

1st – that all dogs should be tied up at sunset and not released till the next morning at sunrise – 2d – that no firing of guns should be permitted within hearing of the camp either by night or day, and that such things should cease wholly at sunset – 3d – That no timber should be cut down for fuel, which would answer the purpose of building, and that when any one wanted wood he should apply to Stephen Winchester and Father Eldridge, who would instruct them when and where to fall trees – It was particularly enjoined on the brethren, to spare the walnut trees, which have been already cut down in great numbers to procure walnuts –

SUNDAY THE 13TH

Windy, warm weather – Meeting held at the "Stand," commencing at 10, a.m. Elder O. Pratt opened the meeting by prayer, and said he would endeavor to occupy the time, by the President's request, till he and Bro. K. should arrive – he then spoke on general matters, for a while, when the President arriving he said he would stop short, but by his request he proceeded. His subject was the necessity of education to the elders of Israel, and to the children in the camp – He was followed by Bro. K., who spoke in corroboration of his remarks, – he said that in Kirtland he studied Grammar for one whole winter, and that positively, he did not know any more about it at the end thereof, than he did when he commenced – unless it was the difference between singular and plural number[79] – He said he did not care any thing about what some folks called grammar; for what he called by that name was the expressing of himself so as to be understood and that was all the Grammar he believed in – He spoke of the late whipping case, and told the congregation that he had called his family together and told them "to hold their tongues and mind their business," which he said was an important maxim, and one taught by Joseph when he was alive, as being necessary to our salvation – He further rehearsed what he said to his family in the late meeting, and spoke at some length on the government of the kingdom of God. – Bro Eldridge, the Marshall, then arose and told the congregation of the late resolutions adopted by the Council. To him succeeded President Young who spoke at some length, sanctioning what Bro. K had said, and then went on treating on miscellaneous matters, and gave a great deal of good instruction – After singing by the choir, the meeting was closed with prayer by prayer by J. M. Grant. Meeting of the council and others this evening, at which some arrangements were made relative to the cattle – some of the committee received &c. &c.

---

79. Heber C. Kimball is here referencing the School of the Prophets that Joseph Smith had convened back in Kirtland, Ohio, beginning in 1833. The first school met in the Newel K. Whitney store with an enrollment that never exceeded twenty-five. The School of the Elders convened in both Missouri and in Kirtland, from 1834 to 1836. The School of the Elders had larger enrollments than the School of the Prophets and, in addition to the spiritual preparation of its members, taught penmanship, English, Hebrew, grammar, arithmetic, and other topics. See Daniel H. Ludlow, ed., *Encyclopedia of Mormonism* (New York City: Macmillan, 1992), 3:1269.

Monday the 14th

Cool fall weather – This morning Wm and Porter started again – also Bro. Winchester, the foreman of this division called his men together for the first time, since they have been organized, and 9 men were chosen to go out mowing hay to-day – Bro. K. congratulated Bro. W. on his calling them together, that he felt blessed, and that it done him good to see it, and told them they must cut as much as 22 tons of hay to-day, which they nearly did, also that he no doubt they would have enough cut at the end of two weeks – Forgot to mention that Jacob Wetherbee went up the river to herd cattle on Sunday – Some of the boys killed a rattlesnake under Bro. Egan's wagon this evening – another item forgotten – got a pair of shoes from Clayton on father's acct. worth $1.50 (one dollar and a half.) Bro. K. Brigham and others were engaged in laying out city lots to-day –

Tuesday the 15th

Went out with the boys cutting hay to-day –there were 15 of them 6 or 8 engaged in mowing, the remainder in raking, – had to build a bridge in order to cross over with the oxen. Toward night it clouded up and had every appearance of rain – 2 brethren (Shurtliff and [Jacob] Houtz) came from the Punkaw village about 200 miles from here near where Bro. Miller is – they bro't letters from him and others – there were also with them 3 interpreters – Bro. Miller's company had killed 5 buffaloes since they have been there, and the brethren saw a number of them about one hundred miles from here, as they were coming down – Bro. K. and others are still engaged in laying out lots –

Wednesday the 16th

Commenced raining this morning about daybreak, and continued thro' the day – consequently there was no haying done to-day – Sister Hovey [Martha Ann Webster], the wife of Joseph Hovey, died this morning – She had been ill for some time – He had recently come from Nauvoo, and had spent a great deal of his time and substance in fitting others out for their journey, before he did himself – the consequence is, that he is very sick himself – His wife left three small children – Bro. K. had him put into Daniel Davis's tent that he might be nearer to us, and thus have better care paid him –

Thursday the 17th

Warm and pleasant – To-day some of the boys were engaged in cutting & drawing house-logs, and finally none of us went into the hayfield – Jacob Wetherbee got back from up the river where he has been to herd cattle – Bro. K. Brigham and some of the council rode down to the new ferrying place attended council this evening, with Bro. K. – Bro. Russel's tent – it had already commenced when we arrived – they were reading a report sent by Bro. Houtz, (one of the brethren who came from the Punkaw Nation with the 3 interpreters) the substance of which, was that Bishop Miller's company were located on a stream called "running water" or Punkaw river, about one mile beyond the Punkaw village, and 200 miles from this place – that they were uniformly used well by the Indians, had good forage for their cattle &c. &c. Bro. Grant, by vote of the council gave an oral report of his visit to the village at the point – He had seen Mr. Sarpee and he was willing that we should remove the ferry boat to the new place that we selected, as he had a Mckinaw boat [a light, open sailboat] of his own that would answer his purpose Mr. Sarpee also informed him that he had lately seen a Dr. Mann, who, he said was at the massacre at Haun's Mills in Missouri, and a regular Mobocrat, who told him that the State Marshall of Missouri, with a posse was on his way here, to arrest the "Twelve"[80] – A vote was taken that no man should go up the river to the place where Father [Thomas] Tanner is herding cattle, to take any cattle without a written order directed to Father Tanner, who was to select the cattle for him, from the foreman of the division to which he belongs, and this in consequence of the cattle being scattered all over the country by men who have been there and taken cattle without the leave of Father Tanner The ferry boat is to be removed to-morrow morning, and Bro. John Higbee is to go to the new ferry to superintend it – Saw a letter written by Sister Billings [Diantha Morley] to Bro. K's folks in which is recorded a specimen of Indian justice – It appears that one of the young Punkaw Indians had shot an arrow into one of Bro. Brigham's cattle for which misdemeanor he was taken and whipt, his pony shot and one of his own eyes dug out – One thing Bro. Grant stated, forgot to mention – that the secretary of War had written to the Indian Agent to have the Mormons leave the Pottawatomie lands on the other side the river as soon as may be –

Friday the 18th

Warm and pleasant, 13 of us in the hay field, mostly busied in stacking hay – a number of the boys remained at home, busied in drawing houselogs, doing chores &c. The brethren of the council, also Brigham Bro. K. and others of the Twelve went down on the bottom about 3 miles from here towards the river, and after each one speaking his mind on the subject concluded to settle there for the winter – Bro. Shirtliff and Houtz do not intend starting back to the Punkaw nation before Monday morning – Father I. Morley was over to-day – he said his tent was pitched on the bank of the river on the other side opposite the New Ferry –

Saturday the 19th

Very windy day – most of the boys except myself went to the hayfield, but soon returned, the wind blowing so hard that they could do nothing Brigham Bro. K. and others of the council went to the newly selected place and commenced laying out city lots which they did

80. Hawn's Mill, located on Shoal Creek in eastern Caldwell County, Missouri, was founded by Jacob Hawn (or Haun) in 1835 and was the site of a massacre in October 1838 when seventeen Mormon men and boys were killed by a mob and another thirteen were wounded. The Saints were expelled from Missouri in 1839. See Alexander L. Baugh, "A Rare Account of the Haun's Mill Massacre: The Reminiscence of Willard Gilbert Smith," *Mormon Historical Studies* 8, no. 1 and 2 (Spring/Fall 2007): 165–70.

about thirty – Jacob W. went up the river, and bro't down 6 yoke of oxen, three yoke of which belonged to father, in order to draw logs for the building of houses.

Sunday the 20th

Fine but windy – Being somewhat indisposed did not attend meeting to-day –

Monday the 21st

Some of the boys went into the hayfield to-day to work at stacking – this being the last day we shall work at the business where we have been – the remainder of our hay we shall get near our winter quarters – wrote two letters for Bro. K. – one to Titus Billings, the other to Elizabeth Glines – To-night about 10 o'clock were routed from our beds by the cry of "all hands repair to the center of the camp," which was done when the men were sent back after their guns, &c. and then Bro. K. proceeded to tell them the object of their coming together – It appears that the rumor that troops were on their way here to arrest the Twelve, turns out to be true – they crossed the river somewhere down in the settlements, and are now on this side, on their way up here – Therefore it is necessary for every man to be properly armed and equipt, and that a guard should be kept up nights to keep all spies from going to and from the camp – These things being attended to and every man told to arm and prepare himself to obey the orders of the foreman of the Division to which he belongs, the meeting was dismissed – They got the news thro' the medium of Mr. Sarpee who lives at the village –

Tuesday the 22d

Windy day – This morning at 10 o-clock, the men in the camp were all requested to meet at the Springs in the valley below our camp – President Young then addressed them and told them the object of our coming together, which was to organize ourselves into companies for self-defense – A vote was then taken, whether we should retain the Old officers of the Nauvoo Legion as captains of companies &c. or choose new ones – the vote was unanimous in favor of the former proposition – Bro. K's boys and myself attached ourselves to the company of artillery, under Captain [Norton] Jacobs [81] – A vote was finally taken whether we should remove immediately to our winter quarters as affording us a better place for convening and self-defense, it was decided in the affirmative, and that we commence to remove to-morrow, one division at a time, the brethren assisting each other in so doing – The companies were dismissed into the hands of their respective officers, with the caution to be on

81. The Nauvoo City Charter, authorized by the Illinois state legislature in December 1840 and in effect on 1 February 1841, provided for the creation of the Nauvoo Legion. Like hundreds of other city militia throughout the nation, the Nauvoo Legion was a legal entity, an American construct, subject to the military laws of the state and of the nation. As such, it answered ultimately to the governor of the state as its commander-in-chief. Joseph Smith served as its lieutenant general and local leader until his death in June 1844. With the revocation of the charter on 29 January 1845, the Nauvoo Legion ceased to function as a legal, state-sanctioned militia. The reconstitution of the Nauvoo Legion here in Nebraska was

the alert, and ready at a moment's warning to be called out by night or by day as occasion may require – The captains dismissed their companies with the same admonition –

Wednesday the 23^D

Rainy misty day. rather inauspicious for our removal. A number of the brethren with teams came to our assistance, and we arrived at our winter quarters about 1 o'clock P. M. which is three miles from Cutler's Park – We are located on the second shelf of the River Bottoms, which is laid out in the form of a city, 5 acres in each block, each block consisting of 20 lots – The city as laid out occupies or takes in, from 6 to 800 acres of ground – We are located on the south side of the road across which, and opposite to us is the lot on which we intend to build – Father's tent and wagons are placed on the other side the road close to the lot where he intends to build, which adjoins Bro. K's lot – There is a running stream of water within 50 rods of us which empties into the river about ¼ of a mile from here. Bro. Shirtliff and Houtz have not yet gone – they intend starting to-morrow – Geo. B. is to accompany them – taking a team of Bro. K's to help them along with their goods. Wrote two letters for Bro. K. – one to Father Billings, the other to Bishop Miller, of which George is to be the bearer. Bro. K. told Bro. Miller, (in his letter) to load his wagon with such things as he saw fit, and, if possible, to procure him 3 or 4 buffalo skins – to send back by George when he returns – Father Cutler is encamped on the banks of the river, and his hay is all stacked there also – the grass on our camping ground is nearly all mown down –

They brought considerable news, and next morning came to our tent and remained for an hour or more, telling the particulars of the late battle between 100 of our brethren and 1000 of the mob who came to attack the city, and were kept at bay by the little force, who compelled them to retreat, with considerable loss, as supposed, although the mob would not acknowledge the loss of a man. There were three killed on the brethren's side and three wounded. The action lasted an hour and twenty minutes, and took place between Winchester street and Squire Wells's house—in the neighborhood, where my father had built his first house. The place was then called Commerce. The mob had six cannons, besides their small arms; the brethren five cannons. President Young, my father and a number of the Twelve, and some others were present at our tent to hear him relate the affair, after which Dr. Richards read the articles of the capitulation of the city of Nauvoo, which took place on the 17th inst.

Woman's Exponent, vol. 13, no. 15,
1 January 1885, p. 115

---

strictly a matter of wilderness defense. It would later be more formally reconstituted under the laws of the Territory of Utah as a territorial militia. It was mustered in for service during the so-called Utah War of 1857. For more, see Richard E. Bennett, Susan Easton Black, and Donald Q. Cannon, *The Nauvoo Legion in Illinois: A History of the Mormon Militia, 1841–1846* (Norman, OK: Arthur H. Clark, 2010), 264.

C. C. A. Christensen (1831–1912), The Battle of Nauvoo, *c. 1878, tempera on muslin, 76½ x 113½ inches. Brigham Young University Museum of Art, gift of the grandchildren of C. C. A. Christensen, 1970. This armed conflict claimed the lives of four men and resulted in the forced evacuation of all remaining Mormons still in Nauvoo in September 1846, the so-called poor camps.*

THURSDAY THE 24TH

Cool cloudy weather – This morning Geo. Billings started, in company with Bro. Houtz and Shirtliff, for the Punkaw Nation – the boys were busied some in building yards for cattle, the others in drawing families down from Cutler's Park. The yards are built opposite us on the other side of the road – This evening Squire [Daniel H.]Wells and Wm. Cutler arrived from Nauvoo – they have been 6 days coming from that place – they came in a buggy – one object of their coming is to get teams to send back for the poor brethren, who are not able to come without assistance – They bro't considerable news[82] –

FRIDAY THE 25TH

This morning Bro. Wells and Cutler came to our tent, and remained for an hour or more telling the particulars of the late affair at Nauvoo – There was a regular battle took place there on Saturday the 12th inst. between 100 of the brethren and 1000 of the mob who came

82. The Nauvoo poor camps were the last remnants of Latter-day Saints to leave Nauvoo in the fall of 1846. Driven out of the city at the point of bayonet and cannon fire, the Nauvoo poor camps numbered some nine hundred people who were totally unprepared for the exodus west. Driven out in September, they crossed the river to Montrose, Iowa, where they huddled in refugee camps, waiting for rescue parties that Brigham Young dispatched from Winter Quarters and Council Bluffs in October. Most of the poor camps spent the winter at Garden Grove, Mount Pisgah, or Kanesville. See Richard E. Bennett, "Eastward to Eden: the Nauvoo Rescue Missions," *Dialogue: Journal of Mormon Thought* 19 (Winter 1986): 100–108.

to attack the city[83] This little force kept them at bay and finally forced them to retreat, with considerable loss, as supposed, altho' the mob would not acknowledge the loss of a man – The action lasted an hour and twenty minutes and took place between Winchester street and Squire Wells' house – the mob having 6 cannon besides their small arms, the brethren 5 cannon – On the part of the brethren there were three killed and three wounded – the former were W[illia]m Anderson and his son about 14 years old, and Bro. [David] Norris a blacksmith – Brigham Bro. K. Dr. Richards and a number of the Twelve and some others were at our tent hearing him relate the affair – After he had got through, Dr. Richards read the articles of the capitulation of the city of Nauvoo, which took place on Saturday the 17th inst. at 3 o'clock P. M. – These were that the brethren should surrender their arms, (with the proviso that they should be returned to them when they crossed the river – That the property of the citizens should be respected, as well as their persons, and particularly that the women and children should be unharmed, and that they, (the Quincy Committee) would use their influence that no outrages should be committed of any kind. The treaty was negotiated between [Joseph L.] Heywood [Almon W.] Babbitt and [John S.] Fullmer [the Nauvoo Trustees] on their own part and Colonel [Thomas Patterson] Brockman (a Methodist preacher) commander of the forces of the mob and the Quincy Committee on the other side. They (the mob,) further agreed that 10 men (including the Trustees and their clerks) should be suffered to remain in the city long enough to transact the business of the church, and assist in hastening the removal of the remainder of the brethren as speedily as possible–

Saturday the 26th

Fine and pleasant – one thing forgot to mention – that the [Nauvoo] Temple had been struck by lightning not long since. It demolished one of the carved faces that stand on the top of the pilasters

Sunday the 27th

Council held to day near Bro. Taylor's tent – did not attend being somewhat indisposed – Squire Wells related to the people the circumstances that lately transpired at Nauvoo, and said that there were a great many brethren there in very indigent circumstances, who would not be able to come away without assistance – Consequently the Council determined to raise teams and send back for them[84] – it was thought advisable first to get all the teams they could of

83. The Battle of Nauvoo was fought in September 1846 between anti-Mormon vigilante groups and mob extremists led by Thomas C. Sharp and others on the one hand, and forlorn Mormon defenders on the other. The battle lasted approximately three days and took the lives of at least four men before ending in an unconditional surrender of the city. It also resulted in the desecration of the Nauvoo Temple and in the expulsion of the poor camps, discussed earlier. See Richard E. Bennett, "Barbarously Expelled: The Infamous Nauvoo War of September 1846," in *History of the Saints: The Mormon Wars*, ed. Glenn Rawson (American Fork, UT: Covenant Communications, 2014), 77–89.

84. The three primary rescue camps were the Murdock, Campbell, and Luman S. Shurtliff companies that hastened back from Council Bluffs to the Mississippi in October 1846. They were successful in rescuing

those who had built houses on the other side the river, at Mt. Pisgah, Garden Grove, because they, being in the great measure prepared for the winter, could better spare their teams than we, who have not yet built a single house, except the one that Bro. K. brought down from Cutler's Park – Helen has been quite unwell, for a few days past, but is now getting better –

Popping the Question

I told her that her marble brow,
O'er which her auburn locks were straying,
Was like a drift of purest snow,
Where golden sunset rays are playing.
I told her that her soft blue eyes
Would shame the brightest spheres of heaven,
That walk the chambers of the skies,
Upon a moonless summer even.
I swore no sunny cloud could vie
In snowy softness with her bosom,
And that her cheeks had stole their dye,
From wild rose and magnolia blossom.
I vowed that unto her alone,
My burning heart had worship given;
That should she on its homage frown,
'Twould then to dark despair be driven
And then I gazed upon her form,
And pres'd her small white hand with fervor –
And asked her if, 'mid calm and storm,
She would be mine, and mine forever?
And I swore I'd keep my vows,
As true as rule, or square, or plummet;
But – she placed her finger on her nose,
And told me that – I "Couldn't Come It."
Promised I in your Album to write,
If so, will at my vocation;
For promises often unite
Your sex to "the Lords of Creation"
Well, now that I've written a verse,
I might as well scribble another,
To tell you it needs a good nurse –
And this is its poor foster brother!

virtually all members of the poor camps. For more, see Wendy Top, "'The Poorest of the Poor and the Sickest of the Sick': The Shurtliff Poor Camp Rescue," in *Far Away in the West: Reflections on the Mormon Pioneer Trail*, ed. Scott C. Esplin, Richard E. Bennett, Susan Easton Black, and Craig K. Manscill (Provo, UT: Religious Studies Center; Salt Lake City: Deseret Book, 2015): 81–97.

A

Journal

Kept by H. K. Whitney, during the journey and sojourn of the Church of Jesus Christ of latter day Saints in the wilderness,

A. D.

1846-7.

(No. 4 Continued.)

Journal 4

28 September 1846–10 March 1847

A
JOURNAL
Kept by H. K. Whitney, during
the journey and sojourn
of the church of Jesus
Christ of Latterday
Saints, in the
wilderness,
A. D.
1846-7.
(No. 4.
Continued.)

Monday the 28th

Windy day – Squire Wells did not start back to-day, as he intended – We are yet busied in assisting others down here. John Davenport and Jacob Frazier went down the river about 3 miles, and cut 4 acres of hay to-day – It is Bro. K's intention to get only 20 tons of hay besides what they have already got stacked at the other place about 6 miles back, which consists of about 120 tons belonging to this division. The wind was so high to-day that my tent was blown down – The brethren have very good success in fishing, quite a number of catfish have [been] caught out of the river since [we] have been here –

Tuesday the 29th

Cool weather – father's boys are engaged in cutting houselogs on the opposite (main) shore. – Bro. King and Jacob Frazier went out to mow – Squire Wells and W. Cutler started for Nauvoo to-day –

Wednesday the 30th

Rather cloudy and misty weather – This morning, Bro. King and Jacob, and Spencer went out to mow – Spencer went in the place of John Davenport, who having seen a yoke of father's cattle day before yesterday, that had been lost for some time – went in pursuit of them – About noon, Hosea Cushing, James Smithies, and myself took a wagon and went into the hay field for the purpose of stacking, but it being pretty late when, we arrived we did not stack any, but concluded to cache up what had been cut, and stack it to-morrow – John D. came where we were, but he had not found the cattle – It rained a little as we were starting for home, but it soon cleared off pleasant –

Thursday the 1st of October

Fine day – This morning Bro. King, John D., George Rhodes, James Smithies, Jacob Frazier and myself went out haying – 4 engaged in stacking, the other two in mowing – Played the violin at a party held at father's tent this evening on the anniversary of little Maria's birth-day –

Friday the 2d

Fine weather yet – This morning, the same persons as yesterday went into the hay field except George Rhodes, who went up to the other camp with two yoke of oxen, to assist some of the brethren to come down – Father's boys have been engaged in building a canoe to-day, which they nearly finished – Mr. Beach and another man from the point, here to-day, selling onions, which they sold at $1.50 per bushel – they also had some soap with them –

Saturday the 3d

Beautiful day – To-day four of us, viz: – James Smithies, J. Davenport, H. Cushing, and myself went into the hayfield – no mowing done of any consequence – principally engaged in stacking – Bro. Pack arrived here on Thursday last – he had been down in the country to procure a carding machine, – he brought back with him, besides the machine two barrels of whiskey which he sells at 75 cts. a gallon[85] – We had a very severe frost, to-night, for the first time this season – The Band or part of them met this evening – I joined them, and played with them – I am to play the instrument, formerly used by A[ndrew] Cahoon, who expects to start shortly for England.

We had had considerable rainy, windy and disagreeable weather. A few days after our removal the wind was so severe that our tent and a number of others were blown to the ground.

Woman's Exponent, vol. 13, no. 15,
1 January 1885, p. 115

Sunday the 4th

Fine and pleasant. Forgot to mention that Bro. Lathrop and another brother arrived here yesterday from Miller's camp; they had been stript of nearly all they possessed, and moved away from Bro. Miller's, some distance, – when they concluded to come down here, supposing it to be only thirty miles – they travelled 6 days, and arrived here at last, having nothing to eat during the time, except a wild goose a rabbit and a turtle, that they killed on their route – Bro. K. called his family together this morning for the purpose of instruction, which was listened to with respect and deference by all the family – There was also a meeting held at the "stand" a short distance from here. Bro. O. Pratt preached a good sermon to the people was informed [?]–

Monday the 5th

Rather windy day – Jacob F. and Wm King went out to mow – J. Davenport assisted in building a bridge, the others in drawing houselogs –

Tuesday the 6th

Tolerable warm day – This morning 4 of us, viz: – King, Cushing, Jacob W. and myself went into the hayfield for the purpose of stacking, which we intend shall wind up the haying business for this season – John D. and James Smithies engaged in drawing houselogs, also father's boys are rafting the same across the river – Bro. Lathrop started for home to-day – he is situated on the Missouri bottoms, on the river, like ourselves, about 100 miles above here

---

85. For more on the Word of Wisdom, see note 31.

where he intends to winter[86] – It is the intention of the brethren to turn out generally on Saturday next, and get in all the cattle, and send them up there for winter keeping – Almon Babbitt and wife arrived here this evening from Nauvoo, he brought considerable news – he said that the mob had complete possession of the place, Temple and all – they had several mock ceremonies with different individuals – they baptized Daniel Davis three times – he (Bro. B.) saw Father in Nauvoo, who was obliged to leave secretly and speedily for St. Louis – Bro. Babbitt, stated that the mob had plundered a number of buildings, among which was the house of Bro. Heywood, who was stript of nearly all he possessed. – They, (the mob,) defaced the Temple, considerably, both inside and out. Some Indians were here this day, and to night we judged it necessary to have a guard out, on account of the horses, as they have threatened to do us all the injury they could, in consequence of our cattle having got into their corn, while we stayed at the Springs –

He brought considerable news; said the mob had complete possession of the place, the temple and all. They had several mock ceremonies with different individuals—had baptized Daniel Davis three times. He saw Bishop Whitney, who barely escaped, and was obliged to leave Nauvoo secretly and speedily for St. Louis. He stated that the mob had plundered numbers of buildings, among which was the house of Bro. Joseph Heywood, who was stripped of nearly everything he possessed. They had defaced the temple considerably, both inside and out. The shore of the city and all the approaches to the city were strictly guarded to prevent the ingress of "Mormons," and when any man was found they immediately baptized him and sent him over into Iowa. Mr. Babbet [Almon W. Babbitt] was advised by the council, which had met to arrange some difficulty between some of the brethren, to remain with us, but he seemed not very anxious to do it.

Woman's Exponent, vol. 13, no. 17,
1 February 1885, p. 131

Wednesday the 7th

Cloudy misty weather – the boys mostly busied in drawing houselogs – Bro. K. Brigham and the Council went up to the "Big Herd" to day to arrange some difficulty between some of the brethren – Bro. Babbitt was advised by the council to move on here this winter – he seemed not very anxious to – do it – A gentleman by the name of Pickett came on with Bro. B. He joined the church since we left Nauvoo, and has taken quite a conspicuous part in the affairs of that place within a few months past, which have transpired between the "New Citizens"

86. The Mormons at the Missouri were cattle rich and money poor. Brigham Young's own herds numbered 1,264 oxen, 146 horses, and 828 cows. Heber C. Kimball's herds counted no less. Thomas L. Kane reported "no less than 30,000 head of Latter-day Saint cattle." The more accurate number, however, is probably closer to 10,000, the largest herd of which—the "Big Herd"—was located several miles north of Winter Quarters. For a more complete study of Mormon livestock, see Gary S. Ford, "Cornelius P. Lott and His Contribution to the Temporal Salvation of the Latter-day Saint Pioneers through the Care of the Livestock" (master's thesis, Brigham Young University, 2005).

and the Old, or, what amounts to the same thing, between the Mormons and Anti-Mormons. Bro. B. says the shores of the river and all the approaches to the city are strictly guarded to prevent the ingress of Mormons, and when any one is found, they immediately baptize him and send him over the river into Iowa – father himself barely escaped re-baptism by speedy flight[87] – Towards night it rained a little, which, however, did not last long – Most persons in the camp that have been afflicted with the ague, bilious fever, &c. during the past season, are gaining their health rapidly, as cold weather approaches – Band met again this evening, meet regularly every Wednesday and Saturday evenings for practice –

Thursday the 8th

Fine day – We commenced to put up a house this morning, and raised it 4 or 5 logs high to-day – Not very well to-day –

Friday the 9th

Rather cloudy this morning, considerable appearance of rain – it, however, soon cleared off – King, John D., and myself went into the woods about 3 miles back, by the old camp ground, to get "necessary" timber, which we partly built – Bro. Babbitt and wife started back this morning – John Smith went with them to meet his mother, who is about 150 miles back near Mt. Pisgah. Mr. Pickett did not go back with Bro. B. – he intends remaining with us and going over the mountains with us in the Spring –

Saturday the 10th

Tolerable fair day, tho' rather cloudy this morning – Three of our boys, viz: – J. Davenport, J. Frazier, and H. Cushing, and two of father's boys, viz: – Jacob Wetherbee and S. Wiltbank went up to the Big Herd in search of cattle – the majority of the men in the camp also went out on the same business – most of them remained there over night, and slept on the ground, not being able to find their cattle, which were scattered all over the country – James Smithies and myself went after a load of wood. King remained at home to repair the fence, &c.– Jackson Redding, returned from the Pawnee Village this evening, whither he had been by appointment to assist some families to remove back here, whom Bishop Miller had left sick and destitute –

Bishop Miller had now become a confirmed apostate. He had drawn away a few weak and disaffected persons and some, who, like himself, were corrupt at heart. They were

87. For more on the indignities performed on the poor camps and other Latter-day Saints who were late in leaving Nauvoo, see Richard E. Bennett, "Eastward to Eden: the Nauvoo Rescue Missions," *Dialogue: Journal of Mormon Thought* 19 (Winter 1986): 100–108. See also Bennett, "Barbarously Expelled, 77–89.

afterwards distinguished as Millerites. Many of those who had traveled in his camp returned to headquarters.[88]

Woman's Exponent, vol. 13, no. 17,
1 February 1885, p. 131

SUNDAY THE 11TH

Commenced raining this morning, and continued at intervals thro' the day – no meeting held in consequence of the foulness of the weather – Forgot to mention that Miss Eliza Ann Peirson, a niece of Dr. Richards, died last evening at his tent – She had left father and mother far behind, to join the saints of God in the wilderness, to suffer and die among them for the gospel's sake – She was a worthy exemplary young person, and the remembrance of the many happy hours I have passed in her society, together with her sisters and friends, will never be obliterated, while time shall last – She was from Richmond, Massachusetts, where I became acquainted with her during my sojourn in the E. States[89] – This afternoon the brethren drove into the camp all the cattle they found during their search yesterday which covered a large space of ground, altho' several hundred are yet missing – Immediately every man commenced selecting out his cattle from among them, some found one, some two, while others were so fortunate as to find nearly all they owned – Bro. K. recovered 32 of his oxen, and 6 cows and heifers – father, a good share of his cattle –

MONDAY THE 12TH

Cool weather but the rain has ceased – Discovered that the cattle had all got out of the yards during the night. We all went out in pursuit. J. Redding and myself went 3 or 4 miles up the river on horse back – By night, we had found all that escaped except 3 or 4.

TUESDAY THE 13TH

Cold windy weather – To-day J. Smithies and myself went into the hayfield, and got a load of hay from the stack we learn that there has been a stack of 70 tons lately burnt down – caused by the owner attempting to burn 'round it – King and Jacob W. went into the woods

88. Associate presiding bishop and remarkable trailblazer George Miller became highly critical of Brigham Young's leadership the further west the pioneers traveled. As a fellow and very vocal member of the Council of Fifty, Miller's plans for the westward exodus increasingly clashed with those of his leaders. Miller's temporary settlement at Grand Island, and then later among the Ponca near the confluence of the Missouri and Niobrara Rivers, did not sit well with his several hundred followers, who became ever more critical of his authoritarian style of leadership. Miller and James Emmett eventually broke with Young and the Saints in January 1846. Section 136 of the Doctrine and Covenants—the "Word and Will of the Lord"—was given, in part, in response to Miller's criticisms. Leaving the Saints, Miller first became a follower of Lyman Wight in Texas and later of James Strang in Wisconsin. He is buried in Marengo, Illinois.

89. Miss Pierson was one of the first to die at the Missouri. Upwards of a thousand more would perish over the next two years.

for shingle timber – This evening Cushing returned from the village below on this side the river, whither he had gone in search of cattle – he brought home a peck of potatoes, which he bought down there at the rate of fifty cents a bushel he saw quite a large camp of the Omahaws, whose tents were made of buffalo skins, and were nearly as white as our canvas tents – There is considerable noise and tumult in the village below, in consequence of the Indians receiving their payment from the U. S. – the amount of money paid to them is $50,000, which was brought up by land, accompanied by a guard of 12 men[90] – The wind was so high, that my tent, together with a number of others, was blown down, and we were not able to put them up again till evening, when the wind ceased – Quite a number of the brethren are engaged in making brick, that we may have good chimneys for our housing – they have the materials here for making first rate brick – clay, &c. it is said that the Indians are killing our cattle in great numbers, down below here, and they have been here with beef to sell, – no doubt the relics of some of our cattle

Wednesday the 14th

Quite rainy this morning – it, however, soon cleared off pleasant – John D. J. Frazier and myself went into the woods for shingle stuff, which we get in length 2 ½ feet – King, Cushing, Smithies and others engaged in building the house, of which they laid the last log to-day, and finished, all except the roof thereof – one of father's buildings is also finished except the roof, which is intended for a store-house – Bros. Wm Murray, Harvey Green, and Dr. [Joseph] Hovey arrived this evening from Nauvoo – they have been three weeks on the road – it appears by their statements that the mob have been pretty busy, plundering houses, ripping open feather beds and scattering the contents in the streets, &c.– They have also defaced the Temple considerably, inside and out, such as knocking the horns from the oxen in the font running about the streets and imitating the blowing of horns with them, and doing other acts of sacrilege too numerous to mention.[91] Bro. Murray's family are about a mile from here down on the bottoms, and are waiting for a bridge to be built across the creek, before they can get here to us since hearing the above, Bro. Hovey informs me that the mob have torn down the altars and pulpits in the Temple, and converted that edifice into a meat market –

Thursday the 15th

Very windy – Bro. Murray's family arrived here to day, after the bridge having been built, about a mile back – Bro. K. King, myself and others engaged in working at the building,

---

90. In return for ceding their lands to the United States, the various Indian tribes were paid treaty money by the federal government, in this case $50,000 to the Omahas. Unfortunately the Native Americans were often swindled out of these payments by liquor traffickers, fur traders, and various other unscrupulous individuals.

91. This has reference to the Nauvoo Temple baptismal font, which was situated on the top of twelve stone oxen, representative of the twelve tribes of Israel. Modern Mormon temples still feature such a font construction.

– Hosea and George went with the herd – Bro. W. Woodruff was brought into the camp this afternoon from the woods, severely injured by the fall of a tree – Brigham, Bro. K. O. Pratt, Dr. Richards and Joseph Young laid hands on him, after which he appeared much relieved –

Friday the 16th

Cold and windy – this morning John Davenport and myself went on horseback down on the bottoms 3 or 4 miles in search of cattle – returned without any success – J. Smithies and George Rhodes went out with the herd – Bro. K. King, Hosea, and Jacob F. to work at the house, the roof of which was nearly completed, we cleared out the inside of it and the family moved into it this evening – Bro. K. took two of his tents down and spread them over the roof – mine was left standing – Bro. K. moved his wagon over to the building. Bro. [Stilman] Pond and family arrived this afternoon, all quite sick with the ague The Indians are located in great numbers about 10 miles below here, where they intend to remain this winter – they have had for some time in contemplation a grand buffalo hunt, which they have abandoned in expectation of living and sustaining themselves by the killing of our cattle instead, which they are frequently detected in driving off – severe heavy frost to night –

Saturday the 17th

Beautiful day, the sky cloudless and serene, tho' somewhat cold – To-day the most of us here engaged in working on the building making a chimney &c. from sod – James S. went after a load of hay – commenced to build another house by the side of the other, which is to [be] petitioned into two rooms, the fire place being between the two houses – fathers boys have moved some of their things into their house, altho' it is not yet finished.

Sunday the 18th

Fine day, and tolerable warm – Meeting held to-day at the "Stand" – not feeling well, did not attend – The subject of our molestation by the Indians was taken into consideration – it was thought to be necessary to build our houses in a more compact body and form our wagons in a circle, that we might be better able to defend ourselves against their encroachments – this was the advice given by the Interpreters who attended meeting with some Indians at the Stand – it was further deemed proper to send out different companies in different directions after cattle – the brethren were directed to take any horse they might find running loose in furtherance of that object – J. Redding is to be the Captain of one company which is to consist of 21 men – Bro. W[inslow] Farr and Z[era] Pulsipher are also appointed to go on the same business, as captains of companies –

Monday the 19th

Clear and cold weather – Our cattle with a great many others bearing the mark "H. C. K." on the left horn, and that of "H." on the left rump were sent up the river this morning to

Bro. Lathrop's encampment, 70 miles from here – The following is a list of cattle bearing the above mentioned mark, "H. C. K." viz: –

H. C. Kimball	28 oxen.
" " "	12 cows
Jackson Redding	6 oxen.
Asa Davis	2 "
Howard Egan	1 "
Richard Slater	2 "
Daniel Davis	5 "
Ellis Sanders	4 "
William Murray	6 "
" "	1 cow.
Harvey Green	4 oxen.
" "	2 cows.
Orlando D. Hovey	2 oxen.
Joseph Hovey	3 "
Sister Canfield	2 "
James Brinkerhoff	4 "
Alva Tippetts	2 "
J. M. Grant	5 "
Alfred Randall	2 "
	93 head.

The following cattle marked "H. W." on the left rump were also sent to Bro. Lathrop for winter keeping –

N. K. Whitney	16 oxen.
Bro. More	4 "
J. C. Kingsbury	4 "
Bro. Pond	4 "
	28 head
	93
Total amount of cattle sent up the river in Bro. K's. name.	121 head

comprising 104 oxen, and 17 cows.

The cattle were sent off under the charge of Jackson Redding, Jacob Wetherbee, Jacob Frazier and George Rhodes, J. Redding, being the foreman. Wrote a letter for Bro. K. to Lathrop instructing him the particulars about the cattle, &c., and requesting him to do the best he could by them. – He also sent him 103 lbs. flour bag and all – After we got the cattle off, Bro. K. observed that it was a good job taken off from our hands, – we did some little on the house to-day – towards evening James Smithies and myself went after a load of hay – Hosea Cushing assisting Bro. Corbett in getting shingle stuff.

Tuesday the 20th

Quite warm to-day for the time of year – King & myself engaged in building a fence to form a new yard for our cows. The boys who started yesterday morning with the cattle, sent back word that they needed more help consequently, Hosea Cushing started this morning to overtake and go with them – A general turnout was made this morning to go out and drive in cattle in conformity with the arrangements made at the meeting on Sunday – In the afternoon, the men in the camp that were left were summoned to go down on the bottoms and put out the fire, which was raging greatly and had already burnt a number of haystacks, but notwithstanding all our efforts we could not entirely subdue it – King and myself worked at it till sunset. Bro. K. went down and burnt round our stack in order to save it. The brethren at last succeeded in turning the fire in such a direction that it should not do much injury – The brethren who went out in search of cattle this morning, returned with a large number of them this evening and put them into Father Cutler's yard, which was appointed as the place of rendezvous, where the brethren might come and each select his own cattle – I believe there were some of father's or Bro. K's. drove in –

On Tuesday morning a general turnout was made to go and drive in the cattle, in conformity with the arrangements made at the meeting. They spent a number of days hunting them, and all that were found were put into Father Cutler's yard, which was appointed as the place of rendezvous, where the brethren might come and each select his own cattle. In the afternoon of the same day, the men who were left in camp were summoned to go down on the bottom and put out a fire, which was raging greatly, and had already burnt a number of haystacks.

Woman's Exponent, vol. 13, no. 17,
1 February 1885, p. 131

Wednesday the 21st

Fine day – This morning, by request of Bro. K. went down to the Ferry, 6 miles from here, to assist Sister Hyrum Smith to move up here – found them just crossing the river – Little John Smith and myself drove up the loose cattle, and arrived at the camp a little after dusk – the family all got here soon after –

Thursday the 22d

Warm and pleasant – the brethren still out in pursuit of lost cattle – Abram Lowsey [Abraham Losee (1814–87)] and myself went out bee hunting – took along a gun also in hopes of finding some game – returned tired and hungry at evening, without any success – Bro. K.

found 3 of his cattle this evening, which had been drove into Father Cutler's yard – Bro. K. learned this evening from a brother who came down from the herding place, that one yoke of his best steers had been killed by falling down a steep place into a creek, one being drowned, the other choked to death, not being able to disengage himself from the yoke

Friday the 23d

Fine and pleasant – This morning early a meeting was called at the stand, for the purpose of making arrangements to send out for cattle – King, started soon after with a number of others for the rush bottoms 20 or 30 miles above here to assist in finding lost cattle – Bro. K. has found one or two more of his to day which were driven into Father Cutler's yard this evening – The Indians are quite plenty with us here, loitering round the meat market, to get the refuse meat, entrails, &c. A meeting was again called this evening at the Stand, and arrangements made for a guard nights &c. on account of the vicinity of the Indians – assisted the girls in washing to-day at the river – John D. and his father returned to-day – they have been up the river 6 miles getting logs, and have got a number nearly ready for rafting down here – they brought home a fine turkey which they had killed, and of which they say there is an abundance where they have been –

Saturday the 24th

Beautiful day – in fact the weather two or three days past has quite resembled that of an Indian summer James Smithies and myself went down after a load of hay – our stack of hay is diminishing quite rapidly since we have quit herding and kept our cows and oxen in yards at home, of which there are 10 of the former, & that were not sent up the river & two yoke of oxen that were retained for our use about home – Father's Cutler's men are drawing logs to-day for another of Bro. K's. houses – done some little at the house to-day, putting up logs, &c. get along rather slow in building as most of the boys are absent, there being but three of us at home at present, viz: – John D. James S. and myself – This day Bro. K. bought a cow of Mrs. Simeon Carter, also a yoke of steers of S. Markham. This evening 40 wagons from Bishop Miller's company arrived here, on their way down to Missouri to get provisions &c., for an outfit in the spring[92] – With them came George Billings and Hans Hansen – both bringing back the teams belonging to Bro. K., that they took away – it was Hans' intention to proceed to Missouri with the rest of the brethren, but Bro. K. would not permit it, the cattle that he (Hans) took away being so poor – Bishop Miller himself came down with the company, also Bro. Shirtliff and others –

Sunday the 25th

To-day meeting held at the Stand – it was announced by President Young that father was close by and the idea of sending after the goods with teams was taken into consideration – it

92. For more on the so-called Missouri lifeline, see note 47.

was also suggested that the brethren who had not built houses should henceforth build on the line of the city and in as compact a body as possible, that it may answer instead of a fence to prevent the Indians from stealing, &c.–

Monday the 26th

Fine day – Another lot of cattle was sent off this morning to the rush bottoms 20 or 30 miles above here – The following is a list of cattle sent up marked "H. C. K." on the left horn, and "H." on the left rump

H. C. Kimball______	15 oxen.
" " " ______	2 cows.
" " " ______	5 calves.
Samuel Moore ______	3 oxen.
Widow Miller______	6 " (4 of which are marked "13. D." on the left horn
" "	1 cow.
" "	1 calf having the above mark
Joseph Hovey______	1 ox
Bro. Babcock ______	2 "
Solon Foster ______	" "
Widow Gheen______	4 "
" " ______	3 cows.
Mrs. Hyrum Smith ______	15 oxen.
" " " ______	7 cows
" " " ______	3 heifers,
" " "	2 calves.
" " "	2 steers
Total amount sent up in Bro. K's name	72 head

Bro K. and Brigham went with the cattle besides a number of others, John Davenport went with them also. To-day, father and Orson arrived from St. Louis also Bro. Wooley and Wright – Bro. Brigham and Heber being absent, nothing as yet done about sending after the goods which amount to about 55 or 60 tons the most of which are probably by this time at St. Joseph's –

Tuesday & Wednesday the 27th & 28th

Nothing worthy of notice transpired these two days except that Bro. K. and Brigham do not yet return.

Thursday the 29th

Brigham and Heber arrived this evening – but none of our boys came back with them This evening a council was held at Father's house, at which Brigham, Heber, Father, and some others were present, – the principal subject of the council on this occasion was the sending after the goods.

Friday the 30th

Pleasant day – Hans with a team started after a load of ox yokes which the boys had not sent home – Bro. Wooley started to go down the river to see about the goods. –

Saturday the 31st

Fine day – This morning another lot of cattle were sent off to the rush bottoms one of father's boys, Henry Forsythe and one of Bro. K's. G. Billings went with them, the latter taking a wagon intending to remain there to herd. The following is a list of cattle sent off.

H. C. Kimball ______	2 bulls
Hans. Hansen ______	1 heifer
D. Davis ______	1 cow
Bro. Babcock ______	1 "
Wm Morris ______	2 "
Wm Murray ______	2 "
Ellis Sanders ______	1 steer
J. M. Grant ______	1 ox
Wm Clayton ______	18 "
" ______	5 cows
Total –	34 head (the last named marked "W. C." on both horns –

The above mentioned are marked "H. C. K." on the left horn, with the exception of Bro. Clayton's, and are all marked "H.", on the left rump The following having the Mark, "H. W." on the left rump were also sent up to the bottoms, viz:

N. K. Whitney		10 oxen
" "		4 cows
" "		3 heifers
" "		1 calf
J. C. Kingsbury		2 oxen
" "		2 cows
Thomas Moore		2 oxen
" "		2 cows
Stillman Pond		2 oxen
" "		2 cows
		30 head
		34 "
Total amount of cattle sent off in Bro. K's name.		64 head

Sunday the 1st of November

Fine warm day – a meeting was held at the "Stand," at which was taken into consideration the propriety of sending off teams to to [*sic*] St. Josephs for the goods – the intention is to start some of the teams to-morrow morning – Bro. Miller's teams started down into the country to-day for provisions – forgot to mention that the Ferry-boat has recently been removed to this place – It was said to-day at meeting that the Pottawatomie agent had forbid us to cut any more timber on the other side the river – Bro. Joshua Holman expired to-day after a short illness of about a week –

Monday the 2d

Cloudy cold day. Wrote a letter for father this morning, to Bro. Wooley at St. Josephs, giving him directions about the disposal of goods, &c.– Eight teams started to-day to bring them up – last evening a load of corn (17 bbls:) arrived for Bro. K., which he transferred to father Cutler's hands, all except 3 bushels, – this day a load of the same, (15 bbls.) brought by Bro. Wm Cobert [William Covert (1808–99)]. – Father Cutler's men laid the foundation of another double log-house, this afternoon, for Bro. K. – father has also got another log-house completed, except the roof James Smithies and myself went after a load of wood about a mile and half from here across the creek – Wm King and John Davenport arrived this evening about 10 o'clock from the rush bottoms about 20 miles above, where they have been herding cattle – they brought down the wagon taken up by Geo. Billings – we have got the last of the hay stack down on the bottom, and shall hereafter be obliged to go 7 miles for hay at the "Division" haying spot beyond the old camp ground.

Tuesday the 3^{d}

Fine day, and almost as warm as a summer day – engaged in topping off the roof of Bro. K's. second building, which consists of two rooms – Father Cutler and men engaged in putting up logs for the third building – and done something at the chimney of the 2^{d}, also, to day Hans engaged in sodding the roof of Bro. Ks. first log building – Eighteen teams started to-day also, for the goods – Bros. Wm. Murray and Samuel Myers brought 2 wagon loads of corn, the former having 23 barrels, the latter 15 –

Wednesday the 4th.

Fine day – tho' rather windy – engaged in drawing sod to build chimney, and to cover the roof of the house –

To-day father Cutler's men were engaged in building the new house which is now raised 5 logs high –

Thursday the 5th

Cloudy – about 3 P. M. it commenced raining and continued at intervals through the day and night – engaged yet in drawing sod for the roof and chimney – James S. building the latter – Hans to work at the former – John D. and King engaged in making doorways and chinking the house – Bro Murray bro't another load of corn consisting of 25 small bbls.

Friday the 6th

Fine day tho, rather muddy from the rain of yesterday – Bro. Winchester making shingles for Bro. K's second house King and John D. to work shingling the roof thereof one side of which they finished – another new house was started yesterday for Bro. Smithies and Egan. Bro. S. Myres [*sic*] brought a load of corn consisting of 11 small bbls. [bushels] which was given to father – Bro. Clayton and Geo. Grant returned from the village on the other side the river to day, whither they went on business for the church on Wednesday – Bro. C. informs me he never saw such a swindling operation as that practised on the Indians down there, they receiving their payments in money and then followed by a gang of sharpers who watch their opportunity, get them drunk, and then gamble with them and cheat them out of all their money – Bro. John Kay came down here from the Punkaw nation – he has been out with them hunting, since he left here and will rejoin them in 6 weeks from this time –

Saturday the 7th

Fine day – Engaged in roofing and sodding the second house – into one room of which we moved this evening, the other room being occupied by Sister Kimball and Mary Kimball – we congratulated ourselves considerably upon being able to live in a house once again, as we have got thoroughly tired of living in tents Sarah Ann's wagon and mine was moved over to this side the road where our house is – there has been a small house built for Bro. Hovey, near where our tent stood. – this is the fifth building of Bro. K's. besides the storehouse – Father has got the brick chimney to his double log-house finished – Bishop Miller's teams have not yet come up from the country –

We continued to use our wagon as a bedroom till the 30th, when it was wanted to bring produce from the country. By this time quite a number of houses had been put up. This one contained a number of rooms, built in a row, between my father's and Bishop Whitney's main buildings. One room was used by father for storing provisions, etc. My sister-in-law, Sarah, with whom we had tented so long, occupied a room adjoining ours, though it was not yet ready for her to move into. We lived in ours one month before it was entirely finished.

Woman's Exponent, vol. 13, no. 18,
15 February 1885, p. 139

Sunday the 8th

Warm and pleasant – The Omahaws are going through our settlement this morning, their horses loaded down with tent-poles, and baggage of different kinds on their way north to the "Grand Hunt," that was spoken of before – Bro. Clayton was at their village yesterday and found out that they had a horse of his in their possession they promised to return it if he would give the one that had it an old gun, to which he acceded, and they promised to bring the horse to-day and receive the pay for it, which, however, they did not do – Bro. Hosea Cushing arrived here from the Big Herd, at Lathrop's camp which was further from here, than Bro. Lathrop told us, it being 160 miles, instead of 70 miles – The rest of the boys are expected back to-morrow, having been gone about 3 weeks Monday next

Monday the 9th

Quite rainy at intervals thro' the day. James Smithies and myself went after a load of wood. The remainder of the boys got back here to-day, viz: – J. Redding, J. We[a]therbee, Geo. Rhodes and J. Frazier, looking as if they had seen rather 'hard times' Bro. K. put up the logs of another house on the end of the double one that Father Cutler is building for him – this is intended for Wm. Kimball, making the 6th building Bro. K. has raised besides a number of others for different persons not in his family –

Tuesday the 10th

Fine day, tho' rather muddy from the rains of yesterday – James Smithies and Jacob Frazier went after a load of wood – the rest of us engaged in building a 7th building on the end of the one that we now live in, which I suppose is intended for S. Ann. Bro. Murray brought a load of 20 bbls. of corn to-day –

WEDNESDAY THE 11TH

Cloudy misty day. – but no rain – engaged in building a chimney for the other room of the house in which we live – James S. and Geo. Rhodes went out to our old haying place, for a load of hay – Charles Decker arrived about noon bringing the news that Wm. and Daniel were about 7 miles from here – the latter arrived about 5 P. M. – a brother by the name of [Walter G.] Sterrit came with them, driving one of Bro. K's teams – Daniel brought Sister Powers with him – father had a lot of corn (30 bbls –) brought to him to-day by Brother [John] Freeman

THURSDAY THE 12TH

Tolerable fair this morning – John D. Hovey and myself went after crotches and other stuff to make a stable – before we got back it commenced raining, and continued with little cessation through the day and night. Bro. K., Wm John D. Bishop Miller and myself went over to Brigham's house, which is just finished, in honor of which we spent the evening in dancing, Bro Kay sung a few songs, and the company dispersed, having had a real good "house warming" – Bishop M. Peter Hawes and L[ucien] Woodworth slept at my house to-night on the floor – the latter is quite sick with the fever. To-day the store-house for the goods was commenced – they are building it beside father's second house on this row –

FRIDAY THE 13TH

Tolerable clear day, tho' rather cold – Wm and myself unloaded a load of corn, and then took a walk round the city, as he had never seen this place before – In the afternoon, Bro. K. Wm. King D. Davis and myself were engaged in working on Wm. Kimball's building – which we got ready to put the roof on – The brethren, for the last two or three days, have been in council with Bishop Miller, trying to take an action on his case before he goes back into the Punkaw Nation – L. Woodworth stayed at our house also to-night again –

SATURDAY THE 14TH

Beautiful day – John D. and myself engaged this forenoon in tearing down and rebuilding the house built for Bro. Hovey on opposite side the street This afternoon Daniel Davis and myself went after a load of wood with the horses, one of which Wm. got in part payment for Heber's house and lot in Nauvoo The rest of the boys engaged in chinking some of the other buildings, except Jacob Frazier, who has been at work yesterday and to-day for Dr. Richards – Forgot to mention that Bro. K. sent up 2 yoke of oxen to the rush bottoms by Bro. [Benjamin Franklin] Stewart, a day or two ago –

Sunday the 15th

Cloudy, but no rain this morning George R. and one of Sister H. Smiths men started up to the rush bottoms with the following cattle, viz: –

N. K. Whitney – 2 cows marked with the mark "H. W."

Mrs. Hyrum Smith – 3 cows marked "H. C. K."

This evening Porter and I bringing along Emeline's sisters, their mother having died on the way – Rained when Porter came to night – Bishop Miller, and some of his company, also left this morning, with whom was Hans –

The bishop had just returned from the country, where he had been, with others of his company, for produce. He left for home with part of his company on the 15th. Many of the brethren had gone down into Missouri to work or to trade for provisions, which consisted, mostly, of corn and bacon; the latter, with cornmeal cakes, was our main subsistence during the winter. Vegetables, and many of the necessaries of life were not obtainable. Indian meal cake and puddings we considered very nice when used as rarities, as we were accustomed to doing in the east, but when we had little or no change, they became somewhat nauseous, particularly to the sick and delicate.

Woman's Exponent, vol. 13, no. 18,
15 February 1885, p. 139

Emmeline was then the wife of Bishop Whitney, and her little sisters and brother were received and cared for, as were other members of his family—being under the charge of Sister Emmeline and Mother Whitney.

Woman's Exponent, vol. 13, no. 19,
1 March 1885, p. 151

Monday the 16th

Rainy, wet weather, which continued through the day – This morning early, George Grant and myself went with Porter on the river in a canoe to hunt his cattle which he left last night with his wagon, on the other side the river – found W. W. Phelps over there camped waiting or an opportunity to come over – Returned, bringing over Porter's wagon and cattle on the ferry boat –

Tuesday the 17th

Cool and cloudy, – rained a little this afternoon – Wm. Smithies, Jacob Frazier and myself went with three teams after a load of poles to make hayrick, &c., &c.– The store house is nearly ready, or will be shortly for the reception of the goods by the time they get here

Wednesday the 18th

Cold but clear weather – Wm. moved into his house to-day – James S. and myself went after a load of hay 7 miles from here, beyond the old camp ground 4 miles –

Thursday the 19th

Cold and heavy frost last night. Nothing worthy of notice to-day –

Friday the 20th

Fine day – assisted Wm in repairing fence The most of the boys over the river getting out puncheon for floors to the houses –

Saturday the 21st

Cool day – James S. and myself went after a load of hay – the boys engaged in laying the floor to the store-house – This evening H. Egan, Bro. [Roswell] Stephens and [Samuel Gully, or] Gulley came in from the army – Bro. E. told me they had been to Santa Fee [*sic*], and that most of the brethren in the army – had gone from thence to California. The three brethren came back I suppose, for counsel – a number of the teams came in with goods to-day, which cannot be opened, till the storehouse is completed –

Sunday the 22d

This day Bro. Wooley arrived from St. Joseph – Meeting held at the Stand – did not attend – understood that it was talked of at the meeting to send off a lot of men early next Spring also a few families, and the remainder remain here – Wm.[,] Porter, and myself took a walk around the city this afternoon – first time that we (three) have had a social walk and "chat", since we left the city of Nauvoo – There seems to be a particular dispensation of Providence in our behalf; for, although, we have had several cold nights and frosty ones, the weather has been remarkably mild for winter, and we have not, as yet, experienced the first snow storm – as is usual in other countries

Monday the 23d

Daniel Davis and myself went after a load of hay with the horses. The rest of the boys, to-day also engaged at work on the storehouse making floor. Bro. John Kay came back this evening – he would not to go on alone, the rest of his company having left him and gone ahead –

Tuesday the 24th

Cool day – severe frost last night – Daniel Davis took a team and went after the ox yokes about 12 miles above here – This evening Bro. K. and Brigham met with 2 men from the Salt

Lakes where they have been settled for 16 years – they narrated their adventures, gave an account of the climate &c., which was quite interesting indeed[93] –

Wednesday the 25th

Very cold day – last night the heaviest frost we have yet experienced – The most of us, viz: – H. Egan, J. Davenport, D. Davis, J. Frazier, and myself engaged in cutting and drawing wood from the bottom close by – Bro. K. cautioned the folks this evening against using our wood lavishly, sitting up late at nights and keeping a fire burning, as (he said,) before the winter was out it would be a very scarce article, and even now it cost him the same as two dollars a cord –

Thursday the 26th

Fine day – rather unwell myself – the boys put up the logs of 2 more houses to-day thus making the 9th building one of which is intended for Bro. Howard Egan –

Friday the 27th

Fine day. – Wm., D. Davis, H. Egan, Jacob Frazier and myself went after a load of poles. This evening Bro. Benson got back from the eastern country, where he has been on business – I learned that a brother who went with him and had some pecuniary expectations from some of his friends, was taken up for insanity because he belonged to the Mormons, and in order to cheat him out of his property

Saturday the 28th

Warm and pleasant – D. Davis went to the Old Fort of Council Bluffs for a load of brick, which he is to get from among the rubbish of the place – J. Frazier and myself went after a load of hay – King engaged in shingling the roof to Bro. K's. building.

Sunday the 29th

Fine day – Meeting held at the Stand, at which it was determined that every man should immediately turn out and assist in making the race way in order that the mill may be finished speedily. Bro. K. called his family together for the purpose of giving them good instruction.

---

93. These two men were likely Justin Grosclaude and a Mr. Cardinal. The former was a trader for the American Fur Company, while Cardinal, an expert trader and trapper, claimed a knowledge of most of the Indian languages and all the best trails to and over the Rockies. Both men advised against Brigham Young's plan to go up the Platte River to the west in favor of traveling up the Niobrara River, several miles to the north. Brigham Young to George Miller, 25 November 1846, Brigham Young Papers, Church History Library. See also Bennett, *Mormons at the Missouri*, 151.

MONDAY THE 30TH

Cloudy, misty day. – Daniel Davis, J. Frazier & O. P. Rockwell, started to go into the country, for produce; the latter, being furnished with $50, is to receive one half of that which he brings up from thence – D. Davis took the wagon which my wife and myself have formerly held in possession, consequently, we moved our bed into the house to-day – Brigham and Bro. K. went to the "Point" to-day, to transact some business pertaining to the church with Mr. Sarpee – Wm., J. D., and myself commenced the building of another log-house, which is intended for Bro. Wallace – this is the 10th building, beside the storehouse, which was originally built at the old camp ground, the timber transferred here, and the house rebuilt. – H. Egan busied in drawing stone from the river

TUESDAY THE 1ST OF DECEMBER.

Fair weather this morning, but in the afternoon, the wind changed to the north, and it became quite cold weather – Wm, H. Egan, J. Davenport and myself to work on Bro. Wallace's house, the logs of which we put up to-day – This evening, Brigham and Heber returned from the "Point" – Father has not yet got the goods open, altho' the storehouse is finished except the making of the doors.

WEDNESDAY THE 2D

Fair day – Wm, H. Egan, and myself engaged in building a fence to form a sheep-yard. – Three of the boys at work to-day on the mill-race –

THURSDAY THE 3D

Fine day – Wm. Egan, and myself also at work at the sheep-yard to-day, which we completed. Very cold weather, for the last two days –

FRIDAY THE 4TH

Tolerably fair day – did not do anything myself to-day, in consequence of a severe pain in my right side –Wm. and H. Egan drove a lot of sheep down here to our yard, which they took from Father Lott's sheep-yard – Father, Bro. Wooley engaged in unpacking opening, and marking goods.

SATURDAY THE 5TH

Quite pleasant to-day – This morning Wm. H. Egan and myself were engaged in branding sheep on the forehead with the mark, "H. C. K.", which we did to the amount of 50 in number – The remainder (6) Wm. and myself drove back to Father Lott's yard – Bro. Davenport took 14 sheep from there also – These sheep are church property, and those that take them to keep, have the wool and half the increase while in their possession – Some little snow to-day – the first of any account this fall or winter –

SUNDAY THE 6TH

Fine day – no meeting held at the stand to-day – This evening, a meeting, previously appointed, was held at father's house that he might instruct the bishops of the several wards in their duties – being unwell, did not attend –[94]

MONDAY THE 7TH

Rather cool to-day – To-day, Abigail Pond died, – her two sisters, Harriet and Jane died a day or two ago. Wm. H. Egan, George Rhodes and myself engaged in cutting and drawing 5 loads of wood – This evening, after returning from work, Bro. Egan moved into his house.[95]

TUESDAY THE 8TH

Pleasant day – Orson and myself engaged in mudding up my room – Peter and Geo. Rhodes went after a load of hay – The rest of the boys put up another house for Sister Miller, and topt off the one next to our own, which is intended for Sarah Ann – To-day they commenced trading at the store-house –

This, like the majority of the houses, was covered with sod, and the chimneys were built of the same. Each room had one door and a window with four panes of glass, but no floor. I was rather unfortunate, first, in having a chimney that seldom drew the smoke, particularly when the weather was cold enough to need a roaring fire in front of a good sized back-log, and then being prostrated on my bed from the 23rd of January till along in March; it gave me the opportunity of cultivating the qualities of patience and calmness under new vicissitudes, from which there was no alternative, only to endure them with as good grace as possible, for many of the Saints were still without a roof to cover them; but I shed many unbidden tears during the smoking period, lasting one month, when finding that our fireplace built of sod was about to tumble down, they had some brick brought from the rubbish of the old fort of Council Bluffs, and built a new one. Thus ended our trouble from that quarter. We had been accustomed to trials from smoke, heat, wind and dust, and many other things of an unpleasant nature during camp life, and we took considerable pleasure in fixing up our little homes. Our floors

94. The calling of twenty-two so-called battalion bishops at Winter Quarters derived in large measure from Brigham Young's promise to the Mormon Battalion recruits that in exchange for their sacrifices of army-issued payments, the church would provide for and protect their wives and families. This marked the beginning of "pastoral" bishops to preside over and provide for relatively small groups or wards of members, so characteristic of modern-day bishops within the church. Several other bishops were called on the Iowa side to preside over much smaller groups of Saints scattered throughout the region.

95. Between June 1846 and May 1847, at least 723 Latter-day Saints perished at Winter Quarters, Garden Grove, Mount Pisgah, the Punkaw village, and other Iowa settlements. The comparable figure for 1847–48 was a minimum of 280. See Bennett, *Mormons at the Missouri*, 147.

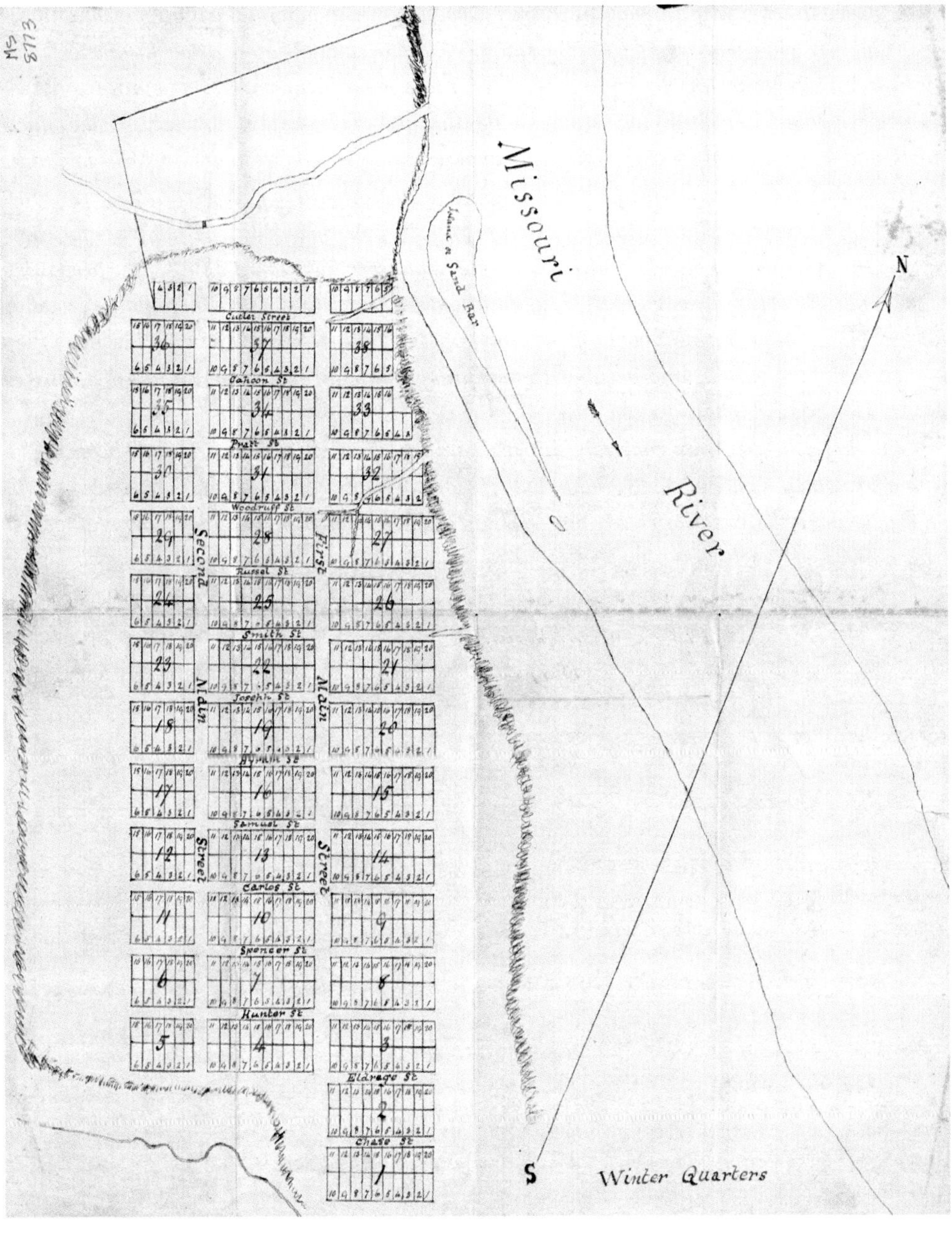

Plan of Winter Quarters of the Camp of Israel on Their Journey to the West of 1846–1847. *Hand-drawn plat map in ink by Thomas Bullock. Thomas Bullock Papers, courtesy of Church History Library.*

Editor's note: *Winter Quarters, 1846–47. An educated guess would place the Council House in block 22 not far from Brigham Young's home, which probably was on a corner lot in block 25. Other public buildings included a store, a carding-machine house, a hostel for visitors, and possibly a few small schoolhouses. Source: Thomas L. Kane Collection, Brigham Young University Library.*

we managed to cover with canvas or pieces of carpeting, which had outlived the storms and the wear and tear while journeying from the states. We made curtains serve as partitions to divide the bedrooms, repositories, etc., from the kitchen. Most of our furniture we had made to order—such as cupboards and bedsteads—they being attached to the house, also tables, chairs and stools, and an occasional rocking chair, relics of other days, graced our ingleside. I was fortunate in having one of the latter, which I had brought with me. And here I received my "setting out" in crockery ware, etc., which, though not very extensive, was deemed quite immense for those times. Our marriage taking place just as we were about starting from the states, the presenting of these needful articles was postponed till a future time, expecting, as we then did, to cross the Rocky Mountains before building houses to inhabit. Two or three pieces I have still, which I keep in memory of the various and peculiar scenes through which we have passed together; as well as the loved ones who have passed away.

The larger houses were generally shingled and had brick chimneys and puncheon floors, with a six lighted window to each room. Father's largest house contained four good sized rooms on the ground and two upstairs. My bro. William and family lived in one room, my mother, her

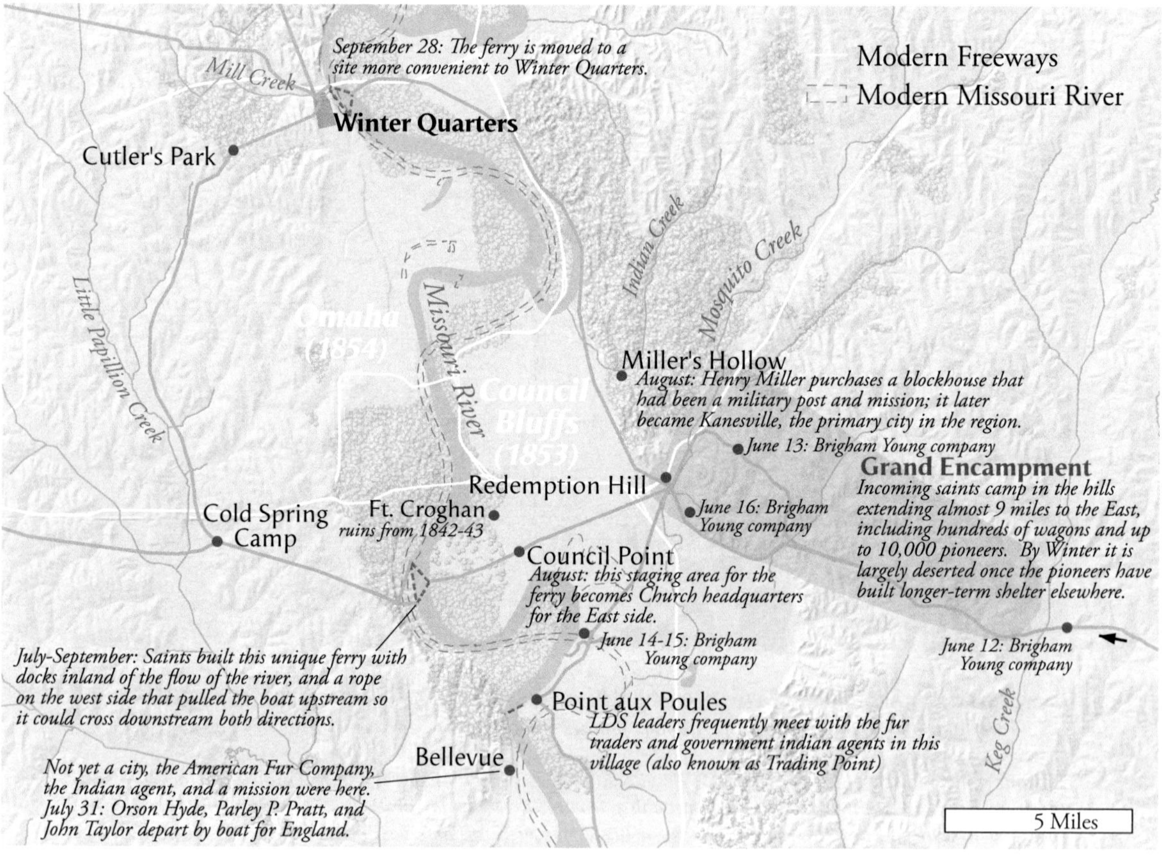

Map of Saints settling Council Bluffs region. Courtesy of Plewe, Mapping Mormonism, *75.*

four little boys, three or four young men and two young women who had been adopted, and two of father's wives occupied the rest; the women assisting in sewing and housekeeping. My mother had been for some time in very feeble health, and her youngest child, who was so sick with whooping cough, when starting from Nauvoo, was taken care of by Mary Ann Sheflin, one of father's wives who lived in the row. She, having charge of him most of the way on the journey, she loved him as though he had been her own child.

Woman's Exponent, vol. 13, no. 18,
15 February 1885, p. 139

Wednesday the 9th

Warm day for the season This morning early, learned, that during the last night a party of Indians, came from the other side the river which they crossed on the ice attacked a small party of the Omahaws; who are encamped near us, and severely, if not mortally wounded two of their number, viz: – "Big Head," the chief of the nation, and his squaw – Mary, an Indian interpretess with the Omahaws, says that it was the Iowas who committed the outrage – The Omahaws, being very much frightened, to-day moved their encampment, and pitched their tents near Brigham's house on Main Street – The two invalids were taken to his house to have their wounds dressed Big Head was shot through the head and arm; his wife through the arm only, which is considerably mutilated, and I understood, that it was the intention to have it amputated Wm and myself went after a load of wood, also for a load of puncheon – Bro. H. Egan went down to the "Point," after a cow – Most of the hands at work on Sister Miller's house[96] –

Thursday the 10th

Cool day – This morning the following cattle marked "H. C. K." on the left horn were sent up to the rush bottoms under charge of Milo Andrews and another man

H. C. Kimball	3 cows.
Richard Slater	1 "
H. Egan	1 "
Mrs. Martin	1 "
The following marked "13D." and "W.G." on the left horn were also sent up to the rushes.	
Sister Gheen	4 oxen.
" "	1 cow
Amount of cattle sent up in Bro. K's. name.	11 head

96. Well known in Native American history were the atrocities performed between tribes. In 1846–47 the depredations performed by the Sioux against the Omaha defy description. Most of their victims were shot through the head or heart while still asleep. The Sioux then cut off the noses of the dead as a sign of spite and contempt. See the Diary of Appleton Milo Harmon, Winter 1846–1847, 10, Church History Library.

Wm and myself went up to Father Lott's and got 10 more sheep which we also branded with the mark "H. C. K." on the forehead – We also got a load of wood from the island opposite here.

FRIDAY THE 11TH

Fine day – Wm, H. Egan, J. Davenport, George Rhodes and myself engaged in drawing wood from the island, which we selected from among the flood-wood – the last load of corn which Bro. K. received came from Bro Ira Ames, and consisted of 19 bushels.

SATURDAY THE 12TH

Tolerably cool – George R. and myself went after hay – the remainder engaged at work upon Bro. K's. houses, and Sarah Ann's home, the roof of which was put on to-day, and covered with dirt. The foundation of the stable was also laid to-day, and covered with dirt. The foundation of the stable was also laid to-day. This evening, the Indians encamped near Brigham's, had a great pow-wow among them, screeching and yelling in a horrible manner – on account of their having just received intelligence that a large number of their warriors, who went on the hunting expedition a short time since, have been killed off by the Sioux. –

SUNDAY THE 13TH

Fine day – Geo. Billings arrived from the herd last evening – Meeting held at the "Stand" to-day – Luke Johnson present, – he had just come on – lost his wife at St. Josephs H. Egan and myself went to-meeting – Brigham was speaking, when we arrived – he spoke at some length about the people's complaining of the store affairs not being conducted in a right manner, he told them that Bishop Whitney was pursuing a righteous course, and doing the best he could for the benefit of the people and Saints at large – Bro. A. Lathrop, who has the charge of the herd about 100 miles above here, arrived this evening –

Brother Luke Johnson was present. He had just come on—had buried his wife at St. Joseph. There was quite a rejoicing among the old Kirtland Saints, to see Bro. Luke Johnson among them again. He stayed one night at father's house. His sister, Marinda Hyde, who was living on the river, came there with him.

Woman's Exponent, vol. 13, no. 19,
1 March 1885, p. 151

MONDAY THE 14TH

Warm day – during last night, quite a heavy fall of snow – the most at any time this season Forgot to mention that yesterday, two of father's boys, viz: – Jacob Wetherbee and Henry Forsythe, and one of Bro. K's. boys, viz: – John Davenport started to go to Missouri to work This morning Wm, H. Egan, G. Rhodes, and myself went down on the bottom for the purpose of obtaining logs, for a stable, but not finding them, we returned, bringing two loads of wood instead – afterwards we split a number of logs we already had – Peter at work on the mill-race – Bro. Smithies chinking and daubing Sarah Ann's house. To-day Bro's. Brigham, Heber, Benson, Cahoon, and Ira Eldridge went down the river about 8 miles to the place where Sarpee used to trade, to make arrangements for the building of houses for the Omahaws, that being deemed a proper place for them to settle, themselves – It is so well fortified by nature, that they can discern the approach of an enemy at some distance – This morning Geo. Billings went back to the herd taking two mules with him

Tuesday the 15th

Fine day – not very well to-day – busied in looking over and rectifying my journal –

Wednesday the 16th

Cool day – Bro. K. received 7 bushels corn by the way of Bro. Bird – busied to day in cleaning out the old storehouse, in order that we may use the logs of which it is built, for a stable – Luke Johnson stayed over night at Bro. K's house – to-day Sarah Ann partially moved her things into her new house This morning Wm. and myself got our fur caps from the store –

Thursday the 17th

Cool day – H. Cushing and myself went after a load of wood. George R. after hay – Luke Johnson took supper with us at S. Ann's house –

Friday the 18th

cool weather – George R. and myself went after wood

Saturday the 19th

Went after wood again to-day – Wm., Egan, and Smithies yet engaged in building a stable, the covering of which they have nearly completed –

Sunday the 20th

Remarkably warm day – meeting held at Bro. K's. house, Joseph Nobles, the Bishop of this Ward presiding, at which arrangements were made to relieve the poor, establishing a school in this ward, &c.–

Monday the 21st

Cold severe weather – George Rhodes, H. Cushing, and myself cut and drew 4 loads of wood from the woods to-day – Wm. Egan, and Smithies finished the roof of the stable to-day

– This evening, Porter, Daniel and Jacob F. arrived, their wagons being left on the other side the river for the night.

TUESDAY THE 22D

cool day – This morning a number of us went over the river, and pulled over the wagons by hand on the ice – The following are bills of articles purchased and brought from the country –

Mr. D. D. Kimball

Bo't of Smith & Donnell.

			$
2	setts cups and saucers.	50c –	1.00
2	curry-combs	20c –	40
1	chamber	38c –	38
6	common bowls	8½ c –	50
4	lbs. coffee	12½ c –	50
4	" sugar	12½ c –	50
3	brooms	10c –	30
1	roll black ribbon		.37
10	lbs. salt	1½ c –	15
1	gallon whiskey		40
St. Joseph Mo. Dec. 8, 1846.	Rec'd Payment, Smith and Donnell		$4.50

Mr. D. D. Kimball

Bo't of Nave & McCord.

			$
3	Sacks 2 15 1 20c		.50
10	bushels white beans	50c	5.00
1	sack salt		3.00
3	buckets 33⅓		1.00
1	comforter		.50
8	lbs. butter	10c	.80
	Rec'd. Payment,		$10.80

Nave & McCord

Oregon, Dec. 11th, 1846. –

Porter also brought a load of pork, which Bro. K. is to have – but do not know the amount as it is yet unweighed – Quite unwell to-day with the pleurisy –

Wednesday the 23d

Warm s. wind to-day. John Whitney and myself took a span of mules and went about 3 miles for a load of wood – Jacob F. and George R. went after 2 loads of hay – In addition to the above named articles Daniel also got the following goods –

Mr. D. D. Kimball

Bo't of Midleton & Berry

	$
30 bushels beans 50c	15.00
Bought of Cosby 12 bushels beans 50c	6.00
" sack	.15
Bo't of Powell 9 ½ b. beans.	4.70
152 lbs. flour	3.00
Bo't of Meek's 16 b. meal 25c	4.00
Matten 1 tea-kettle – .85	
	33.70
	4.50
	10.80
Sole amount of articles bo't in the country by D. D. Kimball	$49.00

Thursday the 24th

Very fine day – busily engaged in making preparations for Egan and Daniel to go into the country – Bishop Miller arrived again this evening from the Punkaw Nation

Friday the 25th

Beautiful weather – being Christmas we had a little party this evening at Heber C's, which passed off finely under the direction as O. P. Rockwell – George Billings arrived this evening from the rush bottoms – Hosea Cushing started this morning with some sheep to go to the lower herd –

Saturday the 26th

another, beautiful, Spring-like day – Yesterday and to-day council held daily and nightly, almost without intermission; father, Bro. Miller and W. Clayton attending, nothing having been done in the store for these two days – This being mother's birthday, father, this afternoon, produced his large glass, which has been in the family for years, and each one of the family was called upon to give some sentiment or wish in favor of our mother. The "union"

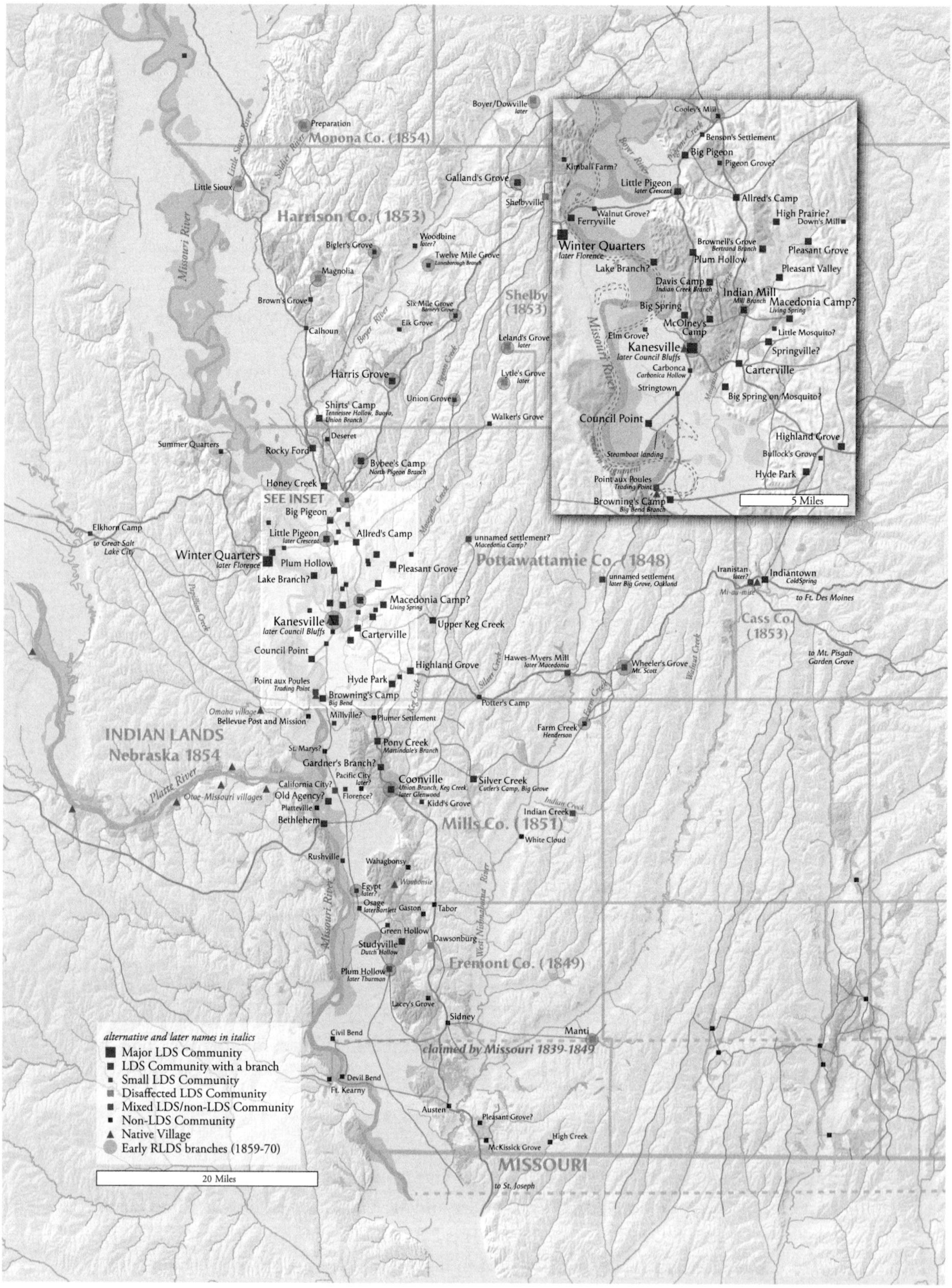

Map of settlements in the Middle Missouri Valley. Eight to nine thousand Latter-day Saints settled on both sides of the Missouri River Valley in the region of Council Bluffs from 1846 to 1848. They resided not only in Winter Quarters and in Kanesville (Iowa Territory) but also in tiny groves, hollows, and out-of-the-way settlements, as shown. Courtesy of Plewe, Mapping Mormonism, *77.*

or meeting did not last above an half hour, but it was the most satisfactory festival that I ever recollect to have spent in that brief span of time.

Sunday, Monday, Tuesday & Wednesday

Nothing worthy of notice has transpired these four days, except that I have been too unwell with a pain in my side to do much in the way of labor – Daniel Davis and H. Egan started for the country on Saturday the 26th – To-day (Wednesday) George Billings starts taking with him another yoke of red cattle, marked "H. C. K." on the left horn, and "H." on the left hip –

Thursday the 31st

Cold day – they finished the well last evening which was dry by Bro. Smithies and George R., and is about 35 feet in depth – feel a little better than I did yesterday, H. Cushing when he returned from the herd brought me 200 brick from the rubbish of the "old Fort" of Council Bluff for the purpose of building me a fireplace, the one built of sod being about to tumble down Bishop Miller, who has gone down into the country, is expected back daily.

Friday the 1st of January, 1847.

Considerable snow on the ground. To-day made out a list of the company and family of H. C. Kimball – This evening Bro. K. again gave up his kitchen room for the purpose of dancing – Brigham and some of his family were present, besides a numerous assembly of the brethren and sisters. – This evening like the Christmas one, passed off finely under the direction of O. P. R. and every one departed to their homes about 1 a.m. apparently well pleased and gratified with our scene of festivity –

Saturday the 2d

Cool weather – added a few more names to the list of the company and family of H. C. Kimball – nothing else worthy of notice to-day. –

Sunday the 3d

Pleasant day – By invitation Bro. K. went and preached at Bro. J[ohn] Scott's house across the creek in Bishop [Addison] Everett's Ward – Wm, Hosea C., Jacob F., and myself attended – Bro. K. spoke on miscellaneous subjects, and gave a great deal of good instruction.

Monday the 4th

Tolerably fair day – This day spent in making arrangements for Merit R[ockwell] and King to start to Bro. Lathrop's with provisions –

Tuesday the 5th

This morning tolerably fair weather Wm. Porter and myself started on horseback, for the rush bottoms, in company with 3 wagons, driven by Merit R. Father Lott, and Edmund Ellsworth, who were all going to Lathrop's camp with provisions – they stopt at a cabin near the old Fort, while Porter Wm. and myself went on up to the rush bottoms where we arrived about dusk – There we found G. Billings and others who are herding cattle – The only house there we stayed in to night which was a miserable hovel indeed – our bones the next morning feeling the effects of the unevenness of the puncheon floor –

Horace, Wm. and Porter started on horseback for the rush bottoms, in company with three other brethren who were going with wagons to Bro. Lathrop's camp (who was there to take charge of the cattle that were sent to the rush bottoms) with provisions. Our boys went for the purpose of driving back some beef cattle—cows and calves, etc., but the weather was so excessively cold that they concluded to return without them.

Woman's Exponent, vol. 13, no. 19,
1 March 1885, p. 151

Wednesday the 6th

Very cold day – we had come up for the purpose of driving back some beef cattle, cows and calves, &c. but the weather was so excessively cold we concluded to return without them – accordingly having breakfasted as we had supped, the night before, in the open air we started for home – on arriving at the Fort, we found that the brethren had not started with their wagons on account of the cold – after stopping a short time with them we started for home where we arrived towards evening –

Thursday the 7th

This day, was by far, the coldest and most severe of the season We could chop wood at the door scarcely 5 minutes without freezing – The first fair day, Geo. Billings is to come down bringing all the cows that have just come in – Bro. K. and father together sent 10 gallons whiskey to Bro. Lathrop by Merit Rockwell and Wm. King

Friday the 8th

More moderate weather than yesterday – To-day Porter went by Bro. K's. request to tell Merit and King to return, having concluded not to send them to Lathrop's, at least till warmer weather

Saturday the 9th

Tolerable cold day – Porter returned to-day, – he overtook the boys a little way beyond the first herd, going on. – they are to be back to-morrow.

SUNDAY THE 10TH

Cold day – Bro. K. preached to-day in Bishop Lutz's ward, at Bro. Leonard's house, did not attend, being busy helping father at home. To-day Merit and King returned, bringing back with them their wagon and things.

MONDAY THE 11TH

Very moderate weather, in comparison with the last two or three days – Geo. Billings and David Davis came down from the herd, bringing 2 cows and 2 calves for father.

TUESDAY THE 12TH

Quite cold. This day, H. Egan and D. Davis arrived from the country. The following are lists of articles, brought by them from the country. –

St. Josephs, Mo. Jan 1847.

Mr. Egan,

Bo't of Smith & Donnell.

			$
45	lbs. Salaratus	8c	3.60
3	sacks salt	$2.50	7.50
	Rec'd. Payment,		$11.10

Smith & Donnell.

Savannah, Jan. 3, 1847.

Mr. Davis,

Bo't of M. Tootle & Co.

				$
1	1 piece Linsey	55½ yds.	25c	13.87½
2	2 " prints	33¾ 34"	67¾ " 14½ "	9.82
1	pair blue blankets			9.00
2	bolts Domestic	29½ 32 yds.	61½ " 10 "	6.15
2	" Drilling	31 " 30 "	61 " 12 "	7.32
2	bolts binding	10c		0.20
12	doz. buttons	10c		1.20
1	hank thread			.85

1	bbl. sugar 249½ 15½ off 234.	25.74
1	barrel ___ ___	.25
1	sack coffee 162½ & 11	17.87½
5	lbs. pepper 20c	1.00
8	" coffee 12½	1.00
24½ bushels wheat 37½c		9.19
	Rec'd. Payment,	$103.47

M. Tootle & Co.

Mr. Davis Jan.1, 1847

Bo't of Cosby & Others.

			$
75⅓	lbs. soap	3½c	2.65
3½	bushels beans	60c	2.10
½	bushel onions	25c	.25
21½	lbs. tobbacco	5c	1.05
21¼	gallons honey	50c	10.60
1	barrel ___		1.00
19½	lbs. butter.	10c	1.95
			$19.60

Expenses for the second trip.

	$
Ferriage	0 – 40
2 doz. sheaf oats	0 – 40
Ferriage	0 – 25
Corn	0 – 20
"	0 – 30
Breakfast	0 – 25
Corn	0 – 25
35 lbs. flour 2c	0 – 70
Salaratus	0 – 05
1 turkey	0 – 12½
black lead	0 – 12½
1 bottle & whiskey	0 – 22½
Meat	0 – 37½
Lard ____	0.12½
Corn ____	0.25

Help ____	0.25
13 bushels corn	1.45
Breakfast	0.25
Ferriage	0.25
Supper	0.30
Ferriage	0.40
For Keeping at Jackson's	1.75
	$8.67½
	19.60
	103.47
	11.10
sole amount of things bo't	$142.84½

Wednesday the 13th

Almost like spring weather this morning – Hauling wood and hay was the most that was done – This evening had quite a convivial party at Bro. Smithies, consisting of all the male members of the family.

Thursday the 14th

To-day as fine weather as yesterday – To-day Geo. Billings and David Davis went back to the herd taking with them 2 cows one marked "H. C. K." and other "H. W." – The boys engaged in hauling wood & hay.

Friday the 15th

Cold day – Wm., with the carriage went to the "Point", taking 5 or 6 passengers, – to attend a ball to be given at the house of Mr. Beaubin. Porter also went down.

Saturday the 16th

Cold as usual – Lyman has been to work drawing wood, hay, &c. with father's team, in order that he may go down to Missouri with the same next week to get a load of such things as father shall need on the journey in the Spring – To-day Wm returned from the Point.

Sunday the 17th

Tolerably warm this morning, but in the afternoon it turned quite cold and stormy. Bro. K. called his family together and gave them good instruction –

Greg Olsen, Winter Quarters. *Used with permission. A setting of winter reflection and revelation, Mormonism's Valley Forge was a place of sickness and death, peace and faith.*

Monday the 18th

Decidedly the coldest day of the season – the thermometer showing it to be 4 degrees colder than we have yet experienced. Made out another list of the members intending to travel in the 2d company under H. C. Kimball in the ensuing spring – Bro. J. Pack and myself went round to warn them to meet at the council house tomorrow night for organization – The 1st company under Brigham Young, met there this evening, for the same purpose – This evening a fire was discovered under the hearth in Bro. K's. room – we took down the better part of the chimney in order to get at the fire, which we put out, and rebuilt the chimney, this taking till half past 4 in the morning – Bro. K. felt very thankful that the fire did not occur

in the night when we were all asleep, as there was 5 or 6 lbs of powder in a chest near the fire-place, in addition to the danger incurred by the fire otherwise –

Tuesday the 19th

Tolerably warm; but became rather cold towards evening. H. Egan and George Rhodes started for the country with 2 teams one with 4 mules the other with 2 horses, Truman [?] and Orson also with 1 team – This evening, pursuant to agreement, a large number of those who had attached themselves to the 2d company under H. C. Kimball met at the council House on Main Street –

Bro O. Pratt first rose and read the names of those who have already given in their names, which were 200 in number –

Bro. K. then arose and said, – That he had not called them together exactly for the purpose of organization but to give them some instruction, and to let them know by what rules they must abide, if they wished to go in his company. – He then proceeded to state that those who wished to go with him, must prepare themselves to obey the law of God, and forbear from stealing one from another, also swearing, and other things prohibited by the Celestial Law – and that those who could not make up their minds to abide by these precepts, had better never start from this place, but go down into Missouri, where they belong –[97]

A revelation, or the will of the Lord, was then read (by O. Pratt), as received through President Young, pertaining to the rules and regulations by which we are to be governed during our journey in the ensuing Spring[98] –

There are to be companies of tens, fifties, and hundreds; each company with a captain at its head, and these to be controlled by a President and 2 counsellors. The revelation embodied or contained the remarks made by Bro. K., and other matters, A vote was then called whether the people would covenant to obey the principles therein laid down, which passed unanimously President Young also made some few remarks substantiating what Bro. K. had said – Another thing spoken of was, that every individual who was on the journey should to the utmost, use his influence in assisting the widows and wives of those in the army, also

97. This mention of the "Celestial Law" was in reference to the law of consecration. First practiced in the early 1830s by the Saints in Ohio in obedience to divine command (see section 42 of the Doctrine and Covenants), the law of consecration or celestial law called for a higher commitment to obedience. This law included, at one time, the consecration or dedication of private properties to the church, and the receiving back of property and means as part of one's stewardship. Although the business management or United Order element of the law was later replaced in 1838 with the law of tithing, the law itself was still enjoined upon the Saints. There was no private ownership of lands and properties at Garden Grove, Mount Pisgah, or Winter Quarters—all belonged to "the Lord." Brigham Young fervently believed that only in living this higher law which they had covenanted to follow in the Nauvoo Temple would their exodus succeed. Their present "errand into the wilderness" was all a Puritan-like covenant exercise in obedience. For what is still the finest study of the interchange of early Mormon theology and economics, see Leonard J. Arrington, *Great Basin Kingdom: An Economic History of the Latter-day Saints, 1830–1900* (Cambridge: Harvard University Press, 1958).

98. See "The Word and Will of the Lord," section 136 of the Doctrine and Covenants. This is the only canonized revelation of Brigham Young. In addition to setting up the organization of the vanguard companies to the West, this revelation also discoursed on the reasons for the martyrdom of Joseph and Hyrum Smith and on the placement of the keys of governance in the church, specifically with the Quorum of the Twelve Apostles. While it said nothing about their eventual destination, it did say much about their behavior as a people of God. Sustained by all the scattered Saints on both sides of the Missouri River, the Word and Will of the Lord brought great comfort and assurance to the Saints in their desperate, scattered situation and firmly established "Brother Brigham" as their chosen apostolic leader, even though it would be almost a year before he was sustained as president of the church. For more on the effects this revelation had upon the Saints in early 1846 at Winter Quarters, see Richard E. Bennett, "'My Idea Is to Go Right Through Right Side Up with Care': The Exodus as Reformation" (Leonard J. Arrington Mormon History Lecture Series No. 3, 6 November 1997, Utah State University Press, 1998).

to remove, lest their cries should ascend up to Jehovah against us – Some other business of minor importance being transacted, the meeting was dismissed with a benediction by Bro. Kimball.

WEDNESDAY THE 20TH

Fair weather with "sunshine clear" – The "Twelve" held a council at Wm. Kimball's room to-day. –

THURSDAY THE 21ST

Beautiful day for this time of year – Busied in taking the names, and list of the property, of those who have attached themselves to Pres. K.'s company. – To-day Jacob H. went up to the herd to get some cattle –

FRIDAY THE 22D

Tolerably fair day – still occupied in writing on the list of company 2^{d}.

SATURDAY THE 23D

Wife quite unwell; but better than she was yesterday. Tolerably, fair day – still at work writing –

SUNDAY THE 24TH

Beautiful day – Wife so unwell, as to be obliged to keep her bed – did not attend meeting in consequence – held at the council house –

MONDAY THE 25TH

Fine day – still occupied in writing on the list – Helen not much better to-day than usual – To-day Bishop Miller and son returned from the country with a load of produce to take home with them.

TUESDAY THE 26TH

Warm day – A meeting of the 2^{d} company, under H. C. Kimball was held at the Council House at 10 A M. – I arose and read the names of those who had joined the company; also those who had given in a list of their property –

President Young then moved that Bro. Kimball nominate his own officers, which he proceeded to do – The following are names of those who were elected unanimously, thro' his nomination

Alpheus Cutler –	President.
Winslow Farr –	Counsellor.
Daniel Russell –	"
Henry Herriman –	Capt. Hundred
Isaac Higbee –	" "
Shadrach Roundy –	" "
John Pack –	" Fifty
Milo Andrews –	" "
Geo. B. Wallace –	" "
Harrison Burges –	" "
Alva Tippetts –	" "
Levi Riter –	" "

Each of the above named individuals spake, returning their thanks to the brethren, for the honor conferred upon them – stating their intentions to be [*sic*] to magnify their office – The captains of Fifties were enjoined to organize their companies, and appoint captains of Tens. Afterwards, Bro. K. spoke at some length – using the parable of a vessel being cracked, and remoulded in to its proper shape by the hands of the potter – Every one has got to take an equal share of the burthen of taking on the poor &c. – I want those who constitute the officers in any company, should act as fathers in Israel, and accommodate themselves to the minds and wishes of the people – I feel sometimes, as tho' like a barrel I should burst with care and anxiety for the brethren, and would like an additional band fastened to me. There has got to be a pioneer company to start from here, and those who can go, will go; and those who can stay, will stay; and this to be subject to the decision of the Presidents.[99] Those who stay, will remain to cultivate the ground. It is necessary for every one to prepare himself with axle trees to their wagons, &c., inasmuch as there is no timber for a long way after you leave here – Moved by President Young, and stated by President Kimball, that inasmuch as Bishop Miller being here is about to return with his family to this place, we build him a house – carried unanimously. – Wm. Pitt moved that John Kay also return, seconded & carried – Meeting of the company adjourned sine die. A party, including a part of the Quorum of the Seventies, came off at the Council House to-day commencing at 3 o'clock P. M. and continuing till towards morning. – did not attend, in consequence of wife being sick.

He speaks of a party, including a part of the quorum of seventies, which came off at the council house the same day, commencing at three o'clock p.m., and continuing till nearly morning. Another one was held Wednesday evening by others of the seventies, and on Thursday

99. Similar to the Nauvoo exodus, their plan at Winter Quarters was for a vanguard company of the Twelve Apostles and other skilled pioneers to leave Winter Quarters early in April for the Rocky Mountains. This company was to be followed in June by a much larger "Emigration Camp" or "Big Camp" consisting of men, women, and children and as many of the wives and children of the Mormon Battalion families as possible. The vanguard company numbered 148 souls; the Big Camp, ten times that number.

evening, the latter, Horace speaks of attending and most of my father's family. There were many parties held there during the winter, and a dancing school was started about the 8th of February. In all these I had no participation, being prostrated by sickness from the middle of January until spring.

Woman's Exponent, vol. 13, no. 22,
15 April 1885, p. 170

Wednesday the 27th

Fine day – George Billings and Jacob F. came from the herd with 8 head of cattle, including one bald faced ox for Bro. K., and a cow for J. C. K. – Party held at the Council House to-day also, commencing at 9 a.m. also pertaining to the Seventies –

Thursday the 28th

Warm day – attended a party given at the Council House this evening – most of Bro. K's. family attended – wife considerably better, but not so much so, as to be around yet, or to set up – Meeting of the officers of the 2d Co. held at Bro. K's, room, but the officers not all attending, it was concluded to defer it till to-morrow at 10 a.m.

Friday the 29th

Fine day – Bishop Miller started to-day for the Punkaw – Meeting of the officers held at Bro. K's. room pursuant to agreement at 10 a.m. –

Present –

H. C. Kimball –
A. Cutler –
W. Farr –
M. Russell –
Henry Herriman –
Isaac Higbee –
S. Roundy –
John Pack – –
Geo. B. Wallace –
Harrison Burges –

Bro. K. stated it to be necessary for the company to be furnished with a clerk – and that it devolved upon the Presidency to appoint him – Bro. James Sloan was elected to that office – Another thing stated by Bro. K. was, that those, upon whom the duty principally devolved, i.e. the Presidency, and authorities, should travel as nearly together as possible in one company – in order that every thing might be more convenient, when they were obliged to assemble for Council –

The next thing taken into consideration was, who should stand as Captain of 1st H. Bro. K. observed, that as Bro. Herriman was a senior President of the "Seventies," that the right would naturally fall on him – He further said, that he thought that the choice of officers was as good as could be made, and could not be altered for the better – The Brethren tho't so too – Bro. Herriman observed that, he meant to do the best he could, wherever placed – Bro. Harrison Burgess came in soon after, and stated that he had a line for Bro. K., which was the resignation of Levi Riter of the office of Captain of Fifty – Bro. K. gave the article of resignation to Father Cutler for his disposal. – Father Cutler observed that it would be at the disposal of the Captains of the 1st Company where to place his men, and in what order – Bro. Henry Herriman was elected to the office of Captain 1st Company – It was concluded, through Bro. K's. suggestion to entitle our body, "The Second Division of the Camp of Israel" –

Father Cutler observed that he would rather leave it to Bro. K. where the Bishops Whitney and Miller should be placed, which was between the two Divisions – Bro. K. observed, "it makes no difference where we are placed, whether in the 1st, 2d, or 3d companies, and that when he made the nominations of his officers, he looked for those who would act as fathers in Israel; and he wished them to treat this people as a child, and nurse them, and be careful of their feelings. – Father Cutler observed, that he thought it best that Bro. K., Bishop Whitney, himself and other furnish a list of those intending to journey in each family respectively. It was proposed by Brother Farr, to ascertain through Bro. Herriman, the number of those in a family, intending to go west. – Bro. K. observed, that he did not expect that <u>all</u> of his folks would go in the 1st company; excepting those immediately connected with him. Bro. K. told the brethren it was their duty to get all the names they could, and that just as soon as the Hundreds were filled up, that there should be at least 30 men drawn out of each for pioneers – Bro. K. observed that the reason of Levi Riter's resignation, was, that he had a calf in the east, in Pennsylvania, and that was <u>hitched</u> to $1500, & he wants to go back and get it, and take his family, with him, because he is discouraged, &c.; and he, (Bro. K,) wants to have the brethren hang on to him by the prayer of faith. Father Cutler observed that it would be his mind, that the officers stand in their order, as they were elected. – Bro. Herriman chose his two captains of Fifties, – viz: – John Pack and G. B. Wallace – Bro. K. observed to Father Cutler, that we need not depend on any <u>regular</u> order, till we get organized in the Fifties; because there would be draughts upon them, for pioneers, artillery, hunters, &c.– It was said that Bro. John Scott will have the command of the artillery – Isaac Higbee chose his captains of Fifties, viz: – Harrison Burges & Alva Tippetts. – Shadrach Roundy chose his captains of Fifty, viz: – Milo Andrews

Bro. K. observed that the selection might be made to-morrow, of those selected to go in the different companies – He also said, that, in travelling, we should generally be governed by circumstances, & that he intended to imitate Brigham in his order of travelling, and that it would be a long time, before we would be governed by any definite rule – Bro. K. observed that he knew the people were more tired on this last journey, than they ever were before and quoted the Carlos Granger story as illustration of the idea [100] – Proposed by Bro. K. that we meet to morrow evening at Daniel Russel's house to give in our returns – Bro. K. observed that we all, with Father Cutler, bow down before the Lord, touching the case of Bro. Levi Riter, that he may be tied up in his designs to go east and take his family with him, which was accordingly done, and the meeting was dismissed

George Billings went back to the herd to-day –

Saturday the 30th

Beautiful weather – Helen yet quite sick, also, Mothers Kimball and Whitney – A few of the brethren, pursuant to agreement, met at the house of Daniel Russel on Main St. – I presented my list, and about fifty of the names of the 1st hundred was selected – but little other business was done, and the meeting adjourned – to meet at the same place on Tuesday evening. Bro. James Sloan being away in the country. I have yet to act as clerk for the company. –

Sunday the 31st

Fine day – Bro. K. preached in Bro. Cutler's ward to-day – did not attend, wife being so unwell – forgot to mention that H. Egan and George Rhodes got back from the country last evening – The brethren have commenced building Bishop Miller a house, which they intend to have ready for him, against his return from the Punkaw.

Bill of the articles bought by H. Egan on the 3d trip.

Corn______10c___	$15.00
2 bbls. flour__375c__	7.50
1 sack salt____	2.40
24 bushels meal__25c__	6.00
16 plugs tobacco 12½c__	2.00
4 " " 9c__	.36
10 lbs. butter 10c__	1.00
Amount______________________	$34.26

Expenses of the 3d trip –

	$
Supper and breakfast for 2.	.50
Breakfast____ "	.25
Pork____	.12½

100. The Carlos Granger story Heber C. Kimball mentioned may refer to Granger's recently leaving the Saints in early 1847 and subsequently moving to Missouri. By 1850 he was living in Schuyler County, Missouri.

Jon McNaughton, Winter Quarters. *Used with permission. Upwards of 1,200 Latter-day Saints perished at Winter Quarters between 1846 and 1848.*

Supper and breakfast__	.25
Shoeing 2 horses__	1.25
Corn and hay__	.75
Breakfast and corn__	.18¾
Ferryage Monattany [?]__	.20
Bacon____ ____	.50
Oats__________	.25
Supper & breakfast__	.37½
Ferryage Nishna Botana__	.50
Cooking & lodging	.25
Supper & breakfast__	.25
	5.63¾

MONDAY THE 1ST OF FEBRUARY.

Warm in the forenoon, but the night sat in extremely cold – To-day Wm. King started for Lathrop's camp with a load of provisions. –

TUESDAY THE 2D

Fine day – This morning at 20 minutes past 6, Sister Kimball gave birth to a boy, who was called Solomon after his grandfather –

Porter started on Saturday last for Punkaw to assist Bro. Miller in removing here – wife's health improving slowly – To-night a company meeting held at Bro. D. Russel's, did not attend in consequence of Helen's illness.

My mother gave birth to a son, whom they named Solomon, after his Grandfather Kimball, which event is mentioned in my husband's journal.

My room was a few doors from my mother's, where I was still bed-fast; but the weather being fine I was conveyed in an easy chair and placed by her side, where I passed two pleasant days, being carried back at eventide. She was in excellent spirits, and before my arrival, the first morning, had composed several verses on the birth of this, her seventh son. They breathed a prayer that his life might be long, and his wisdom great, like unto Solomon's of old, before he had allowed the love of women to surpass the wisdom God had given him.

She was gifted in that line, had it only been cultivated in an early day. Her appearance, at that period of her life, bespoke anything but a sad and heartbroken woman, though there were several of father's wives living under the same roof with her.

Woman's Exponent, vol. 14, no. 2,
15 June 1885, p. 11

WEDNESDAY THE 3D

Fine day – H. Egan and George Rhodes again started for the country – Bro. Isaac Higbee, Captain of hundred, called and got the roll of papers pertaining to the company business to give to Bro. James Sloan – captain of the company – Party, consisting of Brigham's family held at the Council House[101] – Bro. K. with some of his family attended – Father called me into the store to-night, to make selections of such things as I may want for the journey. – wrote 3 letters to the Punkaw nation, for Bro. K. directed to – Bro. Billings, Shirtliff and Sister Glines – sent by Porter –

THURSDAY THE 4TH

Fine weather – Vilate Young & Charles Decker married this evening – no party at the Council House to-day – dancing school to commence on Monday next

FRIDAY THE 5TH

The party, of what is called the "Silver Greys," came off at the Council House to-day and night, consisting of all the old people that could be found in the camp[102] – In the forenoon, the band went round in a carriage playing, the bride & bridegroom accompanying –

SATURDAY THE 6TH

Beautiful weather – This evening at 11 o'clock, mother gave birth to a boy – she is pretty comfortable, also Sister K. Helen's health slowly improving, Yesterday and to-day, so well as to be able to go and see her mother This evening, a meeting held at Daniel Russel's, – sent up a list of names by Isaac Higbee, Captain of Hundred –

SUNDAY THE 7TH

Very warm day – Meeting held at the council house to-day – did not attend – wife not so well to-day, as yesterday – afflicted with the toothache severely to-day and canker in the mouth – Mother and Sister K. quite comfortable –

---

101. The "Council House," located in the center of Winter Quarters, functioned as the social, ecclesiastical, and political heart of Winter Quarters. Most deliberations of the Twelve Apostles, of the Winter Quarters high council, of the bishoprics, and of the various committees were held here. It served as a model for the future Council House located in Salt Lake City on the southwest corner of South Temple and Main Street.

102. It would be a great mistake to conclude that life in Winter Quarters was all dark and gloomy and full of sickness and death. To help pass the time, there were dancing schools, choirs, day schools, and concerts. The "Silver Greys," much like Pitt's brass band, were a musical consortium made up of older, gray-haired men who played various musical instruments and put on concerts and balls throughout the winter of 1846–47 on both sides of the Missouri River.

Monday the 8th

Fine weather – nothing worthy of importance – the parties still continue at the Council House –

Tuesday the 9th

Beautiful weather – The Bishop's convivialities commenced at the council house to-day, under the direction of Bishop Whitney as head bishop of the Church. attended myself with the Band and played – the day and evening passed off finely, spent in praying, singing, dancing, &c. Bro. K. called his children (infants) together for the purpose of blessing them, which was done by Brigham Bro. K., and father, Dr. Richards acting as clerk, I not being present –

The same evening he makes mention of my father's calling his wives together, who had infants, for the purpose of blessing them, which was done in my mother's room, by B. Young, father and Bishop Whitney, Dr. Richards acting as clerk. There were seven in number—four had been born at Nauvoo, one at Richardson's Point, Iowa, and two at Winter Quarters. The eldest was my mother's son, Brigham Willard, born January 29th 1845. The names of those mothers were Sarah Peek, Clarissa Cutler, Emily Cutler, Sarah Ann Whitney, Lucy Walker. The two latter were the wives of the Prophet Joseph, whom father had taken for time only. Still Joseph Smith [III] of Lamoni, Iowa, declares that polygamy was neither taught nor practiced by his father, and that it was "foreign to the gospel his father died in the service of," when there are a dozen or more of his wives still living in Utah, besides scores of men and women who can testify that this principle was taught and practiced by him, and that he commanded others to enter into it. "None are so blind as those who will not see."[103]

Woman's Exponent, vol. 14, no. 2,
15 June 1885, p. 11

---

103. Helen Mar is here addressing the fact that Joseph Smith III, eldest son of Joseph Smith Jr. and Emma Smith, and first president of the Reorganized Church of Jesus Christ of Latter Day Saints since April 1860, had been taught by his mother that her husband never practiced polygamy. This long-held view was ever hotly contested with the "Brighamite" or Latter-day Saint church. Joseph F. Smith, son of Hyrum Smith and nephew of Joseph Smith and later sixth president of said church, affirmed as early as 1869 that his uncle, Joseph Smith, had married at least sixteen wives. Robert Flanders, in his path-breaking study on Nauvoo, proved beyond doubt that Smith had indeed practiced plural marriage. More recently, Todd Compton has provided convincing evidence that Joseph Smith had at least thirty-four wives. See Robert Bruce Flanders, *Nauvoo: Kingdom on the Mississippi* (Urbana: University of Illinois Press, 1965) and Todd Compton, *In Sacred Loneliness: The Plural Wives of Joseph Smith* (Salt Lake City: Signature Books, 1997).

Wrote Joseph F. Smith to his cousin in 1869: "In all kindness cousin Joseph . . . [I] testify that your testimony denying plurality of wives is not from God. . . . The obligation which rested upon your father to establish this order of Patriarchal marriage beyond the power of destruction seemed like a weight to crush him to the earth but knowing the redemption and exaltation of the human race depended upon it, notwithstanding the bigotry of his friends, the opposition of his own house, the universal tradition of the Christian world, and the laws of Illinois against it, he felt to rejoice that he was enabled to fulfil his mission and place beyond the power of men to destroy an institution which would redeem the female sex from degradation and exalt mankind to celestial glory and increase." See letter of Joseph F. Smith to

Heber C. Kimball (1801–68), apostle, member of Brigham Young's First Presidency, and father of Helen Mar Kimball Whitney. Photograph by George Edward Anderson, circa 1850. L. Tom Perry Special Collections, Harold B. Lee Library, Brigham Young University, Provo, Utah.

Wednesday the 10th

Fine weather still – the Bishops party continued on to-day and ended this evening at 10 P. M. – father did not attend much on the account of mother's illness, who is not so well to-day as usual – Helen's and Sister K's improving –

Thursday the 11th

Spring weather – To-day the party of "Silver Greys", who had not previously been at the Council House, met there to enjoy themselves – attended also to-day with others of the Band –

Friday the 12th

Beautiful weather – This morning, went round and notified all those who had sent up cattle to Lathrop's herd – intelligence having been received thro' Bro. E. C. [?] Richardson that the Sioux had come among the people up there, stolen several horses, killed several cattle, &c., &c. The meeting was for the purpose of sending men up to Lathrop's camp to assist in guarding the cattle horses, &c.

Saturday the 13th

Fine day – This day a party held at the Council House, consisting of some of the "seventies," or bench makers, This morning, a number of those appointed, started for the camp of Lathrop, to guard the horses and cattle.

"Cousin Joseph Smith [III]," 9 October 1869. Church Historical Department Letterpress Copybooks, vol. 2, CR 100 38, Church History Library.

Sunday the 14th

Fine and pleasant – This morning at 11 a.m. – a meeting of the family was called at H. C. Kimball's room. – Present – H. C. Kimball, father, and a number of both families. –

The meeting was opened by singing; and prayer by Bro. James Smithies – I arose and read, by Bro. Heber's request, a revelation, given March 7, 1831, which was addressed to the church, and intended for their guidance at that, and also at this time [104] – Another hymn was then sung, and Bro. Heber arose and said: –

I have almost always something in my mind to say, according to the circumstances in which I am placed – My health is quite poor at this time, having taken cold, and I have a severe pain in my side – My body feels as if it was shattered to pieces with fatigue – but I care nothing about it – I have no fear of death – I have no fears about seeing my heavenly Father – but I want to live for the good of this people – life is sweet – why is it sweet? – for the sake of good saints – the cordial endearments of my friends and children – I can meet any body half way, for I have so ordered my life – that I am not afraid of death. I am now forming a character for another world, when I shall come forth with a new body in the resurrection, – and I want to cultivate the principles of charity – that I may conform to the will of God – that I may be able to have victory over Death, Hell, and the Grave that I may be able to say: – "O Death, where is they sting, O Grave, where is thy victory! and when I gain the victory, aint every thing mine – I want the brethren to exercise all the faith and calmness in their power – and I feel as tho' I could hardly set up – as I dreamt the other night, to have my net prepared, to catch all I can; and every man should have and women have nets among you, each one according to his or her capacity – You have all got an idea that Christ has gained the victory for you but I tell you, that you have got to gain the victory yourselves, or you will have it to grapple with hereafter. I presume there is not a person in this room, great or small, but what think that they have as much to grapple with, every day, as I have – There has been a great many parties lately, and I thought that I would have one to-day, You are all my family here to-day – Bishop Whitney belongs to <u>my</u> family, and I belong to <u>his</u> family – and I want all selfishness banished from among you – I know there is faith enough in this place, among you, to make me feel happy from the crown of my head to the soles of my feet. – I should not be surprised if I should not live two months; – still, I do not know but that I shall – but there is no one knows how I feel, by myself. I have no testimony that I shall die for fifty years to come – I want to go to a land of liberty, where we can be free from mobs and strife, in which we have been all our lives – Some profess to have knowledge of all things behind the vail – but I profess no such thing – what is in futurity, I neither know nor care; but I do care for the present; and all who look up to me for counsel as children, as husbands, &c., should be faithful – I do not say that any of you are disobedient; but your minds want stirring up by way of remembrance – not to tell you what you don't know, but you are run down like

---

104. Likely section 45 in the modern LDS edition of the Doctrine and Covenants, which is dated 7 March 1831. It deals primarily with the signs of the last days, the Second Coming of Christ, the establishment of the New Jerusalem, and Christ's ensuing millennial reign.

watches and I want you to wind them up two or three times a day – It does not hurt a watch half as bad to run, as it does to lay dormant; therefore, do not let your minds, like watches, lay dormant – I want you to lift up your hearts to God for me, – and if I have not done as well by my children as any other person; then I will leave it to Brother Whitney, as he is a Judge in Israel – and he is such as appointed by the revelations of God. – There have been parties at the Council House lately, & perhaps I shall have a party, one of these days, myself – I want my family to learn to govern themselves, so that, when they are in the midst of an extreme, even in dancing, they could quit, right straight – You should never let your appetites control your judgments, but your judgments your appetites – Now, if there is any one in my family, that wish to put any one in my place, to govern it, let them try it – and I will go somewhere else – Daniel, and my boys are all faithful – Now, Bro. Whitney, I have got it on to you.[105] –

Father [Bishop Newel K. Whitney] arose and said: – I suppose, as I am the oldest person in the room, you may look upon me in some degree, as a father – I don't know that I can say any more in essence, than what your Father Kimball has said – He has spoken of several things, especially of faith, which if acted upon, will redound to your glory. – Bro. Heber has spoken of the parable of the watch – it is a good one – and if we keep the watch wound up, we cannot sin; for if a man has the spirit of truth and righteousness, he cannot sin – and when he is possessed by the opposite spirit he cannot do anything correct. In the case of drinking whiskey – I have watched myself, and found out that I could not do business as well, as when I was in full possession of my faculties. – When we have a bad spirit, and call upon the Lord, we will find that he is a great deal further off than we would imagine. – Bro. Heber touched upon doing right – I believe that there is no man in the whole circle of my acquaintance, that intends to do better, and work righteousness, more than Bro. Kimball; nor one that comes nearer to the point in so doing. Therefore, it behooves you to hold up his hands, and as he advances in knowledge, so will you the same – as his vessel is filled, he will pour it on to your head. – God is no respecter of persons – but he sets men on earth to teach his people as masters are set to instruct little children – God will instruct his people from time to time, as they can bear knowledge, and when we have fulfilled the things one messenger has given us, another will come with fresh intelligence. – I have no doubt, but what many of you here, will live to see the "Ancient of Days" come – even Old Father Adam[106] –

---

105. The law of adoption was a social and religious order and temple-related ordinance that sealed faithful Latter-day Saint men and their families to presiding General Authorities of the church, such as Brigham Young, Heber C. Kimball, and other members of the Twelve Apostles. Not an adoption in the current sense of children being adopted to their parents, the law of adoption was a theological construct, a part of the chain or spiritual linkage of one generation to another in the eternal family of God. See Gordon Irving, "The Law of Adoption: One Phase of the Development of the Mormon Concept of Salvation, 1830–1900," *Brigham Young University Studies* 14 (Spring 1974): 291–314. See also my *Mormons at the Missouri*, 191–94. For more recent studies on this topic, see Jonathan A. Stapley, "Adoptive Sealing Rituals in Mormonism," *Journal of Mormon History* 37, no. 3 (Summer 2011): 53–117, and Jonathan A. Stapley, *The Power of Godliness: Mormon Liturgy and Cosmology* (New York: Oxford, 2018).

106. Mormonism is a premillennial religion that believes in the Second Coming of Christ who will be accompanied by the Twelve "who were with me at Jerusalem" and by Adam, the Ancient of Days, at a special council to be held at Adam-ondi-Ahman, near Far West, Missouri.

We are now in the Dispensation of the fullness of times; and every ordinance, or office that has been practised in the church of former days, will be revived in this Dispensation, even to the offering of sacrifices.

Malachi says, "before the great and terrible day of the Lord, I will send Elijah, the Prophet, lest there be not faith enough on the earth, and I smite it with a curse; and for that reason was Joseph Smith sent, – to turn the hearts of the fathers to the children &c., to prepare them for the coming of the Lord – and so he will continue to send us intelligence by messengers, till at last, Old Father Adam, himself, shall at last appear to see his children. – We are too apt to judge our brethren unjustly – and we should be very careful how we do so, when we know that they are governed by the spirit of God. – We should mind & keep the helm of the ship in our hands; lest the helm slip a little, a storm come on, and we lose our latitude and longitude. – but if we have the Spirit of God, we never shall get out of our latitude or longitude. – We should be careful and keep the spirit of God on our sides – for the path will grow brighter and brighter until the perfect day. – Now brethren, do you not think that it would be a heaven on earth, if there was perfect confidence among you, – and this is heaven, and all the heaven that we have, will be, that which we make ourselves. – I have sometimes thought of the words of the Psalmist – "How pleasant it is for brethren to dwell together in unity." &c.– A two-fold cord is stronger than one: and take it in a family and see the necessity, as well as the beauty of union. – What shall I say more, brethren? – I could sit down and chat with you, I suppose, and answer almost any question or principle. – I always rejoice when I am able to throw light upon any mind, that is seeking intelligence. – Bro. Kimball was observing that he had done the best he could, and I verily believe it, – under the circumstances. It is our duty to mind the admonitions of the Spirit, lest we be shoaled on the quick-sands of evil. – Now I say hearken to the admonitions of your father; for his teachings are good – and as to this dancing, – when we dance, we should do it as much by the spirit as we would pray.

The Almighty does not intend that a man will stay on his knees 24 hours praying, but he is willing that we should have our recreations, but we must not get giddy, nor transcend the bounds of reason and right; or we will get out of the way and have to fall back and hunt up a position of right again. Peter sums up the case in a few words – "Add to your faith virtue, and to your virtue knowledge, and to your knowledge temperance, and withal be patient, and last of all Godliness and brotherly kindness; and if ye observe these things, ye will not be barren nor unfruitful in the knowledge of our Lord and Savior Jesus Christ." –

I know I have my faults, as well as yourselves; and my principal fault is impatience – and when I preach, I always hew to the line, if the chips fly in my face – and now I feel to bless you all in the name of Jesus Christ. –

Bro. Heber arose and said – I have been much edified by the conversation of Brother Whitney – and we always had the same feelings in common – and our views always met, and our thoughts flow in the same channel, but I don't know why it is so, – Don't you see that there should be temperance in every thing – dancing, eating, and drinking – Now I love to dance myself – but let us learn to be subject to government in all things – I am your head, your lawgiver, and king, and will be, to all eternity, and I am responsible to my head and

President – and you are responsible to me, your file leader. – I believe that some of my old progenitors, of whom I have no knowledge, will appear and tell me when the time shall come for me to rise up and administer in the ordinances for them, and I shall receive a great deal of knowledge from them, which I could not receive directly by revelation – Now, this idea you never thought of did you boys – and I want you to keep it secret within the walls of your own breasts – I want to have power, when I see my brother or sister, to tell Death to depart, and it shall depart – Every one has the greatest obstacle to govern himself – and I have greater trouble to govern Bro. Heber, and put self down, than any thing else. I always want a clerk to attend my meetings, so that like to-day, we can have a record to look back upon for our edification – I never felt better in my mind, but my body is ailing – I do delight in intelligence, and delight to see an intelligent mind. I do not know what I know, unless by the utterance of the spirit; and if you wish to know anything of me, put a paper in your pocket, and minute down things, that you may ask me questions, and I will answer them, – and it will not impoverish me; for, like a barrel of cider, I shall increase in quantity as you draw from me – Now, I want you all to mind and not tell secrets out of my family; for I have things that I dare not tell; and so has Bishop Whitney. Now I feel to bless you in the name of the Lord, and I expect if you had gone to the Council House, you would not have heard any more than you have here – and I feel as if we had had a good time. – It would not do for me to stand and wait for my wife to come up and do my work for me – Bishop Whitney is as honest a man as there is this side of heaven – and I want you to receive his counsel as one of the Judges in Israel, and what he has said to-day, is the word of God – My feelings are good towards you all – I know that you are all exalted above a great many that are just as good as you are. –

Father arose and said – Bro. Kimball has mentioned the idea of minuting things down, in order that you may ask questions – it is a good idea; for I had rather set down among a parcel of house-blocks, than some folks – I love intelligence – and some folks don't let their minds run higher than their ancles – and it is a perfect torment for me to sit down and talk with some folks – Many a time, I have sat down and talked with folks on trivial matters and have actually got some new ideas by asking a little question, before now – Some folks, from diffidence, are backward in asking intelligence – but no gentleman would laugh or sneer at another when a question was asked, even if it was an ignorant one. Bro. Kimball asked the brethren and sisters if they had enjoyed the party as well as the one at the Council House, – they all answered "Yes." – A hymn being sung, the meeting was dismissed with a benediction by Bishop Whitney.

After dismissal, Bro. Kimball observed that he would like to have his children to learn to calm themselves – and he hoped that they would mind and keep the watch wound up – and when they lost time, refer to the Chronometer – Bro. K. dismissed them also with his blessing –

MONDAY THE 15TH

Good weather – To-day – Bishop Miller and Porter returned from the Punkaw, the former bringing a part of his family – his house not quite finished when he arrived – Bros. Egan, M. Rockwell, and Geo. Rhodes arrived to-day also. –

TUESDAY THE 16TH

Pleasant weather, as usual long back – attended a party at the Council House, given by President Young to his adopted children, we had a good time – I went by invitation, as a musician – with some others of the Band – We had a first rate dinner, and spent the time very agreeably – Towards evening a couple of brethren from the army arrived – viz: – Thippetts, & Wolsey. they had journeyed thirty days without eating any thing except their game on the road – they were invited in to supper by Bro. Brigham – they had been robbed on the road by the Indians, and divested of most of their apparel – They said that most of the brethren are located about 300 miles from Santa Fe, and this side of the mountains, where they intend to remain this winter – a number of them have died by various diseases, the ague and fever,

C. C. A. Christensen, Winter Quarters, 1846–47 *(ca. 1880). Gift to the Church of Jesus Christ of Latter-day Saints from the five children of Jeanette Taggart Holmes.*

&c. the names of those who had died, were read over by Brigham, and among them, was the name of Joseph Richards, the son of Phinehas Richards.[107] –

List of articles bought by H. Egan on the 4th trip –

		$
7 bbls. flour 3.75c__		26.25
3 " " 400c__		12.00
Paid for corn____		10.00
for grinding	bush.	1.50
	_24_	
42½ lbs. tobacco_		5.31
1 gross matches_		1.00
2 kegs lard_		5.00
1 sett spinning wheel irons		.25
4 papers tacks__		.25
2½ bushels potatoes_		.62½
Paid Caulkins____		1.00
" H. C. Kimball__		3.00
		$66.18½

Expenses of the 4th trip____

	$
cooking and lodging__	.37½
Ferriage 3 wagons Nishna Botana_	.75
2 doz. Oats___ __	.16
14 lbs. bacon 3c_________________	.42
Ferriage Monattany[?] 2 wagons___	.40
Cooking and lodging _____________	.25
Supper & breakfast___	.25
Ferrying Monattany[?] 2 wagons___	.40
Corn_____________________ ___	.25
Supper________________________	.25

107. John H. Tippets and Thomas E. Wolsey had just endured a harrowing overland journey on horseback of several hundred miles through dangerous Indian territories from Pueblo, Colorado, to Winter Quarters. They brought with them money and letters from the Mormon Battalion to their families at the Missouri River. Of the 500-plus men who served in the Mormon Battalion, approximately 150 wintered at Pueblo because of sickness. David Boone, "The Mississippi Saints: A Unique Odyssey of Southern Pioneers," in *Far Away in the West: Reflections on the Mormon Pioneer Trail*, ed. Scott C. Esplin, Richard E. Bennett, Susan Easton Black, and Craig K. Manscill (Provo, UT: Religious Studies Center; Salt Lake City: Deseret Book), 160–86.

6 doz. oats________________________	.50
17 lbs. bacon_3c___	.51
Ferrying Nishna Botana 3 wagons_	.75
Cooking & lodging_	.37½
" " "	.25
Breakfast________________________	.25
	6.14

Wednesday & Thursday – 17th and 18th.

Fine weather – Today – Thursday, H. Egan and Geo. Rhodes again started for the country – Luke Johnson and Sister Hyde here with us at this time

Friday the 19th

Snow storm with frost and north wind – Luke Johnson stayed with O. P. Rockwell at Bro. K's. house, Sister Hyde with Sarah Ann.

Saturday, the 20th

On rising this morning, discovered that we had, during the night, by far the heaviest snow-storm of the season, with considerable frost –

Sunday the 21st

Quite cool, but pleasant overhead, and the sky clear, and serene – Family meeting held at Bro. K's room. Bro. K. quite unwell – Bro. [Nathaniel Thomas ?] Brown preached, also, Bro. K. and father – did not attend.

Monday he 22d

Fair day – nothing worthy of notice,

Tuesday the 23d

The Bishops with the poor and soldier's wives of the several wards met at the Council House, to enjoy themselves – commencing at 2 P. M., and continuing till morning attended with some others of the Band. –

Wednesday the 24th

Snowed considerably to-day as well as yesterday – My wife's health improving slowly – she has lately been afflicted with the canker she has now been sick 5 weeks last Sunday – Luke Johnson and Sister Hyde are in the place yet, as they are not able to get back home, in consequence of there being no path or road yet made down on the other side the prairie the snow having completely blocked up all the roads.

Wrote two letters for Bro. K. directed to Hiram Kimball and Dr. [John. M.] Bernhisel – to be sent by Daniel Davis, who is soon to start for Nauvoo

Thursday the 25th

continues yet snowing – went with Bro. K. to Father Cutler's house, and read the letter, lately written to H. Kimball at Nauvoo. – Hiram is to send on some mill irons, by Daniel Davis, and Wm. Cutler who is also going along –

The company of Pioneers will probably start for the mountains in about 4 weeks, in order to get to our place of location, in time to put in a Spring crop – Some of the Twelve will also go at the same time –

Friday the 26th

Snowing as usual – and first rate sleighing for two or three days past – Daniel Davis not going immediately Bro. K. concluded to send his letter by Peregrine Sessions who starts for Nauvoo to morrow

Saturday the 27th

Nothing worthy of notice, except that it is thawing gradually. –

Sunday the 28th

Fine day – Bro. K. preached at his room – did not attend – troubled considerably with the canker in my mouth – also my wife, who is now getting quite smart once more –

Monday the 1st of March

Beautiful weather – Ellis Eames, a player on the violin, came up from the Point – a number of the Band including him and myself went round in a sleigh this evening, (Porter driving,) and serenaded several places in the town – Bro. K. was along with us – we stopt a[t] Bishop Hunter's and played a tune – and then by the invitation of Bro. K., went to his house, where we spent some time in dancing, &c. & retired –

Tuesday the 2d

Thawing some to-day – This evening Bro. Kay arrived from the Punkaw nation – having left his family and some others 50 miles from here, not being unable all [*sic*] to get home, in consequence of their feed for cattle having failed –

Wednesday the 3D

Thawing very fast – To-day, a number of the Band went round & raised a contribution for Bro. Kay, in corn, meal, &c. We got 9 bushels of the former, Played with some others of the Band, for the Quorum of High Priests, whose parties commenced yesterday –

Thursday the 4TH

Clear weather, but muddy – This morning, Bro Kay and James Clayton, started with their provisions, to go back where the former had left his family – also this morning, Ellis Eames, J. Redding, Merit Rockwell, two ladies, and myself went down to the Point, in Bro. K's. carriage (about 16 miles,) and attended a party, given at Beaubins, a half-breed – I took my flute to assist Bro. Eames in playing – had a very good time – good supper, &c.,– &c.–

Friday the 5TH

Very bad going, warmer than yesterday Returned to-day – rather dangerous crossing on the ice however, got over safely, pretty well tired out, having been up all night, as well as several nights previous playing with the Band – On my arrival, had an invitation from Porter, to attend a party at Phineas Young's house, but declined –

Saturday the 6TH

Pleasant – John Kay, with some of his family arrived this evening – also, from Missouri, H. Egan, J. Frazier, and Geo. Rhodes –

Sunday the 7TH

Warm and pleasant – Meeting at Bro. K's room – he not present –

Monday the 8TH

Cold severe weather – Meeting of the Pioneers of Bro. K's. Co. held at the Council House this morning – nothing done except making selections of numbers – it is the intention for, some to start on Monday next – the majority, however will not go under 2 or 3 weeks.

There was a meeting of father's company of pioneers, held at the council house, Monday morning, it being the intention for some to start soon, though the majority were not to start under a week or so. Here Horace and his brother Orson, concluded to go with the pioneers in place of their father, and assist in putting in crops, till the ground, etc., that the families, when they came on, might have something to move to. All were busy now preparing, and laying in their supplies for the journey.

Woman's Exponent, vol. 14, no. 4,
15 July 1885, pp. 30–31

Tuesday the 9th

Tolerable fair weather – To-day H. Egan, Merit Rockwell, and Jacob Frazier, started for the country after a load of, corn –

Wednesday the 10th

Very fine weather – nothing of any importance to-day – except I have concluded to go with the pioneers. –

Drawings of
H. K. Whitney
loaned me by Art.
E. W. P.

20
$18\frac{3}{4}$
$17\frac{1}{4}$
3

59

Journal 5

11 March–20 July 1847

Diary of

H. K. Whitney

loaned me by Art.

E. W. P.

[Number 5]

Thursday the 11th

Warm, spring weather – Geo. Billings came down from the herd to-day – I went for father to Bro. Clayton's, to see about a wagon that he and father are jointly getting repaired, to send with the pioneers – Bro. C. thinks of sending one man, viz: – Thomas Corbett – and father expects Orson and myself to go for him – that is, to go on and assist in putting in a Spring crop, till the ground, &c., that the families, when they come on, may have something to move to. – Porter intends going with the pioneers, also Luke Johnson, who came up to-day from below, 6 miles from the Point – Went by father's request, and engaged a pair of boots of Bro. Washburn, to be made next week – Forgot to mention that, last evening I again went with father into the store to make a purchase of some articles –

Friday and Saturday, 12th and 13th

Fine days, but nothing worthy of notice occurred –

Sunday the 14th

Good weather – By father's request, went and copied an important document, which took me the greater part of the day & night.[108]

The revelation on plural marriage was the "document" referred to, the bishop having the only one in existence, which he afterwards gave to President Young, retaining a copy.

Woman's Exponent, vol. 14, no. 4,
15 July 1885, pp. 30–31

Monday the 15th

Pleasant and warm – The pioneers and the 2^{d} Division met this morning at the Council House – they met to arrange themselves in cos. of Tens, &c.

---

108. The "important document" Whitney refers to is the 1831 revelation to Joseph Smith on eternal/plural marriage, currently found in section 132 of the LDS Doctrine and Covenants. Secrecy was enjoined in the copying of the document since many in the camp did not yet know of, or understand, the practice of plural marriage. Only gradually was the "principle" introduced. Helen Mar later wrote of her husband's role in writing down this revelation as follows: "The first copy of the revelation upon celestial marriage was in Bishop N. K. Whitney's possession, when Emma Smith demanded it; but he was too much of a practical and business-like man to neglect to retain an exact copy of the original, which she destroyed as soon as it came into her possession. She thought that this act would put an end to the practice but she was disappointed in her wicked idea. In the winter of 1847, when settled at Winter Quarters, President B. Young, never having had the revelation, asked the Bishop for this copy, which was the only one in existence, and he could hardly be expected to publish it until after he came into possession of it. Previous to letting the President have it, the Bishop got his son, H. K. Whitney—my husband—to copy it for him. The day and circumstance I distinctly remember, for he told me that his father locked him in his store while he wrote it, in order that no one should disturb him." Helen Mar Whitney, *Plural Marriage as Taught by the Prophet Joseph Smith: A Reply to Joseph Smith, Editor of the Lamoni (Iowa) Herald* (Salt Lake City: Juvenile Instructor Office, 1882), 26–27.

Tuesday the 16th

Fair weather – Busy preparing to go with the pioneers. Went by invitation with a number of the Band, to see a noted flute player, McRary, by name.[109] – He professes to be a Choctaw Indian. Geo. Billings come down from the Herd. he is also going with the pioneers. –

Wednesday the 17th

Beautiful weather. My boots were finished to-day – went also, and got a coat made, and done several things, preparatory to the journey. Bro. H. Egan returned today from the country. – Bro. Clayton, to-day, surrendered a quantity of church property into Father's hands at the store. – Got several things to-day of father at the store. – Bro. Corbett laid in his supplies, and brought the wagon to father's yard, that we might lay in, ours also – went to a meeting of the Band again, at James Clayton's this evening – they met to make some arrangements about a concert to be held at the Council House to morrow evening.

Thursday the 18th

Fine day – nothing of importance to-day – the concert came off this evening at the Council House – I attended a short time, and left about 11 o'clock – not feeling very well, – Bro. Clayton in consequence of illness, also, did not attend – There is a disease, called by the folks here, the "black-leg," [black-canker or scurvy] getting quite prevalent in the camp – It commences with a sharp pain in the ancles swells, and finally, the leg gets almost black, and in many cases it proves fatal – There have a great many died, within the last month – It is caused, in a great measure, by the want of vegetable food – and having to eat salt food.[110] –

He mentions the black scurvy, which had begun its work, and already many cases had proved fatal. It would commence with dark streaks and pains in the ends of the fingers or toes, which increased and spread till the limbs were inflamed and became almost black, causing such intense agony that death would be welcomed as a release from their suffering. It was caused by the want of vegetable food and living so long on salt meat without it.

It was now a year or more since the majority had left their homes and civilization behind, and our trail was marked by the lonely mounds of the dead, who had made a happy escape

109. Occasionally traveling performers came into town, musicians such as the enigmatic mulatto Choctaw, William McCrary, who presented a flute concert at the Council House in February, and then again in March 1847. A magician, oneman band, traveling sideshow, and musician all in one, this charlatan and opportunist called himself "Adam, the ancient of days returned," and even convinced some men and women that he was a modern prophet. Bedding several women on the Iowa side, McCrary, who was at one time baptized, was later excommunicated and eventually ridden out of town. See also glossary. A recent study on early Mormon race relations speculates that McCrary may even have been ordained to the priesthood and that his later excommunication may have played a role in the development of the priesthood ban on black Latter-day Saints. See W. Paul Reeve, *Religion of a Different Color: Race and the Mormon Struggle for Whiteness* (Oxford: Oxford University Press, 2015), 128–33.

110. Scurvy was caused by the want of fresh fruits and vegetables, which the Latter-day Saints knew but were powerless to do much about.

from the sufferings and want to which we were so many years subjected, through the wickedness and injustice of man.

Woman's Exponent, vol. 14, no. 4,
15 July 1885, pp. 30–31

FRIDAY THE 19TH.

Fair day – Wrote for Bishop Miller, a document addressed to the President and Quorum of the Twelve, stating the advantages there would be in our taking a south-westerly course, in pursuit of a location for the Saints. – viz: – the mildness of the climate, the chance that we would have in raising cotton, corn, sugar-cane, &c. &c.–

SATURDAY THE 20TH

Beautiful weather, though somewhat windy – my rifle was fixed today, by Bro. Pettit but on examination, was not well done. – doing all we can, myself and Orson, to get ready to go with the Pioneers, as Monday next is named as the intended day for starting. –

SUNDAY THE 21ST.

This morning, a large number assembled at the Stand, at the sound of a bell, to hear Brigham give instruction, which was good. – Bro. Kimball called his private family together this evening, and blessed them, to the number of thirty-six – my wife and myself did not attend, not feeling well. An epistle from Heber C. Kimball was read to his family, containing advice to Wm. and Daniel, (who are to remain here,) concerning bringing up the different families and children under Bro. K's. charge.

MONDAY THE 22D.

On rising this morning, discovered that it had snowed considerably during the night. – A different arrangement was entered into by the Council to-day, pertaining to our removal west – it is now the intention to leave all the families here except those who can fit themselves out, for another season, and the pioneers go on to the mountains and put in a fall crop, and then some of them return for their families, so as to bring them up by the ensuing Spring.[111] –

111. The 1847 plan was very much like that of '46 in that a small pioneer vanguard company would go on ahead and, upon reaching their destination, plant a fall crop—in this latter case at the base, or in some valley of, the Rocky Mountains, with the larger companies of families following in their wake. Without such crops, the pale of starvation loomed over their entire enterprise.

Tuesday the 23d.

Pleasant overhead, but muddy under-foot – my wife's health quite poor, yet, – she is afflicted at present with a severe cough, having taken a hard cold – It was in contemplation, yesterday and to-day, having a public meeting at the Stand, but the weather having been so damp, it was given up – The new arrangements with regard to our removal, will probably protract our departure somewhat. –

Wednesday the 24th.

Tolerable fair weather – nothing of importance to-day – Brigham Bro. K., and father took a ride in their carriage, for the purpose of loaning some money to make up the deficit in the soldiers money, &c., &c.–

Thursday the 25th.

Good weather – Meeting held to day at the Stand – the Mill, which was commenced some time ago, is now about finished, or nearly so, so that they are about ready to grind wheat, corn, &c.–

Friday the 26th.

Every one, as usual, making ready to go with the Pioneers, though it is very uncertain when we shall start. –

Saturday the 27th.

Warm day, and sultry – J. Redding and myself went about 5 miles up the river on the other side hunting – got nothing except a prairie chicken, the weather being too fair to shoot geese, ducks. Luke Johnson came up again, to-day from below, on Brigham's horse.

Sunday the 28th.

Quite windy, but still, a very warm day – Meeting held at the Stand, to-day – afflicted with a severe cold on my lungs, also, in my head – my wife tolerably well to-day – Bro. K's. family, & father's, all well and enjoying good health. –

Monday the 29th.

Fair weather – a number of the brethren that are going to remain behind, started for the "Old Fort," ten miles above here, for the purpose of putting in a crop up there. – A number of families are also preparing to remove to that place – A concert was held this evening at the Council House by the Choctaw Indian, Wm. Chubby, alias McRary, who performed on the flute, saucepan, &c.–

Elk Horn River Ferry. *Lithograph by Piercy,* Route from Liverpool to Great Salt Lake Valley. *Utah State Historical Society.*

Modern Elkhorn River southwest of Norfolk, Nebraska, just upstream from the Cowboy Trail crossing near Broken Bridge Road. Photo looking northward (upstream). Wikimedia Commons.

TUESDAY THE 30TH.

Warm day – it is supposed, that we will start to-morrow or next day – Bro. Kimball has six waggons fitted out – ready loaded to start Bro. Corbett, Orson and myself flying round to-day, to get ready to start. – about ready to grind at the mill – The names of those going in Bro. K's, wagons, are as follow: – Howard Egan, Heber P. Kimball – Wm. King, Cloward – Hosea Cushing, Robert Byard – George Billings, Edson Whipple – Philo Johnson, Carlos Murray – O. P. Rockwell, Jackson Redding. –

WEDNESDAY THE 31ST.

Fine day – nothing of importance to-day. –

THURSDAY, FRIDAY & SATURDAY, 1ST, 2D, & 3D OF APRIL.

nothing doing except helping off the Pioneers – the boys commenced fencing, in front of the houses, to-day – Bro. Clayton has concluded not to send Bro. Corbett, consequently, Orson and myself have to "go it alone". – It is the intention to start most of teams on Monday, who are to go up to the "Elk Horn" river, and there wait till all shall come up. – Brigham and Brother K. will not start on Monday, as there is to be a conference here to commence on Tuesday the 6th inst.

SUNDAY THE 4TH.

Fine day. – A meeting of part of father's and Bro. K's. families was called together at Sarah Ann's room – Present – Heber C. Kimball, N. K. Whitney, Wm. Kimball, H. K. Whitney, O. K. Whitney – Vilate Kimball, Sister Noon, Sarah Ann, Helen M., Mary Kimball, and mother – eleven persons in all – We all clothed ourselves, except Orson and Helen – and father opened the meeting by prayer. We all then stood up in a ring, offered up the signs of the Priesthood, Bro. K. being mouth – after sitting some time, listening to good instruction from Bro. K. and father, we stood up again in a ring, father being mouth, and also offered up the signs of the Priesthood.[112] – Bro. K. expressed his feelings at length, about circumstances

---

112. Prayer circles or rings were an extension of Mormon temple devotions in which men and women who had been endowed in the Nauvoo Temple prior to their departure from Nauvoo would come together in a circle to pray for the sick, the diseased, and those otherwise afflicted. Similar prayer rings were once common in the outdoor Methodist camp meetings of the Second Great Awakening. See D. Michael Quinn, "Latter-day Saint Prayer Circles," *BYU Studies* 19, no. 1 (Fall 1978): 79–105; Hugh W. Nibley, "The Early Christian Prayer Circle," *BYU Studies* 19, no. 1 (Fall 1978): 49–78; and Bernard Weisberger, *They Gathered at the River: The Story of the Great Revivalists and Their Impact upon Religion in America* (Boston: Little, Brown and Company, 1958), 20–40. For the Latter-day Saints, however, these prayer circles, in which the participants dressed in white temple robes, held special temple connotations, covenantal meanings, and renewals.

It should also be noted that other forms of temple ordinances and practices were carried on at Winter Quarters, most notably that of sealings or eternal marriages, but not living endowments. Willard Richards's octagon, sometimes unceremoniously dubbed the "potato heap," served not only as a post office

Parley P. Pratt (1807–57), Mormon missionary, apostle, theologian, and trailblazer. Church History Library.

in his family – He said, "that he just felt," (and he arose as he spoke and picked up a stick by the stove) "like knocking the brains out of a person who attempted to come into his family, and sow discord among them – that he was aware that persons, even in his own family, would arise and try to promote disunion, and strive to alienate their minds from him in his absence, but," said he, "persons that do this, will be cursed, and go to hell, don't you think so, Bro. Whitney?" father replied "yes." – He further observed, "that there was not that person living in the world, in whom he placed more confidence, than he did in Bro. Whitney, and that there was no person living in the world, who would have so much influence in his (Bro. K's.) absence, as Bro. Whitney – and he recommended him to them as a worthy, good, and exemplary man, to counsel them in his absence. He told his wife Vilate, that if any person should presume to come into his house and speak against him or any member of his family while he was gone, to arise and command them to leave the house in the name of Heber C. Kimball – Many other things were said, and much good instruction given by our fathers, and meeting was adjourned till evening, Bro. K. cautioned us not to mention the matters to any one, but to meet as silently as possible, Agreeably to adjournment, we met this evening, and conversed till about 9 o'clock – after we had clothed ourselves, we stood up in a ring, and offered up the signs of the Priesthood, Bro. K. being mouth – afterward, Bro. K. and father alternately blessed each member of his family, and the meeting dismissed bout 11 o'clock, after having enjoyed one of the happiest, (and apparently the brightest) periods in my existence. –

April the 4th, he mentions the calling together of a portion of his father's and my father's families—eleven persons in all—to a meeting for prayer, and also for instruction from father

and hospital but also as a place for the conducting of temple marriages, and perhaps celestial or plural marriages as well. For more, see Bennett, *Mormons at the Missouri*, 188–92.

and Bishop Whitney. This was held in the room occupied by my husband's sister, Sarah Ann, next door to mine, and being now convalescent I was able to attend.

Woman's Exponent, vol. 14, no. 7,
1 September 1885, pp. 53–54

Monday the 5th.

Rained considerably last night, accompanied by thunder and lightning – quite wet under feet this morning – cleared off fair this afternoon – first rain of the season – 4 of the 6 wagons belonging to Bro. K. started out this afternoon and went three miles, as far as the hay stacks – The number of boys who remain of Bro. K's. family are as follow: – viz – Wm. Kimball, George Rhodes, James Smithies, Jacob Frazier, Peter Hansen, and Daniel Davis. – Father, Jacob Wetherbee and myself loaded my wagon this afternoon – meeting held again this evening, at Sarah Ann's room – wife and myself did not attend – only those who were not there last evening.

Tuesday the 6th.

fair day – nothing of particular importance to-day – except the usual preparations for leaving. Conference held this forenoon at the Stand.[113]

Wednesday the 7th

Warm day – made the last grand packing arrangements to-day. –

Thursday the 8th.

Started with my wagon about 11 a.m., myself and Orson, and went three miles to the hay-stacks, where the rest of the boys were – Bro. and Sister Kimball went with us. Brigham and his camp were 3 or 4 miles from here ahead. – Porter came up on horseback, and informed us that P. P. Pratt had just arrived from England, & that John Taylor and O. Hyde were soon expected.[114] Left my wagon, and went back home to spend the night, in the carriage, with Bro. K., Sister K., Father, and Egan, leaving my wagon in charge of Orson and John. – Orson, soon however came back on horseback, and also spent the night.

---

113. One reason why the already-selected pioneers for the westward expedition did not leave earlier was so that they could convene a general conference of the church, the only one held at Winter Quarters. This conference was dedicated to the preparation of all things for the pending exodus and to fortify spiritually those who were to stay back.

114. The apostolic mission of Parley P. Pratt, John Taylor, and Orson Hyde to England was primarily designed to bring back tithing funds from the British Latter-day Saints. The mission failed for various reasons, particularly embezzlements of funds by one or two local leaders. However, they were successful in bringing back telescopes, theodolites, sextants, and other surveying instruments that would be of great value during their journeys west. In addition, they brought with them several faithful Latter-day Saints from Britain.

Friday the 9th.

Fair weather for travelling – Before starting yesterday, Father Lott blessed Orson and myself, and give us many good promises, of health and safety – that we should return to our friends again, &c. &c., Bro. K. Father, Brigham and Dr. Richards started this morning, and went on in Bro. K's. carriage – Orson drove the team, and I rode Bro. Brigham's horse as far as his camp, where we arrived about noon – 7 miles from home – went on 3 miles further and camped by the side of a beautiful spring, having made 10 miles to day. – Orson on guard tonight

[***Editor's note***: Helen, who did not go west in the vanguard company, had many harrowing experiences of her own back at Winter Quarters such as follows:]

My mother's babe was a little over a month old when father left with the pioneers. A little black eyed, rosy cheeked girl, between twelve and thirteen, had been given to them a few days previous to father's leaving, whom they adopted as their own. Her mother had died on the journey from Nauvoo, leaving a number of little children, that were taken by different families. They came from England, and the father was rather a worthless sort of man, and seemed to care very little for children.

The members of my mother's household numbered fourteen, including herself. Three of them were young men who were adopted into father's family—Peter Hanson, George Roads and Jacob Frazier, and three young women—Harriet Sanders, father's wife, Jenette Murray, a cousin of mine, Mary Forsgreen, Lucy and myself and five little brothers made up her private family. Wm., her eldest, acted as guardian, and attended to the wants of the families under his charge. Brothers Daniel Davis and James Smithies were his assistants, and helped to raise gardens and provided the needfuls to sustain life. The younger boys attended to herding the cows, and they were occasionally nearly frightened out of their wits by Indians, who wanted to drive away their cows. One day my little brother Charley went out with them and had the misfortune to lose his only hat, and had to go without for a time, till he was so badly tanned that he was usually called the half breed, and when asked his name would invariably answer, "Charley half-a-breed." He was only five years old, and supposed that to be his real name. His hair was very heavy and nearly black, and his skin was fair, but after becoming so thoroughly tanned, no one could believe him to have been otherwise than dark.

We had a varied and peculiar experience from the time that we were left, till the return of the pioneers. Things looked rather dark, and to all appearance there was no earthly source to which we could look. When one meal was eaten, how the next was to be obtained was something of a puzzle. But when things looked the darkest, and want seemed most imminent, some way or other we were provided for, and relief came sometimes in a way most marvelous. But to return:

As I have previously mentioned, the scurvy was raging in our midst, and a good many had already died in consequence. Only a very few potatoes could be obtained at that time of the year, and for what we did get we had to pay a high price. I, being among the poorly ones, was indulged in this luxury, and which I shall never forget, with the nice tea, which mother had purchased of Aunt Sabra Granger, it being superior black tea, that which Col. Kane had sent her.

Woman's Exponent, vol. 14, no. 10,
15 October 1885, p. 78

Saturday the 10th.

Fair day as usual. Father did not, at first intend going on with us, but finally concluded to go to the "Horn" by Brighams and Heber's requests. – travelled about 15 miles to-day, and encamped on the prairie, near a ravine, where we could get water, about 6 miles from the "Horn". –

Sunday the 11th.

Fair day – travelled on, and arrived at the "Horn" about 2 P. M., and crossed the river on a raft, drawn on the opposite side by cattle, with the assistance of ropes on either side – Bro. Bullock, Dr. Richard's clerk, took down the number of wagons, as they crossed, which amounted to seventy-two – went about a mile, after crossing, down the stream, and encamped for the night – the wagons formed in a line, our horses being hitched to stakes, and fed on cotton-wood trees, besides their allowance of corn – Bro. K. told the brethren this morning, that he hoped that they would not go hunting or fishing, for if they did so, they should not be prospered, as this was a day set apart for the service of the Lord, not for trivial amusements. – stood on guard to night the last watch.

Monday the 12th.

Fair day – Brigham, Bro. K., father, Porter, Bro. Benson, O. Pratt G. A. Smith, Dr. Richards, and a number of others went back to Winter Quarters. – before starting, it was agreed by the council, that the remainder of us left behind, should travel on, about 12 miles to the Platte river, in order to get across an extensive bottom that intervened, lest it should rain, and make it bad going – accordingly, we travelled on and encamped on the banks of the Platte, the sun being about 2 hours high formed our wagons in a kind of semi-circle under Stephen Markham's supervision, who has the cannon in charge[115] – Orson stood guard to-night the first watch. Bro. M. called the people together this evening and told them it was the wish of the "Twelve", that some ones should go ahead and look out for a good track to follow – Father [James] Case, J. Redden, and two other men appointed to go, or volunteered. – Father thought of returning when the rest of the brethren do, in two or three days. – they want to

115. Upon making camp for the night, the seventy-two wagons in this advance company were drawn in a circle, with the front wheels of one interlocking with the rear wheels of the other, with all horses and other animals remaining inside the corral, and with the pioneers sleeping in their wagons or tents. The corral was meant to prevent Indian thievery of their livestock and to serve as a defense against other forms of attack.

have him go ahead with them to the mountains. – but his present business will hardly admit of that. – Little John came with him as far as the "Horn", and went back with the rest of them to-day. –

Tuesday the 13th.

Fair weather – Busied myself in arranging my journal, which had got somewhat behind-hand. – Father Case, J. Redden, and the two others appointed, went out, returned and reported this evening that they had rode for 20 or 30 miles, and found a low marshy country, in general.

Wednesday the 14th.

Warm as usual – We are still lying here inactive, except the taking care of our horses & cattle, as the Twelve have not yet got back.

Thursday the 15th.

Still fair weather – the "Twelve" arrived this afternoon, having been gone 4 days – with them came Father, C. L. Whitney, Bro. [Jesse] Little, (who has just arrived from the east,) & Wm. Clayton, (who is going on with us,) – father and Lyman will return to-morrow, and we also intend to start on our journey. – Bro. Little brought several valuable presents, sent by him, from Colonel Kane to Brigham, Heber, Porter, Father John Smith, and some others – among other things, he sent a riding whip to Don C. Whitney, my little brother, – Father and Lyman brought Orson and myself 2 letters, (dated Saturday 10th, inst.) one being written to me by my wife, the other from mother, addressed to her two sons, Pioneers – Orson wrote a letter back this evening to Maria – and I one to my wife, which however, I did not finish this evening, but intend to early in the morning. –

Friday the 16th.

This day gloomy, windy, and cold – forgot to mention that Ellen Sanders came back with Bro. K. when he returned – about 8 o'clock the camp were called together and organized, 2 captains of 100's, viz: – Stephen Markham and A. P. Rockwood were appointed, also 5 capts. of 50's, and 14 captains of 10's. – There are 143 men and boys on the list of the pioneer company; 3 women, and Lorenzo Young's 2 children, 73 wagons – O. P. Rockwell has gone back to camp with Bro. J. C. Little – Bishop Whitney, Lyman Whitney, Wm. Kimball and J. B. Nobles return from here to Winter Quarters –
The following is a list of all the names of this pioneer company, viz: –

[***Editor's note***: In the original journal, groups of names in the following list were combined together using brackets. For convenience, I have shown combinations by single-spacing the text.]

1st. Ten

1 Wilford Woodruff

2 John S. Fowler
3 Jacob Burnham

4 Orson Pratt

5 Joseph Egbert
6 John M. Freeman
7 Marcus B. Thorpe

8 George A. Smith
9 George Wardle 9 [in this group of ten]

2nd Ten

10 Thomas Grover
11 Ezra T. Benson

12 Barnabas L. Adams
13 Roswell Stevens

14 Amasa Lyman
15 Sterling Driggs
16 Albert Carrington

17 Thomas Bullock
18 George Brown

19 Willard Richards
20 John C. Little 11

3rd Ten

21 Phinehas H. Young
22 John Y. Green
23 Thomas Tanner

24 Brigham Young

25 Addison Everett
26 Truman O. Angel

27 Lorenzo Young

28 Bryant Stringam

29 Albert P. Rockwood
30 Joseph S. Scofield 10

4th Ten

31 Luke Johnson
32 John Holman

33 Edmund Ellsworth
34 Alvarus Hanks

35 George R. Grant
36 Mellen Atwood

37 Samuel Fox
38 Tunis Rapplyee

39 Harvey Pierce
40 William Dykes
41 Jacob Weilar 11

5th Ten

42 Stephen H. Goddard
43 Tarlton Lewis

44 Henry G. Sherwood

45 Zebedee Coltrin
46 Sylvester H. Earl

47 John Dixon
48 Samuel H. Marble

49 George Scholes
50 William Henry

51 William Empy 10

6[th.] Ten

52 Charles Shumway
53 Andrew Shumway

24 Thomas Woolsey
55 Chancey Loveland

56 Erastus Snow
57 James Craig

58 William Wordsworth
59 William Vance

60 Simeon Howd
61 Seeley Owen 10

[7th Ten]

62 James Case
63 Artemas Johnson

64 William A. Smoot
65 Franklin B. Dewey

66 William Carter
67 Franklin G. Love

68 Burr Frost
69 Darius Ensign

70 Franklin B. Stewart
71 Monroe Frank

72 Eric Glines
73 Ozro Eastman$_{12}$

[8th Ten]

74 Seth Taft
75 Horace Thornton
76 Stephen Kelsey

77 John S. Eldredge
78 Charles D. Barnham

79 Almon M. Williams
80 Rufus Allen

81 Robert T. Thomas
82 James W. Stuart

83 Elijah Newman
84 Levi N. Kendall
85 Francis Boggs

86 David Grant$_{13}$

9th Ten

87 Heber C. Kimball
88 Howard Egan

89 William A. King
90 Thomas Cloward

91 Hosea Cushing
92 Robert Byard

93 George Billings
94 Edson Whipple

95 Philo Johnson
96 Carlos Murray$_{10}$

10th Ten

97 Appleton M. Harmon

98 William Clayton

99 Horace K. Whitney
100 Orson K. Whitney

101 Orin Porter Rockwell
102 Nathaniel Thomas Brown
103 Jackson Redden

104 John Pack
105 Francis M. Pomroy

106 Aaron Farr
107 Nathaniel Fairbanks$_{11}$

11th Ten

108 John S. Higbee
109 John Wheeler

110 Solomon Chamberlain
111 Conrad Klineman

112 Joseph Rooker
113 Pery FitzGerald

114 John H. Tibbets
115 James Davenport

116 Henson Walker
117 Benjamin Rolfe$_{10}$

12th. Ten

118 Norton Jacobs
119 Charles A. Harper

120 George Woodward

121 Stephen Markham
122 Lewis Barney

123 George Mills
124 Andrew Gibbons

125 Joseph Hancock
126 John W. Norton 9

13th. Ten

127 Shadrach Roundy
128 Hans C. Hanson

129 Levi Jackman
130 Lyman Curtis

131 John Brown
132 Matthew Ivory
133 David Powell

134 Hark Lay
135 Oscar Crosby 9 Blacks

[14th Ten]

136 Joseph Matthews
137 Gillroid [Gilbard] Summe

138 John Gleason
139 Charles Burke

140 Alexander P. Chessley
141 Rodney Badger
142 Norman Taylor

143 Green Flake (Black) 8 Men in 14th. Ten

The names of the females in the camp are Ellen Sanders, Harriet Young, and Clarissa Young. – the names of the children are Sobiski Young & Perry Decker, making a total of 148 souls in the pioneer company –

The following are the names of the Captains of 50's, as appointed at this organization, viz: Addison Everett, Tarleton Lewis, James Case, John Pack & Shadrach Roundy. – The Capts. of 10's are as follows, viz: – Wilford Woodruff, Thomas Grover, Phinehas H. Young, Luke Johnson, Stephen H. Goddard, Charles Shumway, James Case, Seth Taft, Heber C. Kimball, Appleton M. Harmon, John S. Higbee, Norton Jacobs, Shadrach Roundy, Joseph Matthews. Stephen Markham was appointed captain of the Guard, and ordered to select out of the camp 50 men for guard, in whom he could place confidence, who are to be as a standing guard, to attend to the wagons each night, 12 of them to stand at a time, and to have 2 sets each night, that is, 12 each watch, to stand half the night. – In cases where the horses and cattle are tied at some distance from the wagons at night, an extra guard is to be detailed, – the standing guard not being permitted to leave the immediate neighborhood of the camp. – About 2 P. M. the camp started, proceeded about 3 miles and encamped in a line 600 yds from timber, where there is plenty of cotton-wood, and some rushes – The country in the vicinity of the "Elk-Horn," is one of the most beautiful I ever saw – The bluffs on the east, are nicely rolling, and beautifully lined with timber, and some very nice cedar groves – The "Horn" is a beautiful stream, about 150 feet wide, and 4 deep, and some few fish are to be found therein.

The names of the women were: Harriet Young, Clarissa D. Young, and Ellen Sanders Kimball. Horace speaks of Brother J. C. Little, who was among the late arrivals, bringing some valuable presents from Colonel Kane to President B. Young, Father, Porter Rockwell, Father John Smith, and Aunt Sabra Granger, an old nurse in Father Whitney's family, to whom he sent a box of black tea. He remembered a number more. Among them was Don C, my husband's little brother, to whom he sent a complete and valuable set of fishing tackle, having seen him often during his (the Colonel's) sickness at Cutler's Park.

About 2 p.m. the camp started, and Father Whitney, J. C. Little, William Kimball, Joseph B. Nobles, Lyman Whitney, little John Whitney, and others returned to Winter Quarters, bringing the last mail from the Platte. We were glad to learn that they had gone on, thinking it would hasten their return home, besides their stopping so near made it seem much harder than as though they were traveling on. But we were not slow to improve the opportunities to correspond. Every messenger was the bearer of letters and tokens of affection while they remained there, for we did not know when we should have the chance again. How far they were going, or how long would be our separation, no one could tell. They were going beyond the trackless wastes of the Great American Desert—to what was then an almost unknown country, among the wild beasts and red men of the Rocky Mountains. Nor were they to turn back till they found some suitable spot where they could form a colony, and make homes that they thought would not be coveted nor encroached upon by their white brethren, who had so mercilessly driven them from their midst. The outlook was indeed a gloomy one, and needed all the faith and hope that could be mustered to sustain us under the circumstances, for death was sweeping away its victims, and want and suffering seemed to be staring us in the face, which required courage, and a mighty effort to obtain the requisite amount, to be able to bear up under it. That was among the saddest chapters in my history; and it made so vivid an impression that though years have elapsed, and erased many a scene of later date they have not been able to obliterate it from my memory, nor can I ever dwell upon it without weeping. But the Lord was very merciful, and it was only through His interposition that so many were spared to meet again in the flesh. For all we were brought into tight places, and many even to the point of death, there came deliverance when most needed. There was always a bright star of hope glimmering between the heavy clouds as they bore down upon us, till at last it seemed as though the very heavens were being opened to pour down a healing balm upon the wounded and disconsolate—proving that "Earth has no sorrows that heaven cannot heal."

Woman's Exponent, vol. 14, no. 8,
15 September 1885, pp. 57–58

Saturday the 17th

Cold this morning – wind northwest – at 9 o'clock we started on our journey, wind blowing very high, which made it quite disagreeable; as it was a sandy road – we have travelled a little north of west, yester-day and to-day – went 7 miles and encamped near a beautiful grove of cotton-wood this evening a trader from the Pawnee village encamped near us – he had one wagon loaded with buffalo robes – at sunset the bugle sounded for the people to come together – Pres't. Young said it was necessary to have a military organization before we left this place – It was moved and carried that the 2 divisions be formed in to one regiment under Colonel Markham – there was also 2 Majors appointed, viz: – John Pack and Shadrach Roundy – Bro. Tanner was appointed to the command of the Guard – each Capt. 10 to command his own 10, in case of an attack from the Indians – Bro. K. has taken Wm. Clayton into his mess – he writes his journal for him – Ellis Eames went back in consequence of sickness, as he said, but I think he is weak in the faith – Orson and Myself enjoy tolerably good health –

SUNDAY THE 18TH.

This morning high winds from the south, and very cold – To-day being set apart by the Lord for his people to rest, we do not intend to travel – 3 wagons loaded with furs passed this morning; also 4 or 5 pack-mules passed a short time afterward, going to the settlements – Bro. K. wrote a letter this morning to his wife by Ellis Eames. – It was so cold to-day, that it was thought wisdom not to call the brethren together to meeting – The "Twelve" retired into the woods to counsel together – about sunset Pres't. Young called the captains together and gave them the following instruction: – "At 8 o'clock and 30 minutes, the bugle will sound, and all should retire to their wagons and bow before the Lord and offer up thanks to Him, before going to bed. And that all fires should be extinguished at that time – also, the bugle will sound at 5 in the morning, when all should arise and offer up their thanks to the Lord, and at 7 o'clock be ready to start, also at the same sound or signal of the bugle – all the spare hands should walk on the off side of their respective wagons, with their rifles loaded – The weather cold thro' the day.

When the pioneers were twenty-five miles from the Elk Horn, they met some traders with wagons and pack mules, loaded with furs, on their way to the settlements, and Ellis Evans [Eames], who complained of ill health, returned with them, bringing some letters. One from father, dated Sunday, April 18th, stated that he, like the majority, was suffering from severe cold, and was worn out, having found no chance to rest, as yet, but they had no thought but to go ahead in the name of the Lord God of Israel.

Woman's Exponent, vol. 14, no. 11,
1 November 1885, p. 82

MONDAY THE 19TH.

Fair weather this morning, calm & pleasant – at 5 a.m., the bugle sounded for all to rise and pray –, and at 7 o'clock the camp was in motion, with orders to travel in two rows, or double file – We passed over a beautiful level prairie, in sight of the river Platte – our course to day is mostly in a western direction – We passed a number of beautiful lakes on our route, between us and the river – the brethren shot a number of ducks as we passed along – at 1 o'clock and 30 minutes we stopt to feed, near a bend in the River, after travelling 15 miles – while there, O. P. Rockwell, J. Redden, J. C. Little & Thomas Brown arrived from Winter Quarters, and brought a number of letters for some of the brethren, – among them were 1 for Orson and myself from mother, and 2 for me from my wife dated Saturday the 17th – at half past 2 we started on our journey and went 6 miles, and encamped in a circle, in order to have our horses and cattle, in the centre to secure them from the Indians, the guard being placed on the outside of the wagons – this evening quite cloudy – wind fresh from the south – Bro. John Higbee, and several others went down the river 2 miles with the boat and sein[e] to seek a place to fish – after being absent 2 hours, returned – they only caught 2 fish of any account – Bro. Egan sat with me this evening in my wagon writing, Orson having gone out with the fishermen. –

Tuesday the 20th.

Tolerably fair weather this morning – Blew very hard during last night – the wind in the south-west this morning – arose this morning as usual, at 5 o'clock, at the appointed signal started at 7 o'clock and 15 min. – and travelled along the Platte on pretty much the same kind of land, or extension bottom as we did yesterday, the soil being sandy – travelled in single file to-day – went 6 miles and crossed a small stream called "Shell Creek 1½ or 2 miles from its mouth – it runs S. E., and empties into the Platte River – went 4 miles further and stopt at noon to feed on the edge of a ravine or slough, where there was plenty of clear water – for ourselves and teams – Bro. Markham, John Higbee, Luke Johnson and others, went ahead of us this morning to seek a fishing-place, taking 4 wagons, (including the "Revenue Cutter," by which name the leather boat is known in the camp [)] – Started about 1 P. M., travelled on, and encamped again on the banks of the Platte River, about 4 P. M., opposite an island,

Modern photograph of the main channel of the Platte River. Courtesy of Kenneth R. Mays.

which abounded in cotton wood, of which we all cut a plentiful supply for our horses, to eat during the night; – having made about 18 miles to-day. – The River Platte is much larger than I had thought, varying from ½ to 1 mile in width but is not navigable, it being of but little depth[116] – Soon after our arrival here, this afternoon, the fishermen, who went ahead this morning, came into camp – they had been about a mile & a half above here, fishing in a lake of some extent, and had caught upwards of 200 fish, (mostly Carp,) which were distributed, this evening, among the brethren – Our course of travelling to-day, has been a little north of west – While on the route to-day, before we crossed "Shell Creek," bridge a number of the brethren went to the right, about 1½ miles, to see a village or settlement of "prairie dogs," When they returned, I saw Bro. J. Matthews pass my wagon with one attached to his saddle – Porter and others went also in pursuit of 3 deer to-day, but could not get near enough for a shot at them.

Wednesday the 21st.

Orson and myself arose punctually at the sound of the bugle, this morning at 5, and returned thanks to the Lord – the wind blowing strong from the east – rather cloudy, and has the appearance of rain – most of the ox teams started at 7 o'clock, – and some of the horse teams, soon after – We belong to Appleton Harmon's company of 10, and are included in John Pack's co. of 50 – Our wagon travels next to Bro. Pack's – We started about 10 minutes before 8 o'clock – (some part of the times to-day, we travelled in single file, and some part in double file) after going 4 or 5 miles we met a "dozen or so" of the Loup Band of Pawnee Indians, and among them was their chief, whose name is "Sisketuk"[117] – he rode a mule; the rest were on foot. They came forward, and shook hands with us, as we passed. – Went about 2 miles further, when the tire to one of Bro. K's wagons, came off, and our line of wagons halted, while it was being repaired, which occupied about 15 minutes – We then proceeded till we came parallel to the trading house of Mr. Sarpee, on the south side of the Loup Fork, (a stream which empties into the Platte about 6 miles below,) leaving it to our left about ½ mile. There is a temporary encampment of the Loup Band of Pawnees, near the trading house – we went on about a mile and stopt at 1 P. M., arranging our wagons in a semi-circle, fronting, and near to a slough, about ½ mile to the northward of the Loup

---

116. The Platte River route was one of the most traveled by pioneers heading west. The Platte River was also one of the least navigable because of its shallow, twisting, unpredictable nature. Running east from the mountains in Colorado, it flows into the Missouri River. It was named "Platte" (translates to "flat" in French) by French explorers in Nebraska. Merrill J. Mattes, *The Great Platte River Road: The Covered Wagon Mainline Via Fort Kearny to Fort Laramie (Great Plains Photography)* (Lincoln: University of Nebraska Press, 1987), 6.

117. A Plains Indian tribe, the Pawnee once numbered approximately 10,000 at the beginning of the nineteenth century. For centuries they had dominated the Platte River country in eastern Nebraska, but their numbers were decimated by disease and intertribal warfare. By 1846 their numbers had been cut in half and even fewer by 1873, when forcibly ejected from their lands for a new home in Oklahoma. Today the Pawnee number approximately 3,200 and are headquartered in Pawnee, Oklahoma.

Artist unknown, Pawnee Indians Looking Out for Enemies.

Fork, having, as Father Case said, travelled 12 miles.[118] There was a guard placed on the outside of the wagons, to prevent the horses and cattle from getting out of the enclosure, as a large number of Indians, had come from over the river, and were lurking about the camp – Pres't. Young distributed food among them, given by the brethren for that purpose; also, some salt, lead, &c.; notwithstanding, they considered that we had not given them enough. – Brother Shumway told them, (through an interpreter, a young Indian,) that we were not like the other "Pale Faces," rich, but that we were poor, and had been driven from among other white people, because of our religion, and that we believed in the "Great Spirit" like unto themselves – he told them if we had more we would cheerfully give it. Cheffelan, the "Grand Pawnee" chief was there, also "Sisketuk," the chief of the Loups – the former is quite an aged man, and to him were all the presents given by President Young, he being the main chief over the whole nation – they appeared to be fearful that we would kill or drive away their buffalo, as we passed through the country, though Bro. Shumway told them we would not – their chiefs brought a letter, from Mr. Sarpee, at the trading house, recommending them (the chiefs) as good men, and certifying to their good behavior to the white people – it

118. The decision of the Mormons to travel on the north side of the Platte River and to advance right through the Pawnee village owed much to "Father" James Case. A former employee at the government-operated farm near the Pawnee village, Case had converted to Mormonism, had spent much of the past year at the now abandoned farm and adjacent Presbyterian mission and knew the area and the Pawnee well. He also knew that his farm associates had stored a large cache of hay and provisions near the village. Thus, in addition to traveling a course not used by the California and Oregon immigrants (i.e., on the north side of the Platte River), Case made the argument that it would be better to confront the Pawnee sooner rather than later and, by providing them with ample gifts and by building on his past associations with them, ensure a relatively positive relationship between the Pawnee and the Mormons. Such a calculated gamble paid off, since the Mormons experienced very little difficulty with the Pawnee and, for that matter, with any other tribe. For an excellent study on the Pawnee Indians, see George Hyde, *The Pawnee Indians* (Norman: University of Oklahoma Press, 1951, 1974).

was addressed to President Young. We all started again about half past 2 P. M., – soon after it commenced raining, and continued about 2 hours pretty hard – the wind did not blow very hard, till the rain ceased – towards evening it veered round to the north and it became quite cool – travelled 8 miles further and encamped on the banks of the "Loup Fork," near the water's edge, about 6 o'clock P. M. Soon after our arrival the brethren were called together by Colonel Markham, who stated that, in consequence of the Indians being dissatisfied with us, he wished to call out a guard of 50 men to guard the camp during the night – Pres't. Young moved that 100 men should be called out, one half standing one half the night, and the other half, the other half the night, – Colonel Markham then called upon all those who would volunteer, to step out one side, which, was done, and they were soon arranged in companies of 10's, with a captain of each – Orson and myself are to stand the latter part of the night, J Redden being my captain – It appears considerably like rain again to night, – the heavens black and lowering – 1 company of 100 was detailed for a picket guard.

Thursday the 22d.

Orson and myself arose at 1 a.m., and he went on the picquet guard I was stationed close to the camp. – Strong north east wind and quite cold. felt rather "dumpish" this morning, both of us – Brigham & Heber both stood guard the 1st part of the night – Started this morning at 10 minutes to 8, and travelled over the most interesting part of the country I have yet seen on the route – On our right, about ½ a mile distant was a gentle, and continued elevation of ground, while close to our left, the "Looking Glass" creek, (appropriately named, on account of the transparency of its waters,) flowed gracefully by. – It was at the mouth of this creek that we encamped last night – we went on 1½ miles, and forded it, tho' the water came pretty near up to the wagon bed – travelled on without any particular incidents till we arrived about 12 M., at another stream, called "Beaver Creek," where we formed our wagons in the usual manner, and we stopt to feed our horses & cattle – It is much warmer now than it was this morning, altho' the wind is yet quite strong from the north-east – Beaver Creek runs about south from this place, tho' I do not know how far it is to the mouth I referred to my usual authority, Father Case, who told me we had travelled about 10 miles this forenoon, about half past 2 P. M. we started again on our journey – before crossing Beaver Creek, we put a couple of blocks under our wagon bed, that the water might not run in – most of the other wagons did the same, as it is quite deep – there is a very steep descent on both sides, and after we had got over, we had to pull up the hill with a rope, besides the assistance of the horses, as it was very muddy as well as steep – we went on and travelled over a beautiful country till we arrived at the missionary station 6 miles below the village, which was deserted last fall by the Pawnees, in consequence of the Sioux making an irruption among them, and burning a great share of their buildings, in fact there are but few now standing, they spared the Missionaries house – we arrived here, about ¼ to 6 o'clock P. M., and found most every convenience for encamping, that heart could desire. We found a large quantity of corn-stalks, and quite a large haystack, from which we took a quantity for our cattle and

Loup Fork Ferry. *Lithograph by Piercy,* Route from Liverpool to Great Salt Lake Valley. *Utah State Historical Society. Loup Fork was a tributary of the Platte River and served as a rendezvous place to assemble the wagons of Saints together before heading west.*

horses – the Station is beautifully situated on a small eminence, bounded on the south by the Loup Fork, which is about 1 mile distant, and on the north, east and west, by a range of hills or bluffs, from the height of which a person can command a view of the whole adjoining country, up and down the river for miles – There is also a beautiful murmuring rivulet called Plum Creek which flows by on the north side of the station, between it and the bluffs, affording as good water for drinking as I ever have seen in the country – The white people, sent here by Government, have enclosed quite a large tract of land, with a good fence, which is now standing – they being obliged to leave, when the Indians did, Missionaries & all – from the appearance of things they left in a hurry, as there are various implements of husbandry scattered around, viz: – Ploughs, harrows, carts, hay-racks, &c.– We formed our wagons in two lines, each opposite the other – Amasa, Heber, J. Pack, Bro. Shumway, & Porter, preceded us to this place on horseback, to look out a location for the night. – We came about 7 miles this afternoon, having made 17 miles to-day – Our course to-day, has been very near west – The people were called together soon after our arrival, to hear some instruction from Pres't. Young – He told them he did not want any of them to take any thing away from here, except what they brought with them, not a farthing's worth, excepting fuel, feed for their horses & cattle, &c.– He then spoke about a guard being appointed tonight – he said there should, at the least calculation, be 20 men on watch at a time, (making 40 in both watches) – he also warned the brethren about putting all their horses and cattle into the yards, where they could be better guarded, than to be scattered indiscriminately, one in <u>one</u> place, and another in <u>another</u> – He further said that if we had an attack from Indians, it would be from the <u>Sioux</u>, not the Pawnees, for the <u>latter</u> knew that the <u>former</u> were in the country and were watching them – that the Sioux when they came to make an attack, always came down a little ravine that lies north-east of us[119] – he moreover told them it was necessary that the cannon should be got out, and that they should practice the gunnery or cannonading business a little, (that is, without firing) which those appointed to that business, did, for some time this evening. The farmer's buildings where they lived are across the creek about ¼ a mile, – there the Sioux also burned a number of buildings, including a blacksmith shop – our wagon is nearly opposite the Missionaries' building – near this place we shall probably ford the "Loup Fork," and some of the brethren are going in the morning in search of a suitable fording place – It has been quite warm and sultry, the latter part of the day.

119. The commissioner of Indian Affairs reported in 1843 that there were 12,500 Pawnees and 25,000 Sioux in the eastern Platte regions. By far the Sioux were the most feared. *Report of the Commission on Indian Affairs* (28th Congress, 1st session, vol. 1, serial 431, Senate Documents), 277–78.

Charles Belder, Indian Tribe War Dance *(n.d.). Wyoming State Archives.*

FRIDAY THE 23D.

arose this morning at the usual hour. Brigham, Heber, W. Woodruff, Bro. Benson, Amasa Lyman, Luke Johnson, A. P. Rockwood, James Case, J. Redden, O. P. Rockwell, Joseph Matthews, and one or two others rode out this morning on horseback, in search of a suitable fording place on the Loup Fork – The rest of the brethren remain here in camp, except a picquet guard, who stand some distance up the ravine, spoken of above, as being the place through which the Sioux would most naturally come to make an attack – The weather remarkably warm and sultry – Orson and myself unloaded our wagon, and re-arranged the things therein, & filled our bed-tick with hay from the stack – Orson also made a seat of boards, which he found here, to put in the fore part of the wagon, to ride – The brethren in the camp mostly busy washing, repairing their wagons, &c.– The brethren who went out in search of a fording place, returned at half past 10, and the people were called together to learn the result. – The orders were, for every team to take 2 or 3 or 4 rails (in order to make a raft), into their wagons and instantly proceed on the journey – and for every 10 to travel together, horses and ox-teams – Pres't. Young told the people if they wanted any iron, &c. to purchase it of father Case, as he had not been paid up by the Government for the services he had rendered them as a farmer, while he lived here – We started at ½ past 1 P. M., travelled about 2 miles, and crossed a small creek, name unknown, – soon after we descended a small bluff, and came on to the 1st shelf of the River bottoms – here, to our right on the hill, we saw the vestiges of an old Pawnee village, burned down by the Sioux, some 4 years ago – we travelled 2 miles further, and came to the place selected for the ford, or ferrying place – Bro. Tarleton Lewis had been sent ahead to dig down the bank to the river, and to make preparations for building the raft, – however, there was nothing done to-day-about the raft – I, with some others, assisted Bro. Pack, to take his wagon over, with part of his things, – this was done by means of a rope attached to the wagon tongue, and pulled him across, with the

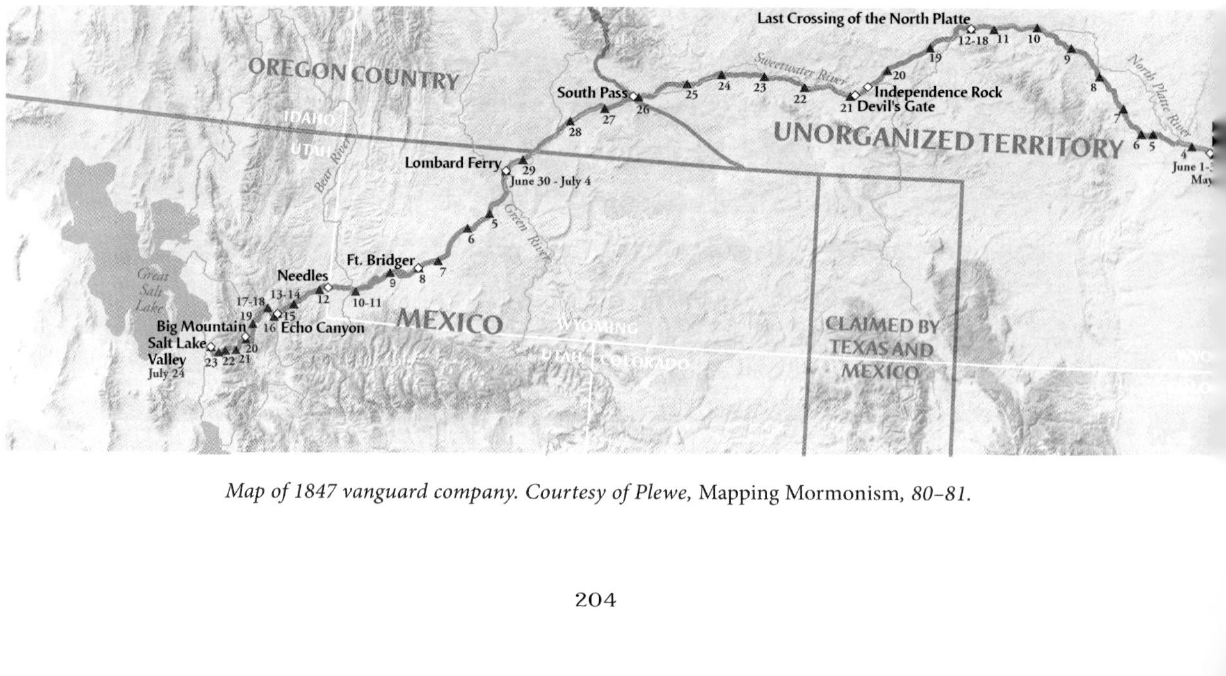

Map of 1847 vanguard company. Courtesy of Plewe, Mapping Mormonism, *80–81.*

assistance of horses – Bro. W. Woodruff and O. Pratt also got across with their carriages with some difficulty, the bed of the river being quicksand, – one or two other wagons crossed also, I believe – the remainder of us went up the hill, a little distance beyond the ford – and encamped on the banks of the river, about ½ a mile east of the Pawnee village, which was also burned by the Sioux last fall, while the former were out hunting A meeting was held this evening, and Thomas Wolsey was appointed to see to the building of 2 rafts, one for each division, to-morrow morning – On either hand as we came along to day, we discovered places where there had been patches of corn raised by the Indians – made 4 miles to-day, travelling a little south of west – a number of the brethren bought wagon tin, and other iron in different shapes of Father Case, some of which they found at the blacksmith shop, and some concealed under ground by the whites, that the Indians might not find it – do not feel very well to-night, in consequences of having waded so much in the water this afternoon to help people over – there is a very strong current, here, and in fact, almost irresistible. –

SATURDAY THE 24TH.

Very warm day, and but little air stirring – The brethren commenced crossing the river this forenoon, in different ways, some putting their effects in the leather boats, and taking their empty wagons over the river with their horses and cattle attached – The horses and cattle were driven back and forth loose in order to establish a firm track, as it was discovered that the sand packed together and formed a more substantial foundation by travelling frequently over it. Stakes were planted at intervals across the stream as a guide for the crossing – Before going over, Orson & Myself went and took a view of the ruins of the Pawnee village which was an interesting sight, indeed, and gave me singular feelings. – The village is situated on the northern bank of and immediately fronting the river – it is irregularly formed, or laid out, is 1¼ a mile in extent and comprises upwards of 200 lodges, a great share of which have been burnt down by the Sioux, as already mentioned above – We visited 2 or 3 of those

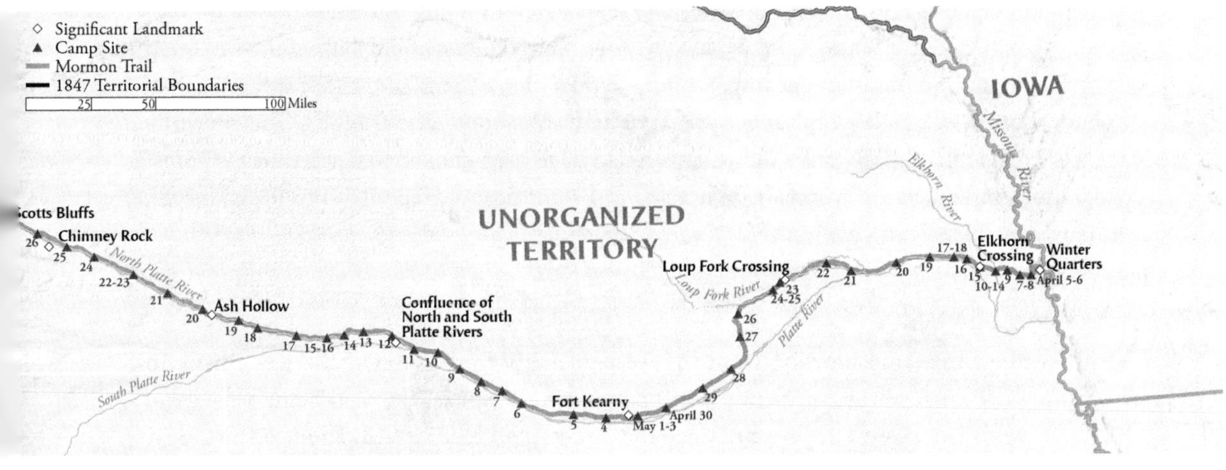

which were standing, and were much struck with the ingenuity manifested in their formation – The largest one that we visited is about 45 feet in diameter – Around the inside are 16 posts, which uphold the fabric, also 8 large ones in the center, and a man can stand upright in any part of the room – across the roof are laid transversely, cotton-wood, or willow poles, all verging towards the center – to these straw is bound with withes, and on the top of this layer of dirt a hole being left in the center of the roof through which the smoke can escape, and the fire being in the center of the lodge, perpendicular with it – around the inside the circle is a bench, formed by digging about 2 feet into the ground, and is about 2 feet in diameter. There the braves are accustomed to sit during their councils or deliberations, with their faces all turned towards the center – Immediately opposite the entrance is a seat, large enough to contain one man connected with, and projecting from the said bench – this is the seat of the chief, and leaves him in advance of his warriors. also about 2 feet – The entrance to the lodge is from 8 to 10 feet in length, and wide enough to admit 4 men abreast – The village is fortified partially, there being an embankment thrown up of about 4 feet in height, on two sides, with a ditch on the outside of that – During our visit, we discovered a number of relics portraying the manners and customs of the Indians, among which was a number of buffalo skulls, on the heads of each of which were drawn 3 or 4 lines, perpendicular done with a kind of red paint, besides other devices of different kinds – We also noticed a large number of holes, some of which were open – they were about 10 feet in depth & are used for storing away provisions, &c. These are called "Cachets" The orifice is about 2 feet across, and at the bottom, the concave is 15 feet in diameter. In there we saw vast quantities of corn which they had here stowed away, for future use. Back of the village about a mile in the bluff, is quite a large graveyard, which, however, I did not visit for want of time – We elevated our load by putting 3 or 4 rails lengthwise across the box, and putting our loading on the top thereof – we crossed the river with out accident, and reached the opposite shore, about ½ past 1 P. M. Aaron Farr assisting us over by putting his horses forward of ours, and we doing the same by him – All the camp got over by about 2 o'clock – all the rest of the wagons went on, Aaron Farr and ourselves remained on the shore, to rearrange our loads, and allow the bottom of our wagon box to dry, before we reloaded. We then went on west about 4 miles up the "Loup Fork" & found the brethren encamped on the banks thereof in a line, and fronting a small pond, about ¼ of a mile from timber – We got here sun about ½ hour high – This morning one of President Young's horses was discovered to have been choked to death during the last night, in consequence of having been hitched to a stake near a deep pit – into which he fell, and was unable to extricate himself –

Sunday the 25th.

Fair weather; the wind blowing from the west tolerably fresh – Spent the day chiefly in watching my horses, which I turned out this morning to graze, the feed being very good here, as grass has taken a fresh start since the last rain – meeting held about 6 P. M. near Brigham's wagon – did not attend, A. Farr and myself being out on the prairie watching the horses – Some arrangements were made about the guard they being enjoined to watch closely the horses and cattle that they do not break loose – It was also suggested by Pres't. Young, that each 10 form a mess of itself, and eat together, thereby saving a great deal of food, that would otherwise be wasted. Another meeting was called this evening, in order to make choice of hunters to hunt buffaloes, &c., when we should arrive where there was game – There were 7 horsemen chosen, also 9 footmen, exclusive of 8 of the "Twelve", who were also allowed the privilege of hunting, when they saw proper – Thomas Wolsey was appointed captain, he having had considerable experience in hunting buffalo This morning a number of the brethren discovered through a spy-glass, on the opposite side the river what had the appearance of 3 white antelopes grazing – an extra guard was detailed to night, to watch in the place of the regular guard, in order to give them time to rest, as every man of them has had to stand guard every other night – the watch consisted of 12 men to-night, 6 being on at a time – Orson stood the 1st watch, together with 5 others, including J. Redding, who was captain or foreman of the 1st watch. –

Monday the 26th.

This morning was awakened at daybreak by the bugle sounding an alarm for the people to gather together – it appears that 2 of the guard surprised 2 Indians in the act of coming into the camp – they were crawling stealthily along on their hands and knees, when they fired at them; immediately 4 men, making 6 in all jumped to their feet and run as fast as they could for the timber – after sunrise, the impressions of several moccasin tracks were plainly to be seen in the sand on the shore of the river – The men were all rallied, and a guard kept up till daylight – Bro. Wolsey, and others, from the shape of the track, judged it to have been caused by the moccasin of a Sioux. Fine breeze from the west, this morning – Just after sunrise, the bugle again sounded, for every 10 to meet again together in a family capacity, and have prayers – Bro. J. Pack officiated for our 10 this morning – Started this morning at 8 o'clock, travelling over a flat, and rather wet bottom for about 3 miles, when we ascended a gentle hill, which brought us on to the 2d shelf, (or table, as it is sometimes called,) of the river bottoms The land is much dryer, than on the shelf below, – we went 8 miles, and stopt to feed and water about ¼ to 12 M., near a pond of water, ½ a mile from the river – nearly opposite to us, on the other side, we discovered the traces of what had once been an Indian village, apparently, having been deserted some time since – near the site of the village were some objects which had the appearance of being graves – started again at ½ past 1 P. M., travelled about 6 miles over a beautiful rolling prairie, without the occurrence of any particular incident, and encamped, sun about an hour high, in a semi-circle on the banks of a small stream, called Grand fork on the open prairie, their being no timber in sight, except a few willows standing on the bank of the stream, which we used for fuel – Our course to-day has been a little south of west – we are about 1½ miles from the river, and have made about 14 miles to-day – about sunset, 2 horses, belonging to Dr. Richards & J. C. Little, were discovered to have strayed away from the camp, and notwithstanding 10 or 12 men went out in pursuit,

& were gone till 11 o'clock at night, they could not be found. Among those who went, were Brigham, Heber, Amasa Ezra T. Benson, O. P. Rockwell, Joseph Matthews, & 5 or 6 others – Porter & others, discovered some signs of buffalo to-day.

Tuesday the 27th.

Warm, south wind this morning – at 8 o'clock a.m., we again commenced our journey – Before starting, this morning, O. P. Rockwell, Thomas Brown, Joseph Matthews, & John Eldridge, again went out in pursuit of the lost horses – we travelled for some distance over a prairie, covered with dry grass, but at length emerged on to ground which had been burned over, and was covered with green grass, affording quite a contrast to that left behind – went about 12 miles, and stopt at 2 P. M., on the prairie, in a kind of hollow or flat bottom, surround by a gentle rise of ground – there was no water here, but the brethren dug 2 or 3 holes in the ground, which, however, did not furnish but very little for our horses & cattle – there was no timber in sight. The camp was again in motion about ½ past 3 P. M., Just as we started, John Brown, one of the appointed hunters, killed an antelope – travelled 4 miles & encamped, at ½ past 5 P. M., in a semi-circle, on the banks of a small stream, called by Brigham Patience creek, which supplied us with clear and pure water, though there was no timber of any kind; notwithstanding, we managed to cook enough for supper, by a small fire which we made from a little underbrush which we found in the vicinity – Brother Wolsey has been out hunting to-day, and saw 8 deer some distance from him, but did not go in pursuit, fearing that the Indians might cut off his retreat to the camp – Just before we arrived here, Brigham, Amasa, Col. Markham, and 1 or 2 others, rode back to hurry up the ox-teams – Just after we encamped, we had quite a gale of wind, accompanied by thunder and lightning, and some little rain, which however, did not last long – Our course to-day, (according to Professor Pratt,) has been a little east of south, having travelled about 16 miles – This evening, a horse belonging to Col. Markham, was shot by the accidental discharge of a gun – the circumstance was this: One of the brethren, John Brown, went into the wagon to get his coat, (not knowing that the gun was there,) and while pulling it out it caught the lock of the gun and went off, passing though the wagon cover the bullet took effect in the foreleg of the horse, breaking the bone literally to pieces, and rendering him entirely unfit for future use – this is the 4th horse that has been lost & killed since Saturday last – Bro. [Lewis] Barney narrowly escaped being shot at the same time, the ball passing within one foot of him, as he was going between the wagons – O. P. Rockwell, Thomas Brown, Joseph Matthews, and John Eldridge returned this evening – they had been back, within 1½ miles of the place where we encamped on Sunday, last – here, as they were riding along, they discovered something crawling along in the grass at a distance, – supposing it was a wolf, Porter was about to elevate his piece at it, when the Indian, (for such it was,) arose to his feet, with a number of others, making 15 in all – who had been hiding in the grass – they manifested an intention to take their horses, pretending to wish to shake hands, asking for tobacco, &c.– but the "boys", when they showed too much familiarity, kept them at a respectful distance, telling them to

"Pukachee", &c.– One of them came up to Bro. Matthews, and put out one hand to shake hands with him, while in the other he held a little behind him, a bow & arrow already strung for use – Thomas Brown, noticing this, and also that he kept his eye on the bridle bit of the horse, rode up to him, and in a very stern manner, told him "to leave", which he did, going off a little distance – The Indians, seeing their determination of character, did not offer to molest them, till they had got some distance, when they fired 6 shots at them, which happily took no effect, altho' "the bullets", as Bro. Matthews said, "whistled pretty close around their heads" – They convinced themselves that these Indians had the horses of which they were in pursuit, as they found the place whence the horses had been taken; from the fact that they could see the tracks, and also the trace of a rope drawn over the ground, that was attached to the neck of one of the horses – as they fired at them they continued to retreat, gradually towards a dense thicket, and here, in the opinion of the boys, were the horses concealed. They recognized two or three of the Indians, as being among those whom we saw when we stopt at noon on Wednesday last near Sarpee's trading house, thus leaving no doubt but that they were Pawnees, & not Sioux – The sky to-night, cloudless and serene notwithstanding the threatening appearance of the weather at sunset.

Wednesday the 28th.

Cool, north, wind, and somewhat cloudy, this morning – we did not start as early as usual, this morning, some of the teams being pretty well tired out from yesterday's travel – We crossed the creek on which we encamped about 9 o'clock, after first digging down the banks, and after waiting 1 hour for the remainder of the teams to cross, we started on our journey at 10 a.m., travelled nearly in a S. direction about 11 miles, and stopt to feed about ¼ past 2 P. M., about 100 yards from the Main Branch of the Platte River – opposite is an island, beyond which flows the Main channel – about the time we started this morning, Brigham, Heber, W. Woodruff, Amasa, & O. P. Rockwell, Thomas Brown Joseph Matthews, Thomas Wolsey, John Higbee, Phineas Young, & Roswell Stevens, (hunters,) went ahead on horseback – at half past 3 P. M., the camp was again in motion – travelled 4 miles further, & reached our place of encampment for the night, at 6 P. M., – We did not encamp immediately, having to wait for the ox-teams to come up, which were a mile or two back. J. Brown shot a wolf to day – the only game killed, opposite our camping ground to-night, also, is an island, the main channel flowing beyond, a small part of the stream running this side, as it was where we stopt this noon – the island is well timbered with cotton wood, and about 100 yds in front of us – after a while the ox teams came up, and we all formed our wagons in a circle, about ½ past 6 P. M., having made 15 miles to-day. – Our course this afternoon has been near west. – The last 2 or 3 days, as we passed along, we have discovered numerous buffalo skulls lying on the prairie – Just as we arrived this evening, the staple in the center of our neck-yoke broke in two, there being a flaw in the iron – Bro. J. Higbee discovered the skull of a man in a partially decayed condition about a ½ a mile back – stood on guard to-night the last watch, from 12 o'clock till daylight.

Thursday the 29th.

This morning the sun rose bright & clear – Started this morning at sunrise, before breakfast, without feeding our horses & cattle, in order to get ahead a short distance, where the grass is more luxuriant – went 2½ miles, and stopt at ½ past 6 in the road, without forming into any particular order – here we got breakfast, having taken wood along for that purpose; also, baited our horses, &c. The place is about ½ a mile from the river – saw an antelope, as we started this morning – at 10 minutes past 8, were again in motion – travelled 3 or 4 miles & crossed a stream called "Wood Creek" – travelled on over a prairie covered with dry grass, and stopt at 1 P. M. to feed, near a pond of water, ½ a mile from the river, having come 10 miles – here we again found green grass for our teams – Started again at 3 P. M., and travelled alternately over green and dry grass, (the road being very dusty, and a strong wind from the south which made it very disagreeable – went about 8 miles and encamped at sunset near the River, in a circle opposite Grand Island. This island we saw yesterday for the first time, when we stopt at noon to feed – It is said to be 75 or 80 miles in length – as near as we could judge we travelled near a south-west course to-day – Fresh buffalo tracks were discovered a little way back of here by some of the hunters. There are plenty of rushes here in the timber – made 18 miles to-day – This evening quite cool, the wind being in the north – rather cloudy, and misty overhead. –

Friday the 30th.

Clear & cold, the wind being in the north – The wagons in our 10 started at 20 minutes to 8 a.m. – went a short distance, and waited ¾ of an hour until the remainder of the teams got under weigh. Travelled over rather an uneven prairie a little south of west, and stopt at 12 M., on the banks of a clear and beautiful stream, with a gravel bottom, ½ a mile from the river – Some few deer were seen by the hunters, to-day. The grass here is of the highest and most luxuriant growth, we have yet seen – There have been 3 fresh buffalo tracks seen to-day by the hunters. – a number of them are out in pursuit of game – travelled rather slowly this forenoon, as we accommodated ourselves to the <u>pace</u> of the ox-teams, making about 8 miles – at 20 minutes to 2 P. M., we were again in motion – went 8 miles and encamped on the open prairie, a mile from the river, and still farther from timber, which was on Grand Island opposite – Bro. Pack, J. Redden & myself walked to the banks of the river for wood, but could find only 2 or 3 little sticks – Pres't. Young gave the boys the liberty of dancing a little this evening, as it was very cold, the wind being in the north – reached this place about 6 P. M. & encamped in a circle, having made 16 miles to-day. The last of the 1st bag of corn for the horses, was used this evening. The wind blew very strong from the north all night.

Saturday the 1st of May.

Cold morning; the wind still in the north – Col. Markham not being very well; the command devolved upon Major John Pack – We were ordered to go in succession this morning every

10 by itself, with its captain at its head. started at ½ past 5, went 6 miles and stopt to feed on the bank of the river at 10 minutes past 8 a.m. Sometime before we arrived here, we saw through a spy-glass 3 buffalo grazing on the top of the bluff to our right some 5 or six miles – a – 2 or 3 footmen went out in pursuit, also 3 horsemen, viz: – Porter, Thomas Brown, & Luke Johnson – Just before we arrived here, saw a large herd some distance in advance of us, also about 5 or 6 miles to our right – Bro. O. Pratt counted 74 by the aid of his spy-glass – They are now quite visible from our present stopping place – The thermometer last night stood at 41 degrees – Our course, this forenoon has been due west. Here, although we found but little wood, we managed to get breakfast – it is about 50 yds across the channel to Grand Island at this place, – travelled about 4 miles and crossed a slough or pond, which puts up from the River about 12 o'clock M. Soon after Porter, T. Brown & Luke Johnson returned – they had wounded, as they supposed mortally, 2 buffaloes, – which however managed to get away from them – about 1 o'clock P. M. we descried, at the distance of 5 or 6 miles, to our right, on the side of the hill, or bluff, 2 or 3 herds of buffaloes grazing; an immediate halt was made, a band of 10 or 12 horsemen (hunters,) speedily collected, and made arrangements for the chase. They soon got ready and started – Bro. Heber soon followed. The wagons travelled along slowly, being in full view of the chase. The horsemen took a circuitous route, in order to head the herd, but were prevented from doing so immediately by an unforeseen occurrence. – An antelope passing by near us, was shot at by one of the brethren, (a footman,) but the shot did not take effect – Directly, the animal made towards the bluff, seeing which, two dogs went off in full chase. – The 3 went right among the buffaloes,[120] which alarmed at the appearance of the dogs began to move off – Soon after the horsemen made their appearance upon the brow of the hill – Now commenced a scene which defies all description. – Every spy-glass that could be found in the camp was put into immediate requisition, and the scene became one of intense interest to us, all as spectators – as soon as the buffaloes discovered the approach of the hunters, they increased their speed, (which before had been slow,) to a full gallop and passing along the side of the hill, were followed by the hunters in quick and hot pursuit leaving a cloud of dust in their rear. – Most of the hunters by riding in among them, succeeded in getting a fair shot although they did not all prove fatal, a number of the herd making their escape that were shot through the body – Bro. Heber rode in among them, made a shot at one and brought him down His horse partly alarmed at the discharge of the gun, and partly at the sight of the animals, suddenly started, and came very near throwing him – Porter rode up to one, (by way of experiment,) & shot him full in the forehead, but without making the least impression, the hide of the skull-piece being an inch thick besides being covered with a large mass of coarse matted hair as we discovered after the animals were brought in. The chase ceased about 4 P. M., and the hunters

120. By 1847 the number of buffalo on the Great Plains stretching from what is now Saskatchewan to Texas and from the Loup Fork to the foothills of the Rocky Mountains numbered almost forty million. The rapid decline and near extermination of the buffalo occurred in the years following 1865—one of America's greatest environmental tragedies. See Frank Gilbert Roe, *The North American Buffalo: A Critical Study of the Species in Its Wild State*, 2nd ed. (Toronto: University of Toronto Press, 1951).

came up to us about 5 P. M., The fruits of the day's work were as follow: – 1 bull, 3 cows, & 6 calves – making 10 buffaloes, – Some of the hunters not yet returned, who went out on foot this morning, 5 wagons were immediately unloaded & sent out to bring in the game – we moved on, and encamped at half past 6 P. M., near a pond or slough ½ a mile from the River, with which it communicates in times of high water – made 18 miles to day, we arranged our wagons, as usual, in a semi-circular form – this place is about a mile above the head of Grand Island, which is plain to be seen from here – there is little scattering timber here, growing on the banks of the pond, but there is very little grass, as it has been grazed very closely by the buffaloes, and prairie dogs; we passed through a town or village of the latter, commencing about 5 miles back, and as far as we can yet see ahead, it continues – The brethren of the camp are, this evening, somewhat concerned about Bro. Joseph Hancock – He went out to the bluffs this morning before breakfast, and has not yet returned – a little after dark, the wagons, sent out after the game returned – and the meat distributed, ¼ of an animal being given to each 10 –

The little meetings which the sisters held twice or three times in a week, were begun in the month of May, while we had the privilege of Sisters Eliza R. Snow, Zina Young and a few others, who went with the first company that left Winter Quarters in June for the Rocky Mountains. The spirit that began to be poured out while they were with us, continued to burn in the bosoms of those who met often one with another, and the love of God flowed from heart to heart, till the wicked one seemed powerless in his efforts to get between us and the Lord, and his cruel darts, in some instances, were shorn of their sting.

At the time when numbers were laying sick with the terrible scourge that was carrying off so many of the Saints, being made easy prey for disease and death in consequence of the weakened condition to which they were reduced by long privations and exposure, and death seemed determined to lay them low, my

Emmeline B. Wells Whitney (1828–1921), journalist, editor, poet, and fifth general president of the Relief Society. Courtesy of Church History Library.

mother would go from door to door ministering food and consolation to the sick, and pouring out blessings upon them, during which time she scarcely touched food herself; at mealtimes she would only take a cup of milk, saying, when urged to eat, that she had no room for it. She seemed to grow stronger in body, and had an abundance of nurse for her babe; in blessing she was blessed, and there were others enjoying a portion of the same spirit, and by their united faith and works, with fasting and prayer, the sick were healed and made to rejoice more abundantly in the mercy of their Lord, that they were numbered among those who were to come up through much tribulation and be made white in the blood of the Lamb.

There were many great and glorious manifestations—some had visions, and by the gift of tongues there were things foretold, some of which we have seen the fulfillment of, and others that are coming swiftly upon those who have turned away and are uniting their voices and influence against that Zion which we were told should be established in these mountains, where the laws of God were to rule, and the honorable of the earth would come to dwell within its borders, because the wicked were allowed to rule elsewhere, and peace was taken from the earth, except it were in Zion, a place where righteousness would reign, and naught should molest or make afraid in all the holy mount.

Many were the things revealed by the spirit concerning the judgments that would be poured out upon the nations after they rejected the gospel, and smote and slew others of God's messengers who should be sent out to proclaim the gospel of salvation to an erring world, and the righteous would barely escape, and many of them would be called upon to lay down their lives in their struggle for the truth; also of the wars that were right at our doors, famine, pestilence, etc., and the anguish that would rend the hearts of the suffering and bereaved; that the time would be when hunger would overcome every tender feeling, and even mothers would eat their own babes. Many terrible things were so clearly portrayed to the minds of those who were present and understood as they were spoken, by the gift and power of the Spirit, that we felt to pray the Lord to close the vision of our minds.

Frequently, without eating or drinking, we would meet in the morning, either at my mother's, or some other of father's houses, and spend the day singing, praying and prophesying; occasionally some of the brethren who could leave their work united with us and received great blessings in connection with the sisters; many consoling things were spoken by the spirit concerning our brethren, the pioneers and battalion, to the truth of which they testified when they returned.

Sisters Presendia Kimball and Frances Swan Kimball, also Emmeline Whitney, now editor of the WOMAN'S EXPONENT, were gifted in the interpretation of tongues. The two former, with a few others, met at the house occupied by Sister Presendia and Laura P. Kimball, and while conversing upon some of the spiritual manifestations the same power rested down upon them, and an open vision appeared to Frances. I have not heard it related for years, but as nearly as my memory serves me, they that were there said she arose, and her countenance beamed with a brightness like unto one transfigured; her voice and language was heavenly, and grace was in every movement, as she stood there and related over scenes in the experience of some of those sisters, which were some of the most acute trials that had been their lot to pass through during their earth-lives, or while being driven from place to place in Missouri, Illinois, and at various times since they took upon themselves the name of Latter-day Saint. She seemed to be addressing one or more personages, who recorded each one's story as they were told them, only one entering their presence at a time, Frances being voice for them, as well as for the personage, who, in return, addressed them with a look of approval, and with a countenance beaming with joy and satisfaction, they were welcomed, and a bright crown of glory was placed on each one's head, attended with words suitable to their station and the occasion. Sister Frances had known little or nothing of their previous experience, and had never heard the incidents related, but she described them as accurately as if told by themselves.

I heard the vision related, but Sister Presendia could do it more justice, no doubt, as she witnessed the whole, and at best I have retained but a faint remembrance of it, not having been present at that meeting.

Woman's Exponent, vol. 14, no. 13,
1 December 1885, p. 98

Sunday the 2d.

Clear and cold – the wind yet in the north. severe frost last night. During last night a buffalo calf was shot in the leg by one of the guard, and caught by a negro in the camp[121] – it had probably smelt, & followed up the wagons, that went out after the game – It was killed this morning –We were all very glad to see Bro. Hancock make his appearance this morning, as we had about given him up, thinking that he had been taken by the Sioux Indians, who are supposed to be not a great way off – He had killed a buffalo cow, (a small piece of which he brought in with him,) and had sat up all night to guard it – He saw 3 wolves, (one of which he shot,) which attracted by the smelling of the meat, came up near his fire. Thus, 12 buffaloes were killed, by the hands of inexperienced hunters, and it seemed as if the Lord assisted us by his almighty hand, for there was a number of brethren who were entirely destitute of meat, &c.– The remainder of the meat, this morning, was divided into 14 parcels, one to each 10. The brethren are principally engaged in cutting halters out of buffalo hides, drying or <u>curing</u> their meat, or guarding the cattle & horses, which are suffered to <u>run loose</u>, one being selected out of each 10 for that purpose,– Brigham, Heber, Amasa, Bro. Benson, Luke Johnson, O. P. Rockwell, H. Egan, J. Matthews, John Brown, Phineas Young & Lorenzo Young started about 1 P. M., in quest of a more suitable camping-ground, where the grass is more plenty for our stock – they returned in about 2 hours, having found a place – we all started at ¼ past 4 P. M. – travelled about 2 miles & encamped at 5 minutes past 5 P. M. on the banks of a slough, or pond (which <u>puts up</u> from the River,) about 400 yds. from the same – Before we started one or two of the brethren went out with Bro. Hancock after the buffalo he killed and left behind – they found it, but it was so mangled by the wolves that they only got part of it – The air quite chilly this evening – not much wind stirring – 2 antelope were

121. The "negro" mentioned here was either Green Flake, Oscar Crosby, or Hark Lay. These three black slaves from Mississippi had joined the vanguard company in Winter Quarters. Approximately eighty enslaved blacks and thirty free blacks migrated to Utah by 1850. Reeve, *Religion of a Different Color*, 143.

killed by the brethren, while they were out after the buffalo. We found the grass here some what more plenty than at the place we left – it is called buffalo grass, being a mixture of dry & green, & the cattle eat it quite greedily – Our wagons are formed, as usual, in a semi-circle – we brought a little wood along with us, as there is no timber of any kind about the place – The river at this point is nearly 2 miles wide. –

Monday the 3d.

Somewhat cloudy this morning – the wind in the south-west – we have noticed for a day or two back, large fires ahead of us, and suppose it to be caused by the Indians. – This morning, at ½ past 9 o'clock, a band of 20 hunters went out on foot in pursuit of buffaloes. – It is the intention to remain in our present encampment to-day, to give the hunters a chance to kill what game they can – 15 men also started up the river to find out a good track for us to pursue when we shall start again – They started about 10 o'clock a.m., and returned at 2 P. M. – They had been about 12 miles – Bro. Wm. [William] Empy, as they were travelling along, saw a number of antelope and pursued them – he was about a mile in advance of the remainder of the brethren, when, ascending a hill, he saw in the valley beneath, between 2 & 300 Indians – He judged from their appearance & situation, that they are aware of the vicinity of our camp, and are there awaiting our approach – The others saw the Indians afterwards, – in all probability, they are Sioux – they have put fire to the prairie, in almost every direction – Bro. Benson and E. [Erastus] Snow were at the head of the expedition – as soon as they came in, orders were given to have all the horses brought in, & for 20 horsemen to go in pursuit of the hunters, in order to have them return immediately, peradventure, we might need their assistance if we should be attacked – a few drops of rain fell this afternoon – Orson went, as one of the horsemen after the hunters – they started about 3 P. M. – there were 23 in all. Some of the hunters got in at ½ past 4 P. M., – and the last of them not until dark – They had separated, and hunted in parties, so that only a part of them saw the men who were sent out after them – The latter came in about sunset. – The hunting party brought in 3 antelope, the others 2 buffalo calves, one of which Orson & John Y. Green killed. –

Tuesday the 4th.

Warm and pleasant, the wind being in the south-west – The brethren of the camp were called together this morning for the purpose of hearing some instruction from Pres't Young. It was in substance as follows: – That each member of this camp should seek for the others' interests, as much as if they belonged to the same family, and this is the way we have all got to feel, & it is the way the whole world have got to feel, who are saved in the kingdom of God. – That, in case that the right or left wing of our camp should be attacked, all the people would huddle to that particular point, & leave other parts unguarded, not understanding the regulations of the camp; therefore every 10, in case of an alarm, should gather immediately around its own captain – That the captain of each 10 should drill his company as often as circumstances & opportunity would permit. – By request of Pres't. Young, the rules

& regulations adopted some time ago, were read by Bro. Bullock, the clerk of the camp, & a vote taken to ascertain if the brethren would conform to, and abide by the same, which was unanimous in the affirmative. – Col. Markham called for 10 volunteers, to constitute an addition to the guard, which were soon made up, making 60 men in all. – We started about 9 a.m., went a little way & stopt to organize the companies in the order of travelling for the day – We started again at 11 a.m., 5 wagons constituting each 10, travelling abreast – went about 2 miles, & met a trader from Fort Laramie – he had come over the river to see us, leaving 8 of his companions on the other side – We all stopt our wagons in the road, and almost all the men in the camp wrote letters back to their friends to send by the trader, who gave his name as Charles Barkman – Orson wrote a few lines to "A. M. W.", which he enclosed in a letter I wrote to my wife – They were bound to Weston, a place near Ft. Leavenworth, & from thence the trader promised to forward the letters to Mr. Sarpee at the Point, who would, in turn, forward them to our friends at Winter Quarters. – I wrote in a great hurry, as the trader was very impatient to depart & rejoin his comrades.[122] The brethren gave him near a bag-full of bread, &c.– & he sold Bro. Philo Johnson a buffalo robe for 1½ lbs. coffee. When he went back over the river, Bro. Pack, T. Wolsey, & John Brown accompanied him on horseback to see the capt. of the company about the transfer of the letters, & also to make some enquiries about the road – after a detention of about ½ hour, we went on & stopt to feed about 4 P. M. forming in a circle – Here Col. Markham called the companies together to drill them, which occupied about ½ hour – While here Bro. Pack, Wolsey, & Brown returned & made report of what they had seen & heard – They (the traders,) advised us to cross the river here, as there was plenty of grass for our cattle, & innumerable herds of buffalo that side, whereas, this side the river, we would find the prairie all burnt in every direction, besides, when we get to Fort John we would be obliged to ferry over the "North Fork" of the Platte River. A vote was taken whether we should travel this side or not, which passed in the affirmative, as it was judged best to make a track of our own, for the brethren, coming on hereafter to follow. – We started again, sun about an hour high, travelled in single file till a little after sunset, & encamped on a running stream, about ¼ mile from the river – Bro. K named it Buffalo creek, from the fact of his seeing a large herd of buffalo about a mile ahead, just as we arrived at this place – We have formed our wagons in a semicircle on a plot of dry grass of about 5 acres, the rest of the prairie being burnt for miles all around – In fact to-day we have passed over nothing but burnt prairie. The wind to-day has been chiefly from the south – Our course has been near south west, having come 9 miles Forgot to mention that the cannon was fired last evening &

122. "I have to write (as you can discern) as fast as I can hurry may [my] hand over the paper," Horace scribbled in one of the few letters he wrote to Helen Mar while traveling west, "because the man is waiting to take the letters back. . . . We are now, according to my reckoning, 240 miles from Winter Quarters. . . . I feel in my heart that we shall see each other again, in the Lord's own due time. . . . I pray for you night and morning regularly . . . in your approaching trial [childbirth]. . . . The country where we now are is infested with Sioux Indians, and it would be dangerous to send back a single messenger . . . Farewell my dear wife for the man is just starting. I remain as ever your affection [*sic*] husband, H. K. Whitney." Helen Mar Kimball Whitney Papers, MSS 179, Special Collections and Archives, Merrill-Cazier Library, Utah State University, Logan, Utah.

this morning, to apprise the Indians that we were prepared for them, if they should meditate an attack upon us. –

Wednesday the 5th.

Clear day – strong wind from the south west – we started this morning about 10 minutes before 7, crossed the creek on which we encamped, & travelled over a flat, marshy bottom, which had been burned entirely over, except here & there small patches of dry grass – at half past 11 we halted to feed, near a kind of marsh, which furnished us with water for our horses & cattle having come 9 miles – after remaining here 1½ hours, we moved on. – We were considerably annoyed with dust & ashes to-day, as we passed along, the ground having recently burned over – Travelled about 5½ miles further, & came to fire – it being immediately in front of us on our route, & the wind blowing very strong it was thought best to go no further; so we retraced our steps about ½ a mile, & encamped in a circle on the bank of the river, opposite an island, on which we found a few scattering cotton-wood trees. It is only 2 or 3 rods across to the island, so we took our horses over to give them browse – The river at this place is near 2 miles in width – On the opposite side is a high range of bluffs, not far from the river, which appear to be covered with green grass – a large herd of buffaloes was seen there this evening. – We reached this place & encamped about 5 P. M. – Just before we arrived, John Brown, Luke Johnson, Amasa Lyman, & Jack Redden each killed a buffalo calf – Joseph Matthews killed a buffalo cow – Bro. K., Porter, and John Higbee, pursued a calf which they took alive & brought into camp, uninjured, except being a little lame in one leg – It was killed this evening. 4 horsemen, & 3 men in the Revenue Cutter started to bring in the game, which amounted to 6 calves & 1 cow, including the one captured alive – We have pursued a due west course to-day, having come 14 miles – The men brought in the game about sunset – The captains of 10s were called upon this evening to go & get their share of the meat. –

Thursday the 6th.

Clear weather fresh breeze from the south-west – the sun arose cloudless & beautiful – we had quite a shower of rain during last night, which seemed quite providential for us, as it extinguished the fire on the prairie, which, when we retired to bed, was brightly burning. – We started this morning about ½ past 5 o'clock, before breakfast, in order to get to a place where we could find grass for our stock – We went 2 miles and halted, having come about ½ a mile beyond the place where the prairie was burning last night, before the rain fell – As we passed along, we saw 3 herds of buffaloes to the right about 3 miles. – we also saw a number of antelope on our route this morning. – Soon after we saw the antelope, the dogs frightened a hare, that had been laying in the grass, which immediately bounded off at full speed – This is the first one I ever saw, & Pres't. Young said it was the first one he had ever seen in this country – Bro. Roswell Stevens shot an antelope as he was running, just as we arrived. We are about ¼ a mile from the river – we brought our wood along with us, as there is none near this place – here we got breakfast – Moved on again at ¼ to 9 a.m., went 2 miles & saw

Artist unknown, Buffalo on the March. *Herds of stampeding buffalo could number in the tens of thousands and could be heard from miles away. Woe to the traveler who got in their way.*

the largest herd of buffaloes we have yet seen on our route – they were only ¾ of a mile to the right of us – here we also saw the first drove of elk, on the journey. – Porter shot at one of the latter before the wagons came up, but missed him – Jack Redden shot an antelope as 2 were passing within 15 or 20 rods of our wagons – being headed & driven towards us from the River by Luke Johnson – they were going as fast as they could run, one a little behind the other, – the former was killed instantly, being shot through near the back-bone – the latter escaped, notwithstanding several shots were fired at him – halted to feed at ¼ to 12, having come 6 miles, – we are now ¼ of a mile from the River. Just before we arrived, Luke Johnson caught a small buffalo calf alive – By the advice of Pres't. Young it was set free. This noon Col. Markham called the members of the 6th 10 of the Night Guard together, in order for them to choose a captain & be organized, ready to go on duty to-night – travelled near a west course this forenoon – We were in motion again, about 1½ P. M., saw numerous herds of buffalo on both sides of the river, & in fact, we were in sight of them all day, travelled on, at pretty good speed, without much stopping, and encamped on the banks of the river, opposite an island, in a circle, about 6½ P. M., – the river here & all the way we have come to-day, is interspersed with numerous groups of islands, of different sizes – we have made 15 miles to-day. – Just before we arrived, 4 buffaloes, which had been down to the river to drink, came directly across our path, 20 or 30 rods ahead of the foremost wagon – still a little further on, we came across one lying down in a ravine, which was so poor it could not run – it was a cow – we left it uninjured, as also, all others that we saw to-day, as the orders are, not to slay any more till permission is given by the authorities of the church – Bro. K., with some others, has been ahead on horseback, & reports that the grass is grazed close to the ground by the buffalo, thus affording but little chance for our cattle, &c.– This evening we can scarcely turn our eyes in any direction on either side of the river, but that we can see herds of buffalo, & ahead of us a mile or so, the plain is perfectly black with them. The sun set clear in the west, this evening, & it has every appearance of being fair weather – not much air stirring The river at this place, inclines to the north-west, & our course this afternoon, has been about west, northwest – at noon to-day, whilst we halted to feed, Pres't. Young lost his new spy-glass, which came from England – he thinks he lost it out of his pocket, while himself & Heber C. were out driving in some of the cattle, that were following off a herd of buffalo – The river is about a mile in width here –

On the morning of May 6th I was delivered of a beautiful and healthy girl baby, which died at birth. Thus the only bright star, to which my doting heart had clung, was snatched away, and, though it seemed a needless bereavement, and most cruel in the eyes of all who beheld it, their sympathies were such that, by their united faith and prayers, they seemed to buoy me up to that degree that death was shorn of its sting, till I could say, "Thy will, not mine, be done." Three weeks of suffering followed, when I was dressed one day, but I took cold and was again prostrated, and lay in a critical state for another three weeks, a part of that time in a cold clammy sweat, until everything on me was as wet as though it had been drenched in cold water, and death seemed determined to claim me, but I was saved for a purpose. Before I was able to sit up, the scurvy laid hold of me, commencing at the tips of the fingers of my left hand with black streaks running up the nails, with inflammation and the most intense pain, and which increased till it had reached my shoulder. Poultices of scraped potato, the best thing, it was considered, to subdue the inflammation; it would turn black as soon as applied, and for all they were changed every few minutes for fresh ones, it was all to no effect. By this time I had lost all faith, and patience, too, and, with a feeling of desperation, I arose, and, taking the wrap and everything with it, I threw it with such force that it went into the fireplace on the opposite side of the room, saying, "There you can stay, for I will never do another thing for it!" and to my great surprise I had no occasion to, as the pain and disease had left me, and from that moment I felt no more of it. Still there were other obstacles in the way of my full recovery; though I was free from pain, I remained in a feeble state for some time, so that I had to lie down a goodly portion of the time.

Woman's Exponent, vol. 14, no. 10,
15 October 1885, p. 78

Friday the 7th.

The air, this morning, keen & cold, the wind being in the north-west – It was concluded not to start early this morning, as a number of the teams are pretty near exhausted with yesterday's travel – Saw an object moving across the river this morning, which, on examination with a spy-glass, proved to be an elk. –The brethren were called together this morning, to hear some instruction from Pres't. Young: he stated, that he wished that some of the brethren, who had spare horses would raise one or two to draw the cannon – that he supposed, when they left Winter Quarters, that it was furnished with a team; but behold, when they had got out here, a long way from home, the men, who had given the horses for that purpose, wished to take them away for their own use – that his own horses were completely tired out in drawing it, & he thought it not more than right that others should step forward & assist – that he wanted a man to drive the team, who would not permit 8 or 10 men & boys to ride on the cannon, that being the case, he thought two horses could easily draw it. Bro. Roswell Stevens furnished one for the day, to put along side of one they already had. – Pres't. Young slightly reproved Bro. Erastus Snow, (who had charge of the cow-herd yesterday) for neglect of duty – the latter retorted, in no very measured terms, when the President proved

Orson Pratt (1811–81), apostle, scientist, and Mormon theologian. Lithograph by Piercy, Route from Liverpool to Great Salt Lake Valley. *Courtesy of Church History Library.*

by a number of individuals, that he was absent from, when he should have been present with, the herd – Notwithstanding, Erastus continued to excuse himself; but Pres't. Yong rebuked him very sharply, telling him that if he had been only a year or two in the church, he would be excusable; but, as he had been for a number of years therein, he ought to know better than to give way to a rebellious spirit; for he had seen a number of men go to the Devil from the same cause, like unto Warren Parrish & Sylvester Smith, who apostatized at Kirtland, several years ago – a vote was taken, that all those, who believed Bro. Snow was in the way of his duty yesterday, should say "Yes" – contrary, "No" – It was unanimous in the negative.[123] – Pres't Young advised that, in travelling, every captain should remain with his company of 10, or, if he left, to appoint a man to act in his place – that it was his mind that no more game should be killed, either antelope, buffalo, or any thing else, "for," said he, "my opinion is, that if we do slay when we do not need, we will need when we cannot slay." – He further said, that men & boys should not, out of mere bravadoe, venture near a herd of buffalo, for some time or other they would get injured or nearly killed by them, & then they would begin to take the hint, & wish they had obeyed counsel, & kept away – I stood guard this morning on the outside of the camp, to prevent the horses & cattle from straying away. – We started on our journey, about 11 a.m., travelled in a north-west direction, about 7 miles & encamped at 3 P. M. in a circle on the bank of the river opposite an island – here we found the grass quite plenty, compared with that of the place we left to-day – Thomas Brown & Porter went back this morning to our noon stopping-place of yesterday in search of Pres't. Young's spyglass; they returned this evening, having been successful – As usual, we saw numerous herds of buffalo to-day on our route – A large number of them coming from the river whither they had been

123. To Brigham Young's way of thinking, the Latter-day Saint pioneers would find their place if they followed their God. Remembering well his participation in the 1834 "Zion's Camp" expedition that marched from Kirtland, Ohio, to near Independence, Missouri, which ended in the death of several men through disease and lack of preparation, Brigham Young was constantly concerned with the behavior of those in the "Camp of Israel." In his revelation back at Winter Quarters in January entitled "The Word and Will of the Lord," Brigham Young made it very clear to his people that unless they kept the commandments, "judgments would come upon them" and "your faith fail you and your enemies triumph over you" (D&C 136:42). To Young, the Mormon exodus was more a trial of faith than only a trail to follow. And as for why Erastus Snow was so roundly rebuked, he had lost Brigham Young's spyglass without owning up to it as Brigham Young felt he should have done earlier.

to drink, crossed our track this afternoon, not far ahead of the foremost wagon – a young calf, belonging to the number, got tired, & laid down in the grass – Bro.[Francis] Pomeroy caught it, but let it go again. – They do not seem to be much frightened at our appearance, as they will allow us to come within a few rods of them without running away – In fine, they are getting to be quite troublesome, as our cattle, smelling them at some distance will follow them off – The weather continued cold through the day – a few drops of rain fell this afternoon, after we had arrived at this place – This evening the companies were all called out for drill exercise, & were inspected by Col. Rockwood, the aide-de-camp of the Lieut. Gen., as the latter was not present. –

Saturday the 8th

Fine, clear day, the sun shining brightly in the heavens – I stood on guard an hour this morning in Orson's place, to prevent the cattle & horses from straying off – Started at 9 o'clock a.m., travelled along In sight of the Platte River, over rather an uneven, barren country – seeing on our route, as usual, numerous herds of buffalo, on both sides of the River – stopt at 1 P. M., on the banks thereof to feed & water, leaving our wagons in the road, as they were arranged in the order of travelling – the weather this forenoon quite warm & sultry, there being but little air stirring – Porter shot a buffalo heifer just before we stopt – a few minutes after we arrived here, a number of buffalo came quite near to our wagons – Amasa Lyman made a shot at one of them, but it did not take effect – we came about 7 miles this forenoon – The grass is grazed close to the ground over which we have travelled to day, &, in fact it resembles a barn or cow-yard, more than any thing else – Started again at ½ past 4, having been detained here longer than we expected, on account of 2 horses straying away among the herd of buffalo – the brethren who went out in pursuit, had to follow them 2 or 3 miles at full speed, before they could recover them travelled 4¼ miles, & encamped at 6 P. M., in a semi-circle, on the bank of the river having pursued a N. W. course most of the day – Bro. Clayton ascertained the distance we had travelled to-day, by counting the revolutions of the hind wheel of the wagon in which he rode – this he done by means of driving a nail into one of the spokes, which would strike a saw that projected from the wagon bed at every revolution of the wheel, which he first ascertained to be 14 feet & 8 inches in circumference, The plain or bottom, over which we have hitherto been travelling, terminates abruptly in a high range of bluffs, about a ¼ of a mile in advance of our camping-place, & these we have to ascend, before proceeding further – as, according to what Bro. K. says, who has been ahead, 1½ miles they stop immediately to the water's edge – The ground here, like that over which we have travelled to-day, is nearly devoid of grass – there being no wood in the vicinity, we were obliged to use buffalo <u>excrement</u> instead as <u>fuel</u> – slight, cool breeze from the south-east, 2 buffalo calves killed this afternoon – one of them was shot by Thomas Brown, the other was caught by T. Pomeroy – nothing else of importance to-day –

Sunday the 9th.

Strong wind from the south-east. Started at 10 minutes to 8 a.m., travelled over a rugged sandy road, along under the bluffs, which come near to the water – went 3½ miles & encamped in a semi-circle at 10 minutes past 10 a.m. – I took my horses to the island opposite, & cut down cotton-wood trees for them as the ground here is also barren of grass – Orson & myself partially unloaded our wagon, to shake the clothes, &c. as every thing very dusty, & also to get at our clean clothes, as we have not changed for 2 weeks or more – The bluffs here are perfect masses of sand, and bear the appearance of having been thrown, or helaped [*sic*] up by the wind, being of different, & irregular forms & sizes – a meeting was held this afternoon. – Bros. Amasa Lyman, Wilford Woodruff, Ezra T. Benson, O. Pratt & Erastus Snow spoke at some length – The latter made an apology for being so hasty & impetuous in his expressions on Friday morning last – I did not attend meeting, having other business – taking care of the horses, &c. Pres't. Young Heber, W. Woodruff, Amasa Lyman, E. T. Benson, Porter, & a number of others went ahead on horseback some distance this afternoon to look out a track, view the face of the country, &c.– They returned about sunset, & reported it to be pretty much as it has been for a few days back – that is, quite barren. This evening Bro. Wm. Clayton planted a guide-post in the ground, ¼ of a mile in advance of our camping ground place, which announced the distance from thence to Winter Quarters, to be 300 miles according to his reckoning – by mine it is 297 miles – the wind having veered round to the north it is quite cool this evening.[124]

Monday the 10th.

Somewhat cloudy this morning, though it cleared off towards noon, & became quite warm. Started at 9 a.m., went about 2 miles & crossed a small creek, called by Bro. K. Skunk creek which flows with considerable rapidity – Travelled till 12 M., over a sandy, wet bottom, & stopt to feed, near a kind of marsh, about ¼ of a mile from the River, having come a few rods over 6 miles – The grass here is coarse, rank, & dry – Porter & Thomas Brown went out in pursuit of a wild horse this forenoon, & have not yet returned – Bro. Joseph Hancock killed a fine buffalo heifer just before we arrived at the creek above mentioned – This morning, before starting, the Twelve, (or a portion of them,) planted a guide-post in the ground, at the camping-place – on one side of the board was written the following inscription – "Look in this – 316 miles from Winter Quarters – Camp of Pioneers, bound Westward – May 10, 1847." – On the other side was written, – "Look in this, & you will find a letter" – We started again at 2 o'clock P. M., – "O. P. R." & Thomas Brown soon after overtook us – they had been unsuccessful in their pursuit of the wild horse – they followed him to the bluffs, after ascending which they lost sight of him – it is supposed to be one lost by some band of emigrants going westward – passed over pretty much the same kind of ground we did

124. While such guideposts were not exclusive to the Mormon pioneers, the vanguard company of Latter-day Saints used them as an essential form of communication to the advancing companies in the rear.

Mormon Train in Camp. Lassoing the steers preparatory to yoking up for a start. *Utah State Historical Society.*

this forenoon – travelled 3¾ miles & encamped in a semi-circle on the banks of the river, opposite an island which affords abundance of cotton-wood – the grass here has taken quite a start, as it has probably not been visited by the buffalo for a week or more – Bros. P. Young & J. Hancock shot a deer near here this evening – We made 9¾ miles to-day, Bro. Amasa Lyman shot a hare to-day – We have seen but few buffalo to-day, & consequently have hopes that the grass will be better after we get a little farther along – We think that the vast herds of buffalo, we have been accustomed to see daily for some time back, are gradually retiring to the eastward. On the island opposite I discovered a number of small pine trees or shrubs – Capt. A. Harmon is busily engaged in constructing an apparatus, by which we can ascertain the number of miles we travel each day – It is to be found by means of a wheel with 60 cogs, a screw, &c., & is to be attached to the side of the wagon in which Wm. Clayton rides, communicating with the hind wheel of the same – travelled near a North-west course to-day – The sky this evening serene and cloudless – there being a slight breeze from the south-east The place we left this morning, (according to Prof. Pratt,) is in latitude north 41 degrees.

Tuesday the 11th.

Fine, clear morning, the wind being in the south-east. – I took my horses this morning to a marsh in the rear of the camp about ½ a mile, on the margin of which the grass is quite green & luxuriant. – A number of the brethren went out about ¼ of a mile, & dug into a hole, near which one of the brethren had shot at a wolf this morning: after digging about 15 minutes, they found 4 young wolves, which they brought alive into the camp – they afterwards killed them. – We are now, from all accounts, not far from the junction of the North & South Forks of the Platte River. – The bluffs ahead, on both sides of the river, judging from their appearance at a distance, make a gradual curve, & approach each other from the north & south, – At ½ past 9 a.m., we recommenced our journey – I saw no buffalo to-day, although there were numerous vestiges of their having been here within a week or two – we travelled in a north-west direction, as usual, over a sandy, wet bottom halting on our route a few minutes on the banks of the river to water our horses & cattle, & encamped at 3 P. M., in a circle, about ½ a mile beyond a small running stream which we forded & about the same distance from the river, on the banks of which is the nearest timber. Soon after we arrived, I went back to the creek, to try my luck at fishing, & returned in about an hour without any success, as there were but few fish in the stream, and those very small. Bro. James Davenport, the blacksmith in our Division, put up his forge this afternoon, near my wagon, in order to make some repairs for the brethren. – Orson mended one of our wagon-bows, which was broken the other day – the air is quite chilly, the wind being still strong from the south-east – made 8½ miles to day. – The grass here is quite fresh & good, compared with what it has been where we have lately travelled, & we have hopes that we will find it still better, as we progress on our journey – I do not know of any game having been killed to-day, except a hare that was shot by Bro. Roswell Stevens this afternoon, near this place, just before we arrived. – some of the brethren dug a well, which supplies us with good drinking water – this is very convenient, as otherwise we would be obliged to go to the creek ½ a mile distant – Bro. Heber came to me this evening & invited me to take a walk with him – we went out about a ¼ of a mile, on the prairie, where we remained near ½ an hour in conversation on different matters, – past, present, & future – Among other things he spoke of the anxiety he had for our friends whom we have left behind in Winter Quarters, & in particular of the affection he had for his wife Vilate & all his family – also of the great friendship he cherished towards our family – that he verily believed, he had the prayers of father & mother for his welfare – he spoke in the highest terms of Vilate & Sarah Ann, praising them for their steadfastness integrity, and uprightness in sustaining him, whenever he felt weighed down with care & perplexity – He gave me a great deal of good advice – said he hoped that I would continue to dignify myself and become a mighty man of honor before God & all men that the "steps" that I had taken should redound more to my honor & glory, than if they had been taken "for time and all eternity", as I was in a manner, acting for a number of persons, viz: – Joseph, father, himself & myself, inasmuch as the former had promised that our two families should dwell near him in the eternal world. – That he hoped no discord would arise between our two families, as we were bound by double ties, & he did not wish them ever to be severed.[125] – He then

125. In this remarkable prairie conversation between Heber C. Kimball and Horace Whitney, Heber refers to how the two families were doubly connected both biologically and spiritually one to another as well as sealed in marriage to the Prophet Joseph Smith. No doubt this has reference to Joseph Smith's sealing for eternity to Horace's sister Sarah Ann as well as to his wife Helen Mar, Heber C's marriage for time to Sarah

spoke of the prospects ahead – that in about 2 months he thought we would reach our place of destination – that he had never thought of getting there in time to raise a spring crop, but would, in all probability in time to plant turnip seed, make gardens, build a few houses &c. & for those who went back to return in the fall – he would like to have Orson & myself build a house, so that in case father should send on any of his family this season, they might have a home & a shelter – After talking some few minutes longer, he proposed that we should pray – We accordingly knelt down, & he made a beautiful prayer, which, for a sincerity & depth of feeling cannot be surpassed – he manifested so much paternal feeling towards his family, in the desires that he offered up before the Lord for their happiness & welfare, that, if they could have heard him, they would have been immediately banished by the conviction that they lay closely entwined around his heart – he prayed for father & mother, for my wife, and finally for the saints in Winter Quarters, & throughout all the world – that the Twelve might have wisdom to guide this people aright even in the present undertaking, that we might be enabled, through the assistance & guidance of the Lord, to reach a land where we could build & inhabit, plant vineyards & eat the fruit thereof, & have a place to set our feet "where there would be none to molest, nor make afraid." – After he had closed, he asked me if I wished to pray? – which I did, & we arose and retraced our steps to the camp, after having enjoyed one of the happiest, (& apparently the briefest) meetings that I have experienced in a long time. – Bro. Heber, almost daily is accustomed to go ahead on horseback, & survey the track look out good camping places for the night, &c.– Sometimes he is attended by a few of the hunters, at other times almost unattended – I neglected to mention that Prof. Pratt took an observation to-day noon, & ascertained us to be in latitude 41 deg; 7 min; & 44 sec. north – at this place. –

We never dreamed, when commencing those little prayer meetings—coming together so frequently and enjoying the outpourings of the Holy Spirit—of having to meet and contend with the opposite; but so it was. The love and union that prevailed seemed to enrage the evil one, and, not being able to cause a division among us, he vented his wrath upon the little ones.

At one of the meetings which I attended at Sister Presendia's, there was a powerful manifestation of the Holy Spirit, and many comforting words were uttered, and prophecies of blessings which it was our privilege to obtain, if we would unite in fasting and prayer.

Previous to this the merchants, Davis and Kimball, who rented one of my mother's rooms, having sold out their stock, had gone back to Nauvoo, and her house was the place appointed by the voice of the Spirit to hold the fast meeting, and the great blessing to be gained thereby was the administration of an angel or angels. I had a promise that day that I should be healed by the power of God. Up to this time I had remained feeble and unable to sit up but little, or to walk to a neighbor's without having to lie down, and this I desired more than anything else of a temporal nature. In obedience to that spirit Mother Whitney, her daughter, Sarah Ann, Sisters Louisa [Laura] Pitkin, Presendia Buel, Sarah Lawrence, Frances Swan, Harriet Sanders, Persis

Ann and the recent birth of their child, and the fact that the Whitney family was spiritually adopted to apostle Heber C. Kimball and his family.

Persis Goodall Young (1806–94), woman of faith. Courtesy of Church History Library.

Young and two or three others who were there, all being my father's wives but Sister Persis and Mother Whitney, met the next morning without eating or drinking. But no sooner had we begun to offer up our united prayers than the devil commenced his operations on the three little ones that were there, mother's Brigham and her little babe, and Sarah Ann's son, who was born on the journey from Nauvoo. It would be one and then the other. The eldest was playing in the room adjoining, and without any known cause, he commenced screaming; floundering and going into the most frightful contortions, which obliged us to stop and administer to him and rebuke that spirit in the name of Jesus, when the child quieted down and went to sleep. We had no sooner begun again to seek in prayer for the promised blessing, than we were again interrupted by my mother's babe screaming, and it had lain sleeping peacefully till then. He was operated upon in a similar manner to the other, so we were under the necessity of again stopping to administer to him, when he was immediately relieved, and went to sleep. But just as soon as we commenced again to struggle for the blessing that had been promised, the third one was seized, and this continued through the day, and every time the evil spirits were rebuked by the power of the priesthood, which had been conferred upon us in the house of God in connection with our husbands. This only stimulated us to persevere, and that wrestle continued between the two powers, each seeking the supremacy, till finally we became satisfied that we would have to part with one of those little ones before we could obtain the coveted blessing. Therefore, when the day was nearly spent, and we had witnessed the workings of the two powers—one just in proportion to the other—the mothers concluded to call Bishop Whitney and relate this day's experience and leave the decision with him, whether or not we had been directed by the right spirit. We broke our fast, and the bishop came about dusk and spent the best portion of the night in answering questions and explaining doctrines and things which the sisters had never before understood. He had previously expressed some fears that the sisters might be out of the way, seeing them meet together so often, but he changed his mind, for he was filled with the Holy Spirit the moment he entered the house. His mind was clear and like a fountain, and we only had to ask and receive, for our faith was such that it would take no denial. He told us that we were nearer obtaining what we had sought for, and the Lord was nearer than we had any idea of, and that our desires would have been realized had we given up one of those children. He said it was only through similar struggles that any great manifestations from on high were ever obtained. There were things that he uttered that night that he did not know of himself, but by the Spirit some choice truths were revealed through him, and they were of a most consoling nature to women, particularly to those who were making a willing sacrifice in helping their husbands to accomplish the great and mighty purposes which the Lord had commanded them to do, and they were promised that eventually all that were true and faithful would enjoy all that their hearts desired, or could conceive of; their trials and sufferings here would be swallowed up in the glory they had attained to through obedience, and they would be enthroned and reign as queens in the presence of God, eternities without end.

I, being very weary and sad in spirit at the close of the day, had lain down, and I fell asleep while he was talking. I was quite young, and not having been healed as I had been told I should be, my faith was considerably shaken; but the things I heard Father Whitney say before I dropped to sleep comforted me to that degree that I forgot my disappointment in the hope of that happiness which I believed would be mine, in connection with those I loved, in a day to come.

Sister Persis Young came early the next morning, saying that she had been impressed by the Spirit to come and administer to me, and I would be healed; that she could not sleep, and she had come there in obedience to that Spirit. She had been so long under its influence that she shook as though palsied when she laid her hands upon my head with my mother. She rebuked my weakness, and every disease that had been, or was then afflicting me, and commanded me to be made whole, pronouncing health and many other blessings upon me, nearly all of which have been literally fulfilled. From that morning I went about to work as though nothing had been the matter. Thus did the Lord remember one of his unworthy handmaidens and fulfill the promise that had been given by the gift and power of the Holy Ghost.[126]

Woman's Exponent, vol. 14, no. 14,
15 December 1885, pp. 105–6

WEDNESDAY THE 12TH.

Fair weather – the wind still strong from the south-east – We started this morning at 20 minutes past 9 – travelled, as heretofore over a sandy soil, without the occurrence of any particular incident, & halted at ¼ past 1 P. M. to feed, on the banks of the "North Fork"

126. In the midst of so much darkness and death in Winter Quarters that difficult winter and spring of 1846–47, and in the absence of so many men off with the battalion and Brigham Young's advance company heading west, many faithful, temple-endowed women took it upon themselves to dispel the devil and heal the sick and speak in tongues by right of their faith and power in the priesthood that had been conferred upon them before they left Nauvoo. These sisters did so not because they believed they held the priesthood, as they believed their male brethren did, but because they had a special commission of faith-based authority in this, their greatest time of peril and need. For more, see Bennett, *Mormons at the Missouri*, 173–89. See also Jonathan Stapley and Kristine Wright, "Female Ritual Healing in Mormonism," *Journal of Mormon History* 37, no. 1 (Winter 2011): 1–85.

of the Platte River – It is the general opinion, that we passed the junction of the North & South Forks during yesterday's travel as we noticed a heavy body of timber, which apparently marks the progress to the N. E. of another large stream, a number of miles beyond the one, along which we are now travelling – Our course this forenoon has been about "N. N. W.", having come 8 miles, according to the piece of mechanism, lately constructed by Appleton Harmon. – It is with considerable satisfaction, that we have at last discovered a mode of telling the distance we travel each day, as hitherto, we have principally relied upon conjecture, through which, we have, no doubt, overrated the distance somewhat, since we left Winter Quarters – at the place where we slept this noon, there are a number of ravines or hollows, in which the grass was quite green & luxuriant – Since writing the above, I learned that Prof. Pratt in his observation yesterday noon, discovered our coming ground of last night, to be 2½ miles above the junction of the 2 "Forks" – He also took an observation this noon – showing that we are in latitude North, 41 deg. 9 minutes 44 seconds, being 10½ miles above the junction – at ½ past 3 we were again in motion; travelled 4 miles & encamped at ¼ to 6 P. M., in a circle, near a bayou that sets back from the river at this place – opposite us is quite a group of islands, which however, afford us no wood, as there is but little growing upon them, except shrubs & low bushes – We have travelled about the same direction we did this forenoon, with the exception that, when we went round a bend in the river, we verged a little to the south-west – the travelling has been very dusty and disagreeable, as the wind has continued strong from the south-east throughout the day – made 12 miles today – The grass is tolerably good here, especially near the brink of the bayou above mentioned – Thomas Brown & Joseph Matthews killed a fine buffalo heifer this afternoon – I have seen no buffalo to-day on the route, & in fact no live game of any kind. – This evening we are about 15 miles above the Junction of the 2 Forks. –

Thursday the 13th.

Cold, gloomy morning, the wind being in the north-east, & the sky overcast with dark heavy clouds. – We started this morning at 9 a.m., travelled along the river on a sandy bottom, (our course being near west,) & stopt to feed, a few rods from the river, near the edge of a ravine, where the grass was very good – having come 4 miles in 2 hours, as we halted at 11 a.m. – I neglected to mention that ½ a mile from last night's place of encampment, between that & the bluffs to our right, was an old deserted Indian encampment – it had the appearance of their having been here some part of the winter, as well as the Spring – here they had dressed their buffalo skins, &c.,– a number of the brethren found some very good moccasons [*sic*], which they had here cast off, & substituted new ones – from the formation of them we have no doubt but that it was a Sioux encampment – Bro. Barney Adams found a buffalo skin that had been partly dressed. – We were again in motion at ½ past 12 M., – very dusty, disagreeable travelling – at 4 P. M., we reached the banks of a stream about 30 yds. wide, which, running along under the bluffs in a western direction, makes near here, an abrupt deviation from its course, & runs to the south, emptying into the river about 350 yds. hence – This we forded, after being detained some time on its banks, & encamped at 5 P. M. between it & the river, having made 6¾ miles this afternoon, & 10¾ during the day – Here we found the grass greener & fresher, than we have before seen it since we came into the buffalo country In advance of our camping-place to night about a mile west, is a high range of bluffs, that seem, as well as I can judge at that distance, to come near the waters' edge – These extend unbroken, far to the right, in the direction, from which we came to-day – Saw a number of buffalo this afternoon, grazing, along the side of the bluff, as we passed along. Porter, Thos. Brown, & a number of others went out in pursuit. They returned this evening, about the time we encamped – they did not kill any of them, as, when they got to them, they found they were so poor, that their flesh would scarcely be fit for use – There is no wood near here, – a number of the brethren brought some with them – those, who did not, were obliged to resort to the only resource for fuel, viz: – "buffalo chips" – The weather has continued cold & gloomy throughout the day, the wind being yet strong from the north-east – we have pursued near a due west course during the whole day. –

Friday the 14th.

Dark & cloudy – wind in the N. E. – has considerably the appearance of rain – about 9 a.m., it commenced raining, & continued, at intervals, till about 2 P. M., – this morning early, 11 buffalo were seen to come down to the river to drink – Bro. John Higbee made 2 shots at them, but secured none. About ½ past 10 a.m. we started on our journey, soon after which, the rain, that had ceased a little while before, poured down with redoubled vigor – Bros. Brigham, Heber, & some others, as usual, preceded us on horseback, to look out the route – after travelling 1 mile, we came to a point, where the bluffs projected boldly over the water's edge – These we went round, bearing gradually to the south of west – after proceeding 6¼ miles, we stopt to feed at 20 minutes to 2 P. M. just as we emerged from a valley, with high bluffs on either side, & again came in sight of the river, about a 1½ mile distant – Here we found the grass quite good. Started again about 3 P. M, – travelled, along under the bluffs, over an uneven, rugged sandy soil, which was quite hard on our cattle & horses, as the wagon wheels would sink quite deep into the sand – went about 2¼ miles, & encamped in the form of the letter "S" about 4 P. M. There have been 2 buffalo bulls killed to-day – one of them was shot by Amasa Lyman & Thos. Brown, the other by Luke Johnson & Eric Glines & Porter – the latter made the first shot – Neither of them were brought into the camp – the Revenue Cutter started at dusk after one of them 1½ miles from here, but, it being so dark, the men concluded to leave the wagon, & return to the camp on foot, on account of the difficulty of travelling through the sand heaps at night – There were also 3 antelopes & 1 badger killed to-day, which were brought into the camp. Thos. Brown, Phinehas Young, & J. Higbee each killed an antelope, & the latter killed the badger – this evening we are near ½ a mile from the River, which is the nearest water – there is no wood; therefore we are obliged, as usual, to burn buffalo chips. – The stream, near the camping place we left this morning, is the largest tributary, of the North Fork, we have yet seen on our route – Pres't. Young named it, "North

Bluff Fork" – An alarm was raised by the guard during the night, that there were Indians in the vicinity of our camp, – a number of the brethren, myself included, arose & fastened our horses to stakes at the back of the wagons – it proved to be a false alarm – The weather this evening, still cold & gloomy – Made 8¾ miles to-day – It is reported this evening by Brigham, Heber, & those who went ahead, that in a little way from here it is very difficult travelling on account of the sand banks, which are very deep.

Saturday the 15th.

Cold & stormy – the wind in the north – started on our journey at 9 a.m., went about ½ a mile, & began to ascend the bluffs – after winding around among them, alternately ascending & descending large hills or banks of sand which had here been drifted by the wind, we at length again emerged on to the bottom about ¼ of a mile from the river – Here we stopt to feed at 20 minutes to 11 a.m., having come 2½ miles – Here we found the grass greener & higher than any place we have yet seen – in fact, as we advance, the better we find it – It has rained almost incessantly from the time of our starting till the present. – The sand through which we travelled this forenoon, is so very deep, that even in descending a hill it was hard work for the horses to draw the wagons, in some places the wheels sinking nearly to the axletree. – I saw Brigham & Heber this morning start ahead on foot, before the foremost wagons, probably to look out the track – at ½ past 12 M. we were again in motion – this afternoon travelled altogether on the bottom, seeing a number of buffalo on the bluffs to our right – we had no rain during the remainder of the day, but the weather continued cold & gloomy, & the northwest blasts howled & swept by us, more resembling a cold day in winter, than one in the genial month of May – We went about 4½ miles & encamped on the bottom in a circle, ¼ of a mile from the River. All the wood we could find, we picked upon the bank of the River, as we passed

Albert P. Rockwood (1805–79), seventy, trusted bodyguard of Joseph Smith and Brigham Young, legislator, and prison warden. Courtesy of Church History Library.

The pioneer roadometer. By using this instrument, the pioneers were able to precisely measure distances traveled every day and allowed William Clayton to publish his Latter-day Saints' Emigrants' Guide.

along – We found plenty of grass at this place – We have, this afternoon pursued a west course, having come 7 miles – The brethren have dug 2 or 3 wells here, which are quite convenient, saving us the necessity otherwise of going to the river – A number of the hunters went out hunting this afternoon – Porter among the rest; who shot a buffalo, returning to the camp about 10 o'clock at night, with the game which the Revenue Cutter brought in –

Sunday the 16th.

Rather cold this morning, the wind still being in the north – Brigham, Heber, & some others went ahead this morning, on horseback to look out a good track for us to pursue, when we shall start again – they returned about ½ past 12 P. M. with the report that, about 3 miles ahead, the bluffs terminated abruptly at the bank of the river, & that we would be obliged to go around them some 4 miles, before we could again come to the River bottoms – This afternoon we noticed to the north of the camp, about 1 mile on the side of the bluffs, 3 buffalo bulls grazing – Bro. Eric Glines made 4 shots at one of them, all of which hit him – he moved off pretty fast after the 4th shot, but soon his head began to droop, his knee to totter, & then he fell at length upon the ground – Bro. Wm. Clayton & myself, when we saw him fall, went up & took a view of him – he was a very large one – Bro. Luke Johnson & Thomas Grover with the assistance of some others skinned him & took out the entrails – One of the brethren took his brains, which are very good for dressing hides – While Bro. Clayton &

myself were out a meeting was held at the camp-ground – Bro. Heber, Dr. Richards, Cols. Markham & Rockwood, I understood were the speakers – The substance of the instruction given was, that if the people expected to be blessed & prospered, they must obey the counsel given to them through the servants of God, & also, that every man should attend meeting at the sound of the horn – Bro. Heber observed, that he would rather the brethren would not hunt on Sundays, unless in case of necessity, but he did not feel disposed to find fault with them – The rules & regulations of the camp, adopted April 16th, were read, & the meeting dismissed – Bro. E. Glines also killed a female antelope today, which on being opened, was discovered to contain 2 young ones nearly grown. Bro. Appleton Harmon finished the piece of mechanism spoken of above to day, by adding one wheel to the apparatus – this he has been to work at, by odd spells, for some time back – we are now able to ascertain the distance of each days' travel, by referring to our "Rodometer" only once, at the close of the day; while previous to this we have been obliged to notice it at the end of each mile[127] – Porter wounded severely 2 buffalo this afternoon one of which he shot in the shoulder & broke the bone thereof so that he was obliged to limp away on 3 legs. – The latter part of to-day's transactions I am now writing by the light of a candle, presented to me this evening by Bishop Edson Whipple – It is made of tallow taken out of a buffalo shot by Luke Johnson & Eric Glines day before yesterday – It renders a very clear & beautiful light, & is not at all inferior to our beef tallow candles in brilliancy – This evening it is quite cold, & unpleasant – as the nights usually are –

Monday the 17th.

Cold weather this morning, the wind being in the north-west – This morning, near Pres't. Young's wagon, a small stake was planted, in the ground, with a broad plank breadthwise, on one side of which was written the following with red chalk: – "North Fork Letter Box, May 16, 1847. 7½ a.m." – On the other side – "C. C. Rich & Company, Pioneers." – Bro. Wm. Clayton also placed one near my wagon, with the following inscription: – "From Winter Quarters, 356¾ miles, May 16, 1847. – From the junction of the Forks of Platte River 41 miles. N. B. – The last 70 miles have been measured, & it is our intention to measure the

127. *William Clayton's Journal: A Daily Record of the Journey of the Original Company of "Mormon" Pioneers from Nauvoo, Illinois, to the Valley of the Great Salt Lake* (Salt Lake City: Deseret News, 1921), 16 May 1847, 152. Disagreement persists over who actually invented the famous pioneer roadometer. Howard Egan was sharply critical of what he perceived as Harmon's claim to invention. William Clayton also took offense at Harmon, who he thought was "trying to have it understood that he invented the machinery, . . . which makes me think less of him than I formerly did. He is not the inventor of it by a long way, but he has made the machinery." *William Clayton's Journal*, 14 May 1847, 149. But Harmon says nothing whatsoever about the matter in his journal. The definitive article on the topic is Guy E. Stringham, "The Pioneer Roadometer," *Utah Historical Quarterly* 42 (Summer 1974): 258–72. Stringham argues that to Orson Pratt must go whatever credit is due, because it was he who Brigham Young suggested should "give this subject some attention." His concept of a continuous screw amongst a series of cogs and wheels doubtless reflected his mathematical genius and ability. Nevertheless, it was Clayton's stubborn insistence and sense of precision that initiated it all. According to Stringham, the original was long ago lost or destroyed, although a duplicate of the original is on display at the Museum of Church History in Salt Lake City.

whole route as far as we go – and as often as circumstances will allow, we shall put up a board with the distance on." –

At 25 minutes past 8 a.m. we started – proceeded about 1½ miles over the bottom & came to a small rivulet, which runs down from the bluffs, & empties into the river a short distance hence – Here we began gradually to ascend the bluffs, travelling along the brink of the stream a short distance to the north, & then crossing it – after travelling in a winding, circuitious manner over a a [*sic*] rugged, deep sandy road, we at length, gradually attained the summit of the bluffs, which we here descended abruptly, & once more emerged on to the bottoms, after having come 4 miles – We then passed along under the edge of the bluffs, which are quite broken, with here & there a valley intervening. Passed over 4 small clear rivulets, which apparently having their sources from springs, flow from the bluffs through the valleys above mentioned, & at length find a termination at the river about ½ a mile hence – We proceeded 2¾ miles over a wet quicksand bottom, & stopt to feed at 20 min. to 12 near several little marshes or sloughs, having made 6¾ miles – The ground here is one entire quicksand marsh between us & the river – One of Pres't. Young's horses got into the mire, from which he was extricated with some difficulty by the assistance of a rope – Started again at 2 P. M., went ½ a mile & crossed a creek which also runs from the bluffs into the river – proceeded a mile & crossed another creek – still 1½ mile further & crossed another – all making their way from the bluffs to the river: – On the other side the river, opposite this latter stream, the bluffs come boldly to the water's edge – From this place, we gradually wended our way, from the river towards the bluffs – after having come 10¾ miles since morning, we stopt at 4 P. M., to wait for the Revenue Cutter, which is back some distance, bringing up 2 buffalo & an antelope, killed this forenoon: – one of the former by John Brown the other by Luke Johnson & Joseph Hancock – the antelope was shot by Amasa Lyman. – The Revenue Cutter soon arrived with its freight, which it deposited here, & went back a mile after another buffalo that Porter had killed. – We were detained here about 1 hour, & started on again at 5 P. M., without waiting for the boat – we now bore gradually towards the River about 2 miles, & encamped in a circle about ½ a mile from the same at 6 P. M. – Here we found the grass usually good, but no wood or water – The latter difficulty we soon remedied by digging into the ground about 4 feet, & found plenty of the sparkling liquid – Some of us had brought along a quantity of cedar wood, which we found on the bank of the river yesterday, opposite our last camping place, so that we managed to cook our suppers without much trouble – Saw quite a number of buffalo, antelope, and other small game on our route to-day – we travelled near a west course, having come 12¾ miles. – Opposite our present place of encampment, on the other side the river, is a bold rugged shore, the bluffs for some distance up & down the river projecting over the water's edge. – Throughout this afternoon the weather has been clear & pleasant, without much wind. –

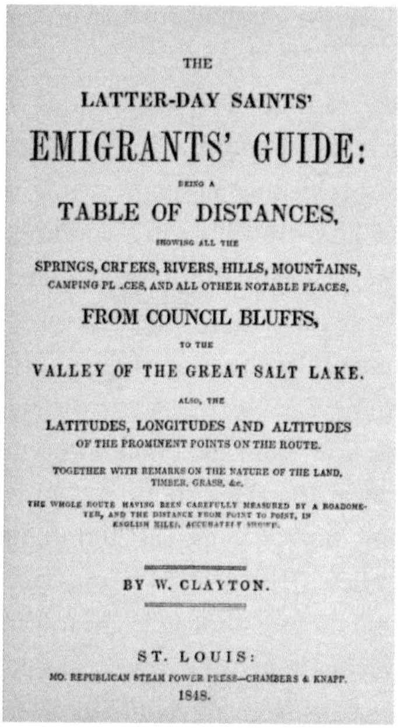
THE
LATTER-DAY SAINTS'
EMIGRANTS' GUIDE:
BEING A
TABLE OF DISTANCES,
SHOWING ALL THE
SPRINGS, CREEKS, RIVERS, HILLS, MOUNTAINS,
CAMPING PLACES, AND ALL OTHER NOTABLE PLACES,
FROM COUNCIL BLUFFS,
TO THE
VALLEY OF THE GREAT SALT LAKE.
ALSO, THE
LATITUDES, LONGITUDES AND ALTITUDES
OF THE PROMINENT POINTS ON THE ROUTE.
TOGETHER WITH REMARKS ON THE NATURE OF THE LAND, TIMBER, GRASS, &c.
THE WHOLE ROUTE HAVING BEEN CAREFULLY MEASURED BY A ROADOMETER, AND THE DISTANCE FROM POINT TO POINT, IN ENGLISH MILES, ACCURATELY SHOWN.
BY W. CLAYTON.
ST. LOUIS:
MO. REPUBLICAN STEAM POWER PRESS—CHAMBERS & KNAPP.
1848.

William Clayton, The Latter-day Saints' Emigrants' Guide.

TUESDAY THE 18TH.

This morning the sun rose cloudless and beautiful – fair prospect of a warm day. – The captains of 10s were called together this morning at Pres't. Young's wagon, to receive some instruction. – It was in substance as follows: – That when we are already in possession of plenty of game, we should not kill it needlessly, for it is a sin in the sight of the Lord to waste flesh. – That if the horsemen, (hunters,) would go ahead & assist in seeking out roads, &c., they would be of much more utility to the camp, than in pursuing every antelope or hare that crossed their path. – That there were men among us in responsible stations, who cared no more for the interests of this camp, than the horses which they rode. – That the spirit of the hunters, as now manifested, would lead them to kill all the game within a thousand miles as inconsiderately as the butcher would apply the knife to the throat of a bullock. – Pres't. Young, after some other remarks pertaining to our duty, dismissed the captains, telling them that they must teach their men by their good example; for the latter would do well enough, if the former would only set them the proper pattern. – Soon after meeting, at ¼ past 8 a.m., we recommenced our journey, Brigham, Heber, & others preceding us on horseback – We travelled over a dry sandy road along the banks of the river for 3¼ miles, & crossed a creek of considerable width, near its mouth – this also comes directly from the bluffs at the north on our right – On the other side the river, (which is about ½ a mile in width at this place,) opposite the mouth of the creek, we noticed a high range of rocky cliffs, which advance to the water's edge, & extend up & down the river for more than 2 miles – On the sides of these, growing in the sandy crevices of the rocks, are immense numbers of small cedar trees or shrubs. – We proceeded about the same distance, & stopt to bait at 10 minutes past 11 a.m., – near the river, which here makes a considerable curve to the north-west, – which has been our general course this forenoon – having come 6½ miles. – Soon after we arrived, the sky, which before had been quite serene, became overcast with clouds, & a few drops of rain fell accompanied by thunder & lightning. – We again started at 1 P. M., travelled over the bottom along the river, as usual, about 3½ miles, & came to a creek which we crossed near its mouth – proceeded ¾ of a mile further & crossed another, which runs in a winding direction into the river ½ a mile hence – went a little way farther, & stopt at 2 P. M., to wait for some of the teams, which are quite a distance behind – Here we were detained about ½ an hour, when we went on & encamped in a circle at ½ past 5 P. M., having come 9¼ miles this afternoon, & 15¾ miles during the day – We are encamped this evening on a small creek, the banks of which we were obliged to dig down before we forded it being but a little distance from the river – It rained a little at intervals, during the afternoon, & this evening it is cold & cloudy, the wind, which has been from the south west this afternoon, having veered round to the north – we have pursued near a west course this afternoon – I learned this evening from Bro. Wm. Clayton that the 1st streams we crossed this morning, opposite the cedar bluffs above mentioned, (which are thus called in Capt. Fremont's journal,) was named by Pres't. Young, "Rattlesnake Creek," – from the circumstance of one of those reptiles attempting to bite Bro. Wolsey near there, which he afterwards shot. – It is in contemplation by Brigham, Heber, Dr. Richards, O. Pratt, & others to form a map of the route we are now travelling, therefore they wish Bro. Clayton & others keeping journals to be very exact in noting the relative distances between creeks, bluffs, &c.[128]– A meeting of the brethren of the camp was called this evening by Col. Markham, in order to give them some instruction relative to their various duties. – It was voted & carried that at the sound of the horn in the morning 4 or 5 men, at the discretion of the captain, should go out of each 10 to hunt up cattle & horses. – Col. Markham said that a great many of the brethren were so selfish that they would not go out of their way 10 rods, to drive to camp their brother's cattle or horses, when they could as well do it as not; thus saving him a great deal of needless labor & travel. It was proposed by Pres't. Young, voted & carried – That if any man should stop his team in the road, without due cause, – thereby detaining the whole camp from proceeding, he with his team should be obliged to travel in the rear of the hindmost wagon the whole day – Pres't. Young also said that every captain, in travelling should remain with his 10, or if he was obliged to leave, to be gone 5, 10, or 20 minutes or go 20 rods from the wagons, to appoint one to act in his stead during his absence, who should, in all cases, be as implicitly obeyed as if he were the captain himself. – Col. Rockwood observed, that he thought it very ungenteel for a man to stop his team when crossing a stream to water them – thereby hindering the whole camp, & usurping privileges that could not be granted to all. – Pres't. Young proposed that to-morrow morning, we should start on before breakfast, & travel till we came to a good baiting place as there is but very little grass where we are now encamped – which proposition was seconded & carried unanimously – & the meeting was dismissed. – It is now about 10 o'clock at night, & I am about to close my book & retire to rest, after "summing up" the occurrences of the past day,

---

128. The roadometer was essential for the completion of what came to be William Clayton's *The Latter-day Saints' Emigrants' Guide*. When the thought struck him to compile such a guide is unknown; however, Clayton kept a precise journal of the trek west, meticulously noting tables of distances, hollows, creeks and almost everything else of note. He also provided suggestions for campsites, watering places, and forage sites, as well as longitude, latitude, and altitude readings. Such a guide would prove invaluable to future companies of travelers, both Mormon and otherwise. With the approval of church leaders, five thousand copies of his guide were eventually published in St. Louis in February 1848. See W. Clayton, *The Latter-day Saints' Emigrants' Guide*, ed. Stanley B. Kimball (St. Louis: Chambers & Knapf, 1848; Gerald, MO: Patrice Press, 1983). Wilford Woodruff once commented on the great care the pioneers took in recording their travels: "It should be understood that we are piloting a road for the House of Israel to travel in for many years to come. Therefore it requires the greater care." Scott G. Kenney, ed., *Wilford Woodruff's Journal, 1833–1898 Typescript* (Salt Lake City: Signature Books, 1983), 3:185.

Jean Jensen, Evening in Ash Hollow—1847. *Oil on canvas, 24 x 48 inches. Used with permission. Ash Hollow was a rest stop on the Mormon, California, and Oregon Trails.*

just as it has commenced a slow drizzly rain, the wind having again changed from the north to the south. –

WEDNESDAY THE 19TH.

Gloomy, cloudy morning, with but little air stirring – We started at 5 minutes past 5 a.m., – proceeded 2¾ miles, & crossed a creek which issuing from the bluffs, runs into the river ¼ of a mile hence, forming, in its course through the bottom, a number of ponds or sloughs – After going on near ¼ of a mile, we crossed another – we proceeded ¼ of a mile further, & stopt to bait & get breakfast, near the river at 20 minutes past 6 a.m. – having come 3¼ miles – The majority of the wagons have stopt about a ½ a mile back – Soon after we stopt, Heber rode by on his way back to his wagon – he had been ahead alone to look out a road over or around the bluffs, which, ahead a short distance, seem to come to the water's edge – On the opposite side the river just before we arrived at this place, we again noticed a number of cedar trees growing out of the bank – We found the grass here, but little better than that we left this morning – it rained a little, soon after our arrival – Started again at 20 minutes to 9 a.m., proceeded 1¼ miles, & came to a mountain stream running from a valley between the bluffs into the river – after crossing this, we came to the foot of the bluffs, which we began to ascend – after reaching the summit, we moved on, winding through a narrow defile, with lofty pyramids of sand, towering far above us on either side. – It was with great difficulty that our horses came through, the sand being so deep, that a number of them were stalled in the passage – at length, we began gradually to descend, & reached the bottom again, having come ¾ of a mile over the bluffs, not a great way from the foot of which, we crossed another small creek, & stopt to bait at ½ past 10 a. m., after going a short distance beyond it, having come 6 miles. – It yet continues to rain, & bids fair to last throughout the day. Started again at 10 minutes to 3 P. M., proceeded 2 miles & encamped at 4 P. M., in a semi-circle, fronting the river, having come a west course, making 8 miles to-day – It rained, with little intermission, till evening. –

Thursday the 20th.

Cold, cloudy morning, the wind being in the north-west – We started at 8 a. m., proceeded ¾ of a mile, & crossed a creek, running in a winding direction from the bluffs into the river near here – after travelling 7 miles over a rather wet bottom, caused by the recent rain we stopt to feed on the banks of the river at 11 a.m. – On the other side the river is a high range of bluffs, (with vast quantities of cedar trees growing on their sides,) extending for miles up & down the river. – Immediately opposite us is an opening in the bluffs, of 50 rods in width comprising a vast area of ground, extending back some 4 miles from the river, the extremity of which, as also the 2 sides, being bounded by a lofty range of hills – at this place the "Oregon trail" strikes the North Fork – winding along through the valley from the south it comes to the river, where it makes an abrupt turn to the west, & passes along under the bluffs near the water's edge – This place is named in Capt. Fremont's journal, "Ash Hollow."[129] – as there is quite a grove of ash trees growing there – I ascertained the above intelligence from John Brown, who with 3 others, viz: – O. Pratt, Amasa Lyman & Luke Johnson went over in the boat & visited the spot – The former had been there previous to this time, while emigrating to the west with a band of brethren last summer[130] – They brought over with them a branch of the choke-cherry tree, which they there found growing; also a specimen of rock, which is something the nature of soapstone. – We again started at 2 P. M., went 3¼ miles & crossed quite a large tributary of the "North Fork ["], running from the bluffs at the north into the river, near where we forded – it is about 6 rods in width it is named Castle Creek We went on 4¾ miles further, & encamped at ½ past 5 P. M. – in a kind of circle, near to, & opposite a small creek about ¼ of a mile from the river. – Here we found the grass quite good – we picked up plenty of cedar wood for fuel as we passed along the river banks – we have come 8 miles this afternoon, & 15¾ during the day – This evening the weather is still cold & gloomy, the wind being yet in the north-west, & the sky overcast with clouds.

Friday the 21st.

Fine, clear morning, the sun shining brightly above us. – This morning Bro. Wm. Clayton placed a guide post near my wagon, announcing the following, written with red chalk:

129. Ash Hollow, a notable milestone of the California, Oregon, and Mormon Trails, is named for a growth of ash trees and is a four-mile-long, 250-feet deep wooded canyon in present-day Garden County, Nebraska. Not far from the North Platte River, this prairie oasis was well sought after for its shade, supply of firewood, and pure water.

130. John Brown had led a company of Mississippi Saints in 1846 along the Platte River and as far west as Fort Laramie inadvertently in advance of the main vanguard company of pioneers. When they finally heard that the Saints were still back in Winter Quarters, they steered south and spent the winter of 1846–47 in Pueblo. See note 139.

"From Winter Quarters 409 miles – From the junction of North & South Forks 93¼ miles – Cedar Bluffs (south side the River) 36½ – Ash Hollow (south side the River) 8 – Camp of Pioneers, May 21, 1847. – According to Fremont, this place is 132 miles from Fort Laramie; – Wm. Clayton. N. B. – The Bluffs opposite are named 'Castle Bluffs.'" – According to my computation, we are 406 miles from Winter Quarters, being 3 miles less than Bro. Clayton's, as in the first part of our journey, we all depended upon conjecture as to the distance. – We started at 25 minutes to 8 a. m., & travelled over a wet bottom, in sight of, & not a great way from the river, beyond which, as usual, extending to the west as far as the eye could reach, is a lofty range of broken, rocky cliffs, with room sufficient between them & the river for quite a wide path, which is the "Oregon Trail", mentioned above – we proceeded 7¾ miles & stopt to bait at ½ past 11 a. m., about ½ a mile from the river – Here the grass was quite green & luxuriant, having taken a fresh start, since the recent rains, which have evidently visited this place in great abundance, as almost every little hollow in the ground is full of water. – Porter & Luke Johnson, as we passed along this forenoon, discovered through a spy glass on the opposite side the river, an object which had the appearance of being a horse – Bro. Clayton also looked at it, & supposed it to be one – This noon, a short time after our arrival, Brigham & Heber pursued 5 wolves, 1 old one, & 4 young ones – Heber killed 2 of the latter, 1 with the end of his whip-stock, the other with a bone, Brigham holding him by the tail the while – the remaining 3 made their escape, taking refuge in their hole – At ½ past 2 P. M., we were again in motion – travelled in a N. W. direction over the bottom 4¾ miles & ascended a small bluff or rise of ground, over which we passed ¼ of a mile, & then once more descended to the bottom – went 2¾ miles further, & encamped in a circle ½ a mile from the river at ½ past 5 P. M., making 7¾ this afternoon, & 15½ miles to day – just before we arrived at this place, 1 Indian a squaw (probably Sioux,) rode within 2 or 300 yards of our wagons – they came from the direction of the bluffs at the north – a number of the brethren rode out to them on the prairie – they remained here till we were encamped, & then rode off in the direction whence they came – a man was detailed out of each 10, to go out with a gun and guard the cattle & horses, in obedience to Orders issued by Col. Markham, soon after our arrival. – Bro. Wm. Clayton came very near treading upon a rattlesnake this afternoon, that lay in the path – one of the brethren took it on a stick and threw it some distance from the road, that it might not injure the cattle – there was one killed yesterday, which I neglected to mention. – Bro. Heber yesterday saw a very large wolf, the skin of which, he said he had no doubt, if he had in the eastern country, he could sell for 10 dollars. Our general course to-day has been a little north of west. – This evening Orson and myself used the last of our first bag of flour – During our travel this afternoon, one of the brethren picked up a large bone in a state of petrification – It was generally believed to belong to some animal of the mammoth species.[131] – Latitude this noon 41 deg. 24 m. 5s.

131. Nebraska is well known for its mammoth and mastodon fossils. While the state has no known dinosaur bones, it is rich with proboscidean bones and fossils, or fossils from animals with trunks, found in ninety out of Nebraska's ninety-three counties. See Megan R. Rooney, "Fossils Discovered in Ninety Counties in Nebraska," *Daily Nebraskan*, 18 April 2007.

SATURDAY THE 22^D^.

Pleasant morning, & warm wind from the south. – We started at 8 a.m., & travelled near a W. course, occasionally winding alternately to the bluffs & river, & came to a stream called Crab creek, about 2 rods in width, with a quicksand bottom, running from the bluffs at the north south into the river; this we forded near its mouth, after coming 5½ miles this morning – Just after we crossed this creek, we saw a strange dog, a little way from the road, which we suppose belongs to the Indians – We proceeded 1¾ miles, & stopt to bait at ½ past 11 a.m., ½ a mile from the river, having made 7¼ miles. – Nearly opposite us, on the other side the river, growing on the summit of the bluffs, is quite a large number of cedar trees, interspersed here & there, extending a number of miles up the river. – We found the grass here tolerably good, being a mixture of dry & green – While we were here, Porter rode in on horseback & said that from the summit of a bluff to our right could be seen in the distance, on the other side the river, a towering precipice called "Chimney Rock" – Bro. Clayton took his spy-glass & went to take a view of it. We started again at 20 minutes to 2 P. M., went 4½ miles over an uneven bottom, & began to wind around the Bluffs gradually ascending at the same time through a hollow, while the summits of still higher sandcliffs towered far above our heads on either side – after travelling about 2¼ miles we again came to the bottom – While passing along through this place, we noticed numerous sand beds which apparently marked the former progress of mighty rushing torrents, descending from the hills above to the river below – these vary from 3 to 6 rods in width. A number of bones of different animals in a state of petrification were picked up this afternoon by the brethren – after reaching the bottom we found the grass quite good, while previous to this, the ground over which we had travelled this afternoon, was a dreary, barren waste – we proceeded & encamped in a circle, near the river, at ¼ to 6 P. M. – having come 8¼ this afternoon, & 15½ miles during the day, & 83¼ miles during the past week – Just as we arrived at this place it began to rain accompanied by considerable wind, which however did not last a great while – Our course has been near west, this afternoon – Wind this evening in the N. E. – a young gray eagle was taken from its nest in a cedar tree near the summit of one of the bluffs, Just before we arrived at this place – George R. Grant caught it – it measured 46 inches, with its wings extended, from one extremity to the other. – This evening, soon after our arrival, Bros. Wm. Clayton, John Pack & myself took a walk to view a high range of broken, detached bluffs, that lie to the north-east of us about a mile – The first one we visited, we had considerable difficulty in ascending, having to assist each other in reaching the summit which we at length attained nearly out of breath – From this point we could command a view of the whole country, for many miles up & down the river – In the distance to the south-west, we could distinctly see some 20 miles distant, Chimney Rock, towering far above the surrounding hills & valleys – Beneath us in front, (from the summit to the base of the cliff being about 60 feet,) the bottom gradually sloped to the waters edge about 1 mile distant – The scene to us was truly one of magnificence & grandeur, & almost baffles description – The clay of which the cliff was formed, had become almost as hard as adamant on the top owing to the climate, winds, the ravages of rains, & old Father Time, while on the sides hung bouncy[?], large fragments that had detached themselves from the crags above, & fallen partly down, & some entirely to the base – We noticed also large clefts, in one of which an eagle, or some other large bird of prey, had built its nest – at the rear of us were numerous hills & valleys of different sizes & forms – The whole scene, was one of romantic solitude, & inspired me with singular feelings, & reminding me forcibly of the descriptions I had read in my boyish days, of the fortified castles & watch-towers of the olden time – We had an opportunity of viewing it to the greatest advantage, as the setting sun, throwing its lengthening rays upon hill, dale, mound & river, made the sight inexpressibly grand & solemn – after remaining here a few minutes we descended at the west end, (the same place where we got up,) & went to another bluff, ¼ a mile distant with a valley intervening – This we ascended also on the western side, with considerable difficulty, & found it still more remarkable than the other, being still 30 feet higher, making 90 feet from the summit to the base, & about 200 feet above the level of the river – The top is somewhat oval in spots, in others rather flat, & is sufficiently large to admit of 30 persons to sit & dine with ease. – We observed some very singular plants & shrubs growing there, that we had never before seen – at the eastern extremity is quite a large cedar tree, near a foot in diameter – We plucked some of the former, & also a branch of the latter, which we brought with us to the camp – We also noticed the vestiges of horses, which had been here not long since, probably owing to some of the Indians having visited the spot on horseback, which is accessible on the eastern side, by pursuing a winding direction – after

William H. Jackson, Approaching Chimney Rock along the North Platte. *Wyoming State Archives.*

Frederic Remington, Indians Reconnoitering from a Mountain-top. *Although their movements were scouted out by both the Pawnee and the Sioux, the Mormon vanguard company was never attacked by either tribe.* Harper's Magazine, *November 1898. Wyoming State Archives.*

being absent about an hour, we returned to the camp a little after sunset, having been much interested, & well paid for our trouble in exploring the spot which was named by Pres't Young, "Bluff Ruins." –

Sunday the 23ᴰ.

Tolerably pleasant, with a warm breeze from the south – This morning, Brigham, Heber, & others went to take a view of the bluffs, & the surrounding scenery. – Bro. Nathaniel Fairbanks, while on his return from the spot, was bitten on the leg by a rattlesnake – He managed to walk to the camp, about a mile, without assistance or remedy. Bro. Luke Johnson administered to him a dose of Lobelia, which soon caused him to vomit – Tobacco was also applied to the spot bitten, & hands were laid on him by a number of the brethren, when he seemed to be much relieved – This was the first case of the kind I had ever seen. – Bro. F. told me that he had not been bitten more than 3 minutes before he felt a pricking sensation in his mouth & hands, & a kind of numbness, (or torpidity) pervading his whole system – a meeting was held near Prest. Young's wagon, commencing at 11 o'clock A.M., The horses were all previously brought in, & staked in the circle, & outside near the wagons – Pres't Young opened the meeting by prayer, & Bro. Erastus Snow arose & spoke at some length of the great works we might accomplish, by persevering with faith and fortitude that

Prairie rattlesnake. Although the vanguard company encountered hundreds of these reptiles, no one died from snakebite. Wyoming State Archives.

which we had sat out to do – Pres't. Young arose & said that Bro. Snow had spoken to give him a chance to rest, as he was quite tired with his trip to the Bluffs – He then proceeded to give us various instructions with regard to our duties; said that he was satisfied with the conduct of this camp, but still there was a chance for improvement, & he hoped that the brethren would not indulge in profane language, but on the contrary, keep the name of the Lord sacred, & bow before him in prayer, morning & evening. – Many other things he said, of interest to us all, & the meeting, after some others of the brethren had spoken, was dismissed about 2 P. M. – about 5 P. M. – it began to blow very hard from the north, & the sky, which had for some time begun to be overcast with clouds, had considerably the appearance of rain – it commenced to rain very hard, just before dark & continued till ½ past 9 P. M. The wind blew a perfect hurricane from the north-west nearly all night – Bro. Fairbanks is a little better this evening.

Monday the 24th.

Cloudy & cold, the wind still strong from the north-west – This morning Dr. Richards put up a small post with a board attached, on one side of which was written, – "Ancient Bluffs 'Ruins' Post Office, Pioneers, May 22, 23, 24, 1847." – On the other side – "456¾ miles from Winter Quarters." – On one edge was written, "Letter Box", on the other, "W. R.", & "G. B. C." – We started at ½ past 8 A.M., travelled a N. W. course over a bottom somewhat wet in places, owing to the late rains, & stopt at ¼ to 1 P. M., near the river to bait, having come 10 miles. – On the other side the river, some miles above, is a large mass of rock, oval in form, situated on an elevated range of small hills – it has a solitary appearance indeed, standing some distance from any peak as high as itself – On the top is a small object, resembling in form, the cupola of a church steeple. A short distance to the left of this mass is another, considerably inferior in size, & of an entirely different appearance, resembling somewhat, in my ideas, an Egyptian pyramid – From this place is also visible in the distance, Chimney Rock. There were 2 Indians in camp this noon, though I did not see them – At 3 P. M., we again started; proceeded 5¼ miles and came opposite to the lone mass of rock, first mentioned above – Just before this one of my horses, (the mare,) "gave out" & we stopt to rest – Bro. Pack, Hancock with their wagons & Captain Tanner with the cannon also stopt – I went ahead some distance on foot, to get the remainder of the wagons to halt, as we had for some time noticed a party of Indians travelling up the river on the opposite shore – The camp moved 1¼ mile further, & encamped in a circle ½ a mile from the River, at 6 P. M. having made 6½ miles this afternoon, & 16½ during the day. – Orson pursued near a W. course this afternoon. drove up with our wagon, soon after the rest of the wagons were arranged in a circle. – The Indians when they saw us encamping, halted a few minutes on the opposite banks of the river, as if in consultation, & then one by one began to cross the river in single file – after all getting over, (the number being 35, men, women and children,)

Unidentified Indian on horseback. Wyoming State Archives.

they went up the river a piece and halted – Pres't. Young commissioned Col. Rockwood & Father Sherwood to go & see them, to converse with them where they were & find out if they had any thing they wished to exchange in trade – The two soon returned, accompanied by 2 chiefs, & 2 other Indians – they had a U. S. flag with them – they went through the exercise of cannonading in their presence, which pleased them very much – a number of others soon after came into the camp – The horses were all laryetied out, & a guard placed to watch them till 10 o'clock, as a number of them had given out on account of to-day's travel. The Indians are encamped within ¼ of a mile of us, & the old chief with his squaw are to remain near our camp, in a tent provided for them – There was considerable provision of different kinds given to them by the brethren, as that was what they seemed most to stand in need of – I have heard of no trades effected with them, except one, & that was John Higbee's exchanging horses with one of them – Orson is on guard this evening, watching the horses, as we have ours laryetied out with the rest. – Tolerably cool air this evening. –[132]

Tuesday the 25th.

Beautiful morning; the sun rose bright & clear – fair prospect of a warm day, though a severe frost last night – we started at 10 minutes past 8 A.M., – about the same time the Indians, who had been round the camp during the morning, recrossed the river – there were some very fine looking men & women among them, & they were all apparently arrayed in their best garments, as if for a visit – a number of the brethren made trades with them, exchanging meal for buffalo robes, &c.– One of them followed us a little way, & exchanged his horse for a mule with Col. Markham – We passed over a small ridge, & came to the bottom near the river where we stopt to feed at ½ past 9 a.m., – having come 2½ miles – We found the grass here quite good – the reason of our halting so early, as a number of horses were almost spent with yesterday's travel – At 11 a.m. we were again in motion – travelled over a flat, wet bottom, very little elevated above the banks of the river – went 4¾ miles & again halted to bait at ½ past 1 P. M. near a slough or marsh, about ½ a mile from the river – on the opposite side the river is a high broken range of bluffs, & apparently not more than 4 miles distant to the S. W. we can distinguish Chimney Rock, which appears from here similar to a church steeple – this is encompassed on all sides by bluffs & crags of different sizes & forms, presenting a beautiful & grand appearance – we have pursued near a W. course, having come

132. The Dakota Sioux were by far the most feared of all the Plains Indian tribes, numbering at least twenty-five thousand. Ever since the Mormon pioneers had left the Pawnee Indian village, the Sioux had very likely been scouting them out. This visit of thirty-five men, women and children was likely a cordial but careful foray not only to obtain provisions but also to check out the Saints up close, to ascertain their numbers, supplies, weapons and above all, their intentions. Thomas Bullock mentions that the pioneers showed them their six shooters and fired off their cannons. Wilford Woodruff recorded that they all wanted to come into camp, "behaved well," and departed after breakfast the next day. See Kenney, *Wilford Woodruff's Journal,* 3:183, entries for 24 and 25 May 1847. For two excellent studies of the Sioux, see Guy Gibbon, *The Sioux: The Dakota and Lakota Nations* (Malden, MA: Blackwell Publishing, 2003); also Royal B. Hassrick, *The Sioux: Life and Customs of a Warrior Society* (Norman: University of Oklahoma Press, 1988).

7¼ miles – a few minutes after we had halted Porter rode up with an antelope before him on his horse, which he had killed this forenoon – we moved on again at 3 P. M., travelled W. 4¾ miles over an uneven, wet soil, & encamped in a circle at 10 minutes to 6 P. M., 1½ or 2 miles from the river, having come 12 miles to-day – Here the ground was quite wet & marshy, as it is almost as low as the river itself, although the grass is very good in places – The weather throughout the day has been warm and sultry, – The brethren dug a number of wells each about 4 feet deep, soon after our arrival at this place. – Bro. Fairbanks is slowly recovering, though his leg is yet considerably swollen – the Indian dog, spoken of as being first seen on Saturday morning, still continues to follow the camp, & is getting quite domesticated, as I saw him lying near the wagons this evening – Latitude this noon, 41° – 41 m. 46 s.

WEDNESDAY THE 26TH.

Pleasant morning, & cool breeze from the north-west – We continued our journey at 8 a. m. travelling W. N. W., as usual, over a low, wet sandy bottom & stopt at 12 M., to bait, about 1 mile from the river having come 7¼ miles – Here we found a beautiful plat of green grass, the discovery of which we hailed with considerable satisfaction. – Bro. O. Pratt took an

Mormon Trail—Chimney Rock. *Lithograph by Piercy,* Route from Liverpool to Great Salt Lake Valley. *Church History Library.*

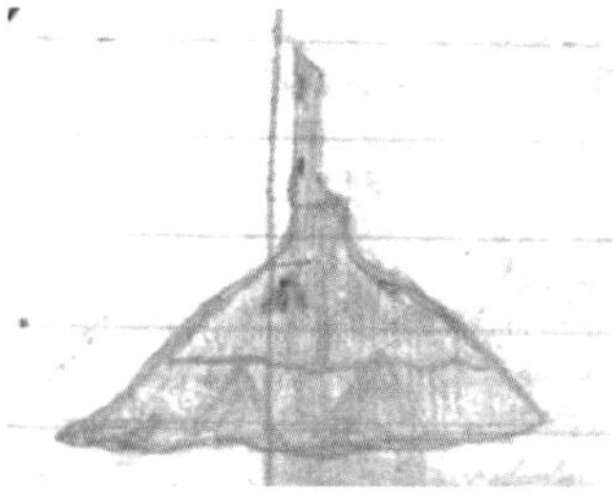

observation last evening to ascertain the distance between our camp & Chimney Rock – He also took one this forenoon, when we got opposite, to the north of it; though I believe, as yet, he has made the calculation of the distance for neither – We are now able to take a more conspicuous & correct view of Chimney Rock than we were yesterday – It is situated on a small eminence, gradually sloping to the water's edge – It is formed of clay, & not of rock as I supposed, & the base or foundation, on which stands the object appearing like a Church steeple spoken of above, considerably resembles in shape a volcano – The bluffs & crags in the background are much loftier than itself – We again started at 25 m. past 2 P. M., proceeded about the same direction we did this forenoon, over a wet bottom abounding with green grass – travelled 5 miles & encamped at 5 P. M., on the banks of the river, opposite a high broken range of bluffs & crags of different shapes & sizes, resembling in majestic grandeur those we have lately passed – Latitude this noon, – 41 deg., 45 min. 58 sec. – I learned this evening, that Professor O. Pratt, in his trigonometrical observation at 12 M., ascertained the distance from Chimney Rock, from the nearest point at which we passed it to the north, to be 3 miles – the altitude of the same 260 feet – The sky this evening is somewhat overcast with clouds, the wind being about W. There were 4 antelope killed to-day by the following hunters: – John Brown, 1 – Joseph Hancock, 1 – Porter – 2 – By request of Bro. Heber, I took a walk with him this evening out on the prairie near half a mile – Here we knelt down, & each prayed alternately for our friends & relatives, whom we have left behind in Winter Quarters, & also for one another, & the Saints at large – after an absence of about ½ hour we returned to the camp. Bro. Heber had been all day riding in advance of the camp, searching out roads &c.– He attempted to find one over the bluffs, in which he said had he succeeded, we would have been 3 miles ahead of our present camping place as that route would be much nearer than the one we pursued, had it been practicable – It rained a little at sunset. –

The above illustration is a representation of Chimney Rock, as described above, the summit of which was distinctly seen by us at the distance of 42 miles, as we were approaching it from the east.[133]

[***Editor's note***: Meanwhile, back at Winter Quarters, Helen's reminiscences reveal the difficulties they experienced on their own trek after leaving Winter Quarters:]

My mother's and Sarah's babies which were so peculiarly operated upon by the destroyer continued sick from that time, and it seemed as if death was determined to claim one or both. Sarah Ann's appeared the worst some of the time, and then it would be my mother's, and the

133. Chimney Rock is a prominent geological rock formation in Morrill County, western Nebraska. Rising nearly 300 feet above the surrounding North Platte River Valley and its peak being 4,200 feet above sea level, it can be seen from thirty miles away. During the nineteenth century, it served as the most famous landmark along the Oregon, California, and Mormon Trails and was often heralded by weary travelers as the halfway point to their western destinations. Due to wind and continued erosion, today's Chimney Rock is not as high or quite as pronounced as when the Mormon pioneers first viewed it.

witnessing the young mother's grief, who plainly saw her infant failing day by day, so touched my mother's tender heart that she made up her mind to make an offering of her own little darling inasmuch as the Lord required one of them, praying as she made the sacrifice, that He in His tender mercy, if it would be acceptable in His sight might take hers and spare Sarah's. Did this not mark her as one of the elect of God, who fought manfully against the flesh, the world and the devil?

In those scenes we were supplied with that spiritual armor necessary to sustain the combat with the inveterate and subtle foe, whose power and devices were being made manifest in our midst. From the moment that my mother made this offering her babe began to improve, and only a few days before another pure spirit had taken its flight from this sorrowing vale of tears, and another doting heart was almost broken as she followed its little body to that lonely spot on the hillside which had been dedicated as a burying place for the dead. There weary pilgrims could rest for a season, and the dear little innocents, whose spirits ascended up to the Father, bearing record of the inhumanity and wrong which had been met with in this world by those who rendered obedience to the truths revealed by the blessed redeemer for the salvation of the human family, and had been driven from their homes in the bleak month of February 1846 to suffer in the wilderness in so cruel and heartless a manner. The sweet comforter was still with us, and from that date the destroyer was stayed in our house.

Among the marvelous instances of faith which I witnessed, was in the family of Bro. Lyman Whitney, a brother of the bishop. Lyman was then at work in the state of Missouri. One of his babes—its mother being his second wife—was lying sick unto death. She told us that it had not swallowed anything for two days, and its eyes were dried up so that it had not been able to close them for some time. My mother, Mother Whitney, Sarah Ann, Sister Presendia, myself and one or two more, were called to go and administer to the sick babe. Sister Presendia first moistened its eyes with milk and water, then it was washed and anointed, and as many as could, laid hands upon it, and all of us unitedly raised our hearts to God in its behalf, Presendia being mouth. We had no sooner said amen, than it opened its eyes and began to wink and look around, and soon after it took nourishment. The mother and her sister who were living together, were both charged to watch it closely and not leave it alone for a moment, or the destroyer would grasp it. They watched it faithfully through the rest of the day and during that night, but as it appeared so much better in the morning, they, not realizing how the destroyer was lying in wait for it, left it sleeping in its cradle long enough to go into an adjoining room to breakfast. When the mother returned she found it struggling in the arms of death. Then she fully realized the meaning of the words of warning which had been spoken by the spirit and power of the Holy Ghost.[134]

134. It was a common belief at this time among the Saints that Satan was the cause of at least some of their sicknesses and afflictions, if not death itself. Such a conviction intensified at Winter Quarters when nothing seemed to stem the tide of suffering and death. Hence, the importance of casting out devils not only as a means of spiritual deliverance but also for physical protection. For more on the sickening pall of death the Latter-day Saints suffered when over one thousand died between 1846 and 1848, see Bennett, *Mormons at the Missouri*, 289.

I remember instances wherein the evil one entered persons that were not sufficiently posted—not having had enough experience to be able to distinguish the difference between the operations of the two spirits—good and evil. There are those living—sister E. B. Wells being one of the number—who will readily testify to these statements. The following I heard from Sisters Presendia, Laura, Christine, Sarah Lawrence Kimball and others. The circumstance transpired one evening at the house of Sister Miller, whose name is now Finch, where a meeting was being held. A few sisters who came had not been present at any of the previous meetings; and two or three of them it was said, had made light of them, and the gift of tongues, etc., which the sisters testified they had frequently enjoyed with a great outpouring of the Holy Spirit. Satan, it seems, came also, and they aver that his face and shoulders were plainly visible through the window. They not only saw him, but heard his awful footsteps as he walked around the outside of the house, after which there were individuals attacked, and the power was so terrible, that it was only by mighty faith and the power of the priesthood that the destroyer was rebuked from their midst. At his first appearance, some who had never before witnessed a conflict with the evil spirits, as may naturally be supposed, were frightened nearly out of their wits, at the sight of his highness, and they took a sudden unceremonious leave while the strong and valiant held the ground, till the victory was gained, and the evil one cast out. From this circumstance went forth a false rumor concerning the meetings of the sisters, started by those who, not having mingled before with them, pronounced it all from the devil.

At an evening meeting held at my mother's, one of the sisters, who had met with us but little, feeling the spirit resting upon her to speak in tongues, arose and began talking—at first very quietly. In a moment her voice changed, as did also her countenance, and her movements were such that there was no mistaking the spirit which was operating upon her. Two or three who were present had the gift of interpretation, and they said with one accord that she uttered nothing but the most wicked blasphemy. But this lasted only an instant as sister Laura Pitkin, who came into the church at the beginning, arose and took hold of her arm, and in a quiet but commanding tone bade her sit down. She dropped into her chair as suddenly as though she had received a blow, and covering her face with her hands groaned aloud, as though realizing what she had done. No one spoke or moved, and in a moment after she arose and left the room. From that she felt so humiliated, and crushed in spirit, that she could not be induced to again rise to speak in a meeting.

Many were the manifestations that were had from above and beneath, which were similar to what the Prophet had witnessed, but which previous to that time, I had taken but little notice of. Joseph said that the devil could talk in any tongue and that he could appear like a gentleman, or in any form he pleased. Also that no one would ever enter into the celestial kingdom without having to meet and combat with that power, either in the flesh or after they had passed out of it, and that his forces would be strengthened and increased just in proportion to the progress that was being made by his opponents. This is easily enough understood by Latter-day Saints, or by anyone who has undertaken a reformation or to accomplish a victory in the right direction.

The slight experience that I gained at that early period gave me a little insight, though in a very small degree, into the workings of the two powers. Afterwards when I was out from under that spiritual or heavenly influence, I made this expression, that I wanted no more light or spiritual manifestations, for fear I should have to meet the prince of darkness. But I had to meet him, a year or so from that date, and I went through a schooling that brought conviction, and impressed indelibly upon my heart the truth of this work, and that Satan, with all his power and cunning, was a deceiver; also that our thoughts were unknown to him only as we uttered them, and therefore we had the advantage over him, when wise enough to keep silent, and we could pray to the Father in our hearts, who was all powerful, and able to read the thoughts and desires of His children.

The experience had at Winter Quarters taught me that it was only through obedience and great humiliation, more especially through fasting and prayer, that we could obtain any great manifestations from on high, or the power to enable us to overcome the adversary.

Could we as a people, lay aside the world, and bring our own evil natures into subjection to that spirit, which would make us of one heart and one mind, and valiant to do all that is required of the Saints of God. I know that we would not be long as we are now, bending under the yoke of oppression, but would soon become that people whom we have been told from the beginning, should be honored, not only by the noble, but by the Great Lawgiver of the whole earth.

Woman's Exponent, vol. 14, no. 15,
1 January 1886, p. 118

I have barely touched upon the scenes that came under my notice during the absence of the pioneers, but am able to testify to the enjoyment of many happy seasons after the mighty struggle with the destroyer was over, and we were again in the enjoyment of health, a blessing that some could appreciate more fully than myself. Some of the little circle that met often one with another to obtain that solace which the comforter alone could give, have passed on to another state, leaving one here and another there to testify to the outpourings of the Holy Spirit that sustained and cheered them during those trying scenes.

Two are still remaining in the family of the late brother John Pack—Sisters Julia and Ruth, who will bear witness to these things, and that there were no repinings such as we read were indulged in by the children of Israel. We could say with one accord as did the prophet Job, though reduced in worldly circumstances or reproached and cut off because of our seeming wickedness, yet in the midst of all our sore calamities we were buoyed up with a holy hope, and were confident of a glorious reward from Him who is the searcher of all hearts and has promised that the meek shall inherit the earth.

The unbeliever may scoff but we know that it was the Holy Spirit—the Comforter, and that faith born of it, that sustained and buoyed up the drooping spirits and lightened the cares and toils of the weary under the varied and trying circumstances that were calculated to dishearten any but Latter-day Saints, who possessed that living faith that enabled the soul to look forward to a glorious future, trusting to that Mighty One whose power had preserved and led them thus far and had delivered them "out of the seventh trouble."

Woman's Exponent, vol. 14, no. 18,
15 February 1886, p. 138

Thursday the 27th.

Warm & pleasant. – We started at 8 a.m., & proceeded over a level bottom in a W. N. W. direction, & stopt at ¼ to 12 M. on the banks of the river having made 8 miles – The ground over which we have travelled this forenoon, abounded in green grass. – Porter killed 2 antelope this forenoon Amasa 1, which were brought into camp soon after our arrival – To the W. S. W. of our present stopping place there is another high range of broken detached bluffs, at the extreme right of which, is a large, high mass of crags, thrown together as if by some convulsion of nature, resembling in form the old battlemented castles we read of, of the olden times. – We were again in motion at 2 P. M., took the same course we did this forenoon, travelling over a tolerably dry bottom, & passed the craggy precipice referred to above, which, coming boldly to the water's edge, rears its lofty summit near 300 feet above the same – The top & sides thereof abound in numerous cedar trees & shrubs – We encamped to the N. W. of it some 2 or 3 miles, on the banks of the river, forming in a circle, as usual – at ¼ to 5 P. M., having come 5¾ miles this afternoon, & 13¾ during the day – There we found the grass plenty & luxuriant, as it has been on the ground over which we have travelled to-day. – At this place the river makes an abrupt turn in its course, to the north, so that our camp, this evening, is situated in a bend of the same. An antelope was shot this afternoon by John W. Norton, which, on opening, was discovered to contain 2 young ones. The sky this evening, is considerably overcast with clouds, which have every appearance of rain, the wind being N. E. The last bluff spoken of, is the termination at the river of the range of them called "Scott's Bluffs."[135] – Latitude at this point, 41° – 50 m. 52s. – I learned this evening, that at the place where we encamped last night, the width of the river is 792 yds, as ascertained by an observation of Professor O. Pratt. Rained a little this evening about at dusk. –

Friday the 28th.

Cloudy & misty this morning, with a slight, drizzly rain. – The brethren were called together soon after breakfast, & a vote taken, whether we should immediately proceed on our journey, or wait till the rain should cease – The former alternative was adopted. – We started at 11 a.m., although it had not cleared off, proceeded 1 mile & came to the mouth of a small clear rivulet in some places 2 rods in width, with a gravel bottom, flowing from

135. First charted in 1812 by an expedition of fur traders, Scott's Bluff is the most prominent in a cluster of bluffs in western Nebraska. Named after a fur trader named Hiram Scott who contracted an illness and was left there by his partners to die in 1828, Scott's Bluff is today a national monument in remembrance of his suffering.

the N. N. W., which course we pursued about 4 miles & came to the source of it which is a spring – Brigham, Heber, & some other including myself, walked for some distance along its banks, – we observed numerous schools of fish in it of different kinds – there is a number of beaver dams across it, & also houses that these animals have built on its brink. – We also noticed the vestiges of camp fires, probably made by Indians We had been gradually nearing the bluffs; we now, however, commenced travelling towards the river, going a little south of west, over a bottom, covered with alternate patches of green & dry grass. – We encamped on the banks of the river, in a circle at ¼ to 5 P. M., having come 11½ miles to-day The grass here is not as good as usual – The weather cold & cloudy this evening, the wind being in the N. E. –

Saturday the 29th.

The clouds dark & lowering, with a drizzly rain, similar to that of yesterday morning. – The horn was blown about ½ past 10 a.m., for the brethren to get up their cattle, & horses, as it had some what the appearance of clearing off fair – Some of them had wandered a considerable distance, so that as much as an hour elapsed, before they could be bro't to the camp, & put before the wagons – after which the brethren in the camp were called together, & Pres't Young arose and first told the captains of 10s to call their respective companies around them, which was done, & Thomas Bullock, the clerk proceeded to call the roll. – and found 2 absent, who had gone out hunting this morning, viz. – Joseph Hancock & Andrew Gibbons. – The President then said, – "I will take this for my text: I shall revolt at the idea of going with this company any further with the spirit that they now possess. From this I shall make my discourse." – He then proceeded to say that the practices, some of the members of this camp had indulged in for a few days past, would ultimately lead them to ruin & death, viz: – playing at cards, dominoes, checkers, dancing, levity, &c.– That these recreations were no harm within, & of themselves, if the people just knew when to stop, & break off immediately, & when they retired to their beds, not forget to bow before the Lord & thank him for the privilege of dancing – That by & by, they would get to playing at cards, one would accuse the other of cheating, then the next thing would be a knock down, & from thence would draw weapons on each other, & shed blood – such, he said, were the inevitable consequences of such a course, if not checked in the bud.[136] – That the Devil knew better than to go so far as to make a man deny the Priesthood in this camp, but was content to make him commit these lesser offences, that would make him forget God, & finally lead to that result. – He then called for a division of the camp, that is, for the Quorums of the Twelve, High Priests,

136. It was from the excess of lightmindedness that the "Lion of the Lord" recoiled. Remembered William Clayton of what Brigham Young said: "If any man had sense enough to play a game at cards, or dance a little without wanting to keep it up all the time, but exercise a little and then quit it and think no more of it, it would do well enough, but you want to keep it up till midnight and every night, and all the time. You don't know how to control your senses." *William Clayton's Journal*, 193.

William H. Jackson, Mitchell Pass at Scotts Bluff. *Jackson drove his own ox team across the western United States in 1866, making sketches like this along the way. Bretney Collection, Wyoming State Archives.*

Seventies, elders & members, to form in a body by themselves – He then exhorted them separately to the observance of their duties, & called upon them all to covenant to desist from trivial & bad practices, & to serve faithfully the Lord with their whole hearts, which they did unanimously by raising their right hands. – He then moved that to-morrow be a day devoted to fasting & prayer to be conducted by the Bishops, as himself with his brethren the Twelve & some other wished to retire apart by themselves – after he had ended, Heber, Bros O. Pratt, W. Woodruff, & Col. Markham each spoke a few minutes in confirmation of what had been said, & the meeting was dismissed.[137] There were present of the Quorum of the Twelve 8 – High Priests 18 – Seventies 78 – Elders 8 – besides the members. The meeting lasted near 2 hours. – We started at ½ past 1 P. M. – travelled in a S. S. W. direction over rather an uneven bottom, & encamped in a circle at ½ past 5 P. M. on the banks of a small creek, running parallel with the river, about ¼ of a mile from the same – having come 8½ miles to-day. – Just before we arrived here, we noticed a number of cotton-wood trees growing on an island

137. Brigham Young's jeremiad at Scott's Bluff harked back to his Word and Will of the Lord revelation at Winter Quarters five months before. He firmly believed that they were on a divine errand, that the success of their journey depended on their obedience to covenant, that they were being tried and tested, that as with Zion's Camp thirteen years before a scourge awaited the rebellious, and that if they were not strictly obedient the entire church would suffer. See Bennett, *We'll Find the Place*, 158–60. His 'scotch blessing' bore almost immediate fruit. Thomas Bullock said as much in a letter to his wife shortly thereafter. "I expect you will think there is a reformation in me," he said, "when you know that I have commenced reading the Bible through. I have already read as far as the 7th chapter of Judges, and express my gratitude to God . . . that I have already received much light and intelligence in things of which I have been a long time dark." Thomas Bullock to Henrietta Bullock, 14 May 1847, Thomas Bullock Letters, Church History Library.

opposite, being the first timber we have seen for a long time – Here we found the grass tolerably good. – It commenced raining about ½ past 4 P. M., & continued near 2 hours.

Tonight the clouds are dark & lowering, & have the appearance of more rain. – We have come 74½ miles during the past week, & are 511½ miles from Winter Quarters this evening.

SUNDAY THE 30TH.

Cloudy morning, though not very cold. – Agreeably to the arrangements of yesterday, a fast & prayer meeting was held this forenoon, commencing at ½ past 8 a.m. & lasting till ½ past 10 a.m. – The time was chiefly occupied in confessions & prayer. – The meeting was held under the supervision of the Bishops, the Twelve not being present. – After this, the horses were all drove in to camp & fastened some inside, others outside the circle, & the brethren again repaired to meeting, which commenced at 20 minutes past 12 M. – A number of the brethren arose & addressed the congregation, relating their past experience, confessing their sins, &c., after which the sacrament was administered & the meeting was dismissed at ½ past 1 P. M., as it began, about this time, to rain. – The Twelve were not present this afternoon, having retired, with some others, by themselves to counsel.[138] – The rain did not last long, for it soon cleared off fair, with a fine breeze from the N. W., & continued so the remainder of the day. On the opposite side the river, are a number of small hillocks, situated on the sides & summits of the bluffs, which, the sun throwing his glancing rays athwart them, appear from here like buildings composing a large village. – It again rained a little this evening about dark.

MONDAY THE 31ST.

Fine, clear morning, with a slight breeze from the west. – quite a heavy frost last night. – We continued our journey this morning at ½ past 8, & travelled along near the bluffs, (which are principally composed of huge sandbanks,) in a W. N. W. direction, over an uneven, rugged, sandy road, in some places almost entirely destitute of vegetation, noticing, during our route, numerous cotton-wood trees growing on the opposite side the river. – After going about 8 miles, we changed our course to a little south of west towards the river & halted to bait at ½ past 12 M., about 1 mile from the same, on the edge of the upper shelf of table of the

138. The entire camp was in a repentant spirit this day, due in large measure to Brigham Young's recent chastisement the day before. This may also explain why the Twelve separated themselves from the camp, put on their temple robes, and formed a prayer circle "a little south of the camp" some distance away. Wrote Orson Pratt of their apostolic effort to seek divine benediction for the camp: "We went out on the bluffs, and selecting a small circular, level spot, surrounded by bluffs, and out of sight, we clothed ourselves in the priestly garments, and offered up prayer to God, for ourselves, for our families, and all the Saints: President Young being mouth. We all felt well and glad for this privilege of assembling ourselves together in a retired spot for prayer." Elden J. Watson, comp., *The Orson Pratt Journals* (Salt Lake City: Elden Jay Watson, 1975), 30 May 1847, 413. Clearly the temple was very much in the minds of church leaders during the exodus west.

bottoms (the lower one, having been recently burned over, affording plenty of green grass,) having come 9½ miles. We again started at 3 P. M.; proceeded near the same course we did this forenoon, over a deep, sandy bottom, which made it very hard pulling for our horses and cattle: we travelled 7¼ miles, & encamped in 2 lines at ¼ to 7 P. M., on a creek, in some places 2 rods in width, which runs from the hills above in a S. E. direction into the river, from which we are about a mile distant. – This stream has a sandy bottom, & high banks on either side for some distance. – We passed by a number of green & dry cottonwood trees this afternoon, being the first we have seen this side the river for some time since. – John Higbee killed a deer (buck) this afternoon. – The place where we are now encamped is almost a barren, sandy desert, with here & there a few, scant tufts of grass, thus affording a very poor chance for horses & cattle, which were mostly laryated, or turned out loose during the night. Latitude this noon, – 42° – 04 min. – 30 sec. – The distance we have travelled to day is 16¾ miles. –

TUESDAY THE 1ST OF JUNE.

Beautiful morning, the sun rose cloudless & beautiful. – We started this morning at 9 still travelling over a desert, sandy road, & pursuing a W. N. W. course – we stopt at 11 a.m., near the river to bait, having come 4½ miles. – There is a little ravine here, into which we turned our horses, as the grass in it is quite green & luxuriant. – We again started at 1 P. M. travelling over nearly the same kind of ground, interspersed here & there with shrubs, & encamped in a semi-circle at ¼ past 6 P. M., on the banks of the river, opposite Fort Laramie having come 12 miles – This is situated in an extensive valley, apparently 1½ mile from the river, environed on all sides except that next the river by a lofty range of bluffs, while in the distance can be seen to the S. west, the dusky outlines of the "Black Hills," towering far above the surrounding scenery. – Not having visited the Fort, I am not able at this time to give a description of it, but Porter who went over & returned this evening, says that it is built in an oblong shape, of dirt, & surrounded by a wall, being connected therewith on the inside – there are here at this time 18 men composing the inhabitants, mostly Frenchmen – On the opposite bank of the river, is a square or oblong built edifice, formed of dirt, for what purpose I know not, though some think it was intended for a yard to keep horses in – at this place the river is divided into 2 branches, one running each side the fort in an eastern direction – the one running on the south side is called the Laramie Fork of the Platte. – Just as we arrived here, 2 brethren came from the Fort to visit us – they had come here from Pueblo 2 weeks since – they had been, (3 families of them,) 15 days on the journey, having come with ox teams, a distance of 257 miles.[139] – the brethren also informed us that some travelers, who arrived here about a week ago from "Sweet Water", said that the snow in that region was 2 feet deep 12 days since, & on the mountains, in places, 15 feet deep – they had come through in 6 days, being obliged to leave their wagons behind, & come ahead on horses, the

139. The "Mississippi company" of forty-three converts in nineteen wagons led by John Brown and William Crosby, had left Monroe County, Mississippi, in April 1846 with directions to join the main pioneer camp

road being entirely blocked up and rendered impracticable by the snow at that place - They further told us that the soldier brethren at Pueblo, who went there as invalids had mostly recovered from their sickness, & were intending to start from there the 1st of June, to come to this place, join our body, & proceed on the journey with us to the west.[140] - The brethren spoken of above, are Robt. [Robert] Crow, & his son-in-law, whose name I did not learn - they had managed to winter their cattle on dry grass at Pueblo, although they had plenty of corn stalks, which they had on their hands this spring, the former being in good condition at the time. - about 3 weeks ago, a band of Crow Indians, came to the Fort, & took all the horses away belonging to the inhabitants - this was done in the day-time immediately before the eyes of the guard they had watch at the time, who of course could not resist them, they being so numerous. These excursions they are in the habit of making every Spring. - This tribe, I am informed, altho' a roving tribe, generally inhabit the country adjacent Sweet Water. - Pres't Young called the captains of 10s together this evening, to impart to them the nature of the business to-morrow, which was, that 2 men should be selected out of each 10, to act as a standing guard, to watch the cattle, &c. while we remain here - that every wagon should be overhauled, & things that were superfluous taken out of them, such as old iron, ploughs, &c., as he thought that 10 of the latter would be a sufficient number for the whole

---

somewhere near Grand Island along the Platte River later that summer. However, not knowing that the Saints were delayed crossing Iowa and would not be following the initial plan of heading west to the Rockies in 1846, the Brown company concluded they had missed the advance companies and headed further west to try and catch up. Upon hearing the disappointing news that the main body of the Saints would winter at the Missouri River, they opted to winter at Pueblo, where they arrived 7 August 1846, two months before the arrival of the sick detachment of the Mormon Battalion. The following June 1847, seventeen of the Mississippi company led by Robert Crow met up with Brigham Young and the pioneers at or near Fort Laramie. He then dispatched Amasa Lyman down to Pueblo to lead the rest of the Pueblo group to the Salt Lake Valley. Thus some Mississippi Mormons, including three black slaves who had set out with Brigham Young's company from Winter Quarters (separate from the Pueblo Saints)—Hark Lay, Oscar Crosby, and Green Flake—were in the now enlarged party that arrived in the Salt Lake Valley on 22 July 1847. Others followed on 29 July 1847. Brown then returned to Mississippi later that fall and in 1848 brought out another company of thirteen families, numbering fifty-six white and thirty-four black persons who arrived in the valley in October 1848. Most settled Cottonwood, presently Holladay, Utah, named after John D. Holladay from Mississippi. Many of these southern Saints also helped settle San Bernardino in 1858 under the direction of Amasa Lyman and Charles C. Rich. See Carol Ann McQuilkin, "Journey of Faith: Mid-Nineteenth Century Migration of Mississippi Mormons and Slaves" (master's thesis, California State University, Fullerton, 1995). See also Leonard J. Arrington, "Mississippi Mormons," *Ensign*, June 1977, 46–51, and John Zimmerman Brown, ed., *Autobiography of Pioneer John Brown, 1820–1896* (Salt Lake City: self-published, 1941).

140. The group here referred to is the so-called sick detachment of the Mormon Battalion. After reaching Santa Fe, many had come down too ill and otherwise exhausted to complete the grueling overland march to San Diego. Colonel Alexander Donovan, commandant at Santa Fe, and Lieutenant Colonel Philip St. George Cooke, agreed to send a sick detachment of eighty-nine men, eighteen women, and several children on a three-hundred-mile detour to Pueblo, seventy-five miles west of Bent's Fort. Their orders were to intersect with the main body of the church in the spring of 1847 somewhere west of Fort Laramie. Meanwhile, the main body of the Mormon Battalion reached the shores of the Pacific in January 1847, without ever firing a shot in combat, just in time to celebrate Mexico's surrender of California to the United States. See Boone, "The Mississippi Saints," 160–86.

company, also some wagons are to be left behind. – He himself the Twelve & some others is going over the river to-morrow to make arrangements about getting a flat boat for us to cross with, as they have one here – Some of the brethren are intending to-commence burning a coal pit to-morrow. – I stood on guard to-night the last watch, from 12 o'clock till daylight, in Bro. Fairbank's place, who has not yet entirely recovered, altho' he is gradually gaining his health – at the place where we are now encamped, are a number of large ash trees growing on the banks of the river. – about midway of one of these, we noticed this evening the body or corpse on an Indian infant, closely enveloped in a buffalo robe, placed between two large boughs or branches, & lashed firmly to the same with thongs of raw-hide – This, I am informed is the mode of burial, peculiar to some tribes, the body being thus secured from the attack of wild beasts. We found wood in abundance at this place: as it is growing on all sides – A band of Crow Indians are daily expected here who are coming in with pottery, furs, &c.– By my computation, the distance between us & Winter Quarters, is 540¼ miles. –

In the early part of June a merchant, Amos Davis, brother of Daniel Davis, and Mr. Kimball, brother to the late John Kimball of Salt Lake, arrived from Nauvoo with goods and groceries and the best of wines, liquors, etc. My mother rented them her dining room for a store, and boarded them. This was an opening as unlooked for as if manna had rained down from heaven.

Woman's Exponent, vol. 14, no. 10,
15 October 1885, p. 78

Wednesday the 2d.

Pleasant morning, & bids fair to be a warm day. – The Twelve & some others went over the river this morning to make arrangements to procure the ferry boat. – Thomas Brown, Orson & F. Pomeroy went out of our 10 to guard cattle this forenoon, & I alone this afternoon, Orson having gone over to the Fort. – While out, I noticed an ash tree, containing the body of another Indian infant, this, being enveloped in a buffalo robe, rested on a piece of bark lashed thereto, which was placed breadthwise two large boughs, about midway of the tree. – John Higbee & some others have been fishing to-day in the Laramie Fork. – After drawing the sein a number of times, they caught 60 or 70 fish of different kinds, viz: – Carp, catfish, salmon, suckers, &c.– About noon the Twelve returned, bringing the flat boat with them, a number of the brethren towing it to the mouth of the Laramie Fork, thence up the river opposite our encampment. – We were obliged to pay them $15 for the use of it. – Bro. Wm. Clayton, has been over to the Fort, informed me that he saw 30 or 40 Indians there, – these are mostly connected by blood & marriage with the man who has principal charge of affairs there, whose name is Bordeaux – I also learned that from that place can be seen snow on the Laramie Peak of the Black Hills which lie to the S. W. – This evening it is tolerably cool. The time to-day has been principally occupied by the brethren in washing, repairing of wagons, &c.

THURSDAY THE 3D.

Somewhat cloudy this morning with a strong wind from the N. E. – The brethren commenced ferrying at sunrise this morning. – About ½ past 8 a.m. Bishop Whipple, F. Pomeroy & myself went over the river & took a view of Ft. John, as also of the ruins of Ft. Platte, of which I shall give a minute description hereafter. While there, we saw & conversed with 1 of 3 men who had come in last night from St. Joseph, Mo. He told us that there were 2000 wagons belonging to emigrants, between here & that place on their route to Oregon, 14 of which would probably be in to-day, as they travelled in separate companies of 100, 50, & as few as 11 wagons in number.[141] Yesterday Professor Pratt by an observation with the quadrant, ascertained the river here to be 108 yds. in width & Laramie Fork at Ft. John 46 yds. wide, both streams running with great rapidity. Amasa Lyman, Roswell Stevens, Thomas Wolsey & John H. Tibbetts started for Pueblo this morning – they are going in order to conduct the soldier brethren to us at the place where we shall stop to hunt a week or 2, probably somewhere in the vicinity of Sweet Water. – Porter, Thomas Brown, Joseph Matthews & John Brown crossed the river & went ahead on horseback to seek a good road.

---

141. OVERLAND EMIGRATION TO OREGON, CALIFORNIA, UTAH 1840–52

Year	Oregon	California	Yearly West Coast Total	Cumulative West Coast Total	Utah	Cumulative Grand Total
1840	13	–	13	13	–	13
1841	24	34	58	71	–	71
1842	125	–	125	196	–	196
1843	875	38	913	1,109	–	1,109
1844	1,475	53	1,528	2,637	–	2,637
1845	2,500	260	2,760	5,397	–	5,397
1846	1,200	1,500	2,700	8,097	–	8,097
1847	4,000	450	4,450	12,547	2,200	14,747
1848	1,300	400	1,700	14,247	2,400	18,847
Pre-gold rush subtotals	11,512	2,735	14,247	14,247	4,600	18,847
1849	450	25,000	25,450	39,697	1,500	45,797
1850	6,000	44,000	50,000	89,697	2,500	98,297
1851	3,600	1,100	4,700	94,397	1,500	104,497
1852	10,000	50,000	60,000	154,397	10,000	174,497

Adapted from John D. Unruh Jr., *The Plains Across: The Overland Emigrants and the Trans-Mississippi West 1840–60* (Urbana: University of Illinois Press, 1979), 84–85.

Fort John, 1844, *precursor to Fort Laramie. Wyoming State Archives.*

– About 1 P. M. it commenced raining very hard, accompanied by considerable hail, also thunder & lightning. This detained the operations at the Ferry about 1 hour, when the rain ceased, although the weather yet has quite a threatening appearance. Thomas Grover has the superintendence of the ferryiage of the 1st Division, & John S. Higbee that of the 2d Division. – My wagon & horses were ferried over about sunset, being the last wagon in the 10, & the ferryage was suspended till morning, 17 wagons yet remaining on the other side. – It again commenced raining just before I crossed the river, & yet continues, it being now about 9 o'clock in the evening. We are formed in a circle on the banks of the river, near the ruins of Ft. Platte, in which most of the brethren put their horses to-night. – Porter & those sent ahead, returned this evening, having been some 8 or 10 miles up the river, & reported the route to be generally even & practicable Latitude at Ft. John, 42° – 12 m. – 13 s. – I will now proceed to give a description of Ft. Platte & Ft. John, which I have hitherto omitted for want of time[142] – The former is in a state of ruins, & is situated on the banks of the N. Fork, about

142. Situated at the junction of the North Platte River and Laramie Fork, Fort Laramie had been a fur trading center since 1834. In 1841 the American Fur Company erected a more substantial post, renaming it Fort John in 1842. By 1847 it was a well-established commercial trading post, complete with high timbered walls, corner towers, and two massive doors looking out over the vast plain before it. Not to be confused with the city of Laramie, Wyoming, Fort Laramie today is a well-preserved historical site situated seventy-five miles north of Cheyenne, near the Wyoming-Nebraska state line. See David W. Lupton: "Fort

a mile from the latter fork – The walls are composed of lumps of clay, apparently dried in the sun, & are about 8 inches thick & from 12 to 20 inches long, laid up like unto brick – the height of the walls is about 10 feet – they measured on the outside east & west 144 feet; north & south, 132 feet. On the east, west, & south, running from the main walls to the center, are 16 rooms, each opening to the interior. – 15 of them are 15½ by 16 feet inside, with window holes resembling port holes. – On the north side there is a large room called by the French "Corell", a place for keeping their horses & cattle, the size of which is 98 by 47 feet. – The thickness of these walls is 30 inches, which are covered with lime, or something of the like nature. – The entrance is on the south & North-east corner, the Old Oregon road running 1 rod from the South-west corner towards the North Fork. – We next visited Ft. John – this is beautifully situated on a small-eminence on the banks of the Laramie Fork, about 1½ mile above its junction with the North Fork & commands an extensive view of the whole adjacent country – we were very kindly received by Mr. Bordeaux the proprietor, who conducted us through the interior of the Fort, & gave us some information relative to the same[143] – The construction of this is similar to that of Ft. Platte, as far as the general outlines are concerned. The number of men employed here is 38, although only 18 are here at present. – The length & breadth on the outside are 168 by 116 feet. – On either side east & west are 5 rooms & 3 each on the north & south sides, making 16 rooms in all, including 10 dwelling rooms on the east & west, &1 on the north side. – of the 3 rooms on the south side 2 are occupied as store rooms, the remaining 1 as a blacksmith shop – The place where the horses & cattle are kept is on the eastern side, & is quite similar to that of Ft. Platte. – Mr. Bordeaux informed us that Ft. John was built about 7 years since, some time previous to the erection of Ft. Platte, which, he with others, had purchased of another company – The country in this vicinity is subject to long droughts, as he informed me till quite lately, there had been no rain for near 2 years. –

FRIDAY THE 4TH.

Pleasant, & cool morning owing to the rain last night. – Wind in the West. – The last of the wagons got over the river this morning about 8 o'clock. The Twelve, with a number of others, went up to the Fort, to bid adieu to the inhabitants, & to pay for the use of the boat – they returned at 20 minutes past 11 a.m., – A number of Indians & squaws from the Fort, paid a visit to our camp this morning. – We continued our journey at 12 M (the 2d Division going ahead, & our 10 being foremost,) & travelled a north-west course about 2½

Platte, Wyoming, 1841–1845: Rival of Fort Laramie," *Annals of Wyoming* 49, no. 1 (Spring 1977): 83–92, and Fred E. Woods, "Fort Laramie . . . Halfway to Our Mountain Home (1847–68)," *Annals of Wyoming* 80, no. 3 (Summer 2008): 17–32. See also Elliot Coues, ed., *40 Years a Fur Trader on the Upper Missouri: Personal Narrative of Charles Larpenteur 1833–1872*, 2 vols. (1898), 1:23.

143. The thirty-two-year old James Bordeaux was an experienced trader, voyageur, hunter, and explorer. With him at the Fort were his Sioux Indian wife, Marie, and two of their children, along with some twenty other Sioux men, women, and children. See John D. McDermott, "James Bordeaux," in LeRoy Hafen, *The Mountain Men and the Fur Trade of the Far West, 1965–1972*, 5:68–69. Wilford Woodruff called Bordeaux "a Frenchman" and "a gentleman." See Matthias F. Cowley, *Wilford Woodruff: History of His Life and Labors* (Salt Lake City: Bookcraft, 1964).

William H. Jackson, [Francis] Parkman Approaching Old Fort Laramie, 1846. *Wyoming State Archives.*

miles, & then began to take a west course, passing along between the bluffs & the river. We halted to bait at 25 minutes past 1 P. M., having come 3 miles – At this place the grass was the most luxuriant that we have seen it for a long time – here to our right a short distance, the river winding in a serpentine direction, glides gracefully by, while immediately to our left are large crags & masses of rock, as it were, suspended over our heads – on the sides of these are numerous cedar trees, as also plenty of ash-trees growing in the vicinity – We again started at 25 minutes to 3 P. M., – travelling over a deep, rugged, sandy road, we gradually ascended the bluffs; after going about 8 miles in near the same direction, we came to a place where the road led down a long & steep descent to the bottom below, which, after reaching, & proceeding ¼ of a mile, we encamped in a circle at ½ past 5 P. M.; having come 8¼ miles to-day – Just as we arrived we had quite a thunder shower, which however, did not last above ½ an hour. – We are encamped within a short distance of the river, on the margin of which the grass is quite green & high – there is also plenty of wood in the vicinity, chiefly white ash. – a man by the name of Myers who has lived in this country 9 years, started from Ft. John, (or Laramie, as it is sometimes called) with us this morning, intending to prosecute the journey in our company – He has 2 wives, (squaws,) at Pueblo, also a number of children. – he had been hesitating between 2 decisions, whether to return to Pueblo, or proceed with us & finally determining to pursue the former course, he had travelled about an hour on the route, this morning, when, suddenly changing his mind, he retraced his steps to our camp, just as we had got ready to start. – He is, at present, travelling with the family of Bro. Robert Crow. The names of the three families who came with Bro. Crow from Pueblo, inclusive his own, as also other individuals travelling with him, are as follows: – Robert Crow, Elizabeth Crow, Benjamin B. Crow, Harriet Crow, Elizabeth Jane Crow, John McHenry Crow, Walter H. Crow – George W. Therlkill, Matilda Jane Therlkill, Milton Howard Therlkill, James Wm. Therlkill – Wm Parker Crow, Isa Vinda Eugene Crow, Iraminda Almarene Crow, Archibald Little, James Chesney, Lewis B. Myers. – The foregoing names, are arranged in a company by themselves, & belong to the 2^{d} Division, thus forming the 15th 10 belonging to the camp of Israel. – They have with them the following wagons & stock: – 5 wagons, 1 cart, 11 horses, 12 yoke oxen, 22 cows, 7 calves, 3 bulls. I neglected to mention that Porter, this morning, exchanged a horse at the fort for 2 cows with their calves, & 1 two year old heifer – Thomas Brown also at the same time exchanged a horse for a pony. –

SATURDAY THE 5TH.

Rather cloudy this morning, though tolerably warm. – It is the intention hereafter to put up guide boards at the end of each 10 miles we travel. – At 20 minutes past 8 a.m. we continued our journey; after travelling north of west over an uneven, sandy bottom; about 4 miles, we ascended a high bluff, & went ½ miles over a cragged, rocky road, when we again descended

James Bordeaux (d. 1878), proprietor at Fort Laramie and longtime fur trader for the American Fur Company, with Marie, his Sioux wife. Wyoming State Archives.

a steep & narrow declivity, & came to the bottom below, which, however, is considerably elevated above the river. – The summit & sides of this bluff abound in numerous pine trees, a number of them growing in the clefts of the rocks. Leaving the river, we now began to pursue a due west course through extensive valleys & narrow defiles, with lofty banks on either side, obscuring a number of sandbeds, which apparently marked the former course of mighty rushing torrents, descending from the mountains. – Near 1 of these, (a small rivulet issueing from a spring close by & running over a portion of it at this time,) we halted to bait at 20 minutes to 12 M., having come 6½ miles. – Our halting place this noon is in a beautiful valley, encompassed on all sides by cragged precipices & small hills, & apparently, "shut out from all the world beside." The Spring spoken of above is called by Captain Fremont "Warm Springs", & is in Lat. 42° – 15 m. – 6 s. – Rained a little at intervals this forenoon. – While here, there were 3 men came to us on mules – these belong to a band of emigrants, who, with 11 wagons are in the vicinity, & have taken a different & main road from the Ft., than ourselves, & consequently, are ahead of us. – We again started at ¼ to 2 P. M., went a short distance, & came to the place where the road made by these emigrants, intersects our own – after going about ¾ of a mile, we again turned to the north-west, & soon began to ascend another long, steep, & stony declivity, after which, we emerged on to a beautiful, rolling prairie, – here we could discover the emigrants, travelling ahead of us some distance – we could also plainly discern snow on the Laramie Peak of the Black Hills, as well as vaporous clouds shrouding a portion of its sides & summit – After having come 7 miles, we again descended a steep, sandy hill, at the foot of which is a sand-bed – this we travelled over

C. Hall, Laramie Peak and Black Hills in Distance (1853). *Wyoming State Archives.*

some distance. – About 3 miles beyond this we came to the place where the emigrants had encamped for the night – Passing them we proceeded ½ a mile further, &, crossing a small stream, which apparently has its source in springs, we encamped on the banks thereof in a circle, at ½ past 6 P. M., having come 17 miles to-day, & 53 during the week; being this evening, 25¼ miles distant from Fort John, & 565½ from Winter Quarters – Our place of encampment this evening, is also in an extensive valley, surrounded by high hills. – We have not seen the river, since we left it this morning, – It is my opinion that the "Black Hills" are so named from the fact of their tops & sides abounding in pine trees & shrubs, which, seen at a distance, have, in appearance, a dark color. –

SUNDAY THE 6TH.

Tolerably pleasant this morning, though the sky is somewhat obscured by clouds. – It rained considerably during the past night. About 8 oclock, the emigrants, spoken of above, passed our camp. A prayer meeting was held this forenoon, commencing at ½ past 8 a.m., & ending at ½ past 10 a.m. – Being busily engaged in writing, I did not attend – the meeting was adjourned for one hour. Orson is engaged this forenoon in washing some of our clothes. – The brethren again came together, pursuant to adjournment, at ½ past 11 a.m., & the meeting was opened by singing, & prayer by Elder E. Benson, after which Elder O. Pratt arose & said, that as it had the appearance of rain, the President thought best that the meeting be adjourned, or dismissed; "accordingly," said he, "consider yourselves dismissed with the blessings of Heaven." – Soon after 21 wagons, belonging to emigrants, passed our encampment, in addition to the 11 that went ahead this morning, making 32 wagons in all. – The shower did not last more than ½ an hour, when it again cleared off pleasant, though quite warm. – It is the intention to proceed 5 or 6 miles this afternoon, as we learn that, otherwise, we shall be obliged to travel over 20 miles to-morrow, before we can come to a convenient camping place, on account of the scarcity of water. – We accordingly started at ½ past 2 P. M., – we travelled 3¾ miles over an uneven, sandy road, somewhat wet in places from the recent rains, & halted about ¾ of an hour, while some of the brethren went ahead to find a suitable camping place for the night. After going about ¼ of a mile further, we passed the encampment of the last company of the emigrants, when, after proceeding a mile, we encamped in a circle, at 5 P. M., on the banks of a small stream, having, this afternoon, come 5 miles. Our course has been, most of the time, a little south of west, through a beautiful picturesque country, abounding in rich, woodland scenery, principally consisting of cotton-wood & willow. We are situated, this evening, in a small valley, encompassed by a gentle elevation of ground, on which are growing in abundance green grass & wild sage. – The latter plant we have noticed for a day or two on our route. – To the south west of us a short distance, on the banks of the creek above mentioned, is quite a dense forest of trees, consisting also principally of cotton-wood. – Porter informed me that while out this afternoon on horseback, he saw 6 or 7 elk. He also wounded a deer, & has gone out with others, this evening, expecting to get it with assistance of dogs – after a while he returned, not having been successful in the pursuit. – The first body of emigrants, consisting of 11 wagons are encamped ¼ of a mile ahead of us. Two of them were at our camp this evening, & conversed with Pres't. Young, & a number of the brethren for some time. One of them, whose name is Burroughs, is an old acquaintance of Luke Johnson, & was formerly from Shalersville, Ohio. He said that they had a pilot with them, whose name is Gabriel Freedom, who is well acquainted with the route. Bro. Burr Frost did considerable blacksmithing for the last company of 21 wagons, who are encamped back about a mile.

MONDAY THE 7TH.

Fine morning – I arose at sunrise, & stood on guard, watching cattle in Orson's place. – We started at ¼ past 7 a.m. the emigrants preceding us a short distance. We pursued a N. N. W. course 5 miles, over an uneven, sandy road, & came to a steep descent, which we were obliged to dig down, before going further – we proceeded 2¾ miles & halted to bait[144] at ¼ to 11 a.m., near a place where small springs issue from the ground. – We found the grass here quite scant. – We saw the dead body of an antelope by the roadside, killed by the emigrants who are in advance of us. – While here 13 more emigrant wagons passed us, making 45 in all ahead, all of which have 3, 4, & 5 yoke of oxen attached to them. – From here the snow is plain to be seen on Laramie Peak, which lies some distance to the south-west of us, we being now as near it as our route will probably bring us. – we again started at 1 P. M., going a short distance we ascended a hill, & came to a beautiful rolling prairie, almost literally covered with pine trees of different sizes, though the ground is quite stony, as we noticed huge fragments of rock on either side as we passed along. We also discovered on our route 2 dead bodies of an antelope & a red-tailed deer, suspended to a tree. We took them along with us. I learned that Porter killed the antelope & Lewis B. Myers the deer. – Our course this afternoon has also been North of West; &, with little exception, over a rough, hilly, rocky country. Descending a steep hill, we at length encamped in a circle at 4 P. M., having come 5¼ miles this afternoon, & 13 during the day. Our situation, this evening, is in a beautiful valley, (partially surrounded by high hills,) near a beautiful murmuring rivulet, with a large forest of trees & shrubbery, growing on its banks. The grass here is the highest & most luxuriant we have seen since we left Winter Quarters. About 2 rods from my wagon, is a very large, clear, & cold spring, affording as good water as I ever drank; & to say all in one word, the place seems to me a perfect paradise. – The 2d company of emigrants, I am informed are encamped about a mile ahead of us. It rained a little soon after our arrival – at the same time Orson went out on guard to watch horses & cattle. I learned that one or two more deer were killed this afternoon, but did not ascertain by whom. The stream on which we are encamped to night, is called by Fremont in his journal, "Horseshoe Creek." – It rained a little during the fore part of the night, Orson stood on guard the latter part from 12 till daylight.

---

144. An archaic term, "To bait" meant to stop for rest or for food during one's journey.

Tuesday the 8th.

Pleasant morning. We started at 25 minutes past 7 a.m. – I, with a number of others, went ahead with pick-axes, spades, & hoes to make the "rough places smooth", & remove obstructions in the road, which leads over a rocky mountainous country. We walked 4¾ miles, & crossed a creek where 2 companies of emigrants encamped last night. Here we stopt at ½ past 10 a.m. & waited till the teams came up – We found John Higbee here, who had exchanged his Indian horse with one of them for a cow & heifer. We walked 2 miles further ahead of the teams, & came to another creek, on the banks of which we halted to bait at ¼ to 12 M., having come 6¾ miles. One of the daughters of Bro. Robert Crow had one of her limbs considerably injured, by accidentally falling out of the wagon, & one of the wheels running over it. This noon I feel quite fatigued with my walk & labor on the road. I understood there was a number of buffaloes seen this forenoon. Lewis B. Myers killed an antelope this morning. We started at 10 minutes past 1 P. M. proceeding, as usual, over a rocky hilly country, alternately ascending & descending high hills, without the occurrence of any particular incident & finally came to another stream about 2 rods wide – quite deep & rapid. – On its banks & adjacent, is another large forest, similar to the one where we encamped last night. Here we encamped in a circle at 10 minutes to 6 P. M., having mad [*sic*] 8¾ miles this afternoon, & 15½ during the day. Our course, generally thro' the day has been N. N. W. – The weather, which this forenoon was quite pleasant, became very cold this afternoon (the wind being in the north,) so that a fire feels, this evening, quite comfortable. Porter killed a deer this afternoon. John W. Norton also killed an antelope. – This evening 5 mountaineers came to our camp on horseback – they are on their way from Fort Bridger to Fort John, & are encamped this evening about 1¼ mile from here.

Wednesday the 9th.

Pleasant morning, though quite cool weather. We started at sunrise, went 1¼ mile & stopt to bait on the same creek. Here we found the mountaineers encamped. They have 2 squaws with them. They had also one or two carts loaded with buffalo skins & other peltry of different kinds. Some of the brethren are intending to send letters back by them. These men were well acquainted with Lewis B. Myers, (who travels with Bro. Crow's family,) & told him that on crossing the Platte River, 3 or 4 day's journey before us, they had made a leather boat, which they hung up in a tree, & that we might use it for ferrying; therefore, it was thought expedient, to send some men ahead & secure it, – before the emigrants should reach the river; – accordingly, 19 wagons started from here this morning, for that purpose, being under the supervision of Capt. Tarleton Lewis. The remainder of us started at 25 minutes past 7 a.m. – We had not gone far before we were overtaken by another band of mountaineers, 4 in number, – these had with them a dozen or more ponies & mules, the most of which had packs on their backs. After going 2¼ miles we crossed another creek. Just before you arrive at this, the earth assumes a reddish appearance, which continues a number of miles. We halted to bait at 20 minutes to 1 P. M., near a sand-bed where had formerly been a stream, having come 11¼ miles, over, as usual, a rough, hilly country. We again started at ¼ past 2 P. M. proceeding a N. W. course as indeed we have the whole day, & finally encamped in a semi-circle, at ¼ past 6 P. M., on the banks of a stream about 2 rods in width, running with considerable rapidity. Just as we arrived, we could see in the distance ahead, ascending a hill, the wagons sent ahead this morning – The mountaineers also passed us & pursued their journey to the west – these came from the Arkansas River, & are on their return to the Mountains. We have travelled 19¼ miles to day, being the longest ascertained days' journey we have accomplished since we left Winter Quarters.

THURSDAY THE 10TH.

Beautiful morning. The weather being quite warm & pleasant. – Bro. Heber told me that he thought, that in about 5 weeks we would reach the place of our destination, viz: – the Salt Lakes, we being now near 300 miles from Ft. Bridger, which is about 100 miles from the former place, where, he said, there was only one inhabitant or settler, viz: – a farmer who settled there last fall – this information he obtained, I suppose, of the mountaineers. He also informed me, that yesterday he saw a natural curiosity, viz: – a toad, having bothe [*sic*] tail & horns. We started at 20 minutes to 8 a.m. & pursuing still a N. W. course, after going, as usual, over a rough, hilly country, 4½ miles we crossed a small rivulet. We proceeded about 2 miles & crossed another, when after travelling 2¼ miles further we halted at 20 minutes past 11 a. m., on the banks of another stream called North Buffalo Fork, having come 8¾ miles. At this place the grass was tolerably good. We again started at ¼ to 2 P. M., – proceeded 4¼ miles & again came to the river, after descending a long, steep, hill – we went 4¾ miles further on the bottom, in a western direction, & encamped in a circle at ¼ past 6 P. M., in a beautiful grove of cotton wood trees, having come 17¾ miles to-day. Near here is a beautiful stream, about 3 rods in width, which, running with great rapidity empties into the river a short distance hence. It is called Deer Creek. By an observation made this evening from the fixed star "Arcturus," its latitude was ascertained to be 42° 52′ 50″. – about a mile above, Bro. [Albert] Carrington & others discovered, this evening, an extensive mine of bituminous (pitch) coal, a specimen of which I procured of him – this is different in its nature from the anthracite (stone) coal. Latitude this noon at North Buffalo Fork 42° 51′ 5″. I understood from J. Hancock, that a portion of the stream on which we encamped last night, (called by the French "a la Prele") runs thro' a natural tunnel of rock arched over, for about 20 rods, the span being large enough to admit a man to walk through it. – I caught 3 fish this evening of very good size 1 catfish & 2 suckers, & in fact Deer Creek abounds in fish of different kinds. There were 4 antelope killed to-day by different individuals.

FRIDAY THE 11TH.

[***Editor's note***: In the original journals, Horace Whitney's handwritten entries for 11 and 12 June are not in sequential order. For reasons not given, these pages follow his entry for 28 June.]

Bright & beautiful – I stood on guard this morning in front of my wagon to prevent the horses from recrossing the creek. We continued our journey at ½ to 8 a. m., & travelled in a western direction along the river, most of the time on a level, sandy bottom, occasionally ascending a small elevation of ground, & halted to bait at 12 M. a short distance from the river, having come 9¼ miles. During most of our route this forenoon, we have noticed a considerable number of cotton wood trees, interspersed here & there, growing on both sides the river – near a cluster of these we have stopt this noon. There have been 4 antelope killed this forenoon – 3 by Ed. Ellsworth, F. Pomeroy, & J. Hancock. the other by whom I did not ascertain. We again started at 10 minutes past 2 P. M.; still pursuing a west course along the river, we crossed 2 small streams on our route, when, after travelling alternately over the hills & bottom, we turned to the right of the road some distance & encamped at 6 P. M., on the banks of the river near a small grove of cotton wood, having come 7¾ this P. M. & 17 miles during the day. – about a mile above us part of 2 companies of emigrants are encamped – these are now crossing the river by means of a boat they brought along, assisted by a raft they have here constructed. The majority of them, however, I learned from 2 of their number this evening, had gone up the river on this side, probably intending to cross where we do. I learned this evening that there were 3 more antelope killed & brought into camp this evening, 2 of which were killed by Henson Walker, making 7 in all – there were a number killed not brought in. Latitude at our stopping place this noon, 42° 51′ 47″. After our arrival I stood on guard in Orson's place, watching cattle.

Saturday the 12th.

Fine morning, with a cool breeze from the west. Some of the brethren, this morning, tried to find a fording place, near here, but were unsuccessful. All the extra men in the camp went ahead to make a bridge over a creek. Bro. J. Hancock, while on guard this morning, shot an antelope. – We started at ¼ past 8 a. m., & following the course of the river a little south of west 3 miles, we crossed a creek over a bridge built by the brethren who went in advance, among whom was Orson. At this place we saw an antelope that had been wounded in the leg by some of the hunters, & moved slowly & with considerable difficulty. Bro. T. Grover fired a shot at him, which did not take effect, however, the animal soon fell exhausted, & he cut his throat. – We proceeded 1¼ mile and crossed another small stream, after which, going 3 miles, we halted to bait at ½ past 11 a.m., about ¼ of a mile from the river, having come 7¼ miles. Here the grass was quite scant. We noticed considerable snow on the bleak, high hills to our left, as we passed along this forenoon. – as before proceeding further we have to cross a deep ravine, the men were called upon to go with spades & dig it down. While here, Bro. Alexander P. Chessley rode up on horseback. He came from our wagons that went ahead on Wednesday last. He said that they were about 3 miles above here, as also a number of the emigrants. They had undertaken to ferry over the river 22 wagons for the latter, for $1.50 each which amounts to $33 they being paid in flour at $2.50 per hundred, also meat & bacon. When he left they had taken them all over except 3 wagons – this is done by means of the "Revenue Cutter," & 2 logs that they had hewn out, the wheels on each side a wagon being placed in the cavity. He reported that the hunters had killed 3 buffaloes, & Porter, J. Brown, & Lewis B. Myers one black bear & 3 cubs, beside a large number of antelope that had been killed. He also reported the river to be quite rapid & deep, & but little grass where they were encamped. Soon after his arrival Heber, Bro. Benson, O. Pratt, Col. Rockwood & a number of others (including himself,) went to search a suitable fording place near here. – They soon returned unsuccessful, & we again started at 25 minutes to 2 P. M. & proceeded a little south of west over an uneven, sandy soil 3¼ miles & crossed a narrow, deep stream, after which we went ¾ of a mile & encamped in a semicircle on the banks of the river at ½ past 4 P. M., having come 11¼ miles to-day, 98¾ miles during the week, being, this evening, 124 miles from Ft. John & 664¼ miles from Winter Quarters. Our 19 wagons are encamped about ½ a mile above, the men being yet engaged in ferrying over the emigrants. – I have heard of only 4 antelope being kill to-day in the 2d Division. The grass here is quite plenty & good – The nearest timber is about ½ a mile below us on the bank of the river. This evening 6 horsemen, (emigrants,) encamped about ½ a mile below us. I saw 2 of their number, who informed me that they belonged to another company of 24 wagons which are back about 10 miles. This evening the brethren are considerably alarmed about Bro. Tunis Rappleye, who soon after our arrival, on a wager, get out to go up to the bluffs opposite (about 5 miles distant,) to procure a snowball & bring it to the camp by 8 o'clock. A number of men were rallied to go in pursuit of him, & the horn was sounded several times, as also guns fired at intervals for his benefit. About 11 he returned: he succeeded in getting the snowball, but could not bring it to camp, as it dissolved before he arrived. –

Sunday the 13th.

Pleasant morning, though the weather throughout the day was quite warm & sultry. The emigrants started from the other side of the river about 9 a. m. – About ½ past 9 a. m. a meeting was commenced & held till noon – A number of the brethren spoke & prayed, & last of all, Brigham, Heber, & O. Pratt addressed successively the congregation. President Young spoke principally of the liberty & light of the gospel. That very few knew what the phrase meant. That we should always try to do that which would result in the most good, & that a man could not know that, unless by revelation from Heaven. That it is enough for us to know what is necessary to be done to-day to be of the most utility, without thinking of the course necessary to be pursued for the same purpose to morrow or next day. Heber spoke of the necessity of our cultivating union one with another, & banishing all selfishness from our hearts, that we may become acceptable servants in the sight of the Lord. – Elder O. Pratt's speech principally related to the utility & necessity of the improvement & cultivation of the time & talents God has given us, showing that a contrary course would result in the depravity of our morals. After the meeting was dismissed, all the officers in the camp met together at Pres't Young's wagon to counsel upon matters relative to our crossing the river to-morrow. It was proposed by the President; that a quantity of poles should be procured this afternoon, that with their assistance, 4 wagons might be lashed together abreast, & drawn across the river without danger of being overturned, accordingly 3 or 4 wagons immediately started off in pursuit of them. (poles.) Bro. Heber, with the aid of the Revenue Cutter swam over a number of his oxen this afternoon. Col. Rockwood, the Commissary, also this afternoon, distributed equally among the brethren in the camp, the provisions got of the Gentiles in payment for ferryage, which were to each person as follows, viz: – Flour 5½ lbs., meal 2 lbs. & a small slice of bacon. The 1st Division are intending to take the freight of the wagons over in the Revenue Cutter, the 2 Division by means of a raft built this afternoon for that purpose.

MONDAY THE 14TH.

Tolerably warm day, with considerable wind. This morning very early the ferryage of the wagons & goods commenced – a number of wagons were drawn across the river with a rope, the current setting towards the opposite shore, some 2, 3, & 4 abreast. a number of them were overset, rolling over a number of times, before reaching the shore, but mine, which was lashed together with 3 others, was brought over safely this morning. Some took their wagons over on rafts, also their goods. I was stationed with Col. Markham & 2 or 3 others to assist in pulling over the wagons as fast as the ropes were attached to them; though part of the time I was engaged in driving cattle attached to the raft which we had to tow up stream some distance. This afternoon we had a very heavy hail & rain storm, accompanied by considerable wind. – Bro. J. Higbee & myself happened to be up the river at the time, towing the raft, & we were obliged to seek the shelter of the nearest bushes, as we were some distance from the wagons. About sunset, I brought over my freight in the Revenue Cutter, which after taking out, I put it again into the wagon, together with some of Bro. Luke Johnson's things, whose wagon is on the other side the river. My horses I had not yet got over, therefore I procured another span, & took my wagon back ¼ of a mile from the river to an elevated plot of ground covered with green grass, trees & bushes, where about a dozen of wagons had already preceded me – This was done in consequence of the river's rising so rapidly, as we were somewhat fearful that the shore would be inundated with water during the night. – As my wagon was full of goods, after eating some supper given us by the brethren, Bro. Luke Johnson & myself laid down before the fire in the open air, covering ourselves with buffalo robes. After a while, Orson, who had been over the river, came back & slept with us. I have done the hardest day's work to-day I ever recollect to have done in my life, & this evening I feel quite worn out with cold & fatigue. I learned there were 24 wagons brought over to-day. Bro. Heber has been quite busy to-day in overseeing the ferryage; I also noticed him assisting in taking over the raft. 4 Frenchmen or traders came up on horseback, soon after I brought over my things, & at their request, were ferried over to the other side the river in the boat, & went down to a camp of the emigrants 4 miles below here.

A letter written by Father Whitney to his sons Horace and Orson, then with the pioneers, which he wrote June 14th, 1847, and directed as follows:

"Camp of Israel in the West." MY SONS HORACE AND ORSON:

Upper Platte Mormon Ferry. *Lithograph by Piercy,* Route from Liverpool to Great Salt Lake Valley. *Courtesy of Church History Library.*

*"I have just started a team for the mountains. * * * I intended to have sent two or three teams and wagons, but the mill dam going down stream a few days since, I could not procure breadstuff for more than one wagon, and that is in charge of Bros. Archibald Hill and Stillman Pond. They have for you near two hundred pounds of flour and one small cheese, say eight or ten pounds, if you need it. Should you not want all the flour, take as much of it as will do you and let them keep the balance, as they are rather scant of breadstuff. If my team should meet you on your return you will give Bros. Pond and Hill a list of all my property which you may have left the other side of the mountains, and in order that they may get possession of it, and take care of the same until I come, and give them all the instructions you can about matters appertaining to my business, etc., in that country, as they have gone expressly to attend to my business, as also their own. It is a general time of health in this place, but there are quite a number of poor on our hands, which makes it rather hard times; but as we have a large quantity of grain growing, we hope we shall be able to do better by them by and by. We have been hindered in starting a company early, as anticipated when you left, in consequence of not being able to procure a supply of breadstuff sufficient to warrant it, and some other reasons might be assigned.*

"We have concluded to fit out but one company to the mountains this season, and it is expected that it will consist of not less than from four to five hundred wagons, from the present calculations, and the most of them will be under the necessity of taking the greater part of their grain unground.[145] *Bro. Eldredge takes a pair of small millstones with him, and the necessary irons, etc., to set a mill in operation by horse power or otherwise, in a short time after his arrival at the place of destination.*

"Our mother has written you at some length, she says, and it is therefore unnecessary for me to touch on any matter except business, but would say that you have our prayers night and day for your prosperity in all things, as also all of your company, that you may prosper and return safe to us this fall, and I am sanguine you will. But remember to be prayerful and show yourselves approved before the Lord, and heed the counsel of those whom the Lord has ordained

145. Newel K. Whitney's letter refers to the "Big" or "Emigration" Camp. Numbering 1,448 men, women, and children in 566 wagons under the direction of Parley P. Pratt and John Taylor, the Big Camp left the Elkhorn River 15 June 1847. They arrived safely in the Salt Lake Valley beginning 28 September 1847, one of the largest companies ever to cross the great plains. See Bennett, *We'll Find the Place*, 254–55, 276. See also Susan Ward Easton [Black], "Pioneers of 1847: A Sesquicentennial Remembrance" (unpublished document, Church History Library).

to give counsel, and it shall be well with you. This from your father, who blesses you in the name of the Lord.

"This is confidential, but you can show it to H. C. K. if you choose.

"N. K. WHITNEY.

"P.S. Give my good wishes to Bros. Brigham and Heber and all the others; tell them things are right in the main, and it is a hurrying time, as usual, or I would have written them; but I suppose their families have written them fully on all matters. May the Lord bless you all.

"N. K. W."

Woman's Exponent, vol. 15, no. 1,
1 June 1886, p. 6

Tuesday the 15th.

Somewhat cloudy, with a strong west wind. I felt quite unwell this morning, owing to being in the water & the hard labor of yesterday, therefore, I did not assist in ferrying to-day, but busied myself in taking the things out of the wagon, & laying them on the ground to air & dry. The wind was so very strong down the stream, that they could not ferry with the usual rapidity, but by night they had got over, as I understood 20 wagons, – which were all brought over on rafts. Bro. Robert Crow lost a horse that he was attempting to swim across the river, in consequence of his feet getting entangled in a laryette that was on his neck at the time. There was quite a large rattlesnake killed near here this afternoon, in the body of which, on examination, was found a large mouse or mole that he had swallowed. – I heard Bro. Benson say this evening, that there was a Missourian, belonging to the last company of emigrants, lately come up on horseback, who informed the brethren that he saw, as he was passing along above the head of Grand Island, a large collection of wagons travelling along on the North side of the Platte River – these, we suppose to be the 2d company of Pioneers, that were to leave Winter Quarters about the middle of May last.[146] There is a rumor, (how true I know not,) – that there are, at this time, 1000 wagons of emigrants, (Gentiles,) on the road between here & Ft. John or Laramie, consequently, it is the intention to leave some of the brethren here to ferry them over, & for this purpose, Col. Rockwood went round, & notified the officers of the camp that there must be 20 men, (10 out of each Division) Start early to-morrow morning, take some provisions with them, also the necessary implements, such as axes, broad-axes, & adz, & go where they could find suitable timber, & build 2 canoes. – Orson went over the river, to take care of the horses, & did not return to night.

Wednesday the 16th.

Somewhat cloudy, with a strong wind from the west. The men spoken of above, went down the river about 3 miles this morning, & returned this evening with the 2 canoes – a boat is

146. Likely referring to the Big or Emigration Camp. See note 145.

Artist unknown, Ferrying Wagons at the Platte—Mormon Ferry. *One of the more successful Mormon enterprises along the trail, the Mormon Ferry near today's Casper, Wyoming, ferried hundreds of wagons both Mormon and Oregon/California-bound settlers in their westward journeys. Courtesy of State Historical Society of Wisconsin.*

to be formed of these, by putting them a certain distance apart; & then placing puncheons across them. I learned this evening that 3 companies of emigrants, have come up on the other side the river & are a little way down the river – The occupants of 10 or 12 of their wagons, who are opposite us wish to be ferried over this evening, & they offer, if we will do it to night to pay us .50 cts. extra on a wagon, more than we got of the others, which would amount to $2.00 each – but this, I believe, was not done, as the brethren were mostly tired out with to-days' work. I do not know the number of wagons brought over to-day, but understand there were but few, as the wind blowing very strong down stream, rendered it impossible to do so with much rapidity. – There is a company of about 21 wagons of emigrants, down the river about 3 miles near where our brethren were at work to-day – these have managed to cross the river on a raft built by themselves, as we learned from 3 of their number, who visited our camp this afternoon – It is the intention to ferry over the emigrants to-morrow, as also the remainder of our own wagons – the cattle are to be swam over – Orson returned from the other side the river towards evening, bringing over the horses with him, by swimming them.

THURSDAY THE 17TH.

Pleasant morning though somewhat windy. I stood on guard the whole day, watching the cattle. All of our wagons were got over about noon, & we all moved up the river about ½ a mile & formed in a circle on its banks. There were also, I believe, 5 or 6 wagons of the emigrants ferried over this afternoon. J. Redding & myself, while out on guard this afternoon, saw a rattlesnake, which he shot. I understand this evening from Bro. Heber, it is the intention to pursue our journey to-morrow. after having occupied 4 days in crossing the river. The air is quite chilly this evening, the wind having veered around from the west to the north. It is also quite cloudy, having the appearance of rain.

FRIDAY THE 18TH.

Pleasant morning, though somewhat cool, the wind being in the north-west. There are 3 companies of emigrants to be ferried over. We are now engaged in rafting over the 2d company. the business having been kept up during the whole night. It is the intention for all to remain here till we shall have commenced bringing over the 3d company, that we may thereby draw the pay for the whole: leaving 10 men to complete the work, whose names are as follow: – Thomas Grover, John S. Higbee, Benjamin F. Stewart, James Davenport, William Empy, Luke Johnson, Appleton Harmon, Francis M. Pomeroy Edmund Ellsworth. The vessel which was constructed by means of the 2 canoes was finished, & launched about 1 P. M. – It is called the "Twins of the Black Hills" – & with it we are able to transport wagons & goods with much greater rapidity across the river than we have hitherto done.[147] We all got up our horses & cattle at 11 a. m., to see if there were any missing & found there was not – Most of the brethren are engaged in ferrying over the emigrants, a number of whom are quite sick – they have lost 2 of their number since they left Ft. John. I went fishing awhile this afternoon, but caught nothing, the river being too high – I believe it is not the intention to leave this place to-day, as contemplated yesterday.- The weather through the day continued quite warm & sultry. Those who are to remain behind were called together this evening to receive some instruction from Prest't. Young, relative to their duties - I did not attend in time to hear it, but arrived just at Bro. Bullock was reading to them a document containing rules for their guidance & conduct, in which they were exhorted to take care of their healths,

147. Under normal conditions, crossing the North Platte at this point where it was usually four to six feet deep and sixty yards wide would have been a relatively simple matter. However, the heavy snows of the winter of 1846–47 and a quickly warming spring had swollen the Platte far beyond its banks. Then a hundred yards wide and up to fifteen feet deep, the Platte posed a formidable challenge; hence the need to ferry the wagons across. Completed in two days, their makeshift ferry consisted of two twenty-four-foot cottonwood canoes, each two and a half feet wide, placed parallel to each other, reinforced with cross timbers. Equipped with a rudder and good oars fixed for steering, it was quickly dubbed "Twins of the Black Hills." The new ferry soon paid handsome dividends as non-Mormon companies offered to pay $1.50–$2.00 per wagon to ferry them across. Church leaders assigned Thomas Grover and several associates to stay back and operate the ferry for the rest of the season. For more on the "Mormon Ferry," see Dale S. Morgan, "The Mormon Ferry on the North Platte: The Journal of William A. Empey, May 7–Aug 4, 1847," *Annals of Wyoming* 21 (July–October 1949): 110–67; see also *We'll Find the Place*, 183–84, 198–200.

& not expose themselves to the cold & wet, as they had now a good boat to use – That they should build themselves a small house on a gentle eminence on the other side the river, both to live in, & to secure them & their effects from the Indians, in case a war-party should come this way. That they should attend strictly to their duty of ferrying over the emigrants, & not be around hunting, &c. but implicitly obey the instructions given them by their captain or foreman, Thos. Grover. That in case that general emigration should cease, they were to return to Ft. John & there remain till their families came up in the next company that is expected on soon, & then come on with them to our place of destination. In conclusion, Prest. Young remarked to them, that if they would obey the counsel given above, they should all be blessed, "for," said he, "I promise you that in the name of the Lord." – A number of the emigrant wagons that were ferried over during last night & to-day have gone ahead – an Irishman, Archibald Little by name, who has hitherto been travelling with Bro. Robert Crow's family, went off with them being hired at $20 per month to go & drive team, &c.– Bro. E. Glines remained also behind, though rather against counsel, to wait for his family. There have been 3 antelopes killed to-day – 2 by Joseph Hancock, 1 by Lewis B. Myers.

Saturday the 19th.

Pleasant morning, though rather cool. We started this morning at 10 minutes past 8, 1 mile above the place where we encamped the other side the river, on Saturday the 12th inst. We proceeded in a western direction, (leaving the Black Hills & river to our left,) over a sandy, hilly, country, without the occurrence of any particular incident, & stopt to bait at 1 P. M., in a small valley, – where the grass was tolerably good, though there was no water, – having come 11¼ miles – after remaining here near an hour, we again started at 2 P. M., – proceeded ¾ of a mile, & came to a quite an extensive sheet of pure water, which is called the "Cold Springs," & issues from springs in the ground beneath – Here we stopt a few minutes to water our horses & cattle – we then proceeded a little south of west over somewhat similar ground to that of this forenoon, (except, indeed, in some places we noticed huge masses of rock lying beside the road,) & encamped a little after sunset in a circle, in an extensive valley, enclosed by lofty hills, near a small rivulet which winds through it, apparently having its source in springs not far off – This, although quite transparent, we found had an extremely insipid brackish taste, but we were obliged to make use of it for want of better. – There was but little grass here, & in fact, scarcely any vegetation, except the "Wild Sage", which I have before spoken of as being quite plentiful in this part of the country – Neither was there wood of any kind, therefore we were obliged to resort to the only alternative – "Buffalo Chips" instead as fuel – Lewis B. Myers killed to-day 3 antelope, 1 deer & 1 buffalo bull, though the latter was in such poor condition that he did not bring him in – Porter also killed a buffalo this afternoon about 2 miles from here – He & Benjamin Rolfe have gone out this evening with a team to bring it to camp. We have travelled 21½ miles to-day, being the longest, ascertained distance we have made per day, since we left home – & are this evening 146½ miles from Ft. John, & 686¾ miles from Winter Quarters. I was chosen last evening as one of the night guard, to stand in the place of Francis M. Pomeroy, one of those selected to remain at the ferry – Our turn comes on every 3d night under Capt. Jacobs. John Pack is to succeed Appleton Harmon, the former captain of our 10, he being also one of those who tarried at the river.

Sunday the 20th.

Clear, cold morning – Porter returned with the slaughtered buffalo at 1 a. m. I arose a little before sunrise, & we started at 6 a.m. & proceeding a west course, over, as usual, an uneven, sandy soil, we at length halted to bait & get breakfast at 20 minutes past 7 a. m. on an extensive, undulating plain, near a pure & murmuring rivulet – sweet to the taste, & quite dissimilar to the one we left this morning, having come 3¾ miles. Here we found the grass green & luxuriant. We were obliged to use the roots of wild sage for fuel by which to cook our breakfasts, which here grows rank & abundant. We all feel considerably concerned about Andrew J. Gibbons, who left us yesterday noon at the cold springs in search of game, & has not since been heard of. John W. Norton went back on horseback in pursuit, & found him with a company of emigrants not far back. We again started at 10 minutes past 10 a.m. – went 9 miles & again stop to bait at 3 P. M. near a small, clear stream, which abounds in fish of various kinds & sizes – We continued our journey at 5 P. M. & passing over a hilly, sandy country, the features of which were rather uninteresting, we crossed a deep, narrow, & rapid stream, running in a serpentine direction, after having come about 5 miles – We then proceeded 1¾ mile, & turned to the left ½ a mile from the road & encamped in a circle a little after sunset, on the brow of a gentle eminence, in front of & about 100 yds. from the same creek we last crossed – On the margin of this, we found the grass very good – We have made 20 miles to-day. Andrew J. Gibbons came into camp on foot this evening, soon after our arrival. He had come from Willow Springs, 10¼ miles back since 3 P. M. he informed us that a company of emigrants have encamped there for the night. I permitted my horses to run loose to-night, as they have had, comparatively, a poor chance to feed since we left the river. W. Woodruff & J. Brown, who left us at the springs above named, & went ahead to hunt, &c. did not return to-night. The cannon was fired at 12 o'clock, so that in case they had lost their way, they might know from the report the direction to the camp. –

Monday the 21st.

Bright & beautiful morning, though as the day advanced, the weather became quite warm & sultry. We started this morning about ½ past 8 a.m., & continuing near a west course, we travelled over a deep sandy, & comparatively level road, occasionally passing over rough, knobby places, & came to the banks of "Sweet Water," at ¼ past 12 M., – Here we halted to bait having come 7½ miles[148] – This stream is quite deep & rapid, & at this place is about 5 rods in width, running in a serpentine direction through the valley, environed by stupendous

148. The Sweetwater River is a tributary of the North Platte River. Running 238 miles through the state of Wyoming, the river was named for its desirable taste. In the early 1800s it was called "Eau Sucrée" (meaning Sugar Water) by French trappers. The Americans called it the Sweetwater River.

lofty hills. Directly in front of us, apparently 1½ mile distant, is a lengthy high mass of rock, somewhat oval in form. It is situated on the east side of the river, about midway of the plain & has quite an isolated appearance, standing, as it does, some distance from the hills by which it is surrounded. This is called Fremont & others, "Independence Rock" & is named in the former's journal, as being 650 yds. in length, & 45 yds. high. On the summit are numerous large fissures, or clefts between the rocks - also hollow cavities forming natural reservoirs, in which there was considerable water. The road winds between it & the river, there being but the space of 2 or 3 rods between each - At the extremity next the river, on the sides of the rock, are inscribed in different colors, with paint, &c., numerous names & dates, done by Oregon emigrants, who have passed here at different periods.[149] A number of these names are inscribed near the summit, others at different distances below. - To this place I had come

A Wyoming Travel Commission photograph of Independence Rock. Wyoming State Archives.

149. Independence Rock—"The Great Register of the Desert"—was so named because so many pioneer companies arrived in its vicinity on or near Independence Day, the Fourth of July. An isolated granite outcropping in the Sweetwater Valley, Wyoming, it stands 6,028 feet above sea level with its northern summit reaching 136 feet above the surrounding terrain. Its mass covers an area of almost twenty-five acres. Robert L. Munkres, "Independence Rock and Devil's Gate," *Annals of Wyoming* 62, no. 1 (April 1968): 24–25.

Artist unknown, Independence Rock Looking West, 1850. *In the distance is Devil's Gate.*

ahead on foot & made the above observations, during our halt this noon, it being 1¼ mile distant from our stopping place. I felt quite fatigued after having ascended and travelled over it which occupied about 1 hour, & I then sat down to wait for the teams to come up. – It rained a little while I was here. Near here are a number of ponds and lakes, the shores of which are covered with a substance of mineral, somewhat the nature of alkali – a number of the brethren have collected large quantities of it, which makes a good substitute for salaratus.[150] There was a woman buried near here lately by the emigrants. The camp was again in motion at 3 P. M. – we went about a mile beyond the rock, & forded the river without accident, although the water came considerably above the bed of my wagon. On this side the river we also noticed a huge, solitary rock, scarcely less singular in its appearance than the one I had just visited, though varying in form, resembling somewhat a sugar loaf. I neglected to mention that at Independence Rock Bro. Clayton put up a guide board, which announced the distance to Ft. John to be 175¼ miles. We now proceeded over a level, sandy, country a little s. of w., & encamped sun ½ hour high in a semi-circle fronting the river; beyond which a short distance is a lofty range of rocky, massive bluffs, standing in bold relief against the evening sky, while on this side, between us & the river, is a beautiful plot of green grass, & behind us to the left a gentle elevation of ground, about ¼ of a mile down the stream is a narrow pass through which the rushing torrent runs, the course of which can be heard at considerable distance. On either side of this is a rocky, perpendicular descent of some 200 feet, formed by crags piled on crags, presenting to the eye at once a scene of romantic interest & grandeur. We have made 15¼ miles to-day – There have been 2 antelope killed to-day, one by Porter the other by Henson Walker . The chasm or pass between the rocks above named is called "Devil's Gate" – Latitude at Independence Rock. 42° 30′ 16″[151] –

150. Saleratus is a yeast-like alkaline substance made of sodium bicarbonate (baking soda) that appeared along the shores of the small lakes in the region and which the Native Americans called "Indian Bread" because of its loaf-like appearance. Travelers often scooped it up by the bucketload to use in leavening bread and light cakes.

151. Just west of Independence Rock lies Devil's Gate, a natural gorge running between two high, rocky ridges some 380 feet high and 200 yards long. Named by the Shoshone and Arapahoe Indians for a long-ago mythical beast who, when wounded, dug out the gorge with its horns, this narrow cleft has been carved out by the Sweetwater River over eons of time. It is virtually impassable and required wagon companies to travel either north or south of this rocky prominence.

TUESDAY THE 22D.

Fine morning, & fair prospect of a warm day. – I stood on guard last night the last watch. We started about ½ past 7 a.m., & following the course of the river over a sandy, dusty road, we stopt to bait at 12 M. on the banks of the same, having come 10 miles. Opposite us on the other side is a high range of broken rocky bluffs, while a little to the right is a wide area of ground between them, extending as far as the eye can reach, relieved by a single object, viz: – an oblong mass of rock, which stands at a considerable distance from any thing similar to itself – Otherwise than this the features of the country around have a uniform aspect, with this variation that, occasionally may be seen one rocky peak towering far above its fellows. – The grass here on the margin of the river is very good – The weather is very warm & sultry. We crossed 3 small creeks this forenoon – 10 emigrant wagons passed us soon after our arrival at this place – 2 horsemen, who were in the company, informed us that a young man, one of their number, was lately drowned at the ferry on North Fork, in attempting to swim his horse across the river. We started again at 2 P. M. & travelling s. of w. alternately over sandy bluffs & bottoms, we forded 2 small streams, near their confluence with the River, & finally encamped a little after sunset on the banks of the same, having come 20¾ miles – The features of the country which we have travelled this afternoon, are similar to those of this forenoon, as we observed all the way to our right across the river & occasionally also to our left, lofty, rocky, & broken ranges of mountains. About 3 miles back from here we passed another isolated mass of rock, similar in form, though inferior in size to "Independence Rock," & in fact we begin to be sensible that we are fast approaching the far-famed Rocky Mountains, which extend from the northern to the southern limits of the United States Territory & Mexico – at this place the grass is plentiful & luxuriant; although we have no fuel except the wild sage root, which here grows higher than any I have before seen. I know of but 2 antelopes having been brought into camp to-night, killed by Joseph Hancock, & Lewis Barney – We passed the 10 emigrant wagons also about 3 miles back, where they have encamped for the night. It is the intention to get as early a start to-morrow morning as possible, on account of the wish of the Twelve to get ahead of the emigrants. Latitude at noon, 42° 28′25″ –

WEDNESDAY THE 23D.

Warm & sultry. We started at 7 a.m., & travelled a west course some distance from the river over, as usual, a deep, sandy road. noticing on our right as usual, a high unbroken chain of mountains. after going about 1½ mile, we crossed a small creek, when proceeding 7 miles, we halted to bait at 20 minutes past 11 a.m., in a beautiful valley, abounding with green grass, opening upon a pass rocky cliffs elevating their towering forms on either side – at this place we again came to the river, which flows within a few rods of our halting place. We started at 1 P. M., – went ½ a mile, & turned to the left, leaving the river & the defile or pass spoken of above to our right – thence we pursued a west course over an excessively sandy road, which was very hard travelling for our horses – The features of the country remain about the same

– high rocky mountains [Granite Mountains] on our right, while 5 or 6 miles to our left are lofty hills covered in places with snow. – After going about 8 miles we descended a gentle elevation & again came to a river, along which we travelled ½ a mile further, & encamped on its banks in a semi-circle at 6 P. M. having come 17 miles to-day. In advance of us at a great distance can be seen the outlines of mountains, loftier than any we have yet seen, – the setting sun throwing its glancing rays athwart their summits, reveal them to our eyes covered with snow. There is a company of 10 emigrant wagons encamped this evening about a mile in advance of us – these left the ferry a day or two previous to our starting thence. – Orson went on guard to watch the horses & cattle soon after our arrival. The weather, which this forenoon was quite warm and sultry, is now somewhat cold, the wind having veered – round to the north – Opposite our camping place this evening, is another of those isolated, massive, irregular piles of rock, thrown together in huge fragments, as if by some convulsion of nature – It is situated, at the entrance & near the center of a wide area of ground, forming a pass, with lofty crags & precipices towering above it on either side. Another lot of emigrants are encamped about a mile back – Joseph Hancock & Lewis Barney killed 2 antelope to-day –

Thursday the 24th.

Somewhat cloudy & cool this morning. We started at 6 a.m., – turning to the left, & leaving the river to our right, we pursued a west course over a somewhat uneven, sandy road 5 or 6 miles, & came to springs which issue from the ground, & have a sulphurous taste – in them we found the ice quite thick – we also noticed a number of salaratus beds, occupied with water – Here, too, we overtook a company of emigrants consisting of 10 wagons, & passed them, after travelling behind them some distance – after proceeding a little further on, we overtook another small company of them – behind these we travelled some 8 or 10 miles, & descending quite a steep, sandy hill, we again came to the river, having made 17¾ miles to-day – Here we encamped at ¼ past 3 P. M. in a semi-circle in an extensive valley or plain, surrounded by high & sandy hills – The grass here is tolerably good, & there was also considerable brushwood growing on the banks of the river, which we used as fuel – at this place we have again to ford the river – The emigrants whom we have travelled with the latter part of the day passed our camp & went ahead – also those whom we left behind came up soon after our arrival & went ahead a short distance & encamped for the night on the other side the river – another company soon after came up & encamped back a short distance. There were 4 antelope killed to-day by J. Hancock, Charles Burk, Henson Walker, & Lewis B. Myers – This evening another sad accident happened in our camp – Bro. John Holman, while driving up the horses, made a motion with his gun at one of them, as if to frighten him, & in so doing, the lock caught in his pocket & the piece discharged taking effect in the horse's flank – He died during the night – He belonged to Pres't. Young and was considered the best horse in the camp – We put our horses on the island opposite this afternoon, as the grass there was better than here –

William H. Jackson, South Pass—High Rolling Plateau with the Wind River Mountains to the North. *Bretney Collection, Wyoming State Archives.*

FRIDAY THE 25TH.

Clear day, with a strong wind from the west. We started at 7 a.m., the emigrants ahead, having preceded us – after fording the river to the island, & travelling over it near ¼ of a mile, we again crossed the river to the main shore – Leaving it now to our left, we travelled 3 miles over a hilly, sandy road, & came to it once again – We now pursued a west course alternately ascending & descending rugged, stony hills, & occasionally travelling over the bottoms along the stream, & halted on its banks in a beautiful grassy plain at 25 m past 11, surrounded by lofty, & sandy hills, having come 8¾ miles – Just before we stopt, we crossed a small creek, which empties near here into the river. We again started at 1 P. M. & went about 2 miles, where we found the company of emigrants encamped, who went ahead of us this morning – We now again began to bear away from the river, & pursuing a west course over lofty, sandy, rocky hills & valleys alternately & crossing 4 small spring creeks, we at length encamped at ½ past 6 P. M. in a small & beautiful valley on the banks of a clear & murmuring rivulet, having come 11½ miles this afternoon, & 20¼ during the day. I noticed during our route this afternoon, on the summits of the highest hills we passed over 2 or 3 extensive ponds of water, formed by the melting of the snow – Bro. Jacob Burnham passed my wagon with a handful of the latter that he had picked up in a ravine, & gave me a portion of it, which seemed quite a curiosity to be seen in summer. The banks of the stream on which we are encamped, abounds on either side in extensive shrubbery or underbrush, which answers to us the purpose of fuel. This evening my eyes are quite sore, in consequence of the dust blowing all day in our faces the wind being in the west – The air is quite chilly this evening.

Saturday the 26th.

Clear, cold morning – so much so that we were obliged to don our over coats. – We started at 8 a.m., & pursuing a west course 4 miles we came to a stream having the appearance of being a Fork or a branch of Sweet Water running south – about 1½ miles beyond we crossed the same stream twice, first to an island & then to the main shore, running in general about the same direction – On the banks of the first of these we noticed quite a large bank of snow, apparently 8 or 10 feet deep. Travelling over a rough, sandy, & hilly country, we halted to bait at 20 minutes to 1 P. M., after having first forded another deep & rapid stream, running also serpentinely in a southern direction. This we take to be the middle Fork of Sweet Water. We were obliged, (the most of us,) to elevate our wagon beds on account of its depth – We have made 11 miles this forenoon. – To the south-west of us at this place can be seen at a distance 2 huge, high rocks, standing apparently a few rods apart – These are mentioned in Fremont's map & journal as "Table Rock." The banks of this stream on either side are fringed with abundance of shrubbery & underbrush – Only a few rods from my wagon this noon, in a kind of ravine, is a huge bank of crusted snow – the vegetation advancing to the very edge of it – & has the appearance, like that we saw to-day on the first stream we crossed, of being 8 or 10 feet deep. It is indeed, to me quite a singular sight, as the weather having become much warmer than it was this morning, & the sun pouring his burning rays upon us, afford us the opportunity of visioning a striking contrast between the 2 extremes, heat & cold – It is the general supposition that we cannot now be far from the entrance or foot of the "South Pass" which is 20 miles wide.[152] – While here this noon, Bro. Eric Glines rode up on a mule – he had come from the place where we left the brethren since Wednesday last. He reported that they had transferred the ferry down the North Fork about 8 miles, & that a number of the brethren were engaged in burning coal pits.[153] We again started at ¼ to 2 P. M., & journeying, as usual, over a sandy & somewhat hilly country, we encamped in a circle at ½ past 6 P. M., on the banks of the same stream we crossed at noon, in a small valley, encircled by gentle, undulating hills, having come 18¾ miles during the day, & 129¾ miles during the week, & are this evening 276¼ miles from Ft. John, & 816½ miles from Winter Quarters – Latitude

152. South Pass, elevation 7,412 feet, is located in a broad, low region of southwest Fremont County, Wyoming. The "Cumberland Gap" of the West, South Pass was discovered in 1812. So named to distinguish it from Lemhi Pass in present-day Montana, by the 1840s it had become the favorite passage over the Continental Divide. The pass is like a saddle with prairie and sagebrush, allowing a broad, nearly level route between the Atlantic and Pacific watersheds. Will Bagley, *South Pass: Gateway to a Continent* (Norman: University of Oklahoma Press, 2014).

153. This region of Nebraska, and more particularly areas to the northeast, features coal veins that appear on the surface. In the twenty-first century, Wyoming has become the greatest coal-producing region of the United States, surpassing even Appalachia in tonnage of coal annually extracted.

this noon, 42° 22′ 42″ The stream here on either bank abounds in green bushes & shrubbery of different kinds, affording us fuel. I have heard of only 2 antelope being killed to-day by Lewis B. Myers, & Sterling Driggs . To the north-west of us a great distance, we can discover a lofty range of mountains, whose summits are covered with snow. The grass here is tolerably good – The air this evening quite chilly though but little air stirring – about dark it was discovered that Bro. Heber, Geo. A. Smith, O. Pratt & one or two others who had gone ahead this afternoon to seek a good camping place, had not yet returned. – Accordingly, Brigham, Phineas Young, Porter, Colonel Markham, Howard Egan, & one or two others rode out after them – they had not gone far before they met Heber on his return – he had expected to meet our wagons coming on – he said that ahead some distance on a small stream were 10 men with pack mules encamped, on their way to the States. With these, or near them, the remainder of the brethren, (O. Pratt & others) had tarried for the night.

SUNDAY THE 27TH.

Fine, clear morning, though somewhat cold – I stood on guard 1 hour watching cattle. We started this morning at 9, & soon after crossed the "dividing ridge," which separates or forms the boundary between the waters flowing east & west into the Atlantic & Pacific Oceans. We now began to descend instead of ascending as we had done for a long time – after going about 4 miles we came across one of the mountaineers above referred to whose name is Major Harris,[154] – he has been in this western country some 20 years, & is familiar with all its localities – He has the appearance of being about 40 years of age – He did not give a very favorable account of the country in the vicinity of the Salt Lake, but spoke in high terms of a valley north of there 40 miles called Cash [Cache] valley, which is some 70 miles in length, & from 15 to 30 miles in breadth[155] – Bear river runs through it at right angles, on the west side of which the soil is sandy, & barren, except considerable wild sage, while on the east side, there is less wild sage, & quite a heavy body of timber, such as cotton wood, box elder, &c. He had quite a number of newspapers with him, some of which are published in Oregon: Among the rest was one dated Feb. 13, 1847, published by Samuel Brannan at a place in California called "Yerba Bueno" – The name of this is the "California Star" – I noticed in it a horrid account of

154. Moses "Black" Harris, so named because of his swarthy, dark complexion, was a native South Carolinian born approximately 1804 in Union County. In all likelihood, he was a member of W. H. Ashley's first fur-trading company up the Missouri in 1822 and in another Ashley party in 1825 led by Jedediah Smith. He had circumnavigated the Great Salt Lake as early as 1825, visited the headwaters of the Yellowstone in 1826, and traveled through the Wind River Valley in 1828 and 1829. He later led several expeditions of rendezvous parties west from St. Louis. After 1840 he became a trusted, if rather expensive, guide for Oregon emigrant trains. A stranger and an enigma even to his fellow mountain men—"a bird alone" in the wilderness—he was known for his tall tales and colorful yarns, the West's most famous entertainer around a campfire. He died in St. Joseph, Missouri, in May 1849 of cholera. See Jerome Peltier, "Moses 'Black' Harris," in Hafen, *The Mountain Men,* 4:103–17.

155. A rich agricultural region in northern Utah, Cache Valley was discovered in 1818 by Michel Bourdon. Its name was derived by fur trappers who hid (French *cacher*) their goods in caches in the region. Mormons began to settle the area in 1852 and established Logan as its central city.

William Gilbert Gaul, On the Way to the Summit. *The Donner-Reed party set out for California the same year the Mormons left Nauvoo: 1846. Delayed by a series of mishaps and mistakes, it became snowbound in the High Sierras in the winter of 1846–47 and resorted to cannibalism to survive. Sam Brannan discovered some of their grisly remains when heading east to meet up with Brigham Young's vanguard company.*

the condition of some emigrants who in attempting to go over the mountains last fall, were frozen to death, while the survivors being destitute of food, were obliged to consume the bodies of their friends, to such an extent of hunger & suffering were they reduced.[156] – This man's comrades have gone on to the east – he, himself talks of going back west. He advises us to take a northern route to the place of our destination, instead of going by Ft. Bridger, there being more feed on the one than the other – We proceeded about 2¼ miles further west & halted to bait at ¼ to 12 M. after crossing a small, clear rivulet abounding in small fish – having come 6¼ miles. We again started at ¼ past 2 P. M., – we travelled in a western direction over comparatively a level, sandy road, without the occurrence of any particular incident & encamped in a circle at 6 P. M. on the banks of a small spring creek, called "Dry Sandy" having come 15¼ miles to-day – This stream at this time does not run, but on the contrary lies apart in kind of springs – The grass here is somewhat thin, though very good. Major Harris has come back with us this far, & stops here to-night – This stream, as also the one we crossed this noon are probably tributaries of the Green River – The weather the latter part of the day, has been unusually warm & sultry. – Latitude this noon, 42° 18' 58". I have heard of but one antelope being killed to-day – done by Porter. We are still in full view of lofty mountains covered with snow. Between these we can distinguish a large hollow, & near there is probably the source of "Sweet Water." This evening Bro. Heber again called upon me to take a walk with him – We went a short distance from the camp & knelt & prayed alternately for the members of the 2 families to which we belong in W. Quarters, & for all the Saints there & elsewhere – Major Harris has a large number of skins to sell at the following prices, viz: – elk skin, $3 – deer do. $1.50 – ready-made pants and hunting shirts, $4. –

MONDAY THE 28TH.

Beautiful weather this morning. I stood on guard last night from 12 till daylight – The horses and cattle are considerably scattered this morning in consequence of the scarcity of grass – We started at 20 minutes this morning past 7 a.m., & pursuing a west course over a dry, even & sandy road, & halted to bait at ½ past 12 M. on the banks of the Little Sandy River, having come 13½ miles – This stream is now as large as Sweet Water, being considerably swollen by the melting of the snow in the mountains – The banks are lined with shrubbery, & near its margin, the grass is tolerably good – The opposite banks are composed of sand & are quite high – The weather has grown extremely warm & sultry – We left Mr. Harris this morning at the Dry Sandy – he intends waiting there for other emigrants to come up – a number of the

156. The Donner or Donner-Reed party set out for California in a wagon train in 1846. Slowed by their choice to follow the Hastings Cutoff, which crossed the Great Salt Lake Desert, the party did not reach the high Sierras until November 1846. Impeded by heavy snowfalls and afflicted by starvation, some of the immigrants resorted to cannibalism to survive. Tragically, of the eighty-seven members of the original party, only forty-eight survived to reach California. For the standard early study of the party, see C. F. McGlashan, *History of the Donner Party: A Tragedy of the Sierras* (Mineola, NY: Dover Publications, 2013; originally published in 1880). For a more recent study, see Peter R. Limburg, *Deceived: The Story of the Donner Party* (Pacifica, CA: IPS Books, 1998).

brethren exchanged, ammunition, & clothes of different kinds, particularly shirts with him for elk, & deer skins – he would give one of the latter for a "hickory" or calico shirt, or for 2 boxes percushing caps – I perused a paper this morning that I got of Dr. Richards, called the "Oregon Spectator", dated March 4, 1847, published at Oregon City. The principal news contained therein, refers to the suffering condition of the emigrants, & petition to the people of Oregon to step forward & assist them, a number of them being entirely destitute of clothing, horses & cattle, wagons, &c., &c.– We forded "Little Sandy," & pursued our journey at 4 P. M. – went west about 2 miles, & turned a little aside from the road & encamped in a circle at 6 P. M. on the banks of the same stream having come 15½ miles over a tolerably level & sandy road – Just before we arrived there we were met by Mr. Bridger & two others on horseback, – the former being the proprietor of the Fort, from whom its name is taken – They retraced their steps to camp with us to-night. Along the banks of the river on quite an extensive bottom, we found the grass quite green & high. In the distance to the west we can distinctly see this evening a line of trees marking, as we are told, the progress of "Big Sandy River" with which this running west, effects its junction, apparently a number of miles hence. – There is plenty of shrubbery & underbrush on the banks of the stream, which affords us abundance of fuel. – There were but 2 antelope killed today that I have heard of – one, a young fawn by Joseph Rooker, the other by Bro. Marble . – An interview was held with Mr. Bridger this evening at which the following information was obtained – That we were about 200 miles away from the "Salt Lake", his fort being half the distance. The country of which he gave us a description is situated between the 2 lakes of Eutaw & Salt, consisting of a valley of 100 miles in extent. – The soil is good, producing wild flax in abundance, also white & red clover, & is peculiarly adapted to the growth of corn & wheat – Between the 2 lakes, 3 large streams coming from the mountains, traverse the valley, & empty into the Salt Lake. These abound in various kinds of fish, & their banks are heavily lined with timber, consisting of pine & oak, also quite a number of groves of sugar maple, which have been used for the making of sugar these 20 years. – That Gold, silver, copper, iron, sulphur, saltpeter, &c. are found in abundance in the mountains, he giving a description of a number of places where the above minerals were to be found – That near to the road is a spring that issues both fresh & salt, hot & cold waters alternately. He also gave a description of another valley country some 200 miles south of that, stating it to be similar to the one just described, & that wheat & corn are there raised in great abundance by the Indians. – In fine, he gave a minute description of the whole country, which differed materially from the account given us by Major Harris – The above, though not minute, is the substance of the information gleaned from the statements of Mr. Bridger & the 2 others – they are now on their way to Ft. John – They moreover told us that it would be necessary for us to start back, at least, as early as August, else we would be in danger of perishing with cold, & that the grass would, in this region, be cut off by the

The Big Sandy River. Wyoming State Archives.

frost, if we deferred our departure to a later period – Orson & myself bathed this evening in the river.[157]

TUESDAY THE 29TH.

Pleasant, though somewhat warm & sultry through the day – Mr. Bridger & his two comrades left us this morning at about 7 o' clock, on their way to Ft. John – Soon after, we started – travelled a west course over a sandy, level road, noticing on our right & left the "Big" & "Little Sandy" Rivers, & at length forded the former stream, probably 2 or 3 miles above its junction with the latter. – Here we halted to bait at 11 a.m. having come 6¾ miles. – This stream is somewhat muddy and quite high at this time, being at the place where we forded it some 60 yds. wide – about half the teams stopt the other side as the grass was somewhat better there than here – We again started at 1 P. M., – travelled S. S. W. over a comparatively

157. Contrary to some popular misconceptions, Jim Bridger, then forty-three years old and a trusted mountain man, knew all about the country south of Salt Lake and spoke well of it. He was far more positive and encouraging of a settlement in the Salt Lake Valley than Moses Harris had been. Said Norton Jacob of Bridger's views: "The information obtained concerning the Utah country is very encouraging." Journal of Norton Jacob, 28 June 1847, Church History Library. For more on Bridger's positive statements, see Bennett, *We'll Find the Place*, 192–94.

C. Hall, Green River. *Wyoming State Archives.*

level, sandy & in some places, quite stony, road occasionally ascending & descending small hills, & encamped on the banks of the "Big Sandy" River, sometime after dark, in a circle, having come 17 miles this afternoon, & 23¾ miles during the day, the longest ascertained day's travel since we left Winter Quarters – The river here takes a serpentine course, though its general direction is west. – The opposite banks are quite high – but little or no timber growing around – grass of the slim "wiry" kind in plenty – There was, that I have heard of, but one antelope killed to-day, shot & brought in this evening by Henson Walker. – Latitude this noon, on "Big Sandy" 42° 6′ 42″

Wednesday the 30th.

Warm & sultry – We started this morning, about 8 & pursuing a S. W. course along the river distance over a sandy & somewhat uneven road, with a range of low, sandy hills to our right, & encamped at noon on the banks of "Green River," having come 8 miles – We found on our arrival, that the emigrants who were ahead of us had all got across, & were encamped some 5 miles above here – This we learned from 2 horsemen whom we found here – Immediately each Division was called together & men selected by Cols. Markham & Rockwood to make 2 rafts, & stand guard – I was chosen, with a number of others to do the latter duty, & to stand ½ a day alternately while we remain here – the 2 rafts were completed by evening – we

Sam Brannan (1819–89). Flamboyant Mormon leader, explorer, journalist, and California's first millionaire, Brannan disagreed with Brigham Young's choice of the Salt Lake Valley as the right place to settle. A highly enterprising gambler and businessman, his financial adventures turned sour, and he eventually died penniless. Courtesy of Religious Studies Center, Brigham Young University.

found no difficulty in getting timber for their construction, as there is plenty of cotton wood growing on the banks of the river. This stream run[s] S. E. at this place & is quite deep & rapid, & at this place, about 100 yds. in width – From all appearances it has this spring been considerably swollen beyond its banks, the bottoms being covered with weeds, flood-wood, &c., left by the receding of the waters. – During this afternoon, we were all much surprised by the unexpected arrival of Elder Samuel Brannan, who was at the head of the company of brethren that went round by sea last year, from New York City to California– He was accompanied by 3 men, 2 of whom had come thro' with him from the latter country – with 1 of these I was well acquainted – His name is Smith, & I believe is some distant relation to our prophet Joseph – He left Nauvoo (where I made his acquaintance,) some 2 years since for Oregon. One of the other 2 men, was one of the individuals we saw with Mr. Bridger the other day – the other man I did not know. Elder Brannan gives a very favorable account of the climate, soil, &c. of California, & appears quite anxious that we should immediately go there and take possession of the country, before it becomes occupied by others – He had left Yerba Bueno April 13th – This place is situated on the bay of San Francisco, & from all accounts, bids fair to become in time a flourishing city – He brought a number of news papers with him, which he distributed among the "Twelve" – Among these was a file of his own, entitled the "California Star." 12 or 14 in number, Mr. Smith informed me that in Oregon they had 2 seasons, wet & dry – The former continuing 7 m, the latter – 5 months, the winters being quite mild. – I stood on guard this afternoon, & at sunset, with others, drove the horses & cattle to camp–[158]

158. A fellow Latter-day Saint, the thirty-eight-year-old Sam Brannan had led a group of Mormons on a ten-thousand-mile ocean voyage from New York City around the southern tip of South America to Yerba Buena (San Francisco) onboard the *Brooklyn.* Brannan had just traveled eight hundred miles overland on horseback from San Francisco Bay. Having compared the arid shores of the Salt Lake with the golden shores of California, Brannan was convinced the Saints should go all the way west to the Pacific Ocean. His eyewitness account of the blighted Donner-Reed party certainly held the attention of his newfound visitors. However, Brigham Young was as skeptical of the man as he was of his message and gave his visitor little or no encouragement. Brannan's *California Star* was San Francisco's first newspaper. Brannan later left the church and became California's first millionaire through gambling and horse racing but died

Thursday the 1st of July.

Fine weather, though somewhat windy – The brethren, this morning, commenced ferrying at a very early hour, & by night had got over about 10 wagons, chiefly belonging to the 1st Division – The raft belonging to the 2d D., on trial, proved to be too unwieldy for use, consequently they commenced to-day to build a new one, which was nearly finished by night – however, the old one was used through the day. Orson stood on guard last night, the first watch. He also stood the fore part of to-day, watching horses & cattle, myself the latter part – Within 2 or 3 days past, a kind of fever has appeared & is quite prevalent in our camp, there being more than 20 men prostrated with it at this time, a number of whom are unable to sit up. – Quite a number of cattle & horses were also swam over to-day. –

Friday the 2d.

Fair day – a number of horses & cattle were swam over the river this morning, mine included. I crossed the river & with 2 others stood on guard all day to prevent the horses & cattle from straying away. Here I tried my luck at fishing & caught a good sized salmon, weighing between 2 & 3 pounds, with which kind of fish this river abounds. Towards evening the remainder of the horses & cattle were swam over. – The ferryage commenced early as usual this morning, & this evening, there are but about 18 wagons remaining on this side, including my own – There is no lack of musquitoes at this place, on account of the river, having so recently overflown its banks, & they "present (or put in) their bills" this evening, like a creditor to a debtor, greatly to our annoyance. –

Saturday the 3d.

Tolerably fair this morning, though considerably windy, with a slight rain this afternoon. – The wagons were all got over safely by about 2 P. M. – Brigham & Heber went ahead to seek a good camping place for the night – After their return we started about 3 P. M. &, proceeding a south course along the river over an even, sandy road, we at length descended a steep hill & came to an extensive bottom, where we encamped in a line at ½ past 4 P. M. on its banks, having come 3 miles. Here we found the grass quite good, though somewhat thin & short – plenty of underbrush for fuel, & swarms of musquitoes in proportion – On this side the river the banks are low & even, on the opposite high & sandy. We have travelled the past week 65½ miles, & are this evening distant from Ft. John 341¾ miles, & from Winter Quarters, 882 miles. – Latitude at our ferrying place on Green River, 41° 52′ 37″

---

in obscurity and poverty in 1889. The "Mr. Smith" who accompanied Brannan may have been Charles C. Smith, a distant relative of Joseph Smith. In Nauvoo he had associated with criminals and men of bad character. Much has been written on Brannan, including Will Bagley, "'Everything Is Favorable! And God Is on Our Side': Samuel Brannan and the Conquest of California," *Journal of Mormon History* 23, no. 2 (1997): 185–209. For arguably the most colorful biography of Brannan, see Paul Bailey, *Sam Brannan and the California Mormons* (Salt Lake City: Westernlore Press, 1943).

Artist unknown, Mormon or Temple Butte, *east of Fort Bridger on Black's Fork of the Green River. Wyoming State Archives.*

This evening the brethren of the camp were called together at Pres't. Young's wagon to receive instructions, pertaining to our future movements. – President Young then stated that it was necessary that some individuals should go back to meet the next company of brethren, in order to pilot & assist them on the road, & that it would be advisable to select those for that purpose that had families who would need their help, in preference to single men, who had no such demands upon them. He said he was willing that 6, or even 8 or 10 individuals should go, as they deemed proper. – At length the following men were chosen or volunteered their services, viz: – Phineas H. Young, Aaron Farr, George Woodward, Eric Glines & Rodney Badger . – President Young proffered them the use of the wagon which has formerly drawn the "Revenue Cutter" – they are also to take 3 horses with them, 1 for riding the other 2 to draw the wagon. – He then stated his wish that there should be a meeting held to-morrow, commencing at 9 a.m., & this to be under the supervision of the Bishops, as himself with some of the brethren of the Twelve intended to accompany the 5 men as far as the river, to see them safely across & also to draw ashore the rafts we have left behind. – That he wished every man in the camp punctually to attend meeting at the time appointed, except those who were stationed on guard, & that there should be no fishing, hunting, &c. on the Sabbath Day. He further said, that when we arrived at Ft. Bridger, there would probably be some trading done, & that there would be men chosen for that purpose, but that if a man wished to make a trade for himself, let him do it & step aside, & not stand in the way of others who also wished a chance – that he himself had been hindered from trading by the latter circumstance, & that if they would let him trade at the Fort first, both the men & boys would get better bargains, "for," said he, "if there is any burthen to be borne, I would rather bear it, & I consider myself better able to bear it than any other man in the church, & would rather, by throwing out $10 as a bait, lose it at once, than that any of you should lose twenty-five cents – these are my feelings, & God knows it, & so does every man who knows my heart."

Sunday the 4th.

Warm & pleasant, with but little air stirring. – The horses & cattle were all drove down to a bottom about a mile from here, where the grass grows much more luxuriant than at this place. – Agreeably to yesterday's arrangement, a speaking & prayer meeting was held to-day, commencing at 9 a.m., – soon after, the 5 men spoken of above started back, being accompanied by Brigham, Heber, & some others as far as the ferry. – About 3 P. M., the latter returned, accompanied by 12 of the soldier brethren from Pueblo, who had left that place the 24th ultimo – these men were originally 13 in number, one of whom, William Walker, meeting with A. Farr this morning at the Ferry, has gone back with him to meet their families – they had left the Ferry on the North Fork of the Platte, on Monday the 28th inst. – Their destination is Ft. Bridger, where they are going in pursuit of horses stolen from them near Pueblo, by French traders a part of which they recovered at Ft. John – 2, a horse & a mule being yet missing. – When they arrived, they formed in a line on horseback, near Pres't. Young's wagon, where, by his suggestion, 3 loud cheers & 4 "hosannahs" were given for their safe return to us. The remainder of their company, they left at the North Fork, who were intending to start the next day after their departure – these had 21 Government wagons – there was also a company of Mississippi brethren with them, consisting of 40 or 50 wagons[159] – Among those who arrived here this afternoon, were 3 of my acquaintances, viz., John Buchanan, James Oakley, & Thomas Williams, the latter being at the head of the pursuing expedition. – They informed us that the brethren at the North Fork Ferry, had been threatened by three Missourians with being mobbed, but on Luke Johnson telling them to commence as quick as they pleased, for that there was plenty of assistance near at hand, (referring to the company from Pueblo,) they thought best to desist & say no more about it – We also learned that the emigrants after getting over the river cut their rafts loose & let them drift away, being so deficient in charity that they were not willing that numbers of their own companies should cross over without paying heavily for the use of them. Bro. Amasa Lyman is also at the Ferry there, with the remainder of the brethren – he had met them on "Horse Creek," between Pueblo & Ft. John, about 75 miles from the latter place. – An ox, belonging to Bro. Robert Crow died this afternoon. – Orson & myself used the last of our second bag of flour this evening. I omitted to mention that we got our horses reshod at the Ferry on Green River, by Bro. Burr Frost.

159. For more about the Mississippi company, see note 139.

MONDAY THE 5TH.

Pleasant morning, though it clouded up, & rained a very little this afternoon. We started at 8 a. m., & pursuing a south course along the river about 3 miles, we left it & bore to the right of it, & going a south west course over a stony, sandy, uneven road, we encamped on the banks of the "Black's Fork" about 5 P. M., having come 20 miles. – This stream is a tributary of Green River, & at this place winds serpentinely in a S. E. direction, being about 8 rods in width, & quite deep & rapid. – I know of no occurrence of interest to-day, except the killing of an antelope by Lewis B. Myers. The grass here is tolerably good & there is also plenty of underbrush for fuel – A few musquitoes though not so abundant or voracious as on Green River. – This evening to the south west, we can discern, at a great distance, a lofty range of mountains covered with snow. – The twelve brethren from Pueblo, as also Elder Brannan & his 2 comrades, have travelled with us to-day & intend doing so as far as Ft. Bridger, though I know not how much farther. – This stream also abounds in fine fish of the salmon kind – I caught a small one this evening. –

TUESDAY THE 6TH

Pleasant weather – though a strong wind from the south-west – We started about 8 a.m., pursuing a south west course, over an uneven, rugged road for 3½ miles, we crossed "Ham's Fork" – going still 1½ mile further we forded another stream, called also "Black's Fork" – We now continued our route in the same direction, over, as usual, an uneven, sandy & stony soil, & encamped again on the banks of Black's Fork", (after first crossing it,) at 6 P. M., having come 18¼ miles – These streams are of uniform size & rapidity, being both tributaries of

Fort Bridger, 1850. *Courtesy of Church History Library.*

Jim Bridger (1804–81), one of America's greatest plainsmen, scouts, guides, and fur trappers, encouraged Brigham Young to consider the Salt Lake Valley as a permanent place to settle. Utah State Historical Society.

"Green River" – Just before we arrived here, we met 2 men with 3 pack-horses, who informed me that the distance to "Ft. Bridger" is about 15 miles – The grass here is tolerably good – also plenty fuel to be obtained from underbrush growing on the banks. My eyes feel quite sore this evening, owing to the excess of dust encountered to-day in travelling.

WEDNESDAY THE 7TH.

Fine weather, though windy & very dusty travelling. – We started at ½ past 8 a. m., & travelled S. W. over, as usual, an uneven, sandy, stony road, & stopt to bait at 1 P. M. on the banks of Black's Fork, having come 9 miles. – This stream we have crossed twice on our route this forenoon, its course being very crooked. – A short time previous to our halt, while descending a hill the reach [pole from the rear axle to the bar above the front axle] to our wagon was broken in two. – as we happened to have a spare one with us the damage was soon repaired. We again started about 2 P. M. & continuing the same course, we arrived at Ft. Bridger, sun about an hour high, & encamped in a circle about ½ a mile beyond it, having come 17¾ miles to-day. After coming in sight of the Ft. we crossed 7 small, rapid streams, before reaching our camping place – these all unite some distance below, & form the stream called "Black's Fork." – This is not a regular fort, as I at first supposed, but consists of 2 log houses, where the inhabitants live, & also do their trading.[160] – Adjacent to these as also about a mile back, is a number of lodges made of skins – these belong to the "Snake Indians", a few of whom reside here – the majority of them inhabit "Snake River," some 3 days Journey distant from this place. – I saw 2 fine trout this evening, caught by Bro. Truman Angel in this stream – these are the first of the kind I have seen, since I left Massachusetts, in 1844. – The ground where we are situated is somewhat low & wet, owing to the recent over flow of the waters, which accounts for the numerous small streams spoken of above, &

160. Established in 1842 on Black's Fork of the Green River, Fort Bridger was a famous fur-trading outpost and supply point for wagon trains on the Oregon, California, and Mormon Trails. Established by the well-known mountain man Jim Bridger, Fort Bridger was later purchased by the Latter-day Saints and served as a military post in 1858. It was finally closed in 1890. See Fred R. Gowans and Eugene E. Campbell, *Fort Bridger: Island in the Wilderness* (Provo, UT: Brigham Young University Press, 1975).

consists of an extensive plain, abounding in high grass, both green & luxuriant, thus affording the best pasture land, we have seen in a long time. Thomas Williams & his company, who had come on here in pursuit of the stolen horse & mules, were disappointed in their search. The men suspected of taking them, having left here some 4 days since – There is one man here however by the name of Timothy Goodell, to whom, he, with his comrades, attach some suspicion, as being concerned in the affair, but as he has previously borne a good character from the accounts we have received of him from Mr. Bridger & others, as we came along, the majority of the brethren, are inclined to acquit him of any participation in the transaction. However, as he was anxious to leave here immediately, he gave Mr. Williams a horse in place of the mule, rather than to wait here till Capt. Brown with the remainder of the company shall come up – This place is distant from Ft. John, 397¾ miles, & from Winter Quarters, 948 miles. – The latitude of Ft. Bridger is 41° 19′ 13″

Thursday the 8th.

Fine weather, though very windy. This morning, Orson & myself went down to the Ft. & bought 2 pair of pantaloons made of deer skins. He gave for his 3 pints of sugar 2 of coffee 1 bar of lead, & a shirt – I for mine, 3 shirts & ½ box of percushing caps. In the afternoon, Orson went about a mile below there to some lodges & bought 4 pair of moccasons in exchange for some little articles he had. – I got Hans C. Hanson to alter my pantaloons as they were considerably too large. – A trifling difficulty having accurred [*sic*] between Andrew J. Gibbons & George Mills, the matter was, this evening, brought before Pres't. Young for adjustment. – It appears that the former had struck the latter on account of being taunted & reproached by him, who is quite aggravating sometimes – after hearing the case, Pres't. Young called upon the brethren of the Twelve separately for their opinion, which was in substance as follows: – That they considered they were both to blame, but of the two, Bro. George the most so, – after which the President addressed himself to Bro. George & told him, that he was an old man, & should learn to respect himself, & he would be respected, & quit all his boyish notions, & not condescend to the manners of boys but set a good example before them. He then told Bro. Andrew that he was to blame for striking Bro. George, & that it was his duty at all times to respect old age – Both parties finally acknowledged themselves to be in the wrong, & asked the forgiveness of the brethren, which was cheerfully granted. – The President then called upon the captains of 10's to know if they knew of anything to hinder our departure to-morrow. They replied in the negative, accordingly, it was voted & carried that we start early to morrow morning. – Howard Egan, Porter, J. Redden & myself this evening rode down to the lodge of Timothy Goodell, & his comrades, where we spent the evening quite agreeably in their company. –

Friday the 9th.

Pleasant Weather, though quite windy, & dusty, disagreeable travelling – Thomas Williams with 6 of his men started back this morning, to meet Capt. Brown & the remainder of the company – 5 of the men remained & went on with us. Pres't Young returned the horse to Mr. Goodell, which he had given up to Mr. Williams, & told him to retain it, till he should see him again. A number of the brethren have made several trades for horses, ponies, & skins, since we have been at this place. – We started this morning at 9 o'clock – proceeded some 4 or 5 miles over an uneven, stony road, & came to a small spring creek, where we halted a short time to water – a little further on we crossed the same creek, which winds through a narrow valley, with lofty hills on either side – Here we saw, & gathered considerable snow – We now ascended a hill long & steep, after travelling over which 3 miles, we descended the longest & steepest descent I have seen since we left Winter Quarters – after going about 5 miles further a S. W. course over gradually descending ground, we at length crossed "Muddy Fork", & encamped in a circle on its banks at 4 P. M., having come 13 miles. This stream is small, & on its banks are growing a number of scattering poplar trees. – This was also the case on the other stream we crossed to-day – the grass here is remarkably coarse & tall, though quite good. –

Saturday the 10th.

Fine morning. – I omitted to mention, that Elder Brannan, with his 2 comrades, as also Thomas Brown went back with Thos. Williams, & his company yesterday morning. – We started this morning about ½ past 8. & travelling, as usual, S. W. over a mountainous, rocky country, we halted to bait at 2 P. M., in a beautiful & extensive valley abounding in fine verdure for our cattle, having come 9 miles. – A short time before we arrived at this place, we noticed a spring having a sulphurous taste. Here, also, there are 2, one of which has a taste similar to that of copperas; the other resembles that of gunpowder. – An Indian, whom we had seen at Ft. Bridger, followed us to this place – he had three pack-horses – In the vicinity of this place, on a high mountain, Lewis B. Myers took a young gray eagle from its nest – It corresponded in size with the one mentioned some time back, as having been caught by George R. Grant – We again continued our journey at 3 P. M. – we travelled some distance through the valley environed by lofty hills, & at length ascending a long & steep hill, we passed alternately over hill & dale through a beautiful, picturesque country & encamped a little after dark, on a small, clear stream having come 18 miles to-day – Our situation, this evening, is in a beautiful valley, surrounded by a gentle elevation of ground, while, far to the south can be seen a number of the lofty peaks of "Bear River" mountains, whose sides & summits are covered with snow. – John Brown has killed an antelope to-day. – Soon after our arrival, Porter rode up & informed us, that about 1½ mile distant encamped on "Bear River," was a number of individuals who had just came through from California – among these was a man by the name of Miles Goodier [Goodyear] whom I have before noticed as being settled near the "Salt Lake" – the majority of them are bound for the States. – We have travelled during the past week 87 miles, & are this evening distant from Ft. Bridger 31 miles, from Ft. Laramie 428¾ miles, & from Winter Quarters 969 miles. –

Sunday the 11th.

Pleasant weather. – This morning the men spoken of above passed our camp on their way to the eastward. – among them was a gentleman by the name of Craig[161] – His family were in Ray Co. Mo. & thither he was now returning – he had left them in April 1846, & gone to California, where he had purchased, as he informed us, some land, near the head of "San Francisco Bay." – He did not give a very favorable account of the country, although, in spots, he said, there is very good land for cultivation, when once "irrigated". – He made the same statement concerning the country in the vicinity of the Salt Lake – he further said that Mr. Miles, who lived at the latter place had there made a small garden improvement, & that he had eat some of the onions, lettuce, &c. which was quite flourishing when he left – the corn had grown about 3 feet in height. – That notwithstanding all we had heard of the richness of the country, we would find it vastly over-rated, & that if we had formed an idea of its superiority, we should be disappointed. – Mr. Miles himself, gives a glowing account of the country in which he is settled – but it is the general opinion of the brethren that he does this, on account of his anxiety that we should travel through there thereby making a road, & ensuring the passage of other emigrants in that direction, which would result in his advantage.[162] – He, Porter, & one or two others have rode out this morning to find a good road to the Lake – The remainder of his company, 4 in number, including Mr. Craig, after halting here a few minutes, pursued their journey – There is a beautiful spring of water, not far from here, which is as cold & sweet as any I ever tasted. – About 1½ mile distant some of the brethren to-day discovered a spring, which contains matter of an oily nature, & considerably resembles tar in taste – Bro. Carrington calls it "Mineral Tar." The brethren of the camp were this evening called together at Pres't. Young's wagon, to ascertain, as he told them, whether they would take, from here, the North or South road to the Lake – after some conversation & interchange of opinion, the former route was chosen. – Bro. Lewis Barney killed an antelope to-day. –

Monday the 12th.

Fine day, though quite dusty travelling – The majority of the camp started about 8 a. m. – Porter, J. Redden, & one or two others having lost their horses which had strayed away, Bro. Pack & myself waited for them to be found, & we all started about 9 a.m. – proceeded about

161. This group consisted of John Craig of Ray County, Missouri; Samuel Truitt from Shelby County, Illinois; and two unidentified California immigrants. Craig had set out from Fort Hall with only two wagons and seven other men to travel to California in the spring of 1846. Wilford Woodruff learned from Craig's party that a woman he had baptized was among the dead of the Donner-Reed party. See Harold Schindler, "Mormon Trail Series," *Salt Lake Tribune*, April–July 1997.

162. Goodyear Ranch owed its beginnings to Miles Morris Goodyear, credited by historians as the first white settler of Ogden and of the state of Utah. He had taken part in westward expeditions since 1836 but did not erect his ranch or fort in the Weber River country until 1846. Goodyear died in 1849. See Dale L. Morgan, "Miles Goodyear and the Founding of Ogden" (two-part series), *Utah Historical Quarterly* 21 (July, October 1953): 195–218, 307–29.

Cache Cave (or Redden Cave) near the top (eastern) entrance to Echo Canyon. Courtesy of Church History Library.

1¾ mile, & crossed "Bear River." – We now travelled in a western direction alternately over lofty hills or mountains, & through extensive valleys, & halted to bait at noon in one of the latter – having come 9¾ miles – Here we remained about an hour & then pursued our journey – travelling over a somewhat more level road, (though in some places quite stony,) than we did this forenoon, we encamped at sunset in a beautiful valley, abounding in verdure, having come 6¾ [*sic*] this afternoon, & 16½ miles during the day – opposite our wagon to-night is a high mass of rock, while a little to the left is a cave in the rock, the opening of which is 12 feet in width & some 15 feet in extent – & is high enough at the mouth, to admit of a man standing upright. Pres't. Young having been taken quite sick, remained at our noon halting place – a number of other wagons, including Heber's also stopt there – I was attacked this morning with the "mountain fever", as it is called, & was obliged to lie in bed the most of the day, suffering in the meantime, the most excruciating pains in my head & back[163] – This evening I swallowed 2 of Wright's vegetable pills, & the sleep which I was denied through the day, I enjoyed quite soundly all night. – I understood there were 12 antelope killed to-day by different individuals – The cave spoken of above, was named "Redden Cave," as it was first discovered by J. Redden[164] – It rained a little, accompanied by thunder & lightning soon after our arrival at this place. –

TUESDAY THE 13TH.

Tolerably pleasant weather, though somewhat cloudy – During this forenoon, Bro. Heber rode up on horseback from Brigham's camp, which is 6¾ miles back The brethren were immediately called together, & the following companies, (consisting of 23 wagons, including

163. Brigham Young was suffering from "mountain fever" which was probably Rocky Mountain spotted fever or Colorado tick fever. Caused by the bite of wood ticks, this form of typhus could be a fatal affliction. For excellent studies on this topic, see Victoria A. Harden, *Rocky Mountain Spotted Fever: A History of a Twentieth-Century Disease* (1990), and Jerry K. Aikawa, *Rocky Mountain Spotted Fever* (Springfield, IL: Charles C. Thomas, 1966). See also J. A. Aldous and Paul S. Nicholes, "What Is Mountain Fever?," *Overland Journal* 15 no. 1 (1997): 22–23.

164. Redden Cave, also known as "Cache Cave," is located about one mile south of I-80 in upper Echo Canyon, Utah. The cave is famous for the large number of pioneer names and inscriptions carved into its soft sandstone.

Porter's & A. Farr's out of our 10.) viz. Captain Taft of the 1st D., & Capts. Matthews, Brown, & Crow of the 2d D., were chosen to go ahead & make a road instead of going through the "Kanyon,"[165] – under the supervision of Orson Pratt – They started about the middle of the afternoon, taking with them crowbars, & other implements, necessary to remove large obstacles from the path. – Bro. Heber returned this afternoon to Brighams camp. – Dr. Richards, Elder Woodruff & some others dug out a good spring of water near here this evening – My health to-day is much better than it was yesterday, the fever having left me. & my head ceased aching, although, I yet feel quite dizzy & weak. – Most of the brethren in the camp that have been attacked by this singular disease, have partially recovered, though some are yet quite low with it – among the latter is Father Solomon Chamberlain . The President's health is improving, & we shall probably resume our journey in a day or two. – We had a light thunder shower this afternoon, which lasted about ½ an hour – I understood there were 6 antelope killed to-day, although I know of but 5 persons, who killed one apiece, viz., Henson Walker, Sterling Driggs, Charles Shumway, Lyman Curtis, & Shoop [Andrew Jackson Shupe], one of the soldier brethren.

Wednesday the 14th.

Warm & pleasant – The brethren in the camp are mostly engaged in repairing their clothes & wagons, & some have gone out in pursuit of game – Quite dull business this, lying by. – A meeting was held this evening at Dr. Richard's wagon, at which was taken into consideration the propriety of removing hence a short distance, it not being deemed healthy to remain encamped on the same spot of ground for more than three days' time. – It was accordingly voted & carried that we take our wagons over the little creek close by & there again form in regular order – Bro. W. Woodruff, who has just returned from the President's camp, reports that his health is improving, but that Col. Rockwood is yet quite sick with the prevailing complaint. Bro. Woodruff intends to go over in the morning & bring the invalids to the camp in his carriage. – It rained considerably soon after we retired for the night. – I have heard of but 4 antelope being killed to-day, by the following men – Lewis Barney 2, Joseph Hancock, & Norton Jacobs.

Thursday the 15th.

Warm, but somewhat cloudy – Nothing of particular importance occurred during this forenoon. – about noon, Brigham, Heber, & the others who staid behind came up, soon after which, we all got up our teams, & pursued our journey. – It now commenced raining, & in fact, continued showery throughout the day – after going about a mile, we descended a long, & rather steep, sandy hill, – thence taking our course, through a beautiful picturesque valley, bounded on either side by lofty crags, we encamped in the same at ½ past 3 P. M.,

165. ***Editor's note***: Whitney inserted his own footnote as follows: "Kanyon – a confined stream of water, flowing between rocks."

having come 4½ miles – the ground here is somewhat wet in places, & is covered with high grass of the best quality – The eminence to the left of us consists of a rugged mass of rock, of a reddish color, whose tops & sides are studded with innumerable cedar shrubs. – Bro. Geo. A. Smith informed me, that he saw, as we passed along, a kind of gum issuing out of the rocks in the side of the hill – This, Bro. [Albert] Carrington who is both a chemist and geologist, supposes to be of the nature of coal. – The brethren have dug a spring here, which affords very good drinking water. – I called upon President Young, soon after our arrival at this place, & was glad to find him in a state of convalescence, & in tolerably good spirits, though his pale & emaciated countenance plainly testified that he had recently been quite ill in body. – My health is now nearly reestablished, with the exception that I yet feel considerably weak in body. – The following are the names of those who went ahead on Tuesday the 13th inst. under the supervision of Captain Orson Pratt to look out a road, instead of going through the "Kanyon" –

S. Markham
O. P. Rockwell
J. Redden
N. Fairbanks
Joseph Egbert
John S. Freeman
Marcus B. Thorpe
Robert Crow
Benj. B. Crow
John Crow
W. H. Crow
Walter Crow
Geo. W. Therlkill
James Chesney
Lewis B. Myers
John Brown
Shadrach Roundy
Hans C. Hansen
Levi Jackman
Lyman Curtis
David Powell
Oscar Crosby
Hark Lay
Joseph Matthews
Gilburd [Gilbard] Summer[Summe]
Green Flake
John S. Gleason
Charles Burke
Norman Taylor
A. P. Chessley
Seth Taft
Horace Thornton
Stephen Kelsey
James Stewart
Robt. Thomas
C. [J.] D. Burnham
John S. Eldridge
Elijah Newman
Francis Boggs
Levi N. Kendall
David Grant

1st Division	7 wagons	15 men
2d	16 "	27 "
Total –	23 "	42 "

I took supper this evening at Bro. Heber's wagon by his invitation, with himself Bro. Clayton, Howard Egan, & Ellen – Bro. Jacobs showed me a small branch of shrub oak, that he had found growing on the top of one of the mountains in the vicinity. –

Friday the 16th.

On awakening this morning, I discovered it to be raining quite hard, which continued till we started, when it cleared off. – We continued our journey at ½ past 8 a.m. – passed along through the valley & halted to bait, at noon near the base of a high, rocky cliff, having a perpendicular descent of 5 or 600 feet. – Orson went to the summit, & took a view of the

William H. Jackson, Echo Canyon Encampment *(1866). Bretney Collection, Wyoming State Archives.*

surrounding country, which, he said, consisted of lofty mountains as far as the eye could reach – We were again in motion about 2 P. M. – The country now assumed a more beautiful & grand appearance, the huge overhanging masses of rocks to our right, towering for several hundred feet above our heads, &, as it were, frowning down upon us with sullen majesty from their dizzy height [Echo Canyon]– A small murmuring rivulet winds serpentinely through the valley, & this we crossed a number of times – Our road sometimes leading over small hills, & at others over level ground, through dense thickets of willow, &c.– In some places the pass between the mountains became quite narrow, & on looking up we could see huge fragments of rocks projecting immediately over our heads. – Indeed, this pass is so well fortified by nature, that I have no doubt but that 10 men could successfully dispute its passage for a long time against 100 men. – We encamped at 6 P. M., in the valley, having come 16¼ miles – a short distance ahead of us can be seen "Weaver's Fork" [likely Webers Fork] of "Bear River" – I omitted to mention that during our halt this noon, Porter rode up on horseback – he reported O. Pratt's company to be some 20 miles ahead. – Father Chamberlain's wagon axle-tree was broken in two this afternoon, & Bro. Wheeler, this evening, was obliged to go back some 2 miles after him, & bring him up in another wagon. –

Saturday the 17th.

Bright & beautiful morning. – We all got started at ½ 8 a.m. as usual. – The 10 to which Father Chamberlain belonged, remained behind till his axle-tree could be repaired, & his wagon some 2 miles back and be brought up. – We descended a sloping hill, & came to Weaver's Fork of Weber River, when turning sharp to our right, we proceeded 1½ mile, & encamped on its banks about 10 a.m., having come 2½ miles. The reason of our stopping so soon was because President Young was suddenly taken quite ill, & could not endure to travel any further to-day. – We have travelled 39¾ miles during the past week, & are, this evening distant from Ft. Bridger 70¾ miles, from Ft. John 468½ miles, & from Winter Quarters 1008¾ miles. – The river here is bounded in places by lofty banks, & abounds in trout, of which the brethren caught a number, to-day. – The banks on either side are lined with dry and green cotton wood trees – the grass is quite good on the bottoms below – Bro. Heber, Dr. Richards, Bro. Benson, Bro. Woodruff, G. A. Smith, & a number of others this afternoon, went up into the mountains & clothed themselves & prayed in behalf of President Young, that he might soon recover his health. – There are considerable signs of bear here as you cannot walk far without seeing fresh tracks of that animal, & on the sides of the mountains can be seen places smoothly worn, where thy have slid down. – On the summits are a numerous horns of Mountain sheep – My health yesterday & to-day has been very poor, & I have suffered considerably with a fever & head-ache in consequence of having taken cold.–

Sunday the 18th.

Pleasant day – The brethren of the camp were called together this morning, before breakfast, at Dr. Richard's wagon, where Bro. Heber addressed them. – He told them that the President is very sick – that he did not feel as if he was going to die; still he might – that it was his mind that the brethren should stay in camp & not go out hunting, & fishing, &c., but lift up our hearts to God in behalf of the President, & others of the sick & afflicted, that we may be speedily enabled to pursue our journey – He further proposed that a prayer meeting should be held, under the supervision of the Bishops, commencing at 10 a.m. – all the above suggestions were voted & carried – at the meeting held pursuant to appointment, it was also voted and carried that all, except the President, & those appointed to stay here, should pursue our journey early in the morning. I walked down to the river this afternoon, when after fishing a few minutes, I caught a very fine trout, weighing a pound or more. –

Monday the 19th.

Pleasant morning. – this morning about 8 o'clock 41 wagons went ahead (including 3 of Bro. Heber's.) – 15 remain here, including a number of Brigham's and Heber's. – I also stayed behind on account of my ill health by, Bro. Heber's advice. Soon after the main body left, we got up our teams & proceeded about 1½ mile & again encamped. – Bro. Heber, Benson, Woodruff & Egan rode ahead to survey the country – they returned about ½ past 4 P. M., & reported the road to be quite mountainous – about 2 miles ahead W. Clayton put up a guide board with the following inscription: – "Pratt's Pass, to avoid the "Kanyon" – 74¼ miles from Ft. Bridger." – President Young's health is slowly improving. – I caught a small trout out of the river this evening. – Orson & 2 or 3 others has rode on ahead a short distance to view the Kanyon.[166]–

Tuesday the 20th.

Pleasant weather. – Pres't Young also much better, it was thought best to pursue our journey – We started about ½ past 5 a.m.., & after going about 1 mile we crossed the river – Leaving it & the Kanyon behind us, we now pursued a W. S. W. course through a valley over gradually ascending ground, & halted to bait & get breakfast at 8, having come about 4½ miles. A cool stream of water flows by near here – the grass is tolerably good – in about 1½ hours we were again in motion – H. Egan, Orson, & a number of others went ahead to repair the road, which now leads through alternately narrow defiles along the sides & over steep stony hills, & halted at noon to bait having in a small valley, enclosed on all all [*sic*] sides by lofty mountains, having come about 6 miles – The road here makes an abrupt turn to the west, which

166. Following a trail blazed by Orson Pratt, the main company traveled down Echo Canyon and camped on the Weber River near present-day Echo, Utah. Choosing not to go down Weber Canyon because of its virtual impassability, they followed the Donner-Reed trail west, ascended Main Canyon from present-day Henefer, crossed the Hogback (Reed's Pass) Summit, and descended Dixie Hollow before climbing a final hill (Big Mountain) to their camp at the site of the east Canyon Reservoir and eventually down Emigration Canyon. Will Bagley, ed., *The Pioneer Camp of the Saints: The 1846 and 1847 Mormon Trail Journals of Thomas Bullock* (Spokane: Arthur H. Clark, 1997), 228–29nn. See also Bennett, *We'll Find the Place,* 212–13. The final thirty-five miles from Big Mountain to the mouth of Emigration Canyon were by far the most difficult of the entire journey.

course it pursues about ½ a mile & then turns again to south-west – The same, small, cool streams [*sic*] runs near here, & this we have crossed a number of times on our route during this forenoon. – Bro. Heber & Benson rode on to search for a good camping place for the night – after they returned, (having found one,) we again started at ½ past 4 P. M. – going a short distance, & turning to the S. W. we ascended a long hill, & after travelling over, as usual, a rugged hilly road, we descended, – & encamped sun ½ an hour high in a valley, having come 4 miles watered by quite a large stream of pure water which crossed twice before stopping. – Here we found 3 wagons belonging to Bro. S. Goddard, Father Case, & Father Dewey – They had stopt here on account of the sickness, of [missing text]

Observations at Ft. John.

By a mean of several Barometrical observations taken during three days, the height above the land of the sea, was determined to be 4090 feet.

By a meridian observation of the sun, the latitude determined was 42° 12′ 13″.

By a mean of six sights with a good Sextant, the calculated longitude west from Greenwich was, in time, $6^{h.}\ 56^{m.}\ 47^{s.}\ 5$ – equal to 104° 11′ 53″.

Latitude of "Warm Springs," west of Ft. John, 42° 15′ 6″.

Father Sherwood, Dewey, and Artemas Johnson. Their company having camped a little way back from here last night, had gone ahead & left them this morning – we learned that G. A. Smith's wagon had broken down – I caught a few trout this evening. – It is supposed we have come about 14 miles, but we are obliged to depend entirely upon conjecture as to the distance. Bro. Wm Clayton with his wagon having gone ahead. – My health to-day is improving, & I now have hopes of speedy recovery, unless I should suffer another relapse. – President Young, though somewhat tired, is quite comfortable this evening. –

Since writing the above, I have learned we travelled 12½ miles to-day.

Journal

Kept by H K Whitney during the
Journey & sojourn of the
Church of Jesus Christ
of Latter Day Saints
in the Wilderness

Anno Domini

1847.

Number 6

Continued

Journal 6

21 July–30 October 1847

A

Journal

Kept by H K Whitney during the

journey a sojourn of the

church of Jesus Christ

of Latter-day Saints

in the Wilderness

Anno Domini

1847.

Number 6

<u>Continued</u>

WEDNESDAY THE 21ST.

Very warm day. Bro. Heber, Benson, & L. Young rode out this morning to survey the country – they returned this afternoon – they had been to the Kanyon, about 1½ mile from here – there they were obliged to dismount from their horses & explore the passage on foot, – the country being almost inaccessible – Bro. Heber told me that the Kanyon is about ½ mile in extent, & that it was his conviction we would be obliged to pass over a high ridge of mountains covered with snow, where we shall resume our journey. – President Young being much fatigued with yesterday's travel, It was thought best to remain here to-day. Father Sherwood & the other brethren are some better to-day. –

THURSDAY THE 22D.

Cloudy morning, though quite warm. – We again set forward this morning about ½ past 7 o'clock, & taking near a south course through the valley, we crossed the stream on which we encamped 4 times & halted about 9 a.m., having come about 2½ miles – This creek is called "Ogden's Fork" & on its banks are numerous remains of small Indian lodges, hastily constructed of willow boughs.[167] The reason of our stopping is that Father Case's wagon wheel was broken or considerably damaged this morning, while on the road which has been quite stony in places. – Bro. Heber, Benson, H. Egan went back to assist in repairing the damage. – They soon returned, having remedied the matter by tying a pole lengthwise under the wagon, & the brethren relieved him of a good share of his load, by each one taking a portion thereof. We again started on at at [*sic*] 11 o'clock – Our course now lay south alternately over a hilly road and through dense copses or thickets of willow & cotton wood, which line the banks of the stream – at length after ascending a steep hill, we found a letter in the end of a stick placed upright in the ground by the side of the road – Inside this was written the following: –

"Kanyon Creek, Tuesday Morning,
July 20, 1847.

"To Willard Richards, George A. Smith, or any of the Saints: – From this point it is 5 miles west to the summit of the dividing ridge: the road will be of a gradual ascent, & considerably better than the one you have passed over for a few days back – the ravine, up which you will go, is without water, except 2 or 3 small springs, which soon lose themselves beneath the soil. You will pass through groves of "quaking asp," "balsam" & "cotton wood", more than you have seen for many days. From the dividing ridge you will make a more rapid descent – the hill for a short distance, will be quite steep, though strait & smooth,

167. Born in Lower Canada (Quebec), Peter Skeene Ogden (1790–1854), after whom the city of Ogden was named, was a fur trader and explorer in the American/Canadian West. After a brief time with the American Fur Company and later the Northwest Company, he was appointed chief trader for the Snake River country of the Hudson's Bay Company in 1823. During his many expeditions, he explored parts of Oregon, Washington, Nevada, California, Utah, Idaho, and Wyoming. He is buried in Oregon City, Oregon. See Gloria Griffen Cline, *Peter Skene Ogden and the Hudson's Bay Company* (Norman: University of Oklahoma Press, 1974).

Artist unknown, Mormon Trail—Big Mountain. *First view of Great Salt Lake Valley from a mountain pass. Utah State Historical Society.*

we have descended worse since we left Ft. Bridger. You will go down about 6 miles, where you will find a camping place, – grass middling good you will find a small spring about 100 rods after leaving the dividing ridge which soon loses itself in the soil; the bed of the stream remains mostly dry for 2 or 3 miles, where you will strike a stream nearly one third as large as the one where I leave this note. Your road, in descending, will lead through quite a timbered forest, principally aspen, but some underwood of oak & small maple. The soil is extremely rich. About 1½ mile beyond the camping ground above mentioned, you will find quite a lengthy hill to avoid passing through a rough, rocky Kanyon. You will then descend in a ravine for 3 or 4 miles unto a broad, & comparatively level valley, which is probably an arm of a prairie, putting up among the mountains from the Eutaw outlets.

"Most Respectfully,
Orson Pratt."

"Elders Amasa Lyman, Charles C. Rich, & the Saints: – Beloved Brethren, – I leave you an extract of a letter from Orson Pratt, found at this camping ground, for your benefit and guidance. Yours, very truly, Thomas Bullock, Clerk of Pioneer camp, Tuesday evening, 7 o'clock. – The sick are getting better." –

The above letter was read by W. Woodruff to the brethren, while we halted on the brow of the hill, which we soon descended, &, after going about ¼ of a mile & crossing "Ogden's Fork" for the 7th time this afternoon, & the 11th during the day, we encamped on its banks in the valley or ravine at ½ past 3 P. M. – having come 7½ miles to-day. I omitted to mention that we had quite a shower during our halt this morning. This stream abounds in fine trout, of which I caught one to-day, & its banks are studded with plenty of underwood, wild current, gooseberry, &c.–

FRIDAY THE 23D.

Pleasant morning. – We started at ¼ past 7 a.m., & leaving Ogden's Fork in our rear, we turned up a ravine, pursuing a west course over a gradual ascent of ground – The road is rough, rocky, & sidling in many places, & leads through dense thickets of underbrush, & quite a forest of hemlock and poplar trees. At length, after travelling 4 miles we attained the summit of the dividing ridge, mentioned by O. Pratt in his letter – here we had a fine view of the mountains covered with snow, & the open country in the distance beyond – we have passed 2 or 3 springs during our route this forenoon. We now began to descend a long, & for some distance, quite a steep hill, over a rough road made by the brethren by cutting down trees, the stumps of which annoyed us not a little, as we passed along, as well as projecting boughs & prostrate trunks of trees, which lay in our path – we crossed a small rivulet 6 times, which ran along at the base of the hill through a ravine, and after having come 4½ miles down a gradual descent we emerged on to an open area of ground, where there is a good

William H. Jackson, View of the Salt Lake Valley. *Utah State Historical Society.*

spring of water, spoken of also by O. Pratt as probably being an arm of the prairie communicating with the lake. – Here we halted to bait at 12 M., having come 4½ miles. – While here, Bro. John Pack & Joseph Matthews rode up on horseback – they reported both companies of the brethren to be some 14 miles ahead encamped in a valley, apparently about 20 miles from the "Salt Lake", which could be seen in the distance to the north-west. The brethren, when they left them this morning, were intending to move about 4 miles further, & then stop & commence planting seeds in the ground, which, they speak of, as being extremely rich and fertile. – Bros. Pack and Matthews were the bearers of a letter from O. Pratt, G. A. Smith & W. Richards, to President Young, giving the latter an account of the roads ahead, the fertility of the soil, & the general features of the country in their vicinity, &c., &c.– After remaining here about 2 hours we were again in motion – going west a short distance, the valley becoming more confined in its limits as we advanced, we turned to the right, & pursuing a west-n-west course, we ascended a very long & steep hill, on attaining the summit of which, Bros. Pack & Matthews left us & went ahead. – Descending now a west course, another long and steep hill, (some wagons being obliged to lock both wheels,) we encamped at its base at ½ past 5 P. M., near a pure & beautiful stream of water, whose banks are thickly skirted with quaking asp, & cotton wood trees having come 9 miles to-day, I omitted to mention that Bro. Lorenzo Young's wagon, while descending the hill this forenoon, was overturned by some obstacle impeding the passage of the road, & the bows mostly broken in pieces. His 2 little boys, who happened to be in the wagon at the time, providentially escaped uninjured, though a portion of the load having become disarranged inside, rolled upon them, stopping up the entrance, & they were only liberated by cutting a hole in the cover. A short time previous to our arrival at this place, the sky became overcast with clouds, & a strong breeze setting in from the south west, there is quite a prospect of rain this evening. The grass here is rather rank & tall though in places quite good. –

SATURDAY THE 24TH.

Notwithstanding the threatening appearance of the weather last evening, the clouds have cleared away, & this morning, the sun rose bright & beautiful as usual – The majority of the camp were in motion about ¼ past 7 a.m., – Frank Dewey & myself did not start with the rest, our horses having strayed away. Bro. Howard Egan had also lost one of his – he went back over the mountain about 4 miles where he found them all, brought them up, & we got started in about 2 hours after the departure of the rest. Pursuing a west course through the ravine, we crossed the stream 18 times. – going down several steep descents, we at length emerged from the pass, (having come 4 miles,) & were highly gratified with a fine view of the open country and the "Great Salt Lake," whose blue surface could be seen in the distance with a lofty range of mountains in the background, which I should judge to be some 30 or 40 miles distant.[168] There is an extensive, beautiful, level, looking valley, from here to the Lake, which I should

168. The Great Salt Lake, believed to have been formed about 11,000 years ago, is a remnant of Lake Bonneville, a body of fresh water, about 20,000 square miles and 1,000 feet deep. Over time, the lake emptied

judge from the numerous deep green patches must be fertile and rich. The valley extends to the south probably 50 miles, where it is again surrounded by high mountains. To the south-west across the valley, at about 25 to 30 miles' distance, is a high mountain, extending from the south end of the valley to about opposite this place, where it ceases abruptly, leaving a pleasant view of the dark waters of the Lake, – standing in the Lake, & about due west, there are 2 mountains, & far in the distance, another one, which I suppose is on the other side the Lake, probably from 80 to 100 miles distant. To the north-west is another mountain, at the base of which is a long ridge of what I should consider to be rock salt from its white & shining appearance. – of Rattlesnakes there are plenty of a rare size, which probably have their dens in the mountains. The distance from the entrance of "Pratt's Pass to avoid the Kanyon" at "Weber's Fork", to this place, is 41¼ miles – we have travelled 44¼ miles during the past week, & are this evening, distant from Ft. Bridger 115 miles, from Ft. John 512¾ miles, & from Winter Quarters 1053 miles. President Young is slowly recovering his health, &, finally, all those in the camp who have been sick are rapidly recovering.[169] – It commenced raining quite hard about 4 P. M., accompanied by a strong wind from the south-west, which continued about 2 hours, thus setting at naught the opinions & apprehensions of some of the brethren, that rain is not sufficiently incidental to this county for the growth of wheat, corn, &c.– Some of them, indeed, had thought that we would be obliged to irrigate the country by digging ditches, &c., but there is no fear, if we continue to serve the Lord with full purpose of heart, but that he will provide us with every thing essential to our future comfort & happiness. One thing I omitted to mention, viz. There are numerous black crickets of an enormous size to be seen here – On these the bears are supposed to subsist in winter, which devour them with great voracity. They would also doubtless be good for the fatting of hogs.[170] It again commenced raining about 9 o'clock this evening, which, however,

---

through a cut made in the north and nearly dried up. Increasing precipitation later formed the Great Salt Lake, which is currently 1,700 square miles in size, with a maximum depth of 33 feet. The lake has no outlets, trapping the water until it evaporates, leaving the salt behind. Richard H. Jackson, "Great Salt Lake," in *Utah History Encyclopedia* (Salt Lake City: University of Utah Press, 1994), http://historytogo.utah.gov/utah_chapters/the_land/greatsaltlake.html. See also Dale L. Morgan, *The Great Salt Lake* (Indianapolis: Bobbs-Merrill, 1947).

169. Not everyone in the pioneer company was excited at seeing the Great Salt Lake. Their celebration was muted by noticeable restraint at seeing a potential home so void of vegetation. Wrote William Clayton: "For my own part I am happily disappointed in the appearance of the valley of the Salt Lake, but if the land be as rich as it has the appearance of being, I have no fears but the Saints can live here and do well while we will do right." *William Clayton's Journal*, 309. Nevertheless, he was soon calling it "the promised land" as did so many others in the camp (316). Wilford Woodruff, who was at Brigham Young's side when he first saw the valley, remarked that "President Young expressed his full satisfaction in the appearance of the valley as a resting place for the Saints and was amply repayed [*sic*] for his journey." *Wilford Woodruff's Journal*, 3:234, entry for 24 July 1847.

170. The so-called "Mormon Cricket," technically identified as *Anabrus simplex*, is approximately 1.25 inches long. Traveling in hordes as big as a city block or more, they moved up to two miles per day. They not only consumed vegetation but other insect and animal life as well, including rattlesnakes, evergreen trees, and sagebrush. See Frank T. Cowan, *Life Habits, History and Control of the Mormon Cricket*, U.S. Dept. of Agriculture Technical Bulletin No. 161 (1929), 26–27. Such infestations are rare today because most

did not last long. Lewis B. Myers & one of Bro. Crow's sons have gone out hunting taking pack horses with them intending to be gone a month or two, in order to get their supply of meat for the winter – they left here yesterday. –

Sunday the 25th.

Somewhat cloudy this morning, although we had but little rain during the last night. This morning is the anniversary of my birthday and I have completed my 24th year. About 9 a.m., Robert Byard, John Gleason & myself took a walk of about ¾ of a mile to the creek across which the brethren had built a dam, from which the water running, through a narrow dike they had dug, irrigated the land that has been ploughed over and partially planted with potatoes – here we found a number of the brethren bathing in the pure, cold water of the stream.[171] There we continued our course about 2 miles along the bottom, at the base of the mountain, & came to 3 different places, where very hot water, issuing from the mountains, runs down to the valley below, and there forms into as many large pools or ponds. It possesses a salt or sulphurous taste, & is so extremely noxious to the smell, that it is almost impossible to remain in the vicinity long at a time – The brink or bottom of these streams abound in a kind of vertigris or slime of a greenish color, like unto copperas, to which it also bears some resemblance in taste, being of a poisonous nature in the opinion of Prof. Orson Pratt, although the water itself is as-transparent as any I have ever seen, after tasting & viewing the waters awhile, we retraced our steps to the camp, halting, a few minutes to bathe at the dam on our return. There had been a meeting during our absence, which I understand was successively addressed by Elders Kimball, G. A. Smith & Benson on different subjects. – at 1 P. M., by request of H. C. Kimball, the following persons, viz. Howard Egan, Hans C. Hansen, Jackson Redden, Carlos Murray, Thomas Cloward, George Billings, Philo Johnson, Charles Harper, Edson Whipple, Wm. A. King Hosea Cushing, Robert Byard, Orson K. Whitney, & myself, assembled themselves in a grove adjacent to the camp, when Elder Kimball addressed them in substance as follows. – "Most of you here present, have become adopted into my family, except a very few (calling them by name,) & Horace, who has become connected with my family by marriage; but I do not care for that, you are all the same to me, & your interest is my interest, for what's mine is yours, & what's yours is your own. If I have the privilege of

crickets have been destroyed in the maze of irrigation ditches throughout the valley. The famous infestation of crickets among Mormon settlements in 1848 is well remembered in history and folklore. Several contemporary accounts, however, report that the crops were saved by flocks of seagulls that descended upon the crickets, first gorging themselves, then vomiting up the remains, before returning again and again in waves of deliverance. See Bennett, *We'll Find the Place*, 344–49. See also William G. Hartley, "Mormons, Crickets, and Gulls: A New Look at an Old Story," *Utah Historical Quarterly* 38 (Summer 1970): 224–39.

171. The Mormons were not the first to implement patterns of irrigation in the American West but were arguably the most successful by their means of diverting water flow from creeks and streams to flood the parched desert soil. Once so watered, the parched soil proved surprisingly fertile. See Leonard J. Arrington and Dean May, "'A Different Mode of Life': Irrigation and Society in Nineteenth-Century Utah," *Agricultural History* 49 (1975): 7.

building a house, I want you to help me, & and I will help you. Horace will want to build a house for some of his father's family, if they should come up, & there is plenty of timber in the hills. When my family comes up, we may conclude to settle somewhere else, if so, there will be plenty to buy us out, if we shall have made any improvements. – I want you all to be prudent, & take care of your horses, cattle, & every thing intrusted to your care. It would be a good plan, (& probably will be done,) for those who stay here, to go back on the 'Sweet Water,' & kill buffalo, &c., for winter consumption. We shall go to-morrow, if Brigham is well enough, in search of a better location, (if, indeed, such can be found,) if not, we shall remain here. – There should be an enclosure made for the purpose of keeping the horses & cattle in nights, for there are plenty of Indians in the vicinity. I should advise you to keep the Sabbath day holy, whether others do or not. I want you to put all the seed into the ground, that you think will come to maturity. I am satisfied that buckwheat will do as well here, as any other seed we can sow. I want also some peach stones, & apple seeds to be planted forthwith. – Bro. Byard & Hans I would like to have immediately engage in making garments of buckskins, & Bro. Cloward in making shoes, & Bro. Johnson in making hats as soon as practicable. If you wish to go hunting, fishing, or to see the country, select a week day, & not the Lord's day, for that purpose. Do not let us get giddy & high minded, as the Nephites did of old, but strive to work righteousness in the beginning, inasmuch as we have reached the 'Promised Land.' If it is advisable to work in a family capacity, we will do so, & if in a church capacity, we should be equally willing to do that. I am going out on a scout with the brethren, & I shall probably want one or two of you to go with me, & also one or two wagons. I am not going to take any thing back with me to Winter Quarters, only what is actually necessary – even some of my clothes I shall leave behind. I shall leave Bishop Whipple with you, – he is quite a steady & economical man, & as such I recommend him to you. I want every man to be as industrious as possible while I am gone, & get into the ground all the turnip, cabbage, & other seeds you can. In case a storm of snow should come on it would advisable to drive all the cattle among the willows, where they can remain until the snow goes off. I want you all to work together, until such times shall come, when every man will have his inheritance set off to him.[172] – I feel towards you as a father towards his children, & I want you to banish all peevishness from among your midst, & accommodate yourselves as much as possible to each others' wishes. I have it to say, that my boys have been faithful to their various duties on this journey, & other people have noticed it & expressed their opinions that they never saw such an attentive set of men in their lives, & I consider that their conduct is worthy of imitation. I want you to be solemn & prayerful & remember me & my family in your prayers." A number of other good ideas were advanced by Bro. Heber of an edifying nature, & then we closed the meeting by prayer, at 2 P. M. & we all retired separately to the camp, having enjoyed one

---

172. In the early Salt Lake settlement, properties were ceded out by church authorities to the faithful as their "inheritance" for obedience in traveling to the valley. In the absence of any land records office, or any other form of civil government, Brigham Young and the Quorum of the Twelve Apostles were the ultimate ecclesiastical as well as secular authority. See Arrington, *Great Basin Kingdom*.

of the happiest, &, apparently, the briefest interviews, I have witnessed for a long time. A meeting was again held this afternoon, near President Young's wagon where the brethren were successively addressed by Elders Woodruff, O. Pratt, & W. Richards on subjects of a general nature, & in particular of the good fortune that had attended our safe arrival at this place, without the loss of any individual by death or otherwise, while on the road; & also, how admirably adapted to their condition is this location for the Saints, abounding, as the country does in beautiful scenery, & the land being unequalled in the fertility & richness of its soil, for which blessings we should render thanks to the Lord, the Benefactor & Author of all good deeds to those who love, serve, & obey him. About 6 P. M., the meeting was dismissed, & the brethren retired to their several wagons, having had a good time, & a spirit of unanimity & good feeling seemed to pervade the whole camp. – This afternoon, Lewis B. Meyers & William Crow returned from their hunting expedition – they brought in only one deer – they returned sooner than they contemplated, in consequence of one of their horses having strayed away. –

MONDAY THE 26TH.

Somewhat cloudy this morning. – at 4 a.m., in accordance with previous arrangements, the bugle was sounded for the brethren to collect their horses & cattle to recommence ploughing & planting, & also at an interval of every 4 hours during the day, that the teams might be alternately relived from labor, & others substituted in their place. – The brethren being called together, Col. Markham read out a list of names of those selected for farming operations – 15 men were also chosen to go & make a road through the Kanyon, as it is called in the mountains, in order to obtain an easy-access to places where there is supposed to be timber for building. – Orson was chosen as one of the latter, who soon proceeded to the performance of their task, with axes, spades, & other implements necessary for its completion. Most of the Twelve, accompanied by some others, rode out morning, on horseback, to take a view of the country, & after a short absence returned, & again went out. – The brethren, as yet, are engaged in ploughing & planting indiscriminately together on the same plot of ground, though Pres't. Young yesterday advanced the idea that as soon as convenient, lines would be drawn, & each man allotted a portion of land, for his individual cultivation. A tent was pitched upon the site of ground, where the family meeting was held yesterday, & in it, this morning, Bros. Byard & Cloward commenced their respective avocations of tailoring & shoemaking. The Twelve returned towards evening – they had visited the large hot springs about 4 miles above here, in which, Bro. Heber informed me, he bathed himself – they also ascended a mountain in the vicinity & took a view of the surrounding country. Bros. Joseph Matthews & John Brown informed me this evening, that they had visited a mountain to-day which lies 15 or 16 miles west of this place – about 4 miles from here, they crossed a beautiful clear stream, about 5 rods in width, & of a moderate current – this, issuing from the mountains to the south-east, traverses the whole length of the valley, and runs N. N. W. into the "salt Lake". – The soil, if possible, is richer & more fertile than at this place, near the river;

beyond, it is not quite so good. Adjacent to, & on the sides of the mountain, they saw considerable wild sage, – at the base thereof, they found a horse, which they brought with them to the camp, – to whom this belongs, they have no idea. Orson returned this evening, pretty well tired out with his day's work. This evening, Orson & myself made up our bed under the wagon, the weather was so warm & pleasant. –

Tuesday the 27th.

The sky is partially overcast with clouds this morning, although the weather is quite warm. Orson went, this morning, with Joseph Scofield, & others, into the mountains to procure timber for building a boat. Soon after breakfast, 2 Indians, of the Eutaw tribe, came to the camp – they were somewhat slightly clad in skins, & are quite small in stature, as I am informed this tribe usually are[173] – J. Redden exchanged a gun & a shirt with one of them for a pony. They gave us to understand by signs, that there was a large party of their tribe about 40 miles from here. The bugle was sounded this morning at the usual hour, & the brethren assembled together, & the list of names of those selected for farming, again read over, soon after which all hands commenced ploughing, planting, &c.– The Twelve and some others started on an exploring expedition this morning, – before they got out of sight, 4 horsemen were observed at a distance coming towards the camp. Bro. Heber waited a few minutes until they arrived. They proved to be Bros. Amasa Lyman, Samuel Brannan. Roswell Stevens & Rodney Badger. – they report the battalion to be two days' journey distant, on their way to this place, Bro. A. Lyman & S. Brannan joined the expedition. This afternoon 5 or 6 more Indians made their appearance in the camp, & stayed here all night. 16 wagons belonging to the Twelve, & some others, (including 3 of Heber's,) were removed to a spot across the creek, about ¾ of a mile hence, near the site of ground, where it is supposed the future city will be built. The tent was also taken to that place.

Wednesday the 28th.

Warm & sultry with but little air stirring. – The horn was sounded at the usual hour this morning as a signal to recommence the labors in the field. Orson, with our horses, harrowed this forenoon. Elder S. Brannan arrived here this morning from the Salt Lake, which he says is about 30 miles distant – he reports the Twelve to be on their return, who will probably be in this evening – they had taken a good bathe in the Lake, the waters of which he reports to be so extremely salt, that a man could not sink, if he should try. On the margin are vast quantities of salt of superior fineness & quality. Brother Joseph Hancock came into camp

173. The Mormon pioneers chose a particularly safe place to settle. The Ute Indian tribes frequented lands primarily south of what is today called "Point of the Mountain" in northern Utah County, while the Shoshones were more to the north. Sometimes called "diggers" for their propensity to live off ants, grasshoppers, crickets, and weeds, the Utes were a particularly impoverished tribe. See Virginia McConnell Simmons, *The Ute Indians of Utah, Colorado, and New Mexico* (Boulder: University Press of Colorado, 2000).

this morning, bringing with him a red tailed deer he had killed in the mountains. – he also informed me that he shot an elk the other day.

Lewis B. Meyers, Monroe Frink, Orson & myself started about noon on horseback to go back & meet the soldier brethren from Pueblo. We proceeded up the pass, 14 miles from here, & arrived at their camp, sun 1 hour high, which was situated on the "arm of Prairie" mentioned some time since, in O. Pratt's letter. – They had arrived at this place yesterday, & remained encamped to-day. I found a number of acquaintances among the "boys," one of whom was William Squires . – with him Orson & myself took supper in his tent, & I stayed with him all night. – The brethren that had been sick among them, have mostly recovered.

Thursday the 29th.

Considerably warm & sultry, though there was a slight breeze from the east. The camp struck their tents sun about an hour high, & proceeded on the journey the horsemen preceding the wagons to the mouth of the pass, where the former, whom I accompanied, arrived about noon, soon after which, the Twelve, & a number of others arrived from the camp on the bottom, who, after exchanging salutations with the soldier brethren, proceeded up the pass to meet the wagons, which were detained somewhat, on account of 2 or 3 of them "breaking down" The horsemen also remained here in waiting. Lewis B. Myers, Orson, & myself after stopping a short time, started for the camp. – going a short distance, we descended to the 2d shelf; where we found the brethren engaged in making an extensive garden – Here we also halted a few minutes, when we rode on to the camp, where we arrived about 1 P. M., fatigued with our ride, though not regretting our journey – For particulars occurring during my absence yesterday, I am indebted to the able journal, kept by Howard Egan, from which the following is an extract: – "Wednesday 28th. The brethren of the Twelve arrived at the camp this evening, very much fatigued by their journey. They reported seeing a number of large caves in the rocks along the mountains, – one of them they could penetrate on horseback, 40 or 50 feet, They also saw a number of wild goats. Brother Woodruff lost his whip & went back 3 miles, & saw a party of Indians a short distance off. – one of them rode up to him & shook hands with him, & made signs that they were going to the north part of the Lake. The brethren bathed in the Lake, – the waters of which are so extremely salt, that a man could not sink in it, if he should try. On the margin are vast quantities of salt of a superior quality, a sample of which Bro. Young brought home with him. They reported it as one of the most beautiful places they had ever seen. The brethren of the Twelve wished me to notify Bro. Markham to have the brethren meet close by our camp, at 8 o'clock this evening, when they were addressed by Pres't. Young, pertaining to our locating ourselves here. 'To begin,' he said, 'he wanted the brethren to express their feelings on the subject.' Many of the brethren done so – all were in favor of settling here. It was moved & seconded that we should locate in this valley for the present, & lay out a city at this place, which was carried without a dissenting voice. It was also moved that the Twelve act as a committee, to superintend the laying out of the city, &c., the plan of which, I will give in another place. He expressed his feelings warmly to the brethren on different subjects – he was filled with the spirit of God, & spoke with power, which caused the brethren to rejoice." – Soon after Lewis B. Myers, Orson & myself arrived here, it commenced raining, accompanied by thunder & lightning, with a strong wind from the south-east, which continued at intervals through the day – The soldier brethren, who were detained, by the accident above mentioned, happening to the wagons, arrived here this evening, about ½ past 5 o'clock – they came in, in a martial manner in the following order, viz: – 1st, the Twelve, with the officers on horseback, – 2d. followed a body of horsemen, next a company of footmen, who stept to the time of the soul-stirring tones of the fife & drum, – 3d, & last, closing the line, followed 30 or 35 wagons. They passed our camp, beyond which they went ¼ of a mile, & encamped, after first crossing the creek, on the banks thereof in a semi-circle. – I learned of Wm Squires that there were about 14 Government wagons, & about 20 wagons belonging to the Mississippi company of brethren, that accompanied the soldiers from Pueblo, where the former arrived last year from Mississippi. I am informed that the slight rain we have had, has so raised the creek in the Pass, that all the small bridges made by the brethren have floated away this afternoon. A number of other wagons, that had been detained in the Pass by accident, arrived soon after the majority did at this place. –

FRIDAY THE 30TH.

Warm day. – the usual avocations of ploughing and planting were recommenced to-day. The brethren also erected a saw pit for the purpose of sawing lumber, with which to build a boat, intended to be constructed in the form of a batteau. The twelve held a council with the officers of the battalion, after which, they rode up to the hot springs. I got Bro. Cloward to mend my boots to-day. This evening, Orson & myself got up our horses, & moved north ¾ of a mile, to the place where the Twelve & others had located themselves to the number of about 30 wagons. Near here is the site of the future city, including the ground allotted to the building of the Temple, which is to occupy 40 acres[174] – adjacent to this place, flowing west is a small, clear stream, which affords excellent water. Of this place, when surveyed & laid out in the form of a city, I will give a more minute description hereafter. Bro. Howard Egan, & the rest of Bro. Heber's boys are engaged in ploughing, & planting seeds of different kinds. This evening, a general meeting of the camp, (including the soldier brethren) was held at this place near my wagon, which was addressed by Pres't. Young. He told his feelings concerning the soldiers – they had saved the people by going when they were required, & he rejoiced that they are here. He expressed his feelings warmly towards the brethren, & also told his feelings towards the Gentiles. The meeting was opened by "Hosannahs" three times, & closed by requesting the battalion to build a bower to-morrow on the Temple Lot, where we can assemble for meetings, &c.–

174. The original temple lot or square of forty acres was soon reduced in size to a more manageable ten-acre lot. See note 137.

Saturday the 31st.

Fine weather, with a warm breeze from the south. This morning about 11 o'clock, Robt. Byard, Carlos Murray, Samuel Gould & his son, & myself, started on horseback, to visit the "Big Salt Spring, about 4 miles up the valley, north of this place. Proceeding along the base of the mountains about 3 miles, the clouds, which for some time had worn a threatening appearance, began to discharge a heavy rain – we immediately sought shelter under the protecting boughs of a small tree, growing on a slightly elevated point of ground jutting out from the mountain. After remaining here about ½ hour the rain ceased, when we renewed our excursion. Travelling about a mile further we arrived at the Spring. This is situated at the base of quite a high, large mass of rock, from a cavity of which, gushing forth, it forms into a semi circular pool, about 18 feet in diameter. To ascertain the intensity of its heat, I thrust my hand into the pool, & found it very difficult to keep it there, while I counted the number "10." Having satisfied our curiosity at this place, we next visited quite an extensive salt lake, lying about 100 rods to the west. It is near a mile in length, & in places, about the same in width, communicating with the Spring, which is its source, by means of a small outlet, running from the former into the latter. Near the margin of the Lake the water is quite shallow, though it increases in depth, as you advance towards the center. The water itself is considerably cool, & quite salt in its nature. We took a fine bath therein, & felt ourselves very much refreshed, & invigorated by the operation. after remaining here about an hour, we mounted our horses to return. After going near a mile, it recommenced raining, & we again retreated to the tree, under which we had previously found shelter. It continued to rain quite hard for ¾ of an hour, accompanied by a strong breeze from the west, & a slight fall of hail, about the size of a kernel of corn, when it suddenly ceased, & we retraced our steps to the camp, where we arrived without accident about 4 P. M., having been highly edified & gratified by our visit. I learned, on my arrival, that there were between 20 & 30 Indians at the camp below. Bro. W. Clayton informed me that he witnessed quite a fight between 2 of their number, originating, I believe, in some misunderstanding connected with the loss of a horse or gun, which one accused the other of stealing from him. The soldier brethren, agreeably to the suggestion of Pres't. Young last evening, commenced to build a bowery this morning, near this place, on the site of the Temple lot, which they completed this evening. I omitted to mention, that, during our route this morning, between this place & the Big Salt Spring, we noticed several smaller ones, of 2 or 3 of which I have given an account elsewhere, while on a former visit. The brethren have already ploughed 53 acres of land since we have been here, the most of which is planted. The following is a list of the kinds of seeds put into the ground for Bro. Heber's family, viz. buckwheat 3 acres – corn 1 acre, oats 1 acre – turnips ½ acre – of different kinds of seeds ¼ acre – potatoes 1 bushel. – Bro. Pack & G. Billings rode back 6 miles on the road we came, & cut 41 logs for building. – Since writing the above, I learned the particulars, connected with the Indian quarrel above-mentioned, a misunderstanding having occurred between 2 of them about a horse that was traded to 1 of the brethren for a gun, one of them struck the other on the head with his gun. Immediately, an old Indian, whom

I suppose to be a chief, interfered, & horse-whipped both of them. A short time after, the one stricken with the gun, mounted one of their horses, & rode off. He had not gone more than a mile, when they perceived him. Immediately, 6 of them started in pursuit. – After an absence of a few hours they returned, & made signs that they had killed both the refugee & his horse. The former were Shoshone or Snake Indians, the latter, (of which there is also a number,) here) [*sic*] were Eutaws.[175] Between here & the camp of the soldiers, the former are encamped to-night. Bro. Clayton & Orson informed me, that while there, they saw 5 or 6

William H. Jackson, Washakie's Shoshoni Band and Encampment, 1870, Wind River Mountains. *Wyoming State Archives.*

175. In 1847 the Shoshone or Shoshoni ("high-growing grasses") numbered approximately 4,500. Originating in the Great Basin, by the time of the Mormon arrival they were spread across northern Nevada, northern Utah, southern Idaho, and western Wyoming. In 1860 the Shoshone, led by Chief Pocatello, fought against incursions upon their land by new-coming settlers. In 1863, 430 Shoshone were killed in the infamous Bear River Massacre. Today some 12,000 Shoshones have survived, many living in the Duck Valley reservations in Nevada and the Goshute reservation in Utah.

The Snake Indians include Bannock, Shoshone, and northern Paiute Indians. They were so named by Oregon Trail emigrants while confronting these Native Americans along the Snake River Valley of southern Idaho. The Snake Indians fought several battles against encroaching American settlers, including the Snake War from 1864 to 1868.

The Ute Indians, one of the poorest of all Native American tribes, had inhabited the Great Basin for perhaps a millennium before 1847. By the late 1840s, their northern boundary with the Shoshone was

Indians assembled around their fire, over a huge mass of the large, black crickets, peculiar to this country, which, after having first deprived of their legs & heads, & roasted on the coals, they were devouring with great voracity. – The battalion being paraded this evening Pres't Young addressed them. I only arrived in time to hear the latter part of his speech – This advised us of the folly of trading with the Indians here, for if we continued to do so, he said, we would always be molested with them, therefore, we should give them to understand that we were not permitted to trade at this place, but appoint a distant place for that purpose. He also admonished the brethren not to buy Indian and California horses, as they were not near so good as our American ones, neither did we wish to be overstocked with horses, for they were only a trouble to us. He further said that as Captain Brown was about to start for California, in order to procure the amount of pay due to them, he thought it best that he should be liberated from all duties pertaining to the battalion here, that he might immediately make preparations for his journey, & that Captain [Nelson] Higgins, as next officer should take the command. He then called upon them to know if they were "willing to obey Capt. Higgins & himself as their superior officer – to which inquiry they all gave a unanimous assent. – He also gave them leave to disband, (in a manner,) & go to work tilling the ground, &c., like the rest of the brethren, & told them, that although their time had expired, they could draw pay until they were legally discharged.

Sunday the 1st of August.

Pleasant morning, with a strong breeze from the north-west. A meeting was held this forenoon in the bowery, commencing at 10 o'clock – another this afternoon, commencing at 2 o'clock P. M. – Being absent, I did not attend, but learned that the revelation given in Winter Quarters last winter, was read by Dr. Richards, & a note taken that they would abide by the precepts contained therein.[176] The idea was suggested, & finally adopted, that we employ the Spanish mode of building houeses [*sic*] with "adobies" – clay or dirt moulded and dried in the sun.[177] I took supper with Lieut. [William Wesley] Willis at his tent, in company with Elders A. Lyman & G. A. Smith, & slept with J. Buchanan.

---

vaguely drawn at the Point of the Mountain in present-day Utah County, some twenty miles south of the Mormon camp. Most still traveled on foot and already have been labeled "diggers" for their propensity to live off ants, grasshoppers, crickets, roots, seeds, and even weeds. As Father Pierre de Smet, the famous Catholic explorer had written, "There is not, perhaps, in the whole world, a people in a deeper state of wretchedness and corruption . . . their habitations are holes in the rocks, or the natural crevices of the ground." Pierre Jean de Smet, "Letters and Sketches: With a Narrative of a Year's Residence Among the Indian Tribes of the Rocky Mountains," *Early Western Travels, 1748–1846* (Cleveland, OH: Arthur H. Clark, 1906), 17:165–67. Today some 3,000 Utes survive.

176. The revelation read by Dr. Richards was undoubtedly Brigham Young's "Word and Will of the Lord," presented to and sustained by the membership of the church back at Winter Quarters and other Mormon settlements at the Missouri River.

177. With so little timber nearby, the pioneers quickly resorted to using adobe construction for their early homes and fortifications. Adobe construction long preceded the Spanish conquests of North and South

MONDAY THE 2D.

Fine weather, with a cool breeze from the N. E. – This morning, H. Egan, G. Billings, Wm. King, & P. Johnson, started into the mountains with teams for timber. Agreeably to previous arrangements, the 2 camps below commenced to move, to this place, that we may all form our wagons into a circle. Prof. O. Pratt, Father Sherwood, & others commenced surveying the ground for the city. Men were chosen for herdsmen, among whom was Orson. Those not engaged in moving to this place are occupied in ploughing, planting, sawing lumber for a boat, making coal kits, &c., &c.– Brother Benson & Porter, & 3 others started to go back about noon to meet the next company expected soon from Winter Quarters. Bro. Clayton wrote a letter for Bro. Heber, to James Smithies, the amount of which was, that he wished him to forword by the bearer, (Bro. Benson,) the general news in Winter Quarters, particularly, as regarded his (Heber's) family; & also, all letters that may have been written by our friends from that place. – Orson, with the assistance of Hark Lay, is engaged in washing our clothes this afternoon. The wagons of the 3 camps, all arrived, & were formed into a circle about noon, a short distance from here. Wm. Squires slept with me tonight in my wagon. Orson and S.[amuel Bradford] Fox under the wagon.

TUESDAY THE 3D.

Warm and pleasant as usual, tho' quite cold last night. Orson, soon after breakfast, went with Erastus Snow to watch cattle. The brethren engaged in their usual occupations – I understood that the ploughing was about finished. – Considerable of the corn & beans planted has already made its appearance above the ground, & is in a flourishing condition. H. Egan & J. Redden again went into the woods, up the pass, after timber. Pres't. Young informed me this morning, that it was his intention to have the ox-teams start back on Monday next – & the horse teams, in two weeks from that time. – I omitted to mention that L. B. Myers returned from the Eutaw Lake yesterday – he reports it to be about 30 miles distant, & that on the east side of it is plenty of timber – which might be easily floated down the river to this place, which is the outlet of the lake. H. Egan and J. Redden returned about 9 o'clock this evening – they had been back up the pass about 8 miles, where they got cedar with which to make bedsteads, pails, &c.– They report the bridges all to have been carried away. A number of hunters have gone back within a day or two, some 40 miles in pursuit of game, meat being something not seen among us for a long time.

WEDNESDAY THE 4TH.

Pleasant weather, with a slight breeze from the south. H. Egan, J. Redden, H. Cushing and G. Billings with 3 teams went 6 miles to get timber – they returned this evening, soon after dark with 3 loads of good logs, got for the purpose of building a storehouse. Bro. Wm. Clayton,

America. In fact, its origins go back thousands of years. Adobes are mud brick construction from earth and other organic materials and are extremely durable, especially in dry, hot climates.

with the assistance of Wm. King & Orson, was engaged in making a new "Rodometer," as he intends to start back with the ox teams on Monday next. Bro. S. Brannan, J. C. Little, Lieut. Willis, & one or two others, started this morning on an excursion to the south, intending to go to the Eutaw Lake. I learned that a case was brought before the Twelve for trial to-day. – it referred to one of the soldier brethren, W[illia]m. Tubbs, who was accused of improper conduct with 2 females, who accompanied the army. I did not learn particulars, but understood, that the accused acknowledged that he had done wrong & was sorry for it, when the case was dismissed, & he was told to "go & sin no more."

Thursday the 5th.

Warm as usual. H. Egan, G. Billings, J. Redden, H. Cushing, Andrew Gibbons, & Philo Johnson, again, with 3 teams went into the ravine after logs – they returned towards night. Orson & Carlos Murray took off the box, & drew a load of wood on our wagon this afternoon. This evening, Samuel Brannan, J. C. Little, Lieut. Willis, returned from their excursion to the Eutaw Lake, of which, & the adjacent country, they give a similar account to that of Lewis B. Myers. During their route, about 10 miles from here, they saw, lying by the side of the trail, the dead bodies of 2 Indians, supposed to have been killed in the affray mentioned as having occurred on the 31st ultimo. They also discovered the dead body of a horse, with its throat cut, some 6 miles from here – this probably belonged to one of them, & had been first shot, while they were endeavoring to make their escape. – Orson & myself used the last of our 3d bag of flour this evening. A number of Indians came into camp this evening, & stopt for the night.

Friday the 6th.

Warm & sultry. – the brethren, engaged in their usual avocations. This morning, considerable alarm was created in camp by the report that the Indians had left during the night, & taken with them all of our loose horses. This, however, proved groundless, as upon a thorough search, the horses supposed to be missing were found, not being easily seen from the camp on account of the high grass. The preliminary arrangements having been completed, the brethren this morning commenced making "adobies" on the bottom about a mile below here; & during this forenoon, moulded and laid out in the sun to dry, some 750 of them. H. Egan, H. Cushing, G. Billings, Andrew Gibbons, with 4 teams went after more logs for building, consisting mostly of balsam fir – they returned towards evening.

Saturday the 7th.

Pleasant weather. – The hounds to G. Billings' wagon having been broken, were repaired this morning, & H. Egan, G. Billings, Andrew Gibbons, J. Redden, & John Tibbets again went into the woods with 3 teams – they returned about noon, with a quantity of poles, of which they made a horseyard this afternoon, on Bro. Heber's lot, which is situated on the other side the creek, a few rods hence. Hosea Cushing made a hayrick to-day – Wm. King is still engaged in constructing a "Rodometer" for Bro. Clayton. Orson & myself, by request of Bro. Heber, took our team, & went up the pass near here, about ½ mile, & got a load of bushes, with which to cover a blacksmith shop, the first house built of logs, which stands a short distance from here. To-day a number of the brethren made a dam, a few rods above the wagons, over the small stream, which was along on the north side of the camp, after this 2 dikes were made, communicating with the dam, the water of which irrigating the whole camp ground, & laying the dust, renders every thing more cool and pleasant. – I was considerably amused this afternoon by the sight of a whirlwind, which occurred near here – It commenced on the south side of the camp traversing which, it passed up the ravine, to the North-east, nearly overturning a number of wagons, and quite demolishing a bower belonging to Bro. Crow's family, during its progress. It also raised a quantity of dust, which, for some time after the wind had ceased, could be seen, at a vast height hovering over our heads, in apparent proximity to the clouds. This evening, Bro. Heber invited all the members of his family to the dam above here, where he administered to them the ordinance of baptism. – A number of other brethren, (making, I believe, 56 in all,) were rebaptized this evening, by himself & others of the Quorum of the Twelve.[178]

Sunday the 8th.

Cloudy morning, with considerable appearance of rain. This morning, the ceremony of baptism was recommenced, & all who felt disposed, were invited to come forward & receive the ordinance, which they did in great numbers, both men & women. A number of Indians again made their appearance in camp this morning. They came for the purpose of reclaiming a horse one of them had sold to Bro. Joseph Hancock for a gun, which the Indians had some way broken, by accident, & still wished to keep it. By the President's advice, Bro. H. refused to give up the horse, for, if we yielded to their claim in this instance, we might make up our minds to submit in future, to every other demand they might make of the like nature. Meeting was held at the bower commencing at 10 a. m. Bro. Heber first addressed the congregation, – exhorting them to abide by their covenants, & to the observance of various duties devolving upon them as Saints of God. He was followed by Elder W. Woodruff, who gave them a great deal of instruction and advice of a like nature, & the meeting was dismissed at noon, being adjourned until 2 P. M. – I wrote quite a lengthy letter for

178. Rebaptism was a popular ordinance in the early Salt Lake Valley among the Mormon pioneers. Its purpose was to recovenant and recommit the Saints to building up their new Zion in the newfound valleys of the Rocky Mountains. Wilford Woodruff recorded that the first to be rebaptized was a still enfeebled Brigham Young himself, followed by 287 others between 6 August and 8 August. Kenney, *Wilford Woodruff Journals*, 3:250–51. Three-fourths of all baptisms performed in Salt Lake City between 1847 and 1852 were rebaptisms. See Richard E. Bennett, "'I Mean to Be Baptized for Scores More': Baptisms for the Dead among the Latter-day Saints, 1846–67," in *An Eye of Faith: Essays Written in Honor of Richard O. Cowan*, ed. Kenneth L. Alford and Richard E. Bennett (Provo, UT: Religious Studies Center; Salt Lake City: Deseret Book, 2015), 139–57. See also M. Guy Bishop, "What Has Become of Our Fathers: Baptism for the Dead in Nauvoo," *Dialogue: A Journal of Mormon Thought* 23, no. 2 (Summer 1990): 85–97.

Wm. Squires, addressed to A. & V. Brown [?]. – giving them a detailed account of his adventures, & future prospects in this country, & also a minute description of the "Great Valley of the Salt Lake." A council of the Twelve was held in a tent near here, at 11 a.m., at which an "Epistle of the Twelve to the Battalion & Saints in California," was read – this is to be transmitted by S. Brannan, who starts on his return to morrow.[179] Meeting met pursuant to adjournment. Present of the Quorum of the Twelve. – Pres't Young, H. C. Kimball, Willard Richards, W. Woodruff, & O. Pratt. – Sacrament was administered, during which time, Bro. Lorenzo Young made some remarks, – after which Bro. Heber arose & said, – "There is some business to bring before the brethren – 1st, in regard to building the stockade of "adobies," & now the idea is, to call out a company of men to be under a leader, who shall attend to that business. Pres't Young says that men, say that 110 are necessary for the business, 60 to bake, 12 to mould, & 20 to put up walls. I think it best to beat [*sic*] up for volunteers." – The names of 76 men were taken as volunteers. Pres't Young said – "We now propose to put up some log houses, & plaster them up outside – perhaps build one side with logs." H. C. K. motioned that we put the log houses on the line – seconded & carried. Robt. Crow moved that we have 4 gates, one on each side – seconded & carried. Pres't Young said. – "We want 5 or 6 men to assist Father Sherwood in surveying the city. Every man shall be credited what he does in the adobie houses, & then when others come in they shall pay the price for it – we expect every man will have his lot & farm & attend to it himself. A few men came with Thos. Williams when he came to Ft. Bridger, – when they came, they borrowed flour of the Pioneer company – most of them refuse to pay what was borrowed for them – they ought to return the complement." Thos Williams said, "there are only 2 or 3 who have paid their portions. Those were the persons who returned to the Battalion." Capt. Brown said, – "Thos. Williams suggested the propriety of going ahead to overtake the Pioneers, & get back a couple of stolen mules – if Williams had asked for volunteers, he could have had half the Battalion." Pres't. Young said. – "you came, & would not have eat more, if you had stayed. Is there a man who would not have borrowed on the strength of his rations? Brother Rockwood let them have 20 lbs. flour – that we don't want – but the 12th 10 have not 10 lbs. flour among them, & that ought to be paid." He then related the "Tim. Goodell affair."[180] "I anticipate the time will come, that I shall enjoy good health in this valley, & be able to speak to the brethren. I deprive myself of preaching to the brethren, in order to keep this side the vail – if the wind had not blowed so hard, I should have spoken upon the sealing principle. I perceive that I fail – that my bodily strength is decreasing – if I had spoken, it would have hurt me. There are many things that I want to say, before I go. I feel thankful I am here – words & actions

179. These letters defined Latter-day Saint policy for California. The first confirmed Brannan's leadership in California, while the second advised Battalion veterans "to come directly to this place." See Journal History, 7 August 1847. Apparently Brannan took with him not only these letters but also a flag of the Kingdom of God. See Orson Hyde to Brannan, 5 September 1846, as referenced in editor Will Bagley's footnotes in *Pioneer Camp of the Saints*, 252.

180. This likely pertained to the matter of Timothy Goodale having allegedly stolen horses from camp. However, "the majority were inclined to acquit him." See entry for 7 July 1847.

cannot exhibit what is in me – the hand of the Lord is stretched out – he will surely vex the nation that has driven us out. – They have rejected the whole council of God. The nation will be sifted, and the most[?] will come out chaff, & they will go to the fiery furnace – they will go to hell. This is the spot that I had anticipated[181] – they will not have a hard winter here – the highest mountains are near 1¼ mile high – we shall find that sugar-cane, & sweet potatoes will grow here – The brethren from Pueblo, advise us all to build "adobie" houses – there never was a better or richer soil than this – Last fall, we found there were lots of persons who had not 2 weeks provisions with them – if we had come on then, we should have led a people to the mountains to suffer – we told the Pioneers to bring at least 100 lbs. bread-stuff – if men had not bread, let them go where it is – there are some who would lie down & die before they would complain, &, again, others, who would take the blood of man for it – the 1st company were charged to bring a sufficient quantity to last them through the present season, until they can raise – I calculate we shall bring as much as will last us until we can raise food, – we want all the brethren who are going back, to go to the "Salt Lake," & have a swim – it is almost equal to vinegar to make your eyes and nose smart." – after a benediction by the Pres't., the meeting was dismissed at 20 minutes past 5 P. M. – This evening, John Buchanan, myself & one or two others went to the 1st salt spring 1½ mile distant, when we had a fine bathe in the warm water. –

Monday the 9th.

Fine weather – This morning, H. Egan, Andrew Gibbons, George Billings, H. Cushing, & Wm. King with 3 teams, & myself, with my team, went up the pass about 6 miles from here, – when we got 4 loads of poles, & took them to the yard about a mile below here, when the brethren are engaged in making "adobies," with with which to build the stockade or fort – Orson to day assisted in irrigating the land. – Capt. Brown, Samuel Brannan, Wm. H. Squiers [*sic*], & some others started this morning on pack horses for California. – Bro. J. C. Little & some other brethren went with them, intending to accompany them as far as Ft. Hall, – & a few only as far as Bear River –[182]

181. Although neither the Whitney journal nor any of the other primary journal accounts reference Young expressing the words "This is the Place" on 24 July 1847, Horace Whitney does make a significant recording of what he said on 8 August, after two weeks of scouting reports had arrived from in and around the valley confirming his choice for the Salt Lake settlement: "This is the spot that I had anticipated." The term "spot" was his preferred term and finds its precedence in many of his sermons and earlier revelations, most notably that defining the place for the Independence temple: "The place which is now called Independence is the center place; and a spot for the temple is lying westward, upon a lot which is not far from the courthouse" (Doctrine and Covenants 57:3).

182. Their purpose in going to California was to make sure the sick detachments were properly discharged and to pick up their pay, which the Saints used to purchase Miles Goodyear's fort. See Will Bagley, ed., *Frontiersman: Abner Blackburn's Narrative* (Salt Lake City: University of Utah Press, 1992): 63–120.

Tuesday the 10th.

Pleasant morning. – H. Egan & myself, with 2 teams went to the place where we got poles yesterday, & cut 3 loads of logs, which he myself, & Ozro Eastman, with an third team took to the adobie yard about 5 P. M., & found Bros. Heber, Markham, King, J. Redden, Andrew Gibbons, George Billings engaged in laying the basement of a row of log buildings on the east side, which side of the stockade,[183] being immediately on the line, is, I understand to be built entirely of logs. One of these buildings is I believe intended for father. Pres't Young's row of buildings joins Bro. Heber's. – I omitted to mention that last evening Bro. Heber invited H. Egan, Bro. Whipple, William Clayton, Wm. King, Hosea Cushing, & myself to a walk over the creek a short distance hence, to view the building lot he had selected. It is situated on a small, elevated bench of land, which commands a beautiful & extensive view of the valley to the north & south. Bro. Heber informed us that it was his intention to select 2 lots for father, to the west of, & joining his own, – one of which he would probably bestow on me – & next to us Bro. Wm. Clayton could have one if he chose. He said that Most of the Twelve have selected lots in the vicinity of the Temple lot, which consists of 40 acres.[184]– after spending some time in conversation on different subjects, chiefly relating how-ever to the prospect of our return to W. Quarters, he proposed that we should pray – accordingly, he made a beautiful prayer, returning thanks to the Lord, for the preservation of ourselves, horses, & cattle, & for conducting us to a goodly land, possessed a rich & fertile soil, even a "Land of Promise." He also prayed for our friends in Winter Quarters, that they might have no sickness among them – & finally for the Saints throughout the land. After he had closed we again repaired to the camp. – This evening I feel very much fatigued, owing to lifting heavy logs, & chopping down trees, to which I have not been used for some time. This afternoon the weather has been quite cloudy, & towards evening, we had quite a heavy gale that prostrated a few of the soldiers' tents, but this, however, did not last long.

Wednesday the 11th.

Fine day. – I was quite unwell this morning. H. Egan & Orson went into the woods after logs – they returned just at night with 2 loads. The rest of the boys were engaged in laying up logs at the "adobie" yard. – That part of the wall [for the fort], to be constructed of "adobies", was

183. ***Editor's note***: Whitney inserted his own footnote as follows: "The stockade, I believe, is to enclose 10 acres."

184. The temple lot or temple square was considered the center spot of their new city, although it was later reduced in size from forty to ten acres. The apportioning of property among the early settlers of Salt Lake City was based on the law of consecration, not on private purchase or speculation. Church leaders made distributions based on apostolic rank and authority, adopted family sizes and needs, faithfulness, and other related priorities. Brigham Young chose first, opting for the block immediately east of the temple block. Heber C. Kimball opted for the block north, Orson Pratt the block on the south side, and Wilford Woodruff chose the block 40 rods southwest of the temple lot. By 20 August, Henry G. Sherwood's survey of the city consisted of 135 blocks, each containing eight lots of 1¼ acres, large enough to accommodate 1,080 families or from 5,000 to 6,000 people, streets eight rods wide, and three public squares besides the temple lot. Journal History, 20 August 1847. See also Bennett, *We'll Find the Place*, 237–40.

commenced to be layed to-day. – a large band of Indians made their appearance in camp this morning, on horseback – not being permitted to come within the circle, after staying some time, they went down the bottom & encamped about 3 miles below here. 4 wagons, (ox teams,) started for Winter Quarters this morning, under the command of Captain Jacobs. – These, I suppose, will stay on the "Sweet Water", & hunts buffalos till we come up. This afternoon, we were all much surprised & grieved by the unusual occurrence among us, of an afflicting & domestic calamity. The following is a brief relation of the affair.: – Bro. Brown Crow, while getting a pail of water out of the small stream, which flows on the south side of the camp, discovered the dead body of his nephew, Milton Therlkill – (a boy about 3 years old,) lying in the deepest part of the water near the dam. The body was immediately taken out & notwithstanding every remedy, usual in such cases, was resorted to for its resuscitation for an hour or more, they were at last obliged to give up the case as hopeless. The child had been seen playing with a younger brother a short time previous by the side of the stream, hence, they inferred that he must have been in the water some 10 minutes. The grief of both the parents was great; but that of the agonized mother baffles all description. She laughed, wept, walked to & fro alternately, refusing all attempts at consolation from her friends, being apparently unable to be resigned to her domestic & melancholy bereavement. As for myself, I never witnessed a sight that so awakened my sympathy, & I sincerely hope, that I may "never look on its like again."

THURSDAY THE 12TH.

Very warm day. – We did not go after logs to-day. The most of the boys, as usual, were engaged in laying up logs at the "adobie" yard. The funeral or burial of the child of Geo. W., & Matilda Jane Therlkill, took place about 2 P. M. Myself with a number of others, accompanied, as assistants, the mourners to the place of burial, which is on Bro. Crow's lot, about a mile below here, nearly opposite the "adobie" yard. as soon as we marked the grave, we all knelt, & a beautiful prayer was made by Elder O. Pratt in behalf of the bereaved parents & friends – after which, by request of Bro. Crow, he made a few remarks, by way of exhortation & instruction to us all; & concluded by a brief, consoling address to the parents, & friends of the deceased – about 3 P. M. we returned to the camp, when 2 loads of salt had just arrived from the "Salt Lake." It is the best kind I ever saw, being as white as snow, though somewhat coarse. The brethren who brought it in, remained on the shores of the Lake for a day or two, boiling down the salt together with the water, in order to separate it from the particles of dirt, with which, it abounded more or less. a number of brethren started to day on horseback for Winter Quarters.

FRIDAY THE 13TH.

Warm & sultry as usual. – Orson & myself went into the woods with a team this morning, after logs, which we took to the "adobie" yard, where we arrived at 2 P. M. & found that they had got Bro. Heber's row of buildings, consisting of 5 rooms, already built up 5 logs high.

– Dr. Richards & others of the Twelve are building on the end of his houses. H. Egan & John Tibbetts went into the woods for saw logs. – There were 2 additional loads of salt brought in by the brethren this afternoon.

SATURDAY THE 14TH.

Pleasant day. – This morning, John Gleason, Alexander Chessley, & myself went fishing in the slough or large creek, about 2 miles from here – we followed it to the mouth, where it empties into a river about 8 rods in width – here we took a fine bath, in the clear blue water – we noticed in the bed of this river, innumerable particles of a gold color mixed with the sand; we separated a quantity therefrom, & brought it to camp, where Bro. Carrington pronounced it to be izen glass – We also caught & brought to camp some 20 fish of a different kind from that which I have before seen. As it is the intention to start the ox teams on Monday next, all who are then going back, started, this morning, on an excursion to the "Salt Lake." Some others also were permitted to go, among whom was Orson. Bro. Clayton went with his wagon – when they returned this evening, he reported the distance to be 22 miles – The shaft, or screw to the "rodometer" was broken on his return. J. C. Little, Joseph Matthews, John Brown, Lieut. Willis, & John Buchanan, who accompanied Capt. Brown & the others as far as Bear River on their way to California, on Monday last, returned to-day – they had been as far as Cash Valley on an exploring expedition, of which place they give a favorable account, although they say there is no more timber there than here, & that like this being up the ravines of the mountains. Lewis B. Myers also returned to day from the same country – Both parties report the game to be very scarce, neither party having killed any. Some of them visited the settlement made by a man by the name of Miles [Goodyear] before referred to, & report the American corn them to be as high as one's shoulders, & the Spanish corn "tassling out." H. Egan, G. Billings & H. Cushing again went into the woods for logs – While on the road they met with quite an accident – H. Cushing's team being ahead, stopt suddenly, when one of the oxen, of G. Billing's, attached to the wagon immediately behind, ran, with full force, against the reach of the former wagon, which projects considerably out behind – the reach penetrated the breast of the ox near 6 inches, inflicting a wound large enough to admit a man's clinched hand, but notwithstanding, having bandaged it up, we think he will get well. The fortification or stockade has progressed barely during the past week, from the united diligence and industry of the brethren & we indulge hopes to be ready to start back soon after Bro. Benson's return.

SUNDAY THE 15TH.

Beautiful weather as usual. A meeting was held at the "Bower," commencing at 10 a.m. Pres't. Young addressed the congregation on the "sealing principles," or more particularly on the "law of adoption." He told them it did not detract from a man's glory or reputation to be sealed to another but added to them; for he still held those of his own & adopted parent of the same time. Meeting was adjourned at 12 M., to meet again at 2 P. M. Meeting met pursuant to adjournment, & the congregation was addressed by Elders H. C. Kimball & O. Pratt on various subjects. The meeting was dismissed at 6 P. M., with the request by Pres't Young that all those who intend to start back to-morrow, should meet at his tent this evening, at the sound of the bugle, which was accordingly done; & all the soldiers going, brought their guns, ammunition, &c., & surrendered them into the President's hands, for the reception & safe keeping of which, there will be a house built hereafter. I do not know the number of those going, but of those about Bro. Heber, are the following: – Wm. Clayton, J. Redden, Robt. Byard, & Thomas Cloward. It rained considerably, soon after we retired for the night.[185]

Monday the 16th.

Somewhat cloudy, & rained at intervals through the day. H. Egan was engaged in hunting up the cattle this forenoon, – Bros. Byard and Cloward got started to-day, each having a wagon with 2 yoke of oxen attached. – 1 yoke of these Bro. Heber procured of Bro. Huntington; the other of [rest of line is blank] Wm. King repaired the shaft to the "Rodometer" this forenoon, & this afternoon Wm. Clayton, J. Redden, & Howard Egan, rode up, in the former's wagon, as far as the first warm springs, which they ascertained to be 1½ m. distant. Quite a number of wagons also got started for Winter Quarters. Some of the boys went up the hollow, where we have been accustomed to get logs, & got quite a large piece of sandstone, out of which, this afternoon, Bro. Allen is fashioning a grind-stone. – Quite a severe wind & storm soon after we retired for the night. –

Tuesday the 17th.

The sky somewhat cloudy this morning. Bro. Clayton with his wagon, started from here to-day. He is accompanied by J. Redden, & E[dwin Ruthven] Lamb . Bro. Heber, Dr. Richards, Thomas Bullock, H. Egan, S. Goddard, Col. Rockwood went up the pass about 10 miles from here, where they [*sic*] brethren were encamped, called them together, & Bro. Heber gave them some instructions, for their guidance & direction on the journey. – This company is entrusted to the commands of Captains Roundy, & Tunis Rappleye. – Bro. Heber, & the others returned towards night, & he & myself took supper at Bro. Wilkie's tent, after which we took a walk over the creek to look at the city lots, of their situation of which, &c., he gave

185. The Saints had been in the valley for only a few weeks when discussions centered on returning to Winter Quarters. It had ever been their plan to leave most in the valley to build the fort, cabins and other buildings and defenses, cut down timber, put in late crops, fence farmlands, build roads, and in so many other ways prepare to receive the 1,500 Saints in the Big or Emigration Camp now on its way from Winter Quarters to the valley and which was expected to arrive in late September or early October. Meanwhile, Brigham Young, William Clayton, Horace K. Whitney, and several Mormon Battalion members who were anxious to reunite with their families after so long an absence, and other seasoned pioneers would head back to the Missouri River before winter set in so as to prepare for the spring migrations of 1848. Clayton and his company were appointed to head back to Winter Quarters first with a large number of spare ox teams, horses, and empty wagons in case early snowstorms hindered the later parties.

me a better idea than I had before possessed. After we had got, we knelt & prayed by his suggestion; after which we returned to camp. He then called most of his boys together at Bro. Wilkie's tent, where each chose his respective lot, & I wrote their names on the blanks, representing their lots on the city plot or map. Bro. W. Clayton, having left, by request of Bro. Heber, to-morrow, I commence to keep his journal. The brethren, as usual, to day are engaged at work on the adobie wall, which will be 9 feet high & 27 inches thick. Prof. Pratt has taken observations & found the latitude of this place to be 40° 45' 50". The altitude above the level of the sea 4309 feet, & above the Eutaw outlet 65 feet. This evening, after we retired, we again had quite a heavy wind from the south-west, accompanied by some rain, & mingled with the latter last night, it is said there was considerable snow – this heralds the approach of cold weather, &, in the opinion of all, we ought not to remain here much longer. The list of men & teams under the command of Capts. Roundy & Rappleye, as taken by the Clerk, Thomas Bullock, are as follow: – 59 men – 32 wagons – 14 mules – 16 horses – 92 yokes of oxen. –

William Clayton (1814–79), scribe, trail-blazer, musician, and writer.

WEDNESDAY THE 18TH.

Fair weather this a.m. though somewhat showery this afternoon. – Nothing of importance occurred to-day, except the usual work going on at the adobie yard. President Young has announced his intention that we shall start back on Tuesday next, & had his horses shod yesterday, in preparation for that event. I went fishing this afternoon, but caught only one – the rain having come on, I returned to the camp, after about 2 hour's absence.

THURSDAY THE 19TH.

Warm & pleasant. – H. Egan & H. Cushing were engaged to-day in drawing gravel with which to cover the houses – the remainder of the boys were also at work finishing them off. Bro. Heber had his horses shod to-day, preparatory to our starting on Tuesday next. – a party of mountaineers, (consisting of 4 white men & 2 squaws,) arrived in the valley this P. M. from Ft. Bridger. Their ostensible reason in coming here was "to see how we get along," as they expressed themselves; but undoubtedly the real object of their visit was to trade with the Indians. They were encamped this evening, about a mile below us on the bottom. – By Bro. Heber's request, this afternoon, I copied the names of those who had selected lots; as also the number of lots & blocks selected opposite each one's name.

Friday the 20th.

Pleasant weather. – I got Bro. B. Frost to make me a new birch pen to-day. – This forenoon, by Bro. Heber's request, I took a bar of iron to the blacksmith shop, got it cut into, & carried it to the stockade, to be used in constructing a chimney in one of Bro. Heber's room's which is being built by Bro. S. Goddard. – Bro. [Levi] Jackman is engaged in making a door. – They have got the covering laid over the top of one of the rooms, & the remainder are nearly ready for covering. – Bro. J. Matthews is engaged in sawing lumber in the saw pit near by, with which to make the floors. While at the buildings, I wrote a few more names on the blanks of the city plot, by Bro. Heber's request among which were father's & my own. These latter are situated on the East side & opposite the temple block. The laying out of the city is now completed: it is composed of 135 blocks each containing 10 acres, which is also subdivided into 8 lots each containing 1¼ acre. The streets are eight rods wide[186]; there are 3 public squares (including the "adobie" yard,) besides the Temple block, in different parts of the city. – Father Sherwood returned from an exploring expedition to Cash Valley this evening whither he went day before yesterday for the purpose of trading with the Indians. With him came a man by the name of Wells, who has lived sometime in New Mexico, among the Spaniards. I understand the brethren have given him the privilege of choosing a city lot, if he wishes to dwell here. Bro. A. Carrington, John Brown, & one or two others started this evening on an exploring expedition to go to two high mountains, called the "Twin Peaks," lying some distance to the south east of this place. It is their intention to proceed to the base of the mountain, & then encamp for the night, & on the morrow around the same in search of coal, &c.– H. Egan & H. Cushing were engaged to-day, in hauling some loose logs, that lay near here, down to the "adobie" yard, &c., &c.– Orson is quite sick to-day. –

Saturday the 21st.

Fair weather, as usual – Pres't. Young & Bro. Heber moved their wagons & effects down to the stockade to-day. Nearly all of Bro. Heber's rooms are now covered, & the floor of the one appropriated to Ellen Sanders' use is nearly laid. The main part of the day was employed by Bro. Heber, H. Egan & H. Cushing, in packing, unpacking, repacking, & storing away the things in the house. I took my wagon to the blacksmith shop this afternoon, when Bro. Burr Frost repaired the skein to my axle-tree, & also one of the hounds which had been broken, for which service, I let him have ⅔ of a pail of corn.

Sunday the 22d.

Pleasant day, though thunder could be heard in the distance this afternoon, & it probably rained considerably in the mountains. A meeting was held at the Bowery, commencing at 10 a.m. – The congregation was addressed by Elder Amasa Lyman upon the subject of our

186. Horace first wrote "40 rods" but then wrote in the word "eight" above it, the actual width of the city's streets—132 feet.

present situation as a people, the blessings that we had received at the hands of the Lord, our future prospects, &c.– A few remarks were made by Pres't. Young stating the necessity of our holding a conference, in order to transact some church business, which it was important should be brought before the people, before we shall leave this place on our return to Winter Quarters. The meeting was then adjourned to meet again at 2 P. M. on this ground. – In the interim, a council of the Twelve was held under the tree on Bro. Heber's lot. – Pursuant to adjournment, Conference met at 2 P. M. – The following are the minutes of said Conference, as reported by the clerk, Thomas Bullock. –

Sunday, Aug. 22, 1847[187]
2 o'clock P. M. –

A special Conference of the church of Jesus Christ of Latter-day Saints, held in the Bowery, on the Temple Block, in the 'Great Salt Lake City.'

Present – Pres't. B. Young, H. C. Kimball, Wilford Woodruff, A. Lyman, W. Richards, & O. Pratt – also Thomas Bullock & J. C. Little, clerks of the Conference. – Pres't. Young called the meeting to order, & the Choir sung 'The Spirit of God like a fire is burning' – Prayer by Elder Woodruff. – The Choir sung 'From all that dwell below the skies.' – Elder Kimball called for the business to be transacted before this Conference; & requested the brethren 'to be free & open[‘], that it may be well for those who remain, & those who are to come here. – 'It is necessary to transact a few items – to have a Presidency to preside over this place, & appoint such officers as are necessary to watch over & counsel them for their well-being – also the Stockade; shall we continue our labors, & concentrate all our efforts in the building of that, or scatter, & every man work for himself? – Whether we shall cultivate the earth in the vicinity of the city, or go 3 or 4 miles and make farms, & fence them so that our crops can be secure? – Shall we scatter our labors; one man build his house, another fence his lot, another go hunting? &c., &c.– These are matters for your consideration – if the brethren have any interest, we want an expression of it – if they have not, be silent, & we'll transact the business.' –

H. G. Sherwood [city surveyor] said – 'It meets my feelings to cultivate the city, & fence it in with an adobie" fence; & a high one will make a guard against the Indians, & keep the cattle out – I am in favor of fencing in the city, & cultivating it.' –

N. Higgins said – 'The Indians suppose the land is all theirs; & are in the habit of taking a share of the grain for the use of the land.'

Pres't. B. Young moved – 'That the brethren fence in the city, & such portion as they've a mind to in sections, & cultivate it' – seconded by D.[imick] B.[aker] Huntington, –

H. C. Kimball said – 'We've talked considerably about it, & the most prudent & economical way of doing it – it is best to fence in that portion which is tillable, & that which is the most convenient for us – suppose we divide it into 3 sections – the fence is put on the line

187. At the top of this page, apparently still in the hand of Horace K. Whitney, but in red ink, is a note that reads, "The 19th birthday of Helen M. Whitney."

of the city, just where we want it; & that which is not wet enough can be irrigated – Another year, we can raise 100's & 1000's of bushels for ourselves and those who come after us; & they shall pay you a good round price for it – I would rather fence a block of 10 acres & have the crop, than to plant 100 acres for the cattle to destroy – Will you put your mights together, for that which is the best for every man, woman, & child? – will ye do it? – (cries of "yes.") – I say, put our forces together, & fence the city, & sow our wheat safely.' – The motion was carried unanimously. –

Pres't. Young said – 'I move, that there be a President to preside over this place' – seconded & carried. – 'I move that there be a High Council' – seconded & carried. – 'I move that all other officers that are necessary, be appointed for this place.' – seconded & carried. – 'I move, that we call this place, "The Great Salt Lake City, of the Great Basin, North America' – seconded & carried. – 'I move, that we call the Post Office, "The Great Basin Post Office –"' sec'd. & carried. –

H. C. Kimball said – 'I move that we call the River, "The Western Jordan"' – sec'd & carried. –

Pres't. Young said – 'It is the right of the Twelve to nominate the officers, & the people to receive them – we wish to know who is coming in the next company – if Uncle John Smith comes, it is our minds, that he preside.' – He further said – 'Col. Rockwood is my principal man, & attends to all my duties.' –

H. C. Kimball said – 'I move that Col. Rockwood be honorably discharged from his duties as overseer of the Stockade' – sec'd & carried. – 'I also move, that Tarleton Lewis be appointed to that office' – sec'd. & carried. –

Pres't Young said – 'There will be thousands of such instances of men being discharged, & who are never shown on record, as appointed. It is the business of all clerks to write the business that is transacted, & not to ask questions – if I call on men to clerk, it is we who do the business, & the clerk who writes it – if we dismiss a hog, a clerk has a right to write it – it is none of his business to ask questions – Col. Rockwood is my aide-de-camp; I was acknowledged as their general & their dictator – if I appoint him to do a thing & don't tell the clerk, the clerk is not to blame, & when he is discharged, it can be recorded. – The brethren are not requested to labor for naught – you don't know what dangers you are in – I am full of caution – I wish that this people may grow & increase, & become a great nation. It ought to suffice the elders of Israel to go & do as they are told – Is it not necessary that that yard should be secured? that Indians cannot get in? – About 40 persons are going to live in those houses – that would only be ¼ of the whole, & have 3 sides exposed – but common sense teaches us to build it all 'round. – Men laboring here will be glad to buy a cow, some sheep, clothing & other things – Some wealthy men are coming, & will want rooms – the men who build them are entitled to their pay – don't be so devilish hoggish as to be afraid of doing a day's work, without getting pay for it; & I can prophesy in the name of Jesus Christ, that a man harboring such a spirit, will be damned – & I say further, such a man shall not live here – Get up your walls 4½ feet high, & that will keep the cattle out – who is there sick in this camp, through living in your wagons? – Now, if you go & leave those walls, & build up your own house, & I venture to prophesy, that you, or some of your family, will be sick; & you will have to watch over them – I had rather they would sleep in the Bowery than in a close house – We propose to fence in 30 rods square, that in case of necessity, the cattle can be fenced in, – & in the inside, stack up your hay – in the spring, remove the fence – plow a trench about 20 feet from the houses, & the women can raise a multitude of garden sauce – I want to engage 50,000 bushels of wheat, 50,000 bushels of corn, & other grain in proportion, & I will pay you 50 cents per bushel for corn, $1.25 for wheat, .25 cents for oats – Why not I bring glass for you, & you raise grain for me? – raise all you can; you can buy sheep, teams, or a cow or two – we want you to live in that stockade, until we come back again, & raise grain next year – If you only fence in 40 acres, make it so that an Indian cannot see in, & then they won't be tempted.' –

O. Pratt said – 'It will be impossible to fence in this city with a fence, so that an Indian can't see in it – it will take 2300 rods to fence in the whole city, & will take a good many months.' –

H. C. Kimball said – 'There are some creeks that have no names.' –

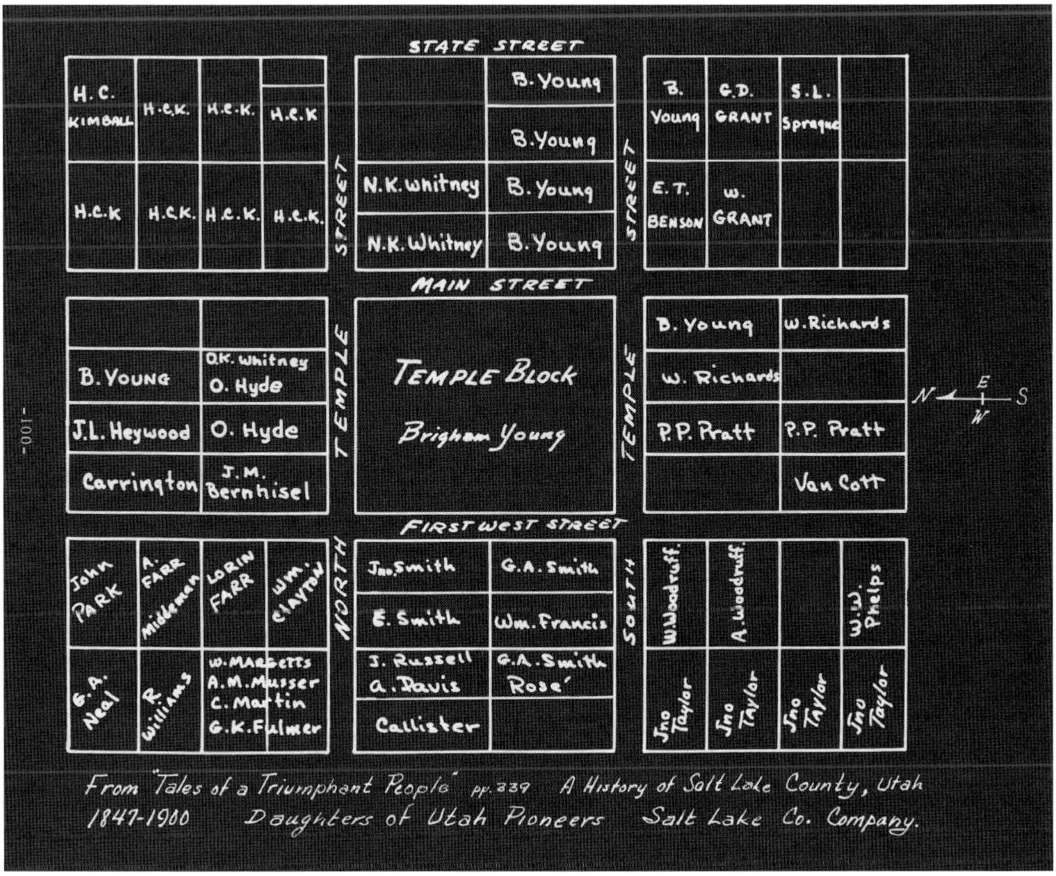

Map of early pioneer leadership of downtown Salt Lake City. Courtesy of Harold B. Lee Library, Brigham Young University.

Pres't. Young said – 'I move, that this creek be called the City Creek' – sec'd. & carried. 'I move, that the large creek about 8 miles south, be called Mill Creek' – sec'd & carried. 'I move, that the little creek a little south, be called Red Bute Creek' – sec'd & carried. – 'I move, that the next be called 'Kanyon Creek' – seconded and carried. – 'I move, that the next be called Big Kanyon Creek' – seconded & carried – 'Now I want to know if the people are satisfied with the labors of the Twelve.'

T. Lewis said – 'I move, that we give them our approbation, that we are satisfied with their labors, & give them our blessing' – seconded & carried. –

Lorenzo Young reminded those brethren who did not pray, that it was a good time for them to begin; & fulfill their covenants that they have now made – 'When we covenant to do a thing, be careful, & always do it.' –

Pres't. Young said – 'I want to know who are going back to Winter Quarters – those who are going to stay – will ye finish that adobie wall? – if so, rise up. – (a number arose.) – I should have no hesitancy in taking 5 men, & build 1 mile of adobie wall, 8 feet high, this fall – Keep it in mind – 50 cts. for corn, $1.25 for wheat, & other grain in proportion.' –

H. C. Kimball said – 'My feelings are for the welfare & well-being of all this people – I am your brother, & you are my brethren – all being born from the same parents; & I am now approximating back again to those feelings, in again being restored to their parents & you should throw it away with selfishness, for it is of Hell – & I say in the name of Jesus, away with it to Hell. – (cries of "amen." –) A man possessed of such feelings stinks worse than a skunk.[188] – I want to cultivate a feeling of union, of peace, towards my brethren; & if they knock me over, I'll try to forget it, & the Holy Ghost will rest upon you; & I shall see the day when the heavens will be opened; & we will render up our stewardships to our Heavenly Father. – Bro. Brigham is going to be greater than he was; he will be greater in strength, in beauty, & in glory – a man don't know how to appreciate a thing, until it is taken away A man don't appreciate a wife, until she is away; nor a wife appreciate a husband until he is gone – Call upon God & we shall increase here – away with the spirit of alienation, & let us be united – I believe I shall have power to thrust every thing beneath my feet, & rise in glory – I wish to God, we had not got to return – if I had my family here, I would give anything I have – this is a Paradise to me – it is one of the most lovely places I ever beheld – I hope none of us will be left to pollute this land – I had rather depart, then do as a great many do.' –

B. Young said – 'I move, that Brother [William] McIntyre be clerk, & keep an account of the public labors' – sec'd & carried. – 'In regard to our starting – get ready as fast as possible, & on Tuesday night we will start out, & see if we are ready to go – 'I move, that we adjourn this Conference to Oct. 6, 1848, at 10 o'clock at this place' – sec'd & carried. – 'I also move, that Edson Whipple attend to the distribution of water over the plowed land.' seconded & carried. –

---

188. In this sermon given just before their return to Winter Quarters, Heber C. Kimball calls for unity within his adopted family and for his "children" to forgo any interest returning to their "gentile" state with families out of the church.

Elder O. Pratt dismissed the Conference by benediction." –

After meeting was dismissed, H. Egan & the rest of the boys, assisted me in taking my wagon, by hand, from the blacksmith shop, down to the stockade. The Twelve held another council, this evening, in front of the buildings. – Bro. Carrington, Brown, & the others returned, during the session of Conference, from the exploring expedition to the mountains, on ascending which, they had found no coal, but plenty of black slate. –

Monday the 23d.

Somewhat cloudy, with a little rain. Geo. Billings & A. Gibbons went after poles, with which to cover the buildings. H. Egan & the rest of the boys were at work on the houses. – Ellen Sanders has moved into her room & the other rooms will soon be finished. – I spent the whole day in copying the "Conference Minutes" of yesterday, into Bro. Heber's Journal & my own. – Thomas Williams & others returned from Ft. Hall to-day[189] – The former was the bearer of a letter from Capt. Brown to Bro. Heber, merely stating his health, prospects, &c. Bro. Heber has recently got a good wagon of Bro. Shelton. This he loaned him for the purpose of assisting in bringing up the families. –

Tuesday the 24th.

Fair weather, till about noon, when it suddenly became cloudy, & we had quite a heavy thunder shower. – The boys mostly busy this forenoon, at work on the houses. – About 2 P. M., it having cleared off, H. Egan & myself, with my wagon, & H. Cushing, G. Billings, & Carlos Murray, with one of Bro. Hebers, [*sic*] wagons, started on an excursion to the "Salt Lake" It is unnecessary to relate particulars, connected with our visit, or give any further description of the Lake; as there has been sufficient mention made of it heretofore; but suffice it to say, that we had a fine bath in its waters, & stayed all night on its banks, together with a number of others, who had come in wagons or on horse back.

Wednesday the 25th.

Bright & clear morning. We arose early, got our breakfasts, & after waiting a short time for H. Egan & George Billings to fill a bag with salt, we started back, & arrived at the stockade about noon, where we found the brethren of the Twelve making preparations to go back, as it is the intention to start about 6 o'clock to morrow morning. After our return from the Lake, we busied ourselves, this afternoon, in getting up the horses, cutting grass for them, that we may keep them up all night, in order to be ready with the rest to make an early start. – Orson & myself packed my trunk with things belonging to both of us & committed it to the care of Bishop Whipple, to whom Bro. Heber has intrusted the charge of his business affairs while

189. Thirty miles south of present-day Pocatello, Idaho, Fort Hall was a trading post on the Snake River. Once one of the Hudson's Bay Company's most southerly outposts, it was eventually included in United States territory after 1846. It later became an important station on both the Oregon and California Trails.

he is absent. We also took the things out of our wagon, & rearranged the load. This evening, we had a beautiful moon, the night being cold & clear.–

Thursday the 26th.

Beautiful morning – as fast as the teams got ready this morning, they started out, one by one; the first about 9 o'clock – I started with my wagon about 10 a. m. & travelled up the pass 14 miles & stopt, about 4 P. M., near a cold spring, on "Kanyon Creek," situated on the "Arm of Prairie", spoken of by O. Pratt in his letter some time since – Here we found some 10 or 12 wagons, which had already preceded us to this place. Brigham & Heber did not start until most of the teams had left the valley, in consequence of being obliged to make some business arrangements before they could leave. – We were considerably annoyed by the dust on our route to-day. Just as I started, I met Lewis B. Myers, on horseback, who, with his squaw, was on his return from Ft. Bridger, where he went about a week since – Bro. Heber & his wagons arrived about sunset. –

Friday the 27th.

The weather to-day was somewhat warm & sultry – We arose early got our breakfasts, & resumed our journey, sun about 2 hours high – ascending the 2d long steep hill over a rough road, we at length attained its summit, having made 4½ miles – Here we halted a few minutes to breathe our horses, & then travelled 4 miles down on the other side, when we reached "Ogden's Fork" – after going a short distance we stopt to bait about 4 P. M. – Then we continued about an hour & then proceeded, & encamped about sunset, having come near 15 miles to-day. – This place is near one of our old camping grounds on "Ogden's Fork". We found the grass here tolerably plenty, though quite dry. Yet there is considerable virtue in it, as there have been little or no frosts. – Bro. Heber related to me, this evening, the following dream, which he'd had a few nights since – He thought himself & father were together near a stream of water. On the margin of the latter, floating along was a large fragment of ice, upon which father stood. – Seeing the danger Bro. Heber told him "to come off, or he would get into trouble"; notwithstanding, he still remained upon the floating mass, & went with it, down the stream. – & at length, was hid from view. Following down the stream a short distance, he saw him swimming as fast as he could for the shore, which he at length attained, & Bro. Heber awoke. – Cold & clear to night, with a bright moon. –

The following are the names of those going back with Bro. Heber's 3 wagons: – Howard Egan, Hosea Cushing, Wm. King, Geo. Billings, Andrew Gibbons, Carlos Murray, Ralph Douglas, Abel M. Sargeant, Wm. Terrill, Albert Sharp, Thurston Larson, & Edward Holden. Bro. Markham is taking back Porter's wagon, by Heber's request. By the latter's suggestion, I have taken Geo. Billings into my mess; he having furnished a quantity of meat, flour, & meal. –

SATURDAY THE 28TH.

1867 Echo Canyon Wagon Train. Charles W. Carter Photograph Collection, Church History Library.

Tolerably fair day. – This morning, we got up our teams & started about ½ past 7 o'clock. Having travelled near 12 miles, we forded "Weber's Fork", & halted about an hour to bait. This stream has fallen considerably since we were last here. We renewed our journey at 3 P. M. – Going about 4 miles along the banks of the stream, we at length turned abruptly to the left, (leaving it in our rear,) & travelled up another pass about 4 miles & encamped a little after dark in it near the creek, leaving our wagons in the road, in single file, the same order in which we travel. – Thomas Wolsey & others went ahead of the wagons in pursuit of game – they saw a number of bears, but did not kill them, as Pres't. Young thought we had meat enough for the present, one of the soldier brethren yesterday having found a Government ox that had strayed away from the valley, the meat of which was divided, this noon, among the Pioneers & soldiers We have made about 20 miles to-day. – After supper, being afflicted with a severe tooth-ache, I retired to my couch, which I made upon the grass in the open air. – It rained considerably during the night.

SUNDAY THE 29TH.

Good weather. We resumed our journey at 25 minutes to 8 a.m., – after proceeding some 12 miles we came to "Redden's Cave", where we halted at 1 P. M. to bait. Soon after our halt, Bro. Benson rode up, with whom, it may be supposed, we were very glad to meet. The brethren gathered around him in a large group, & he proceeded, in a hurried manner, to tell us the news. He said that he had travelled within 40 miles of Ft. John, before he met the company [the west-bound Emigration Camp], which consisted of 566 wagons. He brought a list of most of the names from 13 to 1500 in number. These were divided into 9 companies. – He & Porter had left the foremost company on "Sweet Water", where they had lost a great many cattle by sickness, besides quite a number of horses & cattle that strayed away & were taken by the "Crows". Bro. B. – was also the bearer of numerous newspapers & letters for the brethren. I received 4 from father, mother, my wife, & mother-in-law. Orson also got one – These were dated 14th June. Father's letter informed me that Bro. S. Pond & Arch. Hills were coming to take charge of his business, & that he had sent by them 200 lbs. flour for my use. By the 3 others I learned of the birth of my child on the 6th of May, & of its death soon afterwards.[190] – About 4 P. M. – we again started on – after proceeding a short distance we met Porter on horseback, when, after travelling 8 miles we encamped in the small valley near a creek, about dark, having come about 20 miles to-day. – severe frost to-night. – We were obliged to use wild sage root for fuel at this place.

MONDAY THE 30TH.

Cloudy, gloomy, & cold weather. – We continued our journey at 20 minutes to 8 a m. – After travelling about 6 miles, we came to "Bear River", which after fording, we stopt to bait at 11 a.m. – Orson took Porter's horse, & went from here to the "Mineral Tar" springs, (about 2 miles distant off the road,) after tar. Bro. Heber & myself retired apart, a short distance from the wagons, to read the letters he lately received. These were from Hiram Kimball, James Smithies, Jennette Murray, Mary Forsgren, Sarah Ann, & some others. – After remaining here about an hour, we proceeded on. Having gone about 8 miles, we encamped in a valley at 4 P. M., thus making 14 miles we have travelled to-day. The grass here is quite green & high, & near the wagons are two good springs of water. – Soon after we arrived, it commenced raining a slow, drizzly rain. – Just before arriving at this place, we ascended & descended two long & steep hills, which brought us to the valley where we are encamped this evening. – From the abundance of cedar trees growing on the sides of the hills, we are at no loss for fuel, with which to cook our suppers. – The following are the names of those going back in the present company; –

[***Editor's note***: In the original journal, the names were presented in two columns over three pages. They were combined together using brackets. For convenience, I have showed combinations by single-spacing the text. Presumably, those in their own grouping are those who rode on horseback for the return trip.]

Brigham Young
John Y. Green
Truman O. Angel
Joseph Scofield
A. P. Rockwood
S. H. Goddard

M. Atwood
T. Tanner
A. Everett

A. S. [S. A.] Hanks
Geo. Clarke
J. G. Luce

John Holman
G. R. Grant
D. Laughlin

Wm. Dykes
J. Weiler
David Grant

Thomas Wolsey
Haywood Thomas
Samuel Fox

Willard Richards
Thomas Bullock
B. B. Richmond

190. Perhaps no other entry points to the sometimes matter-of-fact, often unreflective method of Horace's journal keeping than this entry about the birth and death of his first child, a daughter, back at Winter Quarters 3½ months before. See Helen Mar's entry for 6 May 1847.

Harvey Pierce

Ezra T. Benson
Matthew Ivory
David Powell

Erastus Snow
Wm McIntyre
George Brown

Porter Rockwell

Charles Shumway
Andrew Shumway

Burr Frost
Wm. Carter

Wm. Wordsworth
Date Ensign

John Dixon
Simeon Howd

Seth Taft
John P. Wilson
Stephen Kelsey
Charles Parnum

Wilford Woodruff
Dexter Stillman
Wm A. Smoot

J. W. Stewart
Robt. Thomas Nowlin

James Case
J. C. Earl
Judson Persons

Orson Pratt
Joseph Egbert

M. B. Thorpe

George Wilson
Jesse Johnson
John Brimhall
A. L. Huntly
Rodney Badger
W. W. Rust

Jos. Matthews
James Camp
Wm. Park

Green Flake
Benj Stewart
John Crow

P. T. Marshall
C. Rowe
Wm. Rowe

B. L. Adams
A. P. Chessley
Thos. Carrell
John Gould
Samuel Gould

Amasa Lyman
Albert Carrington

John Brown
G. A. Smith
J. J. Terrill

S. Chamberlain
Wm. Terrill

Nath. Fairbanks
C. A. Harper

Perry Fitzgerald
Isaac M. Weston

Ozro Eastman
Monroe Frink
Levi N. Kendall

Stephen Markham
Geo. Mills
C. Klineman

H. K. Whitney
O. K. Whitney

Geo. Billings
Ralph Douglas
Ed. Holden
Wm. Gifford
Albert Sharp
Abel M. Sargent

Andrew Gibbons
Thurston Larson

Heber C. Kimball

Howard Egan

Hosea Cushing

Wm. King

Carlos Murray

comprising 108 men, 36 wagons, 71 horses, & 49 mules. – Pres't. Young called the brethren together this evening for organization, upon which, the following officers were elected Col. Markham, Capt. Of 100 – Barnabas L. Adams, & Joseph Matthews, Capt's. of 50's – Brigham Young, John Brown, Howard Egan, George Clark, George [Deliverance] Wilson, E. Snow, Thomas Tanner, & C. A. Harper, capts. of 10's – Pres't. Young selected his 10, which includes 6 of the Twelve, Col. Rockwood, S. H. Goddard, & J. Scofield. – It was moved that we travel in order. After we had thus organized, Pres't. Young advised the brethren to gather up their horses & tie them, as it was his intention to start as early as 6 o'clock in the Morning, which was accordingly done. – Thomas Bullock, (clerk,) then read a portion of the names of those coming on in the company expected.[191]

Tuesday the 31st.

Pleasant weather. – We renewed our journey at 7 a.m. – After going 10 miles, we crossed "Muddy Fork," the bed of which we found to be quite dry. – Proceeding thence 7 miles, we halted to bait at 1 P. M., after ascending quite a steep hill, & descending to the bottom below. – Here we remained about 2 hours & then started on, & arrived at Ft. Bridger, about 5 P. M. where the wagons halted a few minutes. – We found the numerous small rushing torrents that we noticed when we were here before, were mostly dried up, except the main stream. There were a number of Indians here, – These had several lodges around the Fort. – We proceeded about a mile beyond the latter & encamped for the night, about sunset, having come 23 miles to-day. –

Wednesday the 1st of September.

Tolerably fair weather. – This morning, the several companies of 10's were organized under their respective captains Col. Markham wished me to receive the appointment of captain of this 10, which however, I declined in favor of O. K. Whitney. A government ox, that had been left at Ft. Bridger as the soldiers passed along, was killed this morning, & the meat distributed among the brethren. We continued our journey at ¼ to 8 a.m. – after going 17¾ miles, (crossing "Black's Fork" twice on our route,) we arrived at the ford of the latter stream the 3d time, where we halted to bait at 1 P. M., near one of our old camping grounds. While here, the captains of 10's made out their returns to the captains of 50's – About 2 P. M. we

191. See Bagley, *Pioneer Camp of the Saints*, 276–77.

again took the road – again crossing "Black's Fork", we proceeded 13¼ miles & forded it again, when, after going 1½ further, we encamped a little after dark in a circle on the banks of "Hams' Fork", having come 32½ miles to-day, the longest day's journey we have accomplished since we left the valley. The grass here, we found quite good. – by the order of Pres't. Young, the horses were all staked out. – The night was quite cold, as the nights usually are, altho' the days are warm & pleasant. –

THURSDAY THE 2D.

Warm & sultry. – This morning, 3 mountaineers with pack horses arrived at the camp, – they left Ft. Bridger, last evening at 5 o'clock, & are on their way to Ft. John. We started at 8 a.m., – After fording "Ham's Fork" we travelled 3½ miles & passed one of our old camp grounds on "Black's Fork." – Continuing thence our journey over a barren, desert country, for 19 miles we arrived at "Green River," & encamped on its banks at 4 P. M., having come 22½ miles to-day. – This place is about 4 miles below the ferry, & 1 mile from the place where we last encamped, previous to leaving the river, on our way to the "Salt Lake" valley. – We found an Indian at this place, who said he left "Sweet Water" 2 days since, where there was a body of his own tribe, ("snakes,") encamped. – We learned this from an interpreter, (one of the mountaineers, who stopt with us to night. The Indian also said that he had not seen our wagons on the road. Geo. Billings & myself took a fine bath in the river this evening. – Soon after our arrival, a heavy wind arose, & it suddenly became quite cold. –

FRIDAY THE 3D.

Somewhat cool & cloudy this morning. – Orson last night stood on guard the last watch. We arose early, got our breakfasts, & continued our journey at ½ past 6 a.m. – We proceeded 2 miles, & forded the river which we found to be at quite a low stage of water – Proceeding thence 8 miles, we stopt at 10 a. m. to bait on the banks of "Big Sandy," near one of our old camping grounds. Here we remained about 2 hours, & then proceeded on – after going 17 miles, we forded "Big Sandy," & encamped on its banks, a little after dark, having come 27 miles to-day. – At this place we found Daniel Spencer's company encamped, consisting of about 80 wagons.[192] – They reported the next company under P. P. Pratt, to be encamped on "Little Sandy," 6¾ miles from here, & the other companies scattered at different intervals along the road. – Bro. S.'s company was called together this evening, & addressed successively by Brigham, Heber, W. Woodruff, & G. A Smith, who gave them a description of the valley of the Salt Lake, the extent of our labors there &c. Pres't Young counseled them to go as far as "Green River", & then go back & assist the other companies to come up, some of them being quite needy in consequence of having lost their cattle. The horses were taken up the river about ½ a mile where the grass was good, & several others & myself stood guard

192. Daniel Spencer's company of 362 souls was in the vanguard of the Big or Emigration Camp that left Winter Quarters on 17 June 1847. It was the first of that large entourage to arrive in the Salt Lake Valley on 19 September.

there until midnight, when, by Brigham's advice, the horses were brought to camp & staked out, as we learned 2 or 3 horses had been stolen 2 or 3 nights since by the Indians. The night cold & clear, as usual. –

SATURDAY THE 4TH.

Cool & pleasant. – At 8 a. m., D. Spencer's camp was in motion. A number of our company, having here met with their families, went back to the valley with them. – The following are some of their names: – Wm. McIntyre, Burr Frost, Dayton [Horace Datus] Ensign, Seth Taft. – About the same time, we proceeded on our journey. – After going 7 miles, we encamped at noon, on the banks of "Little Sandy" near one of our former camp grounds. Here we found P. P. Pratt's company encamped, consisting of between 70 & 80 wagons – a messenger having been sent ahead this morning, to detain them here, until we should arrive. – among the acquaintances I found here, were Father John Smith & family, – Sister Thompson & Father Sessions & family. – Most of this afternoon, the Twelve were in council. This evening, the people were again called together, & similar instruction, & information to that of last evening, here given them by the Twelve. – I know of but 2, who are to leave us & go back to the valley, viz. George Mills, & Ed. Holden.[193]

SUNDAY THE 5TH.

Fine weather. – We pursued our journey about 9 a. m. – After going 2 miles, we forded "Little Sandy," thence 13½ miles, we crossed "Dry Sandy" thence 9 miles & crossed a stream, (name unknown,) when, after going a mile we encamped on the same about 5 P. M. having come 26 miles. – Here we found three companies [of the Big Camp] encamped viz: – those of C. C. Rich, Geo. Wallace, & A.[braham O.] Smoot . Among the acquaintance we found, were the following, – James Smithies & family, Peter Hansen, Bro. Pond & family, Thos. More & family, A. Hill, Mary Ellen Harris, Mary Forsgren. The brethren were again called together this evening, & addressed by G. A. Smith, O. Pratt, & W. Woodruff, – similar information & counsel to that of last evening, being given. Prest. Young also added a few words to what

193. The meeting between Brigham Young and Parley P. Pratt "by the blaze of a willow patch" was a highly contentious one. Brigham severely chastised his junior colleague in the Quorum of the Twelve for tampering with the instructions laid down in his "Word and Will of the Lord" on how to organize the companies in the Big or Emigration Camp for their trek west. In Brigham Young's estimation, the camp was far larger than the Twelve had expected or directed it to be, that it was overpopulated with the best provisioned and underrepresented the poor and the halt, and that it did not include nearly as many of the Mormon Battalion families as Brigham Young had promised back at the Missouri River the year before. "When the Quorum of the Twelve do a thing it is not in the power of two of them to rip it up. . . . You had no business to control, alter or direct our organization," thundered the Mormon leader. See General Church Minutes, 4 September 1847, and Journal History, 4 September 1847. Weighing heavily on Brigham Young's mind, however, was more than the organization of the Big Camp; he was also preoccupied with when and how to reorganize the First Presidency of the church, a matter he viewed as increasingly necessary but which Pratt and others of the Twelve did not yet view with the same urgency. For much more on this fascinating meeting and the issues involved, see Bennett, *We'll Find the Place*, 267–74.

Mormon wagon train, from Darryl F. Zanuck's 1947 movie, Brigham Young *(20th Century Fox). Most 1847 wagon teams were ox driven, not horse driven as depicted here. Utah State Historical Society.*

had been said, – that it was his intention we should all remain here to-morrow, & a meeting held at 11 a. m. –

MONDAY THE 6TH.

Pleasant weather. – Pursuant to appointment, the brethren assembled at 11 a. m., & were addressed by E. Snow & others, upon matters similar to those heretofore mentioned. The Twelve met in council this a. m., Bro. Heber sent back Thurston Larson to the valley from here – also Carlos Murray with Layfayette Granger, who has charge of Hiram Kimball's teams. I wrote some in a letter for Heber which is to be sent to Bro. Whipple. A number of the brethren, also left us at this place, to return to the valley with their families – evening quite cold & cloudy. –

TUESDAY THE 7TH.

Morning cold & cloudy & considerable snow to be seen on the mountains, which had fallen during the night. – a messenger was sent ahead this morning to detain Bro. Taylor's camp till we should come up. – We started about 9 a. m. – soon after we had quite a heavy snow storm which continued most of the afternoon – We arrived at J. Taylor's camp on "Sweet Water" about 2 P. M., having come 14 miles – Here we found the brethren, under the direction of Elder Taylor & Bishop Hunter, had made preparations to give us a dinner, which passed off finely, the table being set in an adjacent grove, on the banks of the river. It was a rare sight, in deed, to see a table so well spread with the "good things of this life," in the wilderness, so remote from a civilized country. The remains of the feast, were distributed among the soldiers & prisoners, & the ceremonies of the afternoon, concluded this evening with a dance, which came off to the satisfaction of all parties.[194] – The Twelve were again in council this evening. – The snow has ceased falling, but the weather is yet quite cold. I believe one or two buffaloes, & some few antelopes have been killed, since we arrived in the vicinity of "Sweet Water."

WEDNESDAY THE 8TH.

Clear & cold weather. – We continued our journey at 9 a. m. – after going about 12 miles we encamped at noon, on a small branch of "Sweet Water", where we found Bishop Nobles' fifty encamped – about the middle of the afternoon, J. Grant & W. Snow, with the remainder of the last company arrived here. I wrote again for Bro. Heber this afternoon, in his letter to E. Whipple, to be sent back by Porter, who is to remain in the valley this winter.

THURSDAY THE 9TH.

Cold, clear, & windy weather. – This morning, considerable consternation was created in the camp, by the discovery that between 40 & 50 horses were missing – From the circumstances of an Indian arrow being found near here, & a bell strap, known to have been on the neck of one of the horses, being found & cut into, it was at once concluded that they had been stolen by the Indians – Therefore, about 10 a. m. Col. Markham, at the hand of about 20 men, including Orson, started in pursuit. – This afternoon, 2 of the men returned, being sent back with 2 of the horses, which had been found near the place where Brigham's horse was shot, some 30 miles distant, at evening, 2 or 3 more men came in with 3 horses – These had also been found near the same place, being probably left behind by the Indians in the hurry of their flight. These men informed us, that it was with considerable difficulty they could keep the trail, as the Indians, in order to baffle pursuit, had occasionally separated, left the road, & resumed it some distance ahead. – Owing to this, & other tricks & devices, to which but too

194. John Taylor was second in command to Parley P. Pratt in supervising the Emigration Camp as it moved west. His company was near the rear and was almost the last one Brigham Young visited as he hurried eastward. Eliza R. Snow, a former plural wife of Joseph Smith and one of Brigham Young's "for time-only" plural wives (since their marriage on 3 October 1844) was a key factor in persuading Taylor to put on a sumptuous prairie feast of roasted and broiled beef, pies, cakes, and biscuits for both companies, despite the fact it was snowing heavily. As Isabella Horne recalled, "I can assure you we had a feast indeed, spiritual as well as temporal." Isabella Horne, "Pioneer Reminiscences," 293. Could such a reunion feast explain why Young chose not chastise Taylor nearly as much as he had done Pratt just three days earlier?

well they know how to resort, it is but a mere chance against the most consummate cunning & duplicity, if they are successful in the pursuit. Both of my horses being gone I am entirely broken up as to a team. –

This evening, the brethren assembled themselves together, & were successively addressed, by O. Pratt, B. Young, & H. C. Kimball, who gave them much good counsel & instruction & a description of the valley, similar to that heretofore given to the rest of the companies.[195] – As some portion of J. M. Grant's 100 intend to proceed on their journey to-morrow, it was deemed advisable to send back some of the Pioneers with horses, to assist in hauling their wagons as far as the "Dividing Ridge." A number of them being quite destitute as far as teams are concerned. – The night, though clear, was quite cold.

Friday the 10th.

Fine, clear weather. – Porter & some others returned this morning but brought no horses with them. – The whole of J. M. Grant's Hundred were in motion by about 9 o'clock. – We started soon afterwards, previous to which, however, I wrote another short epistle for Bro. Heber, to E. Whipple, to be sent back by O. P. R. – After going about 10 miles we halted to bait at 4 P. M., on the banks of "Sweet Water." Here we were met by Col. Markham & the remainder of the company, on their return from hunting the horses, in which they had been unsuccessful – having been some 30 miles beyond this place. – after proceeding about 2 miles further, we encamped on the banks of the same stream, having some 12 miles to-day. – Bro. Heber to-day furnished me with 2 horses to put before my wagon, & others, who had lost horses, were supplied in the same manner, with the loose horses. Brigham, Heber, & others who had been accustomed to ride on horseback, being now debarred of that privilege – The grass here was quite good – the night cold & clear. –

Saturday the 11th.

Warm & pleasant. We continued our journey at 8 a. m. – This morning, I put in my pony along side of one of those I had yesterday, before my wagon. The pony I purchased of Ed. Holden a few days since, with whom I exchanged my rifle for the same. – We travelled along through the valley of the "Sweet Water," noticing on our route 2 or 3 dead cattle lying in the road, that belonged to some of the brethren of the different camps. – we also saw quite a number of buffaloes & antelopes; one of the latter was killed by T. Wolsey. – After crossing "Sweet Water" twice, we encamped on its banks at 5 P. M., having come 24 miles to-day. – The grass here was quite good. – The night warm & pleasant.

195. One such glorified report of their new valley home came from George A. Smith. "It feels well," he said to one group of westbound pioneers. "We came over these sages, plains and rocks and found a sweet little valley in the midst of the hills. . . . The soil is of sufficient variety to please every person. If the sisters are in want of hot drinks they can find spring water already heated for them and drink as much as they please . . . with industry, economy and prudence it will be one of the most blessed places in the world. I never was so contented as I was in that valley." General Church Minutes, 3–4 September 1847, Church History Library.

Sunday the 12th.

Fine weather. Last night about 12 o'clock, 2 shots were fired, & considerable alarm created in the camp by the report that there were Indians in the vicinity. A horse, belonging to G. R. Grant, was missing this morning, which was believed to be stolen by the Indians. – H. Egan & Wm King went back this morning, after a horse that yesterday strayed away from one of the 3 mountaineers who accompanied us. – We started this morning at 8 o'clock – Proceeding 8 miles we halted to bait at noon – after remaining about an hour we went on & encamped at 5 P. M. on the banks of "Sweet Water," having come 23 miles. Just before we arrived here, quite a large number of both antelopes & buffaloes were seen at a distance – one of the former, & three of the latter I believe were killed, & brought to camp. – H. Egan & W. King returned this evening, having been unsuccessful in their search for the horse. They reported that they had seen 8 Indians at a distance, who were probably following the camp with the intention of stealing horses.

Monday the 13th.

Warm & pleasant, tho' quite windy. – I stood on guard this morning. – In dividing the meat this morning there was such a large overplus, that it was with considerable reluctance, that the brethren would take any more into their wagons, but it being the President's orders, that no meat should be left behind, they at length agreed to it. – We continued our journey at ½ past 8 a.m. – after travelling 8 miles, we halted at noon to bait. – About 1 P. M., we were again in motion. Passing "Devil's Gate," sun about an hour high, we turned aside from the road, proceeded 2 miles further, forded "Sweet Water," & encamped on its banks in sight of "Independence Rock" at sunset, having come about 20 miles to-day. Here we found the grass better than any we have seen since we left the valley. –

Tuesday the 14th.

Clear weather this morning, though somewhat windy. – We resumed our journey at 9 a.m. – We re-crossed the stream & after gaining the road, proceeded 3 miles & again forded the same near "Independence Rock". Thence going 3 miles, the teams all halted at salaratus pond to get a quantity of salaratus – The bed of this we found to be quite dry & hard, the water having congealed since we were here before. – It was so very solid, we were obliged, in order to procure any, to cut it out with axes. – From this place, Monroe Frink & myself went ahead on foot. – While on the road we saw a number of herds of buffaloes. – 5 or 6 of them came at full speed towards us, & we began to think they were in danger of being overrun & killed by them; until, when they got within 50 yds. of us, they suddenly halted, gazed at us a few minutes, & wheeled in another direction. We walked on 5 or 6 miles further & came to a small creek, where a number of wagons had already preceded us, & encamped, about 5 P. M., the remainder of the wagons came up & encamped. – We have made only 12 miles to-day, owing to the road being very deep & sandy most of the way. – Just before we arrived, a thunder storm arose, which continued the most of the day. The grass here was not very good, but plenty of wild sage, growing both high & rank. Orson & myself stood on guard to night, the 1st watch – Continued cloudy & rained at intervals during the night. –

Wednesday the 15th.

We arose this morning, before sunrise; & although it rained considerably, we started on soon after. – We went 6 miles, & halted to bait at 8 a.m. – Then we got breakfast – Our horses were taken to a spot ¼ mile distant where there was a small stream of water & the feed quite decent. – In about 2 hours we resumed the road. – Going about 6 miles, we again halted to bait at 3 P. M., near a small stream running along at the side of the road – Here the grass was tolerably good – Here we stopt 2 hours also, & then went on – Proceeding 12 miles further & travelling after dark, we encamped near a small sheet or pond of water, having its source in springs. The night was cold & clear, with considerable frost; the rain having ceased, & the clouds cleared away about 10 a.m.. We staked our horses within the circle as the grass here was found to be very scant. We have made about 24 miles to-day. –

Thursday the 16th.

Beautiful, clear weather. I arose before daylight, & took my horses about 2 miles back towards the "North Fork," where the grass was tolerably good. We started about 8 a.m. – after going 12 miles, we forded the "North Fork of Platte River" near our old ferrying place, & encamped on the opposite bank, at 3 P. M. We found this stream quite shallow, the water scarcely coming up to our wagon beds – We took our horses, back from the river ½ mile where the grass was tolerably good. –

Friday the 17th.

Warm & pleasant day. – This morning the following men recrossed the river on horseback in pursuit of buffaloes viz: – Wilford Woodruff, G. A. Smith, Jos. Matthews, John Brown, & Jos. A. After an hour's absence they returned without any game; the reason of which was, they saw no cows; but a number of bulls – the latter they did not wish to kill. – About ½ past 12 M., we were again in motion. – After going 12 miles, we encamped at 5 P. M., on the banks of the River, near a grove of cotton wood trees, where the grass was quite fresh & high. – A number of the horses were taken to the opposite side the river, where the feed was said to be still better. –

Saturday the 18th.

Beautiful weather. – We continued our journey at 8 a.m. – As we passed along the river, we saw a number of large herds of buffaloes, on either side of the stream – one of them was killed by one of the Frenchmen who accompany us. – After going 17 miles we forded "Deer Creek," & encamped 4 P. M. on its banks, near the site of our old camp ground. – This stream we found had fallen considerably since we were here before, being quite low at this time. – There was plenty of good grass here; also fuel; as we encamped on the borders of quite a dense forest of cotton wood. Soon after dark, 2 of the Frenchmen came in with another buffalo, (a cow,) which was fatter than any we have yet seen. – They reported that they had seen, about a mile ahead, a large herd of buffalo cows – it is the intention, I believe, to remain here, till we shall secure some of them. – This evening, while Prest. Young, Bro. Heber, Dr. Richards, Bro. Benson & T. Bullock were taking a walk up the creek in search of coal, Pres't Young and Bro. Benson being in advance, & Bro. Heber a little in the rear, the latter saw a she-bear with 2 cubs walking leisurely along the bed of the stream. He immediately notified the others of the fact, when Bro. Benson took deliberate aim at them over the Presidents shoulders, but the gun missed fire 3 times in succession. The bear, now seeing them for the first time, made for them at full speed. – Noticing this, Pres't. Young fired his pistol & one of the cubs immediately fell, but soon recovered and rose again. Bro. Heber then discharged his piece but apparently without effect. By this time, the animal, continuing to advance with great rapidity, had got within 2 rods of them, when their situation became so evidently critical, that Pres't Young advised an immediate retreat to a neighboring rocky height, which they effected with ease. – The bear seeing them to be out of her reach, turned & went up the hill, sought shelter in a thick cluster of bushes and underbrush, & they lost sight of her & saw her no more – A number of men, with dogs afterwards went in pursuit, but after considerable search, concluded to abandon the enterprise till morning. –

Sunday the 19th.

Fine, clear day – After breakfast, Brigham, Heber, & a number of others again went out in pursuit of the bear seen last evening. – They returned, after an hour's absence, having seen plenty of <u>signs</u>, but nothing of the animal herself. – This morning, also a number of men rode out on horseback in pursuit of game. – A few of them returned unsuccessful this forenoon, – about 3 P. M. we continued our journey – at the same time, Barney Adams rode up & said that some of the hunters had succeeded in killing a buffalo cow & one black tailed deer about 5 miles back. – Accordingly, Col. Markham, with a few other men, (including Orson,) went back after them, taking a wagon along for that purpose. – Three or four other wagons remained here, in consequence of the horses belonging to them, being out with the hunters after game. – After going 4¾ miles we left the river to our left, & travelling 4¼ miles further, we encamped, at sunset, on the banks of "<u>North Buffalo Fork</u>", having come 9 miles. – Here we found the grass rather short but quite good, especially on the banks of the stream. –

Monday the 20th.

This morning, the sun rose bright, & clear as usual. – The hunters, with the wagons, arrived at camp, about 2 oclock this morning, – bringing with them one buffalo-cow, 2 black-tailed deer. – We renewed our journey at 9 a.m. – After proceeding 8¾ miles, we halted at noon on the banks of "A la Prele Creek" – In about 2 hours, we were again in motion – going about 8 miles further, we arrived at a small spring situated in a sandbed. – Finding but little grass here, we continued on, & travelling 7¾ miles, came to a small stream, in which there was considerable water when we passed it before; but at this time, the bed of it was quite dry. As we had a fine moon, we determined to proceed to the next stream 3 ½ miles hence, called "Big Timber Creek", where we arrived at 9 P. M.. After fording which & going up the same a mile or two, (leaving the road in our rear) we encamped at 10 P. M. on its banks, having come in all about 30 miles to-day. – The grass here was quite scant, & but little water in the stream, though we found plenty of fuel in the vast forest that skirts its banks. – This evening a young man by the name of Judson Persons was discovered to be missing from the camp. Upon inquiry it was ascertained that he had last been seen, some 10 miles back, following the wagons on foot. – Soon after our arrival, Wm. King & Geo. Billings went back in pursuit of him – they returned about 1 a.m., with the intelligence that they had been about 3 miles, but could not find him. – It was conjectured by some, that being not far behind the wagons when we turned off the road, he had continued on, not being aware of our deviation from the same. – Orson & myself stood on guard to night, the first watch. –

Tuesday the 21st.

Tolerably fair this morning. – Judson Persons made his appearance in camp about sunrise. He had slept in the bushes last night as far back as the sandbed. – Bro. Heber gave him in charge to Charles Harper. At 8 a.m., just as we were on the point of getting ready to start, some of our men, who had gone out to gather up the horses, gave the alarm, that the Indians were "rushing" them (driving them off.) As some 20 head of them were going over the hill, at full speed we headed & brought them to camp but notwithstanding, they succeeded in getting off with 11 horses. A number of shots were fired at the Indians, but without effect. Bro. Heber & others started off immediately in pursuit of the missing ones. – Soon after, about 200 Indians made their appearance in camp, mostly on horseback – these were commanded by the same chief, who met us with his band below Ft. John, on our way up the Platte River. He & Pres't Young at once recognized each other, & had quite an interview together, he told the President, that he supposed us to be Crows, or the horses would not have been taken, & said that they should be restored to us. – That a few days since they had stolen 45 head of horses from the Crows on the "Sweet Water". – These turned out to be our own horses. Considerable salt was given to them by the brethren, & about 1 P. M. they departed for their camp, about 5 miles up the creek. The horses had been hitched up all the morning, & about 2 P. M., we drove ½ a mile down the creek, & again encamped on the open prairie – Soon after it commenced raining, & continued most of the night. During the afternoon, the missing horses were brought into camp with the exception of one horse & a mule, Bro. Heber recovered his four mules that had been taken – these were all bro't in by different ones, who visited the Indian camp. Bro. Heber returned this evening, from there also. – He was received kindly by the Indians & "smoked the pipe of peace", with some of their most distinguished men. He saw quite a number of horses that were stolen from us on "Sweet Water" including my own. – Pres't Young suggested that we say nothing about these for the present, but when we got to Ft. John, to offer Mr. Bordeau 100 dollars to procure them for us inasmuch as it was deemed inexpedient to try to take them by force, numbering as they do, some 800 men [in] their camp, & comprising upwards of 100 lodges.

Wednesday the 22d.

Cloudy, gloomy, & cold morning. – We started this morning about 8 o'clock. – After going 8¾ miles, we halted to bait at noon, on the banks of a small creek the bed of which was quite dry, although, we found water in a spring in the vicinity. – In an hour we were again in motion. – We proceeded 6¾ miles further, & encamped at 5 P. M., near "Kimball's Spring", on "Horseshoe Creek. In this we found but little water, & the grass, though much shorter than when we were here before, was quite good. – Plenty of fuel from the surrounding forest. – It has continued to rain considerably at intervals through the day. – This evening, Bro. Heber having found a good place to bait our horses, Bro. Benson, E. Snow, H. Cushing Wm. King, & some others & myself took our horses there, where we remained till about 10 o'clock. –

Thursday the 23d.

Fine morning. – I felt quite unwell this morning having taken considerable cold, while out last night. – We arose at daylight, & continued our journey at sunrise. Halting to bait twice on our route we arrived at "Warm Springs," at 10 o'clock in the evening, where we again stopt a few minutes to water our horses, & then turning to the right, took another road to the Ft. from that which we came, being considerably nearer, one way being 14, the other 10 miles. – After going about ½ a mile, we encamped at 11 o'clock, having come about 29 miles to-day.

Friday the 24th.

Pleasant morning. – The brethren got up their teams at an early hour, when they were called together, (each 10 standing apart by itself,) & considerable instruction given them by Pres't Young. A vote was first taken whether the men would obey their officers, & when we get to the Ft. not everybody run there to see what was going on, &c. it was unanimous in the affirmative. – He then cautioned every man to remain near his own wagon, & each captain of 10 to keep his company together. – He severely reproved those who were murmuring against the laws of the camp, & told them if they did not abstain from it, he would leave them on the prairie. – That when they got among the Gentiles, they might swear about us as much as they pleased; but as long as they remain with us, he wanted them to hold their tongues. – Considerable more he said; & finally concluded by telling them that he had scolded them a good deal, & now hoped they would be good boys in future, & blessed them in the name of the Lord. – We continued our journey at 9 a.m., – After reaching the fort, we passed it, & fording the river, near our old ferrying place, we proceeded a mile down the river, & encamped for the night, having come about 12 miles. – At the fort, we found Appleton Harmon, who has hired out there for the winter at the rate of $25 per month.[196] – He informed us that the ox teams left here on Monday last. – They had been somewhat detained owing to 18 of their horses having been stolen by the Indians; 13 of which they recovered. He told us also that on Monday, Luke Johnson, with 3 others, had started back to meet us with a number of horses – The reason that we did not see them, was owing to their having taken the river road. – Brigham, Heber, & others of the Twelve visited the Fortt [*sic*] this afternoon, & had an interview with Mr. Bordeau, the proprietor. He told them, it was rather a dull chance about recovering their horses, but that to-morrow-morning, he would send back a man with any number of men we were a mind to send, to see what could be done. – On inquiry, we found flour to be worth here $45 per barrel, (or 25 cts. a pound), & corn 12½ cts. a pint. The horses were driven down the river a short distance, & strictly guarded. The grass here was tolerably good. –

This evening, a while after dark, the brethren were again called together & 40 men chosen to go on the expedition to-morrow morning, in pursuit of our horses. Previous to this 10 men had been chosen to go ahead & find the Indians, while the others are to follow them up, remaining a little in the rear, to act as a reinforcement in case of necessity. The orders were to recover the horses, "peaceably if they could, but forcibly if they must", being governed, for the most part, by circumstances. – The command of the 2 companies were

Artist unknown, Fort Laramie, *1842. E. Weber and Co. lithograph. Wyoming State Archives.*

196. For more on Appleton Milo Harmon and his significant contributions to the Mormon exodus, see Maybelle Harmon Anderson, ed., *The Journals of Appleton Milo Harmon: A Participant in the Mormon Exodus from Illinois and the Early Settlements of Utah, 1846–1877* (Glendale, CA: Arthur H. Clark, 1946).

intrusted to E. T. Benson & Stephen Markham. Pres't Young then gave some general instructions for their guidance, & the meeting was dismissed.

Saturday the 25th.

Warm, though somewhat cloudy & windy. – Agreeably to the arrangements of last night, the first company of 10 under Col. Markham started at 8 a.m., on their expedition, & in an hour afterward, 40 more, under the command of E. T. Benson, followed in their footsteps. They all returned in 2 or 3 hours, as when they got to the Fort, Mr. Bordeau told them that he believed it useless for them to go farther, because the Indians about the Ft. had sent ahead runners last night to apprise them that we were coming. – It is the general opinion, however, of the brethren, that both the Frenchmen & Indians are leagued together against us in the affair, therefore it was deemed improper to pursue the matter any further. – We learned, this afternoon, more particulars connected with the departure of the ox teams from this place – These were 5 day's journey in advance of us, while Wm. Clayton, J. Redden, & a few others, who had previously preceded them, were 8 day's journey in advance of us. – We shall probably go on to-morrow morning, & are waiting, in hopes that Luke Johnson will arrive with his men this afternoon. – I stood guard this forenoon watching the horses. – Towards evening, Com. Stockton of the U. S. Navy, arrived at the Fort.[197]– With him came Major Harris as pilot. The former is on his way from California to the States. They report a portion of their own company, accompanied by Luke Johnson, & his men, to be about 6 miles distant. Pres't Young & Heber to day bought a number of buffalo robes at the Ft., paying at the rate of $1.25 apiece – Two wagons were sent to bring them over. Orson & myself stood on guard last night, last watch. –

Sunday the 26th.

Fine day. – This morning, a written & minute description of our stolen horses, was given to a.m. Harmon, that, if an opportunity should present itself, he might avail himself of it to recover them for us. – About 8 o'clock, Luke Johnson, John Buchanan, Norman Taylor & J. C. Little arrived with 11 horses, including those they rode. They had been as far as "Big Timber Creek", in search of us, where the same band of Indians that we had seen, undertook to take their horses from them; but on their showing signs of resistance, the Indians betook themselves to flight – Near here, also they met Com. Stockton's company, consisting of about 40 men, with whom they traveled till last night, & encamped with them on the "North Fork", about 4 miles distant. – Pres't Young & Heber each bought a cow at the Fort this morning, paying $15 apiece for them. Heber is also going to take back a cow for a.m. Harmon. – About 4 P. M. having completed our business at the Fort, we renewed our journey. – After going

197. Robert Field Stockton (1795–1866) was a United States navy commodore noted for his role in the capture of California during the Mexican-American War. Second military governor of California, he also later served as a United States senator from New Jersey. He was the first American naval officer to carry out actions against slave ships and was instrumental in the founding of Liberia.

about 3 miles, we encamped at 5 P. M. on the banks of the river where the feed was tolerably good. Com. Stockton intends pursuing the same route with ourselves to the Bluffs, & will probably leave the Ft. to-morrow. He has one wagon with him, in which a number of his men ride, who are afflicted with the measles, while he carries his effects on pack mules. To-day I took Father [Ezekiel] Kellogg into my wagon with his effects – By request of Bro. K. John Buchanan is hereafter to mess with me, who puts in his horse alongside of my pony to work before my wagon –

Monday the 27th.

Fine, cool weather. – Luke Johnson started back to the Fort on horseback after some things that he had forgotten & left behind. We started this morning, a little before sunrise without taking breakfast, after going about 10 miles, we crossed "Raw-Hide Creek", the bed of which was dry, turned aside from the road & halted to bait at 9 a.m. near the river, where the feed was tolerably good – about 11 a.m. we again went on – going 10 miles further, we encamped, at 5 P. M. ½ a mile from the river, having come 20 miles to-day. Soon after our arrival, 2 deer were seen to pass, at full speed, within ¼ mile of the camp. Thos. Wolsey made a shot at one of them, but without effect. – The grass here in places, was good, though somewhat scant. – I sold my buckskin pants to Geo. Duncan to-day for $2.00 – This evening 6 companies of 10's were organized in a military capacity in order that we may be better prepared to defend ourselves against the attacks of the Indians. – The following are the names of the captain of said comp's. Brigham Young, H. Egan, Thos. Tanner, Luke Johnson, Charles Harper, & Geo. Wilson. Besides these, an independent company was formed consisting of those not included in the others. At the head of this was Capt. Brigham Young, whose aide-de-camp was Col. Rockwood & Col. Markham as Colonel & Thos. Bullock as adjutant. – Bro. Heber & myself retired a short distance from camp this evening to pray by ourselves. –

Tuesday the 28th.

Warm & pleasant day. We arose this morning at daylight & were in motion by sunrise – After going near 6 miles we halted at 8 a.m., to bait & get breakfast. The companies of 10s recently organized as a military body, were called together for the inspection of their arms, & to ascertain the number of guns & quantity of ammunition each man had. About 10 a.m. we again started on – Proceeding about 10 miles, we encamped on the banks of the river at 4 P. M. within sight of "Scott's Bluffs," having come 16 miles to-day, at this place we found plenty of buffalo grass, which the horses devoured quite greedily. – Just as we arrived a large herd of antelope passed us at full speed; but notwithstanding several shots were fired at them, only one was killed, shot by S. Goddard. – a small spring creek puts into the river near this place. – Another antelope was killed & brought into camp this evening. We cut a large quantity of grass, & put before our horses to-night, that we may be better prepared for an early start. –

Artist unknown, Fording Laramie Creek *(near Fort Laramie). Wyoming State Archives.*

WEDNESDAY THE 29TH.

Fine weather – We arose, as usual, at daylight & started on at sunrise. After going 5 miles, we passed "Scotts Bluff's," when proceeding about 6 miles further we halted at 9 a.m. to bait & get breakfast. – During our stay here we noticed quite a large body of Indians on horseback, passing along down at a considerable distance on the opposite side the river. About 11 a.m., we were again in motion. During our progress this afternoon, we saw a number of antelopes & buffaloes. One of the latter was killed by Luke Johnson, which was brought on horses to the camp. – After going about 11 miles further, we encamped, at 5 P. M., on the banks of the river, 3 or 4 miles above, & in sight of "Chimney Rock," having come 22 miles. – My pony having become well nigh exhausted, this afternoon I worked George R. Grant's horse alongside of the one belonging to John Buchanan. The grass here was extremely high and good; as indeed we have found it in several places, when when [*sic*] we were here before, it was quite scant, we were obliged to resort to buffalo chips, with which to cook our suppers, being the only fuel that could be found. – A short time previous to our arrival at this place, we observed the Indians, spoken of above, pitching their lodges, & encamping for the night, some 4 or 5 miles up the river, on the opposite side. – Bro. Heber and myself again this evening retired by ourselves for prayer.

THURSDAY THE 30TH.

Warm and beautiful weather. – We arose at the usual hour, and got started ¾ of an hour before sunrise, I put John Brimhall's, and John Buchanan's horses before my wagon this morning. After going 5 miles, we passed "Chimney Rock," when, proceeding 10 miles, we halted at ¼ past 10 a.m., to bait and get breakfast, on the banks of the river, having come 15 miles. – About 1 P. M., we again went on – after journeying 6 miles, we encamped at 5 P. M., on the banks of the river opposite a French and Indian camp, consisting of 8 or 10 lodges, having come about 21 miles to-day. Just as we arrived, we met a Frenchman with a pack-mule loaded with buffalo, taking it to his camp. The man who has charge of this camp, is a Frenchman by the name of Rashaw [Jean Baptiste Richard], who is hired to kill game for the inhabitants of Ft. John. The grass here was unusually good, as also it was all along, through the country through which we have passed to-day, & no fuel except a little flood wood, & buffalo chips. Geo. Wilson killed one antelope & George Billings a wild goose to-day. – Two Indians visited our camp this evening. – Col. Markham went, by appointment, over to the Indian camp to make some trades with them for the brethren. – I sent by him a horn of powder to sell for the money. – He returned about 8 this evening, with the intelligence that the Frenchman had proposed if we would stay here to-morrow, & assist them in hunting buffaloes, they would give us half the game that should be killed – Accordingly, it was decided to accept of the offer, & orders were issued this evening, that no man should leave the camp in the morning, without permission of his captain. –

FRIDAY THE 1ST OF OCTOBER.

Bright & beautiful morning. – Some 10 or 12 Indians passed our camp & went out hunting this morning. About noon, Brigham, Heber, & several others also went out on horseback – they returned about 4 P. M. They had seen quite a large herd of buffalo cows, but when they came to them, they found Geo. R. Grant chasing them, so that they could not get a fair shot at them. Owing to this, and Mr. Rashaw with

Camping on the Platte with Chimney Rock. *Lithograph by Piercy, Route from Liverpool to Great Salt Lake Valley. Courtesy of Church History Library.*

his men not appearing to assist in the hunt, they did not secure any game themselves. Mr. Rashaw said afterward, that it was not, at first his intention to go out himself; but that he had instructed the Indians to kill more than they themselves wanted, & give the surplus quantity to us. – This forenoon, Geo. Billings, John Buchanan, & myself went over to the Indian lodges on the other side the river, where we exchanged a small quantity of salt, powder & a powder-horn, for considerable tallow & meat, a number of others made exchanges of a like nature with the squaws who visited the camp during the day. – About 5 P. M. Com. Stockton's company came in sight, & encamped up the river, 3 or 4 miles. – We learned, this evening, that the Indians who went out this morning, had killed about 20 cows, but whether we will be benefited by it or not, we have no knowledge. –

SATURDAY THE 2D.

Fine weather, as usual. – Some of the brethren bought a number of horses, & Dr. Richards one cow, of the Frenchman. A messenger, (Col. Little,) was, this morning despatched to the camp of Com. Stockton, to ascertain his intentions about accompanying us. The messenger soon returned with the news, that he now intended to cross the river, & take the road to St. Joseph, Mo., as he thought that to be a much nearer road to the States, than the one we are pursuing. – We renewed our journey at 8 a. m. – After going about 5 miles, we halted on the banks of the river while a buffalo cow killed by Thomas Wolsey, & A. P. Chessley, was being skinned & distributed in the camp, – going about 2 miles farther, a young calf was killed by Luke Johnson. We then proceeded 8 miles further, & encamped at ½ past 4 P. M., on the banks of the river, opposite the "Ancient Bluff Ruins," – near which Nath. Fairbanks was bitten by a rattlesnake on our journey out – having come about 15 miles to-day. – Soon after our arrival, a buffalo bull was killed by Thos. Wolsey. We found the grass here, good as usual – plenty of buffalo chips, & but little floodwood for fuel, stood guard last night 1st watch.

SUNDAY THE 3D.

Beautiful morning. We arose at sunrise, & after taking breakfast, & baiting our horses awhile, we continued our journey at 9 a.m. Orson went ahead on the pony; myself on foot; leaving the wagon in charge of John Brimhall, & John Buchanan. After going 2 miles, the road turns to the left, & leads over a sandy bluff. This we avoided, by taking to the bed of the stream, (now quite low,) & went a mile further, where we stopt to bait at noon. A buffalo cow killed by Luke J. & W. Woodruff was brought in here, & distributed among the brethren. – At 2 P. M., we were again in motion. Proceeding 5 miles, we turned aside from the road, & encamped at 4 P. M. having come only 8 miles, owing to the delays occasioned by the killing of buffaloes; as it is considered good policy to lay up a supply of meat while we have the opportunity, most of the camp depending solely upon that for subsistence, being entirely destitute of flour & other provisions. We learned, soon after our arrival, that 2 more buffalo cows had been killed, the one by Amasa Lyman, the other by whom I know not. A wagon was immediately unloaded, & sent out to bring them in. – Orson & Geo. R. Grant killed an antelope this afternoon, that had been previously wounded by Amasa Lyman. The grass here was tolerably good; but no fuel, except our usual resource b. chips.

Monday the 4th.

Warm & pleasant. We arose this morning at the usual hour, & got started at 9 a. m. Proceeding 2 miles, we came to "Crab Creek," where we found a guide-board, with the following inscription. "Camp of Pioneers, stopt here & killed & dried 30 buffalo cows, Sept. 28, 1847." – From this it appears, that they were 6 days ahead of us, & that they left here the above date. We went on 8 miles further & halted at noon to bait on the banks of the river. Here we found two of our Frenchmen, who had gone ahead yesterday, & killed 5 buffaloes near here, 3 of which they saved, the remainder was devoured by the wolves, while they were absent. – Geo. Billings shot a buffalo cow this noon; but, on examination, it proved to be so poor, that we did not take it along. We were again in motion by 2 P. M. Going 10 miles further, we halted on the banks of the river, & encamped at sunset, having come 20 miles to-day. The grass here was good as usual, – no fuel, except buffalo chips. – One of Monroe Frink's horses having failed, I let him have my pony to work this afternoon, in order to enable him to get to the camp with his wagon. – I omitted to mention that this noon, 4 Sioux Indians, including a squaw, visited our camp – These were a portion of a war party, that had been some distance below near the limits of the Pawnee hunting ground, the main body of which had already gone ahead to Ft. John. – This evening, several horses having failed, it was deemed advisable to raise volunteers to go ahead on foot, & arrest the progress of the ox teams. The following are the names of those, who volunteered to go on the expedition, viz. Amasa Lyman, Luke Johnson, John Buchanan, John Brown, John Crow, William Rowe, W[illia]m. Parks, Newton Weston, S. H. Goddard, Alexander P. Chessley, Joseph Rooker, & Kellogg. – A letter was written & signed by the President & Dr. Richards, & given into the hands of Amasa Lyman, who has charge of the expedition, addressed to Tunis Rappleye & John Smith, the captains of the company ahead. This contained instructions for them to stop, kill buffaloes, & dry the meat till we should come up, that they may relieve us of some of our wagons, or, at least, some of the loads in them. –

Tuesday the 5th.

This morning, before daylight, the above named individuals, (most of them being well armed,) started off on foot, on the projected service of last night. – We got our breakfasts, & after waiting awhile for the horses to bait, we continued our journey at 9 a.m. – After going 7¾ miles, we halted at noon on the banks of the river to bait our horses, some of which are failing quite rapidly. – We again started on at 2 P. M. – Proceeding 2 miles we forded "Castle Creek." which was much lower than when we were here before. Going 3¼ miles further, we encamped at ½ past 4 P. M., on the banks of the river, a little below "Ash Hollow" having come about 13 miles to-day. The grass here was plentiful, though getting to be somewhat dry – no fuel, except buffalo chips. – Soon after our arrival, Wm. King, Orson, & some others went over the river to visit "Ash Hollow". In about ½ hour they returned, bringing with them a load of dry cedar wood. We saw plenty of buffaloes on our route to-day, but none were killed that I have heard of. – John Buchanan requested me to take charge of his horse during his absence, & I still continue to work his & John Brimhall's horses before my wagon, both persons intending to accompany me through to Winter Quarters, in the same. – The Frenchmen killed a buffalo cow, & Charles Barnum an antelope this afternoon. I learned this evening. –

Wednesday the 6th.

Beautiful weather. We got started at 8 a.m. – Proceeding 7 miles, we found a letter in a stick by the side of the road, stating, that our boys were here last night about dark, they had also killed a buffalo calf, the skin of which we also found. – We went on 3 miles further, & halted on the banks of the river, at noon, near the base of a sand bluff that comes to the water's edge. At 2 P. M. we again went on, passing over the bluff, through the deep sand, we soon after forded "Wolf Creek," – Here we found John Buchanan & John Crow. The former had been taken sick, & was obliged to stay behind. He stated that the rest left him, last night at 11 o'clock, & were intending to travel all night. – We proceeded 4½ miles further, & encamped at 6 P. M. on the banks of "Camp Creek," ½ a mile from the river, having come 15¼ miles to-day. – The grass here was good – the usual resource for fuel. The Frenchmen killed 2 buffalo cows & 2 calves this afternoon. Orson stood guard to-night last watch. –

Thursday the 7th.

Somewhat cloudy & windy, though a pleasant day for travelling. – We renewed our journey at 8 a.m. – soon after we forded a small creek. Proceeding about 2 miles, we met a party of 3 mountaineers, on their way from Independence, Mo., to Ft. John. They had seen us from the other side of the river, & came over for the purpose of holding an interview. Their whole number, was 8 men; 5 remaining on the other side. The one, who seemed to be their leader, gave his name & title as "Capt. Walker."[198] He imparted to us some news of a general nature, of which we were not before in possession. – Among the rest were the following items, – That the war between the United States & Mexico, which for a short time had suffered some little cessation, was now being prosecuted with renewed vigor – That there had been a more abundant harvest of wheat & corn in the States, than had been before witnessed for several years. – He also stated that packet steamers were now plying regularly between St. Louis & Council Bluffs, & that one had left the latter place for the Yellowstone River, a short time

198. Captain Joseph R. Walker (1798–1876) was born in Tennessee and became a mountain man, scout, explorer, and trader. In 1833 Captain Benjamin L. Bonneville paid Walker to explore the territory west of the Great Salt Lake to California. He blazed the trail from Fort Hall (southeast Idaho) to the Truckee River that would later become the principal route for the California gold rush. In 1845 he was in charge of John C. Frémont's third government expedition to California and Oregon. The pioneers sent letters with him to the Salt Lake Valley in October 1847.

previous to his departure.[199] – That we would find plenty of buffaloes for a hundred or more miles, as we passed along down the Platte River. – He himself intends to proceed as far as Ft. Bridger, &, for ought he knows to "Weber's Fork", near the "Salt Lake". A number of letters were written by different ones to send by him to the valley, – among the rest, I wrote one for Bro. Heber, to Edson Whipple, Ellen, and Mary Ellen. – After spending about an hour with Capt. Walker and his comrade, we bade them farewell, and pursued our journey – Proceeding 3 miles, we stopt at noon on the banks of a small creek, to bait our horses. At 2 P. M., we again went on – going 7 miles further, we encamped at 5 P. M., on the banks of the river, having made 12 miles to-day. – The grass here was comparatively green & high – fuel – buffalo chips, as usual. The bed of the river, at this point was much dryer than at any place we have yet seen. –

Soon after our arrival, this evening our Frenchmen came in bringing with them a letter, which they found in a stick, by the side of the road, near a creek, about a mile below here. – This, on being opened, proved to be from William Clayton. It stated that they had passed here the 1st of October, (being 6 days ahead of us,) & were intending to continue on till they should arrive at some place where there is plenty of wood, & there make a short delay, while they should procure an additional quantity of buffalo meat, several of them being short of provisions. From the letter we also learned, that they traveled from 15 to 20 miles per day; & if this be the case, they must be a hundred or more miles in advance of us. – Appended to the letter were a few lines from Amasa Lyman, stating his determination to overtake them if he had to follow them to Winter Quarters.

Joseph R. Walker (1798–1876), mountainman, explorer, and scout.

Quite an amusing little incident, which I omitted to mention in its proper place, occurred soon after we left our noon halting place. Bro. Woodruff, with his carriage, Dr. Richards, Bro. Benson & a number of others, including myself, had preceded the wagons, about ½ mile, when all at once, we noticed standing by the side of the road, within a few yards of us, a buffalo bull, of some size. Brother Benson rode up close to him, but he would not retreat an inch; on the contrary, shaking his head fiercely, & elevating his back, he manifested evident symptoms of hostility towards

199. Departing from St. Louis on 26 March 1832, the steamboat *Yellowstone* reached the Fort Union Trading Post at the confluence of the Yellowstone and Missouri Rivers (twenty-five miles southwest of Williston, North Dakota) in June of that year. From that time on, the *Yellowstone* and other steamboats sailed as far north as Fort Union when the water levels were sufficiently high.

us, & would, no doubt, have made an attack upon us had we not been so numerous. As it was, he remained firm and immovable like as if he were lord of the soil, & possessed both the powers and inclinations to-dispute successfully this passage of the road. We finally caused him to flee, after the teams came up, by sending our dogs after him. –

I stood on guard to-night, last watch. –

Friday the 8th.

Warm & pleasant day. – We continued our journey at 8 a.m. – After we had proceeded a mile, we forded a small stream, saw the stake, in which the letter, written by Wm Clayton, was found. – On one side of this was inscribed the following: "12 – B. Y. & Council – A. L." – The last 2 letters are initials of Amasa Lyman, & were probably written by him, as he and his comrades passed along. Here, the ox teams had encamped, & there were evident signs that they had remained here a day or two. We proceeded 7 miles further, (crossing 3 more streams in our route,) & halted at noon, a short distance from the river, having come 8 miles. Just as we arrived a large herd of elk made their appearance upon the brow of the hill to our left. Two or three of the brethren went out to get a shot at them, but soon returned without success. Two of our Frenchmen, being mounted on mules, succeeded in killing one of them. – At 2 P. M., we again went on – after going near 4 miles, we came to the base of another sand bluff – Part of the wagons passed entirely over in this the deep sand, & the remainder took to the bed of the stream, (which was quite dry in places,) a portion of the way, & then resumed the road over the bluffs, – I myself waded the river and walked over the wet sand alternately for 2½ miles. – After the wagons had passed over, they forded "Spring Creek," – proceeding a mile beyond this, we encamped at sunset near the river, & one of our old camp grounds, having come 15 miles to-day. Plenty of buffalo grass here, though not so high as we have hitherto seen. Orson & myself feel quite unwell this evening, owing to our using so much meat, as we have not tasted of any other kind of food, for 2 or 3 weeks. My pony continuing to fail rapidly to night, I turned him loose; considering that it was as well for him to live & be stolen by the Indians, as to die by starvation among us. –

Saturday the 9th.

Beautiful weather. We continued our journey at 8 a.m., Proceeding some 4 miles, we passed over another sand-bluff, about a mile in length, when after going 6½ miles further, we came to the base of yet another bluff, 4½ miles in extent. Here we halted about 1 P. M. to bait At 3 P. M., we again went on – After passing over the above named bluff, we proceeded a short distance beyond, & encamped at sunset on the banks of "Junction Bluff Fork," having come 15¾ miles to-day. – & are this evening 202¼ miles from Ft. John. This stream has fallen but little since we were here before – the grass along its margin, was quite good. The usual resource for fuel.

Sunday the 10th.

Still fine weather. Bro. Heber & myself, this morning, made out a list of a large portion of the members of his family, who are to be fitted out, next season, at his expense, with provisions necessary on their journey to the valley of Salt Lake. These amounted in all, including grown persons & children, to 71 souls. We also made an estimate of the quantity of flour they would need; which amounted to about 23000 lbs. – The grass here being better than any we have lately seen, it was deemed expedient to remain here the greater part of the day, in order to give our horses a chance to recruit themselves – Meanwhile, Joseph Matthews was sent ahead to look out a good camp ground for the ensuing night. He returned about 1 P. M., & at 2 o'clock we forded the "Junction Bluff Fork," &, travelling 3 miles, encamped at 4 P. M. on the banks of the river, opposite a small island, where the grass was tolerably good. About the time we arrived, we saw a number of buffaloes to our left, near the bluffs, which the Frenchmen were endeavoring to get a shot at. They succeeded in killing 1, which they brought to camp this evening. –

Monday the 11th.

It commenced to rain about 5 o'clock this morning, & continued without intermission for ¾ of an hour, when it ceased, though it remained cool, & misty through the day, the sun shining at intervals through the clouds, we pursued our journey at 8 a.m. Proceeding a mile, we forded a small stream, near which, in a stick by the side of the road, we found a few lines from Amasa Lyman, stating that they had left here on Saturday morning last; & that, the night before, they had gone to the bluffs to procure a supply of meat – that they got along rather slow, not making over between 15 & 20 miles per day; but were all well & in tolerably good spirits. – Near here we noticed that the ox teams had encamped; from appearances some 4 or 5 days since. – It is the opinion of most of the brethren, that Amasa & his comrades are not now more than 30 or 40 miles ahead of us, & if the ox-teams do not stop, the brethren, weak & faint from living entirely on meat, must, necessarily give up the chase. – We proceeded 6¾ miles further, & halted at noon on the banks of the river, opposite quite an extensive island, covered with bushes & shrubbery. We have travelled along this forenoon in sight of a large cluster of trees, which, in the distance mark the progress of the South Fork of Platte River. It is quite cheering to us, to come once more in sight of, & travel along near the timber, after being so long debarred of that privilege. – At 1 P. M. we again went on – Travelling 4 miles, we encamped at 3 P. M., opposite 2 small islands, having come 11¾ miles to-day. From the appearance of the country ahead, we judge timbers this evening to be but 2 or 3 miles above the junction; but as none of our company have explored the country, near the spot, we have no exact idea of its whereabouts. – The grass here, immediately on the margin of the stream, was quite good; in other places, rather scant. – Quite a number of trees & bushes on the above named islands – & buffalo chips in plenty. – Two buffaloes were killed this forenoon by Geo. Clarke & one of the Frenchmen; &, this afternoon, 2 more were killed near the bluffs, opposite our camp, which, some of the brethren, (including Orson,) went out & brought in on horses.

TUESDAY THE 12TH.

Clear, cool weather. – We started at 8 a.m. – Proceeding 10 miles, we halted to bait at noon on the banks of the river opposite "Brady's Island," which abounds in bushes and some little large timber. – Opposite this place, on the other side the river, is quite a high range of bluffs, the extremity of which, about 2 miles behind and west of us, in our opinion, makes the junction of the 2 Forks. At 2 P. M., we again went on. Travelling 6 miles further, we encamped at 5 P. M., near the margin of a small slough on marsh that apparently has its source in springs not far distant, – We are, this evening, about a mile from the river, near the bluffs. The grass is tall and rank, in general but in places, tolerably good. – Buffalo chips, in plenty as usual. There was one buffalo killed to-day by Dexter Stillman, which W. Woodruff brought to camp in his carriage.

WEDNESDAY THE 13TH.

Clear, cool, and windy weather. – We started on, as usual at 8 a.m. – Going on till noon, we halted on the banks of the main branch of Platte River, opposite a group of islands, abounding in both large and small cotton-wood trees, having come about 8 miles. At 2 o'clock we were again in motion – proceeding 8 miles further, we encamped at ½ past 5 P. M., opposite a small island abounding in bushes. – Just as we arrived, we saw 2 or 3 large herds of buffalo coming down to the water a little in advance of us. Thos. Woolsey, & John Holman went out and each shot a cow. A number of men, (including Orson with the pony) went out to assist in skinning the one killed by the latter, and were gone until 10 o'clock, when they returned Orson bringing in quite a supply of the fattest meat we have seen in some time. Another buffalo was killed to-day I believe by one of the Frenchmen. – The grass here, on the main shore, was quite closely grazed by the buffaloes; on the island it was some better. We have come 16 miles to-day. –

THURSDAY THE 14TH.

As usual, clear, cold & windy weather. – We continued our journey at 8 a.m. Proceeding 6 miles, we halted at noon bait near an island, abounding in small timber & a few rushes which the horses devoured greedily, after subsisting so long entirely upon dry grass. We again started on at 2 P. M. after going 4 miles further, we encamped at ½ past 4 P. M., opposite a group of islands, also abounding in cotton wood trees, & marshes. We have seen numerous herds of buffaloes on either side of the river during our route to-day; at this point, the grass has been very closely grazed by them. The Frenchmen killed 2 cows this afternoon for the benefit of the camp. We are situated, this evening, near the site of one of our old camp grounds [.]

Artist unknown, Fording the (South) Platte. *Wyoming State Archives.*

FRIDAY THE 15TH.

Warm & pleasant day. We started this morning about 8 o'clock. Proceeding 8 miles, we halted at 12 M. to bait, near a slough not far from the river. During our stay here, the prairie got on fire, through the carelessness or neglect of Father Chamberlain. We, however, soon succeeded in extinguishing it, before it had made any material progress. – We again pursued our way at 1 P. M. – Travelling 6 or 7 miles, we passed the spot where Pres't. Young lost his spy-glass on our journey out, & encamped at ½ past 3 P. M. on the banks of the river, – opposite another group of islands, abounding in small timber & a few rushes, – having come 15 miles to-day. – Thos. Wolsey shot 2 cows this evening; the brethren went out after them, but brought in only one, not being able to find the other.

SATURDAY THE 16TH.

Fair, cool weather. – We continued our journey at 8 a.m. Proceeding about 20 miles, without making any noon halt, we forded "Buffalo Creek," (the bed of which was dry,) & proceeding a mile down the stream, we encamped at sunset in a bend of the same, where there was plenty of water, having come 21 miles to-day. At this place we found Amasa Lyman, & his comrades, with the exception of 2, viz. – Stephen H. Goddard, & Father Kellogg. These had left them on Tuesday last, a little above here, determined yet to overtake the ox teams. Amasa, with the remainder, passed here on Wednesday last, & went as far as the head of Grand Island, some 10 or 12 miles below here, where, not seeing any buffaloes, they were obliged to return to this place on Thursday, in order to get meat, & have remained here in waiting for us, ever since. The brethren all looked considerably fatigued with their travels, & were glad, once more, to meet with us. We have but slight hopes of overtaking the ox teams, & these are grounded upon the possibility of their being stopt by Bro. Goddard & Kellogg. – The grass here was tolerably good; & we found plenty of fuel from the scattering trees on the banks of the creek. Two of the Frenchmen came in this evening bringing on their mules part of 2 cows that they had killed. Father Chamberlain broke the iron axle tree of his wagon while descending a steep bank when we forded the creek. –

SUNDAY THE 17TH.

Pleasant weather. There being but few, if any, buffaloes to be seen below here, & a number of our horses having given out, it was determined to remain in the vicinity a day or two, while we could procure some meat, & also recruit the failing strength of our animals. Accordingly, this morning two capts. viz. Luke Johnson & John Brown were appointed to superintend the hunting expedition to be undertaken to-day in pursuit of buffaloes. Each of these chose their men, & started out on foot about 9 o'clock a.m. – Soon after the camp was moved to the mouth of the creek, about a mile below here, & near one of our old camp grounds. Here, for considerable distance around the margin of the stream, the grass was tolerably good; but out from the river some distance it had been closely grazed by the prairie dogs, near a large village of which we were situated. – Soon after our arrival at this place, 2 men, who had seen our wagons from the other side of the river, came over to see us. One of them, whose name is John Shaw, was the leader of a party of 12 men, the remainder of whom stayed the other side.[200] They had 4 wagons with them, & were on their way from Independence, Mo., to Ft. John. The most of them were going out to trade with the Indians this winter. He informed us that he had met Com. Stockton's company 4 days since; they had lost one of their number, who they supposed was shot by the Pawnees. They also killed one of the latter. – Mr. Shaw, after remaining here a short time in conversation, went back over the river, accompanied by John Buchanan, Thos. Wolsey & 2 of the Frenchmen. The latter 4 returned this afternoon. – About noon, a number of wagons were sent out to bring in the buffaloes in case the hunters should succeed in killing any.

MONDAY THE 18TH.

Fine, cool weather. Thomas Wolsey was sent out this morning, to tell the hunters to come in to-night, with what game they had killed, that we might proceed on our way. – We started on at 10 a.m. Proceeding 3 miles, we met a company of horsemen from Winter Quarters, whose names are as follow:

200. John S. Shaw carried on an independent fur trade with the Sioux. Upon returning to St. Joseph, Missouri, in the fall of 1847, he reported having encountered some two hundred Mormon wagons along the trail.

Hosea Stout	W. Martindale
Geo. D. Grant	Wm. Huntington
G. J. Potter	Luman H. Calkins
Wm. Kimball	James W. Cummings
Jacob Frazier	S. S. Thornton
Geo. W. Langley	Levi Nickerson
W. J. Earl	James H. Glines
W. Meeks	Chancey Whiting

16 persons.

Wm. H. Kimball & Geo. Grant each brought a wagon, loaded with provisions & grain for Heber & Brigham. They had been coming from Winter Quarters, 11 days, & were sent from there, by counsel, to our assistance. They had met the ox teams near the ford of the Loup Fork who intended to go on without stopping. – With the horsemen came Stephen H. Goddard, Ezekiel Kellogg, & Jackson Redden. The latter was with W. Clayton when he left the valley. – Orson & myself received a letter from mother, & myself one from my wife, stating that they were all well, &c.– these were dated Oct. 7th. Our folks also sent us a bag of sea biscuit, a small cheese, & a little coffee & sugar, – my wife a little parcel, containing 2 apples & a little tea. After spending a short time in conversation with the brethren, we went on, about 7 miles further, & encamped at ½ past 3 P. M. opposite G [rand]. Island, some few miles below its head; having come 10 miles to-day. The grass here was very good, everything considered. – Thomas Wolsey came in this evening with the intelligence that he had seen one party of our hunters – these he said, had secured enough meat to load the wagons – the other party he had not seen. He told us, furthermore, that they did not intend coming to camp to-night, but would remain near our last camp ground until morning. – That, as he was returning, he saw a large body of Indians across the river, some 5 or 6 miles distant. – It was therefore deemed expedient to send word for our brethren to come in to-night. Accordingly, a little after dark, Hosea Stout, Wilber J. Earl, J. Redden, J. Matthews, Wm. Huntington & W[illia]m. Martindale started out on horseback for that purpose. –

Early in October Bro. William Clayton, with a few others who had preceded the camp of pioneers, arrived at Winter Quarters, weary and worn down by travel, and having been for some time destitute of provisions, and dependent solely upon the killing of wild game for subsistence. They were a sorry looking set, and words would fail to express our feelings when we saw them in such a ragged and forlorn condition, and were told that they must be eight or nine days in advance of the main company; but everyone being interested, they went to work with a will, the women cooking, browning coffee and preparing every good thing that our limited means would admit of. There was no rest nor sleep till everything was ready to start and many a loving message commenced in the midst of it took till far into the night to finish. It had been so long since there had been any communication between us, and some of us were in doubt as to our husbands being with them, as some, we were told, had gone to California, and the feelings that thrilled our hearts under such various and trying circumstances can be better imagined than described; but we did not allow our fears to stand in the way. Everyone did all in their power, and it was something surprising how quickly two wagons were loaded—one for father and another for President Young—with grain and vegetables, all of the latter that could be taken, or whatever could be mustered in the way of provisions. I had two apples, which I packed up carefully with bread, cakes and various little parcels—one apple for Horace and the other for Orson, though this particular circumstance had passed from my recollection till reading of it in my husband's journal with other things received from his father, viz., Wm. Kimball—he driving father's team, and George D. Grant the President's. [In a short letter, hastily written by Sister E. B. Whitney, the present editor of the Woman's Exponent, who acted as scribe, Mother Whitney expresses herself as follows:]

*"We are all well, and hope and pray you are, but we have neither flour nor meal, and have not had any for several days, or we should have baked something to send you so we send you a bag of sea biscuit and a cheese, with a little coffee and sugar. * * The greatest comfort I have had in your absence has been in getting alone to pray for you, that you might be blessed, and I have always been blessed in so doing. I can say that almost my very breath has been prayer for you ever since you left us, that you might return home in safety, and nothing hinder or harm you. * * May the Lord bless and preserve you and return you safe to us, is my constant prayer for you—be faithful and diligent in prayer. I will not write any news, for I shall want to tell you that when you come. I must close, so goodbye.*

"YOUR MOTHER."

Woman's Exponent, vol. 15, no. 1,
1 June 1886, p. 6

TUESDAY THE 19TH.

Fine, pleasant weather, as usual. – We remained to-day encamped. – This forenoon, Bro. Heber, Wm. H. Kimball, & 3 or 4 others went over the river in pursuit of a large herd of buffaloes, that had lately made their appearance in the vicinity. They returned this afternoon, with a cow, which was killed by G. J. Potter & Levi Nickerson . This evening, a little after dark, the hunters, who went out on Sunday morning last, returned, with those who were in pursuit of them – they brought in 3 wagons, which were loaded down with 9 buffalo cows in very good condition.[201] Hosea Stout & his comrades did not find them until this morning. I stood on

201. Buffalo herds had migrated much further east this time of year (the fall) than they were when the pioneer companies left Winter Quarters in the spring. Such migrations were primarily dictated by weather, grazing patterns, grass supply, and prairie fires. Richard Hart, "Where the Buffalo Roamed—Or Did They?," *Great Plains Research: A Journal of Natural and Social Sciences* 11 (Spring 2001): 83–102.

guard to-night, the 1st, & Orson the last watch. – The wolves again to-night entertained us at a distance, with one of their (dis)agreeable concerts. This morning Father Kellogg & myself made search in my wagon for a little bag that had disappeared from his little tin box during his absence. – This contained 2 gold sovereigns but we were not able to find it.

For a time, after the provisions had ran so low that they had to depend on the killing of wild game, for subsistence, they indulged once a week—Sunday—in a thin porridge made of flour and water. After living so much on meat it seemed to create an appetite for tobacco, some who had never previously cared for it were now eager to get it. The scarcity of the article made it so valuable that the boys would make one cud serve them a number of times, and they would lay it away carefully as a most choice morsel. After every other source had failed, and being in a great strait, my husband, knowing that Brother Benson kept the weed for doctoring horses, went and asked him for a little, which he gave him, and when asked what the charge was, he was told that he could return the favor when they got home by coming to his house and singing some songs for him. This was not written down but was related to me verbally.

Woman's Exponent, vol. 15, no. 5,
1 August 1886, p. 34

Wednesday the 20th.

Cold & cloudy weather, with a light, misty fall of rain at intervals during the day. – Bro. Heber intimated to me privately this morning, that search was about to be instituted in my wagon for the recovery of the 2 lost sovereigns belonging to Father Kellogg. This he done, that I should not be taken by surprise. Accordingly about 9 a.m., soon after we had started on, my wagon was ordered out from the road, & the rest went on. Hosea Stout, at the head of a number of men, then came up & forming a circle, he made a short speech of which this is the substance. "That it was well known who had taken the money, & if it was immediately given up, without further ceremony, 'well & good'; if not, every thing in the wagon should be ripped to pieces & burnt, together with the wagon itself, & they would hunt among the ashes for the lost money; & wo be to him whose effects it should be found; for his bones should be left to bleach on this prairie.["] – Neither John Buchanan, John Brimhall, Orson nor myself making any confession, they took all the things out of the wagon, & proceeded to examine every parcel with great minuteness. They had looked over about ½ of the effects, & were about to search my person, when Geo. Grant halloed that the "lost was found." On opening J. Buchanan's nap-sack it was found concealed therein, thus verifying the suspicions of all, that he was the author of the theft. – He himself endeavored to excuse the matter, by saying that this was a portion of 10 sovereigns he had in the valley & he could prove it by Lieut. Willis & others there, but on being asked why he did not tell in the first place that he had the money, he could make no answer. – About this time, Dr. Richards & Bro. Benson rode up, & it being concluded, that without doubt this was the missing money, no further search was made; & the matter was dropt, for further investigation hereafter. – We therefore reloaded our things & went on at a rapid rate, some 3 miles, before we overtook the others wagons, having been detained about an hour by the search. – After having gone about 12 miles, we halted at 3 P. M. on the open prairie to bait our horses; there was no water here, except, indeed, the light misty rain, that continued to fall. At 4 P. M. we again went on – going a little over 2 miles further, we encamped at 10 o'clock in the evening, on the banks of the river near Grand Island on which there was plenty of rushes & good grass for our teams; also wood & water.

Thursday the 21st.

Still cold, cloudy & windy weather. – We continued our journey at 9 a.m. – Proceeding 15 miles, without making any halt, we encamped at 3 P. M. in the bed of the river, (which was dry here,) between Grand Island & the Main shore, either side being heavily timbered, & abounding in rushes & good grass. This was one of the best camp grounds we had had for some time, secured as we were, on every side, from the howling blasts that swept fiercely across the open prairie. We were encamped this evening about ¼ of a mile above the mouth of "Wood Creek," – quite a beautiful little stream whose banks, one either side, were studded with considerable timber. – Frenchmen reported this evening, that they had discovered traces of an Indian camp, & moccasin tracks of no older a date than last night; therefore the brethren were cautioned to watch closely their horses. –

Friday the 22d.

Beautiful, clear weather, though yet quite cool. – We started on at 8 a.m. Going a short distance down the bed of the river, we forded "Wood Creek," near its mouth, – we now began gradually to bear away from the Platte, & after travelling 12 miles we encamped at 3 P. M. on "Prairie Creek," on the open prairie, where there was no timber in sight. The grass here was tolerably good for this season of the year; as for wood, we had brought along a little, knowing the spot where we should encamp, would be destitute of timber. – We are now able to move considerably faster than we have hither to done, in consequence of our reinforcement of horses from W. Quarters. –

Saturday the 23d.

Warm & pleasant day. We were obliged to throw a quantity of grass into this creek before crossing it, on account of the bed of the stream being somewhat miry. – After this it being just sunrise, we continued our journey. – Travelling over a rolling prairie we at length reached the "Loup Fork of Platte River" at 3 P. M. & encamped on its banks, having come 22 miles to-day. – This place is some 3 or 4 miles above the ford of the ox teams, & about 20 miles above our old ford. – The river seems to be much lower than when we were here before. – There is considerable small cotton wood growing on either bank at this point; also on the islands adjacent. – The grass here was not very good being mostly of the tall, rank kind. –

Sunday the 24th.

Clear weather, though extremely cold & windy. – Two wagons made several attempts to cross the river this a.m. which all proved ineffectual, on account of the high winds, & quicksand giving way beneath the horses' feet. – One or two horsemen also while urging their horses across the stream, were thrown from their backs, on account of their stumbling & sinking in the sand; it was therefore decided to defer fording the river, until to-morrow when the wind might cease, & we have a better chance for crossing. Accordingly we drove our teams about a mile down the river, & encamped at 10 a.m. on its banks near a small grove of cottonwood trees, where we were considerably sheltered from the cold wind that continued to blow fiercely through the day. It snowed to-night. –

Monday the 25th.

This morning the weather was quite warm & but little air stirring. We therefore went back to the same place & commenced crossing the river about 10 a.m. Men had been previously sent ahead to stake out a track for us to follow, which, after a few of the wagons had passed over, became quite firm. We were obliged, however, to double teams, & in some cases, a number of men were obliged to accompany the wagons, wading in the water to assist them through. Bro. Heber & myself both did this & were quite chilled through, the water being extremely cold, though not very high, coming up only to the bottom of the lowest wagon beds. We finally got over, without accident, about noon, when we proceeded 8 miles, & came to a small creek on the bottom. Here we noticed quite an extent of ground that had formerly been under cultivation by the Pawnees. After crossing this, & ascending a hill, we encamped at ½ past 3 P. M. upon the site of an Old Pawnee village, which had been burned down by the Sioux several years since – Here we found the grass & other vegetation quite green, affording first rate feed for our horses. We also found plenty of fuel from the ruins of the lodges. This evening, by council, the following men went ahead on horseback to Winter Quarters, to apprise the brethren there that were close by, & that to allay the anxiety that they might feel at our prolonged absence from home: – Amasa Lyman, Luman H. Calkins, J. Matthews, & Thos. Wolsey, John Buchanan, & 2 of the Frenchmen also accompanied them. I wrote a letter for Bro. Heber to Vilate, encouraging her to be of good cheer &c. for we should be with them in about a week[202] –

Tuesday the 26th.

Rather cold & cloudy weather. We arose early this morning, & got started at sunrise. Proceeding 9 miles, we forded a large tributary of the "Loup Fork," about 8 rods in width. Ascending a hill, we now passed the Old Pawnee village, opposite our old fording place. Going a mile

202. It had taken the eastbound companies at least a week to ten days longer to make the return trip to Winter Quarters than anticipated in part because of stolen horses, time spent talking to the various companies of the Big Camp, and other factors.

further, we passed a Missionary station, consisting of 5 or 6 buildings, that had been built since we were here before. It was now entirely deserted; the Sioux having paid it a visit about the last of July, when they tore down the fences & picquets, enclosing the houses, demolished the doors, stove in the heads of flour barrels, & scattered their contents on the ground, & destroyed other property in divers ways too numerous to mention. After leaving this behind, we went on a mile further, & encamped at 2 P. M. near the Old Missionary station, where we encamped on our journey out, having come 13 miles to-day. In an adjacent cornfield, we put our horses, where we gleaned considerable corn that had not been gathered. Some of the brethren also got quite a quantity to eat. Near the field, there was quite a large patch of oats, which our American horses devoured quite greedily, though the Indian ones did not care so much about it. – To-day, Bro. Heber let me have his Prince Horse to work before my wagon in the place of John Buchanan's.

WEDNESDAY THE 27TH.

Rather cool weather. We got started at 8 a.m. Proceeding 6 miles, we forded "Beaver Creek." Thence going 9 miles we forded "Looking Glass Creek" & halted to bait, at 2 P. M., on its banks, having come 15 miles. – At 3 P. M., we again went on – After going about 10 m's, we encamped, at sunset, on the banks of a slough, below "Sarpee's Trading Post," near the place where we were visited by the Pawnees when we halted at noon, on our journey out. – the grass here was dry & poor, – consequently we cut down cotton wood trees for our horses. – We made 25 miles today. Orson & myself stood guard, 1st watch.

THURSDAY THE 28TH.

Cold & windy day. – We continued our journey at 8 a. m. After going 10 miles, we made a brief halt to water our horses, when proceeding 10 miles further, we encamped at 4 P. M., on the banks of "Shell Creek," having come 20 miles. Here the grass was poor, & the brethren again cut cotton wood for their horses, which, however, was not very plenty, the timber on this stream being mostly elm. From this point, we can see this evening that the prairie has been lately burned over as far as the eye can extend. Another stray ox was found, this evening, by the brethren, near here –

FRIDAY THE 29TH.

Warm, though windy weather. The camp was routed by the guard at 5 a.m., & we got started a short time before sunrise. – After a mile's travel, we halted on the banks of the river, where there was plenty of cotton wood trees, of which we cut down a large supply for our horses. A number of men with wagons went ahead from here to select a good camp ground for the night. – After remaining here about 2 hours we again went on. We halted only once during the day to water our horses, & encamped at 5 P. M. on the banks of the "Platte River," having come 25 miles to-day. Here also there was a large quantity of cotton wood which we made use of for our horses. Near here was a "liberty pole," raised by P. P. Pratt & J. Taylor on their journey out.[203] – We have travelled altogether over burnt prairie to-day, & encamped on the same to-night. –

SATURDAY THE 30TH.

Still warm & windy weather. – We arose early, fed our horses heartily upon cotton wood bark, & got under way by 9 a. m. travelling 12 miles we came to the "Elk Horn river." which we forded about 12 or 15 miles above our old ford, & after proceeding a mile down the stream, we encamped at 2 P. M., on its banks, in a large grove of cotton wood, having come about 13 miles to-day. – This stream was considerably high, so that we were obliged to elevate our wagon beds before crossing it. – Immediately after we were encamped, the brethren were called together in the center of the ring, when Pres't. Young said that he wished to know who wanted to go ahead to Winter Quarters, to-night, & if there were any such to arise – none however did. – An expression was then taken whether we should all remain in a body, horsemen & all, & go into town together or otherwise; which resulted in the affirmative. – Pres't Young & Bro. Heber then spoke briefly, stating that they were satisfied with the conduct of the Pioneers during the journey of the past season, & blessed them in the name of the Lord; & soon after we were dismissed with the injunction to provide plenty of cotton wood for our horses during the night. – Bro. Heber let me have a little flour to-night, as my provisions had all given out. –

SUNDAY THE 31ST

They arrived home early the evening following, Sunday, October 31st. When within a mile or so of Winter Quarters "a halt was called, the company was drawn up in order, and addressed by President Young who then dismissed the pioneer camp with his blessing." Many of the brethren and sisters went out to meet them. They drove into town in order and the streets were lined with men, women and children to welcome them "home again."

When we saw them safe back our joy was equal to our sorrows. We could doubly realize why the Lord had so moved upon us to fast and pray, uniting our faith as one in their behalf, as well as for ourselves during their absence; and that it had been nothing less than miraculous that so many were preserved to meet again, saying nothing of the prosperity which had attended us. Many of our people had previously turned their attention to the manufacturing of various articles, such as willow baskets, washboards, half bushels, etc. which they sold to help themselves to a living and preparing for their journey the coming spring.

---

203. Liberty Poles were a common feature amongst most overland pioneers. Bedecked with flags of one sort or another, liberty poles served as rallying places for several Mormon settlements. They were well-known features at Winter Quarters and in the early Salt Lake settlements. See Richard E. Bennett, "The Star-Spangled Banner Forever Be Furled: The Mormon Exodus as Liberty," *Nauvoo Journal* 10, no. 1 (Spring 1998): 21–40. The Mormon banner was primarily a pure white flag.

No picture of despair had been visible, nor were there any doubts entertained of the accomplishment of the journey laying before us, and the building up of Zion in the valleys of the Rocky Mountains. The hand of God had been visible in every trial and to those who sought Him He was ever near.

I will now say to my kind friends and all who have taken an interest in the historical sketches which I have gathered up that the changes which have come to me since I began this pleasant duty, the increase of care and responsibilities thrown upon me through the death of my husband, with various duties which require my attention, I must resign this one at least at the present, as I find it difficult to devote the amount of time and thought which it requires and attend to the tasks incumbent upon me. But I do so with the hope that it will be taken up by some one of our sisters who has more time at her command, as well as ability to do it justice. There are many unwritten incidents which could be related with profit, and prove interesting reading to those who pioneered across the barren, trackless wastes of the great American desert to these once lone and dreary vales of the Rocky Mountains, as well as scores who are not of that number and even many strangers would enjoy reading of those early scenes among the "Mormons." Had I not received this assurance from different quarters in these valleys as well as from outsiders accompanied with urgent requests to continue these sketches, I should have long since yielded to private feelings and discontinued them. I mention this as a stimulus to prompt others to write and give to the world the benefit of their travels and experience with this people, who are so grossly misunderstood and misjudged by the world generally. For every one of us have a mission upon this earth, and it is only the willing hands and hearts, and those who will sacrifice self to the good of others that will gain an everlasting triumph, and be crowned to reign throughout the glorious eternities to come.

Woman's Exponent, vol. 15, no. 6,
15 August 1886, pp. 46–47

Glossary

People Mentioned in the Journals and Reminiscences

Editor's note: The names of the individuals listed below are found within the Horace K. Whitney journals and the selected reminiscences recorded herein from his wife Helen Mar Kimball Whitney. The list is extensive but not exhaustive since a few names are unidentifiable because of missing first names, possible misspellings of surnames, misidentifications with those of the same last name, or because the individuals are very obscure and are lost to history. Other than from the journals themselves, information has been gleaned from reliable primary and secondary sources.

Adams, Barnabas L. (1812–69), was born in Canada. One of the original pioneers to Utah, Adams traveled to the Salt Lake Valley with the Brigham Young vanguard company. On the trek west, he served as captain of the night guard. He was a timberman, furnishing lumber for several buildings in Salt Lake, including the theater and the Tabernacle. He died in June 1869 in Salt Lake City after a logging accident.

Adams, George J. (1811–80), was a Methodist preacher before being baptized into the Church of Jesus Christ of Latter-day Saints in 1840. He served faithfully as a missionary in England and became a member of the Council of Fifty in Nauvoo. After Joseph Smith's death, Adams was excommunicated for advocating that Joseph Smith III, under the guardianship of William Smith, should success to church leadership. He then joined the Church of Jesus Christ of Latter Day Saints (Strangite) and became a member of its First Presidency. After leaving the Strangites, he organized the Church of the Messiah and led an ill-fated effort in 1865 to establish a colony of Americans in Palestine to await the Second Coming of Christ. He died in Philadelphia in 1880.

Allen, James (1806–46), primary recruiter of the Mormon Battalion, had been a captain in the US Army since 1837. A native of Ohio, he graduated from West Point Military Academy in 1829, in the same class as Robert E. Lee and Joseph E. Johnston. He had accompanied Henry R. Schoolcraft in his 1832 expedition to find the headwaters of the Mississippi River. In 1842 he was assigned to Fort Atkinson in Iowa Territory to supervise the Sac and Fox Indian agency. Between 1842 and 1845, he traveled extensively all over Iowa Territory. Allen died unexpectedly 24 August 1846.

Allen, Rufus (1815–87), was born in Litchfield, Connecticut. Baptized in 1835, he became president of the Seventy-Sixth Quorum of Seventy. In 1838 he petitioned Governor Boggs, asking him to put a stop to the attacks against the Latter-day Saints by the mobs. He came to Utah with the Brigham Young company in 1847. In 1851 he opened the Chilean Mission. He died in December 1887 in Riverdale, Utah.

Ames, Ira V. (1804–69), was born in Vermont and joined the church in New York. He moved to Kirtland, Far West, and Nauvoo with the Saints and emigrated to Utah in 1851. He was a merchant and farmer. He died in Wellsville, Utah, in 1869.

Anderson, William (1809–46), was born in Lincoln, Maine. As a youth, he had many spiritual manifestations and dreamed that he was to be a minister of the gospel. He searched many different faiths but was dissatisfied and unable to find the truth for over a decade. He was baptized in 1841 and was ordained a seventy. He then began preaching, and baptized several people. He was one of three Mormons killed in the Battle of Nauvoo in September 1846.

Andrus (Andrews), Milo (1814–93), was born in Wilmington, New York. Baptized in 1832, he was a member of Zion's Camp and was later ordained a seventy. He served several missions for the church, including two to England and one promoting Joseph Smith's presidential campaign. He helped build the Kirtland, Nauvoo, Salt Lake, and Saint George Temples. Nicknamed the "eloquent expounder" for his effective sermonizing, he served briefly as stake president in St. Louis. A polygamist, he had eleven wives and fifty-seven children. He also brought several companies of Saints to Utah, where he served as a patriarch. A road, canal, and railway builder, he died in June 1893 in Idaho.

Angell, Truman O. (1810–87), was born in Providence, Rhode Island. Baptized in 1833 along with his wife, Polly, he was later ordained a seventy. He worked as a carpenter on the Nauvoo Temple before immigrating to Utah in 1847 with the Brigham Young pioneer company. After his arrival, he served as church architect for several years, supervising the building of the Salt Lake Temple. He also played a major role in the building of the Salt Lake Tabernacle and the St. George, Logan, and Manti Temples. He died in October 1887 in Salt Lake City, Utah.

Atwood, Millen (1817–1890), was born in Connecticut. He went to Nauvoo in 1841 to investigate the church and was baptized there. Being a stonemason, he did a great deal of work on the Nauvoo Temple. He was a member of the vanguard and return companies in 1847. He returned to Nauvoo early in 1848 to recover some of his construction tools, later returning to Salt Lake City, where he served as a policeman. On his way home from a mission in England in 1856, he became a member of Captain James T. Willie's ill-fated handcart company. He served as a bishop until his death in Salt Lake City.

Babbitt, Almon W. (1812–56), was born in Massachusetts. He joined the church in 1833 and participated in Zion's Camp. He then served as a stake president in Kirtland, Ohio, in 1841. A lawyer, he served in the Illinois legislature. He was one of the three trustees appointed to liquidate church property in Nauvoo, before leaving for Utah in 1848. There he served in the Utah territorial government. A highly contentious figure, Babbitt was disfellowshipped from the church multiple times. He was killed by Cheyenne Indians in Nebraska in September 1856.

Backenstos, Jacob B. (1813–75), was born in Pennsylvania and was the well-known non-Mormon sheriff of Hancock County, Illinois, at the time of Joseph Smith's martyrdom. His wife, Clara Wasson, was the niece of Emma Smith, and Clara and Jacob were married by Joseph Smith in 1843. On numerous occasions he defended the Saints, often at the peril of his own life. Jacob died in July 1875 in Iowa City, Iowa.

Badger, Rodney (1823–53), was born in Vermont. He joined the church in 1835 and was one of the original pioneers to Utah in 1847. A member of Utah Territory's Nauvoo Legion, he served as constable and deputy sheriff in Salt Lake County. He died in 1853 by drowning in the Weber River while trying to save a family from distress.

Barkman, Charles, was a fur trader whom the Saints met on the Platte River Road as he was heading east on May 4, 1846. He and his company carried letters back to Winter Quarters. No further information is available on this individual.

Barney, Lewis (1808–94), was born in New York. He joined the church in 1840 and was later ordained a seventy. He worked on the Nauvoo Temple, was one of the original pioneers to Utah, and was a hunter for the company. He helped to settle several areas of Utah, Arizona, New Mexico, and Colorado. He died in November 1894 in Colorado.

Barnham [Barnum], Charles (1800–94), was born in Canada. Baptized in 1836, he was one of the original pioneers to Utah in 1847. He died in Salt Lake City in 1894.

Bartholomew, Noah Willis (1808–76), was born in New York. Baptized in 1844, he traveled to Utah in 1848. In 1852 he was elected a selectman in Millard County. The first bishop of Fillmore, Utah, he died there in August 1876.

Beach, Rufus (1795–1850), was born in Roxbury, Connecticut. Baptized in 1839, he became the president of the Twenty-Seventh Quorum of the Seventy in Nauvoo in 1845. He came to Utah in 1847. He later continued west and died in California in 1850.

Bealy, Dr. (dates unknown). No information is available.

Beaubien, Charles H. (1800–64), a French-Canadian fur trader, was born in Nicolet, Lower Canada (Quebec). He migrated to the United States as a very young man. As early as 1820 he worked in the fur business in St. Louis, Missouri, with the Chouteau family, traveling all over the West. After the Mexican-American War, he became an early governor of the new American territory of New Mexico. He died at age sixty-three in Taos, New Mexico.

Benson, Ezra T. (1811–69), was born in Mendon, Massachusetts. He was baptized near Quincy, Illinois, in 1840 and was ordained an apostle at Council Bluffs in 1846. A contractor, postmaster, and hotelkeeper, he came to Utah in 1847 with the Brigham Young company as a captain of ten. In company with Orson Hyde and George A. Smith, he presided over the Saints in Kanesville in 1849, constantly advocating their removal to the Salt Lake Valley. He served several terms as a member of the Utah territorial legislature. He died in September 1869 in Ogden, Utah.

Bent, Samuel (1778–1846), was born in Barre, Massachusetts. Baptized in 1833, he later served as a member of Zion's Camp and moved with the Saints to Far West, Missouri. In Nauvoo, he was a member of the Nauvoo Legion and the Council of Fifty. He also served as the presiding officer of the church at Garden Grove, Iowa, where he died in August 1846.

Bernhisel, John M. (1799–1881), was born in Tyrone, Pennsylvania. A physician by profession, he became a bishop in Nauvoo in 1841. A close personal friend of Joseph Smith, he was a charter member of the Council of Fifty. He immigrated to Utah in 1851. He was Utah Territory's first delegate to Congress, an office he held for ten years. He died in September 1881 in Salt Lake City.

Billings, George Pierce (1827–96), was born in Kirtland, Ohio. He was in the first pioneer company to Utah in 1847. Cousin of Heber C. Kimball, he died in December 1896 in Manti, Utah, and is buried at the foot of the Manti Temple.

Billings, Sister, is likely Diantha Morley (1796–1879), wife of Titus Billings. She was born in Massachusetts and joined the church in 1830 with her husband. She traveled with the Saints and served as a respected midwife. She died in May 1879 in Provo, Utah.

Billings, Titus (1793–1866), was born in Greenfield, Massachusetts. He was baptized in 1830, the second person in Sidney Rigdon's congregation there to join the church. He was a stonemason, a carpenter, and a musician. He moved to Jackson County, Missouri, and participated in the united order covenant there with Edward Partridge, later serving as his counselor in the bishopric in 1837. He took part in the Battle of Crooked River in 1838 and later served as captain and colonel in the Nauvoo Legion. He immigrated to Utah in 1848 and helped found the city of Manti. He died in January 1866 in Provo, Utah.

Bird, Charles (1803–84), was born in New Jersey. He joined the church in 1836. He served as a member of the Nauvoo Legion and also as a bodyguard to Joseph Smith. He was instrumental in negotiating with the native Indian tribes on behalf of the church. After immigrating to Utah, he settled in Mendon, where he served as mayor and justice of the peace. He died in September 1884 in Mendon, Utah.

Black, Miss, is likely Martha (Patsy) Brown (1798–1869), who was born in North Carolina. She came to Utah in 1848. Shortly afterward, she and her family moved west to California, presumably in 1849 in search of gold. She died in 1869 in California.

Boggs, Francis (1807–89), was born in Ohio. He was baptized in 1841. He and his family moved to Nauvoo, where he worked as a carpenter. They followed the Saints to Winter Quarters where he became part of the vanguard company. He lived in several Utah communities and filled a farming and lead-mining mission to Las Vegas. He served one term in the Utah legislature. He died in Washington, Utah.

Bordeaux, James (1814–78), a native of France, came to St. Louis, Missouri, in his youth, where he married an Indian woman of the Oto tribe. After her death, he went west, eager for adventure. An early fur trader called "the Bear" by the Indians, Bordeaux was appointed by Frederick Laboue of the American Fur Company in 1837 to superintend the operation of Fort Laramie, a prime trading post on the Platte River. He was the acting authority of Old Fort Laramie when the Saints first arrived there in 1847. In 1872, Bordeaux abandoned his western interests and moved to Fort Randall on the Missouri, where he had several government contracts with the army. He died in South Dakota in 1878.

Boss, David (1797–1873), was born in Davidson, North Carolina. He came to Utah in 1847. Later, he and his family moved west to California, presumably in 1849 in search of gold. He died there in April 1873.

Boynton, John F. (1811–90), was born in Bradford, Massachusetts. He served a mission for the church in 1832 and was ordained one of the original Apostles in February 1835. Following his excommunication from the church over financial disagreements with Joseph Smith and after two years living in California, he moved to Syracuse, New York, where he died in 1890.

Brannan, Samuel (1819–89), was born in Saco, Maine. He joined the church in Kirtland, Ohio, in 1833, where he worked on the temple. A printer by trade, he published the Mormon newspaper entitled the *Prophet* in New York City in 1842 before leading a company of 230 Saints by ship (the *Brooklyn*) in 1846 to Yerba Buena (San Francisco, California), just as the main body of the Saints were en route to Utah. His attempts to persuade Brigham Young to relocate to California instead of Utah proved unsuccessful. Fiercely independent, Brannan remained in California and amassed a fortune with the discovery of gold there in 1849. Hard living, unwise investments, and divorce led to his estrangement from the church. California's "first millionaire" died bankrupt, sorrowful, and penniless in May 1889 in Escondido, California.

Bridger, James ("Jim") Felix (1804–81), was born in Richmond, Virginia. He was among the foremost mountain men, trappers, trailblazers, and guides between 1820 and 1850. He first traveled up the Missouri River in 1822 and gradually scouted all over the Intermountain West. He was one of the first white men to see Cache Valley and the Great Salt Lake. A friend of many Indian tribes, he founded the trading post Fort Bridger in 1843. The coming of the Mormons was a bittersweet experience for Bridger, ensuring greater trade with incoming settlers but reducing the Indian fur trade. He sold his fort to Brigham Young and the Saints in 1855 for $8,000. He died in Independence, Missouri, in 1881.

Brimhall, John (1824–1906), was born in New York. He was baptized in 1845 and became a member of the Mormon Battalion. He helped to make the first adobe homes in the Salt Lake valley. He died in Glendale, Utah, in December 1906.

Brockman, Thomas Patterson (1797–1859), born in Greenville District, South Carolina, was a merchant, planter, and state militia colonel. He was known for his Unionist sentiments, despite the fact he owned slaves. As a state senator, he supported various measures of compromise and, in so doing helped delay the Civil War. Tragically, both of his sons were killed while serving as Confederate soldiers during that eventual conflict. He died in South Carolina in 1859.

Brown, Elisabeth (1790–1870), wife of Robert Crow, was a cousin of John Brown. She was born in South Carolina. She gave birth to nine children, including twins. She died at Pinto Creek, Utah.

Brown, George Washington (1827–90), was born in Ohio. His mother joined the church in New York, and Brown was later baptized in Sugar Creek, Iowa. He was chosen for the first pioneer company and the return company. After farming in Missouri for two years, he returned to the Salt Lake Valley in 1850 with his mother and siblings. He married and settled in the Wasatch County area of Utah, where he farmed and was later ordained a high priest. He died in Charleston, Utah.

Brown, John (1820–96), was born in Sumner County, Tennessee, and joined the church in Illinois in 1841. He headed a large group of southern Latter-day Saints, including four slaves, who came west from Mississippi in 1846, spending the winter of 1846–47 at Pueblo, Colorado, before joining Brigham Young's advance company in the spring of 1847. He served at least two missions for the church—in the

Southern States Mission and in Great Britain. He served as a member of the territorial legislature and later as mayor and bishop in Pleasant Grove, Utah, where he died in November 1896.

Brown, Nathaniel Thomas (d. 1848), was born in Ohio. He, along with Orrin Porter Rockwell and others, was a hunter for Brigham Young's vanguard company and rounded up lost animals. He returned to Winter Quarters in the fall of 1847, where he was accidentally shot at Council Bluffs, Iowa, in February 1848. Brigham Young purportedly said of him, "Brown's old shoes were worth more than the whole body of the man who killed him."

Buchanan, John (1825–97), was born in Kentucky. He was baptized in 1838 and was later ordained a seventy. He served as a corporal in the Mormon Battalion and immigrated to Utah in 1847. He helped to lead the sick detachments of the battalion to Utah, along with Amasa Lyman. He died in October 1897 in Manti, Utah.

Buel, Prescindia Lathrop Huntington (1810–92), was born in New York. She and her first husband joined the church in Kirtland in 1836. They followed the Saints from there to Missouri and Illinois. Prescindia was sealed to Joseph Smith in 1841 and then to Heber C. Kimball after the martyrdom. Her first husband, with whom she had continued to live after both sealings, refused to go west with the Saints, and she made the decision to leave him. She later had two children by Heber C. Kimball. She died in Salt Lake City.

Bullock, Thomas (1816–85), was born in England and joined the church there in 1840. He was later ordained a seventy and also served as a clerk and scribe to Joseph Smith. He immigrated to Utah with the original Brigham Young company in 1847 and served as the official camp clerk. After his arrival in Utah, he served as the clerk of Salt Lake and Summit Counties, in the territorial House of Representatives, and in the Church Historian's office. He was one of the first four men to publish the first edition of the *Deseret News*. He died in 1885 in Coalville, Utah.

Burdick, Thomas (1797–1877), was born in New York. Baptized in 1834, he served as the clerk of the high council, as well as a bishop in Kirtland. He died in November 1877 in California.

Burgess, Harrison (1814–83), was born in New York. He was baptized in 1832 and was ordained a seventy in 1835. After coming to Utah, he was appointed to serve as a bishop in Pine Valley. He died there in February of 1883.

Burke, Charles (1823–88), was born in Kirtland, Ohio. A carpenter by trade, he moved to Nauvoo in 1841 and helped build the Nauvoo Temple. Burke was a seventy and one of the original pioneers to Utah, and he and his wife helped settle San Bernardino from 1851 to 1857, when they were called back to Utah because of the Utah War. He died in February 1888 in Minersville, Utah.

Burnham, Jacob D. (1820–50), born in New York, was baptized in 1844. His wife and daughter died at Winter Quarters. He traveled to Utah with the Brigham Young company in 1847 but continued on to California. He died apparently while mining for gold in Greenwood Valley in 1850.

Burns, Thomas R. (1824–?), was a private in the Mormon Battalion. He is known to have come west to Utah in 1848.

Burroughs (dates unknown), was a friend of Luke Johnson from Ohio. No further information is available for this person.

Busby, Joseph (1810–99), was born in Pennsylvania. He was baptized in 1841 and was ordained a seventy. He came to Utah in 1848 and, in 1850, was called to serve a mission in the Society Islands. After his return, he served as a foreman in the Utah territorial legislature. He was excommunicated from the church in the early 1880s but was rebaptized in 1893. He died in 1899 in Salt Lake City.

Butler, John Lowe (1808–61), was born in Simpson, Kentucky, and was converted by James Emmett in 1835. A blacksmith, farmer, teacher, fireman, and policeman, he may be best remembered for being one of the principle participants at the election day fighting at Gallatin, Daviess County, Missouri, in 1838. He also served two missions among the Sioux Indians in 1841. After migrating to Utah in 1852, he served as the second bishop of Spanish Fork and died there in April 1861 after a lengthy illness.

Byard (or Baird), Robert (1817–75), was born in Ireland. He was baptized in 1842 and was later ordained a seventy. A farmer and a tailor, he immigrated to Utah with the first pioneer company and later settled in Ogden. There he served as a justice of the peace and as a city councilman. He died in August 1875 in Lynne, Utah.

Cahoon, Andrew (1824–1900), was born in Ashtabula, Ohio. He was the son of Thirza Stiles and Reynolds Cahoon, counselor to Bishop Newel K. Whitney. He was baptized in 1832 and made a bishop in Salt Lake City in 1854. He died in December 1900 in Murray, Utah.

Cahoon D. (Daniel) Stiles (1822–1903), was born in Kirtland, Ohio, the son of Thirza and Reynolds Cahoon. His wife was Jane Amanda Spencer and this daughter born 8 August 1846 at Winter Quarters was Sarah Cahoon. He immigrated to Utah in 1849. He died in Millard County, Utah.

Cahoon, Father (probably Reynolds) (1790–1861), was born in New York. He was baptized in Kirtland, Ohio, by Parley P. Pratt. He held many leadership positions in the church and was mentioned four times in the Doctrine and Covenants. He was a member of the Council of Fifty. He died in Salt Lake County.

Cahoon, William (1813–93), was born in Harpersfield, Ohio. Baptized in 1830, he was a member of the First Quorum of the Seventy in 1835. After crossing the plains in 1849, he worked as a temple carpenter and joiner on multiple temples. He died in April 1893 in Salt Lake City.

Cain (dates unknown). Individual unidentified.

Calkins, Luman Hopkins (1816–93), was born in Marcellus, New York. He served as a member of a bishopric in Winter Quarters. He chose to disassociate himself from Brigham Young and the rest of the Saints and followed "Father" Alpheus Cutler and his band of disciples, who were intent on reestablishing Zion in Independence, Missouri, through an alliance with various Plains Indians tribes. He settled in Fisher's Grove (later Manti), Iowa, for some time. He died in October 1893 in Oregon.

Camp, James Greer (1828–52), was born in Alabama or Tennessee. There is no record of his baptism, but his mother was baptized in 1842 and the family lived in Nauvoo. Camp joined the Mormon Battalion and was sent back to Pueblo with the sick detachment. He arrived in the valley with that company and was also part of the return company. He died in Tennessee.

Canfield, Cyrus Culver (1817–89), was born in Columbus, Ohio, moved to Nauvoo, and served a mission in Illinois in 1843. After serving in the Mormon Battalion, he came to Utah in 1849 and was an early resident of Ogden. He was excommunicated from the church in San Bernardino in 1856 and remained in California, where he became a successful fruit grower. He died in Stillwater, Nevada, in 1889.

Carrell, William Thomas (1819–92), was born in Tennessee. He died in Wayne County, Utah. It is not known how he arrived in Utah in 1847. He is not listed in any of the companies that travelled to the Salt Lake Valley in 1847.

Carrington, Albert (1813–89), was born in Royalton, Vermont. He was baptized in 1841 while living in Wisconsin. Later, he was one of the original pioneers to Utah, where he served in the Utah territorial legislature. A graduate of Dartmouth College and trained in the law, he worked as editor of the *Deseret News* for eight years before being called as a member of the Quorum of the Twelve Apostles in 1870 and later as an additional counselor to President Brigham Young. He served two terms as president of the European Mission. He was excommunicated from the church in 1885 but was rebaptized two years later. He died in 1889 in Salt Lake City.

Carter, "Mrs." (b. 1799). The Mrs. Carter referred to in the text was likely Lydia Kenyon Carter, who married Simeon Carter in 1818. They had three children. After removing to Nauvoo, she was sealed to Heber C. Kimball. She later remarried James Goff in 1851 "for time only," after moving to Utah.

Carter, Simeon Dagget (1794–1869). Born in Connecticut, he was baptized in Ohio in early 1831 and soon served several missions. He was president of the Big Blue River Branch of the church in Jackson County, Missouri, in 1833 before the Saints were driven out. He lived in Lee County, Iowa, during the Nauvoo era and went west in 1849. He helped found Brigham City, Utah, in 1850.

Carter, William (1821–96), was born in England. He was baptized in 1840. He emigrated to Nauvoo in 1841 and helped build the Nauvoo Temple. After being chosen for the first pioneer group, his wife became deathly ill, but Brigham Young promised she would live if he would go west. When Carter returned to Winter Quarters, he found her well. They were later called to settle Dixie, where he directed the work for the foundation of the St. George Temple. He served as a temple worker there, dying in 1896.

Case, James (1794–1860), was born in Connecticut. Before his conversion, he was a former Presbyterian minister who had spent at least a year among the Pawnee at the Presbyterian Indian Mission at Loup Fork River (Plum Creek) in Nebraska. He was, therefore, a trusted advisor to Brigham Young in dealing with the Pawnee Indians. He was one of the original pioneers to Utah in 1847. After his arrival, he served in the Utah territorial legislature. He later served as a missionary in the Indian Territory in Oklahoma. He died in Manti, Utah, in 1860.

Chamberlain, Solomon (1788–1862), was born in Connecticut. He joined the church in 1830 just a few days after the church was organized. But even before that time, he had been preaching the gospel in upstate New York and Upper Canada (Ontario) from pages of the not-yet-published Book of Mormon. He lived in Kirtland, Ohio; Jackson County, Missouri; and Nauvoo, Illinois, and was one of the original pioneers to Utah. He traveled to California to mine for gold in 1850, then returned to Utah. He died in 1862 in Washington, Utah.

Chesney, James Albert (about 1824–69), was born in Missouri. He was a member of the Robert Crow company. He was listed as single and as a laborer in the 1860 Federal Census. He died in Salt Lake City.

Chessley, Alexander P. (1814–84), was born in Virginia. He was one of the original pioneers to Utah. He settled in Provo and there served as a lawyer, constable, and teacher. He served a mission to Australia in 1856, where he died in 1884.

Clark, George Sheffer (1816–1901), was born in Ohio. Baptized in the Mississippi River in 1843, he became a member of the Mormon Battalion and returned to Pueblo with the sick detachment. He was one of only two sick detachment members to catch up to the vanguard company before they entered the valley on July 24. Sick with Rocky Mountain spotted fever, he rode into the valley in one of Young's wagons. He was part of the return company in the fall. He emigrated to Utah in 1850 and settled in Pleasant Grove, where he was the first bishop in Pleasant Grove. He later served a mission to Australia from 1856 to 1858. He died in August 1901 in Pleasant Grove.

Clark, Hiram (1795–1853), was born in Wells, Vermont. Baptized in 1835, he served a mission to Europe and was later called as the first president of the Hawaiian Mission. Unfortunately, his presidency was not a success, and he left the islands discouraged. He died in 1853.

Clayton, James (1824–47), was born in England. He died in November 1847 in Winter Quarters, Nebraska.

Clayton, William (1814–79), was baptized in England in 1837. In 1840 he and his family migrated to join the Saints in Nauvoo. A trusted friend of the Prophet Joseph Smith, in 1842 he succeeded Willard Richards as Smith's clerk and personal secretary. He was present when the Prophet received the revelation on celestial marriage, and, under the direction of the Prophet, he transcribed that revelation as well as others. William crossed the plains with the Brigham Young company and kept a journal in which he meticulously recorded many important events. He wrote several hymns, the most notable being "Come, Come, Ye Saints." He died in December 1879 in Salt Lake City.

Cloward, Thomas P. (1823–1909), was born in Pennsylvania. Baptized in 1842, he was one of the original pioneers to Utah in 1847. He settled in Utah County, where he worked as a shoemaker. He died in January 1909 in Payson, Utah.

Collins, Robert (1822–89), was born in England. He was a member of the seventy and later served in the Mormon Battalion. He died in December 1889 in Salt Lake City, Utah.

Coltrin, Zebedee (1804–87), was born in New York and was baptized in 1831. He served as a counselor in the Kirtland Stake presidency and also as a president of the seventy. He was a man given to dreams and visions. His remembrances of Joseph Smith Jr. were solicited years after he came to Utah in 1847 with the Brigham Young company. In his later life he served as a patriarch. He died in July 1887 in Spanish Fork, Utah.

Coolidge, Joseph Wellington (1814–71), was born in Bangor, Maine. He served as a member of the Council of Fifty and also served for a time as the administrator of Joseph Smith's estate. He died in January of 1871 in Glenwood, Iowa.

Corbett, Thomas (1807–76), was born in England. He died in March 1876 in Salt Lake City.

Covert, William Spencer (1808–99), was born in New York. He was baptized in 1838 and later ordained a seventy. He was endowed in the Nauvoo Temple and migrated in the Heber C. Kimball company to Utah in 1848. He died in November 1899 in Holladay, Utah.

Craig, James (1821–68), was born in Ireland. He was baptized in 1844. Assigned to awaken the pioneer camp each morning with his bugle, he was known as the "Bugler of the Pioneers." In 1861 he was called to help colonize southern Utah. He settled in Santa Clara, Utah, where he later died.

Craig, John (1804?–1870?), of Ray County, Missouri. He was part of a group of overlanders who consisted of Craig, Samuel Truitt from Shelby County, Illinois, and two unidentified California immigrants. Craig had set out with only two wagons and seven other men to travel from Fort Hall to California in the spring of 1846. Wilford Woodruff learned from this party that a woman he had baptized was among the dead of the Donner party.

Crosby, Oscar (about 1815–70), was born to a female slave of William Crosby, one of the Mississippi converts. Oscar, like many Mississippi converts, was apparently baptized at Mormon Springs, Mississippi, sometime before 1845. Brigham Young requested Oscar's help in the first company, and his master consented. After the company's arrival in the valley, Oscar Crosby built a cabin and planted a garden for the Crosby family. In 1851, he helped settle San Bernardino, California. Crosby became a free man in California, and his former master helped him get established. He died in Los Angeles.

Crow, Benjamin Brown (1819–97), was born in Illinois. He resided for a time in Santa Clara, Utah. He died in Idaho.

Crow, Elizabeth Jane (about 1838–?), the youngest child of Robert and Elisabeth Crow, was born in Illinois. Like many in her family, she eventually made her home in California.

Crow, Harriet Brunt (about 1819), was born in Illinois. Death unknown.

Crow, Ira (or Isa) Vinda Exene (1833–51), was born in Illinois. She and her twin sister, Ira Minda Almarene, accompanied their father, Robert Crow, to Utah. Isa married James Charles Humphries. She died in Oregon.

Crow, Ira Minda Almarene (1833–60), was born in Illinois. She came with her father, Robert, in the advance company from Pueblo. She married Francis M. Hamblin in Santa Clara on 16 April 1859. She died in childbirth 1 January 1860 and was buried in Santa Clara.

Crow, John McHenry (b. about 1824), was born in Illinois. As a member of the return company, he later emigrated to Utah again. He never married, and he died in Clover Valley, Nevada, in 1894.

Crow, Matilda Jane (b. about 1825), was born in Illinois. She married George Therlkill. Her 3-year-old son, Milton Howard, drowned in City Creek shortly after the pioneers arrived in the valley. Matilda also delivered the second child born in the valley on 15 August 1847. She died in California in 1906.

Crow, Robert (1794–1876), was born in Tennessee. He married Elizabeth Brown, cousin of John Brown, in Perry County, Illinois, where they joined the church in 1838. Perhaps because of family connections, they and their family joined the expedition of southern Saints that went as far as Independence, Missouri, in 1846 and then wintered in Pueblo after learning that the main body of Saints would not emigrate until 1847. Anxious to meet the Saints in 1847, this small group left ahead of the rest of the Pueblo Saints and arrived at Fort Laramie two weeks ahead of Brigham Young's company. In 1849, Crow attempted to get permission to go to California to search for gold in behalf of the church but was denied. He went anyway and in 1857 led another small company back from San Bernardino to Utah. He died in California.

Crow, Walter Hamilton (1826–1905), was born in Illinois. He was baptized into the church in early boyhood and was active in church work until his death at the age of eighty years. He was the father of nine children. They lived in Washington County, Utah. He died in Woodville, Idaho.

Crow, William Parker (born about 1828) was born in Illinois. He made his home in Placer County, California. He became a successful rancher in California and died there in 1903.

Cummings, James Willard (1819–83), was born in Wilton, Maine, and was baptized in 1841. He served several missions over the course of his life and died in May 1883 in Salt Lake City.

Curtis, Lyman (1812–1898), was born in New Salem, Massachusetts. He was baptized in 1833 and was later ordained a seventy. He helped build the Kirtland temple. He was one of the original pioneers to Utah and was one of the first to build canals there. He settled and named Salem, Utah, after his birthplace. He died there in 1898.

Cushing, Hosea (1826–54), was born in Boston, Massachusetts. He was baptized in 1844. Being a joiner by vocation, he worked on the Nauvoo temple in 1845. He was a member of Utah's Nauvoo Legion. He died from the effects of starvation during the Walker Indian War in May 1854 in Salt Lake City.

Cutler, Alpheus (1784–1864), was born in Cheshire, New Hampshire, and was baptized in 1833. A stonemason by vocation, he used his skills to help construct the Kirtland and Nauvoo Temples. He served as a member of the Council of Fifty and the captain of Joseph Smith's bodyguards. He was a close friend to the Prophet, was a member of the Nauvoo High Council, and helped to carry the coffins of both Hyrum and Joseph. Cutler later rejected the leadership of Brigham Young and was excommunicated in 1851. He then organized his own church (Church of Jesus Christ), popularly known as the "Cutlerites" and believed in returning to Zion in Independence, Missouri with the aid of various Plains Indian tribes. He died in Manti, Iowa, in August of 1864.

Cutler (Kimball Fletcher), Clarissa Crissy (1824–52), was born in New York, the daughter of Lois Lathrop and Alpheus Cutler. She married Heber C. Kimball, 29 December 1845, Nauvoo, Illinois, and had one child by him. She went with the Saints to western Iowa. She later separated from Kimball and was living with her parents there in 1850. She then married Calvin Gilmore Fletcher and had one child with him. They did not go to the Salt Lake Valley but may have become members of their father's Cutlerite Church. She died at Grasshopper River near Thomasville, Jefferson County, Kansas.

Cutler, Edwin (1829–53), was born in New York. He was a son of Alpheus Cutler.

Cutler (Kimball Pratt), Emily Trask (1828–52), was born in New York, the daughter of Alpheus Cutler and Lois Lathrop. In February of 1846, she married Heber C. Kimball and had one child with him. She went with the Saints to western Iowa. In 1848, she separated from Kimball and was living with her parents there in 1850. In 1850, she married Franklin Pratt and later had one child with him. They did not go to the Salt Lake Valley but may have become members of their father's Cutlerite Church. Like her older sister Clarissa, she died in 1852 in Grasshopper, Thompsonville, Jefferson, Kansas.

Cutler, William Lathrop (1821–51), was from New York and was baptized in 1838. He was a son of John Alpheus Cutler. On the trek to the Salt Lake Valley, William served as a captain of the night guard. He served in the British Mission from 1849 to 1850. He died in 1851 in Salt Lake City.

Dalton, Charles (1810–91), was born in Wysox, Pennsylvania. He joined the church in 1838. After migrating to Utah, he served in the Salmon River Mission. He died in 1891 in Ogden, Utah.

Dana, Louis (1805–85), an Oneida Indian chief in upstate New York, converted to Mormonism in 1840. He was a member of the Council of Fifty and, as such, explored parts of the West for a possible new relocation site for the Saints. He was a particularly close friend of Alpheus Cutler and joined his Church of Jesus Christ. After living in Iowa, he moved with the Cutlerites to Clitherall, Minnesota, where he died in 1885.

Davenport, James (1802–83), was born in Vermont. He became a blacksmith and farmer. He and his wife joined the church in 1830 and received their endowments and were sealed in Nauvoo. He was chosen as a blacksmith for Brigham Young's vanguard company and subsequently stayed at the Platte River to operate the church's ferry until the second company arrived. He entered the valley with them and then returned to Winter Quarters. Emigrating with his family in 1851 or 1852 to Salt Lake City, he later moved to Grantsville and then to Cache County, where he died at the age of 81.

Davenport, John (Squire?) (1826–1902), was born in Granger, Kentucky. He was a farmer and a resident of Davis County, Utah.

Davis, Daniel (1808–92), was born in Massachusetts. He joined the church and became a seventy in 1845. He served under Sheriff Backenstos in Illinois. He died in February 1892 in Bountiful, Utah.

Davis, David (1823–?), was born in Pennsylvania. He was baptized in 1835 in Ray County, Missouri, and was married in Nauvoo in 1843. Ordained a seventy, he was endowed in the Nauvoo Temple in 1846 and later lived in Winter Quarters.

Decker, Charles (1824–1901), was from New York. He came to Utah in 1847 with the Jedediah M. Grant company. He was in the first movement of troops in the Utah War. He died in March 1901 in Vernal, Utah.

Decker, Isaac Perry (1840–1916), was born in Illinois. He was a son of Harriet Page Wheeler and one of the two children on the original 1847 pioneer trek to Utah. He was baptized in 1849. He died in 1916 in Provo, Utah, one of the last of the original pioneers to Utah.

Dewey, Benjamin Franklin (1829–1904), was born in Massachusetts. He was one of the original pioneers to Utah. He continued on to California in 1849 but then returned to Utah in 1850. He died in February 1904 in Chloride, Arizona.

Dixon, John (1818–53), was born in England. He was chosen for the vanguard and return companies. In 1850, he served a short mission to the Sandwich Islands. In 1853, he was killed by Indians while hauling wood near Parley's Park.

Donnell, Robert Washington (?–1892) was born in North Carolina and left at an early age for western Missouri, where he established a dry goods business and helped build up St. Joseph, Missouri. He eventually went into business with George Smith. He later established businesses in Montana and New York. He died in New York in 1892.

Douglas, Ralph (1824–1900), was born in England. He was baptized in 1840 and served as a member of the Mormon Battalion. He died in May 1900 in Ogden, Utah.

Driggs, Sterling (1821–60), was born in Pennsylvania. He joined the church in Ohio and immigrated to Nauvoo in 1840. He was one of the original pioneers to Utah. After migrating to Utah, he went to California to help build a settlement of Saints there. He died in December 1860 in Parowan, Utah.

Dunham, Jonathan (1800–45), was born in Paris, New York. Baptized in 1836, he served several short-term missions to various Indian tribes in Indiana, Pennsylvania, Missouri, and New York. He was a colonel and acting major general in the Nauvoo Legion as well as a captain of the Nauvoo police. As a member of the Council of Fifty, he died in 1845 while on a mission to the Indians.

Dykes, William (1815–79), was born in Pennsylvania. He traveled to Utah with the original pioneer company as a hunter. He died in Nebraska in November 1879.

Eames, Ellis (1809–82), was born in Ohio and converted to Mormonism while living in Jackson County, Missouri, in 1834. He was well known as a fiddler. After coming to Utah with the Saints, he became first mayor of Provo, Utah. He later moved to California, estranged from the church. He died in San Bernardino in October 1882.

Earl, James Calvin (1822–21), was born in Ohio. He was baptized in 1838 in Illinois. He was persecuted along with other Saints in Illinois and driven out of the state. He enlisted in the Mormon Battalion but was sent back to Pueblo with the sick detachment. He arrived in the valley with the Mississippi Saints. He and his wife had nine children. He died in Pine Valley, Utah.

Earl, Wilbur Joseph (1817–74), was born in Ohio. He was baptized in 1838. He lived in Nauvoo and was ordained a seventy. He emigrated to Utah in 1848, lived in Springville and Leeds and died in Harrisburg, Utah.

Eastman, Ozro French (1828–1916), was born in Vermont. He was one of the original pioneers to Utah. He died in March 1916 in Idaho Falls, Idaho.

Edwards, William Holliday (1821–46), is found on the member lists of Nauvoo. He had been ordained an elder and endowed in the Nauvoo Temple. He married in 1844 and died at Garden Grove on 13 May 1846.

Egan, Howard (1815–78), was born in Ireland and was baptized in 1842 while living in Massachusetts. He became a major in the Nauvoo Legion and also served in the Nauvoo police force. In 1847 he traveled to Utah with the Brigham Young company and kept a fine diary of the journey. He served a mission to the Indians. He was a Salt Lake City policeman and in 1860 was a Pony Express rider. He died in March 1878 in Salt Lake City.

Egbert, Joseph (1818–98), was born in Indiana in 1818. His family joined the church and eventually moved to Nauvoo. On 6 December 1840, he married Caroline Allred. He was a driver and a cook for Orson Pratt. At one point on the journey, he shot two buffalo but was surrounded by the remaining herd and had to crawl to safety. Exhausted, he returned to camp and other men went to recover the buffalos. He was part of the advance party that entered the valley on 22 July 1847 and also the party that returned to Winter Quarters. He came west with his family again in 1848 and settled in Kaysville, Utah, where he planted some of the first fruit orchards. He died in 1898 in Ogden, Utah.

Eldridge (or Eldredge), Horace S. (1816–88), was born in New York and was baptized in 1836. He came to Utah in 1848 and became a brigadier general in the Nauvoo Legion militia. He served as a member of the Council of Fifty and was a seventy. He was a successful merchant and banker and helped to establish Zion's Cooperative Mercantile Institution (ZCMI). He died in September 1888 in Salt Lake City.

Eldridge, Ira (1810–66), was born in Vermont. He was baptized in 1839. He immigrated to Utah in 1847 in the Daniel Spencer company. He died in February 1866 in Hoytsville, Utah.

Eldridge, John (1821–71), was born in New York. Baptized in 1843, he worked as a carpenter on the Nauvoo Temple. He immigrated to Utah in September 1847 and later served a mission to Australia. He died suddenly while plowing his farm in Charleston, Utah, in May 1871.

Ellsworth, Edmund (1819–93), was born in New York. He was baptized in 1840 and was later ordained a seventy. He married one of Brigham Young's daughters. He immigrated to Utah in 1847 in the Brigham Young company but did not arrive in the Salt Lake Valley until October because he was chosen to remain behind to help ferry immigrants across the Platte River. He served a mission to England and later served as an alderman in Salt Lake City. He moved to Arizona in order to avoid indictment for polygamy but was eventually arrested in 1884. He died in Show Low, Arizona, in December 1893.

Emmett, James (1803–52), was born in Boone County, Kentucky. He was baptized in 1831 by Lyman Wight. After moving to Missouri, he fought at the Battle of Crooked River in 1838. He also served as a member of the Council of Fifty as well as a bodyguard to Joseph Smith. An ineffective, authoritarian leader, he was temporarily disfellowshipped in 1837, then found himself in trouble again when, against the counsel of Church leaders, he led a company of one hundred Saints from Nauvoo to the Vermillion River country. Quitting the church, he traveled to California, where he died in December 1852 in Cottonwood, California.

Empy (or Empey), William (1808–90), was born in Canada. Baptized in 1839, he was later ordained a seventy. He was a member of the original pioneer company to Utah but did not arrive in the Salt Lake Valley until October 1847 because he remained to work at the North Platte ferry. After taking his family to Utah, he served a mission to England. He died in August 1890 in St. George, Utah.

Ensign, Horace Datus (Dayton) (1826–66), was born in Massachusetts and converted in 1843. He was one of the original pioneers to Utah. He helped repair the Goodyear Fort in Ogden after its purchase by Brigham Young. He died in September 1866 in Ogden, Utah.

Everett, Addison (1805–85), was born in Wallkill, New York, and was baptized in 1837. He came to Utah with the Brigham Young company, and after his arrival he helped build Fort Supply near Fort Bridger. Later, he and his wife were called to strengthen the settlements in southern Utah. They worked together in the St. George Temple. He died in January 1885 in St. George, Utah.

Fairbanks, Nathaniel (1824–53), was born in Queensbury, New York. Baptized in 1843, he moved to Nauvoo, where he was ordained a seventy. He was one of the original pioneers to Utah. In 1853, while driving cattle to California, he was thrown off of a mule and drowned near Sacramento.

Farr, Aaron Freeman (1818–1903), was born in Waterford, Vermont. He was baptized in 1832 and moved to Kirtland, Ohio, in 1838. In 1847 he was chosen as a member of the Brigham Young company and traveled with it until they reached Green River, at which point Farr was sent with four others to help guide the oncoming Saints. After he arrived in Utah, being an attorney by profession, he helped establish Salt Lake City's first civic government. He settled in Ogden, where he practiced law and served as a US deputy marshal and member of the territorial legislature. He died in November 1903 in Logan, Utah.

Farr, Diantha (1828–50) was born in Vermont. Her parents joined the church in 1832 and moved to Kirtland, Ohio. They lived in Missouri only a short time and then moved on to Nauvoo. Diantha became a plural wife of William Clayton in 1845. She had three children with him but died in 1850 in Salt Lake.

Farr, Winslow (1794–1867), was born in Chesterfield, New Hampshire, and was baptized while living in Vermont in 1832. He came to Utah in 1850 and settled the Big Cottonwood Creek in 1851. He died August 1867 in Big Cottonwood, Utah.

Fielding, Amos (1792–1875), was born in England and baptized in 1837. He remained in England for several years and served as a Church agent there until 1845. He immigrated to Nauvoo, where he became a member of the Council of Fifty. He traveled to Utah and, in 1875, died in Salt Lake City.

Finch, Sister (Miller). Identity unknown.

Fitzgerald, Perry (1815–89), was born in Redstone, Pennsylvania, and was baptized in 1842. He came to Utah with the Brigham Young company and helped build many forts in the Salt Lake Valley. He died in October 1889 in Draper, Utah.

Flake, Green (1828–1903), a black slave, was born in Anson County, North Carolina. He was baptized in the Mississippi River by John Brown. In company with two other black slaves, Oscar Crosby and Hark Lay, he traveled west in the vanguard company of pioneers. He lived in Salt Lake City for many years before moving to Idaho Falls in 1888, residing there till his death in 1903.

Fleming, Mr. (dates unknown), was a companion to Dr. Reeves. He also appears to be from the Fort Leavenworth area.

Forsgren, John (1816–90), was born in Gävle, Sweden, then spent his early life as a sailor. After his baptism in 1844, he came to Utah in 1847 and was called to be the first missionary to Sweden from 1849 to 1853. He baptized the first convert in Scandinavia: his brother, Peter. In 1852 he was called as president of the Scandinavian Mission. Later, because he began preaching and declaring that he was a prophet, he was excommunicated from the church. He died in January 1890 in Salt Lake City, Utah.

Forsgren, Mary Ann Hunt (born about 1824) married John Forsgrenm who joined the Mormon Battalion. She emigrated in the second pioneer company of 1847 to meet her husband in the valley. Little is known of her after they reached the valley. It is believed that she left Forsgren.

Forsythe, Henry, (dates unknown). No further information is available for this individual.

Fowler, John Sherman (1819–60), was born in New York. He was later baptized and became a seventy in Nauvoo. At Winter Quarters, he was chosen to be in the first pioneer company. After arriving in the Salt Lake Valley, he went with Sam Brannan to San Francisco to meet his wife, who had arrived there with the ship *Brooklyn.* He and Brannan built a successful hotel in Sacramento, where he also ran for mayor. He eventually died there.

Fox, Samuel Bradford (1829–?), was born in Adams, New York. He was one of the original pioneers to Utah but soon afterwards moved to California, where he was stricken with smallpox. He never returned to Utah, but in 1870 he moved to Oregon, where he presumably died.

Frank, Horace Monroe (1832–74), was born in Livingston, New York. At age fifteen, he was a driver with the original pioneers to Utah and was baptized when all the company arrived in the Salt Lake Valley. He was at Sutter's Fort when gold was discovered there in 1848. He later immigrated to San Bernardino, California, became an orange grove owner, and died there in July 1874.

Frazier, Jacob (1824–95), was born in Ohio. He died in September of 1895.

Freedom, Gabriel (dates unknown). No further information is available for this individual.

Freeman, John (1804–71), was born in Lincoln, Kentucky. He was baptized in 1844 and came to Utah in 1847. He died in July 1871 in Kanosh, Utah.

Frost, Burr (1816–78), was born in Connecticut. He became a Mormon in 1842 and was later ordained a seventy. As a blacksmith among the original pioneers to Utah, he was in constant demand. He served in the Iron Mission to southern Utah in 1849–50 and later filled a mission to Australia in the 1850s. He settled with his family in Salt Lake City and died there in 1878.

Fuller, Elijah Knapp (1811–97), was born in Windham, New York. He was baptized in 1842 and later was ordained a seventy. After joining the church, he migrated to Nauvoo. He came to Utah in 1847 as a captain of ten. He helped with the construction of the Salt Lake Temple. He is known for being the man who brought potatoes to Utah. He died in December 1897 in Leeds, Utah.

Fullmer, John S. (1807–83), was born in Pennsylvania. He once studied to be a Baptist minister but converted to Mormonism in 1839. He became a colonel in the Nauvoo Legion. He was also a close friend to the Prophet Joseph and was with him the night before Joseph was martyred. He was one of the three trustees appointed to liquidate church and private properties in Nauvoo. He finally left for Utah in 1848, where he served in the Utah territorial House of Representatives. He died in October 1883 in Springville, Utah.

Gibbons, Andrew (1825–86), was born in Ohio. He was orphaned at a young age and then brought up by a relative of Joseph Smith. He joined the church and moved to Nauvoo. He was then chosen as a member of the original pioneer company to Utah and served as assistant cook. He was called to settle Davis and Iron Counties in Utah and then parts of Arizona, planting orchards all the way. He was a member of the Arizona legislature before he died in St. Johns, Arizona, in February 1886.

Gifford, William (?–1850), was born in Pennsylvania. His parents were early members of the church. William was a member of the Nauvoo Second Ward. He joined the Mormon Battalion and returned to Pueblo with the sick detachment. After entering the valley, he returned with the Brigham Young company to Winter Quarters. Family records place his death in 1850.

Gleason, John (1819–1904), was born in New York. He was baptized in 1838, and became aSeventy in 1843. He was one of the original pioneers to Utah. He was a member of the Nauvoo Legion and also served as county commissioner, justice of the peace, and county clerk. He was known for being a good party host and a fine fiddler. He died in 1904 in Pleasant Grove, Utah.

Glines, Eric (1822–81), was born in New Hampshire and raised in Churchville (Toronto), Upper Canada (Ontario). He was one of the original pioneers to Utah and later relocated to California. He died there in Santa Rosa in 1881.

Glines, James Harvey (1822–1905), was born in New Hampshire. After his baptism in 1843, he relocated to Nauvoo, where he became a policeman. He was also a seventy. During the exodus, he volunteered for the Mormon Battalion, where he served on Colonel James Allen's staff. He was later assigned to the sick detachment. It is not known how he came to be in Winter Quarters ahead of the return company. He moved to Utah in 1852 and died in Vernal in 1905.

Glines, Sarah Elizabeth (1830–89), was born in New Hampshire. She was baptized in 1843, migrated west, and then died in October 1889 in Springdale, Utah.

Goddard, Stephen (1810–98), was born in New York. He was baptized in 1836 and became a seventy in 1845. A policeman and a member of the Nauvoo Legion, he was also a builder and a mason.

He was one of the original pioneers to Utah in 1847. Very musically talented, Goddard formed a choir in Winter Quarters and later became the first conductor of the choir that performed in the Tabernacle in Salt Lake City. Many years later, he moved to California, where he died in San Bernardino in September 1898.

Golden, Christine (1823–96), was born in New Jersey. She became the fifteenth wife of Heber C. Kimball. They were married on 3 February 1846 in Nauvoo, Illinois. She was the mother of J. Golden Kimball. After her husband's death, she moved to Rich County, Utah with her sons. She died in Salt Lake City.

Goodale (Goodell), Timothy (1810–69), was raised in Potsdam, New York, but moved west at age nineteen to become a fur trapper and trader in the Colorado Rockies. He associated with Kit Carson, John C. Frémont, Frederick Lander, and other notable westerners. He encountered the Mormon pioneers in July 1847. He served many years as a guide for those traveling west. Goodale's Cutoff, on the Oregon Trail, bears his name. In 1864 Goodell moved to Montana, where he lived until his death in 1869.

Goodyear, Miles (1817–49), was the first white settler of the state of Utah. Born in Hamden, Connecticut, he joined the 1836 Whitman-Spalding missionary party traveling west along the Oregon Trail. A longtime fur trapper and trader, he built and occupied Fort Buenaventura, along the Weber River in what is now the city of Ogden. The Mormons purchased his farm/fort in 1847 and initially called it Brownsville, after Captain James Brown. The town was later renamed Ogden after another early trapper, Peter Skene Ogden of the Hudson's Bay Company. After discovering gold on the Yuba River in California, Goodyear died in the Sierra Nevada in 1849.

Gould, John (1821–50), was born in Virginia, the oldest son of Samuel Gould. The family joined the church and gathered with the Saints to Nauvoo and then to Winter Quarters. He, along with his father, joined the Mormon Battalion. Both were sent back to Pueblo with the sick detachment from Santa Fe. Both were part of the return company, and both returned to Utah soon after. John and his father were members of Amasa Lyman's southern California exploration company in 1850. John died of cholera on that journey near the Humboldt Sink of Nevada.

Gould, Samuel (1778–1869), was born in Connecticut. He was baptized in 1842 and was supposedly the oldest member of the Mormon Battalion. As a member of the sick detachment, he arrived in Utah in the summer of 1847, then returned to Winter Quarters and later explored California. He later participated as one of the rescuers who were sent out in the winter of 1856 to assist the handcart pioneers stranded in Wyoming. He died in December 1869 in Parowan, Utah.

Gove, Flora Ann Woodworth Smith (1826–?), was born in upstate New York. Her mother, Phebe Watrous Woodworth, converted to Mormonism likely in 1832 and later moved with her nonmember husband, Lucien, with the main body of the Saints to Missouri and later to Illinois. Lucien was baptized in Nauvoo in 1843. That same year, Flora Ann became one of Joseph Smith's youngest plural wives. After Joseph's death, she eloped and married a "gentile" named Carlos Gove "for time." That marriage ended either in separation or divorce, although she had two or three children. Flora reportedly died in Kanesville, Iowa.

Granger, Lafayette (1825–94), was born in Phelps, New York. He died in August 1894 in Scofield, Utah.

Granger, Sabra (1794–1849) was born in New Hampshire. After joining the church in 1832, she moved in about 1836 to Kirtland, Ohio, where she married John Gribble in December 1837. They moved to Far West, Missouri, with the Kirtland Camp in 1838 and on to Nauvoo by 1842. In 1845 she left her husband and assumed her maiden name once again. At Winter Quarters she lived with the Newel K. and Elizabeth Whitney family and served as a nurse. Her place of death is unknown.

Grant, David (1816–68), was born in Scotland. He immigrated to America in 1839, eventually moving to Illinois, where he was baptized. He moved to Nauvoo about 1840 and married in 1843, but his wife died in Winter Quarters. He served as a tailor for the vanguard company and was also part of the advance company that entered the Salt Lake Valley on 22 July 1847. Returning with Brigham Young in the fall, he brought his two children west in 1848. In Utah he practiced his trade and remarried. For a time, he helped raise cotton in southern Utah. He died at Mill Creek, Utah.

Grant, George Davis (1812–76) was born in New York. He was baptized in 1836 by Don Carlos Smith. He followed the Saints to Kirtland, Far West, and Hancock County. He was one of two men who carried the news of the martyrdom of Joseph and Hyrum Smith to Nauvoo. He served as president of the Sixteenth Quorum of the Seventy and a member of the Council of Fifty. He went west with the Brigham Young company in 1848. He died in Bountiful, Utah.

Grant, George Roberts (1820–89), was born in New York. He was baptized in 1845. At Winter Quarters, he became a member of the vanguard company and subsequently the return company. After returning to Utah, he lived in Kaysville. He was a member of the short-lived Salmon River Mission in Idaho, 1855–57, and later moved to Carson City, Nevada. He died in California.

Grant, Jedediah M. (1816–56), was born in Windsor, New York. He joined the church in 1833 and was a member of Zion's Camp in 1834. In 1842 he presided over a branch of the church in Philadelphia before leading a company of pioneers to Utah in 1847. He was the first mayor of Salt Lake City as well as a speaker of the house for the territorial legislature. His son Heber J. Grant later became seventh president of the church. A spirited second counselor in the First Presidency to Brigham Young, he spearheaded the Mormon Reformation of 1856. He died in Salt Lake City in December 1856.

Green, Harvey (1806–75), was born in New York and was baptized in 1831. He immigrated to Utah in 1848 in the Heber C. Kimball company. He later moved to California and died there in August 1875.

Green, John Hyrum (1801–86), was born in England. He was baptized in 1841. He died in April 1886 in Kaysville, Utah.

Green, John Young (1826–80), was born in New York. He was baptized in 1835. He was one of the original pioneers to Utah and drove Brigham Young's team on the trek. He traveled to California in 1848 and later served a mission to Scandinavia. He died in May 1880 in Salt Lake City.

Greene, Nancy Zervia (1829–52), was born in Springwater, New York, the daughter of John P. Greene and Rhoda Young. She died in July 1852.

Griffin, Albert Bailey (1809–96), was born in Essex, Vermont. He was baptized in 1842 and was a seventy. He journeyed west to Utah in 1848. He died in February 1896 in Kanarraville, Utah.

Grouard, Benjamin Franklin (1819–94), was born in Stratham, New Hampshire. He was one of the original missionaries to the Society Islands in 1843. He married a native wife on the island of Anaa in French Polynesia. He returned to America in 1852 and joined a group of Saints in California. He then left the church and became a spiritualist. He died in March 1894 in Santa Ana, California.

Grover, Thomas (1807–86), was born in New York and was baptized in 1834. He served as a member of the Nauvoo Legion and as a bodyguard to Joseph Smith. He helped build the Kirtland Temple and came to Utah in 1847 with the Brigham Young company. After his arrival in Utah, he served in the territorial legislature and was a probate judge in Davis County. He died in February 1886 in Farmington, Utah.

Gully (or Gulley), Samuel (1809–49), was born in Smithfield, North Carolina. A quartermaster with the Mormon Battalion, he vocally defended the Mormon soldiers against ill-treatment by non-Mormon officers. He died while leading a company across the plains in 1849.

Hale, Jonathan (1800–1846), was born in Massachusetts. He was baptized in 1834 and was ordained a seventy. His son, Aroet Hale, was a friend of the Prophet Joseph Smith and kept a very able diary. He died in September 1846 in Council Bluffs, Iowa.

Hancock, Joseph (1800–1893), was born in Massachusetts. He joined the church in 1830 and participated in Zion's Camp in 1834. Nicknamed "Nimrod the Hunter" by Joseph Smith, he lived up to his name as a noted explorer and hunter during the Mormon migrations west. After arriving in the valley, he spent many years traveling back and forth between Utah and California before settling in Utah. He died in 1893 in Payson, Utah.

Hancock, Solomon (1793–1847), was born in Springfield, Massachusetts. He was baptized into the church in 1830, filled several missions, and served on several high councils. He was also well-known for his excellent singing. He died in December 1847 in Iowa.

Hanks, Knowlton F. (1816–43), was born in Madison County, Ohio. He was called to serve a mission to the Society Islands. He died from consumption while journeying to the islands in October 1843.

Hanks, Sidney Alvarus (1820–70) was born in Ohio and lived in Nauvoo along with his brothers, Ephraim K. and Knowlton F. Hanks. In Winter Quarters he was chosen as a scout for Brigham Young's vanguard company. In 1852 he, like his brother Knowlton F., was called on a mission to the Society Islands, where he served until after 1860, often nearly naked and starving. He returned to Utah, where in 1862 he married and lived at Parley's Park. While looking for a lost cow, he froze to death.

Hansen, Peter (1818–95), was born in Copenhagen, Denmark. He came to America in 1843 and joined the church in 1844. He was the third Dane to join the church, baptized after his brother Hans, who was on the first pioneer trek to Utah. He immigrated to Utah in 1847 but did not arrive in the valley until September. He was called to serve a mission to Denmark in 1849 with Apostle Erastus Snow. Once there, he helped to found the Scandinavian Mission and was chiefly responsible for translating the Book of Mormon into Danish. He returned to Utah in 1855. He later served two more missions to Scandinavia. He died in August 1895 in Manti, Utah.

Hanson, Hans (1806–90), was born in Copenhagen, Denmark. He went to sea several times as a boy. On one of these voyages, he was converted to the church and was baptized in the summer of 1842. He was one of the original pioneers to Utah and the only Scandinavian chosen for the company. He died in October 1890 in Salina, Utah.

Hardin (or Harding), John J. (1810–47), was born in Frankfort, Kentucky. He was a lawyer, as well as a general in the Illinois militia. He served in both the Illinois and United States legislatures. He then became a colonel in the Mexican-American War and was killed at the Battle of Buena Vista in February 1847.

Harley, Edwin (1819–1903), was born in Pennsylvania. He came to Salt Lake in 1852. He died in January 1903 in Nephi, Utah.

Harmon, Appleton M. (1820–77), was born in Pennsylvania. He was baptized in 1833 and was later ordained a seventy. He was a Nauvoo policeman and a member of the Nauvoo Legion. As a member of the first pioneer company to Utah and mechanic and blacksmith by profession, he helped construct the famous pioneer "odometer" to measure mileage distances. He also operated the ferry on the North Platte River. In Utah he helped construct sawmills, a furniture factory, and a woolen mill. He died in 1877 in Holden, Utah.

Harper, Charles Alfred (1817–1900), was born in Pennsylvania. He was baptized in 1842. A wagon maker, he was one of the original pioneers to Utah. He helped to colonize Utah and Arizona. He died in Holladay, Utah, in 1900.

Harris, George W. (1780–1857), was born in Massachusetts. He joined the church in 1834 and became a high councilor and a city alderman in Nauvoo. He served as a bishop and high councilor in Council Bluffs, Iowa, and died there in 1857.

Harris, Mary Ellen (1818–1902), was born in New York. She was baptized in 1846. She died in October 1902 in Salt Lake City.

Hatch, Abram (1830–1911), was born in Lincoln, Vermont. His family converted to the church in 1840. He came to Utah with four of his siblings in 1850. Abram settled in Lehi but helped develop many other cities in Utah. In 1870 he was the first legislator to propose a bill granting women the right to vote in Utah Territory. He served as president of the Wasatch Stake for almost twenty-five years. He died in December 1911 in Heber City, Utah.

Haws (or Hawes), Peter (1795–1862), was born in Canada. After converting to the church, he migrated to America to join the Saints. A miller by vocation, he was a member of the Nauvoo Agricultural and Manufacturing Association. He helped raise funds for the Nauvoo House and Nauvoo Temple and helped build the Nauvoo House. As a dissatisfied member of the Council of Fifty, he criticized the leadership of the Quorum of the Twelve in 1849 and was excommunicated. He died in 1862 in California.

Haywood, Joseph L. (1815–1910), was born in Grafton, Massachusetts. He joined the church in 1842. In 1846, when the Saints began to leave Nauvoo, he was chosen as one of three trustees to stay back and take care of the disposal of Church and private properties. He came to the Salt Lake Valley in 1848 and was appointed US marshal for Utah Territory. In 1861 he moved to southern Utah, where he served many years as a Church patriarch. He died in October 1910 in Panguitch, Utah.

Herriman, Henry (1804–91), was born in Bradford, Massachusetts. He was baptized in 1832 and later servedas a captain in the Nauvoo Legion. He died in May 1891 in Huntington, Utah.

Herring, George, was a Mohawk Indian. He and his brother, Joseph Herring, joined the church in Nauvoo and went with the Saints as far as Winter Quarters. However, after a falling out with Brigham Young, he and Joseph left the church.

Herring, Joseph, was a Mohawk Indian. He and his brother, George Herring, joined the church in Nauvoo and went with the Saints as far as Winter Quarters. However, after a falling out with Brigham Young, he and George left the church.

Higbee, Isaac (1797–1874), was born in Galloway, New Jersey. He was baptized in 1832 and soon afterward moved to Independence, Jackson County, Missouri. He gave up some of his land in Jackson County to Joseph Smith to help pay for his legal bills. After fleeing Missouri, he first lived in Quincy and then Nauvoo, where he became bishop in 1841 and justice of the peace in 1843. After migrating to the West, he became the first stake president in Provo. He was later appointed probate judge in 1852. He filled a mission to Europe in 1856 and later died in February 1874 in Provo, Utah.

Higbee, John Somers (1804–77), was born in Tate, Ohio. He was baptized in 1831. He was a gardener, a cabinetmaker, and a fisherman. He was one of the original pioneers to Utah. He died in October 1877 in Toquerville, Utah.

Higgins, Nelson (1806–90), was born in New York. Baptized in 1834, he was later ordained a seventy. He was a captain in the Mormon Battalion and also served in the Nauvoo Legion. He arrived in Salt Lake on July 29, 1847, with a contingent of the Mormon Battalion. He died in Elsinore, Utah, in November 1890.

Hill, Archibald Newell (1816–1900), was born in Scotland and immigrated with his parents to Upper Canada (Ontario) at age three. He and his wife joined the church in 1840 or 1841, and they moved with extended family members to Nauvoo. His wife died at Winter Quarters. There he worked as a teamster for Bishop Newel K. Whitney and became part of the second pioneer company of 1847. He settled in Salt Lake City, where he died in 1900.

Holden, Edward (or Edwin) (1807–94), was born in New Salem, Massachusetts. He died in December 1894 in Provo, Utah.

Holden, Elijah Edward (1826–58), was born in Pendleton, Kentucky, and was baptized in 1845. He served a European mission from 1856 to 1857. He froze to death in Millard County, Utah, in 1858.

Holman, John G. (1828–88), was born in Byron, New York. He was baptized in 1836 and was one of the original pioneers to Utah. A farmer and an alderman, he led a company of Saints to the Salt Lake Valley in 1868. He died in November 1888 in Rexburg, Idaho.

Holman, Joshua S. (1794–1846), was born in Templeton, Massachusetts. A mechanic by profession, he was baptized in Kirtland, Ohio, in 1836. He soon afterwards moved to Missouri in 1838 and then on to Adams County, Illinois, in 1839. By 1842 he was living in Nauvoo, where he became a member of the Nauvoo Legion. He died in November 1846 in Winter Quarters, Nebraska.

Horne, Joseph (1812–97), was born in London and moved to York (Toronto), Upper Canada (Ontario), when he was six years old. He and his wife were baptized there in 1836. He came to Utah in October of 1847 and helped supervise work on the Salt Lake Temple block. He also served as a member of the Salt Lake City council, a justice of the peace, a city poundkeeper, a city watermaster, a school trustee, a Sunday School superintendent, and a member of the high council. He was ordained a patriarch in 1890 and died seven years later in Salt Lake City.

Houston, Mary (1818–96), was born in Jackson, Ohio. In 1846 she was sealed for eternity to the Prophet Joseph Smith (after his death) and for time to Heber C. Kimball. She came to Utah in 1848. She died in December 1896 in Salt Lake City.

Houtz, Jacob (1813–96), was born in Pennsylvania. He was baptized in 1844 and came to Utah in 1847. He served a mission to Prussia in the 1850s. He died in December 1896 in Springville, Utah.

Hovey, Joseph (1812–68), was born in Cambridge, Massachusetts. He was baptized in Quincy, Illinois, in 1839, and soon afterwards he removed to Nauvoo. He lived in Winter Quarters until 1848, when he migrated to the Salt Lake Valley. He helped settle Iron County in 1850. He served in a bishopric in Salt Lake City and as a bishop in Millville for several years. He died in May 1868 in Salt Lake City.

Hovey, Sister, wife of Joseph Hovey, appears to be Martha Ann Webster (1814–46). She was born in New Hampshire, and was baptized in 1839. She died in September 1846 in Winter Quarters, Nebraska.

Howd, Simeon Fuller (1823–78), was born in New York. He left his wife of one month to join the first pioneer company. Though he was also in the returning company, he met his bride in the second company, and they remained in Salt Lake. They later helped settle Parowan and then, in 1856, the Beaver, Utah, area. He died in Beaver.

Hubbard, Charles Wesley (1810–1903), was born in Sheffield, Massachusetts. A farmer, he also ran and built flour mills in each place that he settled. He came to Utah in 1848 with the Heber C. Kimball company and served as bishop in several areas of Utah. He died in Willard, Utah, in December 1903.

Hunter, Edward (1793–1883), was born in Newton, Pennsylvania. After his baptism in 1840, he migrated to Nauvoo in mid-1842, where he became a member of the city council and a financial benefactor for the Saints. Joseph Smith stayed in Bishop Hunter's home for two years while in Nauvoo. Hunter also served as one of Joseph Smith's bodyguards. He came to Utah in 1847. A bishop in Nauvoo, Winter Quarters, and Salt Lake City, he also helped to establish and finance the Perpetual Emigrating Fund. In 1851 he became the third Presiding Bishop of the church. He died in Salt Lake City in 1883.

Huntington, Dimick Baker (1808–79), was born in New York and was baptized in 1835. He served as a constable and coroner in Nauvoo and as drum major in the Nauvoo Legion military band. He was a member of the Mormon Battalion and arrived in Salt Lake in July 1847. He was an early settler of Provo, Utah. He served as a missionary to the Native Americans for many years and also served as a patriarch. He died in February 1879 in Salt Lake City.

Huntington, William (1784–1846), was born in New Grantham, Cheshire County, New Hampshire. After his conversion in 1835, he relocated to Kirtland, Ohio, and later to Missouri. Once in Nauvoo he helped build the Nauvoo Temple and served on the Nauvoo Stake high council. His first wife, Zina Baker, died in 1839, and he then married Lydia Partridge, widow of Edward Partridge. His daughter Zina D. Huntington later became president of the church Relief Society. He died while serving as presiding elder in Mount Pisgah, Iowa.

Huntington, William Dresser (1818–81), was born in Watertown, New York. He was a member of the high council of Nauvoo in 1844. He died in March 1881 in Springville, Utah.

Huntly, A. L. (dates unknown). No information is available.

Hutchinson, Jacob Flynn (1816–67), was born in Milford, New Hampshire. He came to Utah in October 1850 with the Edward Hunter company. He was a tithing bookkeeper and the first bishop of the Gunnison Ward. He died in May 1867 in Springville, Utah.

Hyde, Marinda Nancy Johnson (1815–86), was born in Vermont. She was baptized in 1832. She was the first wife of Orson Hyde and was later sealed to Joseph Smith. She and Orson divorced in 1870. She died in March 1886 in Salt Lake City.

Hyde, Orson (1805–78), was born in Oxford, Connecticut. A former Methodist preacher, he converted to Mormonism in 1831 and participated in Zion's Camp in 1834, one year before being ordained an Apostle in 1835. He briefly apostatized from the church in 1839 but rejoined the following year. In 1841 he dedicated the land of Palestine for the return of the Jews. He also dedicated the Nauvoo Temple in May 1846 and supervised the Saints in Kanesville before moving to Utah in 1852. He served in the Utah territorial legislature as president of the senate and in time became senior member of the Quorum of the Twelve Apostles, but a change in the determination of seniority in the quorum elevated John Taylor to the position of president. He died in November 1878 in Spring City, Utah.

Ivory, Matthew Hayes (1809–85), was born in Pennsylvania. He made a living as a carpenter and mechanic. He was baptized in 1840. He was chosen for the first pioneer company as well as the return company. He emigrated with his family to Salt Lake again in 1856. In 1879, he filled a short mission to New Jersey. In 1885 he was killed by a falling millstone at Beaver, Utah.

Jackman, Levi (1797–1876), was born in Vershire, Vermont. A carpenter by trade, he was baptized in 1831 and worked on both the Kirtland and Nauvoo Temples. He also lived in Missouri for a time before moving to Nauvoo. He was one of the original pioneers to Utah, arriving with the Brigham Young pioneer company. Once in Utah, he became a member of the first high council in Salt Lake City. Later in life he became a patriarch. He died in July 1876 in Salem, Utah.

Jacobs, Henry Chariton (1846–1915), was the second son of Henry Jacobs and Zina Diantha Huntington. He was raised in the home of Brigham Young, served a mission to Great Britain and was ordained a patriarch in later years. He died in Ogden, Utah.

Jacobs, Norton (1804–79), was born in Sheffield, Massachusetts. He was raised a Congregationalist but joined the church in 1841. He worked on the Nauvoo Temple and, in 1844, campaigned for Joseph Smith's run for the presidency of the United States. He came to Utah in 1847 as a captain of ten in the Brigham Young company and kept a very detailed journal. He was a President of the Seventy and served as justice of the peace in Wasatch County. He died in January 1879 in Glenwood, Utah.

Johnson, Artemas (1809–?), was born in Remsen, New York. He was one of the original pioneers to Utah but then returned to Winter Quarters. Presumably, he came west once again and settled in Utah.

Johnson, Luke S. (1807–61), a son of John Johnson, was born in Pomfret, Vermont. He was baptized in 1831 by Joseph Smith Jr. and served a mission in the South in 1832. He became a member of the original Quorum of the Twelve Apostles in 1835. He defended Joseph Smith from his enemies on two specific occasions. Negatively affected by the bankruptcy of the Kirtland Safety Society, in 1838 he was excommunicated. Afterward he taught school and practiced medicine in Kirtland. In 1846 he was rebaptized and in 1847 came to Utah with the Brigham Young company. In 1858 he settled St. John, Utah, where he became bishop. He died in December 1861 in Salt Lake City.

Johnson, Philo (1814–94), was born in Newtown, Connecticut. Baptized in 1841, he moved to Nauvoo in 1842, where he was later ordained a seventy. He enlisted in the Nauvoo Legion. In 1847 he immigrated to Utah with the first pioneer company and, once in Utah, learned the hatter trade. After living for a time in Utah, he settled in Payson, where he died in April 1894.

Johnson (Johnstun or Johnston), Jesse Walker (1820–60), was born in Ohio. He was baptized in 1837 and ordained a seventy in Nauvoo. After volunteering for the Mormon Battalion, he returned to Pueblo with the sick detachment and arrived in the Salt Lake Valley on 29 July 1847. He returned to

Winter Quarters and married the next spring in Missouri. The couple later emigrated to Utah, where he died in a sawmill accident at Parley's Park.

Kane, Thomas L. (1822–83), was born in Pennsylvania. A colonel in the US military, he later served in the Civil War. Never baptized, he nonetheless remained "a friend" to the Mormons for his entire life. Kane was highly instrumental in convincing the Latter-day Saints at Mount Pisgah, Iowa Territory, and at Council Bluffs that President Polk's request for a five-hundred-man Mormon Battalion was a legitimate expression of American interests. Kane rapidly gained the trust of Brigham Young and later played a critical role in the resolution of the Utah War of 1857. Kane County, Utah, was later named after him. In 1872 he returned to Utah and assisted Brigham Young in writing his will that included provision for Brigham Young Academy, Brigham Young College, and other schools. He died in 1883 in Pennsylvania.

Kay, John (1817–64), was born in England. He was baptized in 1841 and became a seventy. He was a foundry man and temple builder. A musician, he was considered the finest singer in all of Nauvoo and helped raise funds for supplies for the church by giving concerts. He died in September 1864 while en route home from a mission to England.

Kellogg, Father Ezekiel (1801–66), was born in New York, was baptized in 1834, and migrated with the Brigham Young pioneer company in 1847. He later returned to the Missouri River Valley and recrossed the plains in 1850.

Kelsey, Stephen (1830–1900), was born in Ohio. He moved with his family in 1842 to Nauvoo. Though only sixteen, he was chosen to be in the vanguard company and later to be in the advance company, arriving in the Salt Lake Valley 22 July 1847. Though his mother was a member, he was not baptized until one day after his arrival in the valley. Part of the company that returned to Winter Quarters in the fall, he found that his mother and a sister had died in his absence. He came west in 1848 with four sisters. In 1864, he was called to settle the Bear Lake area in southeastern Idaho. He died in Paris, Idaho.

Kendall, Levi N. (1822–1903), was born in New York state. He joined the church in Michigan and was ordained a seventy in 1844 in Nauvoo. At Winter Quarters, he was assigned to be a guard for the vanguard company. He returned to Winter Quarters in the fall of 1847 and traveled west to the Salt Lake Valley in 1848. He settled in the Springville area, where he later died.

Kimball, Brigham Willard (1845–67), was born in Nauvoo, Illinois, the son of Heber C. Kimball and Vilate Murray. He served in the British Mission, where he became sick and was excused from further service. He never married, and he died on the plains on his way home.

Kimball, Heber C. (1801–68), born in Sheldon, Vermont, was a farmer and blacksmith. He joined the church in Mendon, New York, in 1832. A tireless convert, he served eight missions from 1832 and 1842. He served in Zion's Camp in 1834 and was ordained a member of the original Quorum of the Twelve Apostles in 1835. He moved to Far West, Missouri, in 1838 and later to Nauvoo. Devoted to his first wife, Vilate, he nonetheless embraced plural marriage, marrying thirty-nine women before leaving Nauvoo. He was one of the original pioneers to Utah. President Brigham Young chose him as first counselor in the First Presidency in December 1847. In 1849 he became chief justice of the provisional State of Deseret and served in the Utah territorial legislature from 1851 to 1858. He died in June 1868 in Salt Lake City after being thrown from his wagon by a lunging horse.

Kimball, Heber P. (1835–85), born in Kirtland, Ohio, was the son of Heber C. Kimball and Vilate Murray. He died in February 1885 in Salt Lake City.

Kimball (Smith Whitney), Helen Mar (1828–96), was born in Mendon, New York. She was the daughter of Heber C. Kimball and Vilate Murray. At age fourteen, she married Joseph Smith as one of his plural wives. After Joseph's death, she married her childhood sweetheart, Horace K. Whitney, with whom she had eleven children, three of which died very young. Before her death in 1896 in Salt Lake City, she authored several pamphlets in defense of the "principle" of plural marriage. Her accounts of the Mormon exodus are abundantly referenced throughout this book.

Kimball, Hiram (1806–63), was born in Vermont. He was baptized in 1843 and married Sarah Granger Kimball, who later became a Mormon advocate for women's rights and an early leader in the Relief Society. He came to Utah in 1850. He was called on a mission to the Sandwich Islands in 1863 but died en route.

Kimball, Lucy Walker Smith (1826–1910), was born in Vermont. Her family joined the church in 1832. They moved to Missouri in 1838, experienced many of the persecutions there, and then moved to Nauvoo. She was sealed to Joseph Smith in May 1843. After Joseph Smith died, she became a plural wife of Heber C. Kimball. She went to western Iowa with the Saints in 1846 and then west to Salt Lake with Heber C. Kimball in 1848. She gave birth to nine children with Kimball and died in Salt Lake City.

Kimball, Sarah Melissa Granger (1818–98), was born in New York. Her family joined the church in 1830 and gathered in 1833 with the Saints in Kirtland, where Sarah attended the School of the Prophets. Her family later moved to Nauvoo, where Sarah married Hiram Kimball. Her idea to form a society to make clothing for men working on the temple planted the seed for the Relief Society, where she later served for forty-two years. She was also a strong advocate for women's rights. She died in Salt Lake.

Kimball, Sarah Peek (Peak or Peake) Noon (1811–73), was born in England and there married William Spencer Noon. She joined the church and migrated to America, leaving her husband because of his alcoholism and dissolute habits. In 1842 she married Heber C. Kimball as one of his early plural wives and had four children with him. She traveled west with him in 1848. She died in December 1873 in Salt Lake City.

Kimball, Solomon Farnham (1847–1920), was born at Winter Quarters. He later served in the cavalry in the Black Hawk War, moved to Arizona, and became something of a prodigal. In later years, he wrote a book called *Thrilling Experiences* about his memories of early pioneers, "sowing wild oats," and the miraculous experiences that brought him back to the church. He died in Salt Lake City.

Kimball, Vilate Murray (1806–67), was born in Florida, New York. She was the first wife of Heber C. Kimball and the mother of Helen Mar Kimball, wife of Horace K. Whitney. She died in October 1867 in Salt Lake City.

Kimball, William H. (1826–1907), the oldest son of Heber C. Kimball and Vilate Murray, was born in Mendon, New York, where he joined the church with his family in 1832. He assisted in the Martin handcart company rescue operations in 1857. Later, he discovered coal in the area now known as Coalville, Utah, and operated a hotel in Parley's Park. He died in December 1907.

King, William (1821–62), was born in Paris, Maine. He traveled to Utah with the Brigham Young company and, after a short time in the Salt Lake Valley, returned to Winter Quarters with Brigham Young. It is believed that he died in Boston in 1862.

Kingsbury, Joseph C. (1812–98), was born in Enfield, Connecticut, and later migrated to Ohio, where he was baptized in 1832 while living with the Newel K. and Elizabeth Whitney family. He arrived in the Salt Lake Valley 29 September 1847. A schoolteacher and farmer, he was also employed in the tithing store. He served in the militia during the Utah War of 1857. He died in October 1898 in Salt Lake City.

Kingsbury, Sarah Ann Whitney (1825–73), was born in Kirtland, Ohio. She was the daughter of Newel K. Whitney and Elizabeth Ann Smith and was the younger sister of Horace K. Whitney. She married Joseph Smith at age seventeen as one of his plural wives. After Joseph's death, Sarah was sealed "for time" to Heber C. Kimball, father of Helen Mar Kimball. However, Sarah continued to be known as Sarah Kingsbury for the remainder of her life. She died in September 1873 in Salt Lake City.

Klineman (Kleinman), Conrad (1815–1907), was born in Bavaria (later Germany). He immigrated to America at age sixteen and was baptized in 1844 in Indiana. He followed the Saints to Nauvoo and Winter Quarters, where he was chosen for the Brigham Young company. He was a member of the return company and later helped settle Dixie and Mesa, Arizona. He was called as a patriarch in 1891 and died in St. George.

Lamb, Edwin Ruthven (1831–1924), was born in New York and was baptized in 1839. He died in March 1924 in Toquerville, Utah.

Langley, George Washington (1818–50), was born in Tennessee. He was baptized in 1842 and lived in Nauvoo and Winter Quarters, where he served as a peace officer. He went west in 1848 and died in Salt Lake City.

Larson, Thurston (1828–1907), was born in Norway. He immigrated to America with his family as a child and joined the church in 1843 in Iowa. He volunteered for the Mormon Battalion but was sent to Pueblo with the sick detachment and arrived in the Salt Lake Valley on 29 July 1847. He escorted many immigrant trains to Utah and made many trips to California for supplies for the Saints. He served as president of the Sixty-first Quorum of the Seventy. A cobbler by trade, he lived in Utah and Idaho and died in Parker, Idaho.

Lathrop, Asahel (1810–91), was born in Tolland, Connecticut. He was baptized in 1836 and soon afterwards moved to Kirtland, Ohio. He later relocated to Missouri and played an active role in the Election Day Battle in Gallatin, Missouri. As a merchant, he operated a successful store in Nauvoo, where he was later ordained a seventy. He died in San Bernardino, California.

Laughlin, David Sanders (1816–56), was born in New Hampshire. He joined the church in Ohio and followed the Saints to Far West, Nauvoo, and Winter Quarters. He volunteered for the Mormon Battalion and became part of the sick detachment. He returned to Winter Quarters in the fall of 1847 and then emigrated to Salt Lake in 1852. He battled a long illness until he died at Cedar Fort, Utah.

Lawrence, Sarah A. (1826–72), was born in Upper Canada (Ontario). Her family joined the church in 1837 and moved to Nauvoo about 1840. After the death of her father, she lived with Joseph Smith's family and was sealed to him with Emma's permission and in her presence. After his death, Heber C. Kimball took her as a wife. In Utah she left him for another man, whom she married. They moved to California, and she later divorced him. She eventually denied ever having been married to Smith or Kimball. She died in California.

Lay, Hark (1825–90), born in Monroe County, Mississippi, and the son of African slaves, was raised in the William Lay household. After his baptism, he was given as a "gift" to William Crosby, a Mormon. Musically inclined, he had a fine singing voice. He was one of the three black slaves brought out to Salt Lake, along with Green Flake and Oscar Crosby. He died in Union, Utah, in 1890.

Lee, John D. (1812–77), was born in Kaskaskia, Illinois, and was baptized in 1838. Shortly afterward, he migrated to Nauvoo, where he served as a city policeman and a member of the Nauvoo Legion. He later helped with Joseph Smith's United States presidential campaign. He was one of the primary planners and executors of the notorious 1857 Mountain Meadows Massacre. As a result, he was excommunicated from the church and was executed at Mountain Meadows in 1877 for his leading role in the mass murders of some 120 men, women, and children. He was reinstated a member of the church in 1961.

Lewis, Tarleton (1805–90), was born in South Carolina and was baptized in 1836. He was one of the survivors of the Hawn's Mill massacre in Missouri in late 1838. A carpenter by trade, he worked on the Nauvoo Temple and served as a member of the Nauvoo Legion. He came to Utah in the first pioneer trek and later mined in Iron County. He served as a bishop in Salt Lake, Parowan, and Richfield. He died in November 1890 in Teasdale, Utah.

Little (also Lytle), Archibald (dates unknown). Thomas Bullock recorded the following incident on 18 June 1847: "Archibald Lytle (a newcomer to the company this day) abused his oxen, striking them on the head and body with the butt end of this whip." Some of the leading brethren tried to help him get the Irishman's wagon up a grade, but he refused their help and continued beating his oxen.

Little, Edwin (1817–46), was born in New York. He was the father of George Edwin Little. He died in Iowa in March 1846.

Little, Jesse C. (1815–93), was born in Maine and was baptized in 1839. During his service as president of the Eastern and Middle States Mission, he served as the chief negotiator between the church and the federal government, including negotiating for the formation of the Mormon Battalion. He was one of the original pioneers of Utah. He served as fire chief, town marshal, farmer, sexton, and cabinetmaker. In the early 1850s, he opened a hotel in Salt Lake City. He died there in December 1893.

Losee, Abraham (1814–87), was born in Canada. He was baptized in 1840 and immigrated to Utah in the Heber C. Kimball company in 1848. He died in October 1887 in Lehi, Utah.

Lott, Cornelius Peter (1798–1850), was born in New York City. He converted in 1834 and participated in the Missouri persecutions of 1838. A skilled rancher, he managed Joseph Smith's Nauvoo farm. While moving west with the original Brigham Young company, he was in charge of most of the ten thousand head of cattle. A farmer and county sheriff by vocation, he eventually became the superintendent of church farms in Utah. He died of dysentery in July 1850 in Salt Lake City.

Luce, John Grant (1817–81), was born in the Fox Islands of Maine. His large extended family was taught the gospel by Wilford Woodruff. He moved in 1841 to Nauvoo, where he was ordained a seventy and served in the Nauvoo Legion. He followed the Saints to Winter Quarters and joined the vanguard company and was incorrectly recorded as Franklin G. Losee. He was a member of the standing guard and gun detachments in that company. After returning to Winter Quarters, he never immigrated to Utah. Instead, he went to Maine and later to Missouri and Illinois, where he died.

Lutz, Albert (1811–98), was born in Pennsylvania and was baptized in 1840. In 1846 he moved to Winter Quarters, where he served as bishop of the Seventeenth Ward. He helped build Kimball's farm and migrated with his family to Salt Lake in 1852. He later served a mission and helped to settle various parts of Utah. He died in October 1898 in Garden Grove, Utah.

Lyman, Amasa M. (1813–77), was born in Lyman, New Hampshire. He was baptized in 1832 and shortly thereafter filled the first of sixteen missions. He served in Zion's Camp in 1834 and became an apostle in 1844. Amasa played a key role in the Mormon exodus by leading many of the sick detachment of the Mormon Battalion to leave Pueblo for the Salt Lake Valley in 1847. He and Charles C. Rich supervised the short-term Mormon settlement in San Bernardino, California, beginning in 1849. He was excommunicated in 1870 for joining in with the anti-Mormon Godbeite movement, for preaching spiritualism, and for publicly denying the Atonement of Jesus Christ. He died in February 1877 in Fillmore, Utah. His priesthood blessings were restored posthumously in 1909.

Mann, Dr. (dates unknown). No information is available.

Marble, Samuel (1822–1914), was born in Phelps, New York. Baptized in Nauvoo in 1845, he was later ordained a seventy. One of the original pioneers to Utah, he settled in Manti, where he served as a city councilman. He also helped operate the Mormon ferry operations in Wyoming. He later moved to Arizona, where he died in March 1914.

Markham, Stephen (1800–1878), was born in New York and was baptized in 1837. A well-to-do farmer, he sold all of his possessions to provide the means necessary for sixty people to migrate from Kirtland, Ohio, to Far West, Missouri. He served as Joseph Smith's private courier as well as bodyguard and was a colonel in the Nauvoo Legion. Stephen sold his house and moved his family into a tent to pay for the lawsuits that Joseph Smith was facing while in Carthage Jail. He was one of the original Utah pioneers of 1847. He captained several groups of Saints on their journey to Utah. He was the bishop of Spanish Fork for several years and died there in March 1878.

Markham, Warren (1824–1900), was born in New York. Son of Stephen Markham, he died in August 1900 in California.

Marshall, P. T. (dates unknown), traveled east with the return company, but nothing more is known about him. He was not a member of any of the first Mormon groups to enter the valley.

Martin, Edward (1818–82), was born in England and baptized in 1837. He immigrated to Nauvoo in 1841, traveled to Council Bluffs with the initial exodus, and enlisted in the Mormon Battalion. He completed the journey with the battalion to California and returned to Winter Quarters. In 1856, on his way home from a nearly four-year mission in England, Martin was made captain of the ill-fated Martin handcart company. Martin married and made a living as a photographer and merchant in Salt Lake City, where he later died.

Martindale, William (1814–73), was born in Indiana. He was baptized in 1840 and traveled to Utah in 1852. He died in February 1873 in Virgin City, Utah.

Mayson (probably Mason), Silas (dates unknown). No information is available.

Matlock, William E. (1812–46), was born in Nauvoo. He died there in July 1846.

Matthews, Joseph (1809–86), was born in North Carolina. He was baptized in 1844, then moved to Nauvoo, where he worked on the temple. He was one of the original pioneers to Utah in the Brigham

Young company. He was one of the original settlers of the Mormon colony in San Bernardino, California. He returned to Utah in 1857 before moving to Arizona in 1880. He died in 1886 in Matthewsville, Arizona.

McBride, Reuben (1803–91), was born in Chestertown, Orange County, New York. He was baptized in 1834. He was the first man baptized for the dead in the Nauvoo Temple. He first came to Utah in 1850 and later served a mission to England in 1857. He served for several years in the Millard Stake High Council. He died in February 1891 in Fillmore, Utah.

McCord, James (1826–1903), was born in Virginia. He went into business with his brother-in-law Abram Nave in Oregon, Missouri, in 1846. They were partners for fifty-two years and established many successful businesses together. He died in St. Joseph, Missouri.

McCrary, William (c. 1811–54)—also known as William Chubby, Okah Tubbee, and multiple other names—was born in Natchez, Mississippi, the son of an African American slave mother and her white master. He married into a Native American tribe and eventually became a Choctaw chief. A traveling minstrel, ventriloquist, lecturer, and self-proclaimed prophet all in one, he joined the church at Winter Quarters. After claiming to be an Indian prophet at Winter Quarters, he was soon afterwards excommunicated for marrying several Latter-day Saint women without permission. His unauthorized marriages may have prompted Brigham Young to institute the priesthood ban on black members.

McIntyre, William (1813–1882), was born in Pennsylvania. He was baptized in 1836 and was later ordained a seventy. He was an assistant surgeon in the Mormon Battalion. He died in January 1882 in St. George, Utah.

Meeks, William (1815–77), was born in Indiana. He was introduced to the gospel by his uncle Priddy Meeks and baptized in 1840. He moved to Nauvoo where he served as a policeman. He went west to Springville, Utah, in 1852. He lived in numerous places in Utah and served as a US deputy marshall. He died in St. George, Utah.

Miller, George (1794–1855), was born in Orange County, Virginia. A carpenter by vocation, he converted in 1839 while in Quincy, Illinois, and helped build the Nauvoo Temple. A very vocal member of the Council of Fifty, Miller was also a remarkable guide and trailblazer. In Nauvoo he also became associate Presiding Bishop of the church. While he revered Joseph Smith's leadership, he crossed swords with Brigham Young, rejecting his leadership and contending that Young was moving west in the wrong direction. Disfellowshipped from the church in December 1848, he joined up with Lyman Wight in his Texas colony before heading north to cast his lot with James Strang in 1850. He died a brokenhearted man in 1855 and was buried in Marengo, Illinois.

Mills, George (1778–1854), was born in England. One of the original pioneers to Utah in 1847, he died of cancer in Salt Lake City in 1854.

Mitchell, Robert Byington (dates unknown), was a subagent for the Department of Indian Affairs stationed at Council Bluffs.

Moon, R. C. (dates unknown). No information is available.

More, Thomas (1801–68), was born at sea between Ireland and New York. He was baptized in 1840 and was adopted into the Newel K. and Elizabeth Whitney family. A carriage maker, he died in December 1868 in Sacramento, California.

Morley, Isaac (1786–1864), was born in Montague, Massachusetts. He was baptized in 1830 and shortly thereafter became captain of the Ohio militia. In 1831 he was called as First Counselor in the Presiding Bishopric of the church. He became a patriarch in 1837. In 1848 he came to Utah and was the first man to settle in what would become the city of Manti. He served as a senator in the territorial legislature from 1851 to 1855. He died in July 1864 in Fairview, Utah.

Murray, Carlos (1829–56), was born in New York. He was a seventy and was one of the original pioneers to Utah. He later traveled to California. He and his wife were apparently killed by Indians in May 1856 in Nevada.

Murray, Helen Janet Jeanette (1826–1901), was born in New York. She was the wife of Hosea Cushing and a cousin of Helen Mar Kimball Whitney. She died in March 1901 in Payson, Utah.

Murray, William Ellis (1802–47), was born in Florida, New York. He died in May 1847 in Snyder, Missouri.

Myers, Lewis B. (1812–93), was a mountain man. He served as the guide and the hunter for the company of Saints led by Robert Crow. After encountering the Mormon vanguard company, he chose to join them and continued to the Salt Lake Valley. Once there, he served as a guide on exploring expeditions and was the first to explore Utah Valley. He settled for a brief time in Ogden before continuing on to California.

Myers, Samuel (1825–1901), was born in Ohio. Baptized in 1837, he was a member of the Mormon Battalion. He died in May 1901 in Glendale, Utah.

Nave, Abram (1815–1898), was born in Tennessee. His family moved to Missouri a year later. He became a merchandiser and in 1846, established a dry goods store with his brother-in-law James McCord in Oregon, Missouri. Their partnership eventually included many other successful businesses in several states and lasted fifty-two years. He died in Missouri.

Newman, Elijah (1793–1872), was born in Virginia. He joined the church in Cincinnati in 1832. He was among those men taken prisoner in Richmond, Missouri, with Joseph Smith. He followed the Saints to Nauvoo and Winter Quarters. He was named to the advance group that entered the Salt Lake Valley on 22 July 1847. He died in Parowan, a settlement he helped establish.

Nickerson, Levi (1814–53), was born in Pennsylvania. He was baptized in 1833 and later served as a seventy. He died in Kanesville, Iowa, in December 1853.

Nobles, Joseph (1810–1900), was born in Massachusetts. He was baptized in 1832 and was later ordained a seventy. A member of the Nauvoo Legion, he was one of Joseph Smith's bodyguards. He was a bishop at Winter Quarters. In 1847 he immigrated to Utah and served as a bishop and as a patriarch. He died in August 1900 in Dingle, Idaho.

Noon, Sister. See Sarah Peek (Peak or Peake) Noon Kimball.

Norris, David (1800–1846), was born in New York. He was baptized in 1840 and shortly thereafter was ordained a seventy. He was one of three Mormons killed in the Battle of Nauvoo in September 1846.

Norton, John Wesley (1820–1901), was born in Lisbon, Indiana. He joined the church in 1838 and was later ordained a seventy in Nauvoo, where he was endowed in the Nauvoo Temple. He was one of the original pioneers to Utah. He served a three-year mission to Australia from 1854 to 1857, then lived for a time in southern Nevada. He died in 1901 in Panguitch, Utah.

Nowlin, Jabez Townsend (1841–93), was born in Tennessee. He joined the church and moved to Nauvoo in the mid-1840s. He volunteered for the Mormon Battalion in Iowa but was sent back to Pueblo with the sick detachment from Santa Fe. He traveled to Salt Lake with the Mississippi Saints and then returned to Winter Quarters for his wife. They later went to Utah and helped establish Provo and the Cotton Mission. He served in the militia under John D. Lee in Iron County and may have been involved in the Mountain Meadows Massacre. He died in Ucon, Idaho.

Oakley, James (1826–1915), was born in New York and was baptized in 1844. He was a member of the Mormon Battalion and one of the original pioneers to Utah. After traveling to California during the gold rush, he returned to Utah in 1851 and died in Springville, Utah, in 1915.

Pack, John R. (1809–85), born in St. John, New Brunswick (Canada), converted in 1836 in New York and moved to Ohio, Missouri, and Illinois. While living in Nauvoo, he was a member of the Nauvoo Legion, the Nauvoo police, and the Council of Fifty. He filled several missions. One of the original pioneers to Utah, he arrived in Salt Lake in July 1847. In 1856 he helped settle Carson Valley, Nevada. He was first principal/president of the University of Deseret, later the University of Utah, which began in his home. He died in Salt Lake City in April of 1885.

Pack, Ruth (1824–1914), was the wife of John Pack. She died in Utah in 1914.

Packard, Noah (1796–1859), was born in Plainfield, Massachusetts. He was baptized in 1832 by Parley P. Pratt and worked as a laborer on the Kirtland Temple. He moved to Nauvoo in 1839 and came to Utah in 1850 and located in Springville, where he was also appointed an alderman. He died in February 1858 in Springville.

Page, John E. (1799–1867), was born in New York. Sometimes called "son of thunder" because of his powerful preaching voice, he baptized almost a thousand converts on his mission to Upper Canada in 1836–37. In 1838 he led the "Canadian" company to De Witt and later Far West, Missouri. They were attacked by a mob along the way, and his wife and two children died. In 1838 he was called to the Quorum of the Twelve Apostles but was disfellowshipped in February 1846 after supporting James Strang's claim as the lawful successor to Joseph Smith. He was eventually excommunicated in June 1846. He died in Illinois in October 1867.

Park, William Asbury (1826–1915), was born in Tennessee and baptized in 1845. He was with the Saints on the exodus and joined the Mormon Battalion. He was a part of the sick detachment and the return company to Winter Quarters. He later lived in Utah, California, and Colorado before retiring to Knob Noster, Missouri, where he died.

Parks, William (1787–1856), was born in Connecticut. He was baptized in 1837. He died in February 1856 in Louisiana, Missouri.

Parnum, Charles (dates unknown), traveled east with the return company, but nothing more is known about him. He was not a member of any of the first Mormon groups to enter the valley.

Parrish, Warren (1803–77), baptized in 1833 by Brigham Young and a member of Zion's Camp in 1834, became for a time a highly trusted scribe of Joseph Smith. He was primarily responsible for operating the Kirtland Safety Society in Kirtland, Ohio. His alleged improper mismanagement of funds contributed to the failure of the bank and led to his disillusionment with and excommunication from the church. He became a bitter enemy of Joseph Smith and the church in Ohio and participated in an armed confrontation with the Saints in 1837. After his excommunication, he formed a short-lived rival "Church of Christ." He became a Baptist minister in 1844. He died in 1877 in Emporia, Kansas.

Patten, Dr. (John) (1787–1847), was born in New Hampshire. A physician by training, he seems to have joined the church in Indiana and moved from there to Jackson County, Missouri in 1833. He was driven with the saints from county to county and out of Missouri to Nauvoo. He later followed the Saints to Winter Quarters but died there suddenly in April of 1847. He is buried in the pioneer cemetery there.

Persons (also Pierson), Judson A. (1828–98), was born in Connecticut. He joined the Mormon Battalion along with two of his brothers and was later sent to Pueblo with the sick detachment. He was a member of the return company, but nothing more is known of him until his death in Sacramento, California.

Pettit, Edwin (1834–1924), was one of the original 1847 pioneers to Utah. Participated in the early San Bernardino settlement with Charles C. Rich and Amasa Lyman.

Phelps, Willam Waterman (1823–86), was born in Homer, New York. He was the son of William W. Phelps and Stella Waterman. He was baptized in 1845 and came to Utah in 1852. He died in June 1886 in Stockton, California.

Phelps, William Wines (1792–1872), was born in Hanover, New Jersey. An ardent abolitionist, gifted intellectual, writer, and newspaper editor in Canandaigua, New York, he moved to Kirtland, Ohio, in 1831. After his baptism, he joined Joseph Smith and Sidney Rigdon on a special mission to Missouri. He was also called to assist Oliver Cowdery in writing and printing books for the church. Excommunicated three different times, he kept coming back to the church, and he came to Utah in 1847 with the Brigham Young company. He became a schoolteacher, a printer, and a speaker of the house of representatives of the Utah territorial legislature. He also wrote several popular Latter-day Saint hymns, perhaps the most notable being "Praise to the Man." He died in 1872 in Salt Lake City.

Pickett, William (1816–93). A strong advocate of settling the Saints in California, Pickett was a close friend and traveling companion to Sam Brannan and an associate of Almon W. Babbitt. He was appointed sheriff of Pottawattamie County (Kanesville region) in 1848 and presumably came west in 1849–50.

Pierce (also Peirce), Eli Harvey (1827–58), was born in Pennsylvania. He and his parents were baptized in Nauvoo in 1842 by Joseph Smith. He was chosen as a teamster for the first pioneer company. On his return to Winter Quarters, he met family members in the second company and returned with them to Salt Lake. He married and helped settle Brigham City, where he later served as bishop. He served only one year of a mission but returned because of illness and died in Salt Lake City shortly after arriving.

Pierson, Eliza Ann (1822–46), was born in Richmond, Massachusetts. She was baptized in 1838. She died in October 1846 in Winter Quarters, Nebraska.

Pitkin, Abigail (1797–1847), was born in Vermont. She was a plural wife of Heber C. Kimball. She died in March 1847.

Pitkin, Laura (1790–1886), was born in Connecticut. She was a plural wife of Heber C. Kimball. She died in November 1886 in Salt Lake City.

Pitt, William (1813–73), was born in England. He was baptized in 1840 and crossed the plains in 1847 with the Brigham Young company. He was the leader of the Nauvoo brass band, which raised money for the trek west and also entertained the pioneers along the way. He died in February 1873 in Salt Lake City.

Polk, James K. (1795–1849), was born in North Carolina. A Democrat, he was the eleventh president of the United States and was in office from 1845 to 1849. He was the "dark horse" candidate the year that Joseph Smith ran for president, and defeated Henry Clay by promising to annex Texas. During his presidency, he greatly increased the territory owned by the United States, including California, Nevada, and what is today the state of Utah. He died in June of 1849 in Nashville, Tennessee.

Pomeroy, Francis M. (1822–82), was born in Somers, Connecticut. He began his career on a whaling vessel and survived a terrible shipwreck. He joined the church in 1844, moved to Nauvoo, and was there ordained a seventy. One of the members of the original pioneer company to Utah, he was chosen to remain to work at the North Platte River ferry (near Casper, Wyoming), so he arrived in the valley later than the rest of the original company. After arriving in Utah, he lived in Idaho and then traveled to Arizona, where he was one of the founders of Mesa. He died there in 1883.

Pond, Francis M. (1828–46), was born in Massachusetts. She was a plural wife of Newel K. Whitney. She died in December 1846 in Winter Quarters.

Pond, Harriet (1835–46), was born in Massachusetts. She died in December 1846 in Winter Quarters.

Pond, Laura Jane (1832–46), was born in Massachusetts. She died in December 1846 in Winter Quarters.

Pond, Stillman (1803–78), was born in Massachusetts. He was baptized in December 1841 and came to Utah in 1847 in the John Taylor company. He lost a wife and several children to disease and malnutrition at Winter Quarters. He died in September 1878 in Richmond, Utah.

Potter, G. G. (Gardner Godfrey) (1811–57), was born in New York and baptized in 1842. Mentioned as a doctor on 1 September 1846, he went west with the Brigham Young company in 1848. He was a leader in the settlement of Mount Pleasant, Utah. He died in Springville, Utah.

Potts, Jacob Harrison (about 1810–?), was born in Ohio. He was wounded at Hawn's Mill and is later found at Winter Quarters. There is no record of his coming west.

Powell, David (1822–83), was born in South Carolina. He was ordained a seventy in Nauvoo. He became part of the advance party that entered the valley 22 July 1847 and the party that returned to Winter Quarters. He came west again with his family in 1853. He later moved to California, where he died near Santa Rosa.

Pratt, Addison (1802–72), was born in Winchester, New Hampshire. He was baptized in May 1837 and was one of the original missionaries called to the Society Islands in 1843. He came back to Salt Lake in 1848 but returned to the Society Islands in 1849. Before his departure, President Brigham Young took him to the top of Ensign Peak, where Pratt then received his endowment. His wife and four daughters followed him to the islands six months after his departure. In 1852 the missionaries were banished, so Pratt and his family joined a group of Saints in California, where he was appointed to preside over the San Francisco Branch. Pratt later became disaffected and left the church to join a group of spiritualists. He died in October 1872 in Anaheim, California.

Pratt, Orson (1811–81), was born in Hartford, New York. He was the younger brother of Parley P. Pratt, who baptized him into the church in 1830. A gifted scientist, writer, philosopher, and theologian, he was part of Zion's Camp in 1834 and became a member of the original Council of Twelve Apostles in 1835. Orson was briefly excommunicated in 1842 because of plural marriage but, upon reconciliation, was rebaptized in 1843. He was one of the first teachers at the University of Nauvoo. He traveled to Utah with the Brigham Young company and was the first to enter the Salt Lake Valley, having preceded the main body by three days. He was also a very learned astronomer, taking measurements of the company's locations by observing the stars. He was a member of the territorial legislature and speaker of the house of representatives. He was president of the European Mission from 1848 to 1851. In 1852 he was editor of *The Seer*, a Mormon newspaper in Washington, DC. In 1874 he became Church Historian, a position he held until his death in October 1881 in Salt Lake City. He left ten wives and forty-five children.

Pratt, Parley P. (1807–57), was born in Burlington, New York. The older brother of Orson Pratt, he joined the church in 1830, was a part of the famous Lamanite mission of 1830–31 and later Zion's Camp of 1834, and was made a member of the original Council of Twelve Apostles in 1835. Like his brother, he briefly apostatized from the church but was soon rebaptized. He came to Utah in 1847. Considered one of the finest writers and systematic theologians of the early Church, Pratt wrote *Voice of Warning* and later *Key to the Science of Theology*. He also composed several favorite Mormon hymns. He was murdered while serving a mission in Arkansas in 1857.

Pulsipher, Zerah (1789–1872), was born in Vermont. Baptized in 1832, he was later called as a President of the Seventy. He migrated to Utah in 1848, where he served as a city councilman. In the spring of 1862, he was briefly disfellowshipped for performing marriage sealings without authorization. Shortly thereafter, he was rebaptized. Later he was ordained a patriarch. He died in January 1872 in Hebron, Utah.

Rappleye, Ammon Tunis (1807–83), was born in New York. He joined the church in 1832 and helped build the Kirtland Temple. He was one of the original pioneers to Utah. After his arrival, he worked for Brigham Young as a head gardener and later helped settle Millard County. He died in December 1883 in Kanosh, Utah.

Rashaw (1810–75). Usually spelled "Reshaw," the name was the American transliteration of the French name "Richard" or "Richaud." Born John Baptiste Richard at St. Charles, Missouri, he established numerous trading posts and other moneymaking ventures in Wyoming and Colorado. On 2 October 1847, Brigham Young arranged for Reshaw to keep some horses until the Mormons returned in the spring.

Redding, Jackson ("Return Jackson Redden") (1817–91), was born in Hiram, Ohio. He was baptized in 1841 and was later ordained a seventy. He served as one of Joseph Smith's bodyguards. Known for his gun-fighting skills, Redding was a fearless enforcer, often acting outside the law. He came to Utah in 1847 in the Brigham Young company. While en route, he discovered Cache Cave (then called Redden's Cave). He served as justice of the peace in Summit and Tooele Counties. He died in August 1891 in Hoytsville, Summit County, Utah.

Reeves, Dr., was a military medical doctor from Fort Leavenworth.

Rhodes, George (1815–80), was born in Thornley, Lancashire, England. He died in July 1880 in Salt Lake County, Utah.

Rich, Charles C. (1809–83), was born in Campbell County, Kentucky, and spent most of his childhood in Indiana, before the family moved to Illinois in 1829. He was baptized in 1832 and moved to Ohio, Missouri, and Illinois with the Saints. While in Nauvoo, he served on the high council and was a member of the Nauvoo Legion and Council of Fifty. He came to Utah on 2 October 1847 and became an apostle in 1849. He was a member of the Utah territorial legislature. Along with Amasa Lyman, he was a cofounder of San Bernardino, California, in the 1850s. He was later directed to settle the Bear Lake Valley of Utah and Idaho. Rich County, Utah, was named after him. He died in November 1883 in Paris, Idaho.

Richards, Joseph William (1828–1846), was born in Massachusetts as the son of Phineas Richards and Wealthy Dewey. He enlisted in the Mormon Battalion as a musician. He returned to Pueblo as a member of captain Brown's sick detachment and died there in November of 1846.

Richards, Phineas (1788–1874), was born in Massachusetts. He was the brother of Willard Richards and the cousin of Brigham Young. Baptized in 1837, he came to Utah in October 1848 and served in the Utah territorial legislature. He also served as a clerk for the high council. He died in November 1874 in Salt Lake City.

Richards, Willard (1804–54), was born in Hopkinton, Massachusetts. He was the cousin of Brigham Young. A Thompsonian (herbal) medical doctor, Dr. Richards was baptized in Kirtland in 1836 and served as first counselor to Joseph Fielding in the British Mission before becoming an Apostle in 1840. In Nauvoo he became editor of the *Times and Seasons* newspaper and in December 1842 was called as the Church Historian and Recorder, a position he held for the rest of his life. He was also a scribe to Joseph Smith. At Carthage Jail, he and John Taylor survived the killing of Joseph and Hyrum Smith. He was part of the first company of Saints to arrive in the Salt Lake Valley in 1847. Founding editor of the *Deseret News*, he served as second counselor in the First Presidency from 1847 until his death in 1854 in Salt Lake City.

Richardson, Ebenezer Clawson (1815–74), was born in Dryden, New York. He was baptized in 1834 and later served as mission president in South Africa, 1857–58. He died in September 1874 in Plain City, Utah.

Richmond, Benjamin Boyce (1825–54), was born in Upper Canada (Ontario) and baptized in Nauvoo in early 1844. During the exodus, he volunteered for the Mormon Battalion and was sent to Pueblo with the sick detachment. He was selected for the company returning to Winter Quarters. He returned to Utah in 1850 and helped settle Springville, Utah. He had three polygamous wives. He died at age twenty-nine in Fillmore, Utah.

Riter, Levi (1805–77), was born in Uwchland, Pennsylvania. He was baptized in 1845 and was called to serve a mission to England in 1852. He died in April 1877 in Salt Lake City.

Rockwell, Horace (1825–93), was born in Belchertown, Massachusetts. He was a brother of Orrin Porter Rockwell and Merit Rockwell.

Rockwell, Merit (1821–?), was born in Belchertown, Massachusetts. He was a brother of Orrin Porter Rockwell and Horace Rockwell.

Rockwell, Orrin Porter (1815–78), was born in Belchertown, Massachusetts. He was baptized near Fayette, New York, the day the church was organized on 6 April 1830. A fearless defender of Joseph Smith and a private enforcer of the law, most suspected him with the attempted killing of Governor Lilburn Boggs in 1842. Porter traveled to Utah with the Brigham Young company and was the bodyguard to the Twelve. After his arrival in Utah, he became involved with the Pony Express and one of the mail stations was located at his home, about twenty-five miles from Salt Lake City. He also served as deputy marshal of Salt Lake City for several years. He died in June 1878 in Salt Lake City.

Rockwood, Albert Perry (1805–79), was born in Massachusetts. After joining the church in 1837, he became a seventy in 1839 and was appointed a President of the Seventy in 1845. A captain, drill officer, and general in the Nauvoo Legion, he also served as commander of Joseph Smith's bodyguards. During the pioneer trek to Utah in 1847, he served as Brigham Young's bodyguard. His daughter was a plural wife of Brigham Young. He served in the territorial legislature and settled in Salt Lake City and became the warden of the territorial penitentiary, later dying in Sugar House, Utah, in November 1879.

Rogers, Noah (1797–1846), was born in Bethlehem, Connecticut, and converted in 1837. Along with Benjamin Grouard, Addison Pratt, and Knowlton Hanks, he served a mission in the Society Islands in 1843. Rogers served as the first president of the mission from 1844 to 1845. He returned to join the Saints in Nauvoo, then died while journeying west in May 1846 at Mount Pisgah, Iowa.

Rolfe, Benjamin William (1822–92), was born in Maine. His family joined the church in 1834 and moved to Kirtland, and later to Nauvoo. Though he had not yet joined the church himself, he volunteered to go with the vanguard company in place of his father and then returned to Winter Quarters in the fall. (His name is not listed, he may have been with William Clayton and the ox teams who left previously.) Returning to Salt Lake in 1848, he was baptized in 1851. He took part in the failed Salmon River Mission. In Salt Lake City he worked as a carpenter and died there in 1892.

Rooker, Joseph (1818–1901), was born in Indiana. He was a seventy and was one of the original pioneers to Utah. After arriving in Utah, he later continued on to Southern California. He died there, in Oceanside, in 1901.

Roundy, Shadrach (1789–1872), was born in Rockingham, Vermont, and was baptized in 1831. While in Nauvoo, he served as a captain of police. He came to Utah on 24 July 1847 with the Brigham Young company and recrossed the plains five times, helping other companies of Saints. He served in the first territorial legislature in Utah. He was called to serve as a bishop in Salt Lake. He died in July 1872 in Salt Lake City.

Rowe, Nicholas Caratat Conderset (1823–1904), was born in Indiana as the son of William Rowe and Candace Blanchard. He was baptized in 1842. He volunteered for the Mormon Battalion but returned to Pueblo with Captain Brown's sick detachment. After returning to Winter Quarters he immigrated again to Utah in 1852. He died in San Pete County, Utah.

Rowe, William (1826–1906), was born in Indiana. He was baptized in 1844 and served as a member of the Mormon Battalion. He died in July 1906 in Thayne, Wyoming.

Russell, Daniel (1799–1859), was born in Springfield, New York. He was baptized in 1839 and died in June 1859 in East Millcreek, Utah.

Russell, Mehitable (1811–92), was born in New York. He was baptized 1832 and died in February 1892 in California.

Russell, Samuel (1812–63), was born in Newstead, New York. He came to Utah in 1847 with the Abraham O. Smoot–Samuel Russell company. He died in November 1863.

Rust, William Walker (1807–94), was born in Vermont. After his wife's death, he and his sons joined the church and went to Nauvoo and Winter Quarters. Trained in medicine, he served as an assistant surgeon in the Mormon Battalion but became a member of the sick detachment when he was kicked by a mule. Also in the return company, in 1850 he moved permanently to Utah, where he practiced medicine in Salt Lake City and then in Payson. He died there in 1894.

Sanders, Ellen (1823–71), was born in Norway. She was baptized in 1842 and, along with her sister Harriet, later became a plural wife of Heber C. Kimball. She died in November 1871 in Salt Lake City.

Sanders, Harriet (1824–96), was born in Norway. She and her sister Ellen were plural wives of Heber C. Kimball. She died in September of 1896 in Meadowville, Utah.

Sargeant, Abel M. (1798–1847), was born in Maryland. He was a member of the Mormon Battalion and traveled to Salt Lake with the battalion in 1847, then continued on to Winter Quarters in order to bring his children back to Salt Lake. Later that year, in October, he and his son died in the Black Hills on the return trip to Utah.

Sarpy (or Sarpee), Peter A. (1805–65), was born in St. Louis, Missouri. Of French Creole ancestry, he began working at the American Fur Company's trading post at Council Bluffs, Iowa, in 1824 and later for the Missouri Fur Company in Bellevue, Nebraska Territory. Sarpy later established a trading post on the Iowa side of the Missouri River called Sarpy's Point or the Trader's Post. About 1846 he began a lucrative ferrying service known as "Sarpee's Ferry." Eccentric and excitable and one who loved horses and liquor, Sarpy became a wealthy man, later opening stores at St. Mary's and Decatur, Nebraska. Sarpy County, Nebraska, was named after him. He died in January 1865 in Plattsmouth, Nebraska.

Schofield (or Scofield), Joseph Smith (1809–75), was born in New York. He was baptized in 1841 and was later ordained a seventy in Nauvoo. He was one of the original pioneers to Utah and used his skills as a carpenter to repair wagons. He served a mission in England in the 1850s. He died in Bellevue, Utah, in March 1875.

Scott, John (1811–76), was from Ireland. He was baptized in 1836. A joiner and a farmer by vocation, he was a member of Joseph Smith's bodyguard and a colonel in the Nauvoo Legion. He came to Utah in 1848 and was the senior president of the Sixty-First Quorum of Seventy. He died in December 1876 in Millcreek, Utah.

Sessions, Peregrine (1814–93), was born in Maine. He was baptized in 1835 and was later ordained a seventy. He served as a bodyguard to Joseph Smith and Brigham Young. He led a company of pioneers to Utah in September 1847. He served missions to Maine and Great Britain and later became the first settler of Bountiful, Utah. He died there in June 1893.

Shaddon, John Winchester (dates unknown). No information is available.

Sharp, Albert (?–1847), was a member of the Mormon Battalion. He died in 1847.

Shaw, John (dates unknown), was a fur trader with the Sioux Indians. On 5 June 1847, he traveled from Fort John to St. Joseph, Missouri, where he reported having met two hundred westbound wagons of Mormons.

Shefflin, Mary Ann (1815–69), a plural wife of Heber C. Kimball, was born in New Jersey on October 31, 1815. She bore him one child before their separation in about 1850. She later married Alfred Walton in Salt Lake City in 1855. The separation must have been amicable, however, for she was buried in the Kimball family cemetery.

Sherwood, Henry G. (1785–c. 1862), was born in Kingsbury, New York. After joining the church, he became a member of the Nauvoo Legion and a city marshal. He traveled to Utah with the Brigham Young company and served on the high council in Salt Lake City. An excellent surveyor, he later helped build the Mormon settlement in San Bernardino, California. He died there in about 1862.

Shumway, Andrew Purley (1833–1909), was born in Massachusetts. Because he was only thirteen at the time of the exodus and his mother had died at Winter Quarters, he received special permission to accompany his father, Charles Shumway, in Brigham Young's vanguard company to the west. Andrew contracted Mountain Fever in Wyoming but was healed by Brigham Young. Father and son also made the return journey to Winter Quarters in the fall of 1847. Andrew eventually settled in Cache County, Utah. He died in Oneida County, Idaho.

Shumway, Charles (1806–98), was born in Massachusetts. He joined the church in 1840 and became a police officer in Nauvoo. He was one of the original pioneers to Utah in 1847 and was later a member of the first legislature of Utah. After bringing his family west, he built gristmills in Utah and Arizona. He died in May 1898 in Shumway, Arizona, which was named after him.

Shupe, Andrew Jackson (1815–77), was born in Virginia. He was a member of the Mormon Battalion. He died in March 1877 in Ogden, Utah.

Shurtliff, Luman (1807–84), was born in Montgomery, Massachusetts. A farmer, missionary, legislator, teacher, hunter, and soldier, he was baptized in 1836 and later was a member of the Nauvoo Legion. He came to Utah in September 1851 as the captain of his own company. He settled in Weber County and was a member of the Utah territorial legislature. He died in August 1884 in Ogden, Utah.

Sloan, James (1792–1886), was born in Donaghmore, Ireland. He joined the church in the 1830s. He served as general church recorder as well as a secretary for the Nauvoo Legion and a personal scribe for Joseph Smith. He served a mission for the church to Ireland and later joined the Reorganized Church of Jesus Christ of Latter Day Saints. He died October 1886 in Sacramento, California.

Smith, Charles C. (dates unknown), was a distant relative of Joseph Smith. While living in Nauvoo, he had associated with criminals and men of bad character. He left for Oregon in 1845. He opened a store at Sutter's Fort with Samuel Brannan just as the gold rush began in California. He and Brannan were among the first to come upon the remains of the Donner-Reed party as they headed west to meet the Saints, hoping to escort them to California. By late 1848 he was on board a ship to Hawaii with the fortune he had made from the gold miners. Nothing more is known about him.

Smith, George (dates unknown), opened a store in Savannah, Missouri, in 1842, with Milton Tootle as clerk. Smith left Tootle in charge of the store in 1845 and opened a new store in St. Joseph, Missouri, with Robert Washington Donnell. They advertised especially to migrants heading west. The Saints bought several supplies from his stores.

Smith, George A. (1817–75), was born in Potsdam, New York. A first cousin of Joseph Smith, he was baptized in 1832, served in Zion's Camp in 1834, and was ordained an Apostle in Far West, Missouri, in 1839 at the age of twenty-one. He served a mission to Great Britain with the other Apostles from 1838 to 1841. He came to Utah in 1847 with the Brigham Young vanguard company. He became a counselor in the First Presidency to Brigham Young in 1868. He was called to settle southern Utah, and the city of St. George was named in his honor. He died in September 1875 in Salt Lake City.

Smith, Hyrum (1800–1844), was born in Tunbridge, Vermont, the older and ever-loyal brother of Joseph Smith Jr. He was one of the first members of the church and was baptized in 1829. He was one of the Eight Witnesses to the Book of Mormon. He served as patriarch to the church after the death of his father, Joseph Smith Sr. He also replaced Oliver Cowdery as assistant president of the church and served in the First Presidency. He was shot to death in June 1844 at Carthage Jail, along with his brother Joseph.

Smith, John (1781–1854), uncle to the Prophet Joseph Smith, was born in Derryfield, New Hampshire. He was baptized in 1832 in an icy stream in upstate New York. He moved to Kirtland, Ohio, in 1833 and soon afterwards was called to the stake high council. He served as a stake president in four different locations—Adam-ondi-Ahman, Missouri; Zarahemla, Iowa; Nauvoo, Illinois; and Salt Lake City, Utah, as well as patriarch of the church from 1849 to 1854, giving over five thousand patriarchal blessings. He died in May 1854 in Salt Lake City.

Smith, Joseph, Jr. (1805–44), born in Sharon, Vermont, was prophet, seer, and revelator of the Church of Jesus Christ of Latter-day Saints, which he founded in April 1830. He translated from ancient records the Book of Mormon and brought forth such other books of scripture as the Doctrine and Covenants and Pearl of Great Price. He built temples in Kirtland, Ohio, and in Nauvoo, Illinois, and taught the eternality of the marriage covenant, the divine destiny of humankind, and the concept of plural marriage to the church. He and his brother Hyrum were murdered in Carthage, Illinois, on June 27, 1844, by a mob of two hundred to three hundred men.

Smith, "Little John" (1832–1911), was a son of Hyrum and Jerusha Smith. He was born in Kirtland, Ohio. His mother died in 1837, at which point his father married Mary Fielding. John was raised in the church and was baptized in 1841. He immigrated to Utah in 1848 and later became the sixth presiding patriarch of the church. He died in February 1911 in Salt Lake City.

Smith (Kimball), Lucy Walker (1826–1910), was born in Vermont. Her family joined the church in 1832. They moved to Missouri in 1838, experienced many of the persecutions there and then moved to Nauvoo. After receiving her own testimony of plural marriage, she was sealed to Joseph Smith in May 1843. After Joseph Smith died, she became a plural wife of Heber C. Kimball. She went to western Iowa with the Saints in 1846 and then west to Salt Lake with Heber C. Kimball in 1848. She gave birth to nine children with Kimball and died in Salt Lake City.

Smith, Mary Fielding (1801–52), was born in Bedfordshire, England. She joined her brother Joseph and sister Mercy in Upper Canada (Ontario) in 1834, and the three of them were there converted to Mormonism in Canada in 1836. After moving to Ohio, she became Hyrum Smith's second wife after his first wife, Jerusha, had died. She became was the mother of Joseph F. Smith, the sixth president of the church. After Hyrum's death, she became a plural wife of Heber C. Kimball. She died in September 1852 in Salt Lake City.

Smith, Sylvester (1805–?), was born in Tyringham, Massachusetts, and was baptized in May 1831. Oliver Cowdery ordained him a high priest six months later. He was a recalcitrant member of Zion's Camp but was later reconciled with the Kirtland high council. He attended the School of the Prophets in 1836. Part of the Kirtland apostasy of 1837, he had left the church by the following year. He moved to Council Bluffs, Iowa, in 1853, and there he was a lawyer specializing in real estate transactions. He was county school commissioner and justice of the peace in later years. He died in Council Bluffs at the age of seventy-three.

Smith, William (1811–93), a younger brother of Joseph Smith, was born in Royalton, Vermont. Baptized in 1830, he became one of the original members of the Council of Twelve Apostles, but he struggled with inactivity and restlessness. He was editor of the *Wasp*, a Nauvoo newspaper. At Joseph's death, he believed Church leadership should stay in the family. With the deaths of his brothers Joseph and Hyrum, he became presiding patriarch to the church but was excommunicated soon afterwards in October 1845. After following James Strang for a season, he joined the Reorganized Church of Jesus Christ of Latter Day Saints in 1878. He died in November 1893 in Iowa.

Smithies, James (1807–82), was born in England. He came to Utah in September 1847 as part of Daniel Spencer's company. He organized the first choir in Salt Lake City. He died there in June 1882.

Smoot, Abraham O. (1815–95), was born in Owen County, Kentucky. He joined the church in 1835 and was later ordained a seventy. He was a policeman in Nauvoo and brought a company to Utah in September 1847. A highly successful businessman, he served as mayor of Salt Lake City, mayor of Provo, member of the Utah territorial legislature, and a justice of the peace. He served several missions for the church and was president of the Utah Stake (then all of Utah Valley) for twenty-seven years. He was elected mayor of Provo City in 1868, serving for thirteen years. A prominent business leader and financier, he was the first president of the board of trustees of Brigham Young Academy, serving for twenty years, and played a key role in that school's founding and financial survival. A longtime president of the Timpanogos Manufacturing Company (later the Provo Woolen Mills), he died in March 1895 in Provo, Utah.

Smoot, William Cockran Adkinson (1828–1920), was born in Tennessee and became the adopted son of Abraham O. and Margaret Thompson Smoot. He was baptized in 1836 and followed the Saints to Far West and Nauvoo. He was made a seventy at a young age. He acted as a guard in the first pioneer company. He was also a member of the return company. Later, he was a missionary to the Indians and brought several immigrant trains to Utah.

Snow, Erastus (1818–88), was born in St. Johnsbury, Vermont. He joined the church in 1833. He was a member of the Council of Fifty as well as one of the original pioneers to Utah. He was ordained an apostle in 1849. He opened Scandinavia to Latter-day Saint missionaries in 1850 and also worked on translating the Book of Mormon into Danish, which was the first translation from English. He served several more missions and also served as a member of the territorial legislature and as a schoolteacher. He founded St. George and served as a presiding authority in southern Utah in 1861. He died in May 1888 in Salt Lake City.

Snow, William (1806–79), was born in Vermont. He was baptized in 1832 and immigrated to Utah in 1850, where he served as a territorial legislator, Church bishop, probate judge, and patriarch. He helped to settle Fort Supply in Wyoming. He died in May 1879 in Pine Valley, Utah.

Spencer, Daniel (1794–1868), was born in West Stockbridge, Massachusetts. He was baptized in 1840 and served a mission to Upper Canada (Ontario) the following year. He moved to Nauvoo shortly thereafter and, after the death of Joseph Smith, served the remainder of Joseph's term as mayor of Nauvoo. He was called a bishop in Winter Quarters and came to Utah in 1847 as a captain of his own company. From 1849 to 1868, he served as president of the Salt Lake City Stake, even though he also served as a missionary to the British Isles from 1852 to 1856. He died in December 1868 in Salt Lake City.

Squires, William (1816–85), was born in England. He was baptized in 1841 and later served in the Mormon Battalion. He traveled to Utah in 1847 and arrived a few days after the Brigham Young company. Shortly thereafter he continued on to California. He eventually returned to Utah and died in St. George in September 1885.

Stephens (or Stevens), Roswell (1808–80), was born in Upper Canada (Ontario) and was baptized in 1834. He was a member of the Nauvoo Legion, the Nauvoo police force, and the Mormon Battalion. He acted as a bodyguard to those of the Mormon Battalion who were sent from Santa Fe with money and letters for the Saints at the Missouri River. In 1847 he was dispatched from Fort Laramie to bring the Pueblo Saints and sick detachments of the battalion to the Salt Lake Valley. He migrated to Utah in 1847 with the Brigham Young company. A skilled frontiersman, he later became a member of the famous Hole-in-the-Rock expedition in southeastern Utah in 1879. He died in Bluff City, Utah.

Sterrett (or Sterrit), William Gibson (1813–73), was born in Philadelphia. He came to Utah in 1847, was a seventy, and died in August 1873 in Pleasant Grove, Utah.

Stewart, Benjamin Franklin (1817–86), was born in Jackson, Ohio. He was baptized in 1844 and was later ordained a seventy. He immigrated to Utah in 1847 in the Brigham Young company but did not arrive in the Salt Lake Valley until September, because he stayed at the Upper Platte Ferry to help the remaining Saints cross over. He was one of the original settlers of Payson, where he served two terms as mayor. He was also one of the founders of Benjamin, Utah, which was named in his honor. He died there in June 1885 after being struck by lightning.

Stewart, James (1827–1908), was born in Indiana. He joined the Mormon Battalion and was a member of a sick detachment of the Mormon Battalion. He returned to Winter Quarters and then went west again in 1851. He died in Fairview, Utah.

Stewart, James Wesley (1825–1913), was born in Alabama. He was one of the men assigned to stay and operate the ferry at the Platte River for oncoming immigrants. After arriving in the Salt Lake Valley, he seems to have been chosen for the return company, then subsequently returned to the valley with the second company. His diary records the hardships of the first winter in the valley. He died in Cokeville, Wyoming.

Stillman, Dexter (1804–52), was born in Connecticut. He was a member of the Mormon Battalion. He died in November 1852.

Stockton, Robert Field (1795–1866), was a United States Navy commodore and was noted for his role in the capture of California during the Mexican-American War. Second military governor of California, he also later served as a United States senator from New Jersey. He helped abolish flogging on US Navy ships. He was the first naval officer to carry out actions against slave ships and was instrumental in the founding of Liberia.

Stout, Hosea (1810–89), was born in Kentucky. He was baptized sometime between 1832 and 1838. Captain of the police in both Nauvoo and Winter Quarters, as well as a colonel in the Nauvoo Legion, he was an active defender of the Saints and a strict enforcer of the law. He served as president of the Eleventh Quorum of the Seventy. Feared by many, he died in March 1889 in Salt Lake County, Utah.

Stringam (or Stringham), Bryant (Briant) (1823–71), was born in Colesville, New York. He joined the church in 1842. A butcher and stockman, it is likely he was chosen for the vanguard company for those skills. In Utah he was appointed a probate judge in Cache County and ran a commissary during the Indian wars. For his last fifteen years, he tended the church's tithing stock on Antelope Island. In 1871, after being three days in a wind and rainstorm while caring for the animals, he took ill and died a few days later at his home near the Jordan River.

Summe, Gilbard (1802–67), was born in North Carolina. He was part of the advance company who entered Salt Lake Valley on 22 July 1847. He later served as a counselor in the general presidency of the deacons quorum for some time. In 1865 he was called on the Muddy Mission to Moapa Valley, Nevada. Summe died in 1867 at Harrisburg, Utah.

Swan, Frances Jesse (1821–94), was born in Scotland. Her family joined the church in about 1840. She became the twenty-first wife of Heber C. Kimball but divorced him in 1851 and married George Clark in 1852 in California. They did not return to Utah for the Utah War as counseled, but she and her husband were instrumental in rescuing Thomas L. Kane from a mob and spiriting him away to Utah to mediate in the Utah war. She died in San Francisco.

Sykes (Sikes), Elizabeth (1822–44), was born in New York. She converted to the church and sometime before 1840 immigrated to Nauvoo, where she was a schoolteacher. She married Wilson Law but died shortly thereafter in March 1844. There was also an Elizabeth Sykes born in England in 1797. Nothing more is known about her.

Taft, Seth (1796–1863), was born in Massachusetts. He joined the church in 1841. He was one of the original pioneers to Utah in 1847. After his arrival, he served as a bishop in Salt Lake. He became one of the original settlers of Manti. He later returned to Salt Lake City and served as a patriarch. He died there in 1863.

Tanner, Thomas (1804–55), was born in England. He immigrated to America in 1831 and was baptized ten years later. He came to Utah with the Brigham Young company. A blacksmith on the trek west, he was also in charge of the cannon. He later became foreman of the church blacksmith shop in Salt Lake City. He died in 1855 in Salt Lake City.

Taylor, David (dates unknown). No information is available.

Taylor, John (1808–87), was born in Milnthorpe, England. He started preaching Methodism at age seventeen. In 1830 he migrated to Toronto, Upper Canada (Ontario), where he was baptized in 1836. He became an Apostle in 1838 and filled a mission to Great Britain with the rest of the Twelve from 1838 to 1841. He and Willard Richards survived the mob's attack at Carthage Jail in June 1844, which killed the Prophet Joseph and his brother Hyrum. Taylor and Parley P. Pratt led a company of Saints west as part of the "Big" or Emigration Camp that followed the Brigham Young company, arriving in the Salt Lake Valley beginning on 5 October 1847. Taylor served as speaker of the house for the Utah territorial legislature. He became the third president of the Church of Jesus Christ of Latter-day Saints in October 1880. A stout defender of plural marriage, he died in hiding in July 1887 in Kaysville, Utah.

Taylor, Norman (1828–99), was born in Ohio. He was baptized in 1844 and was a member of the Mormon Battalion. He was one of the original pioneers to Utah and later moved to San Bernardino, California. He returned to Utah and died in Moab in 1899.

Terrill (Terrell), Joel Judkins (1801–83), was born in Virginia. He was baptized in 1844. He volunteered for the Mormon Battalion but traveled to Pueblo with Captain Brown's sick detachment. After returning to Winter Quarters, he immigrated to Utah in 1850. He died in Ogden.

Terrill, William (dates unknown), was a member of the company of Mississippi Saints that arrived in the Salt Lake Valley on 29 July 1847. He shared a wagon with Solomon Chamberlain on the return trip to Winter Quarters.

Therlkill (also Threlkel), George Washington (1820–1900), was born in Peoria County, Illinois. He married Matilda Jane Crow, and they traveled with her father-in-law, Robert Crow, to meet the southern Saints. He was mauled by a grizzly at some point and recovered while in Pueblo. He died in California.

Therlkill, Milton Howard (1844–47), was the son of George W. and Matilda Jane Therlkill. On 11 August 1847, at three years of age, he drowned while playing at the place where City Creek had been dammed for irrigation. His was the first Mormon death in the valley.

Therlkill, James William (1845–1921), was born in Illinois. He died in California.

Thomas, Hayward (1814–93), was born in Pennsylvania and baptized in 1840. He went to Nauvoo in 1844 where he was ordained a seventy. At Council Bluffs, he joined the Mormon Battalion and later became part of the sick detachment. After arriving in Salt Lake City, he returned to Winter Quarters, driving one of Brigham Young's teams. He returned to Utah in 1851. He died in Pennsylvania.

Thomas, Robert T. (1820–92), was born in North Carolina. The family joined the church in 1843 and moved to Nauvoo, where Robert was ordained to the office of seventy and sent on a mission to the southern states for a year. He was a wagon maker in the first pioneer company. He was in the advance party that arrived in Salt Lake Valley on 22 July 1847. He later helped settle Provo, where he held prominent positions in church and community. He died at Provo.

Thornton, Horace (1822–1914), was born in New York. He was baptized in 1836 at Kirtland, Ohio. He was a seventy. At Winter Quarters, he was chosen for the vanguard company, where he was assigned to be a member of the artillery company, to guard the camp every other night, and to hunt for the company. He was also chosen for the advance company that entered Salt Lake Valley 22 July 1847. He lived in several different settlements in Utah and served in the temples at St. George and Manti. He died at Manti.

Thornton, Samuel Stratton (1817–92) was born in New York. He was ordained a seventy and endowed in Nauvoo. He died in Madison County, Idaho.

Thorpe, Marcus Ball (1822–49) was born in Connecticut. After being baptized, he did not join the Saints until they were at Winter Quarters in 1846. He was part of the advance party that entered the valley 22 July 1847 and the party that returned to Winter Quarters. In 1848 he came west again and then went on to California, finding enough gold to bring his parents and family to Salt Lake City. He boarded a ship sailing east around Cape Horn with the money hidden on his body but fell overboard and drowned.

Tippets (or Thibbetts), Alvah (1809–47) was born in Lewis, New York, and was baptized in 1832. He served as a captain in the Nauvoo Legion and a captain of fifty on the trek to Utah. He died in October 1847 at Winter Quarters.

Tippets, John Harvey (1810–90) was born in New Hampshire. He was baptized in 1832 and was later ordained a seventy. He was a member of the Nauvoo Legion and the Mormon Battalion and was sent to Pueblo with the second sick detachment. He and Thomas Woolsey were then sent to Winter Quarters with money and letters from the battalion. They were taken captive by Indians twice on their way. Brigham Young advised the two to remain in Winter Quarters rather than return to Pueblo. Tippetts, along with Thomas Woolsey, Roswell Stephens and Amasa Lyman, was sent from Fort Laramie to bring the Pueblo and Mississippi Saints to the Salt Lake Valley. He was one of the original pioneers to Utah in 1847. He later served a mission to England, and also served as a church patriarch. He died in Farmington, Utah, in 1890.

Tootle, Milton (dates unknown). He and his business partner, George Smith, opened a store in Savannah, Missouri, in 1845. He played a major role in the growth of St. Joseph, Missouri, supplying goods to emigrants and developing a wholesale business that reached throughout the West.

Toronto, Joseph (1818–83), was born in Collines Isle, France, or Cagliari, Sardegna, Italy. He was baptized in 1833. He died in July 1883 in Salt Lake City.

Tubbs, William (1824–97), was born in Ohio. He was a member of the Mormon Battalion and also served as a seventy. He died in Stewartville, Minnesota, in May 1897.

Van Cott, John (1814–83), a cousin of Parley P. Pratt, was born in Canaan, New York. He was baptized in 1843 and was later ordained a seventy. He came to Utah in 1847. He served as president of the Scandinavian Mission from 1853 to 1856 and served a second mission to Scandinavia from 1859 to 1862. He served as one of the presidents of the seventy and as a member of the Utah house of representatives. He died in February 1883 in Salt Lake City.

Van Wagoner, Halmagh John (1788–1846), was born in New Jersey. He was baptized in 1844. He died in October 1846 in Winter Quarters, Nebraska.

Wadsworth, Abiah (1810–99), was born in Maine, and was baptized in 1840. He died in April 1899 in Idaho.

Walker, Henson (1820–94 or 1904), was born in Manchester, New York, and was baptized in 1840. He came to Utah with the Brigham Young company and became the first bishop and mayor of Pleasant Grove. He was a member of the Nauvoo Legion and also served as a bodyguard for Joseph Smith. He died in January 1894 or 1904 in Pleasant Grove, Utah.

Walker, Joseph R. (1798–1876), was born in Tennessee. He became a mountain man, scout, explorer, and trader. In 1833 Captain Benjamin L. Bonneville paid Walker to explore the territory west of the Great Salt Lake to California. He blazed the trail from Fort Hall to the Truckee River that would later become the principal route for the California gold rush. In 1845, he was put in charge of a John C. Frémont's third government expedition to California and Oregon. He died in California.

Walker, William (1820–1908), was born in Peacham, Vermont. He was baptized in 1835, was ordained a seventy in 1846, and came to Salt Lake in 1847. He served as mission president in South Africa and died in January 1908 in Lewisville, Idaho.

Wallace, George Benjamin (1817–1900), was born in New Hampshire. He was baptized in 1842 and worked on Joseph Smith's presidential campaign in 1844. A wealthy, successful man, he immigrated to Utah in 1847 and later served a mission to England. He offered the dedicatory prayer when laying the northwest cornerstone of the Salt Lake City Temple. He served in many stake presidencies. He died in January 1900 in Granger, Salt Lake City.

Wardle, George (1820–1901), was born in Cheddleton, England. Musically gifted from childhood, he learned to play many instruments and was also trained as a wheelwright by his father. He was baptized in 1839 and emigrated to Nauvoo in 1842. He was a member of the vanguard company and the return company. He returned with his wife in 1848 to Utah, where he founded dancing and music schools in several settlements over the years. He taught Brigham Young and several other leaders of the church to dance and promoted community musical endeavors throughout his life. He died in Vernal, Utah, in 1901.

Warrell (Worrell), Franklin A. (1821–45), was born in Pennsylvania. He was a member of the Carthage Grays. He had threatened the lives of Joseph and Hyrum Smith on the morning of 27 June 1844. Nonetheless, he was placed as a guard at Carthage Jail when they were murdered that day and offered only token resistance to the mob. Porter Rockwell shot and killed him on 16 September 1845 after he and others attacked Sheriff Jacob Backenstos.

Washburn, Abraham (1805–86), was born in New York. He became a shoemaker and tanner. Baptized in 1838, he moved to Nauvoo in 1841. He immigrated to Utah in 1848 and later helped establish Manti. He moved to Monroe in Sevier County, where he died in 1886.

Weatherby (Weatherbee), Jacob (1826–47). A young pioneer at Winter Quarters, he was attacked by Omaha Indians on June 19, 1847, a few miles east of the Elkhorn River and died the following day. His was the first and one of the very few cases of bloodshed between Mormons and Indians at either the Missouri River or all along the Mormon Trail.

Weiler, Jacob (1808–96), was born in Pennsylvania, one of fourteen children. His family disinherited him when he was joined the church in 1841. He moved to Nauvoo, married, and followed the Saints to Winter Quarters, where he was chosen for the first immigrating company. He helped in building roads and bridges. On the return trip, he met his family on their way to Salt Lake in the second company. He returned with them to the valley where he served as a bishop for almost forty years and then as a patriarch for a short time. He died in Salt Lake City.

Wells, (Squire) Daniel Hanmer (1814–91), was born in Trenton, New York. He was a friend to the church for several years prior to his baptism in August 1846. He taught school in Ohio and Illinois. He arrived in Utah in 1848. He later served as an apostle, as second counselor to Brigham Young in the First Presidency, as president of the European Mission, as president of the Endowment House in Salt Lake, and as president of the Manti Temple. He was also mayor of Salt Lake City and a member of the territorial legislature. He also served as chancellor of the University of Deseret and directed the organization of settlements in Utah and Arizona. He died in March 1891 in Salt Lake City.

Weston, Isaac M. or Newton (dates unknown), traveled east with the return company but nothing more is known about him.

Wheeler, John (1802–91), was born in South Carolina. He was baptized in 1840 and was later ordained a seventy. He was made a member of the standing guard for the pioneer company. He later moved to California. He died in Idaho.

Whipple, Edson (1805–94), was born in Vermont. He joined the church in 1840 and served a mission promoting Joseph Smith's presidential campaign in 1844. He was one of the original pioneers to Utah in 1847. He was an officer in Utah's Nauvoo Legion. He lived in Provo for several years. In the 1880s he migrated to Mexico, where he died in May 1894.

Whiting, Chauncey (or Chancey) (1819–1902), was born in Nelson, Ohio. He followed Alpheus Cutler after the death of Joseph Smith and became the second president of the Cutlerite church. He died in June 1902 in Clitherall, Minnesota.

Whitney, Ann Maria (1836–81), was born in Kirtland, Ohio. She was a daughter of Newel K. Whitney and Elizabeth Ann Smith and was a younger sister of Horace K. Whitney.

Whitney, Clark Lyman (1809–51?) was born in New York, the younger brother of Newel K. Whitney. He followed the church west to Winter Quarters and stayed there preparing to immigrate. Before leaving he was hired to build a mill in Texas. There he met former bishop George Miller as he was leaving Lyman Wight's group. According to Miller's account, he easily convinced Whitney that James J. Strang was Joseph Smith's true successor, immediately agreeing to follow Miller to Wisconsin along with at least two wives. He died in Voree, Wisconsin, but his death date is somewhat uncertain.

Whitney, Don Carlos (1841–86), was born in Nauvoo, Illinois. He was the son of Newel K. Whitney and Elizabeth Ann Smith and was the younger brother of Horace K. Whitney. He died in November 1886 in Salt Lake City.

Whitney, (Mother) Elizabeth Ann Smith (1800–1882), was born in Connecticut. She moved to Kirtland with her aunt at about eighteen and there met Newel K. Whitney. She and her husband were baptized in Ohio in 1830. At Nauvoo and later in Utah, she was one of the first female temple workers and served as a counselor in the Relief Society presidency to both Emma Smith and Eliza R. Snow. She died in Salt Lake City.

Whitney (Wells), Emmeline Blanche Woodward Harris (1828–1921), was born in Massachusetts and baptized at age fourteen. She married James Harris at fifteen, and they immigrated to Nauvoo. Harris left her after their infant son died. She taught school in Nauvoo and became a plural wife of Bishop Newel K. Whitney. After his death, she became a plural wife of Daniel H. Wells. A poet and author, she also edited the *Woman's Exponent* for thirty-seven years. She was active in the movement for women's rights both in Utah and nationally. She was called as Relief Society general president at age eighty-two and served eleven years. She died in Salt Lake City.

Whitney, Francis (1805–83), was born in Somerset County, Massachusetts. He was baptized in 1843. In 1845 he left his family and went to Nauvoo. He arrived in the Salt Lake Valley on July 29, 1847. In 1848 he returned to his family and took them to Utah. He died in April 1883 in Huntington, Utah.

Whitney, John Kimball (1832–1915), was born in Kirtland, Ohio. He was a son of Newel K. Whitney and Elizabeth Ann Smith and was a brother of Horace K. Whitney. He died in August 1915 in Mendon, Utah.

Whitney, Newel Kimball (1795–1850), was born in Marlboro, Vermont, and was the father of Horace K. Whitney. He was baptized in 1830 in Kirtland, Ohio, and was appointed bishop there in 1831. A highly successful businessman, he operated the church store there and was in charge of the temple lot in Kirtland as well. Whitney and his wife, Elizabeth, left Kirtland in the fall of 1838, settling first in Quincy and later in Nauvoo, Illinois, where he was called as the second Presiding Bishop of the church in 1844. He died in September 1850 in Salt Lake City.

Whitney, Orson Kimball (1830–84), was born in Kirtland, Ohio. He was baptized in 1841 and was later ordained a seventy. He was a son of Newel K. Whitney and Elizabeth Ann Smith and was a brother of Horace K. Whitney. One of the original pioneers to Utah, he died in Salt Lake City in July 1884.

Whitney, Samuel (1772–1846), was born in Grafton, Massachusetts, and he was baptized in 1835. He was the grandfather of Horace K. Whitney. He died in March 1846 in Kirtland, Ohio.

Whitney (Smith), Sarah Ann (1825–73) was born in Kirtland, Ohio, to Newel Kimball Whitney and Elizabeth Ann Smith. She was a devoted younger sister to Horace K. Whitney. In 1842, at age seventeen, she was sealed for time and all eternity to the Prophet Joseph Smith as one of his polygamous wives. Later she married Joseph C. Kingsbury in an apparent polyandrous relationship. After Joseph Smith's death, she married Heber C. Kimball as one of his many plural wives. She raised five children before she died in Salt Lake City in 1873.

Wight, Lyman (1796–1858), was born in Fairfield, New York. He was baptized in 1830 and was ordained the first high priest in Church history in June 1832. Having a military background, he served in Zion's Camp in 1834 and was responsible for the protection of the Saints in many parts of Missouri. Imprisoned with Joseph Smith in Liberty Jail in 1838–39, he was later called as an apostle in 1841. After Joseph Smith's death in 1844, he led a group of Saints to Texas but was excommunicated from the church in 1849. He died in Dexter, Texas, in 1858.

Williams, Almon (also Almond) Mack (also McCumber) (1807–74), was born in Connecticut or New York. He joined the church in 1843 and received his endowment and sealing to his wife in Nauvoo. After trekking west with the vanguard company, he returned to Winter Quarters but never went to Utah again. He died in Mills County, Iowa, in 1874.

Williams, Thomas Stephen (1826–60), was born in Columbia, Tennessee, and was baptized in 1837. He was a member of the Mormon Battalion. He died in March 1860 in the Mojave Desert, California.

Willis, William Wesley (1811–72), was born in Illinois. He was baptized in 1834 and was later ordained a seventy. He arrived in Utah on July 29, 1847, as a lieutenant with a contingent of the Mormon Battalion. He later served as mayor in Cedar City. He died in April 1872 in Beaver, Utah.

Wilson, George Deliverance (1807–87), was born in Vermont. Baptized in 1834, he was later ordained a seventy. He was a member of the Mormon Battalion and arrived in Salt Lake in July 1847. He built sawmills in several cities in Utah. He died in October 1887 in Hillsdale, Utah.

Wiltbank, Spencer Watson (1824–1902), was born in Christiana, Delaware. He was baptized in 1843 and immigrated to Utah in 1848. He was a seventy. He died in May 1902 in Apache County, Arizona.

Wilson, John P. (dates unknown), was a member of the return company from Salt Lake to Winter Quarters in late 1847. Nothing further is known about him.

Winchester, Stephen (1795–1873), was born in Vermont and was baptized in 1833. He immigrated to Utah in 1849. He was the father of Benjamin Winchester. He died in January 1873 in Salt Lake City.

Wolsey (or Woolsey), Thomas Ezra (1805–97), was born in Kentucky. He joined the church there in 1838 and was later ordained a seventy. He worked on the Nauvoo Temple and was a member of the Mormon Battalion. He was sent with the sick detachment from the Santa Fe to Pueblo. He then traveled alone through dangerous territory from Pueblo back to the battalion on the Rio Grande and guided another sick detachment back to Pueblo. He made another harrowing journey with John Tippetts from Pueblo to Winter Quarters. He remained there and became a member of the pioneer company. He, along with John Tippetts, Roswell Stephens, and Amasa Lyman, was sent from Fort Laramie to bring the Pueblo and Mississippi Saints to the Salt Lake Valley. He later helped explore California. He died in Wales, Utah.

Woodruff, Wilford (1807–98), was born in Farmington, Connecticut. Baptized in 1833, he was ordained an Apostle in 1839 and served a highly successful mission to Great Britain with the rest of the Twelve, baptizing upwards of 1,600 people. He was one of the original pioneers to Utah, arriving in 1847 with the Brigham Young company. A highly spiritual man given to dreams and visions, he was intensely interested in the work of salvation for the dead. He was made president of the St. George Temple at the time of its dedication in 1877; there he performed hundreds, if not thousands, of ordinances for his ancestors. In 1889 he became the fourth president of the church. During his presidency, he issued the Manifesto in 1890, ending plural marriage in the church but saving the temples from government confiscation in the process. He also ended the practice of sealing members of the church to church authorities (the law of adoption) in 1893 in favor of families being sealed to their ancestors, a move which led to the establishment of the Genealogical Society of Utah in 1894. He died in September 1898 in San Francisco, California.

Woodward, George (1817–1903), was born in New Jersey. He was baptized in 1840 and was later ordained a seventy. He was one of the original pioneers to Utah. He settled in southern Utah, and died in St. George in 1903.

Woodworth, Lucien (1799–1867) was born in Vermont. He was an architect and carpenter who moved to New York and later to Missouri in 1839. By 1841 he arrived in Nauvoo and was hired as the architect of the Nauvoo House but did not join the church until 1843. He was an aide-de-camp in the Nauvoo Legion and was admitted to the Council of Fifty in March of 1844. Sometime before May 1844, Joseph Smith sent him to Texas to meet with Sam Houston concerning a possible Mormon settlement in Texas. He eventually went west with the main body of Saints and lived in San Bernardino from 1854 to 1856. His death date is likely 1867.

Woolley (or Wooley), Edwin Dilworth (1807–81), was born in Pennsylvania. He was baptized in 1837 and came to Utah in 1848. He served as a bishop in Salt Lake and as a member of the Utah territorial house of representatives. He died in October 1881 in Salt Lake City.

Wordsworth, William Shin (1810–88), was born in New Jersey and baptized in Pennsylvania in 1841. He was ordained a seventy in February 1846. He was chosen to be a road and bridge builder in the first pioneer company and then made the return journey to Winter Quarters. He went to Utah again in 1856, where he continued to work on roads, bridges, and ditches. He died in Springville, Utah.

Wright, Alexander (1804–76), was born in Scotland, and immigrated to Canada in 1835. He was baptized in 1836 and became a seventy in 1845. He served a mission to Great Britain and was one of the first to bring Mormonism to his native Scotland. He died in Virgin City, Utah, in August 1876.

Yearsly (or Yearsley), David (1801–49), was from Pennsylvania. He joined the church in 1841. He died at Winter Quarters in 1849.

Yocum (or Yokum), William (1805–53), was born in Huntington, Pennsylvania. He was among the wounded in the massacre at Hawn's Mill in 1838 and lost a leg as a result of his injury. He died in November 1853 in Weston, Iowa.

Young, Brigham (1801–77), was born in Whitingham, Vermont. He was baptized in Mendon, New York, in 1832, after studying the church for almost two years. A carpenter by trade with a powerful personality, he served in the 1834 Zion's Camp march to Missouri and helped build the Kirtland Temple. Ordained an Apostle in the original Council of the Twelve in 1835, he remained true to the Prophet Joseph Smith during the Kirtland apostasy of 1837. He led the Twelve's highly successful mission to Great Britain from 1838 to 1841. He was among the first to receive the endowment in Joseph Smith's Red Brick Store in Nauvoo in 1842. In 1846–47 he led the Mormon exodus to the Salt Lake Valley, where he was soon appointed the first territorial governor. He was sustained second president of the church in Kanesville, Iowa, in December 1847. Known as the "Great Colonizer" and "Lion of the Lord," he reestablished the Saints in scores of communities throughout the Intermountain West. He lived to see the completion of the St. George Temple in 1877 and dedicated land for the building of the Salt Lake, Manti, and Logan Temples. A staunch polygamist, he presided over the church until his death in 1877 in Salt Lake City.

Young, Clarissa Clara Decker (1828–89), was born in New York. She was the daughter of Isaac Decker and Harriet Page Wheeler. She was one of the three original pioneer women to come to Utah in 1847, along with her mother, Harriet. Clarissa was one of the wives of Brigham Young. She died in January 1889 in Salt Lake City.

Young, Harriet Page Wheeler Decker (1803–71), was born in Hillsboro, New Hampshire. She was one of the three original pioneer women to Utah who traveled with the Brigham Young company. On the trek to Utah, she was accompanied by two children: Isaac Perry Decker and Lorenzo Sobieski Young. She was also the mother of Clarissa Clara Decker Young, one of Brigham Young's wives. She died in December 1871 in Salt Lake City.

Young, Joseph (1797–1881), was born in Hopkinton, Massachusetts. Older brother of Brigham Young, he once was a Methodist minister in Upper Canada (Ontario) before joining the church in 1832. He was instrumental in the conversion of his brother Brigham Young. Along with Brigham, he served in Zion's Camp in 1834. Upon his return to Kirtland, he became the senior president in the First Council of the Seventy in 1835. He was a member of the Nauvoo Legion and came to Utah in 1850. He died in July 1881 in Salt Lake City.

Young, Lorenzo (1807–95), was born in Smyrna, New York. He was the brother of Brigham Young. He began preaching Christianity but struggled gaining converts because he was reluctant to join with any existing church. He was baptized in 1831 and came to Utah with the Brigham Young company. He sowed the first acre of wheat in the Salt Lake Valley. He died in November 1895 in Salt Lake City.

Young, Lorenzo Sobiski (or Sobieski) (1841–1924), was born in Winchester, Illinois, and was a son of Lorenzo Dow Young. He was baptized in 1849. He was one of the two children who came to Utah with the first pioneer company. He was a farmer and loved gardening. He died in March 1924 in Shelley, Idaho.

Young, Persis Goodall (1806–94), was born in New York. The wife of Lorenzo Young, she attended Hebrew School in Kirtland. She and Lorenzo were driven out of Missouri to Nauvoo, where she separated from him and was sealed to Levi Richards. She went west in 1850. She was sick much of her life but lived until 1894. She died in Kanab.

Young, Phinehas Howe (1799¬–1879), brother to Brigham Young, was born in Massachusetts to John and Abigail Howe Young. As a Methodist preacher, he was introduced to the Book of Mormon and baptized in 1832. He weathered the trials of the Saints from New York through to Council Bluffs. There he was chosen as a hunter and scout for the vanguard company. At the Green River, he volunteered to be a guide for the second company of 1847, later guiding three more companies to the valley. In Utah he worked at various professions while also serving in a stake presidency and as a bishop. Having been married at one time to the sister of Oliver Cowdery, he had made efforts to bring Cowdery back to the church and was with him at his death in in Missouri in 1850. He died in Salt Lake City.

Young, Vilate (1830–1902), was born in Mendon, New York, the second daughter of Brigham Young and Miriam Angeline Works. She was named after Vilate Kimball because of the close friendship between the Youngs and Heber and Vilate Kimball. She married Charles Decker at Winter Quarters in 1847, and they had eight children. She died at Lewisville, Idaho.

Young, Zina D. Huntington (1821–1901), born in Watertown, New York, was the daughter of William Huntington and Zina Baker. With the rest of her family, she converted to Mormonism when she was fourteen years old. With her parents and family, she moved to Kirtland, Ohio; Far West, Missouri; and eventually to Nauvoo, Illinois, where she married Henry B. Jacobs in 1842. She was later sealed to the Prophet Joseph Smith as one of his wives and, after his death, to Brigham Young. Zina not only possessed notable spiritual gifts but, after her removal to the West, she also became very active in public service activities, including establishing Deseret Hospital in Salt Lake City. She became the third Relief Society general president in 1888, serving until her death in 1901.

Index

Page numbers in *italics* refer to images.

C

D

E

K

N

O

P

R

S

Y

About the Editor

Richard E. Bennett, professor of Church history and doctrine at Brigham Young University since 1997 and former president of the Mormon History Association, has published several books and over sixty articles on a wide range of topics in Latter-day Saint history. His award-winning *Mormons at the Missouri, 1846–1852* (University of Oklahoma) remains the definitive study of the Latter-day Saint experience at Winter Quarters (Nebraska), and his follow-up work, *We'll Find the Place: The Mormon Exodus, 1846–1848,* is an equally comprehensive study of Brigham Young's pioneering trek from Winter Quarters to the Salt Lake Valley. Born and raised in Sudbury, Ontario, Canada, he was also chair of the Department of Archives and Special Collections at the University of Manitoba in Winnipeg for twenty years. He and his wife, Patricia, have five children and several grandchildren.